John Betjeman

Letters

Volume One: 1926 to 1951

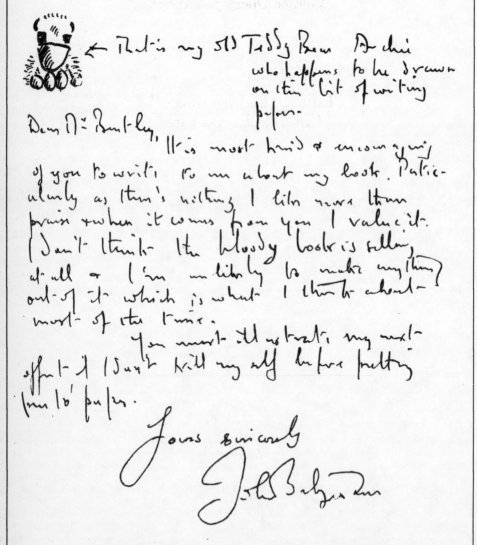

THE ARCHITECTURAL REVIEW

9, Queen Anne's Gate, Westminster, S.W.1

PROPRIETORS

THE ARCHITECTURAL PRESS
LIMITED

TELEPHONE VICTORIA 6936

← That is my old Teddy Bear Archie who happens to be drawn on this list of writing paper.

Dear Mr Bentley,

It is most kind & encouraging of you to write to me about my book. Particularly as there's nothing I like more than praise & when it comes from you I value it. I don't think the bloody book is selling at all & I'm unlikely to make anything out of it which is what I think about most of the time.

You must illustrate my next effort if I don't kill myself before putting pen to paper.

Yours sincerely

John Betjeman

Nicolas Bentley had written to congratulate JB on the publication of his first book of verse, *Mount Zion*, in 1931 (*see page 85*).

JOHN BETJEMAN

Letters

Volume One: 1926 to 1951

Edited and introduced by
Candida Lycett Green

Methuen

First published in Great Britain in 1994
by Methuen London
an imprint of Reed Consumer Books Ltd
Michelin House, 81 Fulham Road, London SW3 6RB
and Auckland, Melbourne, Singapore and Toronto

A CIP catalogue record for this book
is available at the British Library
ISBN 0 413 66950 5

Typeset by Deltatype, Ellesmere Port, S. Wirral
Printed and bound in Great Britain
by Mackays of Chatham plc, Chatham, Kent

For Jock Murray

Contents

Preface

Few men are universally loved for what they are and respected for what they do. My father, John Betjeman, was one of these exceptional people and when he died in March 1984 my mother, brother and I received hundreds of letters, not only from friends and acquaintances, but also from people we did not know, telling us what he meant to them. One wrote, 'He was loved by all of us who never met him but felt we knew him. When I think of him it is entirely with joy – his joy – that he found all around him – and the wonder that was new to him each day, of life and people and the things he loved. And how he managed to make other people see and share this wonder and joy.' Since my father's death I had always determined to write about him at some time in the future. Although it would not have occurred to me to edit his letters had it not been suggested, I realized that selections from his own correspondence might reveal his extraordinarily varied qualities, his fighting spirit, his compassion for people in trouble, his infectious enthusiasm, far better than I could in my own words alone.

Three years ago I went to see the biographer, Michael Holroyd, and asked him, in my naïvety, how one set about editing letters, as though there were some magic trick.

'Where do I *start?* I never even went to university.'

'Neither did I,' he said. 'You just have to love your subject and that's enough.'

Ever since, I have clung to what he said. It gave me strength whenever I felt academically inadequate. There was the time I went to John Sparrow's memorial service in Oxford and found myself having tea afterwards next to an ancient don. He asked me what I was doing.

'Editing my father's letters,' I said proudly.

He replied, 'Mmmm, that should take you about fifteen years, or conceivably twenty.'

Perhaps it should, and, having spent several days in the Bodleian reading through letters, I would willingly have worked there for the rest of my days. Another time I told a boisterous and aggressively feminist literary agent how much I was *enjoying* the work. She looked at

me sternly, as though I shouldn't be, and said, 'Well, I hope you're
going to do it *properly*, because you certainly have an onerous task on
your hands.'

I know I have an onerous task. But I love my father and want to show
the world how great he was: how he was, unlike most of us, interested
in things other than himself; how he revealed the divine in the ordinary
and enriched so many people's lives; how he laughed an inordinate
amount and when he put his head back and opened his mouth and shook
with laughter you couldn't help laughing too; how he joked about the
clergy and obscure denominations (I was not brought up to count my
cherry stones, 'big house, little house, pigsty, barn', but, 'church,
chapel, agnostic, free thinker'); above all, how strongly he believed. I
remember once my brother fell down the ladder from the apple loft at
Farnborough and his best friend Terry Carter came into the kitchen
and said to my parents, 'Paul's dead.' We all rushed out and found him
unconscious, but alive. Later my father walked across to the church and
stayed there for over an hour. I asked his secretary Miss Webb what he
was doing and she said he was thanking God.

I want to show how my father is not categorizable; how his
architectural tastes were catholic and all-embracing, from the stone
dwellings on St Kilda to the wild buildings of Gaudi and the brick
galleries of Jim Stirling; how he did not necessarily love all things
Victorian, as is popularly supposed, but only a carefully selected
proportion; how he never accepted the mediocre and how he was
England's grand champion not of conservation, with all the stuffiness
and fossilizing academicism that the word now implies, but of
safeguarding what he called 'indeterminate beauty' – the last thing on
any official list, because of its indefinable quality.

This volume does not comprise a collection of literary masterpieces.
My father never considered himself to be a 'letter writer'. I have chosen
the letters not merely for their interest but for the glimpses they reveal
of his often quite ordinary life. Some of the letters he wrote to Mr
Boswell of the BBC, for instance, about his expenses, may seem trivial
to some but they were the stuff of life to him and, in consequence, are to
me. I hope therefore that the book unfolds as a biography of a sort. My
father *never* wrote letters with a view to posterity. They are spontaneous, often urgent, but never proselytizing or long-winded – for one
thing he did not have time. Bill Peterson, who is compiling my father's
bibliography for the Oxford University Press, has so far assessed that,
apart from his poetry and his many topographical books, he contributed nearly 2,000 pieces to periodicals and newspapers, and 200

prefaces and contributions to books; that he was on the radio 735 times, including making his own programmes, which he began in 1933; and that, after appearing on television for the first time in 1937, he followed it by 493 further appearances.

This list would have embarrassed him. His great gift to anyone who came in contact with him was to talk about *them*, to bring *them* from the shadows into the limelight, however briefly, and leave them with a feeling of self-worth. He never saw things in terms of his own achievement and seldom kept his own writings. By the end of his life his library included few of his own books. When he was twenty-nine years old, my father was asked to list his chief interests, dislikes and hopes for an anthology. Characteristically he wrote to the editor, 'This has cost me sweat and blood. I cannot write about myself, just as some people can't sign their names.' Among his chief interests he listed: ecclesiastical architecture of the late eighteenth and early nineteenth centuries; box pews and three-decker pulpits; Irish peers, Irish architecture and pre-Celtic Twilight Irish poetry, written in English; Salkeld's Catalogue; branch railways; suburbs; provincial towns; steam trains. His dislikes included aeroplanes; main roads; insurance companies; 'development'; local councils; and materialism, dialectical or otherwise; and his hopes were for a Triumph of Christianity and a town plan for England. He stuck to his guns.

In my connecting commentary I try to fill in the background of each period. In respect of his early life I can add little to what is revealed by my father in *Summoned by Bells*, which covers my first three sections of this volume, nor to Bevis Hillier's excellent and full biography, *Young Betjeman*, which covers the first four up to my parents' marriage in 1933. From then onwards I found myself in virgin territory. As yet nothing extensive has been published about my father from this time and, whereas most editions of famous people's letters are preceded by the publication of a full biography or autobiography, this volume is not. It is for this reason that I felt a commentary was necessary and once I myself reach a certain age in the story I can begin to add my memories of him to those of others.

In this, my first of two volumes, there are inevitably sad gaps. Most of my father's contemporaries have died and few or no letters survive from this early period, written to such close friends and regular correspondents as 'Cracky' William Clonmore (who, my father always said, was the most saintly man he ever knew), John Sparrow, 'Colonel' Kolkhorst, Maurice Bowra, Lord Alfred Douglas, Christopher Hollis, Ronald Hughes-Wright, Frederick Etchells, Osbert Lancaster, Peter

Fleetwood-Hesketh and many more. My brother Paul kept none of my
father's letters written to him at school. Some people never keep letters
on principle, particularly clerics, who like to be free of worldly goods
and leave a clean slate at the end; others, who would like to keep them,
simply can't, because of being on the move. As soon as the writer
becomes famous and his letters valuable the story changes. But my
father was not famous until the end of this first volume.

Throughout his working life he was strapped for cash, and in the
1960s, when his fame was well established, he sold all his papers,
incoming letters and all future ones, to the newly created University of
Victoria in British Columbia, the highest bidder. On his death,
everything which had accrued since duly followed on. In February
1992 I travelled to Victoria, booked into a wooden-balconied bungalow
bed-and-breakfast on a wide cherry-blossom-lined street which led
down to the sea, and walked daily up to the tree-girt sixties university
campus, the style of which my father might or might not have come
round to in time. In the McPherson Library which rambles around the
basement, I found several corridors of grey four-drawer filing cabinets
containing, as it were, my father – an incongruous, though not
inappropriate, resting place for such an Anglophile – the suburbs of
Victoria combine the atmosphere of North Oxford, Wentworth and a
kind of Welwyn Garden City on Sea, all set in startlingly beautiful
surroundings.

In my allotted orange plastic cubby-hole my father's life began to
pour over me. Notes from Oxford friends, garage bills, rockets from
librarians for not returning books, brought instant and vivid reality. I
did not notice time and from that moment to this have loved the luxury
of having my father, and often my mother as well, constantly safe inside
my head. When my mother died in 1986, two years after my father, she
gave me a magic strength. I felt as though I were putting on an overcoat
which was her spirit and which I could keep on for ever. I never felt that
about my father's death, only devastation. Now, ten years later, I feel a
strength from him as well.

I returned to England armed with over two thousand photocopies of
letters to my father (there are approximately fifty thousand altogether)
and set about the great task of reaping his outgoing letters by
advertising, and by writing to hundreds of universities, libraries and
associations in Britain and America, as well as to four hundred and
twenty individuals. Then I waited. The excitement of receiving replies
and copies of letters knew no bounds. It was like Christmas every
morning and this lasted for at least four months. A whole new life began

to evolve. My old schoolmistress, who had taught me forty-five years before, saw my advertisement in the *Newbury Weekly News* and wrote and asked me to tea in order that she might show me her letters. Various treasure hunts began to unfold – the search for letters from my father's friend, the late William Mitchell (whom he nicknamed 'Scudamore'), eventually led me to his brother, Richard Mitchell, a process which had necessitated being in touch with a succession of nine people, over a period of ten days. He wrote, eventually, from a half-timbered house in Essex, depicted on his writing paper, 'We have an attic which contains an astonishing number of things. I did indeed encounter a small and rather ancient attaché case of Bill's containing correspondence and was about to cry "Eureka" when I came across some letters signed "John", but stifled my cry in mid-Greek shriek when I found they were dated 1794.'

Such wild-goose chases, which I could never resist pursuing, were numerous and time-consuming, but pleasurable. I did not heed the advice of Mark Amory, the editor of Evelyn Waugh's letters and diaries, who told me that the whereabouts of all the letters worth bothering with would already be known. Just as I will always back an outsider at the races, so I could never give up on finding a secret cache of my father's letters jammed into a teapot on some high kitchen shelf in a Nottinghamshire vicarage. It never happened.

The only major snag in the whole operation has been my father's handwriting. It is virtually illegible and everyone complains about it – even my father himself, who said that only God could read it. He sometimes had to resort to capital letters for clarity. Despite having lived with it all my life, I am still flummoxed by some passages. The more people I could muster to concentrate on solving a certain word at the same time, the better. It is exactly like trying to do a *Times* crossword clue with someone looking over your shoulder. You try unbelievably hard and sometimes manage to come up with the answer. Occasionally I have just had to put 'illegible' in square brackets. Anything else in square brackets is also my insertion.

Many of my father's letters contain funny drawings and these have been included wherever possible. He usually wrote the date in Roman numerals, but I have made all the dates uniform. He was a stickler for correct spelling and I found hardly any spelling errors whatsoever, except occasionally in names, which I have corrected. If any mistakes occur, they are mine. He was also keen on proper punctuation, but since a lot of his letters were dashed off, he sometimes did not have time to read through them. I have inserted the barest minimum where the sense might be misconstrued without it. I have referred to my father throughout as 'JB' for ease; to my mother before her marriage as 'PC' and later 'PB'; to my brother as 'PSGB'; and to myself as 'CB' in footnotes. Friends and acquaintances of JB's who appear often in this volume are described in the *Dramatis Personae* at the end, together with a thumbnail sketch, rather than a long footnote at their first mention. More often than not they are also mentioned in my introductions and the index will help point towards them.

As for the footnotes, my father hated them and joked about the academic disease of 'Foot and note'. I was determined to have as few as possible but found myself unable to resist imparting the sort of information he would have liked, and they have grown. I have tried to make them as readable and unstuffy as possible. I have not included people's dates unless I think it relevant or necessary to the story, as with the Scott family of architects, which is impossible to understand without! At one point I included the dates of every poet, painter, artist and architect mentioned in the footnotes and the latter began to read like a pompous textbook, which is exactly what my father would have hated. If something in a letter cries out to you for an explanation and has none it means I have been unable to find out anything about it. I have also done my utmost to use the correct spelling of every name but inevitably mistakes creep through.

This edition of the letters is not a definitive scholarly collection. That could run to twenty volumes and take thirty years to complete. The selection I have made and the way I have presented them is designed to tell his story and to paint his portrait in his own words as well as some of mine.

Acknowledgements

I would like to thank the following individuals and institutions for providing letters and for the immense trouble some of them have taken in finding, sorting and copying them:

All Souls College, Oxford, for letters to John Bryson and John Sparrow; Tim Arlott for letters to John Arlott; Sir David Attenborough for letters to Mrs F. L. Attenborough; Beinecke Rare Book and Manuscript Library, Yale University, USA, for letters to Nicolas Bentley, Bess Betjemann, Penelope Betjeman, Hector Bolitho, Maurice Bowra, Tom Driberg, Geoffrey Grigson, John Hayward, Father C. W. Hutchinson, G. A. Kolkhorst, C. S. Lewis, James Lees-Milne, John Lehmann, Brinsley Macnamara, Alan Pryce-Jones, Mrs Pryce-Jones and Martin Secker; Polly Bird for letters to Douglas Goldring; Birr Scientific Heritage Foundation and The Friends of Birr Castle, Ireland, for letters to Michael Rosse; Bodleian Library, Oxford, for letters to Lionel Curtis, Walter de la Mare, E. W. Gilbert, Jim Knapp-Fisher, C. S. Lewis, the Secretary of the Canning Club, Martyn Skinner, Sidgwick and Jackson, Janet Stone and the Revd J. M. Thompson; Joan Booker for a letter to Frederick Booker; British Broadcasting Corporation Archives, Caversham, Reading, for letters to J. R. Ackerley, Mary Adams, George Barnes, Mr Boswell, Malcolm Brereton, Guy Burgess, Lionel Fielden, Miss Kallin, A. Lorimer, E. Molony and B. E. Nicholls; the British Library, London, for letters to Jack Beddington and Evelyn Waugh; Mrs Brooker for a letter to Mr Ibberson Jones; Jan Channel for letters to Anne Channel; Christ Church College, Oxford, for letters to Tom Driberg; Mrs D. Cleverdon for a letter to Douglas Cleverdon; Collins Archives, Glasgow, for letters to Collins; The Council for the Care of Churches, London, for letters to Dr Eeles; Dartington Hall Trust for a letter to the Headmaster; The Duchess of Devonshire for letters to Nancy Mitford; Nell Dunn for letters to Mary St Clair-Erskine; Valerie Eliot for letters to T. S. Eliot; Mark Girouard for letters to Blanche Girouard and Dick Girouard; Ron Gurney for letters to Samuel Gurney; Hamish Hamilton archives for a letter to Hamish Hamilton; Lady Harrod for letters to Sir Roy Harrod; Dacre Harvey for letters to Mrs Simpson Harvey; Lady Dorothy Heber-Percy for letters to Gerald Berners; Lord Hemphill for letters to Emily Villiers-Stuart; Houghton Library, Harvard University, USA, for letters to Sir William Rothenstein; Huntington Library, Pasadena, California, USA, for letters to Oliver Stonor and Patrick Balfour; The

Trustees of the Edward James Foundation, West Dean, Sussex, for letters to Edward James; King's College, Cambridge, for letters to Anne Barnes, Anthony Barnes, George Barnes and Clive Bell; King's College, London, for letters to Arthur Bryant and Mrs A. Bryant; McFarlin Library, University of Tulsa, Oklahoma, USA, for letters to Cyril Connolly; McPherson Library, University of Victoria, British Columbia, Canada for letters to Cecil Beaton, Bess Betjemann, John Edward Bowle, Robert Byron, Randolph Churchill, William Clonmore, Hubert de Cronin Hastings, H. S. Rogers, Camilla Russell, the *Sheffield Star*, the Society of Authors, Sir John Summerson, *The Times*, the *Times Literary Supplement* and Ward, Lock & Co.; Raymond Mander and John Mitchenson Theatre Collection for a letter to Laurie Lister; Merton College, Oxford, for letters to Sir Max Beerbohm; Modern Records Centre, Warwick University, for letters to Sir Leslie Scott; Lady Moyne for letters to Bryan Guinness; Mugar Memorial Library, University of Boston, USA, for letters to Frank O'Connor; John Murray Publishers for letters to Jock Murray; The Trustees of the National Library of Scotland, Edinburgh, for a letter to Lady Kinross; The National Trust for letters to Lady Mander and Charles Wade; Thomas Pakenham for letters to Edward and Christine Longford; Pattee Library, Pennsylvania State University, USA, for a letter to Professor Bickersteth; Pembroke College, Oxford, for a letter to Mr R. B. McCallum; Patrick Perry for letters to Lionel Perry; Myfanwy Piper for letters to John Piper; Harry Ransom Humanities Research Center, University of Texas, Austin, USA, for letters to Edmund Blunden, Elizabeth Bowen, F. Compton Mackenzie, J. C. Trewin and Sir Hugh Walpole; Rare Books Collection, University of Buffalo, USA, for letters to Charles Abbott and Geoffrey Grigson; RIBA Library, London, for letters to Sir Giles Gilbert Scott and H. S. Goodhart-Rendel; Susannah Robinson for a letter to Nancy Mitford; Bruce Shand for letters to P. Morton Shand and Sybil Shand; Special Collections Library, Rare Book and Manuscript Library, Columbia University, USA, for letters to Edmund Blunden; Special Collections Library, University of Durham, for letters to William Plomer; Anthony Symondson SJ for letters to Sir Ninian Comper; David Synnott for letters to Pierce Synnott; Tate Gallery Archives, London, for letters to Paul Nash and Jane and Kenneth Clark; Mary Taylor for letters to Geoffrey Taylor; Trinity College, Dublin, for letters to Frank Gallagher; University College, London, for letters to George Orwell; Wadham College, Oxford, for letters to Maurice Bowra; and West Sussex Record Office for letters to W. Hussey

and the following for their own letters:

Richard Buckle, Patrick Cullinan, John Foster-White, Harman Grisewood, Gregory Halliday, Kenneth Harrison, Lady Harrod, Rupert Hart-Davis, Gerard Irvine, Ron Liddiard, the Revd Paul Miller, Lady Mosley, Diana Peel, Stuart Piggott, Myfanwy Piper, Anthony Powell, Roland Pym, Ruth Webb and Miss Whitaker.

Especial thanks to:

Elizabeth Bolton of Boston University Library, USA; Sally Brown and staff at the British Library, London; John Byrne of Bertram Rota; Mr Cox of King's College, Cambridge; Jill Cronan, Peter Beecham and Jill Kerr of English Heritage; Gillian Furlong of University College Library, London; Olive Geddes of the National Library of Scotland; Vincent Giroud of Yale University Library, USA; Colin Harris of the Bodleian Library, Oxford; Sarah Hodson of the Huntington Library, Pasadena, California; Sidney Huttner of Tulsa University, USA; Brian Kennedy of the Irish National Gallery, Dublin; Sharon Kusnoki of the Edward James Foundation; Peter Lewis of All Souls Library, Oxford; Angela Mace and the staff at the RIBA Library, London; Ian Maxted of Exeter Library; Michael Meredith of Eton College Library; Virginia Murray of John Murray Archives; Kate O'Brien of King's College Library, London; Stuart O'Seanor of Trinity College Library, Dublin; Chris Petter and the staff at the McPherson Library, University of Victoria, British Columbia, Canada; Miss Piddock of Lincoln College Library, Oxford; Mr Quinn at Collins Archives; Miss E. M. Rainey of the University of Durham Library; Louise Ray at the Tate Gallery Archives; Janet Seely of the Council for the Care of Churches; David Sutton of the University of Reading for his Location Register of English Literary Manuscripts and Letters; H. J. R. Wing, Assistant Librarian Christ Church Library, Oxford; the staff at the London Library; the staff at Marlborough Public Library; and the staff of University of Texas Library, USA.

I would also like to thank the following for their time, wisdom and moral support:

Mrs Abbott, Lady Aitken, Tim and Patricia Arlott, Julian and Isobel Bannerman, Hercules Belville, Paul Betjeman, John Bodley, Jackie Booth, Roger Bowdler, Alice Boyd, Lady Mary Clive, Colin and Niddy Cook, Jilly Cooper, Alison Craddock, Gladys Dearlove, Mabel Dearlove, Debo Devonshire, Terence de Vere White, Nell Dunn, Geoffrey Dutton, Father Philip Dyson, Miss Eagle, Madeleine Edmeed, James Fergusson, Charlotte Fidler, John Foster-White, David Fraser-Jenkins, Mark Girouard, Victoria Glendinning, John Grey, Pearl Groves, Dacre Harvey, Jools Holland, Ian Johnson, Brian Kennedy, Mary Killen, Robert and Helen Kime, Paul Knapp-Fisher, James Lees-Milne, Amabel Lindsay, Christopher Logue, Lisa Moylett, the late Lord Moyne, Robin Muir, the late Jock Murray, John Murray, Claire Murray-Threipland, Andrew Parker Bowles, Patrick Perry, Bill Peterson, Stuart Piggott, Anthony and Lady Violet Powell, Alan Powers, Geoff Renard, Dr Robb-Smith, Jacob and Serena Rothschild, Tony Snowdon, Florrie Sprules, Stan Sprules, Dawn Squires, Terence Stamp, Richard Stroud, the late John Summerson, Mary Taylor, Rosie Tullier, Judy Urquhart, Caroline Watson, Queenie Weaver, Miss Webb, Lord Weinstock,

Michael White, Miss Joan Whitaker, Freda Widdowson, Bill Wilkins, Biddy Wilson and Margaret Wintringham

and the following for inordinate kindness:

Alan Bell for reading the proofs; Deborah Bosley for star research; George Chowdharay-Best for his lively scholarship; Maurice Craig for reading and correcting the Irish section; Michael Holroyd for encouraging me; Nickie Johnson, Grand Mistress of the Word Processor, for her secretarial genius; Desmond Fitzgerald for his Irish expertise; Tracy Leeming for her extraordinary tenacity in transcribing and cataloguing; Ron Liddiard for his Berkshire memories; Julian Loyd for Irish detection; David Lycett Green for cataloguing incoming letters; Eve MacSweeney for her friendship; Lucy Manningham-Buller for her generous help; Douglas Matthews for compiling the index; Mary O'Donovan, my copy-editor, and the team at Methuen, for confidence-giving professionalism; Myfanwy Piper for inspiration; Alan Pryce-Jones for solving mysteries; Joan Ryan for three weeks' scholarly assistance; John Saumarez Smith for knowing so much; Alexandra Shulman, my editress at *Vogue*, for giving me a sabbatical; Neil Somerville of BBC Archives for kind help; Nick Startin and Helen Hawkins for keeping me fit; and Nell Stroud for enlightened research.

My undying thanks to:

the ever-patient and kind Geoffrey Strachan, my editor, who steered me through the home straits with a calm, firm hand; Billa Harrod and Gerard Irvine for being grilled relentlessly and for reading the typescript; Mark Amory, Colin Leach and Diana Mosley for reading the galleys; Richard Ingrams for constant encouragement from the beginning and for correcting and commenting on my text; Desmond Elliott for everything; and Rupert, my husband, and David, John, Endellion, Imogen and Lucy, my children, for putting up with me.

Finally, thanks are due to the following for providing photographs of themselves and others (all photographs not credited come from Betjeman family archives):

Anthony Barnes for 16a, 16b, 16d and 24; William Burlington, photographer, for 1c, 2a, 7a and 22a; Camera Press Ltd for 10b, 14c, 14e and 15d; Mrs D. Cleverdon for 15b; Patrick Cullinan for 16c; Nell Dunn for 9a; John Dutton for 3b; Charles Fergusson for 9d, 10c and 19c; Lady Harrod for 11d and 14d; Lady Howe for 12a; Hulton Deutsch Collection Ltd for 13d; Gerard Irvine for 14a and 14b; Lady Mosley for 10e; Lady Moyne for 9c; Virginia Murray for 12c; the National Portrait Gallery for 12b; Patrick Perry for 10d; Myfanwy Piper for 17; Alan Pryce-Jones for 9b; Christopher Sykes for 16e; David Synnott for 10f and 11b; Mrs G. Taylor for 15a; and Eleanor Wilson and Mr and Mrs A. C. Crichton for 20a.

Illustrations

═══════

Part-title illustrations by JB:

1 JB's bear, Archibald Ormsby-Gore.
2 Pentire Head, Polzeath, Cornwall.
3 The Mitford sisters.
4 Penelope before she married JB.
5 PB in the kitchen.
6 Barns near Uffington.
7 PB at Dunsany Castle.
8 'Colonel' Kolkhorst.
9 The Old Rectory, Farnborough.
10 South Church, Aberdeen.

Plate sections photographs:

1a and 1b JB's parents, Bess and Ernie Betjemann.
1c Number 31 West Hill, Highgate.
2a Number 53 Church Street (now Old Church Street).
2b Undertown, Trebetherick, Cornwall.
3a JB in 1925, the year he went up to Magdalen.
3b Magdalen College Dramatic Society, 1927.
4a Lord Alfred Douglas, Nancy Mitford and JB at Brighton, c.1930.
4b Colonel and Mrs Dugdale and friends at Sezincote, c.1930.
5a Philip and Hester Chetwode, JB's parents-in-law.
5b PB in the garden at Uffington with Kitty Fritz, 1934.
6 PB in India, 1933.
7a Garrards Farm, Uffington, Berkshire.
7b Gerald Berners painting PB and her Arab gelding, Moti, at Faringdon.
8 PB driving Moti through Uffington in the dog cart.

9a Mary St Clair-Erskine (later Dunn).   9b Alan Pryce-Jones.
9c Bryan Guinness (later Moyne).
9d 'Cracky' William Clonmore (later Wicklow).
10a Archibald Ormsby-Gore and Jumbo.   10b Maurice Bowra.

John Betjeman – A Chronology

1906 to 1951

1906	Born Highgate, London, 28 August, son of Ernest and Mabel Bess (née Dawson) Betjemann.
1911	Byron House Montessori School, Highgate.
1915	Highgate Junior School.
1917	Dragon School, Oxford.
1920	Marlborough College, Wiltshire.
1925	Magdalen College, Oxford.
1928	Schoolmaster at Thorpe House Prep School, Gerrards Cross, for one term.
1929	Private Secretary to Sir Horace Plunkett for two months.
1929–30	Schoolmaster at Heddon Court Prep School, East Barnet.
1930–34	Assistant Editor, *Architectural Review*.
1931	*Mount Zion* (The James Press).
1932	Conceives *Shell Guides* for Shell Oil Company. *Cornwall Illustrated* (Shell). Lifetime involvement with BBC begins.
1933	*Ghastly Good Taste* (Chapman and Hall). Marries Penelope Chetwode, 29 July.
1934	Moves to Garrards Farm, Uffington, Berkshire.
1934–35	Film critic to *Evening Standard*.
1935–39	Works in Shell Publicity Department, Shell-Mex House.
1936	*Devon: A Shell Guide* (The Architectural Press).
1937	*Continual Dew* (John Murray). Son Paul born.
1938	*An Oxford University Chest* (John Miles).
1939	*Antiquarian Prejudice* (Hogarth Press).
1940	Works for Ministry of Information. *Old Lights for New Chancels* (John Murray).
1941	United Kingdom Press Attaché, Dublin, Ireland.
1942	*Vintage London* (Collins). Daughter Candida born.
1943	Returns to Uffington from Ireland. *English Cities and Small Towns* (William Collins).

	Resumes job with Ministry of Information.
1944	Serves with Publications Branch of the Admiralty in Bath. *English Scottish and Welsh Landscape* with Geoffrey Taylor and illustrated by John Piper (Frederick Muller).
1944–51	Regular book reviewer for *Daily Herald*.
1945	Moves to Farnborough, Wantage, Berkshire. Works for British Council in Oxford and Blenheim. *New Bats in Old Belfries* (John Murray).
1946–48	Secretary of Oxford Preservation Trust three days a week.
1946–78	Serves on the Oxford Diocesan Advisory Committee.
1947	*Slick, But Not Streamlined* (Doubleday, New York).
1947–50	Edits *Watergate Children's Classics* for Sidgwick & Jackson.
1948	*Selected Poems* (John Murray). *Murray's Buckinghamshire Architectural Guide*.
1948–63	Serves on the London Diocesan Advisory Committee.
1949	*Murray's Berkshire Architectural Guide*.
1949–54	Literary Adviser/Editor to *Time and Tide*.
1950	*Collected Poems* (John Murray).
1951	Moves to The Mead, Wantage, Berkshire. *The English Scene* (Cambridge University Press). *Shropshire: A Shell Guide* (Faber and Faber) with John Piper.

Brief chronology of major works
1951 to 1984

(Book titles are in italic, television film titles in quotation marks)

1952	*First and Last Loves*
1954	*Poems in the Porch* *A Few Late Chrysanthemums*
1956	*The English Town in the Last Hundred Years*
1958	*Collins' Guide to English Parish Churches* *John Betjeman's Collected Poems*
1959	*Altar and Pew* 'John Betjeman: A Poet in London'
1960	QUEEN'S GOLD MEDAL FOR POETRY (FOR *COLLECTED POEMS*) COMMANDER, ORDER OF THE BRITISH EMPIRE *Summoned by Bells*
1962	*Collected Poems* (with additional poems) *A Ring of Bells*

1964   *Cornwall: A Shell Guide*
1965   *The City of London Churches*
1966   *High and Low*
      'Journey to Bethlehem'
1967   'The Picture Theatre'
1968   'Contrasts'
1969   KNIGHT COMMANDER, ORDER OF THE BRITISH EMPIRE
      Victorian and Edwardian London
      'Bird's Eye View'
1970   *Ten Wren Churches*
      'Four with Betjeman'
1971   *Victorian and Edwardian Oxford*
1972   POET LAUREATE, 10 OCTOBER
      Victorian and Edwardian Brighton
      London's Historic Railway Stations
      A Pictorial History of English Architecture
      'Betjeman in Australia'
1973   'Metroland'
1974   'A Passion for Churches'
1976   'Summoned by Bells'
1983   'Time with Betjeman'
1984   DIED, TREBETHERICK, 19 MAY

One:

Deeply I loved thee, 31 West Hill!

═══════

1906 to 1926

When the great bell
BOOMS over the Portland stone urn, and
From the carved cedar wood
Rises the odour of incense,
I SIT DOWN
In St Botolph Bishopsgate Churchyard
And wait for the spirit of my grandfather
Toddling along from the Barbican.

'City'

JB's strong and deep-rooted affinity with the city lasted his lifetime. During the late eighteenth century his forebears, who were cabinet makers, had emigrated from Holland to the East End of London. In the 1820s, George Betjeman, JB's great-grandfather, had founded the family firm which produced beautifully worked writing desks, dressing cases and cabinets in workshops in Aldersgate. JB's grandfather, John, brought the firm into the limelight by inventing the Tantalus, an elegant decanter carrier with a lockable cage-like cover. It became an essential addition to middle-class Victorian homes because it prevented the servants from pilfering the drink.

According to the parish records in St Botolph's, Bishopsgate, JB's great-great-grandfather, George, who died in 1813, had usually spelt his surname with one 'n', but by the time the Tantalus took off there was a craze for all things German and adding the extra 'n' was seen to lend cachet to the trading name. Hence JB's father, Ernest Betjemann, always spelt his name thus and when he took over, both the business and its name, Betjemann and Sons, were well established.

Ernest oversaw the new workshops and showroom in the Pentonville Road, Islington, where ever more elaborate artefacts were produced. Malachite and ebony bookends; tortoiseshell and gilt photograph frames and onyx ashtrays, sold at Asprey's of Bond Street and J. C. Vickery of Regent Street; and special orders for larger and larger dressing cases from fabulously rich Indian Maharajahs, came rolling in during Ernest's time.

Ernest had been brought up in the respectable district of Highbury, expressly built for middle-class city workers and small-time tradesmen. In 1902 in St Saviour's, Aberdeen Park, he married a local Highbury girl, Mabel 'Bess' Dawson, the daughter of an artificial flower maker. At first they lived at 52 Parliament Hill Mansions, Highgate, where JB was born on 28 August 1906. Soon afterwards they moved half a mile away to 31 West Hill where, out of his three London childhood homes, JB was happiest. Later the family moved to Church Street in Chelsea, which he never liked, but which excited my socially aspiring paternal grandmother, who enjoyed hovering on the edge of artistic circles.

JB's own evocation of his early life, in his blank verse autobiography, *Summoned by Bells*, is unsurpassable. The abiding passions to which he was true for the rest of his life were crystallized in those years. He loved London where he was born and brought up, he loved Cornwall where he holidayed with the utmost regularity. He loved poetry from as early as he could remember. (His mother read it to him and his father encouraged him to write it.) He loved hot buttered toast, preferably slightly burnt, because Hannah Wallis, the old-fashioned family servant and JB's emotional mainstay, provided mountains of it when he returned from school, and he read his poetry to her while he ate it. (My grandmother, Bess, remembered how she found JB reading poetry to Hannah Wallis, who was in the lavatory with the door locked.) He loved church bells because 'lying in bed of a late summer evening I remember hearing the bells ring out from St Anne's, Highgate Rise – the church where I was christened – they poured their sound deep and sorrowful, over the chestnuts of the Burdett-Coutts estate, through the hornbeam leaves I could see from bed.'[1] He loved paintings from the time when his father had taken him to the Tate Gallery and he had stared in wonder at Frank Bramley's 'Hopeless Dawn'.

He loved architecture the more because his housemaster, Gerald 'Tortoise' Haynes, took him on bicycle trips from the Dragon School in Oxford to discover Norman, Early English and Decorated churches in forgotten villages. From seeing the precise perfection wrought by the skilled artisans in his father's cabinet-making factory, he loved beautifully made objects like clocks and musical boxes. He loved girls with freckles and blue eyes like Mary Bouman who was his next-door neighbour in Highgate. He loved girls with short hair and fringes, girls with turned-up noses and sulky looks and girls whose skin was covered in a soft blonde down, after falling first for his schoolmate at Byron House Kindergarten School, Peggy Purey-Cust, and then for sporty Eton-cropped Biddy Walsham on holiday in Trebetherick. (All the women he idolized had one, or a combination, of these features: my mother; his secretary, Jill Menzies; Myfanwy Piper; my schoolfriend, Sarah Fox Pitt; the Duchess of Kent; Ginnie James.)

He was one of the few people I have known who actually welcomed all forms of creepy-crawly wherever they appeared. He had loved centipedes, beetles, spiders and woodlice ever since he first lay on lawns in Trebetherick and watched them at eye level among the blades of grass or gently lifted a large stone to find another world. He loved being driven very fast, from the time when as a boy he travelled down to Cornwall with his father who cherished his motor cars. (Once, in the sixties, on a very short stretch of road between Wantage and Faringdon when we were in no particular hurry, he said to me, 'See if you can do a hundred,' and I did.) He loved the London Underground and indeed all trains from an early age and would study maps and timetables for hours. In his early teens he would travel all day across London and into the suburbs with his Dragon School friend, Ronald Hughes-Wright. He loved his bear Archibald Ormsby-Gore quite simply because he had and still has a strong presence, which made JB feel utterly safe. His mother had first animated Archie by moving his head up and down while he talked. He was completely dependable. One of JB's maxims was that, unlike people, 'Art never lets you down.' Neither did Archie. 'He's the one tangible thing that doesn't let me down: never loses his temper, doesn't have to go to the lav. He's there whatever happens. . . .'[2]

As a child JB was ultimately happiest in his own company, for doubt about his fellow beings inevitably crept into that sunny Highgate life. His parents argued eternally and he was beaten up mercilessly by arch bullies on the way back from Highgate Junior School. He said later, 'I learned a lot from that tough London boys' school. I learned how to get round people, how to lie, how to show off just enough to attract attention but not so much as to attract unwelcome attention, how to bribe bullies with sweets (four ounces a penny in those days) – and I learned my first lessons in mistrusting my fellow beings.'[3] His feeling of abandonment when the family next door went abroad was absolute. 'I think the saddest moment of my life, as numbing as any subsequent loss, was the time when Bill, Mary and Betty [Bouman] left the district. I was about seven years old. The pavements outside our houses on West Hill, the Heath, our little gardens seemed empty for ever.'[4] He was also saddened when a certain and much-heralded Miss Usher, 'swarthy and in Girl Guide-y sort of clothes', who had arrived to stay for a holiday in Cornwall, had been nice to all his Trebetherick friends, but not to him.

He later discovered that she had not warmed to him because she thought him 'a common little boy'.[5]

Cornwall, however, was usually the healer of all wounds and continued to be so throughout JB's life. Joan Larkworthy (now Kunzer), his 'earliest girl chum', was like a sister to JB. 'I can see him now, arriving that first summer in his little piqué suit at the Haven Guest House in Trebetherick which was run by my nanny's parents, the Buses. I was five and he was four and we played the most extraordinary games and dares. I remember we all went down to the golf course and made John go into the church and ring the bell. Then there were two old girls who lived in Trebetherick called the Miss Poledons. They were daughters of a retired admiral. We used to go round chanting:

> In a dum diddle dum diddle dum dum hat
> Round as a pancake, squashed and flat
> Sat Rotary Rhoda Poledon.

'John forced one of the Miss Poledons to go through the cave at Lundy Bay and she said, "What a disgusting aroma," which made us laugh like drains. Once when he was about fifteen he played in the Trebetherick cricket team against St Minver. He arrived looking very lumpy and peculiar. I remarked on his appearance and he said, "I'm filled with newspaper inside because I'm so frightened of getting hit." '[6]

Ernest and Bess Betjemann made friends with old A. E. 'Hum' Lynam and his wife, May, who had a house at Trebetherick called Cliff Bank and whose brother, Charles Cotterill 'Skipper' Lynam, was headmaster of the Dragon preparatory school in Oxford. Their children, Joc and Audrey, became JB's friends and together with the rest of the Trebetherick gang – Joan and Roland Oakley, Vasey, Ralph and Alistair Adams, John and Biddy Walsham, Joan and Tom Larkworthy, Phoebe and Alan Stokes – they remained close to him through his life. He made them all laugh. He used to lie down by the side of the road in a crumpled position with his mouth open, to see how many passers-by would stop and see if he was dead or not. It was through the happy acquaintance with the Lynams that JB came to board at the Dragon from 1917 to 1920. He burgeoned there; after his initial homesickness he felt safe and happy, cocooned by the avuncular masters. His father encouraged his poetic tendencies: 'Have a shot at getting a poem in the *Draconian* this term,' he wrote (5 May 1919). JB felt inordinately close to Hum and his wife May; long summer holidays spent together in Trebetherick had created a special bond which continued down the generations. Hum gave him a greater faith in God. JB felt he could say anything to Hum and wrote a poem which was printed in the *Draconian* (the school magazine where his earliest published poems and prose pieces appeared).

> Hum and May went out one day
> On a motor-bike painted vermilion;
> Hum was the nut of the latest cut
> And May was the girl on the pillion.

His prowess at acting in both Gilbert and Sullivan operas and Shakespeare plays was openly acknowledged. After his bit parts in *Henry V*, a review in the *Draconian* read, '. . . Having beheld him manufacture out of two small parts, the Earl of Cambridge and the King of France, two separate, distinct and perfect gems of character acting . . . I can't give higher praise than by saying that he ought to play Bottom . . .'

In 1920 JB left the safe cradle of the Dragon and experienced the cold-shower shock of a public school, at Marlborough College. As an only child, he found his relationship with the other boys undeniably difficult at first and his increasing feeling of remoteness from his parents may have made him retreat into a shell and thus become a suitable target for bullying. What *did* happen at Marlborough was that he developed an extraordinary love of the place and the surrounding country and he took great comfort from it, not only then but always. If he had hated his school as much as he later made out, he would not have wanted to return. JB returned throughout his life.

As a family we always lived within striking distance of Marlborough, first at Uffington, then at the tiny village of Farnborough and finally at Wantage. We often visited Christopher Hughes, JB's old Marlborough art master, for whom he retained a lifelong affection. At the Dragon School in Oxford it had been Gerald 'Tortoise' Haynes who had won JB's devoted admiration and who had taken him to look at churches and taught him about flowers and trees. JB dedicated his book *First and Last Loves* to the memory of Tortoise who, he said, had 'first opened my eyes to architecture'. Hughes was the same sort of inspirational teacher and imbued JB with an ever stronger interest in his surroundings. JB's enthusiasm for sketching expeditions was kindled both by his father, who was a good painter, and by Hughes.

When I was a child, JB taught me, as Hughes had taught him, how to effect a cloudy sky by blotting the still wet blue wash with a rolled-up handkerchief. We often went on sketching expeditions. Sometimes we sat on the bridge at Ramsbury near Marlborough, to which JB had been taken as a schoolboy, and tried to draw the beautiful red brick Renaissance manor house in the park beyond. Years later JB recalled, 'No words can express my longing to get inside this house, I think the mystery of its winding drive gave me a respect for the system of hereditary landowning which I have never shaken off. . . .'[7]

In retrospect, some of JB's Marlborough contemporaries remember him as set apart from other boys and somehow different. Though time has doubtless exaggerated this image, he was indeed exceptional in one respect. He was the only boy of his year who took his own set of golf clubs to school and often played on the downs course above the town. He played with his father in the holidays on a regular basis and was better than average for his age. At Trebetherick JB and his gang established their own golf course around the cliffs. Ralph Adams was Treasurer, Audrey Lynam Secretary and JB President. His name appeared on the tickets issued to anyone who came to play. While being hopeless at every other outdoor game throughout his life (except perhaps croquet), he remained a dab hand at golf until well into his fifties.

All through his time at Marlborough JB affected many different poses and succeeded in annoying masters and boys alike with his clever repartee. He found it confoundingly simple to write parodies and could roll off verses at the drop of a hat. 'In those years, the 1920s,' wrote JB, 'games were very highly respected at the school, and a group of those who didn't like them and who longed for an exotic life, produced a magazine called *The Heretick*.'[8] There was open war between the hearties and the aesthetes and perhaps for the first time JB understood the power of the press. His first poem published there was a satire on the increasing breed of 'new country' folk. Gert and Elsie's cottage boasted:

> . . . rustic furniture, no bath, no drains,
> But still it is *so* countrified. A friend
> Can sleep upon the sofa. And they eat
> Off pottery (hand painted). Oh! the pains
> And saving for their game of let's pretend.

JB also wrote a lot for private consumption. Mrs Rossiter, who is now ninety, was a dormitory maid in B2 House when JB was there. 'I remember him as if it was yesterday – he'd say, "Mary, I've written a poem for you, be sure to read it, it's in my chest of drawers."'[9]

His early enthusiasms became his life's grand passions. On 27

November 1923 JB read a paper on 'The Victorians' to the Marlborough Art Society. He used to love spending time in a little-used section of the Marlborough library which contained the leather-bound run of Alfred H. Miles's *Poets and Poetry of the Nineteenth Century*. The memory of these volumes, with their short biographies, clear criticisms and selected examples of the poets, remained with him always. His love for the obscure, which had begun at the Dragon School, blossomed at Marlborough. At the Dragon his great influence had been the poet Charles Dibdin, whose style was echoed in JB's poetry across the decades. At Marlborough it was Lord Alfred Douglas's poetry which excited him. His interest resulted in a correspondence with the poet. JB's father discovered this; he was forbidden ever to be in touch with Douglas again. (In the late thirties 'Bosie' came to stay at Uffington, sad and old with a huge, bulbous, red nose – his past notoriety forgotten.) Apart from his warning about the likes of Alfred Douglas, JB's father also advised him on the value of money 'and its importance to your happiness. I do not mean that money means happiness – it doesn't and has but little to do with it – but it is sure certain that money ill spent, wasted or *over* spent is unhappiness,' he wrote (26 September 1923).[10]

JB's showmanship also began to emerge at Marlborough and by the end of his time there he was confident in his ability to amuse. On his last Prize Day in the June of 1926 he acted as Lady Teazle in *The School for Scandal*, to great acclaim.

JB fostered one or two mild enmities at the time, most notably with his classics teacher, Gidney, but he also made friendships for life. The Blunt brothers, Wilfrid, Christopher and Anthony, remained his friends, but closer still were his *Heretick* collaborators, the historian, John Edward Bowle; Philip Harding who spent every Christmas with us in his declining years; and lastly tall, thin Arthur Elton, who became an internationally acclaimed pioneer of the documentary film. JB described him as 'one of my greatest friends. . . . I remember being delighted at his having such a lot of initials and surprised at hearing he was the heir to a baronetcy and a famous country house. He had always seemed to me so quiet and gentle, and in my middle-class way I supposed persons such as he would be proud and grand. He was a modest man.'[11]

1. JB, 'Childhood Days' (BBC radio talk, 16 July 1950).
2. JB, Susan Barnes interview, 'Betjeman I Bet Your Racket Brings You in a Pretty Packet', *Sunday Times Magazine* (30 January 1972).

3. JB, 'Childhood Days'.
4. JB, 'Childhood Days'.
5. JB, *Summoned by Bells* (1960).
6. Joan Kunzer, CLG interview (1992).
7. JB, Preface to *Ghastly Good Taste* (1970).
8. JB, tribute to Sir Arthur Elton in *North Somerset Mercury* (1973).
9. Mrs Rossiter, CLG interview (1992).
10. JB's papers, University of Victoria, British Columbia.
11. JB, Tribute to Sir Arthur Elton.

Sent to Mrs Grant

PEACE

PART I

I was a quiet eve when I went out
No people to see nor a call nor a shout
I thought of the places I had not seen
As I sat upon the village green
I sat & listend to the church bell chime
And thought in my head discomforting time
 O God be with me
 Yet wretched I may be
And I sat by the village stocks
And saw the waves dash over the rocks
And the sunset made a blood red sky
And I looked at the clouds that were up O so
high

PART II

I went home in the stillnes of the night
And air the moon was giving me light

J. Betjeman

August 23rd

Written at 9 years,
Greg Halledy & Ayral.
Corner guernsed · 1915?

To Gregory Halliday   29 Radnor Walk
20 July 1975   London SW3

Dear Mr Halliday,
I was so sad to hear in your kind letter to me on July 19th of the death of
your uncle Godfrey [Grant]. He was very kind to me when I was about
seven or eight and gave me the first second-hand book which started my
collection. It was Borlase *Antiquities of Cornwall*. It gave me a taste for
the antique which I never lost. I so well remember as a little boy
walking with Godfrey and his sister to Barton and seeing an ivy-
covered ruin, Compton Castle, and also glimpsing an awesome and
dark street called Pimlico which I equated with the slums of Kentish
Town in London. I thank you so much for the childish piece about
peace which you have sent for me to look at. It is just like the stuff that
comes to me in the post. I must have thought that rhyming was poetry.
I am still conscious of the value of quiet.
  Yours sincerely, John Betjeman

The marble workers, Messrs Harry Grant & Sons, of Watcombe, near Torquay, made
inlaid mosaics in floral and other designs for G. Betjemann & Sons. The two firms'
association stretched back for three generations over sixty years. From an early age, JB
often visited the Grant family at their house, Dunmow, in St Marychurch on the edge of
Torquay, with his father, Ernest, who was a director of Grants. He loved the
monkey-puzzle tree in the garden. He sent postcards to Mrs Grant and to her son,
Godfrey, whom he much admired. In 1915 he sent one of the first poems he ever wrote
to Mrs Grant and it was returned to him sixty years later by Mr Halliday, a nephew of
Godfrey Grant.

To Edward Rimbaut Dibdin   B House
                                                   Marlborough College
16 November 1924   Wilts

Dear Sir,
Please excuse the intrusion and impertinence of a complete stranger and
mere schoolboy, but I've found from *Who's Who* that you have written
on Charles Dibdin. I wonder, very much, whether you could give me
some information about a poem by his son, Charles Isaac Mungo.
When I was at my private school I had a book called, I think, *Comic Tales
and Lyrical Fancies* or, at any rate, something like that, by Charles

Dibdin Junior. (The cover had written inside it 'with the author's most affectionate attentions to his dear and dutiful daughter, Mary'.) It was very plain, in boards, with no memorable illustrations and much of the verse – and in fact the style and publication of the book – reminded me of George Colman's comic poems. I lost this book and have naturally never been able to obtain a copy again; but what impressed me about the book was a poem at the end of it call'd 'The Maniac's Funeral'. It was excessively morbid and in heroic couplets, and quite worthy of one of the *Cypress Wreath* albums of about 1840; at the time however I thought it was awfully good and as I am going to read a paper (after the manner of all persons who parade their education before 'Literary Societies') on the minor poets of that Regency Period, I wondered if you could let me have a copy of this poem – 'The Maniac's Funeral'.

I have found little anywhere, save in theatre histories, of Charles Dibdin Junior – although plenty about the elder and Thomas (not Frognall) Dibdin – and any information about his poetic or dramatic merit would interest me very much. Of course, all he wrote may be quite worthless – it is a long time since I read that book – and his verses at the end of T. Dibdin's edition of his father's songs are not anything out of the ordinary. I hope I am not troubling you and please pardon apparent pedantry.

Yours sincerely, John Betjeman

PS Is C. D. Jnr's novel *Isn't It Odd* good?

E.R.D., 'literateur, artist, art expert', had published a biography of Charles Dibdin in 1901.

Charles Dibdin Junior's book was *Comic Tales and Lyrical Fancies* (Whitaker, London, 1825). It includes 'The Maniac's Funeral', which describes a widow's grief at her mad husband's demise:

> The portal open'd wide – where madness sits,
> 'Bays to the moon', or churns, in moody fits;
> A coffin came; age made the bearers slow;
> One weeping woman all the train of woe! . . .
>
> She saw him wooing her consenting smile;
> Then heard him raving with demoniac bile –
> Saw him a corpse, his madness all forgot,
> Felt all her loss, and shudder'd at her lot . . .

Two:

Oxford May mornings!
When the prunus bloomed

═══════

June 1926 to November 1928

The wind among the elms, the echoing stairs,
The quarters, chimed across the quiet quad
From Magdalen tower and neighbouring turret-clocks,
Gave eighteenth-century splendour to my state.
Privacy after years of public school;
Dignity after years of none at all –
First college rooms, a kingdom of my own:
What words of mine can tell my gratitude?

Summoned by Bells

In October 1925 JB went to Magdalen College, Oxford. His two English tutors were the modest and self-deprecating Revd J. M. 'Thompie' Thompson, whom JB loved; and C. S. Lewis, whom he didn't. The latter had no time for aesthetic idlers, nor for jokes. He was particularly annoyed when he was caught out by thinking JB had written a good essay: 'I soon discovered [the essay] to be a pure fake, for he knew nothing about the work when we began to talk. I wish I could get rid of the idle prig.'[1] JB's reciprocal animosity lasted for years after his university days and he later wrote to Thompie (1 January 1935) about Lewis, 'I must get him psycho-analysed out of me.'

Almost immediately on arrival, JB joined the Oxford University Dramatic Society, whose members at that time included Gyles Isham, Emlyn Williams and Peter Fleming. By the following summer he was a well-established character. 'Dear Betchy,' wrote John Fernald, a producer of the OUDS, later Principal of the Royal Academy of Dramatic Art, 'You've been cast for Milieu in Comaye's play *New Country* and for Ford in Denys' play *The Collector*. Will you *please* turn up for rehearsals . . . As I am (grotesquely) producing I want to make *sense* of you.'[2]

JB made his mark and it didn't take long for him to be singled out by Maurice Bowra, the legendary Dean (later Warden) of Wadham College, famous for his brilliant conversation. Bowra recalled that when he first met JB, just after he had come up, he was 'talking fluently about half-forgotten authors of the nineteenth century – Sir Henry

Taylor, Ebenezer Elliott, Philip James Bailey'.[3] Bowra immediately
saw how funny JB was, while JB wrote that Oxford of the late twenties,
'which was when I first came up, seemed to me to be divided, as far as
undergraduates were concerned, between aesthetes and hearties. I was
an aesthete. There would have been no hearties at the parties which I
attended. Maurice's were always dinner parties . . . His most endear-
ing quality was his power to build one up in one's own estimation. He
did this by listening and either agreeing or suggesting a similar train of
thought. In the same way he took one's own troubles on his shoulders.
Firmly and kindly he separated me from those he regarded as
unsuitable.'[4]

JB was also 'discovered' by the notorious 'Colonel' Kolkhorst, the
university Reader in Spanish, who entertained galaxies of undergraduates on Sunday mornings in his rooms in Beaumont Street. He was
called 'The Colonel' because he was so utterly unlike one. His rooms in
Beaumont Street smelt of mice, chicken soup and dogs. To the tune of
'John Peel' JB sang, and everyone else joined in:

> D'ye ken Kolkhorst in his artful parlour
> Handing out the drinks at his Sunday morning gala
> Some get sherry and some get marsala –
> With his arts and his crafts in the corner![5]

Bowra and the Colonel, who disliked each other and were rivals at
collecting bright young undergraduates, were formative figures
throughout JB's life. He both loved and admired them and perhaps
most important of all he laughed ceaselessly with them. As children we
often visited Yarnton Manor outside Oxford, where the Colonel lived
until the 1950s. The large Jacobean and Victorian house was heavily
curtained and at lunch-time it always felt like a nightclub. It was stuffed
with oriental carpets, both on the floor and on the walls. 'Miss Otis
Regrets' rang out from a wind-up gramophone. (After his death in 1954
all his letters and papers were destroyed by relations, who deemed
some of them indecent.)

Through the Colonel and Bowra's gatherings and through his
Marlburian friend, Philip Harding's elder brother, Archie, JB met
many of the friends he remained close to for the rest of his life, including
Kenneth Clark, Anthony Powell, John Sparrow, 'Cracky' William
Clonmore, Patrick Balfour, Alan Pryce-Jones, Hamish Erskine, John
Murray, Mark Ogilvie-Grant, Michael Rosse, Cyril Connolly, Chris-
topher Sykes, Basil Ava, Harold Acton, John Dugdale, Evelyn
Waugh, John Sutro, Christopher Hollis and Douglas Woodruff. At

Magdalen he had befriended Lionel Perry, the witty, handsome 'Golden Boy', a year ahead of JB, and towards the end of 1926 they shared rooms at 142 Walton Street. On Perry's death, JB wrote to his mother Mrs Braddell (24 September 1980) telling her how grateful he was for Perry's friendship: 'I don't think I have ever laughed so much as I did with Lionel. . . .'[6] It was laughter which brought JB and Osbert Lancaster together. Osbert arrived a year later and was introduced to JB by an old Marlburian friend, Graham Shepard, son of E. H. Shepard, the illustrator of *Winnie-the-Pooh*. Osbert warmed to JB instantly and recalled, 'We liked the same jokes, we liked the same people. It started off with hoots of laughter about – I can't remember – some joke figure or other.'[7] They remained rock-like friends for ever afterwards.

In the summer of 1926 Bowra and JB went to stay at the Irish seat of Pierce Synnott, a wackily-dressed and eccentric undergraduate with whom Bowra was in love. His love was never reciprocated, for when Bowra plucked up the courage to put his arm round Synnott he was told to take it away. The three of them drove about looking at architecture and this was to be the beginning of JB's never-ending love affair with Ireland. 'Ireland seemed to me Charles Lever and aquatints come true. I thought it was the most perfect place on earth.'[8] This was also the realization of his childhood dreaming about the mysterious romance of country houses. He wrote to Synnott years later, 'Yours was the first country house in which I stayed (excepting that of Ernie's friend, Sir Henry Webb in S. Wales) and since then how many pairs of linen sheets have received my lustful limbs in what fine mansions.'[9]

In the autumn of 1926 JB's first article was published in the *Isis* and a poem soon after. In 1927 he became a regular contributor to the *Cherwell*, ending up as the editor. A previous editor had been Bryan Guinness, who became a great friend of JB on their first meeting. Bryan was a quiet, gentle youth with a vague, almost haphazard, manner which was utterly beguiling. The Guinnesses were the greatest family in the 'beerage' who had started brewing their special stout in Dublin in the eighteenth century and amassed a vast fortune by the twentieth. Although he later became vice-chairman of the company, Bryan was always a writer at heart and was happiest in the company of artists and writers.

Julian Kennedy Cooke wrote a pathetic note to JB in May 1927: 'I think it would be much more satisfactory if you controlled the *Cherwell* altogether, so I have told the [J.C.] Squire that I am retiring. I feel you are the man for it and that I should always be useless to you if not actively a nuisance. Best of luck old boy; and I should always be ready to make myself useful with the proofs. . . .'[10]

Christopher Sykes, a wildly funny man who later wrote Evelyn Waugh's biography, became JB's co-editor. 'Dear Betjeman,' [JB had by now dropped the final 'n' of his surname] he wrote in a hurried note, '. . . [Edward] James has written an article which passes belief it is so bad and he wants to publish all my worst pictures and Villiers David has sent some infuriatingly silly ideas – so my napoleonic brain has just evolved a most enormous idea – let us have little James to talk about [Harman] Grisewood's 'resonant forehead' if he wants to, but let us write a weekly supplement that will just shatter the rest of the damned paper and finally will eat it up with little James and ugly Villiers – come to Oxford *immediately* and talk it over – it's all a question of time fuck you. Xtopher.'[11]

Although JB had had two mild flirtations, one with a waitress, the other a clergyman's daughter, most of his main introductions (for girls were thin on the ground at Oxford, and according to Osbert Lancaster 'played a very small part in our lives') came through his friends' sisters. Hamish St Clair-Erskine often took JB to stay with his parents, the Earl and Countess of Rosslyn, at Hunger Hill near Coolham in Sussex, a mock-Tudor house with leather thongs which worked the door latches. Although JB was considered to be 'not quite a gentleman' by Lord Rosslyn, his ability to make Lady Rosslyn laugh made him irresistible to her. Hamish's sister, Mary, was fifteen when John first went to Hunger Hill, and they developed an instant affinity, which never diminished in sixty years. They adopted comic literary poses (JB pretended to be translating Virgil for publication) and made each other laugh. JB wrote to Mary (3 January 1974) when Hamish died, 'My mind flies back to happy days pulling the leather-thonged latches at Hunger Hill and to the smell of woodsmoke and tinkle of whisky glasses and Loughie and Vera [the Rosslyns] and you and David [St.C.-E.] very young reading Arthur Mee's *Children's Encyclopedia* or maybe *My Magazine* and your father and his port at that ever-hospitable table and all the time the generous merry company of Hamish so kind and joining in a life which then seemed to be all laughter and fast cars and driving all night in flat country around Coolham . . . I am so grateful to have known him and Hunger Hill days. Vera's violet eyes and constant cigarettes and warm welcome – you and your family and I have Ham and Captain Alan Payan Pryce-Jones to thank for introducing me to it, the dressing up, the turning over the *Tatler and Bystander*, the night winds in those firs around Hunger Hill, you the prettiest girl on earth and Ham the handsomest boy – I am so grateful for having known you all. . . .'[12]

JB realized that his gift to amuse opened many doors and although he already knew he wanted to be a poet, he was certainly unwilling to show it for fear of being thought a bore, or worse, pretentious. He got into the aristocratic set with ease, never at any stage by pretending to be one of them, but by playing up his middle-class background and making what he decided was its comedy into a virtue. He often pretended to be a commercial traveller and signed his letters 'Tinkerty Tonk Old Boy'. He openly admitted to social climbing, and was willingly seduced by country-house living:

> Oxford May mornings! When the prunus bloomed
> We'd drive to Sunday lunch at Sezincote:
> First steps in learning how to be a guest,
> First wood-smoke-scented luxury of life
> In the large ambience of a country house.[13]

Alan Pryce-Jones, always known as 'Bog', later 'Captain Bog' and sometimes 'Hideous', was often in the same party. They had met at Magdalen. 'I was sitting in my rooms,' wrote Alan, 'wrapped in a towelling cloak and reading when the door was opened by a third year man. . . . I was embarrassed at being discovered in what I knew to be a ridiculous garment, but my visitor sat down and began a conversation which lasted, off and on, for over fifty years.'[14]

JB took Alan off on trips to look at architecture in his Morris Cowley car (which at one stage of its crocky career would only turn to the left, meaning that the route taken had always to be circular). Alan lived in Chelsea near JB and they saw a lot of each other in the holidays.

Nearly everyone in JB's circle of aesthetic friends was homosexual – it would have been unusual for them not to be. Louis MacNeice remarked that during that time at Oxford, 'homosexuality and "intelligence", heterosexuality and brawn, were almost inexorably paired.'[15] If you had been through the preparatory and public school system, it was natural to develop crushes (albeit of a subliminal nature) and it would have been surprising if such feelings had not continued at Oxford. Some of JB's friends, such as Harold Acton and W. H. Auden, were more overtly homosexual than others. Auden left countless notes in JB's rooms, sometimes scribbled and sometimes typed on JB's erratic typewriter: 'Where is my book, what happened to you on Sunday at tea?', 'Come and see me tomorrow. . . . Bring *Sanitary Defects* with you, Love Wystan'.[16] This last was a reference to a book on sanitation which

JB had lost; it was a subject in which Auden was interested, as his father had been before him. Their friendship was instant, recalled JB, although to an outsider they were as different as chalk from cheese; JB loved his fashionable friends, Auden was unimpressed; JB thought he knew a lot about poetry, Auden contradicted him; JB deemed his father a philistine, Auden revered his; JB was in love with the landowning classes, Auden was aware of the slum conditions in Birmingham. 'So snobbish was I, so other-worldly he . . . and yet there was an oracular quality about this tough youth in corduroys that compelled my attention. Above all he liked poetry, chanting it aloud after tea.'[17] Auden also 'loved the Isle of Man, its railways, trams and trains, and first encouraged me to go there'.

In this age of gilded hedonism, of long breakfasts and silk dressing gowns, JB's more serious side was kept hidden. He was always worrying about his lack of funds and pursued various obscure routes towards being published, both as a playwright and guide-book writer, inspired by gaps he found in the second-hand bookshops that he so loved to frequent. He loved the smell and feel of old books and he had also begun to like the smell of incense. Oxford introduced him to the Baroque Movement of high Anglo-Catholicism. 'Dear Betjemann,' wrote F. L. Cross from Pusey House, home of the movement, 'Father Sargent has suggested to me that you might be able and willing to serve here this term. . . .'[18] He agreed to serve at Sunday masses. But his religious leanings remained a private part of his life at this stage. He discussed his feelings about Christianity with only a chosen few, one of whom was 'Cracky' William Clonmore, one of his closest friends from the beginning of his Oxford days, who was training to be an Anglican priest at St Stephen's House in North Oxford. JB had been introduced to Clonmore by his room-mate, Lionel Perry, and he was to visit Clonmore's Irish seat, Shelton Abbey, again and again. They shared a deep affection for the Colonel and a fashionable abhorrence of their respective fathers, but also a deep religious conviction. 'It may surprise you a little,' wrote Clonmore (16 April 1927), 'but very nearly from the time I first met you, I wondered whether you were not meant to be a priest. From the practical point of view, if you were to work in a slum you would, I think, as far as I know you, and know anything at all about slums, be very good at the job – there is an infinite amount of work to be done, and every slum district is badly understaffed. I think that people like you and I are better at understanding slum people than men who are more normal and saner. It is not really anything to be proud of, but the way one is made.'[19]

It is ironic that these deep and genuine searchings did not see JB through the obligatory university divinity exam. Having failed this, he was rusticated in the spring of 1928 and took a job in a prep school called Thorpe House at Gerrard's Cross for a term. He returned on a trial basis for the Michaelmas term and was finally sent down for good at the end of the year.

1. C. S. Lewis, diary entry in George Sayer, *C. S. Lewis and His Times* (Duckworth, 1974).
2. JB's papers, University of Victoria, British Columbia.
3. Hugh Lloyd-Jones (ed.), *Maurice Bowra* (Duckworth, 1974).
4. C. M. Bowra, *Memories 1898–1939* (Weidenfeld and Nicolson, 1966).
5. This is one of several versions of JB's lyric.
6. Lionel Perry's papers.
7. Richard Boston, *Osbert: A Portrait of Osbert Lancaster* (Collins, 1989).
8. Bevis Hillier, *Young Betjeman* (John Murray, 1988).
9. Pierce Synnott's papers.
10. JB's papers.
11. JB's papers.
12. Mary Dunn's papers.
13. JB, *Summoned by Bells* (John Murray, 1960).
14. Alan Pryce-Jones, *The Bonus of Laughter* (Hamish Hamilton, 1987).
15. Richard Boston, *Osbert: A Portrait of Osbert Lancaster*.
16. JB's papers.
17. Stephen Spender (ed.), *W. H. Auden: A Tribute* (Weidenfeld and Nicolson, 1975).
18. JB's papers.
19. JB's papers.

To Pierce Synnott   53 Church Street
                                                     Chelsea
21 June 1926   SW3

My dear Master Pierce,
I am so sorry that I have not written to you sooner. Now that I do write,
the accumulated news of some days has left me and I feel myself in the
humiliating position of a John Tayleur – filthy little swine.
    When I had travell'd and talked with [W. B.] Yeats all the way to
Galway – I almost divulge our conversation now – I met my father and
as I said, went to Ballynahinch where I was obviously not wanted. I
fished so much in the heat, with my blood being drained by enormous
flies and poison being put in its place by still larger ones, that I got
sunstroke and arrived in Dublin, on my way back, with my father, with
a temperature of 101. My father said that he was being swindled in
Dublin and insisted on my crossing that night. This I did suffering
agony and vomiting the whole way.
    Now that I am better, it is just possible to cross London and look at a
few of my Greek Revival Churches. (Yesterday (Wednesday) Maurice
[Bowra] suddenly appeared and we went to the Tate and John Sutro
together). I had a good lunch at the Ivy with our Maurice. We met a
man you know in the Tate called Adrian Stokes – nice.
    Christ! Christ! Christ! I am miserable.
    Oh introspection!
    Remember me to them all at Furness; I enjoyed myself so much.
    Love and kisses, JB

> JB had stayed with P.S., his Oxford friend, at his house in Ireland in the company of
> Maurice Bowra. He went on to fish with his father on the thirty-thousand acre estate in
> Galway, owned by the cricketer Ranjitsinhji for whom Ernest Betjemann had made
> artefacts.
>   John Tayleur was an unpopular Oxford character, one of the Tayleurs of
> Buntingdale, a fine baroque house near Market Drayton in Shropshire.
>   John Sutro, rich and eccentric, was an Oxford friend of JB's, who founded the Oxford
> Railway Club which used to hire trains to drive about England. His family was in the
> film industry.
>   Adrian Stokes was a writer and art historian. He became a trustee of the Tate Gallery.

To Lionel Perry

Monday [summer 1926]

My dear Lionel,
I felt that you would appreciate this more than any others of my
acquaintance. I am in the Grill Room not of Oddenino's, nor of the Café
Royal nor even of the Troc[adero] but of the Crystal Palace. Here I am
encased in Paxton's Great Masterpiece looking over the suburbs of
South London – rows of red-brick villas with here and there patches of
green which indicate the position of the local tennis clubs.

Fortunately the only book I have with me is a small red volume dated
1852 of the combined poetical works of Heber, Hemans and Radcliffe.
I shall boat on the lake this afternoon and read Hemans, looking up at
the Crystal Palace like a great waterfall among the trees and repeat that
melodious lady's own numbers:

> Well mark each aromatic flower
> Expanding to the radiant hour.

It *will* be jolly.

Dear [Prince] Albert has left his mark here by appearing in every
little niche round the concert room where the names of great people are
written round the walls in blue and yellow and gold and red –
HERCULES – MENDELSSOHN – MME PAGANINI – APOLLO –
everybody.

Even as I write, a man has entered the 'Grill Room' with real
Dandiacal whiskers.

Au revoir. I shall see you at Oxford. If you are in London my
telephone number is Kensington 41775 and my address 53 Church
Street, Chelsea, SW3.

Love and kisses, John Betjeman

L.P. was at Magdalen with JB.
'Dandiacal' means 'inclined to be a dandy'.

To Pierce Synnott   St Enodoc View
                                                Trebetherick
                                                Nr Wadebridge
11 September 1926   North Cornwall

Dear Pierce,
Thank you for your postcards of Mantua. I should like one from San
Marino if you go there; I am interested in the stamps. As you may
judge, I am in a tiresome mood, but then look at the name of the house I
am living in.

An event of interest has occurred in the village. The wife of a tenant
farmer of my father's has run away from her immoral husband, who is
at the moment beating at the doors of the village saying, 'Have you seen
my missus?' The wife has gone to London – according to the postman
who read the telegram she sent.

How is Jasper? I do hope he is enjoying his holiday as much as you
are.

Store up in your mind, or preserve photographs of all the good Italian
things you see. I do not think Ernie will ever let me go abroad, nor yet
that I shall ever get away from him. The Lord bless you and keep you,
the Lord make the light of His countenance to shine upon you and give
you peace, this time henceforth and for evermore.
    JB

> JB's interest in stamps continued. He used Manx stamps on all his letters in later life.
> Jasper was P.S.'s younger brother.

To Unknown   The Oxford Movement
                                                142 Walton St
20 October 1926   Oxford

Dear Sir,
For two years I have been studying the classical churches of London
that were built under the Metropolitan Churches Acts in the early part
of the nineteenth century – e.g. St Matthew's Brixton, St Pancras etc.
As far as I know, no work has been produced on these beautiful
buildings, and I wonder whether what knowledge I have, could be of
any service to you,
    Yours faithfully, John Betjeman

To Mary St Clair-Erskine   All Souls College [stolen writing paper]

[1926?]

My dear Lady Mary,
Or shall I say mi-lady Mary after the manner of those eighteenth-century English novelists who knew the meaning of passion – pardon me if I mention a word a trifle unorthodox in our modern highly cultivated society but where I would apply it, I can hardly refrain from doing so – a *cause d' amour* – for else I fain 'Lethe-wards would have sunk' in my misery at being inarticulate. *Mea culpa! mea maxima culpa!* that the other day when you graced the quadrangle of our college I could hardly have been so uninterested as I would have wished so I trust you forgave my asking of you to accept the hospitality of my humble rooms. I am sorry you were not feeling well enough to take cocoa, my cocoa and I hope your headache – not, I feel sure, with one of your sincerity a *malade imaginaire* – is better. Will you come to tea next Thursday at four twenty-five for four thirty as I have something important to tell you. My aunt Miss Wilkins will be there.
   Eheu! fugaces – I have been so long composing this I must now return to the half lines and repetitions of Virgil of which the first part is being published next year. Should our tea party be in *every way* successful to all parties, you will, I know, do me the honour of accepting a copy of the book *ex manu auctoris*.
   À bientôt, Austin Puxley Pierce

> John Sparrow was writing a short technical treatise on Virgil's versification with the title 'The Half Lines and Repetitions of Virgil'.
>   JB's signing himself as the fictitious Austin Puxley Pierce marked the beginning of a life of signing obscure names instead of his own.

To Mrs Pryce-Jones   Magdalen College
21 January 1927   Oxford

Dear Mrs Pryce-Jones,
I am so glad you liked the Mowers and I cannot tell you how complimented I am by your confidence in one so humble as myself.
   I feel I must reply to your letter although you told me not to, because it may relieve your anxiety about Alan. I hope I shall not be saying what you have already realised.

Alan arrives in Oxford with talents and the power of conversation: like all people with those two qualities he is very impressionable and very anxious to be universally popular, to become 'a figure' in Oxford life. He finds this will probably be quite easy for him and very naturally he attracts satellites, and 'figures' in Oxford recognise his ability. He has never met so many people with similar tastes to himself before and he is quite delighted: a social life seems to be of more importance than an academic one.

That all happened last term: now he realises, I think, that he has not used much selection in some of his friends. He is bored by the effort required to keep up with all those acquaintances necessary to have as a social star. The star therefore very rightly wanes and Alan feels discontented and tries to find something more valuable to follow.

He will probably, out of mere boredom, continue, for a little, this social life which ruins his finances: but with it all Alan is ambitious and self-contained. He knows as well as I do that the 'social' life is of no real value up here.

He will want to satisfy his own ambition and he is much too much of an egotist (you don't mind my saying so – it is not a fault of his, it is lucky for him) to allow his vanity and his ambitions to be unsatisfied. He will therefore take to the pleasurable (though I am too weak yet to have found it so) discipline of working for exams. His desire to win the Newdigate is the first step in that direction.

Alan is far too vital to take anything second-hand. He would not believe a social life was dull unless he had proved it for himself. Like all young persons he cannot bring himself to believe that other people may have experienced the same feelings as himself and formed conclusions he himself will afterwards form. No one can blame him for that. Really I think it is just as well that things are as they are with him. He has got to go through the social phase. The harder he does it – the sooner it will be over. He is much too balanced and proud underneath for it ever to dominate his life. I am afraid it's awfully hard for you to pay the very heavy price of giving a talented son every allowance you can. But it is worth it, because Alan changes every week now. He is feeling about for some object to be his final end and he is quite certain that he has not got it yet.

In that trite discussion I kept out the thing which will guide him in the right direction – his love for you and all the good that is in him and that his egotism must not crush.

Forgive me if I presume and preach, John Betjeman

Vere Pryce-Jones, Alan's mother, had written to JB asking him to keep 'a rather stern and kindly eye on Alan. . . . I do worship him so, and *know* he could make something Great and Good out of his life if only he does not fritter it away. . . . He is so terribly "casual".' Osbert Lancaster later observed, 'It was like asking Satan to chaperone Sin.'

To Bryan Guinness   Magdalen College
Tuesday [May 1927?]   Oxford

Dear Guinness,
I'm very sorry you braved the squalor of Walton Street and odours of 142 in the rain.

It's good of you to offer me sub-editorship of the *Cherwell* and I should like to accept it provided that it will not take up all my time. I should like to know quite what my relations with the others would be, and I'm very much afraid that owing to a bloody casting reading of *King Lear* tomorrow at eight, I shan't be able to accept your invitation to dinner. I do apologise for my wretched manners in

(i) not sending anything to the *Cherwell* when you'd asked me.

(ii) refusing your invitation to dinner which gives me not a little regret and I hope that I will be able to see you before the end of the term. Shall I call – but I'm snowed up with Essays etc: until Thursday. I'll call on Friday morning if that'll do – sorry to be so vague –

Yours sincerely, John Betjeman

JB and B.G. became lifelong friends on meeting at Oxford.

JB did accept sub-editorship and eventually became editor. The *Cherwell* took on a marked architectural slant.

To Bryan Guinness   [Postcard]

21 July 1927

By Thomas Moore, J. Betjeman, William C. [Clonmore]

> By Avoca's green valley I wandered repining
> And looked for a rest in a Gothick retreat
> Lo there in the West the red orb was declining
> And here was an Abbey enshrouding my feet

'How hallowed' I cried was my endless complaining
Of here I have met with a Gothick reward
I will shoulder my Lyre now the long day is waning
In the finial's shade will sheathe up my sword!

[Second postcard]

Here by Avoca's endless tide
I sought thy Gothick strains
Fair Harp of Shelton, undeserved
I eye thine hallowed fanes
Lost Soul of Erin! in thy glade
I saw thy steeple tall
I watched thy turrets unafraid
I heard thy finials fall

T. Moore, c. 1823
John Betjeman
William

JB and William Clonmore wrote these spoof verses after the great Irish poet and lyricist about Shelton Abbey, Clonmore's father Lord Wicklow's Gothic mansion in Arklow.

To William Clonmore

[1927?]

My dear William,
This is Pierce's notepaper which I have taken from his room. It is very common isn't it? Dear Little Kate [Katherine Howard, Clonmore's cousin]! I am charmed by that postcard and all my old love revives. I've got a drawing of her which I did at Shelton and I'd send it to you save that I love her so much I couldn't part with it. She has good manners and shyness and she's fond of you too – but she likes her netball more than anything.

She quite refines my soul – the other girl debases it. I wish my parents, during their espionage system, could find this letter. William – David's letter is so funny. He's in the Acland Home you know – he strained his knee on something. Oh William! how funny it is to think of you. I'm getting chucked out of the *Cherwell*. Isn't [Roy] Harrod nice? Katie's nicer. Poor old [illegible] there on Sunday.
    JB

None of JB's letters to W.C. has survived save this. They were regular correspondents and made each other laugh outrageously. Mr Newcombe, whom the Earl of Wicklow, W.C.'s father, had employed as chaperone and social mentor to his son, thought JB common and discouraged their relationship, which only served to strengthen it.

'The other girl' could be an Oxford waitress or the daughter of a clergyman, both of whom JB had short and unsuccessful relations with.

To Pierce Synnott   53 Church Street
                                               Chelsea
7 August 1927   SW3

My dear Pierce,
I must congratulate you on your First, although dotty William [Clonmore] tells me it was a great blow to you. It does not surprise me – I hear you are in a bit of a huff with me. I lunched with Maurice [Bowra] the other day and saw [John] Sparrow and [Hugh] Gaitskell in the afternoon. I hope they had a good time that night. We sent a postcard from you to Mark Ogilvie-G[rant].

It is hellish here. I lost my trunk – at least my suitcase was as good as taken from my hand – when travelling from Wilnecote to Bath, at New Street Birmingham station, the other day. Erney [Ernest Betjemann] proposed to make me a twenty-first birthday present of another suitcase back again; he was thwarted by the thing turning up from Bournemouth yesterday. I have to take the dog out at eight o'clock for a ten-minute walk EVERY BLOODY MORNING.

There is a beautiful baroque church at Edgware built by an eighteenth-century Duke of Chandos:

It has high pews, an east end consisting of altar and Corinthian columns supporting a broken curved pediment behind which is an apsidal end painted blue to imitate the sky and containing a dark Renaissance organ with gilt pipes which was used by Handel. The walls and ceiling and west end of the church are covered with very elaborate paintings in the Guido Reni manner but c. 1770. The best thing of its kind I've ever seen in England and at Edgware of all places among a lot of pseudo-Elizabethan bungalows. What a bore I am. Poor old Pierce I don't know where you are so please don't answer.

Your devoted, JB

To Pierce Synnott

6 September 1927

Sezincote
Moreton in Marsh
Gloucestershire

Dear old Pierce,
Dotty [William Clonmore] and I sent you a postcard in four languages yesterday. Thanks awfully for your invitation old boy. I've been away for two weeks from home and I have written to get leave off. I doubt whether I will get it – but I will let you know as soon as I hear. Pray God, that I can come.

I have not heard from Sparrow recently. He said he was going to Cornwall weeks ago – did you see that [Humphrey] Raikes has accepted the principalship of a University in Johannesburg S.A.?

Ernie is getting better but is exceedingly sorry for himself. Bess [Betjemann] is dying of misery and martyrdom. My girl has broken her heart – she sent me some hideous etchings in the picturesque style for my birthday – I put them in the waste paper basket at once. I am in a quandary about her. Pierce, I've got to go to Cheltenham now. I've just heard from Maurice – good bye – for the time. I will write again later.

JB
Remember me to Mrs S!

Raikes was a popular chemistry don at Oxford.
   The etchings were probably sent by the 'plain, dutiful clergyman's daughter' remembered by Maurice Bowra in *Memories*.

To Pierce Synnott   The Nursing Home
                                                 46 St Georges Road
                                                 Pimlico
3 October 1927   SW1

Dear old Pierce,
I hear there has been a terrific lot of bad blood at Naas. Maurice sent a
letter which made me laugh a good deal. Have you seen William
[Clonmore]?
    I am here after an operation on my nose which was very painful and
has – God be praised – kept me away from 53 Church Street for the last
ten days. I shall be out on Wednesday. On Saturday I go to spend a
ghastly few days in Cornwall with my parents. Ernie has got only
'pseudo' angina (although this can kill him, it is incurable) but he also
has structural disease of the heart. This means that he will die in about
five years – just enough for him to wreck my life. I find that my own
pulse rate is very abnormal being 60 to the average person's 72. My
normal temperature is about 97 instead of 98.4. I shall die young, I
think.
    I have had a longish course of reading during these last three days that
I have awoken from semi-consciousness. Among the works I have read
is Butler's *Way of All Flesh*. It struck me as an entertaining book but very
shallow. To what purpose – other than the apparent side issue of the
evils of family life – was it written? He does away with [Christ]ianity by
very old fashioned methods and I cannot believe he thinks the shallow
fatalism that he leaves is an adequate theory of existence. You probably
know all about it, you old ugly, and you'll be able to tell me what is
wrong and what is right with the book.
    I am glad you have not passed that tedious exam. It means that you
will come back to Oxford. If you do not I am doubly sorry I was unable
to come to Naas this vac. Bloody Ernie forbade it – said he couldn't
afford it just after he'd taken his little bit out to dinner and everything
else – and now that his every word has to be obeyed or else he gets an
attack, I thought I would spare putting murder on my conscience. I
hear Urquhart took Sparrow from Naas and didn't like Russborough.
Russborough was nearly perfection. I have found the real perfection at
West Wycombe. There is a church on top of a hill (1760) where Bubb
Doddington is buried, whose proportion, painted ceilings, plaster and
furniture beat anything I saw at Syon House, Brentford. Of course it is
locked, only used in the summer months at 6.30 on Sunday Evening

and rapidly becoming a ruin. The wet pews were cleared away and
yellow chairs are in their place, yet it remains perfect. There are no
postcards of it as it is too little known.

Poor old Lionel Perry looks very ill,
so does Pat Gamble. I met a Mrs
Hubbard that knew you and your
sisters. She looks like this – only
younger.

She was Jack James's mistress – at
least that's what Jack James always used
to say.

Forgive my not having written before, Pierce. My new car, which
although it is only a Morris Cowley, goes very fast, has occupied my
thoughts very considerably.

Ernie has been away shooting for about a week and it has put me out
of temper that he should choose a time when I am away too. Do you
believe in the existence of God? I want nice, definite logical proofs, you
old dear. Remember me to B. and Aunt T. and your sisters and also to
darling, darling Master Jasper.

Only frightfully
good looking
    Yours JB

PS The last part of
this letter might have
been from Ralph Radcliffe
to Tom Douglas.

P.S.'s house, Furness, was at Naas, County Kildare.
  Russborough is one of Ireland's star eighteenth-century houses.
  Jack James was an Oxford friend of JB's who became deputy Master of the Mint.
  JB had been given a Morris Cowley car by his Aunt Edie, Ernest's sister.

To Bryan Guinness   'The Beeches'
                                                       Sandfield Road
                                                       Headington
3 October 1927   Oxford

(This is a little half-timbered heaven furnished with 'fumed oak' and
simple colours. This letter is so untidy that it might have been written
by you.)

Dear Bryan,
I was so delighted with your letter on which mad William had made
comments. I am so sorry not to have replied before. I cannot say how
really I miss you and poor Mark.
   The other day I had occasion to go and see James Lindsay at 46 High
Street. It was very depressing to enter that little yellow cell at the back
of the house and recognise no Gothic ornaments, wrought-iron and
'artistic' shades and not to see that notice in that awful handwriting
about being called for at eight o'clock. I imagine you are not yet back
from Greece. It always pleases me to think of Mark in specially
arranged clothes for travelling, standing by a Greek Pillar at the
Parthenon. *Please tell me what he said when he reached the Parthenon*. I have
been debating on it with myself ever since I heard he was in Greece. It is
the least appropriate setting I can imagine for him.
   The *Cherwell* has again evaded collapse. Do you want some copies? I
have nothing to do with it now but there is a lot of trouble because
Edward James (the editor) has been getting hold of Basil Ava and
[Freddy] Furneaux to help him and has been ousting Villiers David.
There is so much trouble about that it might be any OUDS committee
meeting. There is also another intrigue in connection with the paper.
Ava and Furneaux (who seem to be the lode-stars of Edward J.) have
signed an agreement saying they will edit the *University Review* next
term. They are apparently very good at that sort of thing and it looks as
tho' the *Cherwell* will sink. Edward J. intends to amalgamate the papers
under the name *Cherwell* and by doing away with [Harold] Sissons,
secure 'the friendship' of the ghastly people who run the *Review*. Thank
God I'm nothing to do with the paper now! Old [Christopher] Sykes
has done some excellent drawings, but Mark is much missed.
   I find myself of little importance this term – a legendary hermit up on
this hill who is neither thought of nor mentioned. And you? What are

you going to do or what are you doing? I bought a suit with squares on it the other day, thinking it might turn out like your suits only I find I look like a bookmaker. Poor old Pierce will never leave Ireland now – his first was a great blow to him and his failure for the Civil Service has been the only thing to cheer him up. Haven't got any more notepaper so accept the devotion of
  John B

> JB moved out of College to Headington in October.
>   Basil Ava, known as 'Little Bloody', was clever and a loved friend of JB. (He was killed in action in the last year of the Second World War.)
>   Harold Sissons was managing editor and owner of the *Cherwell*.
>   Freddie Furneaux (Viscount, later the Earl of Birkenhead) was the son of F. E. Smith. Later JB found his literary advice indispensable and Furneaux wrote an introduction to his *Collected Poems* in 1958.

To Unknown   53 Church Street
                                          Chelsea
[February 1928?]   London SW3

Dear Sir,
I wonder if you would allow me to consult the registers and records of your church on Friday next at about eleven a.m.? I am anxious to find information about Revd (I have forgotten the initial) Bates and his wife, a Miss Stanhope and possible relative of Lord Chesterfield.
  Mr Bates was an ardent Hutchinsonian and the uncle of Toplady, as you probably know. He, and his wife especially, were particularly hostile to Toplady when he was a child. As I am engaged on a dramatisation of Toplady's life I wish to find out whether the Bates had any children who might also have plagued his earlier years.
  Yours sincerely, John Betjeman

> JB retained a lifelong interest in Augustus Montague Toplady (1740–78) and his bookshelves groaned with his Calvinistic writings. He was the author of the hymn 'Rock of Ages'.
>   There is no evidence of such a dramatisation in JB's papers.

To John Edward Bowle   Thorpe House
                                                   Oval Way
                                                   Gerrard's Cross
17 May 1928   Bucks

My dear John Edward,
I am surrounded by nineteen shrieking boys; I am settling quarrels and
starting new ones. One blasted little brat is asking me a question now
and I am ignoring him. Another is sulking because I have made him sit
down. It is impossible to write coherently because I have continually to
get up and go into the changing room to stop the bullying. Wait a
moment – oh God. The boys all got wet from cricket today and after we
had changed their socks, I was left in charge of them while they were in
the confined space within doors. How I loathe them all.
    The weekend after next, thank God, is my time off.
    The boys will keep coming and looking at this letter. I shall have to go
for a walk with them soon. Oh Lord – one of them is crying because the
others have tied him up with a rope.
    Yours, JB

    J.E.B. was at Marlborough with JB and went on to become a historian.
    JB took a job at Thorpe House prep school for a term during his rustication.

To Patrick Balfour   Trebetherick
                                                   Nr Wadebridge
4 September 1928   North Cornwall

My dear Patrick,
I said I would write to you and thank you for the helpful letter you sent
to me at the beginning of my visit to Clandeboye. Oh how peaceful
were those first few days, with 'the most intelligent conversationalist
for his age' [Basil Ava] – laughing at Edward James' poetry and getting
the enormous eyes of Bloody to roll round in my direction:

                    Lord Ava had enormous eyes
                    And head of a colossal size
                    He rarely laughed and only spoke
                    To utter some stupendous joke
                    Which if it were not understood
                    Was anyhow considered good.

> He was so very good at games
> He'd even beaten Edward James
> And others of the wealthy set
> Who fill the pages of Debrett.

But the peace was rudely shattered by the arrival of two girls in that Classical library, one of them carrying a gramophone record – a new one to be tried. Then we all started to practise the Charleston. We moved the gramophone into the saloon where there was a parquet floor and tried them. I was miserable. Edward tried to get his own back (not without success) on Bloody and me because we had laughed at his poetry. But it was over in a little while when Edward departed. I found that by altering my plane of thought I could get on quite well with Veronica [Basil's sister].

I am glad you like Bloody – what an admirable sterling character is his!

I have got to go out with a lot of jolly girls now – oh God I wish I were dead.

Yours, JB

JB met P.B. at Oxford. He was to become one of JB's closest friends.

JB stayed at the Dufferins' Northern Irish seat, Clandeboye, County Down, at the end of August. He got on well with Basil's mother, Brenda, who was faintly off her head and thought she was Queen of the Fairies.

To Ward, Lock & Co. Ltd   11 Magpie Lane
                                             Oxford
                                             Magdalen College
11 November 1928   Oxford

Dear Sirs,
I think it would be a good idea if guide-books, instead of following the public taste, should lead it. I can only believe that your guide, let us say, to LEAMINGTON will be of interest to persons connected with the gas industry who take a holiday in the town. For them it is of importance that electric light was abandoned for lighting the streets in 1893.

Unless your author is writing in a spirit of satire, I do not think he could call the glass and iron pavilion in the Jephson Gardens 'handsome'. I do not think he will be able to get even the most prejudiced old Leamingtonians to believe that the unearthly marble fountain in the Pump Room is 'handsome' either. Certainly the Congregational Church is not, as he says, 'handsome'.

He describes many of the entertainments and playing fields of the town as 'excellent'. They very rarely are.

Please do not think that I want to be unpleasant or that I am too modern, but I do believe that nowadays the greater enormities of the Gothic Revival and of Victorian smugness are at a discount.

It seems to me that there never was such a chance of educating taste by means of the guide-book as in this day of motors and a reawakened interest in surroundings. Many of the stucco villas and terraces of LEAMINGTON are very good examples of late Georgian Architecture, while the sham Gothic of the Parish Church is not as bad as your guide makes out (I quote an authority). Were you to have photographs of these buildings and dated accounts of the statelier late Georgian and early Victorian Streets, you would be rendering incomparable service.

Please forgive my candour and possible presumption.

Yours very truly, John Betjeman

The little red illustrated guide-books of England and Wales, published by Ward, Lock and Co., were written around the turn of the century and revised regularly.

Three:

Thirty pounds a term and keep

December 1928 to December 1931

HERE ARE THE MITFORD GIRLS

My undergraduate eyes beholding,
    As I climbed your slope, Cat Hill:
Emerald chestnut fans unfolding,
    Symbols of my hope, Cat Hill.
What cared I for past disaster,
Applicant for cricket master,
Nothing much of cricket knowing,
Conscious but of money owing?
    Somehow I would cope, Cat Hill.

Summoned by Bells

The moment JB was sent down from Oxford, Ernest fixed up a job for him in the City with a firm of marine insurance brokers called Sedgwick Collins and Company. He hated it and lasted only a few weeks there. His social success at Oxford, however, had given him confidence and, after beginning to get his foot in the door of the BBC, he procured a job through his friend, Gerald Heard, as private secretary to the septuagenarian Sir Horace Plunkett, an agricultural expert. However, while JB was 'off sick', his schoolfriend, John Edward Bowle, snitched the job. In a letter to Lionel Perry Bowle tried to exonerate himself: 'John hopelessly overdid treating the job as a joke and Plunkett, who is very clever in spite of his infirmities, was fully determined to get rid of him as soon as he could find a substitute, since he is apparently determined to take the book he is writing seriously, and does not feel equal to the responsibility of looking after John as well as himself. . . . In a word, he [JB] has NO SENSE, and expects as of right that people will look after him simply if he prattles about the place. Lots of people are prepared to do this, but alas, they can't give him money and a job. One must at least *appear* reliable to get and keep anything and I just don't think that J is good for anything if he does not realize this.

'Do get some sense into him . . . I think he would never do for serious journalism as he has not any sane judgement about the rather heavy questions which he would have to write about. Unless he can get a job like Tom Driberg's doing gossip, I don't see him in journalism. He is unaware of his limitations and gets hysterical if one suggests that he has them. This may all sound priggish but as he seems rather on his beam-ends one has to put the thing clearly. You had better put this letter in the fire, as I don't want more bad blood streaming about.'[1]

In April 1929, JB got a job at Heddon Court Preparatory School (in Barnet) by saying that he was good at cricket, which he wasn't. He remembers being visited by Oxford friends Evelyn Waugh and Richard Plunkett-Greene: 'I was teaching the bottom form at football and cricket and divinity and everything like that, and we went out to lunch in the lunch break in a hotel in Barnet and had a lot of very strong beer called Colne Spring, made by Fremlins, and I was so drunk when I came back that I wasn't able to take the game of football, and the boys kindly took me up to my room, and never said anything about it.'[2] His ineptitude at cricket was found out when he was expected to play in a cricket match, boys versus teachers: 'D'you know what Winters told me, Betjeman? *He didn't think you'd ever held a bat.*'[3] And he was finally sacked. He had actually lasted more than a year.

At this period in their lives JB and his Oxford pal, Patrick Balfour (later Kinross), were thick as thieves, and JB used Patrick's house in Yeoman's Row as a London base. 'Old Patrick', who often spent Christmas with us in his later years, looked exactly like a mosquito. 'Mosquito' had even been one of his nicknames at Oxford. He was immensely tall and stick-like, with huge black eyebrows which grew in almost vertical spikes. Although he married, for a brief period, Angela Culme-Seymour, 'the bolter' of Nancy Mitford's novel, *The Pursuit of Love*, he was homosexual, or what JB called 'a hundred per cent'. He and JB much enjoyed shocking each other in their letters. At Balfour's memorial service at St Saviour's Church in Paddington in 1976 JB told the congregation that Patrick was 'the mainstay of our happiness . . . he loved introducing congenial people, or rather people who would be congenial to each other . . . I went to stay with Patrick's family in Skye and we danced reels. There was a highland gathering at Braemar and Patrick, whose much-loved mother was a Johnstone-Douglas, went to the gathering wearing tartan. It was one of those terrible mistakes that only the Scottish understand, and I remember his father, whom he called the Baron, referring to Patrick as a "Piccadilly Highlander".'

In the school holidays, JB preferred to spend time in other people's houses. The place where he most loved to be was Sezincote in Gloucestershire, the ravishing onion-domed Indian palace of a Cots-wold house (designed in the early 1800s by Samuel Pepys Cockerell), where his friend John Dugdale lived and where clusters of the gilded youth would gather at weekends. John's father, Colonel Dugdale, was a staunch Conservative and during the long glittering lunches would gaze out towards his fields, dreaming of hunting. His mother, Ethel, a rabid Socialist, who loved entertaining eminent politicians, became JB's confidante and surrogate mother, and Sezincote his home from home.

Ireland had already become a regular place of pilgrimage for JB each summer. He stayed with 'Cracky' William Clonmore at Shelton Abbey, and with Basil 'Little Bloody' Ava at Clandeboye, County Down. But his spiritual home in Ireland became Pakenham Hall, in County Meath, the home of Edward and Christine Longford who ran the Gate Theatre in Dublin and who kept open house to all the Pakenham brothers' and sisters' friends. Lady Violet Powell (then Pakenham), Edward's sister, remembers JB arriving there for the first time, brought by his Oxford friend and her brother Frank Pakenham, in the summer of 1930: 'They [the Longfords] were bowled over by him. He became more than just a court jester.'[4]

Anthony Powell, who later married Violet and was a frequent guest of the Longfords, remembered how 'John made everybody laugh and exposed the funny side of Irish denominations. Every year at Pakenham Hall there was a tea for the local school and Pansy [Pakenham, who married the painter Henry Lamb], Violet, John and Kathleen Delaney, who was an actress at the Gate Theatre who John had a thing about, dispensed the tea. Father Mouritz, the low-church vicar of Rathgraffe, also came, and inspired John to write:

> 'The Protestant tents are open to view,
> The Protestant ass is tied to the tree,
> The Protestant boys are loyal and true,
> And Father Mouritz is coming to tea.
> Slitter, Slaughter, Holy Water,
> We'll bate the Papishers, every one,
> We'll spit in their faces
> And make them run races,
> The Protestant boys shall carry the gun.

'He would recite his endless rhymes in an Irish brogue:

> 'I never like the AArish
> I never cared a whack
> For a lot of skulking Paddies
> Who'd stab you in the back.
> But of all the stinking Aarish
> With which that land is cursed
> The bloody Earl of Longford
> Is just about the worst.'[5]

Christine Longford wrote in her unpublished 'Memoirs', 'If friends could be marked in arithmetic, in a marking game, as we used to do in the evenings, I would mark John up as the greatest: he gave Edward the most and longest pleasure, either by his company or by letters and books for thirty years.'

JB trekked religiously to Trebetherick in Cornwall each year. Here, among the families of retired Indian civil servants, Harley Street doctors and minor public school headmasters, the Betjemann family, who were in 'trade', teetered on the edge of Trebetherick Society. Their place was assured, however, when, with the success of the business, they bought so much land along the cliff and in the village that they could no longer be ignored. Having always either stayed in the Haven Guest House or rented a house called 'Linkside', in 1929 they decided to build their own perfect holiday retreat. 'Undertown' was a last blast of Arts and Crafts architecture designed by Ernest Betjemann's golfing friend, Atkinson, the architect of the first Odeon cinemas. Its special 'Trebetherick' quality, fine attention to detail and beautiful use of local materials, set a high standard for those which followed and of all the modern houses in the village it remains unsurpassed. The cosy fuschia-ed and tamarisk-ed gardens of Trebetherick with their sunken slate terraces set out for tea in the shade of macrocarpas, were a far cry from the templed parks of some of his Oxford friends, and though he complained about having to spend time with his parents, his deep attachment to Trebetherick never wavered or diminished. (He died there, happy, in 1984.)

JB's time at Oxford had not only widened his horizons but also the gap between him and his father. Although he loved Ernest, JB flaunted a fashionable disdain for the middle-class values which he stood for, of living within his 'hard and cleanly earned' income and of appearing 'neat and presentable' at all times. He was also irritated by the words of caution which came each time Ernest paid off another of his son's Oxford debts.

JB had resolved not to follow him into the family business, which he found uninspiring and perhaps saw as threatening to the friendships Oxford had brought. This decision caused Ernest considerable pain and, for a time, put the relationship on a formal and distant plane. JB was closer to his mother, despite the fact that he complained about her hypochondria to his friends, which was hardly surprising since every other letter Ernest wrote to him contained phrases such as, 'Mother has a slight cold' or 'Mother is dreadfully troubled with neuritis in the left arm'. JB confided in Bess to a certain extent and considered her to be his staunch ally. He told her about his girlfriends.

In June 1930, JB, who was then twenty-four years old, met Camilla Russell while staying at Sezincote and decided to fall in love with her. It was a light-hearted romance and clearly both parties were in love with the idea of love. Her letters to JB in fast chubby writing are bursting with happiness and sometimes imprinted with her lipstick. They begin with endearments such as 'Duckie' or 'Darling Twitchie' or 'My darling old rubbish-heap', and are full of a giggling and breathless feeling of hope, expectancy and social arrangements. Camilla and JB contrived to meet in various friends' houses: '. . . If I can persuade Alistair to make his sister pretend she was there. . . .' she wrote (undated). They became secretly engaged. It was with Balfour that JB first shared the news of his secret engagement. Balfour immediately replied, 'Oh my word, I envy you being in LOVE! I feel old and dried up and that such a thing will never happen to me again. Yes, capitalism is done for and you will be able to get married and all will be lovely – oh I am so glad! It surely will come off, won't it? Meanwhile not a word shall escape my lips. I am so moved by what you tell me. . . .'[6] (This clandestine behaviour was to set a pattern for JB's future engagements for in the eyes of the upper classes he was not a suitable candidate for marriage to their daughters.) Camilla wrote (undated), 'I am looking forward to meeting Evelyn Waugh but I hope he doesn't try and delve into my soul about anything – I am in such a state of nerves and have got such a jumpy conscience that I hardly dare mention your name to anyone in case they should ask me *where* and with *who* and *when* and *why* I saw you last. . . .'[7]

They corresponded, often in picture code, for over a year and their affair, which never got beyond kissing, was eventually ended by Camilla's enraged father who discovered that JB had sent her a copy of James Hanley's recently published and risqué novel, *Boy*. (In the autumn of 1931, Camilla returned to Egypt where her father was the Chief of Police and where she met Christopher Sykes who was to be her future husband.)

In October 1930, JB started working for the *Architectural Review* as assistant editor at three hundred pounds a year. In November, his first collection of verse was published by his infinitely rich friend, Edward James, who collected Surrealist art and in whose company JB witnessed the most startlingly exotic life. In his black-ceilinged and silver-panelled Oxford rooms they had breakfasted on Virginia ham and champagne and read poetry to each other. The result was *Mount Zion* or *In Touch with the Infinite*, whose sub-title (presumably adapted from

Ralph Waldo Trine's devotional work, *In Tune with the Infinite*, then in vogue) was added when they decided to use a picture of a lady with an early upright telephone on the cover. Perhaps the most famous poem it contained was 'Death in Leamington'. JB's passionate interest in typography and book design was kindled by James and together they took much care in the production, using the coloured paper which fireworks were made of. James wrote to JB, 'I suggest that the paper be fairly good and the cover nicely executed, so that while the book may present an epitome of everything that is the worst taste in type and decoration, yet there be an underlying feeling that the whole is well produced. We must not allow the outside world one moment to doubt the deep intensity of our sophistication.'[8]

JB's literary career was about to take off. The editor of the *London Mercury*, J. C. Squire, who had spotted him at Oxford through the *Cherwell*, had already published his poem 'Death in Leamington' and his short story about an obscure Irish peer, 'Lord Mount Prospect'.

1. Lionel Perry's papers.
2. JB, Christopher Sykes interview, Georgetown University Library, Washington DC.
3. JB, *Summoned by Bells* (John Murray, 1960).
4. Anthony and Violet Powell, CLG interview (1992).
5. Anthony and Violet Powell, CLG interview (1992). JB's rhyme about Longford remembered by Maurice Craig.
6. JB's papers, University of Victoria, British Columbia.
7. JB's papers.
8. JB's papers.

To Mary St Clair-Erskine   Sedgwick Collins & Co.
                                              7 Gracechurch Street
December 1928   London EC

My dear Mary,
It's no good asking me what this means that is written on the back –
although I fill in these forms every evening I have not got the slightest
idea of their meaning and my inaccuracy is disastrous. Here is a picture
of me handing round slips in insurance offices – I am the tallest figure.

There you see me quietly waiting and waving my little piece of paper
before being insulted by that nasty looking gentleman at the desk with
his hair parted in the middle and his well-creased trousers. Do you
wonder that I become a little depress'd? Do you wonder that I think of
the peace of Hunger Hill as I gaze out of the Crittall All Steel Efficiency
window at the white tiles of the opposite office? Does it strike you as
unusual that I look forward to wine, cigars and good food as I sit
swallowing baked beans and chicory coffee in an ABC? I am writing
this letter of thanks in the office and the drawing seems to be causing a
considerable amount of disturbance as the clerks continually come up to
my desk with little messages and policies and slips wondering what on
earth I am doing. I must stop.

'The Twentieth year is well-nigh past
Since first our sky was overcast
Oh! would that it might be the last
                    My Mary.'
Isn't that an apt quotation?
PLEASE write to me or telephone to me when you have a spare
moment in London. Then I will propose and Loughie can come in at the
dramatic moment – Goodbye – a thousand thanks.
    John B

> JB's job lasted a very short time.
> The picture was on a separate bit of paper and has now been lost.
> Hunger Hill was M. St C.-E.'s home in Sussex.
> The quotation is from William Cowper's 'To Mary'.
> 'Loughie' was M. St C.-E.'s father, the Earl of Rosslyn, formerly Lord Loughborough.

To Malcolm Brereton   25A Yeoman's Row
9 January 1929   SW3

Dear Sir,
Gerald Heard told me of an idea that I should talk on *Architecture* for the
BBC and that he had spoken to you on the subject. I should be delighted
to give a talk on early nineteenth-century architecture in London or
even on the eighteenth-century styles should you desire it.

Again I am prepared to discourse on Modern English Architecture
although the first-mentioned subject is that upon which I am best
informed; perhaps you will communicate with me.

Yours faithfully, John Betjeman.

> M.B. was a Talks producer at the BBC. He was killed in action in 1942.
> This is JB's first letter to the BBC. Nothing came of it. Gerald Heard, 'but not
> understood', as JB called him, the author, broadcaster, mystic and wit, was an influence
> on JB at the time.

To Mary St Clair-Erskine   As from 53 Church Street
                                           Chelsea
Tuesday 29 January 1929   SW3

My dear Mary,
Nothing will induce me to spell your name 'Marie' – as I don't call you
'Marree'. I shall not toady to these Anglo-Frenchisms. I want to see
your school reminiscences. They will cheer up my lonely office hours
as I wander from company to company buffeted and scorn'd by the vast
commercial world – a world that seeks distraction from the fear of death
and eternity in rudeness during the day and self-indulgence during the
ev'ning. There's a *bon mot* for you to put in your diary. I will disclaim all
credit for it and give it you. There it is – to hum round the dinner table
and make eyes glow with admiration for 'that clever little Mary
Erskine'. Well, it's not a very good *bon mot* and much too laboured. This
is awful, about your leaving the country for six months. Not only will it
mean a plague of those tedious travel letters and those long descriptive
postcards written in pencil: 'This is a *sweet* place and *ever* so old. We
went to the famous *café* here and had *café* and it was only two francs, but
the guide said it was three francs, fortunately I knew it was only two and
was able to explain to the *garçon*. We are having lovely weather – hot sun

and cloudless sky, are you?' All that is crowded onto the part marked 'for correspondence only' in an illegible hand partly rubb'd out in the post. But it will break me up.

I don't know whether I told you that I am going to be a secretary at 'The Crest House, Weybridge, Surrey' on Saturday ev'ning next. Then I retire ever more from the world. But why can't I see you before then? Why can't I look at the Dutch Pictures on Saturday or go out on Friday ev'ning?

I never thanked you enough for your letter and now I must go out with my little leather wallet and scrip and get ready to be insulted. Thank you so much for advertising me so well and kind – sweet girl – the Lord will provide for you. Write and write while you are abroad and don't scruple to tear half or three-quarters of it up after a week or two. Pray accept all the love and devotion of

John B

Mary setting off for the Meet.

Killed.

M. St C.-E. had asked her friends to call her Marie; she was about to set off to Rome with her mother.

    Sir Horace Plunkett, for whom JB was about to work, lived at the Crest House. Gerald Heard had secured him the job.

To Patrick Balfour   Beresford Hotel
                                             Birchington-on-Sea
10 February 1929   Kent

My Dear Patrick,
I chanced to look in the *Tatler* at this bungalow hotel the other day,
when what did I see but a photograph of the Hon. Patrick Balfour
making him appear very red in the nose. I was so sorry not to be able to
have lunch with you the other day and help you, where it was
necessary, with Arthur Pack.

I am at the moment Private Secretary to Sir Horace Plunkett who in
the early eighties was a big man in Agricultural Co-operation. He is still
more than keen on it and being slightly off his head has written the first
chapter of a book of nine chapters no less than seventy-two times. He
says the same thing over and over again and rarely completes one of his
sentences which suits my style of thinking. The pay is fair and the food
and travelling excellent. He is in bad health at the moment and this
hotel is furnished in that Japanese style so popular with the wives of
Anglo-Indian Colonels who retire to Camberley. There is a ballroom
and an 'Oak and Pewter' room which is very pretty.

I was working in the city when Bryan's wedding occurred and could
not accept that invitation I was so proud to possess. If you hear of any
article that needs to be written on architectural or obscure religious
questions you might let me know as I am now reduced to turning an
honest penny to pay off my bills at Oxford.

My dear Patrick, if you are still of my way of thinking in your less
public moments you will do well to go to the roller-skating rink at the
Alexandra Palace on a Saturday afternoon. There are, without
exaggeration, no less than five hundred cups of tea there and an
introduction and a dance can be effected at once. The discovery was one
of the greatest moments of my life. The rink at Margate, near here, is
very good. They come and offer you potato crisps.

Talking the other way, I am amazed at the beauty of Mary Erskine
(Hamish's sister) and I love to contemplate the anger of Hamish if I
were to elope with her.

Tinkerty-tonk old boy. I shall be in London on Wednesday and up at
least once a week from the Crest House, Weybridge, Surrey (Edwardian old-world) and I hope I shall see you. I shall be here until
Wednesday if you care to write but I shall not be offended if you don't.

Love and Kisses, John B

PS I have got a new suit – it is black and very smart and natty.

Bryan Guinness married Diana Mitford, one of the five beautiful daughters of Lord
Redesdale, on 30 January 1929 when she was eighteen.
'Cups of Tea' was a code word for boys.

To Mary St Clair-Erskine   The Crest House
                                                    Weybridge
[Undated]   Surrey

Dear Mary,
A thousand thanks for your letter – as this is the first time that I am out
of bed I am able to enclose your MS and use a typewriter. I am so sorry
that you too have had 'flu. I wonder whether it was of the sort that
produces great aches and pains all over the body and then causes acute
mental depression for three or four days. I think Roman 'flu may be a
little different unless yours was caught in England. I have been reading
a lot of Wells lately. He seems to me to be underrated although he is
entirely a scientist. The *Undying Fire* and *Men Like Gods* are most
stirring. He does appreciate the horror of British Life. I will send you
my poems when I have typed out some copies of them. Mark
[Ogilvie-Grant] has had 'flu.
    John B

To Alan Pryce-Jones   The Crest House
                                                    Weybridge
15 February 1929   Surrey

My Dear Hideous,
Would you be so good as to copy out for my employer and to send to me
those hackneyed lines of Erasmus Darwin which prophesy the use of
the air as a means of transit? This request will give you an idea of our
mental state. I am joining the Society of Friends for a time.
    Andrew Wordsworth in a letter to me the other day wrote as follows:
'I shall never forget the emotion with which . . . I heard Alan read that
beautiful poem ending with the words:
    'It was not here nor there
    Nor perhaps anywhere.'

I do not expect you will have time to write to me. If however you have doubts and speculations about the after-life do let me initiate you in popular philosophy and when I don't know you can ask Gerald Heard. Christopher [Wood] has got 'flu.

Tinkerty Tonk, JB

A.P.-J. arrived as a freshman at Magdalen in 1927 from Eton. On first meeting him, JB remarked on his extraordinary cape-shaped dressing gown; they became friends from that point.

JB went to Quaker Meetings in 1929 encouraged by Gerald Heard, but did not join the Religious Society of Friends until 1931.

Christopher Wood was a rich young man who shared a flat in Portman Square with Gerald Heard.

To Mary St Clair-Erskine   The Crest House
                                                    Weybridge
19 February 1929   Surrey

Oh Fair One,
Supposing someone at that convent were to see the first three words of this letter. You would be suspected of carrying on an illicit romance. A thousand thanks for your letter. I am glad you saw the Pope. You seem also to have been affected by the scenes which must have been very majestic. If the Church of Rome lasts (and I do not give it more than half a century) what you witnessed will indeed be a great historic event. I must say that it seems to me to be very like a last gasp. I am afraid I am being unduly irritating. I will talk to you when I see you again about the questions of after-life and we will have a good long argument. I do however believe that we change to something outside the three dimensions and unlimited but not individual (for individuality implies earthliness and the limits of human consciousness) essence or body or whatever you like to call it for we cannot describe it in words nor imagine it. We experience it, I say again, when we forget ourselves at mass or at the theatre.

I had a letter from your beloved mother the other day all the way from Venezuela and in pencil. Hamish is, I suppose, still the leader of Oxford society. One can hardly expect him to write when he is at Oxford because there are so many things to do and think about. It is only when one returns to oneself that the need for self-expression arises again. I am being clever aren't I? It is part of my ambition to go to Italy when I shall be able. I dislike strong sunlight and any but rainy damp weather but the buildings and the paintings and the statues all around you now, fill me with awe and longing. I wonder what has happened to poor Loughie. I went through Loughborough Junction the other day or rather what once was it. A fearful gloom lay over it so different from your Italian skies. It has suddenly occurred to me that you might write a book like *Elizabeth and Her German Garden* or *The Enchanted April* which is an infuriating thing about Italy saying this kind of thing: 'As I sit here after my *siesta* and watch the lazy *braggadocios* (itinerant weavers) crawling up the dusty hill in their dog-carts, all the sweet charm of this south country comes over me. Old Sienna, who acts as parlour maid and cook in La Villa Boncompagnie tells me that when the sun sets on the lake opposite the peasants say it is as though an enormous *orangi* (orange) had been thrown into the water. Why do people bother to live in those silly, dusty cities when there are all these flowers and glorious Italian evenings!' That might easily (save for the last sentence) be Compton Mackenzie. And yet that style will find its way into every suburban home and on the river Thames in the summer faded typists will read it to the tune of a gramophone. Good bye – this letter seems rather as though I were trying to make conversation. Now for Agricultural co-operation.

Love, John B

> *Elizabeth and Her German Garden* and *The Enchanted April* were written by Countess Elizabeth von Arnim, who became Lady Russell.
> M.StC.-E. toyed with the idea of writing novels and asked JB to read her efforts.

To Mary St Clair-Erskine   Sezincote
                                              Moreton in Marsh
19 March 1929   Gloucestershire

Oh Fair Maria,

This is an exquisite house in the 1800 Anglo-Indian style. I enclose some postcards of it. I have been at the door of death with the after effects of 'flu and jaundice and am recuperating here. I have written to you for a definite reason so you can skip this until you get to the end of the letter and then look at the paragraph that begins with capital letters.

As usual, I am on the rocks. Out of pure kindness of heart I asked someone that I knew at school and at Oxford intimately and whom I had been wont to consider a friend of mine, to take over my wages and secretaryship with Horace Plunkett while I was ill. He was out of a job and penniless. He told H.P., while I was away, that he thought I was too much of a flibbertigibbet for the job and proposed himself in my stead. He then lied to a number of people in which I am happy to say he was caught out but H.P. being mad, as I think I told you, thought he was a good honest chap and much better than me. While he was doing this job in my stead he was offer'd a job on the *Manchester Guardian*. But he refused this because he thought mine was better. I am consequently chucked out and vainly trying to keep alive on nothing. Oh Heaven! I believe I shall end up as a reporter on the *Portsmouth Evening News* – a nice bright job in the hub of the social world.

What of your 'flu – have you been near death like me? If not just pay attention for a moment.

MRS GORDON DUGDALE (sister-in-law of the sweet person who owns this house) and HER DAUGHTER PAMELA (eighteen and to be presented this year, I am told, kind hearted and delightful but I have never seen her) are arriving in Rome on March 25 (about). They are incredibly rich and know no one in Rome – will you mind if they come and see you? I have given them your address. The mothers are huntin' shootin' and fishin' people up at the House (Ch[rist] Ch[urch], Oxford). Write to me and let me know about everything and the glories of St Peter's and the Baroque churches. Hamish is off his head and your mother has returned but I have not heard of her yet.

Fare well and are well, *adieux*, JB

> Sezincote in Gloucestershire, JB's 'home from home' with the Dugdales, was built in 1805 by Samuel Pepys Cockerell. JB had been introduced to the son of the house, John Dugdale, by Lionel Perry.
>
> It was John Edward Bowle who stole JB's job.

To Mary St Clair-Erskine   Heddon Court
                                              Cockfosters
17 April 1929   Herts

Oh fair child,
How terrible it is to think of you covered over with spots and how sad to find the notepaper so badly burnt. I was able to read your letter, tears dropping the while, at the sweet sympathy you show for me. Although you see that this is written from my home address, it is the address of a home that no longer owns me. Because I will not go into business my father has virtually cut me off. May you never know how dreadful it is

to dislike your father, may you never be worried and complained of by your mother and abused and taunted by your father.

I have come here for one night to pack up my things – my father has gone out to dinner but has left a message to say that he may come home early 'in order to talk to me' – this effectually prevents my going out for the evening. The pen trembles in my hand for it is only to tell me that I am undutiful and a cad that he wants to see me at all. Then he will say that I have not got it in me to appreciate how deeply, how terribly, how mercilessly I grieve him by not going into the nice little office he has arranged for me and helping to support him and my mother in their old age. As he has an income of about seven thousand a year when he has paid his taxes and as he spends it all on himself, there is little cause to worry over his future poverty. It makes me sick to think of him.

I am off to be a prep school master in Barnet at a hundred and eighty pounds a year. This is not so bad as I get my keep and will have enough to be independent during the comparatively long holidays. Moreover I am having a book of verse published under the title of *Chapel and Spa* and Longman's, the publishers, have commissioned me to write a book on the obscurer branches of English sectarianism. This will not be as dull as it sounds. In fact it ought to be very amusing.

I seem to talk about nothing but myself. Suffering has increased my egotism. I wallow in the pleasures of Melancholy. You must be sad too with Hamish (bless him!) going to look like a little idiot at a ball in Sicily dress'd up as Emmanuel Swedenborg or someone. Poor old Patrick Balfour – have you seen him? He has been sweet to me in my misfortunes. But now they are over, now smiles wreath this unusually sallow face and I make firmer my resolves to cut out any friends I made at school.

When next I have a permanent address it will be this:

Heddon Court
Cockfosters
Herts.

Can you read it? Write, fair one; this handwriting, the result of a businessman's nib which my father characteristically provides, must try your eyesight. When people of your age get measles they often go blind or have to wear glasses for life. I feel I must lend you a little of my depression. Tell me when you can read and I will send you books, meanwhile remember the unceasing devotion of that pitiable object of charity, John Betj

JB started his job at Heddon Court, Barnet, at the end of April 1929 (he left in July 1930).

    JB's first book of verse, *Mount Zion*, published by his friend Edward James in 1931, was going to be called *Chapel and Spa*. His book on sectarianism never materialized.

To Bryan Guinness   Barnet

2 May 1929

My dear Bryan,
A thousand apologies that I could not come to tea last Tuesday. I am a prep-schoolmaster all over again. Admittedly the job is convenient as it is at Barnet, which is almost London, and the school is fairly good. Michael Dugdale was educated here.

    My vicissitudes have been almost unbelievable since I saw you last in the great hall of Euston Station. By the way I have got a wedding present for you which arrived at my house three days after your wedding. It is too large to send by post, a musical box with bells and drums that plays Balfe and Polkas; a duplicate of one I have myself. I will have it dispatched now that I know where you live. It is brilliantly useless.

    Now look here, old boy, I can get away to dinner any evening. What do you say to a little meal one day with you and your authoress wife? It would by such fun after the prunes and suet of this place. I long to see Miss [Diana] Mitford.

    I feel an awful cad for not having written before but my thoughts are often in your direction old boy so cheeriohski.

    Tinkerty tonk, John B

To Patrick Balfour   Trebetherick
                                                       Wadebridge
5 August 1929   Cornwall
Bank Holiday

My dear Patrick,
A thousand thanks for your letter. I have been very busy this morning avoiding a ghastly day of fishing – picnicking on Bodmin Moor. The

arrival of a letter for me with hubbub gave me an excuse to stay a long time in the lavatory and so avoid going. I have now the place to myself and can criticise to my heart's content the old world floor and older world grate and the crazy paving and bits of brass and pewter. This house is amazingly like Hinges [Hunger] Hill. The doors and the paint used are the same. I wish to heaven it were more comfortable. Bess [Betjemann] is infused with an idea that the maids have too much to do. We are almost reduced to making our own beds although I should have thought that three servants for three people was adequate. I leave here on the 14th.

I hope when I leave to be allowed to stay with you on that night and on the next before I go to Scotland with the Addises for a stay of five days.

Then I will come back and we will have at least a week during which time we can visit the Colonel [Kolkhorst]. I am so glad that you and Evan [Morgan] met him. He is perfection. Yes, I'm glad about Baden Powell.

As to Dinard, I feel that my finances and my time will neither run to it. Wouldn't Aberdeen suit Schruffy [George Schurhoff] better?

Hobhouse must have got into communication with the insulting caretaker at 53 who gave John Edward Bowle a bad boiled egg for his breakfast on three consecutive mornings, the only thing I know of in his favour. She puts down sheets of paper in front of you as you enter the house lest you should dirty the floor. But it is worse here.

I have discovered a rather beautiful girl here aged thirteen and like a Shepperson drawing and my sex becomes rampant. Blue eyes and beautiful voice and figure. I think I must be a bit heter.

Will you let me know if it will be all right on the evening of the 14th? Give my love to Mrs Jenkins and thank her for the collars she sent on. Dear Mrs J. I have to borrow all the notepaper I use, hence this curious shape as the address has been torn off.

Love, JB

Mrs Jenkins was the housekeeper at Yeoman's Row.

To Patrick Balfour   Hartrigge
                                              Jedburgh
17 August 1929   Roxburghshire

My dear Patrick,
I do dislike those uncompromising Scotch females who act like vicious
swans over their lunch on the Railway. The train was full of them from
Pont Street with their powder put on rather badly and with an air of
Martyrdom when they were travelling third and felt that they ought to
have been travelling first but could not afford it. They all wore simply
fearful hats and carried dogs about.

   We have family prayers here which last a good time and then a sung
grace of two verses, we stand up to eat porridge so that by the time
breakfast begins one is quite tired.

   Everywhere the peasants will point out boulders behind which
Burns took down his trousers and ruins where Sir Walter Scott took
down his sheep dog. I think I am being rather witty.

   What I want you to do is to name where you want to meet me when
we cross to Skye in order that I may see about getting there. Is it Fort
William or Mallaig? Tinkerty-tonk, old boy, and good luck to you and
the Colonel. Tell me EVERYTHING please about your visit.

   Love, JB

> JB stayed with a pupil from Heddon Court, Richard Addis, and his family and
> afterwards with P.B. and his parents, Lord and Lady Kinross, on the Island of Skye.

To Lady Kinross   Heddon Court
                                              Cockfosters
16 September 1929 (Morning)   Herts

Dear Lady Kinross,
It was so depressing to leave Skye and wait
about two hours in Kyle of Lochalsh while
men did nothing to the car, still in sight
of the misty mountains, that my temper
became very bad. I saw Heriot Row and
two water colours – very nice – like this:

Which were yours, Patrick told me. I was honestly (g) surprised to see such miracles of taste and technique – not that I thought they would not be good (g) – but that they should be as good as all that. I thought Heriot Row so good – that staircase and the entrance Hall. We could not pass an opinion on the drawing room because the amber light made the walls look white. I saw Miss Pamela's and Miss Rosemary's bedroom with all their childhood treasures and the religious pictures. There was no room for Miss Ursula.

Mrs Jenkins is in mauve this morning. How very gloomy his lordship's study is with all those law books round it.

You will find yourself longing for Skye. As soon as one reaches the mainland the atmosphere changes. It must be psychic, you know, and, talking of psychic, Patrick had a dream, coming down in the sleeper, about Eleanor Glyn. He dreamt she sent him long telegrams about souls and morals which bored him very much and surprised the people at Killyakin Post Office. He told me all this in the sleeper. When we got to Yeoman's Row there was a long letter from Eleanor Glyn all about *Beauty* and *wide open spaces* in answer to a postcard Patrick sent from Skye.

PS Poor old Hew.

Gosh! I did enjoy myself in Skye. School is going to be so awful after it. There is a new games master from Malvern coming.

Guess who these are and fill in the names underneath, cut out coupon and send to Mr Gossip, *Daily Sketch*, and you will receive a thousand pounds for correct solution.

What a vulgar place Gleneagles is, we had a bathe and tea there. I enjoyed it but could scarcely believe such horror existed.

Oh I did like Skye – thank you so much.

Yours respectfully, John Betjeman

Patrick Balfour and JB travelled back to London together after staying on Skye. They stopped at 17 Heriot Row, the Kinrosses' Edinburgh house, which had been the home of Robert Louis Stevenson.

To Patrick Balfour

14 October 1929

My dear Patrick,
The enclosed is an eyelash of one of the boys. It is quite a short one
compared with some of his lashes which are nearly three quarters of an
inch long. He is called Murrant and is very rich.
    Yours, JB

[On the back of the envelope]
Hollom IV wrote the following lines today on R.101 which he passed
over:

> An awful wonder
> Grey from tip to tail
> Moving 'gainst wind
> Nor any sign of sail.

To Alan Pryce-Jones   Heddon Court
                                                   Cockfosters
8 November 1929   Herts

My dear Hideous,

I have recently (My dear Archibald be so good as to leave the
room) been the recipient of the proofs of 'Mount (No, I should

like you to go away entirely, please) Prospect'. When I come to look

through it a second time I found it (Keep your hands away from

your face and go away) dreary as the Alexandra Palace. But still if [J. C.]

Squire still thinks it's funny it brings in money (If you think you

are hiding yourself, Archibald, you are greatly mistaken) to one sorely in need of it. I am reviewing Norwood on Education for the *Architectural Review*. It is a monument of dullness.

Chiefly I had to write to you about this – have you read Random

Records by (Get out of the way) George the Younger. New and

fascinating light on Dr Johnson Gillon and all 'the Club'. Ask Squire. It is a vilely written book in a 'racy' Regency style with jokes worthy of a colonial Bishop – e.g. so our postmen too, are becoming *men of letters!* (in italics – this last).

Hannah More's correspondence is absorbing. I imagine it is quite well known.

I suppose you have heard that Patrick has met someone who has spoken to Lord Guillamore. Ring him up and ask (Sloane 5629).
I am in bed with bronchitis.
Accept the love of

I cannot sign my name because Archibald, a trifle soiled after his fight, has got back again.

> JB's poem 'Lord Mount Prospect' was published by J.C. Squire in the *London Mercury* in December 1929.
> Lord Guillamore was an obscure Irish peer with whom JB had become intrigued when in Ireland.

To Mary St Clair-Erskine   Heddon Court
                                             Cockfosters
21 November 1929   Herts

My dear Maria,
For once I was admitted into 'the world' last night and who should I meet but Hamish while in the distance your father cut me. I thought that if I were to send you a book you would be obliged to write to me when all the excitement of dancing and meeting new pals, chums and comrades was over. I hear lovely stories of the dance you went to and of the success you were. The already pale star of an inefficient preparatory school master must be waning fast.

But seriously, I should very much like to know what you are doing and writing. If you are still writing.

Old Lionel [Perry] has just been up here to see me today. He said he saw you at a ball. Too grand and scintillating I expect you were. It is not often that I see the *Tatler* and it came as rather a shock to come on a picture of you. It was rather like what I have attempted overleaf.

I do not expect you had time to see it. However, when you get back to Hunger Hill you will have some spare time on your hands. Pray accept the loyalty, homage, devotion, affection, admiration and respect of

Your abject servant, John Betjeman

PS Our games master here saw your photograph and fell in love with you. I know you will be delighted and will have a message for him even if you have none for me.

> The illustration has been lost.

To Patrick Balfour   Heddon Court
                                                  Cockfosters
2 December 1929   Herts

My dear Patrick,

Alas! I should have remembered at the time but Wednesday next is December 4th when I am going with Dotty Hope [Anthony Hope-Hawkins] to the 1917 Club dinner. It is a well-established engagement and for all the attraction of the other I cannot put it off. If you are able to come to another arrangement you might ring me up tomorrow morning and let me know.

I am on tenterhooks. Hollom IV follows me about wherever I go. He likes to look at those large copies of the *Architectural Review* with me. He says he wants to ask me a question and somehow he doesn't know how to ask it. In a private way he has told me that twice today. I wonder what the question can be?

I did enjoy myself on St Andrew's night. I should like to hear of her Ladyship's opinion of it. I was delighted to see her in that velvet coat. She is perfection. I often think of Rosemary [P.B.'s sister].

I was very rude to one of the mistresses today. There is rather a bust up.

Farewell love and apologies, JB

On 10 February 1930 JB wrote to P.B.: 'I enclose as a little present to you some of Hollom J.'s verses to me. . . . The Colonel's advice to me has been never to put down on paper anything that could incriminate one, so I have followed his advice.' Hollom's verse read:

> Would that his heart were open to my own,
> I wish I knew his thoughts, and mine were known,
> I wish, and yet I hardly dare, to know,
> Yet so it is, and so it must remain.

To Patrick Balfour   Konigshof Grand Hotel Royal
15 April 1930   Bonn

Dear Patrick,

It is useless to pretend that I enjoy myself abroad. The continual difficulty of overcoming a foreign language which the meanest children in the public gardens opposite can speak with fluency, the constant frustration of natural impulse through inability to communicate with the object of one's desires, overcomes the spirit as much as it mortifies the flesh. For instance I have drunk tea in my life but never have I wanted to drink it so much as in this town. It is obtainable but I do not know how to ask for it; it is waiting steaming hot, but I have not the courage to depend upon my *Hugo's Simplified Course*.

I suppose the buds are appearing now outside the Yeo but here they are out already, indecently forward. If the Sarcophagus [George Schurhoff] were here with his knowledge of German and you with yours of French we might scrape through comfortably. At the moment it is like being cold-shouldered at Harrogate. Dotty is never out of the minster church and Mr Newcome never of his armchair. The overheating of the hotel is unendurable. Dotty and I are going to another town tomorrow which is nearer to the Abbey – only eight miles distant – which we are to visit at eight o'clock on Maundy Thursday morning. But we are only going for two days.

Do you remember how Victorian the evening light was on that road to Inverness last summer? Do you remember the rocks and the small conifers at the edge of brake and brae? This place is like that. Not unlike an oleograph. It is disfigured by festoons of electric wire. Across every field run several cables, up every hill a funicular railway. Nor is that all. Down every dusty road tread the *wanderfogel* or some such word. It is hardly necessary to describe them since they wear velvet and pepperpot hats. When the bells start thundering from the Romanesque churches and the sun sets behind the pine-clad forests up the roads, along the tramway lines march the *wanderfogel* with their arms locked, their hearts and their mouths open. They are going to walk across Germany for their Easter holidays in groups of two.

I cannot go on but I should appreciate a letter to this address. My love to the poor Sarcophagus; if Dotty were not out to tea with a High Church Lutheran lady he would doubtless send his to you both.

By the hall door there is a beautiful tulip.

Love, JB

JB went on a culture trip to Germany with William Clonmore and Harry Newcombe.

To Bryan Guinness   Hotel Gasthof der Brudergemeine
21 April 1930   Neuwied am Rhein

My dear Bryan,
Knowing of your interest in Religious movements or rather of your attention in listening to mine I hasten to tell you from this one of their settlements – in a few words an account of the graveside service of the Moravians. When I have done this I have a disclosure to make to you of no great importance.

This is an eighteenth-century town, a refuge for all early reformation sects who still retain their substantial chapels – the Mennonites, the New Apostles, Baptists, Lutherans and Moravians. The Moravians here have a separate community subject to its own laws and shops. The houses are good simple eighteenth-century: with rococo front doors and the plaster walls are painted now green, now pink, now white. The Brethren's church is an enormous white building within – benches white, organ case white, gallery and boxes white. The congregation and pastor wear black. The unmarried women wear one sort of cap, the married ones another. They sit on one side of the church, the men sit on the other. It is all something like a dream it is so unbelievable. No one visits this town. It is considered ugly, being so 'plain'.

At four o'clock on Sunday morning, the Brethren's band assembled outside in the cobbled street and played their Easter hymn. That woke me up and by five I was in the big white church. We had some hymns – the Moravians are great hymn writers, we have Montgomery and Fenwick of that persuasion in England – and there we assembled in procession and walked behind the brass band to the burial ground about a mile away. There surrounding the graves, neatly divided according to our ages, we hailed the rising sun – the resurrection from the dead, among the rotting houses of eighteenth-century Moravians.

George Meredith was educated at the big school house which collapsed during the war. The women all wear special caps showing whether they are married, unmarried or children. But that is not all, staying in this, the brothers' guesthouse and drinking the brothers' very potent beer is an American Moravian lady. She is Vice-President of the Moravian Historical Society and lives at Bethlehem, Pennsylvania. You must know that Count Zinzendorf revived the Moravians in the eighteenth century and was exiled for it. He was a wonderful but most peculiar man. He went to live in Chelsea in a house, a part of which Whistler went to live in afterwards. It was called Lindsay House and a Moravian designed it for him. There I believe you are going to live.

Here is an account given to me by the Moravian Lady of USA of the architect, Sigismund von Gersdorf, born on 14 September 1692 in Herrnsdorf bei Oberlansity. Mother of the house of Culm. When a boy was page to Elector of Saxony. Joined the army but, being delicate, resigned. Married in 1726. In 1741 went to Herrnhut Moravian Headquarters and was so impressed that he joined them and sent his children to school there. Died in 1777. A grand man. Built much in Germany.

I should think that no one in London (not even the greatest authorities) knows who built that house. Do go to 32 Felton Lane off Fleet Street and ask to see the Chapel. You will find more there. Then get Hutton's *History of the Moravian Church* – a truly stirring work. I am not being funny. You and that delightful missus of yours might become Moravian – you might be another Zinzendorf and save the church, which is in a bad way in England.

I hope the christening [Jonathan Guinness's] was not a failure, although I hold that it ought to have been in some other religious sect – it would have done the Swedenborgians a lot of good – they are in very low water. My affection and Dotty's, whom I see tomorrow, I hope – I return on Saturday next.

John Betjeman

Nikolaus Ludwig, Graf von Zinzendorf (1700–60) was bishop of the refounded Moravian Church.
Lindsay House was (and is) 96–101 Cheyne Walk, divided into separate houses.

To Patrick Balfour   Pakenham Hall
                                                        Castlepollard
1 September 1930   Co. Westmeath

My dear Patrick,
Bess actually gave me the money for my fare over to here on condition
that I returned to Cornwall on the 9th. Well, it is something to be so
much in demand. I was grieved to hear the Sarcophagus [George
Schurhoff] told me you were in Germany on the day I visited London
and stayed one night at the Yeo.

I have something extra special for you and also, by the way, I am
advertising you here cunningly and well and have so advertised you at
Sezincote that we will spend the first weekend we have free when I
return to London in that Indian Palace and I do not know how to begin.
This is it. Lord Trimlestown's seat is called Bloomsbury near Kells and
near this very remote place, as you know. We devised a very clever
scheme for calling on him. We made out a petition to prevent the
demolition of Dublin Places of Worship – which, by the way, are of
course not going to be destroyed – and took it for him to sign.
Bloomsbury is very difficult to find and when you do reach it, is very
small. We asked about Lord Trimlestown in the district and no one had
heard of him. There we found Bloomsbury, an unpretentious William
IVth structure in the Roman Manner and painted light mauve and
brown. We learned at a lodge near the grass-grown drive and ruined
gates that Lord Trimlestown had left it fourteen years ago – 'Those
were grand days,' the old man said. His eldest daughter is a Mrs
Ratcliffe who lives in an even smaller Georgian house near Kells. That
is all. Four of his nine sisters are nuns and the rest have not married very
well. I am so sorry.

On the way back heart-broken and stricken we found an interesting
sight in the roadside. An old man who lived in a wheelbarrow with a
mackintosh and umbrella over the top, all the year round. He was deaf
and drunk but not dotty. I think he was a brother of Lord Trimlestown.

This is an early nineteenth-century Gothic Palace in the remotest
part of Ireland, to right and left rise round towers (hold this page up to
the light and you will see one), ruined abbeys, ruined castles and
prehistoric camps, I am in heaven.

JB

Pakenham Hall was the home of Edward and Christine Longford. (It is now called Tullynally, its original Irish name.)

Lord Trimlestown was inspiration to JB's article in the *Evening Standard*, 'Peers without Tears' (1933).

To Patrick Balfour   Pakenham Hall
                                                          Castlepollard
13 September 1930   Co. Westmeath

My dear Patrick,

Thank you so much for your numerous letters: oh, would that I could come and see you and that glorious company in Scotland. Alas, I had no money before yesterday and now I must go back to Bess in Cornwall who is getting reproachful. I shall return to London on 27 September and go to Heddon Court for the weekend and then start looking for rooms.

I have gathered quite a lot about Lord Trimlestown, his ancestors and his sisters and daughters now living. I have made up a little poem:

> -curry, -brock and -mell are gone,
> Soon 'twill be farewell to Clon;
> Little known they were before,
> They are even less with -more.

The other day we went to the Cavan Tennis Tournament. It was all organised by Lord Farnham who did the umpiring, carried a bucket of sand to the place where competitors serve and arranged that a subscription dance should take place in his house.

His house is called Farnham and, as he has had to sell most of his furniture, it is a little bare but the acetylene gas makes a brave show, so do Lady Farnham (who has an unfortunate habit of winking) and his two daughters Verbena and Verbosa. They all told us it was very sporting of us to come several times. Lord Farnham is just like a pear. Very tall and slim. Do write to him as he is so badly off and Verbena and Verbosa are so pretty. I fell in love with Verbena and danced with her. She is very London.

Dotty is now at the Palazzo D'Inferno, Portugal with Colonel Kolkhorst. You might mention that too.

My dear Patrick I long to see you and wish I could do so before I go to London but funds and reproaches are unsurmountable.

I have had two letters from Bloody in two days.

I think Longford is delightful – amusing, appreciative of our jokes and no loony.

Farewell and write again, John B

Love to the Baroness Hewie, Rosemary, Ursula and Pamela.

> JB finished at Heddon Court in the summer term and stayed with P.B. when he first returned to London.
>
> JB composed endless joke rhymes about Ireland: his verse is a play on the name Clonmore.
>
> Verbena Farnham was in fact called Verena, and Verbosa, Marjory.

To Diana Guinness   2 Culross Street
                                                   Grosvenor Square
5 January 1931   London W1

My dear Diana,

Just as I was taking up my pen to write a Collins Music-Hall to you – what should arrive but a telegram to say *Prospects Rosy Return on Friday Bryan*. Was it a true telegram? Good Lord! Supposing it is.

HERE ARE THE MITFORD GIRLS
IN THEIR LATEST SONG SUCCESS
AT THE
CHISWICK EMPIRE
Am I supposed to be coming really? Glory be!
Love to Bryan and of course to
Pamela Mitford
from
JB

'A Collins' is slang for a thank-you letter, deriving from the obsequious behaviour of Mr Collins in Jane Austen's novel *Pride and Prejudice*. The Music-Hall reference is a JB addition.

To Camilla Russell

28 July 1931

The Architectural Review
9 Queen Anne's Gate
Westminster SW1

Dearest C,

Will you never have any consideration for others who are always considering you? Have you seen about those things yet at Stow?

I want:

> 1 tin of Sanitas
> 1 lb of Borwick's Baking Powder (best – ask Mrs Hobbes for this)
> 1 tin of Keating's Powder
> 3 ozs of peppercorns
> One bottle of Italts [sic] Invalid Port
> 5 Miniature fir trees for a little Japanese garden I am thinking of making in a lid of a biscuit tin.

Please see about these *at once* they are *most important*.

Your most affectionate and loving, Mother

Camilla Duckie,

I enjoyed myself so much at ye olde Manor. I wonder if you can read this message:

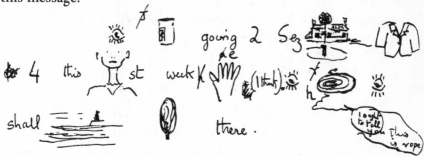

Since I left Little Compton and returned to my slum in London I found out that my basement, besides being infested with large pink rats, is also the arbous [sic] of typhus germs. I think I am dying. As I should like to see you before I die I hope you will understand that message. It may be your last chance.

Remember to wear flannel next your skin during this cold spell. Give my love to Faith Montague (notice the final 'e') if she is still with you. I must say I did like her – she keeps one up to form. I suppose she's just crashed off in a super-charged Mercedes to Bicestershire.

I regard you with the deepest affection (I wrote to your aunt yesterday).

Love and Kisses, JB

> C.R., a nineteen-year-old beauty, was based in Cairo where her father, Russell Pasha, was the Head of Police, but stayed in Gloucestershire with her great-aunt in the summer. JB met and fell for her at Sezincote. He often wrote to her in a scolding tone pretending to be her mother whom they both referred to as 'Red Nose', or 'the Nose'.
>
> Ye Olde Manor was C.R.'s great-aunt Gertrude Harris's house at Little Compton near Sezincote. (It had burned down in 1929 but was restored by 1931.)
>
> The message reads, 'I am going to Sezincote for this next weekend (I think). I hope I shall see you there.'
>
> 'Arbous' may refer to 'arbovirus (arthropod-borne) infections'.

To Camilla Russell   47 Upper Brook Street
14 August 1931   London W1

My darling 'Miller,
In case I do not see you tomorrow – which seems to me extremely likely considering the violent avalanche of circumstances against us – I have got the faithful old Lionel to act as emissary. He is elderly and dear to me and utterly reliable. Give what messages you like to him. I have an awful feeling that our correspondence may be tampered with. Thank God you leave that incommodious little Catball on Sunday. I must know what line to take with your aunt.

If Anthony [Russell] has his heart in the right place he will let me stay at ye olde Ridgewaye next weekend when you are there; I have written to him an appealing letter. In that case we can concoct endless plans. This sudden blow is no more than an incentive as far as I am concerned. Why the Ethel M. Dell are you not allowed to see who you like? I shall come down in a car with Lord Alfred Douglas, Tom Douglas, Norman Douglas, Horatio Bottomley, and Mrs Hearn and set light to Catball when dear little Red Nose and her blasted textiles are in it. I wonder if she is at the bottom of it all? I must confess that I have never loved you so deeply as I do now. It takes circumstances like this to get me on the hop with annoyance. I think I shall have Red Nose exiled from Egypt and from England for receiving and dealing in stolen woven goods.

Would you be so kind as to imprint a piece of paper for me, to go back with Lionel as a token of good faith and fellowship and the work of each for weal of all. I hear that they have balanced the budget. This will only increase class hatred (hatred of the lower classes) because of the ten per cent off the dole and will also do no more than put off the collapse until next year's budget [which] will have to meet an ever greater deficit owing to the . . . oh enough of it. You will be back again then. I shall whisk you off to Ireland when the collapse comes and there two enormous eyes will roll around the emerald fields and purple hills and a cool hand will clasp my clammy one and together we will walk to the Lake Isle of Innisfree or Pakenham or Furness or Shelton Abbey. Darling I love you I love you I love you. Dorothea and Dorothea every day. It's hell. But my God it's exciting, ain't it duckie?

Clean up your little face and go and be nice to everyone, because I love you and don't care what happens.

Love and Kisses, JB

> Lady Russell (Dorothea) had found out about C.R.'s liaison with JB and had whisked her off to Catball, a house not far from Little Compton.
> Anthony Russell was a rich and distant cousin of Camilla who had a house called The Ridgeway.
> C.R. replied (undated): 'Circles and sticks a bird and a tree. When will my Twitchie come back to me. I miss you so much, oh misery me! I love you, *I love you, I love you*, after which burst of affection let me tell you that I am absolutely in the Depths without you, *why* aren't you still here, it is as you say Ethel M. D. Hell now that you have gone and left me to the not-so-tender mercies of Mater. The Pater is being jolly decent . . .'

To Patrick Balfour

Sezincote
Moreton-in-Marsh
Gloucestershire

16 August 1931
Lord's Day

Dear Patrick,

I am so sorry that I have not written to you before but I have felt all the time that when I do write it must be a letter that will amuse you and I have become more and more self-conscious about it until now my letter will read like something from the correspondence of Sir Walter Scott. I suppose you have heard that old Lionel has gone off to be male attendant to old Pratt Barlow and that Dotty is friends with Evelyn Waugh in the arms of the Scarlet Woman and is in a highbrow Papist publishing firm called Sheed and Ward which brings out books on *Cultural Religion, A Study in Inspirationalism*.

Pamela [Mitford] and I had lunch the other day. She was wearing an orange beret and a black blouse and the mountain air had given a Palmolive tint to her cheeks so we went to the Café Royal where we saw G. Heard, whose new book *The Social Function of Religion* has so impressed Aldous Huxley. I have become more friendly with H. Nicolson, speaking of the great. I ought to tell you that I proposed marriage to a jolly girl last weekend and got accepted. It has left me rather dippy. It occurred at two in the morning – suddenly two arms were raised from the floor and put round me, for I was sitting in a chair in an old-world Tudor manor house and then I was accepted and I kissed first the tip of the nose and then the neck and then the forehead and we took off our shoes in order to go upstairs quietly and we turned off the lights and stood on the stone floor of the hall and suddenly two cool little hands were in mine and then a subtly unresisting body pressed against me and I kissed her full on the lips for the first time. Since then there have been other kisses. Patrick, don't say anything about it because the parents are certain to object and with my reputation it would be very trying if it got about. I am counting on the break-up of capitalism for a chance of marrying. The Oxford economists are giving it another six months. Germany and America have another two months. Poor old Maurice Hastings. Neither you nor I have anything to lose and I think it is rather pleasing than not and we are living in the most important times since the Reformation. I wonder whether we will survive the changes that are rapidly approaching. I hear you are writing a novel. I cannot think how you can be well enough if you are abroad. Thank God I am in England. If you want any help over here with the manuscript do give it to me but I suppose you will use A. D. Peters. I have rather more friends again now, thank God, although I was in very low water when you left England. My God, I wish you would come back. Don't say anything about that engagement business, Patrick. It may come to nothing. It may come to something. I have written an attack, in verse form, on the average Wykehamist which is appearing in the *Weekend Review* next week. I wish I knew your address. I go to Clandeboye on Wednesday or Thursday so will you write to me there, if you want to say anything?

Your photographs, especially of the Marboeuf Garage, are all that could be desired and we are shoving them into a town planning number, though God knows when that will appear. The Garage, by a stroke of ill fortune was captured by the *Architect and Building News* just before we got it. Do you want any books? Would you like Gerald's?

Yours with love and kisses, JB

Bobby Pratt-Barlow was a rich kindly musician who was patron to artists, a friend of the Prince of Wales, and did nothing much in life. He lived in Sicily.

Gerald Heard's book was called *The Social Substance of Religion*.

Maurice Hastings, who leased the great house Rousham near Oxford and whom JB called 'Malpractice', was wildly eccentric and jumped the dining-room table on his hunter. He didn't have a penny until he married the American heiress, Rosemary Crane.

P. B. sometimes took photographs for the *Architectural Review*.

To Camilla Russell

as from
c/o Countess of Longford
Pakenham Hall
Castlepollard
Co. Westmeath

26 August 1931

IRELAND

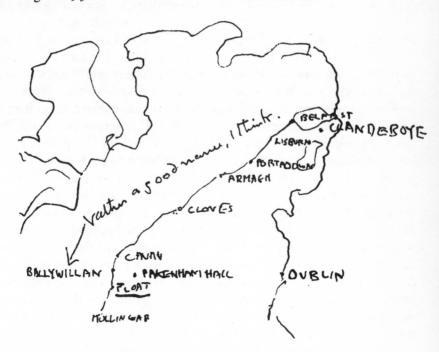

In the twelve a.m. express (all stations) Belfast to Cavan change for Great Southern Railway to Float.

Darling,
Your letter arrived today just before I was leaving Clandeboye for a delightfully obscure journey right through the North of Ireland over

the border and into the dear old Free State which is far better. Cavan where I have forty minutes to wait is the scene of the Protestant v. Catholic riots. I hope I shall see some. I am now in a very decayed first-class carriage jolting through Irish landscape with a glimpse now and then through beech trees of an imposing eighteenth-century house with cracked stable and broken windows doubtless the residence of some insane and obscure peer. The train's bumping makes my writing more illegible than usual but Love will find a way.

Poor darling. I hate to think of what an awful time you must be having. It is infuriating to feel that the only help I can give is thinking of you and loving you – I should like to arrive at  [Catball] in a super-charged, all spring sprocket, steam-valved, streamlined Mercedes and with a small piece of flannel charged with ether, asphyxiate our little friend  [Red Nose] and watch you pack your paintbrushes and lovely dresses, give you a terrific kiss on the lips and seal your eyes with two more kisses and take you away to a large and comfortable house in the Irish Free State where we would live in happy madness and sin until we died. It is extraordinary that you should be made to suffer. I really feel that it is a direct intervention on the part of God and that I have been brought along to rescue you from it. You've got to be calmly and quietly rebellious. I should not wait until Egypt to refuse your mother's wishes but I should take up a line about some domestic detail while your aunt is in the offing to give you moral support. Darling, I know it is very easy for me to make suggestions while I am in Ireland (very lonely and depressed without you and you are right in the wasp's nest). Do your best and remember that whatever happens I love you and you can depend on my bandaging up any physical wounds you may receive and taking you away altogether and arranging that my friends shall look after you if you can't stand it any longer. I love you. I love you I love you. That probably was telepathy on Sunday night for I suddenly became very gloomy at Clandeboye and longed for you and looked up to see that it was ten fifty-five.

I may say Clandeboye was pretty good hell. The Berry family – Camrose who owns the *Telegraph*, *Sketch*, *Rainbow*, *Chum* and about five hundred other papers – was much in evidence.

Maureen [Dufferin and Ava] kept talking to me about you in a very pointed manner. She thinks you are delightful and beautiful. I must confess that I agree with her. There were too many smart, bright young people to suit me. They never went out but played dance records in the library and some kind of paper game which required no mental or physical effort. I felt very Bolshevistic and lay on chairs in the corners of rooms wishing you were with me until Bloody was obliged to say that I was but a shadow of my former self. This was a lie so I got tight last night at the grand reception to Bloody by his tenantry.

Mrs D[ugdale] I expect knows everything. That does not matter at all. She is far too sensible to be any danger. I shall write to her. Don't worry about that. I ought to tell you that Archibald, my bear, has accepted a call to the Congregational Church on Wanstead Flats where he has been doing the duty of lay reader for some years.

He is also very keen on solo dancing.

It gives me considerable pleasure to show him to you.

Talking of illustrations, I would very much like to have some snaps of you that we took at Little Compton – if any of them came out. You are in a bathing dress in one of them.

I shall be at Pakenham until 3 September when I am going to Cornwall – against my will although I shall at least be on the same island as you – to see my mother.

This will be for a weekend. I shall be back in London on Monday 7 September. Write to me as much as you can. I love your letters, you angel, and they brighten the gloom of separation. Until eleven o'clock, farewell, darling. Just think of your eyes miles apart and me miles apart from them. For God's sake arrange something with old Anthony [Hope]. I shall write to him.

Heaps and heaps of love, God bless you, JB

> Basil Ava had married Maureen Guinness in July 1930, the same month in which he succeeded as 4th Marquess of Dufferin and Ava.
> Mrs Dugdale knew of the liaison, but was pleased to get JB's letter. C.R. wrote (undated): 'It *must* have been a bloody good letter that you wrote her, darling, because she is covered with confusion and horror that you could for a moment have imagined she would have said nasty things about you to anyone . . . she's frightfully worried and would almost do anything at the moment! She's ever so much on our side. . . . She kept on saying the whole of this weekend *how* she wished you were here and what a pity it was she couldn't ask you down, but that next year of *course* you will come before Mama gets back!'
> The message reads, 'Darling how lucky we are to [?love] one another.'

To Camilla Russell   Pakenham Hall
                                                          Castlepollard
29 August 1931   Co. Westmeath

My dear 'Milla,
I feel obliged to write so soon on top of the other letter simply to complain of the hellish people staying at Clandeboye, to praise the heavenly people here. There was Seymour Berry about whom I may have complained to you in the past. He is the typical social success – dear old Seymour, so witty you know and so influential – the sort of

chap it's well to keep in with, you know – the son of Lord Camrose. Oh! he's so epigrammatic that the whole table hangs on his words. Then there's dear old Buzzy [Shestel] – both he and Seymour have got six-litre Bentleys, topping little buses, they can rev up and change down in less than twenty minutes – splendid shock absorbers too. Dear old Seymour – dear old Buzzy. I can't understand why little A[va] surrounds himself with them.

Here there is Maurice Bowra coming with his Homburg hat on horizontally and his fists clenched and his untiring energy, kindness and humour. David C[ecil], who is off his rocker and Mary Pakenham, to whom I am devoted, is here also. It was she who heard, when she was a girl at school, another girl say 'Lady Mary – *and* knows it'. Pansy her sister and Henry Lamb – good painter and funny chap who smokes Irish Cigars – Pansy's husband, Evelyn Waugh with his eyes blazing with religious fanaticism and Frank whom you know and Eliza Harman his fiancée, with whom he is walking out, and her sister who seems dim and not unnaturally frightened. The Longfords are delightfully mad this year. Edward (L.) struck a man in the face at the Dublin Horse Show because he was a hearty and sang 'God Save the King' when people were not supposed to. There was a free fight all over the stand and Edward had to leave. There is an old family toy here of whom I am very fond. He looks like this:

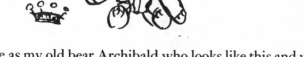

but not so nice as my old bear Archibald who looks like this and who is very interested in Temperance Work at Clacton-on-Sea:

I am writing too much, but I should like to hear from you, and since I am obliged to take another piece of notepaper, duckie, I want to give you some advice. Wash your face, child, and don't go about all anyhow and I think I've told you a thousand times before about curling your

hair. Why don't you take some trouble about your appearance and
DON'T LEAVE YOUR THINGS LYING ABOUT. Take this to the kitchen
for me.

I continually think of your brother [John Wriothesley Russell]. It's
most extraordinary that he is so witty. He would love it over here. I
wish you *both* could come and you especially, as it would make you ill
with laughter. I am unable to digest my food.

We have invented a very good game which consists in taking the first
verse of any of the more awful poems by Kipling and inventing verses in
the manner and from the moral standpoint of Kipling to follow after
them.

Give my love to old Wriothesley and the Pasha and of course, to your
mother, who must send her article to me here now – not to Clandeboye.
Did you get a postcard of Kelmscott? Give my especial love to your
Aunt and don't get depressed because I *know* you will be perfectly safe
with her. For Heaven's sake stay in the manor and start asserting your
thin and not unattractive self.

Yours till death, JB

Wash your face, child.

Buzzy Shestel was a rich American around at the time who had a lot of cars.

To Camilla Russell   Pakenham Hall
                                                        Castlepollard
2 September 1931   Co. Westmeath

My dear, sweet

Here before I leave for Ethel M. Dell in Cornwall (Trebetherick,
Wadebridge) which I think you know, I must write to cheer you up.
Mrs D. was told by me to foster the Friendship scheme so she is double
bluffing. Nothing could be better. She has no secrets from John and she
knows I love you. Do all you can to get John to arrange nice things for
the weekend after next – he's a loyal old thing and will back us up I am
sure – tell him everything if you want to. I shall be leaving Cornwall on
Monday. A word of cheer from you will be welcome, you ugly little

angel. I am so glad you saw old Groundsell [Graham Eyres Monsell] – he's lovely and mad and a kind old thing. This is rather a bore about old Anthony [Hope] being so vague. But anyhow there's Alastair G[raham], Evelyn [Waugh] can arrange it, and there's only sweet little Red Nose to be managed. But she's rather a handful I admit.

I would like to know, duckie, whether I ought to write to Catball or to ye Olde – which is the safer and more likely to escape the prying nose and metallic eye of dear little Dorothea. I hope you're drowning your sorrows over them both. You will be able to make it an excuse for seeing me – we might illustrate it in the *Architectural Review* or would that look too much like love? I find myself becoming very depressed from five thirty p.m. onwards with the thought of you, I want you to be with me so much. I've got an idea (my hat, by the way, that's a bit of all right staying with your dear old grandfather [?]; of course I shall be in London to see you) – take some deadlie Nightshade from ye Olde Worlde Gardeane and mix with it some potion of henbane and hemlock and place it in a cuppe of tea prepared for Red Nose or laye it on a textile and cause her to cut her fingerres. I shall be living, until the end of September at 47 Upper Brook Street (Mayfair 3542), in the rooms of a friend of mine who is in Italy. They keep shouting to me to come to the Mullingar horse show and a bloody girl staying here whom I have skilfully avoided up till now is coming in the same car with me and the Dean [Maurice Bowra]. She is wearing 'smart' clothes, all wrong, and she's damned serious and doesn't realise how important and nice the people are with whom she is privileged to stay. Darling, I do love you so much. It is most odd that you are so much more intelligent than any other jolly girl I come across and as nice as Mrs Dugdale into the bargain. I shall write to her by the next post and tell her to let you talk to her and comfort you, my angel. You must have someone now your Aunt has gone away, to whom it would not be a bad idea to send on my special letter. Darling in the weekend after next I shall be seeing your enormous eyes miles apart (G.W.) and we will be having our old thrilling life of hair-breadth escapes.

Circles and sticks a bird and a tree when will my Miller be wedded to me? Soon, soon. I love you, you hideous little angel. Have you washed your face child? Let me see it –

Love for ever, JB. X I have kissed this.

The letter begins, 'My dear, sweet Miller'.
C.R. wrote (undated): 'I don't think Mrs Dugdale is on our side after all. I haven't seen her, therefore have had no opportunity to find out what she thinks, but Aunt G. says she

thinks the same as *she* does; of course Mrs Dugdale *may* be doing a double-bluff and only
saying that to please Aunt G. and perhaps she really *is* for us all the time, but it's very
difficult to know what to think.'

To Camilla Russell   9 Queen Anne's Gate
29 September 1931   London SW1

My darling 'Milla,
The cover is a bit of all right only Edward James considers the idea of
removing the central portion and having a sort of cut-out with the
illustration showing through which is on the inside cover – and perhaps
some of that transparent paper such as one sees on bills where they can't
bother to address an envelope but spend ages folding the notepaper so
that an address shows through.

The finished effect will therefore be something like what I have
depicted:

If any touching up is necessary I will send you the rearranged proof
before it goes to the printers. We are finding it very difficult to secure
any rustic hedgerow countryside farmstead type. If it is impossible we
will have to get you to draw it.

For ⁓ 's sake don't th it's much of an [All Glory Laud
and . . . . . .] to decorate the cover of such a precious and boring and
slender little volume. I'm fed up with my blasted poetry. I suppose it won't
matter now you have made the announcement, putting your name on the
preface as artist or even to your signing your name on the cover if you can
find a place for it other than on that melancholy tombstone –

dread omen. I had better hear about that soon, duckie. Anyhow it's all settled and your tasteful little drawings – with the exception of that little church which will be replaced by transparent paper – will appear.

I have been enjoying hypochondria in bed just lately, hence my delay in writing to you. I do hope I shall see you before you go but it will have to rest with you, duckie, because I am not sufficiently friendly with Alastair Graham to make a move on my own. Edward James has lent me his house for part of the winter and I shall move into it next week, to be waited on by a negro servant living in and a half-witted housekeeper – it's not my style although I shall be surrounded by Rembrandts and early Corots. I'm a bit tight owing to having seen Randolph C[hurchill]: the Mayfair Lady Killer. More scenes are brewing with my typist who leaves this week. The atmosphere is a bit strained. I wrote to *dear* G.L.H. [Gerald Heard] and said I'd heard evil rumours about you and me but of course didn't believe them. Oh we're bloody clever. Love to your friend and her pale eyelashes.

Love and Kisses, duckie, xxxxxxxooooooooooooo JB

> C.R. was very anxious and excited about the book cover for *Mount Zion*: '*Oh God*, I am excited about it, I am leaping with excitement to think that quite soon your poems and my cover will be passing through the hands of the élite of literary society!!' Sadly, C.R.'s cover was not used.
>
> The message reads, 'For God's sake don't think it's much of an honour . . .'

To Charles Wade   The Architectural Review
                                                       9 Queen Anne's Gate
                                                       Westminster
15 October 1931   SW1

Dear Mr Wade,
When I came over to see you some months ago from Sezincote, you said you would be willing to let me have, for publication in the *Review*, those photographs of the model village in your garden. If you are still willing, I should very much like to have them as soon as possible, and indeed any drawings, should you possess any, because I should like to put them in our December issue, and we get going on that in a day or two.

I hope I shall see you if I ever come to the Cotswolds again, but with the likelihood of a revolution in London, and death by motor accident or rapid disease, any sort of peace seems out of the question.

Yours sincerely, J. Betjeman (*Sub-Editor*)

C.W. sent the photographs and JB's subsequent article, 'Wolf's Cove, Thirlwall Mere and District', on the extraordinary miniature replica of a Cornish fishing village by a pond in the garden of Snowshill Manor, Broadway, Worcestershire, was a howling success. He wrote it as though the village were real: 'However rough the day, the most unseaworthy luggers are safe in the bay. . . .'

JB forwarded a fan letter from Martin Hardie, Keeper of Drawings at the Victoria and Albert Museum, about the article to C.W. (18 January 1932) and wrote, 'It is one of the first complimentary letters the *Architectural Review* has had for years and years.'

To Camilla Russell   3 Culross St
                                              Grosvenor Square
17 October 1931   W I

My dear and sweet Milla,
Indeed I was not angry with you either the other night or the next day. I merely think that saying goodbye is such hell that it is better left out altogether. However I remembered after you had telephoned to me that I had promised to buy some books for your journey. Now it is one o'clock on Saturday – or it will be when I can get away – and the shops will be shut! The only book I have by me that could interest you is the second *Mercury Story Book* and it looks rather like conceit to send it to you since there is a very 'precious' story by your former friend inside it. Still, I *am* conceited.

Don't be depressed by Egypt. The one thing to remember is that S.A. [sex appeal] ain't all that matters and that since you are clever and able to look after yourself you need not become a cavalry officer's wife – for a bit anyway. If I am not forgotten or dead through depravity after your absence *perhaps* you will see your devoted servant again tho' he be balder and even more decayed. There's one consolation in being me and that is that I am not you. I don't think for a moment that you go through the emotional hell that I do when I see those enormous eyes so wide apart, but my God better hell than brawling women in the same house. I wish I were near to help you out with Red Nose. Don't forget to write to me even when I am a drunken memory, which I probably will be when you get the letter. I had a writ for twenty-six pounds yesterday and another for twelve pounds today. I think I must try and insert them into Randolph's housekeeping bill.

Goodbye, darling – it's a pretty hopeless business being in love with you – but wash your face and teeth regularly in the mornings and do not wear the same clothes too long, and avoid all rich food.

You've got all my love, old girl.
Cheeriohski, JB

PS Poor darling – even if this letter sounds odd and I must admit it is curious – you know I sympathise.

C.R. had written: 'I hate not seeing you to say goodbye properly – I hope you didn't think I was rude last night not to, but I thought I would have seen you this morning so didn't bother to bid you a very fond farewell. Were you angry with me?'
JB's infatuation was already petering out.
The *Mercury Story Book* contained JB's 'Lord Mount Prospect' which had first appeared in 1929.
He was at the time sharing a house with Randolph Churchill, which belonged to Edward James.

To Tom Driberg   3 Culross Street
                                               Grosvenor Square
10 November 1931   London W1

My dear Thomas,
Here's this precious little work – I beg the favour of a notice. De Cronin Hastings did the drawings (many of them), he is editor of the *Archy Rev*, as the printers call it. The binding is of the paper used in fireworks (Prime's).
Come in any evening you can. The book is out tomorrow.
Love and kisses, JB

JB had sent his first book of verse *Mount Zion* to his avant-garde Oxford friend, T.D., who had written for the *Cherwell* during JB's time and went on to become a social columnist in the thirties following the literary careers of JB, Evelyn Waugh and Nancy Mitford who he assumed would become famous.
Nearly thirty years later T.D. became JB's invaluable and respected textual adviser.

To Nicolas Bentley   The Architectural Review
                                               9 Queen Anne's Gate
                                               Westminster
1931 [December?]   SW1

That is my old Teddy Bear Archie who happens to be drawn on this bit of writing paper.

Dear Mr Bentley,
It is most kind and encouraging of you to write to me about my book.
Particularly as there's nothing I like more than praise and when it comes
from you I value it. I don't think the bloody book is selling at all and I'm
unlikely to make anything out of it which is what I think about most of
the time.

   You must illustrate my next effort if I don't kill myself before putting
pen to paper.

   Yours sincerely, John Betjeman

> N.B., publisher, artist and author, illustrated *Old Possum's Book of Practical Cats* by T. S.
> Eliot. Some time later he proposed to do an illustrated edition of JB's poems and
> produced four or five drawings. They were thought to be unsuitable and the project fell
> by the wayside.

To Patrick Balfour   The Architectural Review
                                        9 Queen Anne's Gate
8 December 1931   Westminster SW1

My dear Patrick,
Many thanks for your captions which arrived nicely in time. Unfortunately, the somewhat loose wording of your letter met the eye of Mr
Budd, an ardent Evangelical in our correspondence department, and I
have been told to tick you off for it. However, as the captions arrived, it
does not much matter, and it was a pleasure to receive a letter addressed
in terms rarely used in business, except in conversation, and then
always.

   While dictating this, I find it impossible, of course, to particularise
the complaint that was made. However, it cheered up de Cronin
Hastings a good bit, and God knows no one has ever heard of him.

   I am,
   Yours devotedly, J. Betjeman

> Mr Budd was the over-meticulous doorkeeper who clocked everyone's movements at the
> *Architectural Review* and with whom JB had many rows.

To Camilla Russell

21 December 1931

My darling Milla,

PRAISE THE LORD

There once was an elderly bear
Whose head was the shape of a pear
He sat in deep gloom
And longed for the tomb
As he'd lost nearly all of his hair

3 Culross Street
Grosvenor Square
London W1

Archibald has accepted the Incumbency of Raum's Episcopal Chapel, Homerton, E17. It is a proprietary chapel and in communion with a part of the Church of England. It has always been associated with the Evangelical party and he will have to wear a black gown in the pulpit as the Surplice is considered ritualistic. He will distribute Holy Supper at the Lord's Table after the seven o'clock evening service every fourth Sunday in the month. I hope, as do we all in Homerton, Clapton, Walthamstow and Hackney Marshes that his ministry will be successful and fruitful.

I may say, Milla Duckie, that I purposely disregard Christmas so I have not sent you a present although you were probably expecting one. You will however get a present in a week or two which must not be connected with Christmas. Edward James comes back on 10 January so if you write to me, address your letter to 9 Queen Anne's Gate, SW1. I am no longer worth knowing with this doom impending. I am now utterly convinced that capitalism is going to crash and here in England we will be caught like rats in a trap as there is insufficient food, and transport to other countries will be affected. If you want to remain alive I should not come back to your native isle. Send back that horrid Dorothea and she will starve to death. I met a somebody Harris the other day, a girl, daughter of that deaf old Lady who is a friend of Bosie's wife, who seemed to be a cousin of yours.

I go away tomorrow to stay with Richard and Elizabeth [Plunkett-Greene]. Anthony [Hope] will be there. It would be your cup of tea all right. So many rivals for your hand and all unsuccessful?

I think I ought to tell you that I do not like Dorothea at all. I keep thinking of her. She occurs in my dreams. Hot water running into a bath. I have developed a red spot on the end of my nose out of sympathy with you. Milla – she is not at all a nice woman. She has no virtues. I get bored now and then by lunches with Cattani who, I feel sure, is nevertheless no friend of hers.

Old [Christopher] Sykes told me he saw you.

My two new friends are Sir Anthony (Hope) Hawkins and A.E.W. Mason. I only like the old. But all the same I love you very much although I'm sure it's no good. Thank you so much for writing to me – go on doing so despite my inadequate replies. I'm very fond of you – my hat I adore you.

JB

C.R. later married Christopher Sykes.

To Bryan Guinness   3 Culross Street
                                                       Grosvenor Square
28 December 1931   London W1

My dear Bryan,
Thank you so much for the tasteful little diary. Not only is it elegant and a cut above the diaries people I know possess; but it matches the one you gave me last year. I spent Christmas with Richard and Elizabeth [Plunkett-Greene] at Rustington [Sussex]. We got tight and I recited Newbolt's poems, firing off a toy pistol, as a 'turn' at the local Yule-Tide Dance at the Beach Hotel in Littlehampton. Alcoholic remorse set in afterwards.

Will you ask Diana whether it was next weekend she asked me down to Biddesden? or a later date? Or not at all? It was all done on the telephone. My thoughts when they are not with you are with Pamela

Mitford. I hope I am not a bore. Possibly.

Richard is anxious to know whether you still think he is a nice chap. By the way they have had this novel taken by John Murray. That's good, ain't it. Richard thinks you and Diana are very nice. I am not feeling very well. Give my love to Diana and Pamela Mitford.

Thank you so much, old boy.

Yours in His name, John B

JB had fallen for Pamela Mitford whom he had met at Biddesden, where she ran the farm.

Four:

Gentle hills and lanes like rivers

February 1932 to January 1934

"OI STOOD
AMAZED BOI THE
INTRICACY OF THE
CLOISTERS IN GLOUCES-
TER CATH EDRAL"

Fling wide the curtains! – that's a Surrey sunset
  Low down the line sings the Addiscombe train,
Leaded are the windows lozenging the crimson,
  Drained dark the pines in resin-scented rain.
Portable Lieutenant! they carry you to China
  And me to lonely shopping in a brilliant arcade;
Firm hand, fond hand, switch the giddy engine!
  So for us a last time is bright light made.

                                        'Love in a Valley'

Although the country was descending into a slump in the early thirties JB was on the ascendant. A regular wage from the *Architectural Review* gave him a sense of security, and a mild success with the female sex, confidence. His stories and talks for the BBC were being accepted. His poem, 'The Arrest of Oscar Wilde' was published in the *Oxford and Cambridge Magazine*, edited by his friend, Randolph Churchill. Chapman and Hall, of which Evelyn Waugh's father was a director, published his essay on architecture, *Ghastly Good Taste*, the typography of which looked like a Victorian music-hall programme. JB had taken immense trouble over the book, roping in his friend Mary St Clair-Erskine to choose borders with him. Arthur Waugh wrote to JB (29 April 1933), 'I am sure it will be a very good book. I love the turns of your humour and the swift sallies of your wit. . . .' Inside was a long pull-out illustration by JB's close friend, Peter Fleetwood-Hesketh, who had studied architecture under Sir Albert Richardson and later worked in the offices of H. S. Goodhart-Rendel. Like JB, and often with him, he fought to save good buildings and battled all his life against sub-standard development. Though they corresponded much, none of JB's letters to Peter Fleetwood-Hesketh has survived.

    Another pillar in JB's life whom he met at this time through the *Architectural Review* was the architect Frederick Etchells. In 1927 Etchells had translated Le Corbusier's *Vers Une Architecture* which fuelled the fire of the Modern Movement, and in 1929 designed the Crawford office block in Holborn, one of London's first 'modern' buildings. (JB never spoke his name without saying 'FRIBA' [Fellow of the Royal Institute of British Architects] afterwards.) Etchells was part of our lives. During his latter years until his death in 1973, he lived very simply in a cottage in West Challow in Berkshire. Unlike many modern architects he did not take himself too seriously which is why JB and he were lifelong friends.

'The sunset sheds a horizontal ray
On Frederick Etchells, FRIBA,'

wrote JB, and sang it to the tune of 'The Volga Boatmen'.

At the *Architectural Review*, JB made new friendships and strengthened old ones. Its offices acted as a perfect platform from which to launch his burgeoning career. He had got the job as assistant editor through Bowra's friend, Maurice Hastings, a clever and capricious drunk, said to be a Squire Mytton-like character who cracked hunting crops at Rembrandts. His father owned the magazine and it was run by his uncle Hubert de Cronin Hastings who became JB's friend and guru. (Hastings called JB 'Jaggers'.) Although JB called him 'Obscurity' (he was so shy that he had once given a lecture with his back towards the audience), his admiration for him was unbounded. Obscurity's skill at design and layout inspired JB. 'Every page must be a surprise,' he had said. The laying out of the issue was the most important thing. The text was very much an afterthought, just grey matter filling the spaces between the photographs.

JB also met his future wife, my mother Penelope Chetwode, at the *Architectural Review* in 1931 when she brought in her article on the Indian cave temples of Ellora at the suggestion of their mutual friend, the travel writer, Robert Byron. She and JB lay on the floor and looked through her photographs. She began to fall for him. His engagement to Camilla Russell had come to nothing but he was at the time courting Pamela Mitford in a somewhat vague way. This did not deter my mother who, taking hold of the situation, determined to meet him again.

During the early thirties, JB spent almost every other weekend at Biddesden in Wiltshire with his friend Bryan Guinness, who had married the ravishing Diana Mitford in 1929. It was a glorious early eighteenth-century Baroque house of red brick, set in rolling chalk countryside on the edge of Salisbury Plain. Bryan employed a large staff and his house was a Bohemian mecca for the artistic intelligentsia of the day. Diana's sister, Pamela Mitford, who lived in a nearby cottage, was running the farm at the time – 'Miss Pam' the farmworkers called her, as did JB. 'Bryan used to ask me over for dinner –

that's how I met Betch,' remembers Pam (now Mrs Jackson). 'The Huxleys (I hated Aldous) and the Augustus Johns used to come and Lytton Strachey and Carrington and Evelyn Waugh (whom I really disliked); Betch made me laugh. I was very, very fond of him, but I wasn't in *love* with him. He liked me to drive him to Marlborough so he could show me his classroom, and to drive up on to the Downs to the deserted village of Snap; you could see the remains of cottages. . . . Of course he was highly religious and always wanted to go to Matins in Appleshaw, so we'd bicycle there together. Sometimes when I was in London we'd go off to very peculiar churches south of the river, where they sang hymns like "Shall we gather at the river", and then you had to be "saved" at the end of the service. Those who wanted to be saved stayed on and the other people left. We stayed and were both saved. We had to go into a cubby-hole with the parson.'[1]

Apart from her religiosity, JB was in love with Pam's *rurality*. 'He said he'd like to marry me but I rather declined. I think he would have been much too shy to have advanced on one. He wasn't like that at all.'

If the Guinnesses and Mitfords were liberal in their choice of friends, my maternal grandparents were not. The Chetwodes, both from ancient aristocratic families, were definitely 'out of the top drawer' and found it difficult to accept the idea of JB, who was definitely not, in their midst. Philip Chetwode was a brilliant horseman who served in the Cavalry and rose to become a Field Marshal. He was second-in-command under Allenby at the battle of Jerusalem, and subsequently Commander-in-Chief of the army in India. He worshipped his only daughter and she him. He passed on to her his passion for, and deep knowledge of, horses. Hester, his wife who was called 'Star' by her friends, was a beauty, highly cultivated, a bit of a snob and a great friend of Queen Mary. She felt at ease surrounded by servants, whereas my mother from an early age rebelled against her privileged circumstances. She was not allowed near the kitchens, but so strong was her desire to cook that she would steal ingredients and utensils and make fudge over a bedroom fire with her childhood friend, Wilhelmine Cresswell, whose stepfather was also a soldier at Aldershot. As a young lady in India she preferred riding out over the plains of Delhi, to dining with suitable young subalterns in the palace her parents occupied. It wasn't surprising that the Chetwodes were averse to the idea of her seeing 'a middle-class Dutchman'. 'We ask people like that to our houses, but we don't marry them,' Star is supposed to have said.[2]

My mother once said she didn't think she was pretty enough to marry an aristocrat so she decided to settle for a member of the intelligentsia.

In fact she was very pretty and at the time she met JB was already in love with two aristocratic Johns. One of them, Johnnie Churchill, was so passionately in love with her that he dressed in disguises in order to be near her, and gave her a pink sapphire engagement ring, which she kept. The other was Sir John Marshall, the Director-General of Archaeology in India, who had seduced her. He was fifty-five, married, and like a god to her. She admitted being in love with all three Johns at the same time but, after months of dallying, she plumped for JB and asked him to marry her. It was this dominance and self-assurance which melted JB and he accepted. Both were frightened of the wrath of her parents, so the betrothal was top secret. The situation was put in abeyance while my mother, having eventually told her parents that she wanted to marry JB, was parcelled off back to India with them. (None of the early love letters from JB survives. My grandmother had always advised my mother to destroy love letters.)

While my mother was in India, JB met her pretty, raven-haired friend, Wilhelmine 'Billa' Cresswell, at a house party at Sezincote, where she had come as John Dugdale's potential date. The fickle JB found the General's daughter from Snettisham in Norfolk irresistible and Billa found JB a magic antidote to poor dull John Dugdale. They fell in love and scratched their intertwined names onto a garden wall that same weekend. 'John Dugdale was very annoyed,' remembers Billa. JB met her in London the following week. 'We didn't go all the way, we lay on a sofa and kissed and cuddled.'³ And then they were engaged. Only four others shared the secret: Patrick Balfour, Frederick Etchells, Alan Pryce-Jones and Joan Eyres-Monsell to whom Alan was engaged at the time. Joan wrote immediately (undated), 'Darling, darling, darling Billa . . . Betj. told me that you were engaged last night and I am so *thrilled* about it I don't know what to do. It's nearly as exciting as Bogs [Alan Pryce-Jones] and I.

'It is HEAVEN and I think really he is much nicer to marry than Graham [Eyres-Monsell] or anyone (except Alan). . . . Darling, what a heavenly quartet we shall be, Ooooh. It's too lovely to be true. . . . He [JB] said to me, "All my emotions have changed lately," and he said that he didn't love P.C. any more. . . . He really was in the 7TH HEAVEN of happiness about it all. He said he was sorry about Filth [one of JB's nicknames for PC] but anyway he realized their marriage would *not* have been a success and she had not nearly so nice a character as you and that you were funny lovely beautiful witty kind, intelligent EAST END and altogether heaven and absolutely made for him.'⁴

When my mother learned of the situation through a letter from JB, she sent a telegram from India saying, 'Do nothing until you hear from me. I know I can make you happy.' JB was thrown by my mother's desperate plea and backed down. It had been a whirlwind romance. Billa and her subsequent husband, Roy Harrod, the economist, remained true friends of my parents for life.

Before the dust had settled on his feelings for Billa or his enthusiasm to marry PC had been rekindled, JB wrote to Mary St Clair-Erskine, in March 1933, 'I have been rewarded during my visit to Cambridge today by a further acquaintance with Victor Rothschild, your friend, and we talked about you most of the time. He has very kindly given me a beautiful photograph of you and asked me to tell you so. It will annoy Philth very much as she is always inclined to be jealous of my affection for you. It will also console me because I am beginning to think I cannot afford to marry Philth, as she is really an expensive person like you although, unlike you, she thinks she can live in squalor on my few hundred a year and enjoy it. . . . Also I think I should soon become as dim as hell and be known as the common little man Penelope Chetwode married. Please keep this to yourself as I am unsettled about everything and rather wish the night had borne my breath away.'⁵

In April 1933 my mother returned to England and, despite all the waverings, her meeting with JB was euphoric. They planned to marry as soon as possible. My mother bravely wrote to her father to whom she was so close.

'Dearest Penelope,' he wrote back (14 May 1933), 'I have just got your letter of May 4th in which you say you have made up your mind to marry John Betjeman. I cannot pretend to be pleased, but you are a grown woman with more than the usual share of brains, and if after all this time you have had for reflection you are not certain of your feelings you never will be.

'I have told you the risks you are running and it is useless to repeat everything I have said or written – I love you more than I can say and hope and pray you may have chosen right, and that you will be happy.

'I know nothing about the proper time for the announcement – so you must consult with your mother. I am writing to Upton [the family solicitor] to go and see her and begin making arrangements, but from the letter John B's father wrote to me, I fear they can only be very unsatisfactory ones. Bless you darling.

'Your own daddy.'⁶

After a few weeks my mother changed her mind and broke off the engagement. She felt torn in three directions between her duty to, and her respect for, her parents, her overwhelming desire to extend her cultural knowledge of India, and her love for JB. She went to stay with my eccentric and all understanding great-aunt, Polly Stapleton-Cotton, in the South of France. JB was devastated and took refuge at Biddesden, where all the Mitfords were highly sympathetic. Bryan Guinness wrote a supplicating letter to my mother (18 June 1933) saying, 'I have no right whatsoever to interfere in the lives of either yourself or John, and it would be proper for me to apologize before attempting to do so: but I shan't, as it can do you no harm to hear my views, and if they annoy you it will be easy for you to tear up this letter and, no doubt, to forget what it says. . . . Now there can only be two possible reasons for which you have broken off your engagement to him. One is that you do not love him any more. . . . There is however the alternative possibility that you do still care for John and that you have broken off your engagement as a result of parental pressure, conscious or unconscious. If so, I cannot sufficiently express how much I deprecate your cowardice. John is a very great person. He is eccentric and needs looking after: but he has a genius of a very unusual kind. (He is incidentally a very great and old friend of mine, as you know, or I should not be writing this.) Such a person endowed as he is for your service, with great emotional capacity, is not lightly to be cast on one side because your parents were not at the same public school as his. If you are soon to live a life of your own unhedged by the false barriers of snobbery you must stand fast. As for putting your fancy foreign travel before the course of your duty and the inclination of your heart, I would not have believed it possible that the shallowest nature could have urged so basely selfish and mundane an excuse. . . . I can't bear to see John so unhappy – that is why I have been so impertinent.'[7]

In the end, however, it was Nancy Mitford who advised JB to take a radical step. 'Well, *go after her and get her*, don't just let it go like that. You must go out to the South of France and win her back.'[8] So he did.

My mother had already written him many letters saying how much she loved him. 'We both love each other very, very much, with a love that (should we part) will never come to either of us again; the physical stoof is ideal and although it's of only secondary importance it is a thing which only comes once in a lifetime as perfectly as it has to us (I believe extremely few women get complete physical satisfaction from any man); we'll have enough money to live fairly comfortably but, owing to capricious circumstances, we each have very strong interests at opposite ends of the world. It's out of the question for you to give up yours (we'd have no money if you did!) and I'm too weak and SELFISH (that's what it comes to) to give up mine. *Can we effect a compromise?*'[9]

What she wanted was another two years' freedom – she saw marriage as constricting her immediate independence. Once she had advanced enough in her studies she would be happy to marry him. 'After all, people like H. Nicolson and V. Sackville West both do their own things and yet adore each other and get on frightfully well. There's no earthly reason why we shouldn't. And I shouldn't need additional sexual outlets like V. S. West because I'm not at all promiscuous by nature but fundamentally faithful. And if I searched high and low throughout the East and the West among man, woman or beast I'd never find anyone to suit me physically so well as you, of that I am utterly certain!'[10]

After JB's fleeting visit she wrote (undated), 'I know now that it's inevitable we should marry and I swear not to let you down. And once we're married, seeing each other will be quite easy I'm sure, but we MUST keep it all secret for the next year or two.'

In the presence of JB's parents and Hubert de Cronin Hastings, and completely unbeknownst to the Chetwodes, my parents were married on 29 July at Edmonton Register Office, near Heddon Court, where JB had taught, sharing temporary lodgings with John Humphrey Hope. The marriage was later blessed at St Anselm's in Davies Street opposite Etchells's office. Having spent a few days with JB at the Green Man pub in Braxted, Essex, my mother then returned to her parents' house in Grove End Road and pretended to lead her life as before. 'Ooooh, I did enjoy Essex,'[11] she wrote, continuing a subterfuge way of life for a few weeks until the story broke. After an official announcement of the marriage had taken place, my mother wrote to Bryan Guinness in September, 'I expect you were rather surprised to see that we were married two months ago! but my father was very ill with dysentery at the time and I did not want to worry him until he was well again. Both he and my mother have been charming about it and very practical. They were very upset at first and it'll take some time for my mother to recover.'[12]

It was not a good start, for my mother did indeed prefer her Indian studies to JB's affections. She went to Germany for three months, during which time JB felt desperately insecure. He confided his innermost thoughts to one of his great heroes and colleagues on the *Archie Review*, the writer, Philip Morton Shand. My mother also used him as a listening post, and wrote to JB, 'P. Morton Shand is the best person you could have confided in.'[13] Shand's credentials as a marriage guidance counsellor were hardly obvious to the outsider, since he had himself married four times. But he was kind and perceptive, and held both their hands through the storm. Shand had strong views on architecture and its necessity to uplift and amuse, and inspired JB against any kind of pedantry. His extreme eccentricity was irresistible.

'No one would have thought that this nonchalant, tall man with his fair hair, distinguished nose and elegant manners was a conscientious and reliable journalist,' wrote JB. 'Though he had been educated at Eton and King's and spoke French and German well, he preferred quantity surveyors to architects, craftsmen to designers, and simple peasants to complicated suburbanites.'[14]

That P. Morton Shand had approved of my mother's plan to go to Berlin for three months made JB feel faintly better, and he set about finding a house where they both could live on her return. He decided on a small farmhouse in Uffington, Berkshire, and employed a pretty girl with dark brown hair called Molly Higgins to help get it straight. An affair was inevitable and he admitted it to my mother immediately. She wrote from Germany, 'I did not realise until I got yours this mornin' that you were actually in love with Molly H. I thought you might be but did not let myself think that you really were.'[15] She went on to admit that she had had feelings for other people while in Berlin but had never followed them up. By the time she returned for Christmas 1933, the affair with Molly Higgins had faded and my mother was very much in command.

1. Pamela Jackson, CLG interview (1993).
2. C. M. Bowra, *Memories 1898–1939* (Weidenfeld and Nicolson, 1966).
3. Wilhelmine Harrod, CLG interview (1992).
4. Wilhelmine Harrod's papers.
5. Mary Dunn's papers.
6. PB's papers, Beinecke Library, Yale University.
7. PB's papers.
8. Nancy Mitford's papers.
9. PB's papers.
10. PB's papers.
11. PB's papers.
12. Bryan Guinness's papers.
13. PB's papers.
14. JB, 'P. Morton Shand', *Architectural Review* (November 1960).
15. PB's papers.

To Diana Guinness   The Salutation Hotel
                                       Topsham
27 February 1932   Devon

My Dear Diana,
Alone in the cold Commercial Room with a smelly and ancient dog
looking at me and a child practising scales next door, my thoughts are
still with Miss Pam [Mitford]. I have been seeing whether a little
absence makes the heart grow fonder and my God, it does. Does Miss
Pam's heart warm towards that ghastly Czechoslovakian Count? I came
down to this eighteenth-century town alone for a rest. It is built entirely
in the Dutch manner except for a few Regency terraces and closes. It
subsists on Smuggling and in one part you can buy Brandy for three
and ninepence a bottle.

   I do want to see you when I return – which will be tomorrow – and
hear whether this severe test has improved my chances and done down
my rival. I have written a confession of my tactics to Miss Pam today.
Was that wise? Love to Bejooni [Bryan Guinness] who should be
writing a book review as fast as his awkward penmanship will allow.
Peter Watson has gone to Switzerland and I am living in state in his
house alone and fairly happy, save for this insensate haunting for Miss
Pam.
   TELEPHONE TO THE ARCHIE REV when you return.
   Love, JB

      The Czechoslovakian Count was in fact only a friend of Pamela Mitford's and not a
      suitor.

To Lionel Perry   as from 9 Queen Anne's Gate
                                       London SW1

(This paper was the property of H. S. Tuke the famous artist)

29 March 1932

My Dear Old Li,
I have been chary of writing to you before because I was in such a rage
about your peculiar behaviour over Camilla. Now however that I have

ceased to have that affection for her which made us both the scandal of
the Cotswolds I can see only foresight and righteousness in your
treatment of the affair. What put it into my mind to write to you this
morning was that last night I had a special sort of dream in which you
played a most gratifying part and I must say that was extraordinary.
The whole thing happened in Belfast in this dream.

I am staying with Etchells, the architect, and we are contemplating
doing a guide-book to Berkshire which mentions the things worth
seeing in the Georgian and Regency way besides the Gothic and
Norman. There are at present no adequate guide-books to any part of
England. They either give wide-angle views of Public Libraries and
Infirmaries or else they mention in detail what rent the land paid to
Hubert de Burg in 1286 and who the glebe passed to after the
Reformation. With this guide in view we have visited about thirty
churches this Easter, including Mildenhall where they are thinking of
sawing off the tops of the box pews and hanging a light over the Holy
Table. We also visited Waterlionel near Wheatley. I expect you
remember it. It was Easter Sunday evening and they had lighted the
candles for Evensong in their little sconces which were affixed to each
box pew; the two bells were going and the vicar was coming in to
minister at the filthy new Mowbray altar which has been put at the East
End. It was a sight to make your heart long for England i[n] that
horrible place abroad.

I suppose you have heard about the death of poor old Lytton
Strachey and how about a fortnight later [Dora] Carrington borrowed
Bryan Guinness's gun and shot herself down at Biddesden. You may
have heard too that I fell slightly in love with Pamela, the rural Mitford.
I don't know whether I still am. I saw Lucy Byron, Robert's sister,
yesterday and she always makes me want to cry she looks so nice, she is
like a fair-haired Pamela Penelope Perry.

Old Horace Plunkett died the other day and I expect Gerald Heard
will come into a fortune and I expect John Edward [Bowle] thinks he
will too. John Edward has treated me rather badly, you will be
surprised to hear, and I am not seeing him any more. It is all too long to
go into now. Cracky is so Roman Catholic that it is impossible to
understand him and Duff and Sparrow go their own way. Anthony
[Russell] is in Cardiff and without you in the old country, Li, to keep us
all together, there is none of the bonhomie that used to make us one
great Golf Club Bar. You filthy old thing with your round head like an
eighteenth-century gatepost and your incomprehensibility. I am very
much afraid capitalism is going to survive and I am sure I do not know

where we will all be because I for one have been running up bills on the strength of its collapse.

The Longfords have had a letter from [Lord] Trimlestown and they are meeting him for he has come over from Eltham in Kent to Dublin.

Goodbye Li and write to me soon
Boggins is of course in Italian Somaliland
Is your job hell? Worse than Lazard?
Curses on Peter Perry
love from JB

'Waterlionel' was JB's joke name for Waterperry, whose church has box pews. Pamela Penelope Perry was L.P.'s sister.

To Patrick Balfour

The Architectural Review
9 Queen Anne's Gate
Westminster

4 April 1932

SW1

My dear Patrick,
I am going down to Cornwall on Saturday next alone and am to be met there on Sunday by Mr E. O. Hoppé. Together we are going to take photographs on Monday, Tuesday and Wednesday of the larger Georgian Houses of mid-Cornwall. Would you care to come too? If so will you meet me at St David's at two fifty-five? I shall be on the London train. Don't buy a ticket. Evelyn [Waugh] says he will come if he does not get a better invitation. You will understand his reservations when I tell you what you will have to face if you are prepared to come. I will pay for most of these:

1) Meals in a filthy hotel near the house served by 'jolly' people (I will pay for most of these).
2) Hideous village full of 'jolly' schoolmasters – pupils?
3) One daily servant.

Advantages are that no Ernie or Bess will be there, that the scenery is good and that your mother's double will be in the village.

Let me know if you can come, old boy. It would be grand if you could. Yours till death, JB

JB was working on a record of houses for the *Architectural Review*.
E. O. Hoppé was a well-known photographer.

To Nancy Mitford   The Architectural Review
                                       9 Queen Anne's Gate
                                       Westminster
19 April 1932   SW1

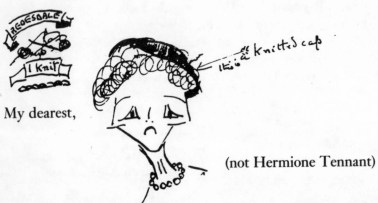

My dearest,

                                       (not Hermione Tennant)

I met Thomas Mitford in the street yesterday all fresh from a wedding.
Your handwriting is like that of a maid. I think the Baccarat Case,
though fascinating, can't be allied to Architecture. However, I am
ringing up Diana [Guinness] to find out if you know about Spain. Diana
is out. I have had to call up what the telephone operator calls Sloone
sex-four-seven-sex. Thomas Mitford tells me that you haven't been to
Spain and that he has. He says, however, that you could review this
book. Two hundred words is quite enough. You have not been to Spain
so it will be all the easier.

The primitive stuff seems to be alone fairly interesting, you might
remark what you think hideous and what not hideous.

Alan Pryce-Jones is back. The book is being sent to you. Write to me
again. I loved your letter.

Love, John B

PS If Pamela Mitford refuses me finally *you* might marry me – I'm
rich, handsome and aristocratic. JB

JB had met N.M. through her sister, Diana Guinness.
    The Baccarat Case was an Edwardian scandal centred around a card game of the same
name at Tranby Croft, involving Edward VII and the Lycett Greens among others.

1a and 1b JB's parents, Bess and Ernie Betjemann.

1c Number 31 West Hill, Highgate, where JB lived as a small child;
he recalled in *Summoned by Bells* how happy he had been here.
The porch was added later.

2a Number 53 Church Street (now Old Church Street), Chelsea, which the Betjemanns bought while JB was at prep school. He said the house was 'poky, dark and cramped, haunted by quarrels and the ground-floor ghost'.

2b Undertown, the holiday house built by the Betjemanns at Trebetherick, Cornwall, in 1929. It has since been added on to.

3a JB in 1925, the year he went up to Magdalen. He later wrote on the back of the photograph, 'What a bloody awful fellow.'

3b Magdalen College Dramatic Society's cast for *Love Lies Bleeding or The Puss in Russian Boots*, 1927. Included are JB (*fourth from right, in beard*) as 'A Lunatic, Ebenezer Stephen Stevenson' and John Dutton (*third from right*) as 'A Best Man, Mr Jolly'.

4a Lord Alfred Douglas, Nancy Mitford and JB at Brighton, c. 1930.

4b Colonel and Mrs Dugdale (*second and third from left*) and friends at Sezincote, c. 1930.

5a Philip and
Hester Chetwode,
JB's parents-in-law.

5b PB in the garden
at Uffington
with Kitty Fritz,
1934.

6 PB in India, 1933.

7a Garrards Farm, Uffington, Berkshire (now called 'Oxfordshire'), where JB and PB lived when they were first married and which they continued to rent for twelve years.

7b PB thought nothing of bringing her Arab, Moti, into other people's houses. Here Gerald Berners paints them at Faringdon.

8 PB driving Moti through Uffington in the dog cart,
with Audrey Talbot and Robert Heber-Percy behind.

To Blanche Girouard

The Architectural Review
9 Queen Anne's Gate
Westminster
SW1

25 April 1932

My dear Blanche, old girl,
I can't think why it is that I have got red ink in this pen – I must have filled it at the wrong ink pot. Pray allow me to thank you and Dick very much for my delightful visit to the Towers. I saw another house called The Towers just outside Lordships Lane Station in Sydenham. It was like this:

It had been built about 1870 and was I should think very suitable for a preparatory school.

I don't know whether you know Streatham, Forest Hill, Gypsy Hill and Upper Norwood, but believe me when you and Dick next go [on] a hike they are easily the most extraordinary and ugly part of London. Especially round the Horniman Museum (LCC Tea in the grounds, ninepence) and the Crystal Palace.

Thank you so much, old girl, and thank Dick, too, for all your kindness.

From that poverty stricken old rip, John Betjeman

B.G., a daughter of the Marquess of Waterford, and her husband, Dick, who was an Oxford friend, often entertained JB to dinner in their house in Upper Berkeley Street which JB nicknamed 'The Towers'. JB always pretended, as a joke, that he was godfather to their son, Mark.

To Alan Pryce-Jones

Statements in these letters cannot be
guaranteed by the medical officers
[stamped all over letter]

                                        The Architectural Review
                                        9 Queen Anne's Gate
                                        Westminster
2 May 1932   SWI

Dear Alan,
I very much appreciate the honour you confer on me in asking me to
write for your little booklet in English and French – provided I am not
supposed to write in French. Believe me, the reminiscence will be slight
and eccentric, for the full horror of my childhood I can hardly bear to
describe.

    The formality of this letter will, I hope, equal the elegance and
conciseness of yours, and until I see you again, allow me to remain
    Yours, JB

        A.P.-J. edited a book of childhood recollections entitled *Little Innocents* to which JB
        contributed.

To Diana Guinness   The Architectural Review
                                        9 Queen Anne's Gate
                                        Westminster
29 May 1932   SWI

My dear Diana,
I have been meaning to write to you for a long time. I shall have to come
to lunch on Thursday. I shall be a little weak as I shall just have had my
internal irrigations – the details of which I cannot bring myself to put
down on paper.

    I am afraid poor old Bosie Douglas must have returned to his old
habits. Here is a letter from him to me:

    I had a glorious weekend at Oxford, the weekend before last. I stayed
    with Richard Rumbold (a ghastly and pretentious undergraduate, JB)

at Christ Church. I met dozens of undergraduates and they were all perfectly sweet to me. I have almost determined to go back to Oxford and take a degree! I am of course *still an undergraduate* which is a cheering thought. I have written a sonnet (I really think one of my best) about my 'come-back' to Oxford after nearly (forty) years' exile. It will be in next week's *Cherwell* . . . I too am in love with someone I saw at Oxford: 'who ever loved that loved not at first sight. . . .'

And that brings me to the point of my letter. That 'Austrian Betjeman', about whom I am continually hearing, and about whose success I have had little reason to doubt, has so stemmed, instead of incited, my passions for Miss Pam that I have gone and fallen in love with another jolly girl. Details later. I long to see you. Love to Bejooni.

Love, JB

PS When will Biddesden be ready? We look forward to doing it in the *A.R.* as soon as it is. Keep it for us won't you. Also what about Zinzendorf's house?

> On reading his poetry when at Marlborough, JB began an innocent correspondence with Lord Alfred Douglas; it was quashed by JB's father, then revived in the early thirties. JB was fascinated by him and annoyed C. S. Lewis by claiming that he was greater than Shakespeare. He was kind to Alfred Douglas throughout his life.
> JB's rival for the affections of Pamela Mitford was an Austrian. Penelope Chetwode was the 'jolly girl'.
> Zinzendorf's house may refer to Lindsay House in Chelsea, 96 Cheyne Walk, where Zinzendorf once lived. JB had said to Bryan Guinness, 'There I believe you are going to live,' and he lived there for two years.

To Patrick Balfour

The Architectural Review
9 Queen Anne's Gate
Westminster
SW1

22 June 1932

My dear Patrick,

Please do not think that because I have not seen you lately I am being wilfully remiss. This love business and the snobbery of the C. [Chetwode] family is leading me a dance – or, should I say, dances, which little PC [Penelope Chetwode] does all she can to alleviate.

As soon as I have had a definite rupture or alliance with her ladyship I shall see you again – if not sooner.

Love and kisses, JB

To Diana Guinness   The Architectural Review
                                      9 Queen Anne's Gate
                                      Westminster
12 August 1932   SW1

My dear Diana,
I have lost my fountain pen and have to use a mapping pen. I am so
sorry to hear that you are ill in the South of France with pleurisy. It is
probably not true but if it is I am very, very sorry for you, not so much
because of your disease, as because you are in the South of France
which has always been in my mind as something worse than
Maidenhead although I admit I have never been there.

What I want to know is when we can do Biddesden for the *Archie Rev*.
I hear G.K. [?] has given permission to the *Studio* but that after all is only
part of the house and can be done in the *Archie* as well.

I had a letter from Valkyrie [Unity] Mitford. She tells me Nancy's
book is good. I saw a very obscure peeress called the Dowager Lady
Downe when I was on a bicycling tour looking at churches near
Wisbech last weekend. We had lunch with her at her Gothick House, in
the open air. I wrote these four lines about her:

> She sat dead calm among the wasps
> Hemstitching at her evening gown
> The Norfolk sunlight floated by
> The Dowager Viscountess Downe.

Love to Bejooni. I hope he is not gambling. Probably you are not in the
S. of France at all. Penelope I now call Beastliness. I do get on very well
but her ladyship finds me commoner and commoner.
    Love to you old girl, from JB

    D.G. and B. Guinness were summering in the South of France.

To Patrick Balfour

24 August 1932

Good old Patrick,

JB drew the above as if it were an extract from the 'Londoner's Diary' on which P.B.
worked. It reads, 'JB. EFFEMINATE MEN. I think it is time something was said in and on
behalf of effeminate men. Though they don't all appeal to me, if treated with sympathy
and understanding they will often yield surprising and pleasurable results [illegible].
PATRICK BALFOUR.'

To John Murray

26 August 1932

The Architectural Review
9 Queen Anne's Gate
Westminster

Dear Jock,
An intelligent friend of mine – a dim once Corpus Aesthete – called
Gilbert Armitage has just completed an excellent pamphlet called
Banned in England on The Law Regarding Obscene Literature (Wishart,
one shilling, *Here and Now Pamphlets*). It is an important and diverting
subject well written about. Could you bring it to the notice of the Editor
of the *Quarterly Review*, that obscure paper? It is out on 1 September. I
have read an advance copy.
    Love and Kisses, JB

JB had met J.M., his future publisher and lifelong friend, at Oxford. Murrays founded
and owned the *Quarterly Review*, which was an extremely influential political
mouthpiece, all through the nineteenth century. Jock's uncle, Sir John Murray, edited it
from 1929 until 1967, when it was wound up.

To Edmund Blunden   The Architectural Review
                                           9 Queen Anne's Gate
                                           Westminster
30 November 1932   SW1

Dear Professor,
Thank you so much for the review. It is definitely alpha plus.
    Do you know the poems of N. T. Carrington about Devonshire?
Written about 1830. One on 'My Native Village' and the first two
verses on a 'Frigate in Plymouth Harbour'. They are excellent. Most of
the rest is effusive stuff about feasting natives of the vale.
    I so much enjoyed meeting you with F. Pakenham and hope I may do
so again.
    If you can, do let me have a reply about Carlton House Terrace. But
if you have no feelings on the matter, don't bother.
    My love to C. S. Lewis whom I shall always remember as a loving
guide, a sympathetic *littérateur* and a beta plus plus man if not an alpha
minus.
    Yours sincerely, John Betjeman

        JB struck up a lasting friendship with E.B. whose work he much admired.
          The reference to C. S. Lewis is sarcastic.

To James Lees-Milne   The Architectural Review
                                           9 Queen Anne's Gate
                                           Westminster
16 December 1932   SW1

Dear Jim,
Get Lord Lloyd to write to *The Times*. I am nobody but we are raising
hell in next month's *Archie Rev*: I have had letters of protest from Aldous
Huxley: *Antic Hay*, Edward German, Max Beerbohm, Sir Henry
Newbolt, Bloody [Dufferin and Ava], Ernest Thesiger, Rose Macaulay, Clive Bell, countless professors, curates, actors, musicians, poets
and novelists and the *Architect's Journal* has had them from MPs, tenants
and architects. We'll do in that bloody fool Blomfield yet. Love to
Unity Valkyrie [Mitford].
    Enclosed is a poem by Brian Betjeman (c. 1863 op. 190?) under the
influence of the Rossettis.
    Love, JB

J.L.-M. was a friend from Oxford days and for ever onwards.

Blomfield had designed 4 Carlton Gardens as a commercial building and had also done drawings for the redevelopment of Carlton House Terrace. There was a considerable outcry at the proposal to demolish John Nash's terrace and to 'substitute buildings of the commercial class in their place'. The reform of the administration of the Crown Lands was asked for in Parliament and in the end the scheme for wholesale redevelopment was dropped.

The poem referred to is missing.

To Robert Byron   The Architectural Review
                                9 Queen Anne's Gate

31 December 1932   Westminster sw1

My dear Robert B,

First let me say how admirable your *book* is. My dear chap, it is the last word on the subject; clearly written, decently produced, well illustrated, stimulating ('This is the best book I have ever read,' Ralph Straus. 'This is the best book ever I have read,' J. C. Squire.) Anyhow I can assume you have hit the nail on the head. It has been sent to Compton Mackenzie to review – his last work before he goes to prison for life.

And now about Byzantine Art. Can you extend your article, if you have not sent it off already, and write captions to the illustrations you want. We are going to turn it into an illustrated article.

If you are in want of a valet, should you be coming to London, I have an EXCELLENT one at my disposal.

Love to LUCY BYRON and to Mrs Eric Byron and to ERIC and to yourself,

From John Betjeman

R.B., the travel writer, wrote a lot for the *Architectural Review* and was the mutual friend who introduced my mother to JB. His book was *The Appreciation of Architecture* (1932). Lucy Byron was R.B.'s sister, Mr and Mrs Eric Byron, his parents.

To J. R. Ackerley   The Architectural Review
                                9 Queen Anne's Gate
                                Westminster

24 January 1933   sw1

Dear Joe,

Here's this blasted thing in black and white, and for goodness sake PAY

DEEP ATTENTION TO IT. It is close reasoning, fascinating as a popular talk, and all-important in a country which has had its day.

The row about *Carlton House Terrace* has raised the unemployment Conservative MPs to a certain pitch of civic consciousness. Sir Arthur Steel-Maitland and Austen Chamberlain are among others forming a committee to prevent the destruction of Carlton House Terrace, but to do little if anything more. This is a merely negative thing which will raise the wrath of the few Labour MPs (Lansbury is on our side) in Parliament, as they will think it, as it really is, merely an effort to preserve a decaying aristocratic neighbourhood.

In company with a great many other people I want to use this little spurt on the part of the Conservatives as a lever for something really important – that is to say, an amendment to the Town and Country Planning Act. As you do not know, the Architects' Unemployment Committee has set to work on the replanning of the slums in the North Kensington area, that is to say at Latimer Road and Uxbridge Road, and has suggested new blocks of flats which will keep the old street lines and also improve the amenities of the district. The plan and elevations they have got out are, of course, only advisory because owing to the exigencies of private ownership it is impossible to bring about a coherent scheme in any part of London. Something must be done to remedy this. The Town and Country Planning Act, which has just been passed and comes into force on 1 April, is really only a short step in this march. It provides for a sort of advisory bureau which Borough Councils and Rural and Urban Councils can come to when they want advice about their building estates, as to what sort of houses to plan, in what sort of material, and in what sort of areas. Naturally, no pigheaded capitalistic Borough Council will wish to consult such a body unless compelled to. Admittedly, when they do consult the body then they come within the powers of the Act, and the Act provides means of compensating private owners and doing away with the harmful effects of private enterprise in a district which is to be developed for the benefit of the public. What we want to get made is an amendment to the Town Planning Act which will make it compulsory for it to be obeyed, and as far as Carlton House Terrace is concerned, we want to transfer the power over the Crown Lands in London from the Commissioners of Crown Lands to the Board of Works. We then want to put the Board of Works within the restrictions of the Town and Country Planning Act, newly made compulsory. Then all these hundreds of unemployed architects, and I believe they amount to thousands, can be set to work to make out an advisory plan for the whole of London, saying what areas should be preserved because they are well-planned already, what heights should be preserved and where, what type of elevation is necessary in what sort of district. If this can be brought about slums can be removed, industrial areas can be separated from residential ones, the traffic can be organised, and London stands a chance of becoming something like the beautiful place it must have been a hundred years ago.

Surely this is a matter for a talk. I do not suggest that I should do it, but I do suggest that someone should as soon as possible, and I do not see how you are going to fit it into the five minutes which you say is all that can be spared. There are any amount of people I can suggest to you to do it, if your own Mr Howard Marshall will not, if you will only apply to me. Arthur Steel-Maitland will *certainly* do it.

I am sending a copy of this letter to old Lionel [Fielden] in order that it may be kept in both your minds.

In the sure and certain hope of a speedy resurrection,
John Betjeman
PS As Parliament reassembles on 7 February Steel-M will be RIGHT IN THE NEWS.

> The talk never happened. J.R.A., who worked for the BBC (which is how JB first met him) had already turned down another crusading idea of JB's. The last programme on architecture had 'bored the listeners almost to death', J.R.A. wrote (25 October 1932).

To Lionel Fielden

The Architectural Review
9 Queen Anne's Gate
Westminster
SW1

24 January 1933

Dear Lionel,
I have sent the enclosed letter to Joe. Please read it, it's damned important, and it looks to me as though the BBC is the best medium we could possibly have for gingering people up into doing something about the present unarchitectural and unplanned chaos in which this city, as well as most others in the country, has been placed.

Yours, John Betjeman

> L.F., who was head of General Talks at the BBC, wrote a memo to J. R. Ackerley asking, 'What is all this bilge?'

To Mary St Clair-Erskine   As if from The Archie Rev
                                            9 Queen Anne's Gate
28 January 1933   London sw1

My dear Maria,
I am so sorry I was so tipsy and distressing the other night. I felt that I
had shattered any illusions you might have had about me. All the time I
have been haunted by the vision of those blue eyes wide with horror at
my shattering their illusions. And then there was Ham [Hamish
Erskine], his brown eyes black with dismay. I can remember it all
through my drink. That turned-up nose of yours looking the other way.
Me becoming human. Ah, if you are not a gentleman *in vino veritas*. By
way of consolation I am sending you a list of clothes you ought to buy
and if I am ever rich enough I shall provide them for you myself.

REQUIREMENTS FOR The Lady Mary St Clair-Erskine
1 school hat
1 school badge
1 pair of gym shoes
1 school tie
1 monitor's brooch
1 hockey stick
1 blouse for everyday wear
1 blouse for sports wear
1 blue serge skirt
1 pair of black woollen stockings
1 school jacket
1 school sponge bag
1 school toothbrush in glass tube
No Teddy Bears
1 pair of school mittens
1 school hairslide
Elastic for hat
Signed, Joan Betjeman
Matron of the Mayfair Ladies' College for Schoolgirl Appeal

Please write and say you have got back your illusions and that I am
not 'human'.
Love, JB

To Wilhelmine Cresswell   The Architectural Review
                                             9 Queen Anne's Gate
                                             Westminster
                                             SW I

Please put 'personal' otherwise the office enjoys my private correspondence.

15 February 1933

Darling East End girl,
Here you have in bluish green and white an offer from a young and literary man. First let me put the objections to marrying me:

a) Loose character, weak and self-indulgent and egocentric. Extravagant and selfish.
b) No birth – parents estranged both from me and one another – and not at all the right class for Generals. No hope whatever of their getting on. 'After all she must marry a gentleman.'
c) Contracted already to someone who undoubtedly loves me and to whom it is going to be horrible to have to be unkind.
d) Income £400 a year. Suppose in the first year I make nothing extra (it is all luck and highly probable) then this with your £100 that makes £500. £500 = £7.12.1 a week.

Now take weekly expenditure supposing we lived within it:

	£7.12.1	
Rent	£1.10.0	This is exceedingly low rent indeed because Etchells is a friend and might not allow us to go on here, especially as he may give up 52 Davies St. No rent under £2 a week.
Wages for a woman	£1	
Gas etc.	£0.10.0	

That leaves £4.12.1 for food, clothes, fares, drinks and any pleasures in a week. It ain't much, duckie, it's only 13/1d a day for everything except rent and wages. It's no joke. Can you stand it? I feel somehow it's almost too much to ask anyone to put up with.

Do really seriously consider it – love apart – and tell me whether you could stick it. *I will quite understand, if you can't.* It's bad enough for one person – but think of it for two. We must count on no outside help. There never is any when you want it. Poverty isn't conducive to a happy married state. Why, I pay two days' food ration in a single night without thinking.

Finally there's no getting away from the fact that I love you, darling Billa, and that I'm wonderfully happy thinking about it and feeling that you love me. My God, I am. It's the most restful and consoling affair I have yet experienced, and it's quite enough really to know that you exist with those extraordinary clothes and that loud voice and that white and painted face. Moreover we're one up on everyone else because we've suffered. There's one thing we must not do and that is let anyone outside the magic circle of Joan [Eyres-Monsell] and Etchells and Cracky know anything about it. Philth [PC] will be furious and doubly hurt if she thinks I am chucking her because of you – which is, after all, the truth. I shall write and tell her that I don't want to marry her – at once. But I shall merely go on the financial tack and the snob tack. The rest must wait until I see her. I shall point out the obvious incompatibility of temperament. I shall hear how she takes that – if she doesn't see any reason for not marrying; if she still really loves me, as I believe she does – then there is nothing for it but a scene. And My God – there will be some! I am frankly terrified. Sir Philip [Chetwode] with a horsewhip and others with their tongues. It's all worth it for you – but it doesn't make your position enviable. We will lose a host of good friends. But why should I be miserable when I know what would be my lot if I was to marry Philth? And if you love me, why should you suffer? – and I? And how I love you darling, darling Billa – but I ought to keep this side out of my letter and so must you keep it out of consideration, and think of my circumstances and position.

We won't really suffer, because we love each other so much, and that makes anything possible. But you must be reasonable and so must I. We must also wait in *absolute silence and secrecy*. Trust no one, but the Big Four mentioned above for God's sake, swear Joan into perfect confidence. The whole game is up if it gets about. Meanwhile I will tell Philth's friends that I don't want to marry her – can't afford it. Dishonesty is the best policy – and the kindest at present. I love you, I love you, I love you. Write to me and tell me what you think. And for God's sake don't leave letters lying about. No one is honest. Few are charitable.

Nothing, no further stage can be reached for at least a month. God bless you, darling, and don't worry – all my love for ever,
    From Betj

W.C. worked in a mission in the East End (very briefly).

Although already secretly engaged to my mother, PC, JB also became secretly engaged to W.C. after meeting her at a weekend houseparty at Sezincote, where she had gone as a prospective girlfriend for John Dugdale, the son of the house.

To Alan Pryce-Jones   The Architectural Review
                                              9 Queen Anne's Gate
                                              Westminster
18 February 1933   SW1

Darling Bog,
I am so sorry I have not written before. Of course I am delighted. You've scored all along the line. But there is one thing you must do before you marry – you must explain that you were once inverted. She won't mind at all. In fact she obviously knows as she is quite aware that old Graham [Eyres-Monsell] and I and all our friends are inverted. I think it is mad not to be honest and clear up the embarrassment of a prickly conscience. Actually inversion is an additional charm. It worked very well with Philth although I have now decided that I daren't marry her – money and emotion and fear getting in the way.

Oh Bog, I *am* pleased – though very sorry for Dotty. You must marry at once. 'Delay has danger' as my favourite poet the Reverend George Crabbe says. Those eyes of hers like tennis balls and that drawl and that undeniable depth and constancy. Of course it's what we all need and those who are supposed to make bad husbands – like you – always turn out the best. And to think of your children and their Uncle Adrian. Bog, I am glad. I have a lot of important things to tell you when you return. I hope you've written a good play. There's no more need to write for money. You will become a great author. I will tell her she must marry you *at once*.

Archie [Ormsby-Gore] has been very drunk lately. He was asked to talk at the Young Men's Welfare Centre in Colchester, last Tuesday and arrived reeling with sherry.

I don't know why he should do this
sort of thing. His Homer is still
unfinished. He has ringworm.

It has been lovely and cold here. The sort of weather that makes me active and today I am going to Whitefield's Tabernacle to write a play about Toplady.

There is a publication called *New Verse* which contains good and bad stuff. It ought to contain some Boggins [A.P.-J.].

I have been asked to toast the Society's health at the OUDS supper. This is very funny considering I was turned out of the OUDS for libelling it. I shall not comply with the request. God bless you, Bog, and come back soon. Abroad is awful.

Love, JB

> A.P.-J. was engaged to Joan Eyres-Monsell, but nothing came of it. (In the event she first married John Rayner. She is now married to Patrick Leigh Fermor.)
> Archie Ormsby-Gore, JB's teddy bear, continued to lead a vivid imaginary life.
> OUDS is the Oxford University Dramatic Society.

To Michael Rosse   9 Queen Anne's Gate
19 April 1933   London sw1

Dear Michael,
Please excuse this rather unexpected letter on what will be, from me, an unexpected subject. I have a friend whose card is enclosed and who is one of the Big Three in the new White Army in Ireland. As you are an Irish Citizen and I expect have opinions about Dev's [De Valera's] actions and politics at the moment, I thought that you might be interested in the enclosed pamphlets about the ACA – the White Army. I suppose it's all right, my writing to you about this, for all people who have property and TREES in Ireland are bound to be a bit anxious now and it looks to me as though their only hope lies in the ACA. Cosgrave's party is full of corruption, though Cosgrave himself is all right and I shouldn't think the Cuman na Gaedheal will ever get in again. The Centre party doesn't count and the IRA is communist, as we all know.

The ACA isn't particularly left wing but it will support Cuman na Gaedheal where it can and put up its own members when it can't. If you would let the Captain (card enclosed) see you either when you are in Dublin or else let him come and see you for half an hour in your Gothick Castle, he would tell you all about it, what it has done and what it wants to do. Could you let him have your opinion at his address in Dublin? He won't insist on a subscription; he merely has you on a list of people who might be interested in the ACA.

Return to England, alas, tonight. Your sister promised to send me a specimen of that writing paper of yours with a Gothick Castle at its head, but I must have made a bad impression, because she hasn't.

I hope your trees are doing nicely. The Captain is a nice man. Do see him. He is interested in Hindu eroticism as well as the ACA.

Yours, John Betjeman

M.R. (the Earl of Rosse) had been at Christ Church during JB's time. He was in the smart set with Harold Acton, Brian Howard, Bryan Guinness, Mark Ogilvie-Grant and Robert Byron.

M.R. had written (undated), 'The President [of the ACA], I think, O'Higgins, called on my agent the other day and was only with difficulty prevented from coming and laying his suit before me! I have no political views myself and though I understand the aims of the ACA are excellent, one is better not involved in any organisation at present.' The Army Comrades Association later became the Blue Shirts. In their early days, as the ACA, they were encouraged by many, W. B. Yeats among them, before anyone knew how they would turn out.

To Hector Bolitho   The Architectural Review
                                                 9 Queen Anne's Gate
                                                 Westminster
15 May 1933   SW1

My dear Hector,
I should be delighted to write about Epstein for your little book on twelve Great Jews. The fee I regard as pretty well all right – especially for art criticism. I can certainly get it ready by August and will go and see old Epstein whom I have not seen for several months.

I hate it abroad otherwise I would envy you. Why don't you go to Essex or Wilts instead of to Trans-Jordan?

Thank you so much for asking me. I hope the book comes off.

Yours devotedly, John Betjeman
PS What about a book on twelve Great Living Edwardians? Alfred Douglas, Henry Newbolt, Anthony Hope, C. F. A. Voysey, Conrad Noel, Stephen Hobhouse, Gerald Balfour, the Bishops (counting as one person) ? ? ? ? or you might call it *Twelve Great Remainders*.

H.B., a novelist, biographer and playwright, was to write on how Jews had contributed to English life. Neither JB's contribution nor H.B.'s book came off.

To Randolph Churchill   The Architectural Review
                                           9 Queen Anne's Gate
                                           Westminster
18 May 1933   SW1

My dear Randolph,
Here are the story by Mary Erskine and two of my poems.
  I shan't be at all surprised if the poems aren't suitable.
  Hope to see you soon old boy.
  Yours devotedly, JB

> JB first met R.C. at Oxford and in 1931 had shared a house with him in Culross Street,
> the London base of Edward James who had gone to America. JB referred to him as 'the
> Mayfair Lady Killer'. He edited the magazine, *Oxford and Cambridge*, at the time, and
> published one of the poems, 'The Arrest of Oscar Wilde', which Geoffrey Grigson had
> already turned down for the first issue of *New Verse*.
>   Mary St-Clair Erskine had written in April: 'It is charming of you to take so much
> trouble. I felt after I had sent you my novelette that it was bad . . . I don't mind not
> getting cash for months if only someone would accept it.' They didn't.

To Penelope Chetwode   The Green Man
                                           Little Braxted
                                           Witham
Lord's Day [?May or June 1933]   Essex

Δεαρ λιττλε λοομπ οφ φιλθι Δοογγ,
[Dear little loomp oph philthi Doong,]
Oh the beauty of this part of Essex. Gentle hills and lanes like rivers,
high fields of green corn on either side of them, yellow plaster and
matchboard houses with red roofs and black barns all round them and
willows and elms everywhere and meadows and ragged robin and
Δοογγωνι [Doongoni] in every ditch.
   This here has an earth closet and no bath but it is clean and silent and
Georgian and I have had lovely food and a comfortable bed. Last night
Oi went to a fair at Coggeshall, an almost unspoiled Georgian town and
there were a lot of people looking loike little Δοογγι [Doongi] larking
about with their boys.

They were the Coggeshall tarts. Oi ave made a great discovery about a place called Pattiswick which I shall disclose to you when Oi see you. It concerns us both intimately.

I went to see one church (Georgian) miles out of the way and it had been pulled down years ago. I went to see another more miles away and it had fallen down. There I saw countless loovely villages and Georgian pubs and terraces and halls.

Langford Grove where Oi am goin ter leckshare is a late Georgian building decorated by the Adam Bros within. It belongs to the Reverend the Lord Byron.

ω Δοογγι ωοι διδ οι μακε γου κροι οι λοονε γερ σω μοοχ. Μοι Γοδ οι λοονε γερ. [o Doongi woi did oi make you kroi oi loove yer so mooch. Moi God, oi loove yer.]

Τιλλ τεα τερμορρερ θεν. [Till tea termorrer then.]

φρομ γερ οων νιννι, νοονι, νιννι νοονι νοονι νοονι νοο. [phrom yer oon ninni, nooni, ninni nooni nooni nooni noo.]

The Green Man became my parents' idyllic hideaway, perhaps before and certainly directly after their clandestine marriage in July. My mother needed to tell her parents where she was staying and used the architect Bailie-Scott who lived nearby as an alibi.

JB was not actually writing in Greek; he simply changed English letters to Greek letters.

Langford Grove was where Wilhelmine Cresswell had been at school.

To Patrick Balfour   The Architectural Review
                                        9 Queen Anne's Gate
                                        Westminster
13 June 1933   SW1

My dear Patrick,
Thank you so much for your book which arrived today and which I
have not read yet. I will try and mention it in the *A.R.*
   I was so sorry Philth and I did not come to your party the other night.
Since then she has chucked me over and gone to France. I have been sick
whenever I have tried to eat and wept tears all night since then. I did not
think I was capable of so much emotion. Cracky caused the rift by
advising her not to marry me. But perhaps it was all for the best, though
I loved her so much that I now feel I haven't got an existence on this
planet. Can't write any more.
   Love, JB

   In fact PC went to stay with her aunt Polly Stapleton-Cotton in Opio, South of France,
   to make her mind up about JB.

To Bryan Guinness   The Architectural Review
                                        9 Queen Anne's Gate
                                        Westminster
4 August 1933   SW1

My dear Bryan,
What a masterly review of Callis' *Themes*! I have just read it. I am so
sorry I did not write when you were in Ireland. I do not know any
people I find better company or with tastes more exactly suited to my
own than Edward and Christine [Longford].
   I pull'd off my affair successfully thank God – after a lot of wavering
on the part of the opposite member of the deal during the last week – I
had to appear confident and contented when I could have sworn I was
going to be let down at the last moment. But the Lord prospering the
righteous, I wasn't and I am a different man from what you saw of me
last. Please swear by all you hold sacred not to tell *a soul* about this. I
cannot over-emphasize the importance of silence. Not even the
opposite party knows you know.
   Philth goes to Scotland on Tuesday and to its filthy snobbish 'Aunt

B' [The Countess of Pembroke] tomorrow.

I look forward to coming down on the eleventh of this month – till then – adieux and thank you for all your kindness in the most hideous stress.

JB

> JB and PC were married on 29 July at Edmonton Register Office, without her parents' knowledge, and she continued living with them as though nothing had happened. She and her father then travelled north for two weeks and stayed with family friends at Garrowby near York, Innes House, Elgin, Morayshire, and Glenconner near North Berwick. They returned on 6 September.

To Jack Beddington 52 Davies Street
17 August 1933 London W1

Dear Beddioleman,

I hate to disturb you during your chickenpoxed holiday but as I am far from a holiday myself and very righteously indignant at being put upon, I beg you in the name of Lansdowne Road, in the name of John Armstrong and all you hold sacred to help me in an almost unbelievable position.

You met our Mr [Maurice] Regan and as you no doubt noticed he is a good simple soul with a mind for figures and without any great qualities of leadership. You might not have noticed however that he is also a person of no aesthetic susceptibility whatever. If you want evidence of this, you need only look at the advertisements for and the productions of the Architectural Press; for instance *The History of the English House* (1936) in the Methuen 1910 style is his production, so also is *English Windmills* in the best Latin Grammar Book style. Any old type and any old binding and any old paper so long as you can save a few halfpence. If you saw his little home and his cousin's uncle's father and other relations who predominate in the Architectural Press you would realise why it is that the *Archie Rev* never quite goes the whole hog despite the valiant efforts of people like de Cronin [Hastings] and why the book department here is a complete flop. I have been co-opted on to the books and my salary raised from three to four hundred a year. I am still editor of the *Archie* in all but name . . . or rather will be next year. I have been told however that I am to get mss and 'generally help' which means that they put all the work they don't want to do or don't know how to do on to me.

All this however is typical of businessmen and all one can expect but here is a thing that has happened which exceeds even the evangelical standards of right and wrong that the Regans prescribe for themselves. The Regan family you must know, hold many though not quite all the shares in the Archie Press through hard work saving halfpence in their youth. There is only one person of whom Maurice Regan and the rest of them are afraid and that is the 'chief' – Percy Hastings, the father of de Cronin. He lives in the country and writes them long letters and comes up occasionally and leaves them all shaking. De Cronin they override and think clever but inclined to go too far. So does the father but not so much. This Percy, however, owing to his financial position has to keep in with the Regans who have so many shares and he has made our Maurice joint managing director, on his own retirement, with de Cronin. I do not wish to be unpleasant about the Regans, but they are not our sort. They all live in Wimbledon, have closed saloons, see no one but each other and are not interested in anything but getting money which they do not know how to spend.

I expect that even you have directors like that. But here is the iniquity that I am bursting to tell you and paragraph after paragraph of necessary explanation has prevented me. Maurice Regan has told the 'chief' all about the Shell Guide and the 'chief' is delighted. He has not mentioned however that the idea was mine, the make-up was mine and that I saw you first and started the whole thing. I do not think he did this with the intention of doing me down but simply in order to prevent my being 'too mad' as he would say and being given authority to arrange the make-up and thus prevent the thing from being a failure. Actually, of course, the thing would be a failure if he had anything to do with the aesthetic side of it. If it is a success the 'chief' will give all the credit to Maurice Regan for having prevented my going too far. At the moment the 'chief' imagines that I merely had something to do with some of the pages.

You will notice in the list of expenses an item called 'author's fee . . . fifty pounds'. As the author, I said to Maurice Regan that it would come in very useful. Maurice Regan knows my strained circumstances at the moment (things have happened of a very interesting nature which I cannot put down on paper but will tell you if I see you) but yet had the face to say that the fifty pounds was part of my four hundred a year. This, however, is beside the point except in so far as it shows you the sort of thing I am up against.

I do not want any more money. But there are two things you can do . . . or at least one of them, which will show the bloody Regans that in the outside world at any rate I am thought a little more of than in the Architectural Press.

1) You have not signed the contract yet. Before you do, could you insert a clause saying THAT ALL QUESTIONS OF MAKE-UP, ILLUSTRATION AND MAPS are in the Hands of Mr J. Betjeman and also that the Letterpress is as well? You can say that you want to do this because you are impressed with my original make-up and have full confidence in me. I don't know whether you have but if you haven't then of course that is that. As an additional reason you can say it is much easier to deal with one person with whom you are acquainted and whose judgements you understand than with a firm. This will do me some good if the 'chief' sees the contract and will also save your guide from any Edwardianisms. It is not as though my make-up on which costs have already been calculated is going to be more expensive. It may be cheaper.

There is one more thing however with which you could save my bacon. If the guide is a success and they continue to pay me four hundred a year and make me do the rest of the guides and edit the *Archie Rev* as well, I will not only be underpaid but also overworked. These guides interest me far more than anything else because I hate urban life and am really cut out for archaeology, make-up and photography and know England pretty well. But it is useless to undertake work like this as a side issue where one is cramped and crabbed by the narrowness of the Regans and I would very much like to have the opportunity of getting away from my present unappreciated position and doing the guides on my own with some other publisher. In that case I should at last be able to escape the shackles of the Architectural Press and be a freelance more or less. I would take my own photographs and thus save a good bit of money and actually visit all the counties. I have chosen Cornwall in this initial instance because I have lived there for much of my life and know it very well. With some other counties it might not be so easy to do it in a half time way. I would therefore demand no more than a living wage . . . less than I get now because I should be doing something I liked . . . and work solely for Shell.

This is all however in the unlikely event of the guide being a roaring success.

Will you therefore insert one more clause in the contract saying that you reserve the right to discontinue the guides, if you wish it, at the settling up of the Cornish Guide and also that you can take them elsewhere if you want to continue them again . . . or rather that, *in the event of their success, you insist upon my remaining their author and I can then dictate my own terms.*

Pray forgive my extremely confidential and frank letter. Perhaps you are a little disgusted at my exposure of all these facts and think I might treat you in the same way. Believe me I would not and it is only an accumulation of examples such as this last of my misrepresentation to the 'chief' and lack of appreciation from the Regans that has made me write this letter.

You see I have become a little disgusted too. I bear the poor dears little ill will because I do not think they know any better and because they are not blessed with imagination. Had they been, the Architectural Press would have been as important as it ought to be. The 'chief' had vision all right, so has de Cronin, poor chap, and that is why he is so depressed much of the time. But he was too wiry in his active days as far as I have heard and got an extraordinary reputation.

If I thought there was any chance of eventually bringing the Regans round to thinking me more sane than mad and paying me a little better and, if not appreciating, at least of not criticising my work, I should not have written thus. But I have waited four years now and nothing has happened.

There you are, Beddioleman, this letter is a cry from the heart and one of the longest I have ever typed. Pray treat it as such and forgive my indiscretion.

Yours in name of Augustus Toplady, author of 'Rock of Ages', with love to Mrs Beddioleman and those beautiful children,

John Betjeman

J. Beddington, the famously innovative and uproariously funny publicity director of Shell, became a mainstay in JB's life. JB called him 'Beddioleman' because an American had once addressed him, 'Well hi, Beddy, ol' man!' in JB's hearing. It also distinguished him from his father, 'Beddy Oldest Man', his brother 'Beddy Middle Man' and his son, 'Beddy Young Man'.

J. Beddington replied: 'I can and will insist that you are to be responsible for the whole make-up and to get the credit for the whole job. . . . I don't see much chance of your getting away from *Archie Rev* to Shell. Further, I am convinced that it would be a great mistake for you at the moment even to try to do such a thing.'

JB had been paid twenty pounds for making a dummy of the first proposed *Shell Guide Book* by Beddington, who commissioned artists such as Graham Sutherland to design posters.

To Bryan Guinness   52 Davies Street
[September 1933]   London w1

My dear Bryan,
Thank you so much for your telegram and pleasant invitation.
Unfortunately that telegram arrived too late for us to make arrangements. I go to Ireland tomorrow. The parents have been told. Lady
C[hetwode] is mad with rage, taking a different line about it every hour,
but the General has been charming as could be and is obviously an
enchanting and great man. I feel like a criminal. Filth is still culture
crazy and rather depressed by the pain inflicted on her parents who
adore her. So I really think it all for the best to encourage her to go
abroad and learn German for a few months while I look about for
somewhere for us to live in the country but not too far from London.
Until she lives alone for a bit she will not know what it is like not to have
a home and I am all for encouraging her. This is a delicate matter but
one has got to take the risk. So if you write you might take up the line
that going abroad FOR A BIT is a jolly good idea and will give the little
thing independence. It is really splendid of her to have married me.
Lady C. is putting an announcement in *The Times* tomorrow.
   Thank you so much for your help in this hellishly ticklish job.
   Love and gratitude, JB

> PB had written to JB in early September from Morayshire, saying how glad she was to be
> Mrs Betjeman: 'It gives me a great sense of security and I feel that I am at [any] rate
> anchored to something (if only a bit of seaweed) in this turbulent ocean of existence.' On
> returning to London and JB and after telling her parents of her marriage, she made the
> decision to go to Germany.

To Bryan Guinness   Alderley Park
                                       Chelford
9 October 1933   Cheshire

My dear Bryan,
Thank you very much for your letter. Thank God, things are running
smoothly and we are both doing nicely.
   Philth goes to Germany on *Sunday evening next*. We leave here on
Thursday morning and on Thursday, Friday and Saturday morning,
Philth will be signing documents and buying things before she goes

away for three months. While she is away I shall be looking for somewhere to live in the country and I think I shall choose the Wilts district. I have already heard of something cheap and good. Can't stand main roads.

But what I really meant to write about was this. Could we come down to Biddesden on Saturday afternoon next and stay for Saturday night returning on Sunday evening? – or rather Sunday afternoon? This will be our last time together for three months and it would be nice in rural and friendly surroundings.

If this is all right will you let me know either here before Thursday or else at 52 Davies Street, London W1.

Don't, please, put yourself out about it – I shall quite understand if, at such short notice, it is impossible.

Love to Nancy and Miss Pam and to yourself for so much sympathy and help in what was so nearly my bereavement.

John B

> After the news of their marriage had broken my parents lived in a series of depressing and cramped London flats before PB left for Germany.
>
> JB was helped with his house search by Christian Barman, an old friend and nominal editor of the *Architectural Review*, who lived in Uffington. He discovered Garrards Farm was to let. JB decided to take it.

To Wilhelmine Cresswell   Alderley Park
                                                   Chelford
10 October 1933   Cheshire

My dear Billa,

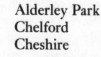

How swell of you to write. It is a most extraordinary thing that I have done. Had to keep dark about it because the F.M. [Field Marshal] was ill at the time of marriage and might have had a relapse. The King is annoyed, I understand. So is Auntie Star but she has given me some gold calf [sic] links to give me social tone.

Dear Billa, P. sends you its love, and, my God, so do I – let me see you in London.

Love, JB

To Bryan Guinness

14 January 1934
Lord's Day

52 Davies Street
but as from the *Archie Rev*
marked Personal

My Dear Bryan,

Forgive my typing a letter, the very nature of whose contents is personal, but I find that the space between the typewriter and the brain is more comfortable than that between the pen and the same object. I am still distressed about my apparently strange behaviour with Our Little Friend. I must here state in clear type that I am not in love with her although I am sure I should be very happy were I in such a state. No. I merely find her a companion of an almost male order of intelligence and sympathy and therefore take pleasure in her company. Her physical charms cannot rival those of Philth.

But what I really wanted to write about was the fact that this evening I met Bill Coghlin our old friend and believe me he is charming. He asked after you with the greatest reverence and affection and I think it would be a good idea if you could tell me when you are free this or next week and we could meet together for luncheon. I will telephone to him at the British Commercial Gas Association with which he is connected. Will you therefore communicate with me at the *Archie Rev*?

I have been offered the job of film critic on the *Evening Standard*, a purely commercial and soul-destroying affair, but on the other hand money is money when there is the upkeep of a wife to be considered and I shall take it if I cannot get an adequate wage (six hundred pounds a year) out of the *Archie*.

I hope you are all right about our little friend as I am or rather not as I am.

READ *BINSEY POPLARS* BY GERARD MANLEY HOPKINS.

Love, JB

When JB refers to 'our little friend' it is possible he meant Molly Higgins, the pretty girl with dark brown hair who helped decorate Garrards Farm in the autumn of 1933. He had confessed to PB in December that he was in love with her.

To Bryan Guinness   9 Queen Anne's Gate
                                                 London SW1

20 January 1934
Saturday before the Third Sunday after Epiphany

My dear Bryan,
Philth is coming back on Thursday and although I cannot say where we
will be living for the first week or two I hope you will forgive my making
a proposal that we should visit you for next weekend. Philth says at the
end of her letter, 'But DO let's go away early on Friday (can you get a
day off?)' – of course I can't as I am very busy these last days but could
get away on Friday evening – 'for the week-end – preferably to Bryan as
he is so sweet and sympathetic and one can do exactly what one likes at
Biddesden'. If therefore it is possible that we should come to Bidders
then that would be very nice. I shall go, I think, to the Charing Cross
Hotel for the coming week as I am very fond of it there and like the sense
of an impending journey there is about an hotel on the railway.
    Cracky calls O.L.F. [our little friend] the C.B. because she looks so
like a choir boy. Religion and sex, dontcherknow.
    Love, JB

> Garrards Farm was in a bad state and needed various alterations suggested by Etchells. It
> was not ready to move into immediately on PB's return. She wrote from Berlin,
> 'Darling, I'm so relieved you say I can come back. I think you'll find it will work alright,
> anyway on my side now. . . . I hope you'll be happy with me but if you aren't you can
> always go off with M.H. [Molly Higgins]. . . . It will be lovely if we can go down ter
> Bryan the first weekend as then we'll be able to motor over to Garrards straightaway.'
> Molly Higgins proved to be no serious threat. My mother made friends with her and she
> sometimes came to stay at Garrards.

Five:

Chalk-built pre-war Uffington

February 1934 to December 1937

Tonight we feel the muffled peal
  Hang on the village like a pall;
It overwhelms the towering elms –
  That death-reminding dying fall;
The very sky no longer high
  Comes down within the reach of all.
Imprisoned in a cage of sound
Even the trivial seems profound.

'Uffington'

In February 1934 my parents moved to Garrards Farm in the village of Uffington in Berkshire, a small and unassuming chalk-white house on the village street. There were brick dressings around the casement windows, from which you looked out across flat, well-hedged, vale country to White Horse Hill and the great sculptured folds of the Berkshire Downs. They rented the house for thirty-six pounds a year from Mr Wheeler, a tenant farmer of the Craven Estate, and brought with them a German maid, Paula Steinbrecher, who spoke no English when she arrived and for almost a year was under the impression that JB's name was 'shut up' since my mother said it to him so often.

They flung themselves headlong into village life. JB became People's Warden at the beautiful Early English Church of St Mary which rose cruciform like a cathedral from the cottages below, and Vice-Chairman of the Uffington Hockey Club under Mr Leahy who ran the village post office and stores. My mother directed nativity plays, lectured the Women's Institute on such subjects as Indian philosophy and how to make mayonnaise, and in a fit of over-ambition decided to stage a play called *The Monkey's Paw* by W. W. Jacobs.

The rehearsals went very badly, remembers one of the actors, Ron Liddiard, whose parents, Cyril and Kit, farmed the perfect hunting country around the small hamlet of Baulking. '"Well, John will be down at the weekend, he'll pull it into shape," said Mrs Betjeman. And sure enough, only ten minutes after his arrival it was going very well. Mr Betjeman was a brilliant director, but then of course he saw a lot of films, being a film critic. I remember once when he brought two comedians called Ralph Lynn and Tom Walls to stay. After church on Sunday morning they went for a walk and called in at the Wentworths who had a smallholding outside the village and made home-made wine. Mrs Betjeman had to get her horse and cart out to pick them up – they were so drunk they couldn't walk.'[1]

JB had a Ford Prefect in which he travelled to catch the London train at Challow Station most mornings. 'He could never start it,' said Ron Liddiard. 'He got in a terrible temper winding it up with the starting handle, and swearing a good deal as it backfired.' My mother preferred to ride or drive her white Arab gelding, Moti, to a four-wheeled dog cart she had bought in the nearby village of Stanford in the Vale, for twelve pounds. She often drove over to Faringdon House, an elegant eighteenth-century pile on the outskirts of the local town. It belonged to the eccentric composer, painter and novelist, Lord Berners. Wide lawns spread out beyond the gravel entrance sweep towards the parish church and a perfect park sloped gently down behind the house to a lake and the level valley of the Thames. As JB remembered Berners: 'His voice was rather low and toneless. He rarely laughed and his brown eyes only looked up for a moment when something particularly impressed him. When he did speak he seldom wasted words. He seemed to have read and appreciated every classic in English, French, Italian and German, yet he never forced his learning on you. His stories were short, extremely funny and fantastic . . . going to lunch or dine at Faringdon, you never knew who you might meet. Most improbable things happened. I remember Lord Berners taking Schiaparelli [the dress designer] to a jumble sale in the vicarage garden at Baulking and I remember our pleasure when she was pressed to buy something in the second-hand clothes stall.'[2] Another time he brought H. G. Wells and Baroness Budberg ('Bedbug' to my parents) to Garrards for a ride in my mother's cart. Berners and his demoniacally good-looking boyfriend, Robert Heber-Percy, were inordinately fond of my parents and they had many friends in common like Nancy and Diana Mitford, John Sparrow and Wilhelmine Cresswell. Visits to Faringdon House fast became an established part of my parents' and subsequently my brother's and my lives, and we had Sunday lunch there at least once a month, until well into the seventies. On hot days my mother swam right across the lake, through the patch of water lilies, with bold regular strokes.

Another well-loved neighbour was Samuel Gurney, who came from the great family of Norwich Quakers, and lived nearby at Compton Regis in a solid mid-Victorian vicarage tucked into the bottom of the

Downs. He drove a Rolls Royce, was a prominent Anglo-Catholic and enjoyed entertaining the higher echelons of the clergy. Sometimes he staged outdoor Masses in this garden, where a stream tumbled down through rocks and there were leafy dells and steep banks of ferns, and religious statues in amongst the gunnera, while at the top of the slope a great open-armed Virgin Mary embraced the scene. My parents met 'Uncle Sam' through the Misses Molly and Edmée Butler and formed a long friendship with him which lasted until his death in 1968. JB leaned on him for theological advice and it was a subject they discussed for over thirty years. In 1934 Gurney wrote a perfectly serious letter to JB about the immorality of foxhunting – a sport JB had never considered taking up: 'The thing [foxhunting] itself outrages conscience. Theologically, of course, every evil produces good results, and every pain and pang swells the treasury of the Passion: but nevertheless it is 'woe to that man by whom the offence cometh'. Its indefinite continuance is unthinkable. It won't really square with the faith. Put it another way. Picture the bright young thing, leaving the altar in the morning, her lips rosy with the Blood of Jesus: returning home at night, her finger dripping with the blood of vixen. Or Jesus, Mary, and Joseph all in at the death and blooded. Have I put it too strongly?'[3]

The Misses Butler who lived at Woolstone Lodge and considered themselves the local squiresses, were also part of our lives at Uffington and always. They saw themselves as my parents' guardians – perhaps more practical than spiritual – and were constantly giving advice about the suitability of certain village girls as staff. The formidable Miss Molly who was the more determined of the two had a face like a boot, a huge bulbous nose and stood with her feet at a quarter to three, while Miss Edmée was retiring, thin and wiry and looked like a shrew. They wore squashed-looking felt hats on all occasions. Miss Molly played the organ at Woolstone Church and was an expert bee-keeper. Miss Edmée was a superlative cook: her spiced shoulder of lamb was a masterpiece and took four days to make. Once my parents were asked to dinner with the Misses Butler when their cousin, who came from Camberley, was visiting, of whom they were inordinately proud.

'Would you like John to change?' my mother asked Miss Molly on the telephone.

'Oh no, he need not bother.'

'Will your cousin be wearing a dinner jacket?'

'Oh yes, but he's used to it.'

During the first months at Uffington my parents found it hard to

entertain on JB's wage from the *Architectural Review*. In April 1934
Ernest Betjemann wrote to my mother, 'If I could I would give you the
most lovely home, Penelope, but I am afraid now I have had another
setback. . . .'[4] (He had just had a mild heart attack.) He sent three
hundred pounds and some furniture, including a dining-room table
made in the Pentonville works. The family firm, though still in
operation, had been a victim of the slump and Ernest had had no income
for four years. Two months later, while talking to his business manager
one evening, he had another heart attack and died. He was sixty-two
years old. JB was in London: 'I'd meant to get off at the underground to
go and visit him. But I was worrying about getting back to my
newspaper on time so as not to irritate the editor. While I was making
up my mind, the train waited rather longer than usual, as if saying, "Go
on, get out." But I stayed on and went to the newspaper instead. My
father died that night. I couldn't eat anything for days. . . .'[5] For all the
mockery JB had made of his father over the last few years to his friends,
a genuine grief and remorse set in. He had bridged much of the gap
which his time at Oxford and his refusal to join the firm had brought
about, and was on fairly friendly terms with his father. He had
accepted Ernest's apparently overt flaunting of a mistress whom he had
kept for years and Ernest, in turn, had accepted his only son's ambitions
to write for a living. He made the effort to read all JB's articles in the
Architectural Review on which he usually made favourable comments
and he praised *Ghastly Good Taste* unequivocally. His praise of *Mount
Zion*, however, had a guilt-inspiring sting in its tail, when Ernest
alluded to the dedication to Mrs Arthur Dugdale. This appeared below
a picture of Sezincote. 'CONSTANTLY UNDER THOSE MINARETS I have
been raised from the deepest depression and spent the happiest days of
my life,' it read. Ernest suggested that 'The dedication would have lost
nothing by the insertion of the words "some of" before "happiest days"
and would have been more complimentary to Mother and I.'[6] It was the
sort of inadvertent error that anyone might have made and I am sure
that JB had not realized how wounding its effect would be. Neither did
Ernest realize how guilt-ridden he would make his son feel.

Later Clonmore wrote about JB to Lionel Perry (19 August 1940),
'You will remember the crocodile tears which were shed over Ernie,
after all the abuse the poor man had to face when alive.'[7] This was
unfair; though JB and his mother had cause for dismay and surprise
when, at the funeral on 23 June in Chelsea Old Church, Ernie's
long-standing mistress appeared, accompanied by several children,
supposedly his. He was buried in Highgate Cemetery where an obelisk

marks his grave, and at St Enodoc Church in Cornwall a wall plaque marks his memory, designed by JB's friend Etchells.

P. Morton Shand and his fourth wife, Sybil, spent Christmas at Garrards in 1934. Although the house only had four small bedrooms, there was to be a constant flow of visitors over the years, including stalwart regulars such as Jim Lees-Milne, Cyril Connolly, William Clonmore, Bryan Guinness, Osbert Lancaster and his wife Karen, Peter Quennell, Frederick Etchells, Lord Alfred Douglas, Lionel Perry and Evelyn Waugh, who thought at one time that he would like to buy a house in what he called 'Betjeman, Berners country'. What is hard to explain today is how much these friends made each other laugh. They seemed to laugh all the time when other artistic sets did not. The group included more than its fair share of funny people. My parents' entertainment value meant that they were constantly asked out to meals or to stay. In July 1935 my mother wrote to her mother in India, 'We are going to stay with Sexy [Cecil] Beaton as John is to be the parson in his film! I am chaperoning Caroline [Paget] who is the heroine (a negress!!), and shall probably do noises-off parts. Sexy is the hero and I believe John Sutro, the villain. It is a serious film from [David] Garnett's *Return of the Sailor*, though why Sexy chose a story with a negress heroine God knows. . . . John was asked to be the parson long ago but refused as he thought he wouldn't have time, but now Sexy says he must be as Oliver Messel (who was doing it instead) has gone to America. The film is only amateur though Thomas Meyer, the director, is professional.' John Sutro had put up the money to make the film at Beaton's house Ashcombe on the Wiltshire/Dorset border. It was dubbed in *The Bystander*, 'the film with the Mayfair cast'.[8]

Oxford friends also visited Garrards Farm, John Sparrow and Maurice Bowra in particular. The latter wrote several mad poems about Uffington life, always referring to my mother as 'Yellow'. They included a long and eventually filthy Tennysonian verse, 'An Idyll', which began:

> At Garrards Farm, beneath the White Horse Hill,
> Lived John and little Yellow, – daughter she
> Of some famed General in the Indian Wars . . .
> John would peruse the works of bygone men . . .
> Sunk in the past was he but not afraid
> To grapple with the present's many needs,
> To play at cricket on the village green . . .
> But Yellow was more active in her ways;

> She physicked horses when they had the thrush,
> Or lectured to the Women's Institute,
> Or knitted jerseys for the godly poor,
> Or taught the middle classes how to cook . . .[9]

It went on to describe my brother's conception in explicit terms. Paul Sylvester George was born on 26 November 1937. 'Colonel' Kolkhorst, being an atheist, refused to be a godparent; John Sparrow accepted, as did Mary Pakenham (now Clive), Tom Driberg and Anne Feversham.

Back in December 1933, JB had written an article for the *Evening Standard* with the help of Patrick Balfour and Randolph Churchill called 'Peers without Tears', and on the strength of it was appointed their film critic. (When he interviewed the film star, Myrna Loy, he persuaded her to say that she liked perpendicular architecture.) The job was well paid and not time-consuming. JB liked the comedians the best, W. C. Fields, Laurel and Hardy and 'Schnozzle' Durante. He did not like the crooning films of Bing Crosby, child stars such as Freddie Bartholomew or musicals about Vienna. He wrote, 'I suppose "I found my heart in St Catharine's, Cambridge" doesn't sound as good as "I found my heart in Heidelberg".'

Once he was settled at Uffington his weekday life at the *Architectural Review* began to pall. In January 1935 he stormed out. However, when his future as film critic began to look doubtful – for he was forever complaining about having to kowtow to the advertisers – he crept back to his old boss Hubert de Cronin Hastings and asked if he might return. Hastings replied, 'The board is damned if it is going to switch everything round again to please you. It admits that you leave a gap. Already you have fulfilled the prophecies of those who shall be nameless, who in their wisdom laughed and said, "In six weeks he'll be wanting to come back." I said, "Nonsense. You've lost a genius. In six months you will be wondering why you were so mad as to let him go." . . .'[10]

Hastings's letter went on to give him kind and avuncular advice to start afresh somewhere else. In August he started working three days a week for the Shell Oil Company at Shell-Mex House under the kind eye of the advertising director, Jack Beddington. Beddington was a renowned talent spotter and through the thirties his team included Rex Whistler, Nicolas Bentley, Edward Ardizzone, Peter Quennell, Graham Sutherland and John Piper, who all designed posters or invented new ways of advertising Shell. JB was meant to write jingles and put together short advertising films, but he also spent quite a lot of time making up jokes with his colleague, William 'Scudamore' Mitchell. 'We were searching for a name for a new kind of motor oil,' Mitchell remembered, 'and John suggested it should be "Beddioline" – after Beddioleman, of course.'[11]

The *Shell Guides*, architectural guide-books to different counties intended for the use of motorists, began to take up more and more of JB's time. In 1933, Beddington had advanced him twenty pounds to produce a dummy for a trial *Shell Guide*. Now he agreed to finance a series. The Architectural Press published JB's first *Guide to Cornwall* which was priced at half a crown, and used a Spirax binding and a variety of typefaces. JB's obsession with typography and layout, inspired by his mentor Hubert de Cronin Hastings, gave the early *Shell Guides* an innovative and distinctive look. JB went on to produce a guide to *Devon* and then commissioned his friends to cover the counties they knew best. Paul Nash wrote *Dorset*, Peter Quennell *Somerset*, Christopher Hobhouse *Derbyshire*, William Clonmore *Kent*, John Nash *Buckinghamshire*, Thomas Sharpe *Northumberland and Durham*, John Rayner *Hampshire*, and Anthony West *Gloucestershire*. JB chose the photographs, did the layout and wrote the captions for these commissioned guides. Robert Byron's *Wiltshire* had a collage of photographs as its cover designed by Gerald Berners, the like of which had never been seen before, but JB was most proud of his design for Stephen Bone's *West Coast of Scotland*, which was printed in purple ink, 'to remind one of heather'. In 1937 JB wrote, 'The *Shell Guides* had at once to be critical and selective. They had to illustrate places other than the well-known beauty spots and to mention the disregarded and fast disappearing Georgian landscape of England; churches with box pews and West Galleries; handsome provincial streets of the late Georgian era; impressive mills in industrial towns; horrifying villas in overrated 'resorts' had all to be touched upon. These things, for various reasons left out by other guides, are featured in the *Shell Guides*. Add to this the realisation that the purchaser of the *Guides* is probably not an intellectual in search of regional architecture of the early nineteenth century but a plus-foured weekender who cannot tell a sham Tudor roadhouse from a Cotswold manor, and you will have some idea of the scope of the books.'[12]

It was Professor J. M. Richards of the *Archie Rev* who recommended that JB should meet John Piper because he was such an 'excellent typographer'. They met early in 1937 and JB recruited Piper to write the *Shell Guide to Oxfordshire*. They saw eye to eye immediately: theirs was to be the friendship of a lifetime and their collaboration on the *Shell*

Guides produced a magic which changed people's perception of England. Their enthusiasm shone through. 'We realized we liked the same things,' said JB. They both saw architecture in terms of the setting rather than a scholarly thing out of context. They had a lot else in common for they were both children of the middle class, they had both refused to go into the family business, and they had both spent much of their childhood bicycling about looking at churches.

By now JB's friendship with the architectural historian, John Summerson, was blossoming. They had met at the top of Fortnum and Mason's in 1934: 'I was arranging an exhibition of Arvold Artoes. John came in and I didn't like the look of him. I was on the floor stapling something together and he just stood there and stared at me. It didn't take long before we laughed. From then on throughout our lives, whenever we met, we always burst out laughing. We had some running squabbles about architecture – I liked Corbusier then, and I was more up-to-date in my views than he was. John called me "Coolmore" because he thought the name suited me. He had discovered that it was the name of my mother's family seat in County Cork. He always called me that at committee meetings. He would say, "Mr Chairman, let's ask Coolmore for his opinion," and no one knew what he was talking about.'[13]

JB often signed his letters to Summerson as 'G. K. Chesterton' or 'Maxwell Fry'. Their discussions about Regency, Victorian and Edwardian architects lasted until JB's death. Summerson, an old Harrovian, wrote in a lecture on JB to the PEN Club, 'He held that Harrovians wrote the best prose, instancing Winston Churchill, Wyndham Ketton-Cremer and, more surprisingly, Sir Bernard Docker, with a few others, me included. . . . He found architecture and architects (especially architects) irresistibly funny . . . what he did not like was the illumination of the obscure by art historians. That destroyed the bloom of obscurity. The twilight which had settled on the Victorian and Edwardian was a beautiful, tragical-comical twilight. It was not an academic problem looking for an academic answer. Hence his antagonism towards Pevsner, which for a time was obsessional. The Pevsner approach was like installing a system of floodlights in a twilight landscape.' JB preferred scholarship to be delivered humanely with humour and wit. Summerson was, in that respect, perfection.

Apart from his work for Shell, JB began to do an increasing number of radio talks for the BBC through his friend, Gerald Heard. He had kept up his contact with Talks director, Malcolm Brereton, to whom he had originally written in 1929. In 1932 and 1933 he had given at least half a dozen talks. In June 1935 Mr Pocock of the BBC wrote, 'We are trying to evolve a technique of short story actually adapted to the microphone. The matter is at present in its early stages, and perhaps it would interest you to consider whether you might not be able to assist us.'[14] In an inter-office memo a month later Pocock wrote to Malcolm Brereton, 'I had a talk with Betjeman this afternoon, and he read to me his story beginning "Just a minute, sir" over the microphone, though of course we had no effects. His idea is not simply to have a story with effects, but effects worked into the plot and taking the place of essential description. This seems to me to be extremely interesting and probably sound. Anyhow, it is well worth looking into and experimenting with. I recommend you to get some of these records – there must be a train, for instance, and probably noises of feet scrunching – and to try out this story. In the meanwhile I have asked him to do another one on similar lines and we might do them both in the same period, with real effects.'[15]

In 1936 JB began to make programmes at the BBC Bristol studios. His voice was becoming familiar to the public and his topographical talks were provoking letters from listeners. In 1937 he gave several talks called 'Town Tours' including Bristol, Bournemouth and Exeter. His talk on Swindon, which was mildly scathing, provoked 'a Swindonian' to write, 'Well, Mr John Betjeman, I hope the next time I hear you broadcast it will be to boost a place not to ridicule it.'[16] William Morris's daughter, May, whom my parents often visited at Kelmscott Manor across the Thames in Gloucestershire, was overjoyed: 'I am glad indeed to hear that you said nasty things about the town of Swindon. There are some very good honest people there but the town is a disgrace, standing on the edge of the beautiful Down country.'[17] One of JB's directors at the BBC was his friend, Guy Burgess, who asked JB to take part in a series on eccentrics: 'I would leave the choice of subject largely in your hands.' JB chose the Irishman Adolphus Cooke.

In 1937 he made his first television film, *How to Make a Guide Book*, in a studio at Alexandra Palace. 'It was a bit like giving a lecture,' remembers Myfanwy Piper, who had made a similar film just before JB under the same producer, Mary Adams, 'Mine was on what you could see in the country from a bicycle. There was a static camera and you were allowed to bring in a few objects with which to illustrate your "lecture". I brought the landlord from the Golden Ball pub in Lower Assenden who was an ex-policeman and the inn sign from the Black Boy on the road at Hurley.'[18] JB told Mary Adams that he did not think the medium had much future unless the camera could get out and about.

JB kept up a lively correspondence with his Arts and Crafts heroes, C. R. Ashbee (and subsequently his widow Janet), and Charles Annesley Voysey, then a widower, whom he often took out to lunch. He was particularly conscious of single people at Christmas. But on being invited to Uffington, Voysey wrote in December 1936, 'I wish I could believe all the nice things you say of me . . . I am atheist and believe as the psalmists and profits [sic] so need no saviour and in consequence hate Xmas . . . I am reminded of my poverty.'[19] JB also made a place for publicly disgraced homosexuals, of whom Lord Alfred Douglas was a prime example. Constantly hard up, Douglas would often ask for favours. 'Dear Moth,' he wrote in September 1937, accepting a dinner invitation, 'I would have to stay the night of course and wonder if you could provide *sleeping accommodation* for one night? I am going through a severe financial crisis. . . . I am daily expecting a small legacy left to me last January by my godmother [Mabel Montgomery, sister of Florence of *Misunderstood*] and until it comes I am "broke to the world".'[20]

JB met T. S. Eliot again in 1937 after a twenty-one-year gap. Eliot had taught briefly at Highgate Junior School in 1916, where JB remembered him as 'the American Master', whom he had singled out as being the right person to receive his manuscript called *The Best of Betjeman*. Perhaps Eliot had noticed some early talent, for in 1936, when he was a director of the publishers Faber and Faber, he began to court JB as a possible Faber author. When pipped at the post for his poems by John Murray, he did not give up. He tried to instigate a book with him on English architecture, and Fabers ended by publishing the *Shell Guides* for a time. Their deep and heartfelt quest for religious enlightenment and their shared sense of humour over odd and obscure aspects of life were bound to make them lifelong friends. T.S.E. stuck an extract from a song he had cut out from a newspaper on a postcard to JB in 1937.

> We must all stick together,
> All stick together,
> Never mind the old school tie,
> United we shall stand
> Whatever may befall
> The richest in the land,
> The poorest of us all
> We must all stick together,
> Birds of a feather
> And the clouds will soon roll by.[21]

On 2 November 1937 *Continual Dew* was published by 'Jock' Murray, the sixth John of the famous and old-established family firm, John Murray, which had published Lord Byron. Jock had been a contemporary of JB's at Oxford, where they had had friends and a love of poetry in common. The little volume, whose title was derived from the Anglican church service, '. . . pour upon us the continual dew of Thy blessing . . .,' included fifteen of the poems from *Mount Zion* and eighteen new ones, some of which had already been published in magazines. As usual, JB insisted on a typographical feast, and also on involving his friends. Osbert Lancaster designed the cover and Hubert de Cronin Hastings did several illustrations; Edward Longford corrected the proofs and the whole was dedicated to Gerald Berners.

1. Ron Liddiard, CLG interview (1992).
2. JB, 'Lord Berners, 1883–1950', *The Listener* (May 1950).
3. CLG's papers.
4. CLG's papers.
5. JB, Susan Barnes interview, 'Betjeman I Bet Your Racket Brings You in a Pretty Packet', *Sunday Times Magazine* (30 January 1972).
6. JB's papers, University of Victoria, Columbia.
7. Lionel Perry's papers.
8. CLG's papers.
9. CLG's papers.
10. JB's papers.
11. Bevis Hillier, *John Betjeman: A Life in Pictures* (John Murray, 1984).
12. Richard Ingrams, *Piper's Places: John Piper in England and Wales* (Hogarth Press, 1983).
13. Sir John Summerson, CLG interview (1991).
14. Copy in BBC archives.
15. BBC archives.
16. JB's papers.
17. JB's papers.
18. Myfanwy Piper, CLG interview (1992).
19. JB's papers.
20. JB's papers.
21. CLG's papers.

To Samuel Gurney   Garrards Farm
                                                      Uffington
9 February 1934   Berkshire

Dear Mr Gurney,
I must write and tell you how much I enjoyed your book [*Lady Talbot de
Malahide*]. Though I did not know your mother, the book was written in
such a quiet and peaceful manner that I read it right through almost
without a stop.
    How wonderful Quaker Norwich must have been. Have you read
The Borough Mayor by R. H. Mottram? It has lovely descriptions of the
town in the early nineteenth century.
    What do you think of the idea of founding a *popular* church
newspaper to cope with the competition of the *Universe* and the
Christian Science Monitor?
    Yours sincerely, John Betjeman

> S.G. was a high Anglican neighbour of my parents who lived at Compton Regis, a
> hamlet near Uffington. The book about S.G.'s mother (who had married twice) did not
> sell and hundreds of copies remain at Compton Regis to this day.
>   JB toyed for fifteen years with the idea of founding what he decided to call *The Church*,
> but it never materialized.

To Lionel Fielden   Garrards Farm
                                                      Uffington
29 March 1934   Berkshire

Dear Lionel,
This is to confirm the statements I made on the telephone yesterday
afternoon. I should very much like to become the film critic on the BBC
if and when, as I hear from critical quarters, Oliver Baldwin leaves.
    I get damned well paid here, but would rather have less pay and more
congenial work. Writing to please the stinking advertisers and inane
stuff about whether Garbo wears silk or linen stockings, are not in my
line – for long. I have told the *Evening Standard* this and I would have no
difficulty in changing on to you as far as they are concerned. The Editor
and I are equally disillusioned about film criticism for an Evening
Paper, perfectly friendly about it, though by no means intimate. The
only thing is I can't reconcile my conscience with my work.

On the BBC I should be able to say what I like and as I have given talks before, perhaps you will consider the application for the post made by

Your respectful chum, John Betjeman

JB was not happy at the *Evening Standard* and was given six months' notice his editor Percy Cudlipp in March. (He appears however to have stayed on until August 1, 35.)
   L.F. replied (11 April 1934), 'I don't think the pay would make it worth your while, since you may not know that it only runs to ten guineas once a fortnight, which is not a very large figure considering the amount of time you have to give to the matter. Secondly, I doubt very much whether you are "a master of the microphone". I think your writing is admirable, but that's quite a different thing, and particularly in the case of film criticism, where we want someone who will ring the bell every time.'

To Alan Pryce-Jones   Garrards Farm
                                                     Uffington
6 October 1934   Berkshire

My darling Bog,
I was staggered by the announcement in *The Times*, particularly because I remember a man called Fould-Springer who had rooms under mine at Magdalen and whom I very much disliked. Ask [C.S.] Lewis to the Wedding. Still you are not enaged to him, are you? As far as I remember you have married enormous riches. Will she be the Baroness Pryce-Jones like Lady Blanche Girouard? You see what I mean.

Oh Bog, Bog, how I miss you and how I envy your SUCCESS. Don't marry without a long period of probation. Think of Cracky, Sarx [George Schurhoff] (who has got a job as Superintendent of the Cancer Hospital in Vienna), Li and all those of our friends who immediately drift away, however much one likes them. Oh God – the difference of being married from being a bachelor. It is like living on another planet.

My God, Bog, have a care – I do hope I shall see you. I am not what I was at all. I find it even quite odd to speak to people I haven't seen for some time. It may even be a strain speaking to you. The fear of death is worse than ever, particularly when one works in a word factory. Avoid all work. I hope your marriage will enable you to do that. They are putting the electric light wires right across our view.

Love, JB

A.P.-J., whose engagement had been announced, married Thérèse Fould-Springer later that year. Patrick Balfour was best man.

To the Revd J. M. Thompson   Garrards Farm
                                                 Uffington
1 January 1935   Berkshire

Dear Mr Vice President,
How very kind of you to help. I will tell you what is happening about my 'sophisticated guide-book'. That list I gave you is only illustrative not final or even tentative. John Sparrow is going to do eighteenth- and nineteenth-century (and twentieth- possibly) memoirs for me. I shall do architecture myself. The History of Oxford was what I wanted you to do – that is to say a short list of books actually dealing with the growth of the University. [A. D.] Godley's *Oxford in the 18th Century* is an excellent example. What books are there on Oxford in the seventeenth, sixteenth, fifteenth, fourteenth, thirteenth, twelfth, eleventh, tenth, ninth, eighth centuries? I don't think there is any need to mention the charm of Oxford types like 'Just Oxford' and 'Dreaming Spires' etc. Perhaps, on the other hand, if you know of any early guide-books it might be fun to mention the first, followed by a few which are still obtainable in second-hand bookshops – I refer to no guide-books later than 1860 (i.e. Arnold's *Oxford and Cambridge*).

I am terrifically flattered by you and Mrs Thompson comparing me to Max Beerbohm. My hat! that's the highest compliment I have ever been paid. I wish Lewis had heard it. I must get him psycho-analysed out of me.

Please come over and see us. I am home from Thursday to Monday always and there's the telephone number on the other side of this paper.

I saw the Warden of Merton in the street the other day, hundreds of scarves and coats and letters for the post. What a nice man. Remember me to Mrs Thompson and [illegible].

Yours ever, John Betjeman

The Revd J.M.T. was Vice-President of Magdalen College from 1935 to 1937 and was JB's much-loved English tutor.

JB was collecting material for *An Oxford University Chest*, which was not published until 1938.

To Jack Beddington   Garrards Farm
                                                        Uffington
14 January 1935   Berkshire

My Dear Beddioleman,

Thank you very much for your telegram. The position with the *Northumberland* guide – and how remote it all must seem to you in your great skyscraper – is now this. The setting-up of the type has cost twelve pounds; we have spent another eighty-eight pounds in blocks and maps which, of course, can be used when whoever we like writes the guide. I think [S.P.B.] Mais's chapter on Castle and Pele Towers might be retained and meanwhile we should get someone to do 1) a competent gazetteer and 2) an article on Northumberland in General. I suggest W. H. Auden but cannot get authority to offer him money without you. So I am going ahead with the other guides. By the time you get this letter Paul [Nash]'s fine piece of work will be in its final page form at the printers, Peter [Fleetwood-Hesketh]'s will be on the way and so will parts of mine. I have been working all January in Devon – a wonderful feat of the imagination composing a gazetteer of every village in the county collating books of all periods with the directory. There will be, besides this huge gazetteer, an article by me on 'The Face of Devon' (written and set up in type) and an article on 'Devon County Families' by Roger Fulford. The text will be interspersed with spells and curses – Devon is still great on witchcraft, I found. As you may imagine this takes every day of the week often till midnight. Carmel [a colleague?] therefore finds me useless but is being as good as he can be. If you think we ought to go ahead with *Northumberland* this year please let me know soon and I will get it written. The other guides are occupying all my time now so there is not really a delay yet but will be in a fortnight.

    Love to Mrs Beddioleman and to you, JB

Paul Nash wrote the *Shell Guide to Dorset*; Peter Fleetwood-Hesketh to *Lancashire*.
JB's *Shell Guide to Devon* came out in 1935 (published by the Architectural Press).

To Rupert Hart-Davis Garrards Farm
11 April 1935 Uffington

My dear Rupert,

Hot from the telephone I take up my typewriter to remind you about Hamish Hamilton and to suggest some reasons stating why I am a suitable young, if that is what you would call me, man for the job.

I was three years with the Architectural Press editing the *Archie Rev* where block-making, type and binding were almost my daily consideration and always my chief delight. I wrote, made up and produced the *Shell Guide to Cornwall* and did the make-up of the other three guides which have just appeared. I arranged the format and typography of my other two books (*Ghastly Good Taste* and *Mount Zion*).

My literary acquaintance is too exhaustive to be pleasurable. Artists flower like primroses along my path. I am bloody artistic and bloody literary.

I am twenty-eight years old.

My disadvantage is that I know nothing about contracts for authors and very little about distribution to booksellers, though this should not be difficult to acquire. On the other hand I think I am pretty shrewd about what is likely to sell well and what has no earthly chance. I can also write and lay out advertisements, a task I have had more than once to do for the Archie Press.

I would like to add in conclusion that I am not, as far as I know, about to be sacked from my job. In fact my editor only today commended me. My reason for leaving or rather wishing to leave is that I am not fond of my work, however good my employer may think I am at it. Nor would you be, old boy, after two years of a world that is comic at first and sickening in time.

Pray God that I may succeed. I would want a salary. At the last extremity I would put up money in order to get a decent return, an unlikely event in the present rather dim state of the firm.

Yours devotedly, John Betjeman

R.H.-D. met JB at Oxford. He was at Balliol College. In 1935 he was working for Hamish Hamilton the publishers. Nothing came of the suggestion.

To Wilhelmine Cresswell   Garrards Farm
                                                    Uffington
14 August 1935   Berkshire

My darling Billa,
Three photographs have come into my hands.

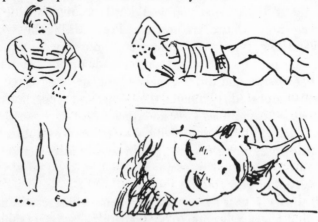

They are so sexy, lovely and exciting that they are no longer in my
hands only, but under my pillow.
Penelope is not best pleased.

Etchells and I are doing a church crawl next week from Wednesday to
Saturday. Etchells is driving and we hope to visit Norfolk. This would
only be for a matter of hours. If you are at Snetters [Snettisham] could
we not ask you out to luncheon? Or dinner? If you aren't at Snetters
then let me know. Love to your mother and to the General – but do
come out with us, duckie. I mean those photographs are burnt on my
brain.
   I leave film criticism this week for a nice three days a week job in
Shell-Mex and two years contract – long in my sort of life.
   It would be nice to see you at Uffington if you will propose yourself.
P. would be quite pleased, contrary to her usual expression.
   Love, John Betjeman

   'Church crawling' was JB's term for visiting every church on the way from anywhere to
   anywhere.
      JB wrote a funny and incisive article, 'Goodbye to Films', in the *Evening Standard*

(20 August 1935) which began, 'Yesterday I wrote my last article as film critic in this paper. When I started off, a pale green bogus-intellectual, a year and a half ago, what a different man was I.'

To Penelope Betjeman   Briarlea
                                                          Colwell Lane
                                                          Haywards Heath
19 September 1935   Sussex

Moi darlin Roomi,

Oi am thinkin of you at the moment quiverin loike a jelly on the English Channel. Oi do hope you won't be orribly sick. Do not bother to write long letters to me as there will be so much for you to see in Rome.

This house belongs to what are obviously Anglo-Indian people not of top drawer variety. Many little pieces of brass have already been put away. One corner in each room is hung with Indian silks halfway up, affixed with drawing pins. The walls are grey and the paintwork is black. The chairs and sofas are covered with black cotton addressed with little pink flowers.

All round there are trees, but you can see the other houses, many of them half-timbered, peeping in and about between. There are electric light standards in the roads.

The garden is small and the house (1860 not unpleasant on one façade) has obviously had a murder committed in it. No sun seems to shine. I dread opening a cupboard for fear of finding a corpse. The rooms are small and high. The bathroom is a mere boxroom and the water is by no means hot.

It has rained since I came last night.

Oi am goin to make a little calendar with twenty-one days and tear off the day, just as we used to do at school.

I wish I were in Rome, I must say, to see the churches. I should be glad if you would tell me whether they had really bad nineteenth-century restoration. Whether nineteenth-century, late classical in Italy is as bad as Gothic Revival over here. Look at some of the less known churches.

May the sun warm you, the rain soften you, the dew refresh you and God bless you. May the little noot [nut, i.e. head] come back burstin with Oriental knowledge and classical coolture until this poor yellow poofball is quoite insignificant besoide it.

Everlastin loove
You ijjas little thing from
Tewpie
PS Oi shall not ave toime to wroite a letter *every* day. Sometimes only
a postcard.

> While PB attended the Congress of Orientalists in Rome with Dr Betty Heimann, JB
> rented Briarlea with Lionel Perry and William Clonmore for three weeks. The three
> were collecting material for *Shell Guides*. JB described the sojourn to Mrs Braddell,
> Perry's mother, on 24 September 1980: 'I don't think I ever laughed so much as I did
> with Lionel when we lived in a house at Haywards Heath called Briarlea. We used to call
> it Brierley Park which gave it a bit of class.'
> The speech bubble reads, 'And this column, Dr Patty [Betty], is oondoubtedly
> influenced boi Drarijjice [?] though we foind it so far west as Rome.'

To Penelope Betjeman  'Briarlea'
Colwell Lane
Haywards Heath
21 September 1935 Sussex

Moi darlin Pedrilloppee,
Oi am reading *The Newcomes* by Thackeray. Can't think why I haven't
read it before. It is indeed a most respectable pious book with a nice lot
of humour.

It has rained almost consistently here while the gales have temporarily subsided. The paths of this dark little garden are strewn with windfalls, but whenever you turn them over they are eaten by wasps.

Poor old Bosie has gone into the courts again and been awarded four hundred pounds' damages against the quack doctor who almost sent him blind. He says he will be lucky if he gets the money.

Give my love to Ram Rajputana Moj Mogul Pitt Bonarjee Jam, a mystical Christadelphian friend of mine you will probably see at the Conference. I expect Dr Betty knows him.

I am going to East Hoathly now where, I believe, the Rector is a Calvinist.

Good boi moi own oogli little thing.

Yew 'ave the low and oigh church prayers of

Tewpie

To Penelope Betjeman

In the G[reat] W[estern] R[ailway] from Challow 9.15 but as from:
                    Briarlea
                    Colwell Lane
                    Haywards Heath
24 September 1935   Sussex

Moi darlin Developpee,

Oi went to the opening of the cinema at Faringdon and did not see Paula [Steinbrecher] as there was such a crowd and we sat at the back. Gerald [Berners] and Stewart Rowe and the Manager sat at a little table with a Union Jack on it before the procession. Gerald had learnt his speech beforehand. He recited it to us several times: 'Ladies and Gentlemen, I am very pleased to be able to open this cinema tonight. For many years now I have been a regular customer at the old Corn Exchange Cinema. Although I enjoyed myself there very much, I do not think its ecclesiastical atmosphere (*laughter from the more expensive seats*) was quite appropriate to films. I think we all ought to thank Mr Elliott (the Manager) for letting us see the films in a building such as this is, in such comfort and elegance.' Stewart Rowe then made a stirring and longer speech and after that Gerald had something whispered in his ear by the manager. Then he stood up at attention and said in a loud clear voice, 'I declare this cinema open.' We had 'God Save The King' and then the films.

Gerald is very concerned about Robert [Heber-Percy] and Hanbury [John Sparrow] and hopes Hanbury will not snitch Robert away or always be ringing him up. I said I thought this unlikely.

I think you may find Lizzie [Peter Watson] in Rome. Give my love to Rajput Ramsur Katmandu-Khan. He and Mahomet Ali and I were great friends when we travelled across Turkestan together wearing nothing on our feet but dried haddock skins and carrying little pairs of magic spectacles for reading inscriptions.

I wish I could see Archie.

And I wish, oh I wish much more, Oi could see little Developpee.

Yours truly, JB

PS Thank yew very mooch, Oi wish Oi was in Rome with yew, for your letter rec'd today.

PPS Your Uncle Arthur is not so well again and your auntie doesn't think she will be able to leave by the end of the week for France.

Booni nooni nooni mooni nooni, yow yow yow yow

Oi will draw you with the Pope temmorrer.

Gerald Berners was possessive of his excessively good-looking companion, Robert Heber-Percy, and nervous that he might prove dangerously attractive to John Sparrow.
'Lizzie' was the name given to Peter Watson in Berners' book, *The Girls of Redcliffe Hall*. Berners was the headmistress, and other 'girls' included Cecil Beaton and Oliver Messel.

To Penelope Betjeman

Room 792
Shell-Mex House
Victoria Embankment
London WC

28 September 1935
Saturday

Moi darlin Udolloppee,

Thank you for your postcard of your second favourite Temple. Love to Ghirlandaio and his bottle nose.

It occurs to me that if I stay with Gerald [Berners] I will have to renew my season [ticket]. Anyhow I will have to do that if I am to get back from Sezincote because I return on October 2nd and my season expires on October 1st. I wish to God Cracky had been more considerate and businesslike and this awful muddle would not have occurred. God knows where I shall be next week. Gerald comes up to London.

I bought a book of engravings and of churches in Brighton (ten shillings – but couldn't resist it) dated 1826. There was one of Thaxted. It had no pews even then. Apparently it is all rot about Robert [Heber-Percy] and Gerald [Berners] lunching with Hitler. They merely happened to be in the same restaurant. We must cross-examine them very thoroughly on what Hitler said to them.

I had luncheon with Bosie yesterday in his new flat, which is in the basement of a back street in Brighton. He thinks it absolutely lovely.

Roger Hinks tells a funny story about King's, Cambridge. A scholar was reading the lessons in chapel there from the first chapter of *Ezekiel*, 'As for the chariot the wheels were so high that they were dreadful.' He read the words as Hamish [St Clair-Erskine] or Peter Watson would say them at a party: 'As for the *chariot*, the wheels were SO HIGH they were DREADFUL.' He could not be had up as he had read the actual words.

I met a charming clockmaker in Ditchling who said that his mother said to him, 'I don't like telephones, I don't like the wireless. In fact I don't like anything that comes through pipes.'

Oi miss yew more and more and more and opes yew miss your loovin, Tewpie

Ghirlandaio was an Italian painter.

JB had a passion for clocks and always carried a chiming pocket watch. All the clocks in his house were maintained to keep perfect time.

In his last letter before PB's return, JB wrote (29 September 1935), 'Moti [PB's horse] wrote to me a short postcard complaining of Archie [JB's bear]. Apparently he (Archie) and Fritz [the cat] have been excavating the new concrete that has been put down in the stables, under the impression that it conceals a Roman pavement.'

To the Headmaster, Dartington Hall   Garrards Farm
                                               Uffington
9 January 1936   Berkshire

Dear Headmaster,

I am writing a guide-book to Devon for the *Shell Guides* and have got Ivan Moffat to write a panegyric about Dartington for the work. I thought Dartington by a pupil might have the so-called popular appeal. I hope you do not mind, but we obviously ought to mention Dartington at length.

Could you let me have a photograph of Dartington – any part of it, detailed or general, that you think will look well in the guide – to reproduce? In the the *Architectural Review* (of which I was assistant editor at the time) we had some illustrations but they were all of the O.P. Milne part as far as I remember.

There is a further detail in which I would be very grateful if you could give me assistance. I notice in *Kelly's Directory* under Ashprington that the village of Tuckenhay has 'extensive stores and quays abutting on the river Harbourne, as well as an old gas house, erected, for lighting the village, by the late Mr Abraham Tucker about the year 1806'. This is too thrilling to be missed if it is true.

Do you

1) Know anything about it?

2) Know of a photograph of it?

3) Know of a local photographer who would take some views of it for me?

Yours very truly, John Betjeman

The headmaster asked to see proofs of the panegyric and knew nothing of Tuckenhay, about which *Kelly's Directory* was correct. In the end there were only a few lines on Dartington in the *Shell Guide*.

To Paul Miller Garrards Farm
Uffington
10 August 1936 Berkshire

Dear Master Paul,
As though I could possibly
forget you. You were
something like that then
and spoke very slowly and had enormous handwriting and by now you
have the correct horror of pseudo-Tudor and I am green, fat and bald
and Heddon Court is a building estate. Thank you very much for *Extra*
which seems to me well above the run of school magazines – in fact I
found it interesting and read it from cover to cover in the train from
Uffington this morning. Your article and the thing on Catalogues, the
Editorial and Mr C. C. Wells's things I liked best. Though it was all
interesting. Attlee doesn't count, as he is a professional. How nice of
you to draw Wilkins's front – there is none of that fearful Blomfield
about it – what a pity Blomfield ever spoiled it.

I would very much like to meet you again and wonder whether you
could have luncheon with me. If you can, what about Rules in Maiden
Lane, Covent Garden on the 12th – that is to say the day after
tomorrow. And we will have some talk about Wilkins and reminiscences of Heddon Court. I am at Shell-Mex from eleven to four thirty
on Mondays, Tuesdays and Wednesdays. The rest of the time I am at
Uffington (Uffington 46). Let me know if we may meet.

Yours, John Betjeman

> JB had taught P.M. at Heddon Court prep school.
> The Wilkins front was at Haileybury College, where P.M. was now a pupil. Sir
> Reginald Blomfield's huge domed chapel, added later, destroyed the symmetry of the
> original front.

To P. Morton Shand Garrards Farm
Uffington
29 August 1936 Berkshire

My Dear P. Morton Shand,
Thank you so much for your two delightful letters, especially the
religious enclosure. What a cad old Mrs Alexander Faulkner Shand is.

If you want them I will give you introductions to the Master of Marlborough, the Headmaster of Canford, the Headmaster of Cranleigh, the Headmaster of St Lawrence College, Ramsgate, and the Headmaster of St Edmund's School, Canterbury, or possibly it is the other school at Canterbury – I cannot remember. I think I got between five and ten guineas not including travelling expenses, but if I tell them to pay you the same as they paid me I do not think you will find yourself out of pocket. Let me know which schools you would like and when you can go and what is your lowest fee and I will write. Love to Mrs P. Morton Shand and those charming children.

All the best to Bruce, old boy,

Love and kisses, JB

P.M.S. was a colleague of JB's on the *Architectural Review* and became his lifelong friend. Mrs A. F. Shand, P.M.S.'s mother, had just cut his allowance short on his marrying his fourth wife, Sybil. He wanted to make extra cash by lecturing on architecture.

To Gerald Berners   3 Foro Romano
6 September 1936   Rome

Dear Gerald,
This is the first night in your house and I must write at once to thank you for lending it to us. It really is a bit of all right with that view of all those ruins and the charming Tito to whom I speak in French, Italian, Deutsch and English very cleverly. There are several things in this house which I have already noticed remind me of you and Robert and take me back to those spreading lawns and the misty Upper Thames and Isis. For instance 1) on the ornaments on the staircase little hats and caps; 2) a robot in the saloon; 3) two huge packs of cards very sinister to look at – undoubtedly cards are connected with magic, you have only to magnify them to see; 4) a tortoise in china; 5) ye olde shippe on upstairs sitting room mantelshelf; 6) mixture of books: *Four Just Men*; Gibbon's autobiography; Wodehouse; Vasari; Lewis Hind (mutilated) on Turner's *Golden Dreams*; *The Seven Gangsters of Brookmere School* with illustrations by H. M. Brock; Gibbon's *Decline and Fall*, etc.

Whenever I find these objects, and I find them all over the house, I have a laugh. I have been reading Firbank and Rome has made me enjoy him. In fact I am delighted to be here.

Joan [Eyres-Monsell] and Pegrilloppy are very cultivated. Never out of the Galleries. We enter every open church. I am taking notes now, like Peyellowppy, so as not to get muddled. Joan is very keen on the churches. This city makes me very fond of Turner. I think you must like him a good bit from the many books you have about him. He is a terrifically good painter, ain't he?

I had influenza two days after I got here and was in bed in the pleasant *pensione* for four days with a badly moulded ceiling to look at, cumbrous German furniture and green wallpaper of a pearlised pattern. The woman in the next room put on the wireless every evening, roving from station to station between what seemed to be bad thunderstorms. The weather here has certainly been poor – but, thank God, not hot and I don't know when I have been so bowled over by the beauty of a place. There is a lot I will have to talk to you about when I see you – Musso[lini]'s improvements for instance. Then I like the V. E. [Victor Emanuel] monument except for the curve at the top – I expect Crystalpalappy will be writing to you. Love to Robert. Tell him I'm dotty about the things to see and will come back exhausted. Cracky has one of Mrs N's letters to Lord Wicklow. Wicklow apparently hardly seems to notice them. His letters are always very short and this is the sort of thing he says: 'Dear Billy, The weather over here has been not so bad. I have had the prayer hall repainted. A Mrs Naish has been writing to me. I think she is mad. I enclose a letter. The rhododendrons are doing well. Affecly yours, Wicklow.'

Affecly yours, John Betjeman

> JB, PB and Joan Eyres-Monsell were on holiday together in Rome, staying in Gerald Berners's house.
> Lewis Hind's book is called *Turner's Golden Visions*.
> Lord Wicklow was Clonmore's father.

To John Murray   Rome

28 September 1936

My dear Jock,
After a terrible struggle with my conscience, in which I gave in to my young publisher who subsequently gave in to me and cleared my conscience for me in the most charming manner, I have retrieved my poems for you.

I must say at once that the young man, Reginald Hutchings, could not have been more generous and delightful about it. He had already canvassed the booksellers and had set up the stuff in galley form. We had no formal contract and I felt a fearful shit. However I said I had agreed with you to reprint *Mount Zion* as well and he said he couldn't do that and without any harsh words we parted. His bill will be about nine pounds. I feel that I ought to pay this or at any rate a large part of it – out of my advance. I do not want to penalise your firm for my own stupidity and cupidity.

As for *Mount Zion*, I feel that the following poems can be omitted and any others you would like to remove:

'Varsity Students' Rag
A Seventeenth-Century Love Lyric
Mother and I
For Nineteenth-Century Burials
Competition
School Songs
Camberley
Arts and Crafts
St Aloysius Church Oxford

I imagine the Westminster Press, Harrow Road, have the blocks. Will you write to Edward [James] about his copyright, if it exists?

I have told Mr Hutchings to send the MSS to you. Do do what you can for him. He is genuinely a good typographer. In fact first class.

I enclose a further poem (expurgated) about Joan Eyres-Monsell's house. I am in Rome (alas) till October 15th: my address is 3 Foro Romano, Rome.

Love, JB

PS I may have written to you last night. In that case that letter of last night's cancelled.

JB had been about to publish some new poems with an enthusiastic young publisher/typographer, R. Hutchings, whom JB continued to help after this first disappointment. He wrote an introduction to a book by John Rayner in 1937 for him, but no trace can be found of its publication.

Continual Dew, published by J.M. in 1937, contained eighteen new poems and fifteen poems from *Mount Zion*; among them were 'For Nineteenth-Century Burials', 'Competition' and 'Camberley'. 'The 'Varsity Students' Rag' and 'The City' reappeared much later in *Collected Poems* in 1958.

Joan Eyres-Monsell's house was Dumbleton in Worcestershire, about which JB wrote two poems. One he recalled from memory in 1976 was a parody of 'A Nuptial Eve' by Sydney Thompson Dobell:

Dumbleton, Dumbleton, the ruin by the lake,
    Where Boggins and Sir Bolton fought a duel for thy sake;
Dumbleton, Dumbleton, the Gothic arch that leads
    Thro' the silver vestibule to where Sir Bolton feeds.
The groaning of the golden plate,
The sickly social shame;
Oh heirs of Dumbleton! The Monsell in thy name!'

The other, entitled 'Dumbleton Hall', was published in *Uncollected Poems* (1982).

To Edward James   Garrards Farm
                                                    Uffington
3 December 1936   Berkshire

My dear Edward,
I am so sorry I was not able to see you that Monday. I would very much
like to see you about *Mount Zion* and to hear your idea. I have
telephoned Wimpole Street once or twice but no answer. Therefore
this goes to Wimpole Street hoping for the best.

Murrays are keen to publish the poems. I'm glad they're doing it
because they will let me have some fun with typography, as you did. A
further thing. Last week Auden wrote to me saying what a corking good
'comic' (I like that) poet I was. Eliot wanted to reprint *Mount Zion* for
Fabers. But Murrays got in first. I am not sorry. It would not have been
fun to come out uniform with Stephen Spender.

I am in London the first three days of every week from eleven to four
thirty either at Shell-Mex or B. T. Batsfords. Let me know when we
can meet. Or you might like to come here? Or not? Or yes? Hope to
God you haven't gone to America. *I've* been abroad lately. I went to
Rome, you know. I must tell you about it.

Love and kisses, JB

> E.J., JB's fabulously rich Oxford friend, had published *Mount Zion*, JB's first volume of
> poetry illustrated by de Cronin Hastings in 1931. It was printed by the Westminster
> Press. James had intended to do an enlarged second edition of *Mount Zion*, including
> additional and new poems by JB with illustrations by Mark Ogilvie-Grant. JB never got
> round to giving James the poems, which James had counted on to recoup his losses from
> the first edition. JB had given away half the copies, imagining that they would not sell.
> E.J.'s idea, in exchange for handing over *Mount Zion* to Jock Murray, was to use some of
> JB's new poems in the magazine *Minotaur*, in which he had a 'direct interest'.
>   JB was overseeing the *Shell Guides* at B. T. Batsford during this time. They published
> the *Guides* in 1937 and 1938.

To T. S. Eliot   Garrards Farm
                                                    Uffington
10 December 1936   Berkshire

Dear Mr Eliot,
It is good of you to take an interest in my poems via Wystan Auden. As I
explained to him, *Mount Zion*, with additions, is about to be reprinted

by John Murray. I should have been tremendously honoured to have had them even considered by Fabers and by you. I should so like to meet you. I just remember that tall young Mr Eliot at Highgate Junior School. You were very nice to me. The only other pleasant person there was a Miss Long, an excellent teacher. I hated the school. They all used to shout, 'Betjeman's a German spy – a German Spy – a German spy' and dance round. I came to the conclusion that I was. There was a horrible sadistic Matron with ginger hair. Mr Kelly should have been shot. He used to shake us till we cried – nasty old man. It was a very bad school and I was pleased to leave and go to Lynam's [The Dragon School] in North Oxford where all the laburnums and bicycles are.

Perhaps we could meet one day when you are free.

Yours sincerely, John Betjeman

PS I enclose a little Christmas Greetings Telegram as a present for you. JB

T.S.E. had taught JB at Highgate School in 1916. Eliot, who worked for Fabers, had been pipped to the post by Murrays to publish JB's poems.

To Wilhelmine Cresswell   Garrards Farm
                                                 Uffington
10 December 1936   Berkshire

Darling Billa,

Thank you all for your nice letter. I am so glad to hear about Mrs Dugdale's plan. I think that the Conservatory could be made into a very nice Long Bar in the Jazz-Swedish style.

Whenever I feel sexless I only have to turn up those photographs Joan [Rayner] took of you, to feel I have read *London Life* from cover to cover.

Yellow has gone to London. But she will be back on Saturday.

If you are really giving a combined Christmas present to Mrs D, what a bloody good idea. Will you let me know definitely and I will send a pound from myself and Yellow will give something too.

Please let me know and I will do this *at once*.

When are you coming to stay again? I long to see you. I wish quite often that we had got married. You are just my cup of tea and we would have laughed such a lot. But Pethrillappy is very nice. I can't have my cake and burn the candle at both ends.

Kindly propose yourself to stay. Yellow is devoted to you as I am.

Love to your mother and the General and Mr Hadley and your sisters.
Love and Kisses, JB xxxxx
PS Hobrilla [Christopher Hobhouse] says you have three thousand a
year.
PPS Who was the 'Sir Cresswell Cresswell who shocked society to its
foundations'?
PPPS Yellow has our cheque book that is why I can do nothing till
she comes back. JB

> W.C., Lionel Perry, Bryan Guinness, William Clonmore and Duff Dunbar had written
> tongue in cheek (undated), '[Mrs Dugdale] has been to Stratford-on-Avon a good deal
> lately and is very anxious to have Sezincote half-timbered . . . if you can spare a few
> shillings we have got the address of a place where we can get some very good composition
> half-timbering 'Oakemax' quite cheap which can very easily be tacked on to the stone.'
>   Hobrilla was Christopher Hobhouse, a lawyer who had written the *Shell Guide to
> Derbyshire* (1934). He was tall, conceited and brilliant and lots of people of both sexes
> were in love with him (he died in 1940).

To T. S. Eliot   Garrards Farm
                                                     Uffington
17 December 1936   Berkshire

Dear Mr Eliot,
Thank you very much for your letter of yesterday. Well that's that
about John Murray but I should love to have luncheon with you and
discuss the future. After Christmas will certainly be best. I come up on
Mon, Tue and Wed of every week and am free for luncheon on those
days. Perhaps you will write here and let me know a date.

Indeed I do remember you at Highgate, though I had not identified
you as yourself until Wystan Auden reminded me. You were known as
the American Master and I remember that a boy told me you were a
poet but I didn't believe it. You had horn-rimmed spectacles, were tall
and with a pale face. You sometimes smiled. Your hair was dark. I have
not seen you since then, nor to my knowledge, a photograph of you.

The particularly nasty people I remember were Pat Blamey, the
Goodwins, Brooks, Holt, the Roomes, Pugsley and that frightful
Matron and round Mrs Kelly. Also a boy called Van Masdyke who
should have been shot and a little squit called Ricardo. I was severely
bullied by a couple called Ibbetson and Robson. I didn't like a man
called Hobbes who left before you came, I think.

I recommend to you a book by a neighbouring clergyman (Revd F. P.

Harton B.D.) called *Elements of the Spiritual Life: A Study in Ascetical Theology* (SPCK ten and six). It has caused me to take more than an academic interest in ecclesiastical matters and you, as a sincere Catholic, will admire it very much if you have not read it already.

Yours sincerely, John Betjeman

The Revd F. P. Harton was the vicar at Baulking near Uffington and later became the Dean of Wells.

To Edward James   Garrards Farm
                                               Uffington
1 January 1937   Berkshire

My dear Edward,

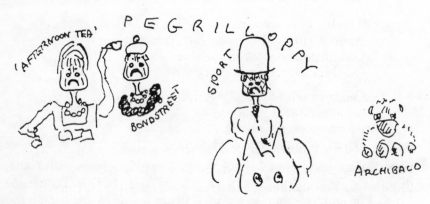

Many thanks for your long letter which, now that it has arrived, is explicit, touching, reasoned, kindly and generous. I must ask you to forgive me for my elusiveness.

It is indeed sad to know that you lost over *Mount Zion* and sadder still for me to remember that I had promised you the next edition with old Mark [Ogilvie-Grant]'s drawings. But it is very good of you to let me reprint some of the *Mount Zion* poems in Murray's new book. I have the great consolation of knowing that Murray's other poet is SIR HENRY NEWBOLT. Eliot, as I think I told you and Auden, wanted my poems for Faber but they were too late and how infinitely more horrible to appear uniform with STEPHEN SPENDER and MACNEICE.

Indeed you may have some poems for *Minotaur* and I am flattered to think they will appear in that beautiful magazine. I think you've been bloody clever with it, old boy, and I was present when your Aunt

Venetia was shown your article on the Queen's hats by Lady Chetwode. I see Jock Gray (Murray) on Tuesday next and we will select some poems to send on to you and will post them on that day.

I hear that large dog is dead. Very sad for you. Penelope, however, very much looks forward to your coming to stay here and we both look forward to seeing you again and having sumptuous meals with you in that extraordinary house in Wimpole Street. How very odd of you to stay at that skyscraper [the Waldorf Astoria]. It looks odious and those culture-crazy Americans buzzing about. Did you know my poem on the death of George V written at the time (not for publication)? It was strongly prophetic:

> Spirits of well-shot woodcock, partridge, snipe
> Flutter and bear him up the Norfolk sky
> In that red house in a red mahogany bookcase
> The stamp collection waits with mounts long dry
>
> The big blue eyes are shut which saw wrong clothing
> And fav'rite fields and coverts from a horse
> Old men in country houses hear clocks ticking
> Ox-thick carpets with deadened force
>
> Old men who never cheated, never doubted
> Communicated monthly, sit and stare
> At a red suburb ruled by Mrs Simpson
> Where a young man lands hatless from the air.

Pyellowppy sends its love. A happy new year. Let us know when you come back. You shall have full acknowledgement in the new book.

Love and Kisses, John B

'Death of George V' was published in a revised version in *Continual Dew* (1937).

To Alan Pryce-Jones

13 February 1937

Garrards Farm
Uffington
Berkshire

Darling Bog,
I will willingly join in with your ingenious right-minded letter and so will Gerald B[erners]. I will telephone to you on Monday next when I come to London.

On Friday evening at eight fifteen I am talking to the ART

WORKERS' GUILD, founded by Morris and with several of his friends still in it. Voysey, C. R. Ashbee, Basil Oliver. They wear cloaks and rags round their necks with rings in them and cameos. A nicer set of old people you couldn't imagine. Coffee at 6 Queen Square, Bloomsbury and talk afterwards. Do come if you can. It will be a revelation to you of a lovely new world. I am talking about the *Spoiling of London*.

Love to Poppy. Pethrilloppy sends its love. It comes up on Tue, Wed, Thur this week.

Could we both have luncheon on Tuesday with you?

Love,

A.P.-J. was drafting a letter to send to *The Times*.
'Poppy' was Marie-Thérèse P.-J.'s nickname.

To John Murray   Garrards Farm
                                                    Uffington
18 February 1937   Berkshire

My dear Jock,
A) The proofs [of *Continual Dew*] you have sent of the antique types are very nice. The fourteen point is better. But there must be the same depth of text on each page, so as to balance. The rest should be entirely decorative. The ornaments which fill up are i) too small ii) not solid which they should be.

There is quite a common ornament like this ● which should do very nicely. The present one is too pale, small and finicky.

B) I have *lost* the two contracts you sent to me! Can anything be done about them? God knows where they are. Will you be kind enough to include in the contract or by writing my veto on review copies being sent to 1) *London Mercury* 2) *New Verse* 3) *Contemporary Poetry and Prose* 4) *Morning Post* 5) *New Stateswoman* 6) if possible, *Times Literary Supplement*. Anyhow I believe poetry sells by word of mouth and not by reviews. What do you think?

C) I enclose a new poem on Slough.

D) Yes, do arrange for an American edition if any USA publisher is fool enough to want to make one.

Yours, John Betjeman

To Bryan Guinness   Shipton MOYNE Post Office
                                                  Tetbury
[1937]   Glos.

Dear Bryan,

Happening to drive through this tremendously unimportant village in order to look at the church, I thought you might like to have a letter from it because of its name.

The church is Victorian and expensive. Family called Estcourt.

The village is lost in elms and it is raining today.

The stamps on the envelope are the first to be sold of this kind from Shipton Moyne P.O. Love to your new wife whom I haven't seen.

Yours devotedly, John Betjeman

> B.G., the son of Lord Moyne, married Elisabeth Nelson in 1936 (he and Diana had divorced in 1934).

To Edith Simpson Harvey   Garrards Farm
                                                  Uffington
8 March 1937   Berkshire

Dear Aunt Edie,

We are going up in the social scale. I have the following report on our name from Holland.

'It seems that there has been some arbitrariness in the use of the name Betjeman, Besteman and Betteman. Some biographers state that in families living in the sixteenth and seventeenth centuries some branches transferred the name Betteman and Betjeman to Betseman. One of the last known Betjemans was Joost Betjeman, who lived in Dordtracht from 1493 to 1541. He was "pensionaries van Dordtrecht" (pensionary or governor) from 1516 to 1537 and the states of Holland were so grateful for his merits, that they rewarded him with a hundred large pieces of wainscot for the panelling of his house. He died as state holder of the margraviate of Bergen op Zoom (a city in the southern part of Holland) in 1541.

'Biographers are not sure whether Jan Betseman was a son of Joost Betjeman. Jan Betseman was appointed one of the first counsels of the "Hooge Road van Holland" in 1582.'

I don't know whether this is anything to do with us. I would like any more information you can rake up.

Love to the Doctor and all
Yours affectionately, John B

E.S.H. was Ernest and Arthur Betjemann's sister who married Dr Simpson Harvey in 1930. Being of a rebellious nature, she had always championed JB during family turbulence and gave him terrific support. When Ernest had refused to buy JB a car while he was at Oxford, she went straight out and bought him one herself. Until her marriage she had suffered through her name being thought to be German and had tended to call herself 'Benjamin' instead.

To T. S. Eliot　　　　　　　　　　　Garrards Farm
　　　　　　　　　　　　　　　　　　Uffington
[1937?]　　　　　　　　　　　　　　　Berkshire

Dear Mr Eliot,
Murrays have let me have this, their last copy, of a repulsive and only surviving edition of Meade Falkner's fine book. It is not up to *The Lost Stradivarius* which is unobtainable. But I do hope it will give you some of the great pleasure it gave me. Don't be put off by the ridiculous dust jacket. I regard it as a return, though a poor one, for two first-class luncheons which will bear fruit. It is a present to you.

If you really want to come here in June or May, say so. I think you would like it – the ecclesiastical life is very strong.

Yours in Calvin's name, John Betjeman

JB sent T.S.E. a copy of *The Nebuly Coat* by John Meade Falkner who wrote *Moonfleet* and Murray's *Handbooks* to Oxfordshire and Berkshire.

To Sybil Morton Shand

9 April 1937   Trebetherick

Dear Mrs P. Morton Shand,
P. Morton Shand might try Hodson's. I had a letter from Hodson asking to do work for them, but I turned down the offer. When I get back to Garrards Farm I will look out for the address. I have not got it here in Cornwall.

Canning wrote to me today and said in the course of his letter, 'Morton Shand was intensely amusing. I still tell his stories everywhere I go.'

I shall be back next week. It was very nice seeing you both at Uffington. Love to P. Morton Shand.

Yours, John B

S.M.S. was to write to JB a few months later in a desperate bid to find her husband a full-time job 'away from his house'.

To John Piper   B. T. Batsford Ltd
                                                         15 North Audley St
13 April 1937   London W1

Dear Artist,
I have seen Mr J. L. Beddington, and he will be very pleased for you to do a *Guide to Oxfordshire*, starting at once, if you can manage it, and letting me have the MS by the middle of December this year.

I don't know how you propose to write the *Guide*, whether in the manner of Paul Nash, or of John Rayner's forthcoming *Guide to Hampshire*, or your own manner, but I expect you would like to know about terms. They are as follows – fifty guineas for your work, ten guineas expenses, and we pay outside photographers for any of their photographs you want to use. We also supply you with a photographer (Maurice Beck: Temple Bar 1234) free of charge, who will be at your service during the month of May, Coronation included.

We have not before had someone writing a *Guide* who is also a photographer, and so when we have got together the photographs for the *Guide*, and when we have seen how many of yours you are using, we might come to some financial arrangement about them. The *Guide* need not be illustrated entirely with photographs, as you know, and if you have drawings, engravings and paintings, let's have them.

I do hope you will do the *Guide*, and that these terms suit you, because I am sure there is nobody who will be better at it than you will, or would, be.

Yours sincerely, John Betjeman

JB met J.P., who was to become his closest friend and collaborator, when J. M. Richards recommended him as an excellent typographer. In October 1937 J.P. wrote to JB, 'The writing's nearly done. What a job. It is worth five hundred pounds. . . . I have also collected another photo or two: Thames Show Fair and Charlbury Harvest Festival with prayer books and pumpkins, which is a good one.'

To Alan Pryce-Jones   Garrards Farm
                                                     Uffington
17 April 1937   Berkshire

Darling Bog,
I meant to write to you ages ago to thank you for that nice letter from the Pulteney [Hotel, Bath]. And then you had gone before we had a chance of talking after the film. Thank God you are both coming to live in England for ever. We will be able to sample churches, Sunday after Sunday. Lord's Day after Lord's Day. We will be able to see that baby [David] with those rabbit's ears on his dress grow up to be fit to sing treble in the surpliced choir of St Cyprian's, Clarence Gate or with those surpliced spinsters of St Mildred's, Bread Street.

I don't at all like the sound of there being no service at Ch[rist] Ch[urch], Newgate Street. My friend Revd T. Hine Haycock, the incumbent, is BROAD to low. His Sunday evensongs were quite well attended when I used to worship at his church. I advise you to keep your eye on the incumbent of St Alban's, Wood Street, if he is still alive. The Rector of St Dunstan's in the East (Broad) will ask you to lunch if you go and see him in the church at twelve any weekday.

We must explore BRISTOL. There is a lot of LOW there. St Mary-le-Port is black-gown Calvinist. Alms are collected in a 'decent basin' (oblations, by the way, are really offerings other than money such as shoes, socks, pocket handkerchiefs and knives and forks, that is why a basin is provided – according to the Lows). Communion can be received standing at St Mary-le-Port (open for half an hour on

Thursday afternoons like St Benet, Paul's Wharf).

My dear Bog, I do miss your company and I am so fond of Poppy and will not forget how sweetly she behaved in Northmoor church. The thing that has happened to me is that after years of sermon tasting, I am, now a member of the C of E and a communicant. I regard it as the only salvation against progress and Fascists on the one side and Marxists of Bloomsbury on the other.

Gerald B[erners] is simplifying the Cadogan letter. He thinks that we may miss the point even for *The Times* if we veil it too much. I don't quite know what he intends to do. Will let you know next week.

I have been asked to write a book on eighteenth-century churches for Chapman and Hall and will get you to collaborate with me. What a delightful task it will be!

You would be doing a great service which will earn you a knighthood like that of Sir [John] Collings Squire, by founding a League for destroying creepers on trees and eighteenth- and nineteenth-century (early) buildings and by helping to save the buildings themselves. If I had an income and the time I would do it myself.

Write to me again and for God's sake come to England for ever soon. Love to Poppy and to that child.

Love, JB

To Alan Pryce-Jones

From Revd Archibald Ormsby-Gore
(MA Oxon)
'Hill Top'
Muckby Sluice
Bag Enderby
Lincs

17 April 1937

Dear Mr Pryce-Jones,
They tell me that you are the Liberal Candidate for this division and, as a Congregational Minister who has seen eighty years' service in the Congregational Union, I would like to tender you an old bear's advice.
Yours truly,
Archibald Ormsby-Gore
PS My grandmother was a Payan. A.O.G.

The Strict Baptist, Archibald Ormsby-Gore, JB's bear, wrote to only a chosen few.
A.P.-J.'s middle name was Payan.

To Oliver Stonor   Garrards Farm
                                            Uffington
25 June 1937   Berkshire

Dear Sir,
I must thank you very much for your kind letter which helps me with
the BBC. I suppose the devils are eating into Georgian Exeter. They
would. Nothing the past has done is reverenced. None of the
self-effacing architectural principles of the past are followed. None of
the planning *Desire de quoquam quicquam bene velle mereri*. But your letter
was a great encouragement.
    The book I mentioned is *Regional Architecture in the West of England* by
Richardson and Gill. Published by Ernest Benn. Remaindered, of
course, because it was in advance of its time. Commins has a copy. It
should not cost more than ten shillings. It was published about ten
years ago. There is a whole chapter on Exeter.
    Though I say it with modesty, a guide-book I did myself to *Devon*
(*Shell Guide* two and six) has a photograph of Barnfield Crescent which is
rather good and other views of Exeter. With apologies for my delay in
answering, I am,
    Yours sincerely,
    John Betjeman
PS How lucky you are to live in Pennsylvania Park.

O.S., a novelist who also wrote under the name of 'Morchard Bishop', was an early fan of
JB's and became a regular correspondent.
    JB gave a talk on the BBC (11 June 1937) about Exeter in the series *Town Tours*.
    Commins was an antiquarian bookshop then in Bournemouth.
    Pennsylvania Park is a regency area near Exeter University.

To Guy Burgess   Garrards Farm
                                           Uffington
8 July 1937   Berkshire

Dear Guy,
I was away when your letter arrived. I should very much like to talk in
your series on Eccentrics. I propose doing Old Nollekens who lived in
London and whose life is in the *World's Classics*. In addition I might hint

at Sir John Soane who was more cracked than eccentric. He too is identified with London. The Duke of Portland is certainly excellent, but I do not know enough about him and one has to be so careful when members of the family are still alive.

It is nice of you to give me an opportunity of talking – I should like to talk from BRISTOL as it is so much easier for me.

Let's meet again. I am in London (Shell-Mex and BP Ltd) the first three days of each week Mon, Tue, and Wed here eleven to four-thirty (T.B. 1234). We might have lunch. I hope your meeting continued as successfully as it started.

Yours, John B

> G.B. (later famous as a spy) worked in the BBC Talks department and had known JB through Oxford friends.
> In the end, JB spoke on the Anglo-Irishman Adolphus Cooke of Cookesborough, one of the most famous mausoleum builders. Cooke had intended to have himself buried near the house – in a mausoleum complete with fireplace and books – but changed his mind and was buried in a stone beehive in Reynella Churchyard. The talk was broadcast on 24 September 1937.

To Mary Adams   Garrards Farm
                                                   Uffington
                                                   Berkshire

Your reference PP(v)MA
My reference Excellent

15 July 1937

Dear Mrs Adams,
I was equally sorry to miss you and hope I did not make an appointment which I failed to keep. Anyhow I am glad I provided the Ally Pally with entertainment. God knows it seemed to need it, lost there between Wood Green and Muswell Hill with Crouch End and Stroud Green spreading pink to the south.

I was interested by television. But I feel, as I expect everyone you see feels and tells you, that these initial stages are a little boring. The value of television seems to me to be its possibility of outside work. I mean, when television cameras can show to millions of people actual scenes of shooting and dying in Spain, then it will become the most valuable propaganda medium in the world. When it can actually drive down the Great Worst Road picking up the noises, and then catch the silence of a cathedral close, it will awaken people to the repulsiveness of their surroundings. Beside this, 'How to Make a Guide Book' seems an unimportant thing, but more important to me than Museums which I simply loathe – except the Soane, Saffron Walden, Dulwich Art Gallery and minor provincial collections.

However I really would like to try to make a programme on 'How to Make a Guide-Book' – but I can't possibly get it out in detail by July 20th as I am overwhelmed with work. You do not say how long the programme is to be. If ten minutes, I think choosing pictures for a guide-book should provide great fun. If more, I must work out other schemes. As I cannot get this done by July 20th, perhaps you would like to defer my activity till later in the year. I hope I am not being inconvenient. *Omnia tempus edax.* [Time, the devourer of all things.]

The last time we met was over Parish Churches. I would have provided an excellent series of talks in my opinion. Parish churches are my pet hobby. As it was, you chose Mr Greening Lambourne, a dull and inaccurate man and I was interviewed and turned down by your assistant – a Mr Wilson with a pink art-silk tie, unless I am mistaken.

Yours sincerely, John Betjeman

M.A. had been with the BBC since 1930 and was a TV producer from 1936 to 1939 (she went on to become Assistant Controller of Programmes in the fifties and was awarded an OBE in 1953). She had written (31 May 1937), 'I don't know whether you have seen the television screen, or whether its problems interest you, but I should very much like you to come up to Alexandra Palace and discuss with us the possibilities of this new medium. We have in front of us a period of experimentation, and we should like to think that you were interested in how it can best be used.'

To John Murray   Garrards Farm
                                                   Uffington
20 July 1937   Berkshire

Dear Jock,
Here is the tap and tracing with the way to draw the drops of water. You might make a test and see whether they fall from the outside or inside rim of the tap. Certainly not the middle.

Leave in 'Plunger', 'Washer', 'Rim of Valve' – they add poignance. Put a rule round and reduce to a suitable width. I should think the deeper the better for the drips. My tracing is possibly not quite deep enough.

I think it ought to look very nice indeed. Perhaps you will let Ted [Edward McKnight] Kauffer know of this. He might incorporate it in his dust jacket.

Yours, John B

JB produced the drawing of a tap which appeared on the title page of *Continual Dew*. Edward McKnight Kauffer was an American designer and illustrator.

To John Murray   Garrards Farm
                                                                    Uffington
29 July 1937   Berkshire

My dear Jock,

Dent's have done the dirty on us. 'As Mr Hadfield understands it' is not as it actually happened. I telephoned to Dent's and they said I could look over the King's Treasuries file. When I called to look over said file, a man came down from the inner recesses and I explained to him what the border was wanted for, showed him the proofs of Osbert's drawings and the poems in them. He said that would be quite all right and there would be a nominal fee. The business of the nominal fee was echoed by the elderly woman assistant also in the shop. I said Murray's would write confirming this.

I think you should point this out to Dent's and say you have had the block made. They have no right to try to shove the blame on to me and to ignore what was actually spoken in their shop.

Supposing all this fails. I send by this post a volume of the *Dome* containing a design by G. M. Ellwood (still alive, see *Who's Who*). If he would give us permission to reproduce his design, we might get him to write out the Exeter poem in the appropriate lettering so that the general effect would be like this:

Very nice, I fancy. I will write to him, if Dent's refuse to give in.

Ellwood is a member of the [Art-Workers'] Guild and I doubt not that I could point out to him tactfully the sort of thing I want and get him to do it. No Guild man costs very much. This would really be better than anything up till now. But I do feel sorry for the way you have been treated by Dent's. I never said *I* would write to them, I said you would.

Yours, John B

J. M. Dent and Sons Ltd, the publishers who founded the Everyman Library, had a showroom on the corner of Bedford Street. John Hadfield looked after Dent's publicity.

Letter published in the Sheffield Star   Garrards Farm
                                                            Uffington
8 September 1937   Berkshire

St Paul's Church

Sir,

As a visitor to Sheffield and a student of architecture, I would like to express a hope that your most beautiful classical church of St Paul's will be rebuilt exactly as it stands on its new site.

It is appropriate that Sir William Kilner, a Yorkshireman, is to save the work of a great Yorkshire architect John Platt II, who designed the tower of St Paul's and whose father, John Platt I, probably designed the body of the church. Sheffield will be following the splendid example set by Lincoln, which rebuilt in the suburbs its fine classic church of St Peter at Arches, formerly in the heart of the city.

May I put in a plea for the re-erection of St James's Church – minus its Victorian improvements? The church, like St Paul's, is in the best Georgian tradition, a tradition which is just beginning to be appreciated after nearly seventy years of neglect. St James's is described as a plain building. But plain does not mean ugly, indeed after much that one sees in modern and Victorian architecture it means the reverse of ugly. Like St Paul's, St James's depends for its effect on subtlety of proportion (which we knew all about one hundred years ago): this does not strike the eye at once, yet as soon as it is gone for ever one misses it.

Both these churches are in a too rare tradition to be lost for ever. They are honest North Country buildings and I hope North Country-men will help to preserve them.

Fortunately the old Ruskinian prejudices against preserving

anything that is not medieval or earlier on the grounds that it is 'barn-like' (are barns so ugly?) and 'of no architectural merit', is almost dead. Sheffielders who are keen on preserving the Georgian heritage of their city should communicate with the Secretary, the Society for the Protection of Ancient Buildings, 20 Buckingham Street, London WC2.

The Society has recently taken under its wing a Georgian Group for the express purpose of saving such buildings as St Paul's and St James's.

Yours etc., John Betjeman

To Mary Adams   Garrards Farm
                                                      Uffington
14 September 1937   Berkshire

Dear Mrs Adams,
I enclose a sketch [overleaf] of a suggestion for a background for my talk on 'How to Make a Guide-Book'. It is meant to represent a village hall. Please note the OIL LAMP, an important feature, which I hope you will be able to get to hang, like a comforting presence shining its radiance on my words.

I suggest that the blackboard background – if one is needed – should be another part of the village hall.

Will you get for me:
a good-sized Cornish pasty
a waste paper basket
a hanging oil lamp
I will bring a collection of rural objects and we can chuck out those that are no good. About six should be the maximum.

The talk would start with blackboard, go on to village hall and end with blackboard. I shall let you have some photographs by Thursday.

I would have liked a Methodist chapel pulpit and background, but this would probably be going too far.

I shall be at Shell-Mex House tomorrow (Wednesday) Temple Bar 1234, if you want me.

Yours sincerely, John Betjeman

The film was transmitted on 21 September 1937.

To Douglas Goldring   Garrards Farm
                                         Uffington
16 September 1937   Berkshire

Dear Author,
A friend of mine and of Robert B[yron]'s and of a good many people on
the Committee of the Georgian Group, is anxious to get the job of
secretary. She is called Miss Wilhelmine Cresswell, The Old Hall,
Snettisham, Norfolk and 16 Great James St, WC1. She has been
secretary of her local (Norfolk) C[ouncil for the] P[reservation of]
R[ural] E[ngland] branch and also can type etc: and has a good
knowledge of eighteenth-century architecture. I think she would be an
excellent person. She has a little money of her own, but like so many of
us, nothing like enough to live on. Can you bring this up at a meeting?
  Yours, John Betjeman

D.G., along with Lord Derwent and Robert Byron, was responsible for forming the Georgian Group in 1937. They were aghast at the number of star Georgian buildings which were being pulled down all over London in the thirties. JB told me that what clinched their determination was the destruction of a house by Wood of Bath in Chippenham High Street which was replaced by a new Woolworths.

'Thank you *so* much for helping me get my job,' wrote Wilhelmine Creswell (30 September 1937).

To Anthony Powell   Shell-Mex House
                                                Victoria Embankment
19 October 1937   London WC2

Dear Tony,

Thank you very much for the suggestions which I have shown to Beddioleman. He says they are very good but ones that always occur to people when they first think of Shell and BP advertising. That means to say that he cannot use them. The doodles one has apparently been done by someone or other before.

What he does like very much is the suggestions for *Times Change* and three of them he is having experiments made with. I am sending back the others.

Roland Young has said that he cannot let us know until tomorrow morning whether he can lunch or not, but anyhow you and I will lunch and let's hope that Roland Young will come too. Meeting here at one o'clock.

I am glad Christine [Longford]'s play was such a success. Love to old Violet [Powell]. What a nice, formal letter this is.

Yours, John Betjeman

JB met A.P. at Oxford and at Pakenham Hall when they were staying with Edward Longford whose sister, Violet, A.P. married. Shell ran a series of advertising slogans entitled *Things Old and Things New* for which A.P. entered some ideas. 'It was a sore point,' remembers A.P. 'Mine were never accepted.'

To Mary Adams   Garrards Farm
                                                Uffington
21 October 1937   Berkshire

Dear Mrs Adams,

Thank you so much for the excruciatingly funny photograph. I shall certainly have it framed. It is the maddest thing I ever saw.

But it gives me an idea. Might not I become a sort of Harry Tate of Television and give talks on 'How to Make a Motor Car' in a nice intimate style, using objects even more ridiculous than those I used for 'How to Make a Guide-Book'. I might do 'How to Make a Television Set', 'What to do with Old Razor Blades', 'A New Use for Carriages', 'How to make an Omelette', 'Interior Decoration in the Falkland Islands', etc. It would be most enjoyable. Think of the objects one could select.

Who on earth is Mr Marshall? [?]

Give my love to MP.

Yours sincerely, John Betjeman

> The photograph was a still from the film of JB holding up his chosen objects.
>   Harry Tate was a celebrated Music-Hall artist, whose most famous comic sketch was 'Motoring'.

To John Murray   Garrards Farm
                                          Uffington
23 October 1937   Berkshire

Dear Jock,

Thank you so much for the book [*Continual Dew*] with which I am delighted. Ted [McKnight Kauffer]'s cover is magnificent. Most appealing and an agreeable contrast with the lovely black and gold inside. The gilt edges are lovely. So is the grey paper. Loveliest of all is the prayer book paper.

> 'If the amount of trouble and money that has been expended on the production of this undergraduate persiflage had instead been spent on some of our young poets, the publishers at least could be congratulated.' Anticipated notice from *New Statesman and Nation*.

You might put that on the cards you intend to send out.

My dear Jock, I feel it unlikely that you will sell more than a dozen copies and I do appreciate the charity, for I can only call it that, which has made you publish the verse in so exquisite a style. You and Lord Gorell will get your reward in heaven.

Didn't I send you a whacking great list of friends on brown paper? I haven't got an address book and it was the best I could do. If I think of some more I will let you know. Let me have some cards and I will enclose them in my letters.

Will you send back, some time, the books from which some of the illustrations were taken?

It's Murray's *Guide to Oxfordshire* not *London*, that John Piper wants to borrow.

With many many thanks,

Yours till death, John B

J.M. had written (11 September 1937), 'We have chosen a blue cloth for the binding. A horrible material which I think you will like.' *Continual Dew* came out on 2 November.

Lord Gorell was Editor of the *Cornhill* magazine from 1933 to 1939, in which some of JB's poems appeared.

To John Summerson
Garrards Farm
Uffington
Berkshire

4 November 1937

The Catholic Apostolic Church, Gordon Square, WC1

The	⎧ Irving		Angels	⎫	Praise
Second	⎨ Drummond		Prophets / Evangelists	⎬	the
Coming	⎩ Baxter / Francis / Northumberland		Priests / Deacons	⎭	Lord

Dear John Summerson,

I think you should know, if you don't already, that [Dunbar] Smith and [Cecil] Brewer's magnificent Mary Ward Settlement in Tavistock Place is coming down. Sir Herbert Baker is erecting a new one in Islington (this I have from the Warden of the settlement). It is said to be Brewer's earliest work and in my opinion, the best of his works that I know. Do get some photographs taken of the dining room, theatre, school rooms and residents' rooms. The place is wonderful. Probably the elevations are at S. and B.'s office in Queen Square (Art Workers' Guild House).

What about this committee we are supposed to be on?

Yours, John Betjeman

JB met J.S. on the top floor of Fortnum's in 1934 where the latter was arranging an exhibition of Arvold Artoes.

The Mary Ward Settlement and its attendant buildings, which were built at the turn of the century, are still *in situ*.

To Wilhelmine Cresswell   Garrards Farm
                                                  Uffington
11 November 1937   Berkshire
Armistice Day

Darling Billa,
Love will find a way. Congratters old girl and to Roy. Love to you both.
Delighted. It's not 38 Beaumont Street, by any chance? There will be
some surprise in Ch[rist] Ch[urch]. It's all rather like Eleanor Bold and
Mr Arabin.

I shouldn't worry about the G[eorgian] Group, which can take care of
itself. Though if you can look after it from Oxford, so much the better.
It's a good idea to have something which keeps your self-respect up
when you are married to the Harrod Curve.

I enclose a letter from my Bristol BBC friend, Francis Worsley. I
wrote to Guy Burgess but so far have had no answer.

Yours with love, duckie, John B

> W.C. had become engaged to the economist Roy Harrod who was a don at Christ
> Church, Oxford. They married in January 1938 and lived at 6 Beaumont Street,
> Oxford.
>   Eleanor Bold and Mr Arabin are key characters in Trollope's *Barchester Towers*.

To Bryan Guinness   Garrards Farm
                                                  Uffington
17 December 1937   Berkshire

My Dear Brigh-yern,
Thank you so much for the play. The Vicar came to dinner last night.
He was for many years a missionary in Korea and translated the signs
on the cover as Yangihang chop chop meaning incense-laden tart. He
has now taken off the play to read and will bring it back this evening. So
at present I can say nothing about it but thank you very much.

P had a fearful time with the child – three days labour then a
Caesarian. But she is all right now – moved from the hospital yesterday
and is at 40 Avenue Road with her parents. So is the son, to be called
Paul Sylvester George. I do hope we will meet in the New Year and be
able to see Mr Anthrax's Moses.

I'm glad you've chosen Mangan's dark Rosaleen for your daughter.
How is your wife?

Give my love to May [Amende].

Sad about the Crystal Palace, isn't it? I haven't properly recovered yet.

Yours with love, John B

Originally called *Honeymoon in Peking*, B.G.'s play was published as *The Fragrant Concubine*.

Paul Betjeman was born on 26 November 1937.

Mr Anthrax was possibly Boris Anrep, the mosaicist who worked for Bryan Guinness at Biddesden.

Rosaleen Guinness was born just before Paul. James Clarence Mangan's poem 'Dark Rosaleen' was a translation from the Gaelic.

May Amende was the parlour maid at Biddesden.

The Crystal Palace was burnt down on 30 November 1936. B.G. dedicated his poem about the Crystal Palace to JB.

To Bess Betjemann

21 December 1937

Garrards Farm
Uffington
Berkshire

Darling Bessie,

A Happy Christmas. But it doesn't seem much good wishing you one if you've still got that wretched lumbago. P telephoned to us this evening to say that you had sent us £5 (five pounds). That was very very generous of you. You honestly shouldn't have sent us so much. Thank you very much indeed. It will be more useful really than any other kind of present – for this is an awful time – with the income tax just coming on again. God bless you.

I am worried to hear from P how ill you are. And now you won't be able to go to the Collinses' for Christmas, I suppose. Poor Bessie. If you'd like it, you have only to say the word and I will come down after Boxing Day and stay a day or two. Now please do this if you feel too lonely and dispirited.

Did our trees arrive? They were sent off all right. I have not seen your letter yet, as P is in London at the Woadery and there is no room for me there what with the Nurse and the Baby. So I am spending the nights down here and going up to London for the day. It gives Betty [Evans] and Gwynne [her sister] something to do to have me to look after.

As soon as I got down, of course, the village boys started bawling 'Noel' outside the door in hope of money. They come in relays every night. I am arranging to have signed receipts so as not to pay twice. It's the most wicked form of begging. They don't even sing in tune – like me.

Poor Bessie. All alone and in bed again. I am thinking of you and praying you will get better soon. And honestly, if you want me, I will come down. P is so much better now that I can safely leave her for a few days.

She wants to have the child christened on Jan 8th, a Saturday. Do you want to come? Woad [Philip Chetwode] and Mrs Woad [Hester Chetwode] will be there, but are not staying in the house. On the other hand we can't put you up owing to lack of space – the Nurse and the Baby in two rooms, P and I in the other. But I could arrange accommodation in the village, if you like. On the whole, if you don't want to meet Mrs Woad, it might be rather a good gesture not to turn up rather than that there should be a few acid remarks! I don't know – I leave it to you. But let me know soon because of getting rooms. You could sleep in my bedroom, I have suddenly thought.

Woad has got it into his head that I am a pacifist, I think. It almost turns me into one. We have a fearful time starting the car in the morning. Cold. I rather like the cold otherwise.

It makes me feel well – touch wood! Driving to the station has been terrifying the last two mornings. I have suddenly come to stretches of frozen rain across the road – the car once turned almost completely round. No harm done and I caught the train, what is more.

You will be interested to hear that the forebears of George Betjeman (1820ish, founder of the firm) are buried in the churchyard of St Botolph's Aldersgate – that parish almost adjoins St Giles' Cripplegate where James Dawson [JB's grandfather] was church warden. I had copies from the St B's registers sent to me. George Betjeman Senior died aged forty-nine in 1813. The name in the registers is spelled six times with one 'n' and twice with two 'n's. I wish I knew which was right. I am having a fine time making these researches during lunch hours in the City. Now I've got to find where my gt-gt-grandparents George and Eleanor Betjeman were married. I hope they *were* married as they had about fifteen children! – all baptised in St Botolph's Aldersgate between 1804 and 1813.

After that I'll make searches in Spalding with you into the Dawsons. It's an easy and amusing game but costs a shilling a time.

You remember that house we loved so much at Stanton Harcourt outside Oxford? You saw it and made me get out of the car. And then we found a moat round it and walked down a footpath to see if we could get a better view. It was a high seventeenth-century square building with all the old windows and was inhabited, but looked very decayed.

It is suddenly to let – a hundred and fifty a year – and some friends of mine are after it. If they get it, we will be able to see it. Apparently it is much older in parts than it looked. The cellars have Norman vaulting. It was a Palace, dismantled and then became a farmhouse and remained in one family called Arnott since the eighteenth century. Old Mrs Arnott died a month ago. She was the last. She was living in it when we saw it. Her husband farmed it like his forebears.

It is apparently even better inside than it was out. The ceilings are painted plasterwork, all the old panelling is painted with seventeenth-century designs and even the lavatories are eighteenth-century and flush away into the moat. At the sale there are to be hundreds of clothes belonging to the Arnott family for sale – the clothes date back to the seventeenth century. All the furniture is contemporary with the eighteenth and seventeenth centuries. What a place! I'm glad you stopped the car and we got out and looked. I will try to go to the sale which is in a fortnight. The house belongs to All Souls College, Oxford. I hope they will preserve it and its surroundings and that my friends get it.

It's getting on for one o'clock now and I must stop as I have to get up early in the morning. I do hope you will be better soon. Don't think I don't write oftener because I don't love you. You must know by now what a rotten correspondent I am.

But when I *do* write – well look at the length of this letter!

A happy Christmas. Keep cheerful.

Much love, poor lonely Bessie, from John

PS The Woads leave Avenue Road on Thursday and I shall be there then until Christmas.

PPS I have just finished the excellent novel, *Cathedral Close*, and send it as our little extra Christmas present.

PPPS Paul Sylvester George is v. greedy and has to have enemas.

The Chetwodes' Avenue Road house had been Alma Tadema's studio. Hester loved its mad style and painted some of the walls black, which she set off with violently coloured cushions. JB always called it 'The Woadery'.

The house JB and Bess had found at Stanton Harcourt was the Parsonage, built in 1675 by Robert Huntingdon.

To G. A. Kolkhorst   40 Avenue Road
23 December 1937   NW8

Darling Colonel,
I enclose a letter from my other self thanking you for that very happy
weekend. I did enjoy myself you dear horizontal-eyed, cube-headed,
wool-dressing-gowned old thing.

The christening is at Uffington on January 8th Saturday at three
o'clock – if that suits you. Cracky will tell you the responsibility you
have undertaken. THE SINS of my child are on your shoulders until he
is confirmed.

Will you please thank Cracky very much for his charming letter
which made us laugh a hell of a lot. This is rather UC [upper class],
writing this way on the *writing* paper, not notepaper, and ONvelopes,
by the way, not ENvelopes. I went into St Mary Moorfields this
afternoon (RC church) and stood at the door amid the crowd – not liking
to go forward to a pew. I then thought I would go out by a door at the
side having noticed a woman go there already. I opened the door, a light
was switched on and a holy but pained face beneath a biretta was
disclosed – it was the priest hearing a confession. Thank God it wasn't
Father Burdett.

I *did* enjoy myself. I did like laughing. Tell wheezy old [Revd] Hugh
[Bridle] about that confessional.

P and the child are doing very well. P is up now and tying up little
parcels for people. Give my love to Sister. I do like her – she does like a
joke. Oh those little china
ducks with pepper and salt
and mustard.

Give them my love. Kiss Yarnton for me. See me more often. I can't do
without you. P sends its love so does little P.

Love and a Happy Christmas and New Year, JB

Nearly all G.A.K.'s papers were destroyed on his death. JB had met him in his first days
at Oxford and he was a part of his life from then on.

JB's reference to the telling use of correct upper-class vocabulary and pronunciation
was a source of constant amusement between G.A.K. and JB. Lady Chetwode, with
whom he was staying, was very correct and abhorred the use of the word 'notepaper' etc.

Hugh Bridle was an Anglican priest. He was a great friend of the Colonel's and Clonmore's and a contemporary of JB's. He taught at Radley College near Abingdon from 1931 to 1940 and he was licensed to officiate in the Diocese of Oxford.

Sister had been nurse to the Colonel's invalid mother and stayed on at Yarnton as housekeeper.

To G. A. Kolkhorst   Garrards Farm
                                                        Uffington
31 December 1937   Berkshire

Darling Colonel,

Sorry not to have replied before. We've all been moving from London hither.

Doubly sorry you can't be a godparent. I suspect old Hugh and Cracky of having got at you.

But if they haven't, I perfectly understand your objections. The service in the old Prayer Book looks alarming. If you look in the Revised Prayer Book (which we shall use) you will find yourself less committed. What surprises me, you dear woollen-clothed old thing, is that you mind so much about the C of E that you show the respect for her you do. You are much more religious than your old cube-shaped head would lead me to believe. You might almost be a Communist!

No, I really do understand. But take a look at the Revised Book Service, before you finally decide. We have got a clergyman godparent to look after the religious instruction part.

Anyhow, whichever way you decide, do come to the Christening which is on Sunday week at noon. And lunch afterwards?

P and the child are doing very well, after the journey down here. The child howls all day, but it is not as bad as traffic and aeroplane noises. God bless you.

Remember me to Sister and Toby [Strutt].

I long to see you again.

Yours, John B

The Colonel had declined to be a godparent to my brother Paul, and continued to do so, despite this letter. Paul's godparents were John Sparrow, Anne Feversham, Mary Pakenham and Tom Driberg. He was christened at Baulking by the Revd F. P. Harton.

Toby Strutt was a friend of the Colonel's whom none of his other friends liked.

Six:

When all the world seemed waiting to be won

======

January 1938 to October 1940

Stuart, I sit here in a grateful haze
Recalling those spontaneous Berkshire days
In straw-thatched
       chalk built,
              pre-War
                     Uffington
Before the March of Progress had begun,
When all the world seemed waiting to be won
When evening air with mignonette was scented,
And 'picture-windows' had not been invented,
When shooting foxes still was thought unsporting,
And White Horse Hill was still the place for courting . . .

'To Stuart Piggott', 1975

'I remember walking along the village street from my parents' cottage in Uffington,' recalled the archaeologist Stuart Piggott, 'and knocking on the door of Garrards Farm. It was tea-time. John opened the door and I explained in an embarrassed manner that we had a mutual friend in Reggie Ross-Williamson and before I had finished the sentence John said, "For God's sake come in, we're having a helluva time with the Prime Minister of Nepal – you've got to come and help me out." From that moment on we were friends. I remember once Gerald Berners brought a house party over from Faringdon which included Gertrude Stein and Alice B. Toklas. They had come to see a touring company playing *East Lynne* at Uffington Village Hall. JB asked me to come over early before they arrived: "I've found a quotation of Gertrude Stein's and I am going to try it on her and see how it goes." When she arrived, JB went up to her and said, "You know, Miss Stein, there's been ringing in my head a line of yours," and JB then quoted something. "I can't recollect it – can you, Alice?" said Miss Stein, turning to her companion. "No, I can't," Alice replied. "You may rest *assured* Mr Betjeman, it is not from one of my *major works*." For years afterwards we made each other explode with laughter just by saying, "It's not from one of my major works." '[1]

My parents felt increasingly happy at Garrards. The pattern of their life was settled; my mother gardened, kept a goat, went everywhere in the four-wheeled dog cart and wrote cookery articles for the *Daily Express*. (She was sacked in the end after the marrow wine she had suggested her readers left to ferment for six weeks exploded in their cellars and backrooms all over England. She had not herself tried out the recipe which a villager had given her.) When JB was not working in London he wrote in his cramped dressing room at Garrards where his curtains were by Voysey and he had to move the bed to open the cupboard where he kept his papers. In the dining room he painted a naked lady with *art nouveau*-ish tulips growing out of her above the mantelpiece. The solid Arts and Crafts table by Betjemann and Co. was surrounded by rush-seated, ladder-back chairs designed by Ernest Gimson, chosen by JB and given as a wedding present by Mrs Dugdale of Sezincote. Most of the rooms at Garrards were decorated with Morris and Co. wallpapers and my mother even had a dressing gown made of the 'bird and anenome' design. When the contents of William Morris's house, Kelmscott, went up for sale in July 1939 after the death of his daughter, May, my parents bid for some Rossetti sketches, which they couldn't afford at fourteen pounds, and a Morris tapestry which went for three hundred and fifty pounds. They ended up with Mrs Morris's Spanish guitar for eighteen shillings, two Philip Webb designed towel rails for four shillings and three Staffordshire horses for sixteen shillings.

When Osbert Lancaster and his wife, Karen, came to stay they often visited Kelmscott and once took part in one of my mother's 'musical evenings' at Uffington Village Hall. Osbert said that he had 'never spent an evening of such continuous and unalloyed pleasure . . .' 'Summer is icumen in' was sung by Adrian Bishop (an Oscar Wilde-ian wit who lived nearby), Maurice Bowra, Karen Lancaster and JB, accompanied by Lord Berners on the piano, my mother on the Hawaiian guitar and Osbert on the flute. The cacophony was unforgettable.

My brother remembers another evening in the village hall when our mother had persuaded a village girl to recite Thomas Hood's socially conscious poem, 'The Song of a Shirt':

> Stitch, stitch, stitch,
> In poverty, hunger and dirt.

She forgot the continuation and kept repeating this same line over and over again with short pauses in between. My brother was also made to recite Belloc's 'There was a boy whose name was Jim . . .', egged on by

JB. He dried up at the end and when prompted said, 'I do not do that part,' which everyone but he thought very funny.

JB became more and more involved in village life. The Revd Hugh Bridle wrote from Uffington Vicarage (30 August 1938), 'Dear Mr Betjeman, I am writing to you as People's Warden to request you to take steps, in conjunction with Captain Piggott, to prevent another incident such as occurred on Sunday morning last at the eleven a.m. service.

'When Mr John Wheeler brought the collection to the chancel steps he deliberately jostled me with his shoulder and if I had not been fairly firm on my feet I should have been knocked over. His manner in church is never very reverent and has been commented on many times, but it must be made clear to him that his action of last Sunday must not be repeated.'[2]

Mr Wheeler farmed the Garrards land as well as his own and in order to make amends for his irreverence gave some land to the Church so that they might extend the graveyard. (Ironically he was the first to be buried in it.)

My mother was also doing what she assumed to be her duty until she was asked not to. 'My dear Penelope,' wrote the Revd F. P. Harton from the vicarage in the neighbouring hamlet of Baulking, 'I have been thinking over the question of the playing of the harmonium on Sunday evenings here and have reached the conclusion that I must now take it over myself.

'I am very grateful to you for doing it for so long and hate to have to ask you to give it up, but, to put it plainly, your playing has got worse and worse and the disaccord between the harmonium and the congregation is becoming destructive of devotion. People are not very sensitive here, but even some of them have begun to complain, and they are not usually given to doing that. I do not like writing this, but I think you will understand that it is my business to see that divine worship is as perfect as it can be made. Perhaps the crankiness of the instrument has something to do with the trouble. I think it does require a careful and experienced player to deal with it.

'Thank you ever so much for stepping so generously into the breach when Sibyl was ill; it was the greatest possible help to me and your results were noticeably better then than now.'[3]

This rebuff did not deter her from carrying out other village duties nor change her devoted attitude to the Revd Harton, who sent her, as recompense, a copy of H. V. Morton's *In the Steps of the Master*.

At the outbreak of war in September 1939 JB joined the Uffington

Observer Corps which was stationed in a small hut in Parrot's Field on the road to the White Horse. Mr Long, the Head Gardener at Kingston Lisle Park, who had served in the First World War, assumed seniority because of his previous experience and did not advise shooting at enemy aircraft – 'In case they shot back,' recalled Ron Liddiard, who also served in the 'x2' Observer Corps. 'I remember one night,' he said, 'I was on duty with Mr Betjeman and the news came through from the centre in Oxford that there were enemy aircraft in the area. So we ran out of the hut to what your father used to call "the urinal", in which all the tracking equipment was kept, and he got hopelessly tangled up in the flexes on the way and fell down shouting, "We're going to lose the war." '4 Ron Liddiard wrote 'Ode to x2', making rhyming couplets for all its twenty or so members.

> . . . B is for Betjeman, of 'charring' he's fond,
> The floor while he's at it, is like a 'girt' pond . . .
> I think you'll agree, we're a reet motley crew,
> But there's no post in Berkshire, LIKE GOOD OLD X2.5

My mother served in the Downs Patrol Division, which involved riding up on to the Downs at dawn looking for parachutists. She once saw a parachute tangled up in a clump of beech trees beside the Ridgeway, but there was nobody in sight.

In December 1939 JB applied for a commission in the Intelligence Department of the RAF. His friend Michael Judd, who was stationed at Peterborough, implored him not to go ahead, as amongst other drawbacks 'the uniform is most unbecoming' and 'the discomfort intense'.

My Chetwode grandfather, while writing at John's behest to high-up contacts in Government and the Forces, asking them to take on JB who, at thirty, was too old to join up through normal channels, was privately urging him to take a job offered by Sir Kenneth Clark. 'Get a written offer of the film job [in the Ministry of Information] and *accept it at once*. Star [Lady Chetwode] says you can tell the Air Force you are *directed* to take it up!'6

JB persevered in the face of this advice but was turned down on medical grounds in January 1940. 'I am afraid it is impossible to make an appeal or find out why you were disqualified. From my knowledge of medical examinations, it was probably caused by your casual remark that you once had been treated therapeutically,'7 wrote H. Beauchamp, a Roman Catholic Staff Chaplain in the Air Force and an acquaintance of JB's, to whom he had written trying to find out why he had failed.

Frustrated in his first choice of the Air Force, he then applied to join the Royal Marines, with similar results. Jack Beddington, his boss at Shell, followed this sequence of events with some bemusement and assured him his job at Shell was still there for a few weeks. But as it turned out, JB, honour satisfied, had joined the Film Publicity Division of the Ministry of Information on 6 February. Michael Balcon sent him a script for a feature film to be called 'Battle of Britain', but they both decided that war films should be left to more peaceful times.

JB's friendship with John Piper deepened over this period and he began calling him what was always to be his nickname, 'Mr Piper'. They had stopped off for tea at a hotel in Much Wenlock when they were collaborating on the *Shell Guide to Shropshire* and were put in a waiting room until a table became free. Eventually a waitress came through and said in a dainty North Country accent, 'Will you two men come forward please.' JB began talking to Piper in the same accent pretending to be a business executive and referring to his colleague as 'Mr Piper'.

Going to Shropshire for the first time, which neither of them knew particularly well, was an eye-opener for JB. 'It was like going to Brazil or somewhere. It was always frightfully funny. He [Piper] always related people to buildings. He liked speculating about vicars and architects . . . we thought that looking at a village meant looking at the church . . . I don't think I've ever felt so confident as I did with Mr Piper.'[8]

Although Piper had met JB a year before, his wife Myfanwy remembers with great clarity her first visit to Uffington on 11 March 1938. 'I'll never forget the date, it was a landmark – a wonderful sunny day and I had *just* conceived; we drove to Uffington and John came out to greet us. Penelope shouted from the background, "You can't have sherry, lunch is ready." We had grilled kebabs of lamb with onion and tomato. I remember being very impressed by the broccoli which was tied up in bundles. There were two girls working in the kitchen being trained by Penelope. We had praline mousse for pudding. I was also very impressed by seeing a house more untidy than our own. I remember the medicine cupboard in the bathroom being crammed full with bottles, far more than anyone else had . . . Of course John and Penelope had lots of rows but they were quite open about them. They once had one when the Connollys were staying and they walked into the bathroom where Cyril and Jean were in the bath together and, oblivious, carried on with the row.'[9]

My mother did not know the meaning of the word embarrassment.

When Gerard Irvine used to stay he was amazed by the way she always left the door open while going to the lavatory.

Betty Evans and her sister Gwynne were the 'two girls' in the kitchen – their father ran the Craven Arms in the village and they went to work at Garrards after Paula, the maid, had gone back to Germany after a year. 'He was a little bit eccentric,' remembers Betty about JB. 'He sometimes went to London wearing one black shoe and one brown. He honestly didn't notice.' [I can corroborate this – he *never* did up his shoe laces because he couldn't tie a bow, so never looked closely at his shoes.] 'I was always having to mend his teddy bear, Archie – he was *always* in the room with him.'[10] Betty was my brother's nursemaid and stayed until she married George Packford in 1942.

By the late thirties JB's fame was beginning to spread beyond the intellectual élite; as a result his correspondence tripled. His output and activity were tremendous. Although he was still working for Shell, he was taking on a lot of extra work to pay the bills. His regular talks on the radio continued; he covered seaside resorts in a series called *Sea Views* and West Country cities in a series called *Built to Last*. Hence he was travelling all over the West Country and conducting an extremely funny correspondence with Mr Boswell of the BBC about his expenses, which were time-consuming to extract and involved much cross-questioning as though you were a minor criminal.

JB's confidence grew. His booklet of poems, *Sir John Piers*, inspired while on holiday with the Longfords (by an early nineteenth-century gambler, duellist and spendthrift, who was the last of the name and resided at Tristernagh in Ireland), was privately printed and distributed among his friends, and 1938 saw the publication of *An Oxford University Chest*, which he dedicated to his mother. It was a mixture of essays, photographs, prints and cartoons about Oxford's dons and undergraduates and included an architectural tour around its buildings. The production was extremely stylish and remains fresh and undated to this day. In 1939 under the auspices of his friend John Lehmann he published a tirade against iconoclasm, *Antiquarian Prejudice*, in the Hogarth Press sixpenny pamphlet series. 'It is a real *tour de force* and I only hope it gets about to the people who should read it; but these things never do. I do think it reads awfully well,'[11] wrote J. M. Richards (14 April 1939), who was by then editing the *Architectural Review*. JB explains that architecture is not just singular buildings but our whole surroundings: 'When we wake up one morning and find the view from our windows shadowed. . . . when we hear of Mr Rudolf Palumbo putting up things which will scrape as much of the London sky as the

LCC will allow . . .' Pages ensue on the iniquities of the 'School of No Thought' architecture which builds before it plans and is based on greed and careerism. 'What will give us time to think?' he ends. 'A Ministry of Fine Arts? A change of government? Or a change of heart?'

Meanwhile JB's poems were becoming more sought after among those friends and acquaintances who were involved with literary magazines. The first number of Constantine Fitzgibbon's *Yellowjacket* contained a poem of JB's, for which he was paid one guinea. Cyril Connolly, who often came to stay at Uffington and whom JB had revered since Oxford days, asked him to contribute poems to the new magazine he had founded, *Horizon*. Connolly and JB were kindred spirits who, as was the fashion, both mocked their fathers, whom they deemed to be philistines. Connolly's was a retired Major who had become the world's leading expert on South African snails, had a face disfigured by syphilis and lived in a Kensington hotel.

When JB suggested to John Murray that he had had another offer for a new volume of poems, Murray snapped them up and in 1940 published *Old Lights for New Chancels*, a title of which JB was not enamoured. The book included 'Pot Pourri from a Surrey Garden', 'Trebetherick', 'Upper Lambourne' and 'On a Portrait of a Deaf Man'. The latter was about JB's father, for whom he now felt a calm affection, tinged with a remorse which never left him.

JB never wrote his poems in a quiet room, shut off from the world. My mother always said he wrote most of them on trains. As well as trains, I remember him writing them in station waiting rooms and on the backs of menus in restaurants. He would write two or four lines and build them up, usually on the backs of envelopes, on flattened cigarette packets and on blank pages in his tiny pocket diaries. When he returned home in the evening he would piece together the disparate scraps, of which some were inevitably lost, and while the idea was still fresh in his mind he would commit it to proper paper, sometimes waiting until the next morning. His poems were never worked on over long periods, except for what eventually became *Summoned by Bells*, which evolved over a period of about twenty years.

It was JB's enthusiasm and love of life that made him so liable to be asked for favours, but also so happy to carry them out. He took tremendous trouble finding jobs for out-of-work friends and answered letters from complete strangers with genuine interest. By the time he was in his early thirties he knew the feeling of being besieged with a mounting pile of unanswered letters and mounting deadlines impossible to meet. It was a situation which gradually worsened throughout his life until he had hardly any time of his own.

JB was always in an insufferably bad temper in the mornings, accusing everyone of getting at him and hiding his clothes. His state of nerves, made worse by this pressure of work and genuine need to make money to support a family, so exasperated my mother that she insisted he see a psychoanalyst to rid him of what she termed his 'persecution mania'. Gerald Berners, who was also seeing one, had been told he had a 'dead bird in his subconscious'.

Friends, acquaintances and strangers showered him with requests. Allen Lane asked him to write a book on churches for Penguin, Sibyl Colefax tried to enveigle him to her society soirées, the Left Book Club wanted him to lecture on poetry, the Town Clerk of Lyme Regis asked for a new Cry for the Town Crier contest and the Secretary of the Georgian Group wrote begging him to attend a meeting at Oxford Town Hall (13 January 1938). 'So – darling John Betche will you, who always do *all* the dirty work, please go? Someone who thoroughly understands architecture must go . . . so there is only you.'[12] Soon afterwards he was playing an active part in saving the beautiful Town Hall in Devizes which was threatened with a modern replacement. The fact that he was at once articulate and passionate about places he loved made him the obvious choice to cause a local stir. His lifelong reputation as a champion of threatened buildings was confirmed at this time.

A reputation as a playwright, on the other hand, was not. Stephen Spender wrote from the prestigious Group Theatre begging him to write a play (8 February 1938). 'You are the only writer to whom we are writing directly to ask for a play, as we feel that, in asking you, we can have considerable confidence that you will produce a play really worth having.'[13] This was one of the few requests he must have refused, for everything else he accepted. Christine Longford asked him to design the sets for a play she was producing at the Gate Theatre in Dublin called *The Absentee*. She was thrilled with the 'gorgeous designs. . . . The Gothic library is peculiarly lovely.' He lectured so often for the Workers' Educational Association that by June 1938 the Swindon branch asked if they could make him an honorary Vice-President. In 1938 he was paid fifty guineas to edit the winter edition of *Decoration*, and complained quite vociferously in the wings about the interference he had had from the Art Editor, Robert Harling. He accepted a fifty pound advance from Hamish Hamilton to edit Graham Robertson's letters (which he had to give back in the end) and twelve guineas from Geoffrey Grigson to write an article for *The West Country Book*.

In 1939 Gerard Irvine, an eighteen-year-old prefect at Haileybury College who admired *Mount Zion* and *Ghastly Good Taste*, wrote to JB out of the blue and asked him if he would drive to Hertfordshire to lecture to the school Arts Society. JB accepted. 'He seldom said no,' said Gerard. 'The thing to remember about John is that he was inordinately *kind*. He lectured about Tennyson I think. He was a terrific success, of course, with all us very self-conscious aesthetes and then, because it was near the end of term, I got permission for him to drive me back to my house at Wotton-under-Edge in Gloucestershire. My father, who was a retired General, liked him but didn't say so; my mother was very surprised by him. Later on when I was going for my scholarship interview at Oxford he took me to meet the "Colonel" and we had lunch at Yarnton which lingered on until tea. . . . I admired his work, I thought he was the cat's whiskers, and I soon discovered that he was talking about the same things that I was feeling but had never said, about architecture, the church and poetry. I modelled myself largely upon him thereafter.'[14] Gerard, who had decided to be a priest when he was seven and was ordained in 1945, has remained close to our family ever since.

During 1939 the artist, Paul Nash, set up a quasi-official committee to compile lists of artists and writers who might be involved in non-combatant war work. The committee consisted mostly of his friends around Oxford: John Piper, P. Morton Shand, Leonard Huskisson, G. M. Young and JB who was asked to second Kenneth Clark. Gerald Berners proposed a list of musicians, Stuart Piggott of archaeologists; Nash and Piper chose the painters and JB, T. S. Eliot and Siegfried Sassoon, the writers. There was faint confusion when Kenneth Clark pointed out that there was already a Central Register of artists for propaganda and camouflage. Nash's idea, however, was for the artists to record various aspects of the war. Sassoon was told by the Ministry of Information that he was already on a list of 'influential authors'. 'I asked what they expected me to do,' Sassoon wrote to JB (15 September 1939), and their reply was this: "In general the Ministry feels that authors can best serve by continuing their ordinary work and addressing the public, through the channels that are open to them." The trouble is that, as you say, most authors have ceased to earn anything since Sept 1st. . . . Anyway I will help if I can.'[15] Three days later Eliot sent JB his list. 'I can't give their ages but they are all under forty. It is important that some should be kept alive for the important work – that is, the work to be done after this war is over (whatever the result). . . . I trust that you will be one of them.'[16]

JB's admiration for the great church architect and last Gothic Revivalist, Ninian Comper, burgeoned through the 1930s and he finally met him in 1937. He described how one of Comper's pupils, Martin Travers, took him to dinner with the architect: 'The house was a Georgian Gothic building, set among trees in a large garden with a lake and a view over the miles of Surrey from Beulah Hill. There I learned the catholicity of Comper's taste, his admiration for the English Regency, his learning in ecclesiastical art; there I saw those careful notebooks, full of sketches and photographs, records of his journeys in Italy, Greece, North Africa and Spain and motor-caravan tours in France. . . . We went on talking about architecture, literature and people till the lights twinkled out over Croydon in the summer evening.'[17] In July 1939 JB invited his two favourite architectural veterans, Voysey and Comper, to dinner together in Hatchett's in Piccadilly; they had never met. John Summerson made up the four. Comper did most of the talking, about ecclesiology and church dimensions. Voysey wrote afterwards to JB (12 July 1939), 'I want to thank you very sincerely for your princely hospitality of last night. I only wish Comper had allowed you more time to talk.'[18]

Meanwhile the Betjemann family business had been trundling on. In June 1939 the manager, Horace Andrew, had written to JB, 'I would like to have your opinion on the enclosed advertisement for our new cocktail glass. If you think it worthwhile, would you be good enough to supply a little descriptive matter? I am not sure that I like the title, "The Nineteenth Hole Cocktail Glass". What do you think?'[19] JB's response was prompt and he suggested it be called "The Dormy Glass". Mr Andrew was apprehensive, however, and thought that only golf-players would appreciate the name.

In December 1940 Viscount Cranborne, Under-Secretary at the Dominions Office, wrote to John requesting that he proceed to Dublin as Press Attaché. At the beginning of December 1940, Penelope Aitken, the daughter of Sir John Maffey (later Lord Rugby) and JB's future employer as Ambassador, visited the Ministry of Information where JB was working. 'I met John Betjeman, who is arriving over as your Press Attaché,' she wrote to her father. 'I think he should be very good . . . The couple have a big reputation here, both rather eccentric and intellectual; he has written poetry and books on architecture and was also a film critic on the *Standard*. He should be the sort of whimsical person the Irish will like and he likes them. I think he's a good choice.'[20] Years later JB admitted to Penelope Aitken that when she had walked into the room that day, he had thought her so beautiful that it had made him go weak at the knees and he had to go and lie down when she left.

JB's heart also fluttered when he met Joan Hunter Dunn, the martinet who ran the canteen at the Ministry of Information. Her name fascinated him and he remarked to Osbert Lancaster that she must be a doctor's daughter and live near Aldershot. He was right on both counts and his subsequent poem, 'A Subaltern's Love-song', which begins

> Miss J. Hunter Dunn, Miss J. Hunter Dunn,
> Furnish'd and burnish'd by Aldershot sun,

was published by Cyril Connolly in *Horizon* in February 1941.

1. Stuart Piggott, CLG interview (1992).
2. JB's papers.
3. PB's papers, Beinecke Library, Yale University.
4. Ron Liddiard, CLG interview (1992).
5. Ron Liddiard's papers.
6. JB's papers, University of Victoria, British Columbia.
7. JB's papers.
8. Richard Ingrams, *Piper's Places: John Piper in England and Wales* (Hogarth Press, 1983).
9. Myfanwy Piper, CLG interview (1992).
10. Betty Packford, CLG interview (1993).
11. JB's papers.
12. JB's papers.
13. JB's papers.
14. Gerard Irvine, CLG interview (1992).
15. JB's papers.
16. JB's papers.
17. JB, 'N. J. Comper', *Architectural Review* (1939).
18. JB's papers.
19. JB's papers.
20. Lady Aitken's papers.

To Paul Nash   Garrards Farm
                                                  Uffington
Eve of Epiphany 1938   Berkshire

Dear Paul,
I am reading William Allingham's wonderful diary with its verbatim
conversations full of life and jokes, with Rossetti, Leigh Hunt, Morris,
Ned Jones, Carlyle, Tennyson, Browning and every great Victorian
literary and artistic figure. It is every bit as entertaining as Boswell.
Published by Macmillan 1907. London Library has a copy for certain.
I write because there's a frequent reference to 3 Eldon Road Hamp-
stead, where Allingham and his wife Helen (Old Water Colour Society)
lodged or lived. Is the numbering still the same? If so, yours is the
house: P. 352. May 1 1887, 3 Eldon Road, Hampstead. The Russell
Scotts call. With Clara and H to Kate Greenaway's new house,
Frognal: pleasant large studio. . . . etc. etc.
    In that year there are several conversations recorded notably with Dr
Martineau (82) about Gladstone. In 1889 W.A. moved to Eldon House
and in that year he died. He spent most of his time in Surrey round
those years and Eldon Road seems only to have been his London house.
    Thought you would like to know this. Allingham wrote:

> Up the airy mountain
> Down the rushy glen.

He was an Irishman by birth. From 3 Eldon Road he went to Mrs Alma
Tadema's new house, Grove End Road. . . . follows a description of it.
Penelope and parents lived there till three years ago. Coincidence.
    Love to Margaret [Nash]. Written to [Frederick] Muller.
    Yours, John B
    PS From further reading I think Clara Martineau lived at 3 Eldon
Road and the Allinghams used to stay with her. She was a daughter
or niece of James Martineau and his sister Harriet Martineau (see
D.N.B.)

P.N., the painter, was an old friend who had written the *Shell Guide to Dorset* (1935) for
JB.
    As children, my brother and I learnt lots of nonsense rhymes composed by JB, such
as:
        Up the airy centipede, down the rushy Platt [a path in Wantage] .
        I've got to go to Swindon to buy myself a hat.

To Cyril Connolly   Garrards Farm
                                                               Uffington
28 January 1938   Berkshire

My dear Cyril,
I have just finished reading your 'YEAR NINE' in the *New Statesman and
Nation*. I am always writing to you to say 'this is the best you have done'.
I must say it again. I never realised what powers worthy of Swift you
had. I always thought you were the wittiest of writers we had. But I
didn't know it was in you to make a picture of such ghastly horror as
'YEAR NINE'. It has something of Yahoos about it. My goodness Cyril,
you are a clever old thing. The *New Statesman and Nation* has got a bit
[illegible] lately, but 'This England' should be edited by someone who
sees a joke and can make one. At present it rams points home in a
clumsy manner which are much better expressed directly in other parts
of the paper.
    Once again, old boy, congratters and love from us both to you and
Jean, John B

> C.C., the writer, often stayed at Garrards Farm. JB had been about to cancel his
> subscription to the *New Statesman and Nation* but C.E.M. Joad's piece on 'Faith' and this
> one of C.C.'s, induced him to change his mind.
>   'Year Nine' was a futuristic dystopian fantasy on State Art.

To Myfanwy Piper   Garrards Farm
                                                               Uffington
28 January 1938   Berkshire

My darling Prefect,
Thank you very much for the return of the book and for your lovely
postcard. I couldn't get any suitable opera tops illustrations. So I have
made the Oxford poem more sophisticated, less spontaneous, sexy in a
sexless way. The quotations were, most of them, from the *Cherwell*.
Your postcard arrived from Stroud on Wednesday. Very nice. But
what do you mean about Beddy's devotion [illegible]. I think the
thimble mentioned in your letter is an inkwell.
    Goronwy Rees of the *Spectator* told me that a *lot* of people think you
beautiful. I like to think that you were at St Hilda's and had a senior girl
keen on you who got a second in Mods and a third in Theology, like the
girl in the verses.

I am so glad you like the verses. It is most odd how you have undone an unpublishable gush of verse in me.

When I was at Stroud – at Stinchcombe with Evelyn Waugh – I looked across the Severn Valley to Wales.

I can't be grateful enough to old Karl Marx [J. M. Richards] for introducing me to John Piper, the best photographer and topographer I have ever met, nor can I thank J.E.C.P. [J. Piper] enough for bringing you into my life.

Pengellow [PB] and you must meet.

What sort of ribbon was that with which you did up the book? I am keeping it in anticipation. Oh what a lovely note on your opera tops postcard. What lovely language!

Ever your adoring fag, JB

> JB had sent his poem, 'Myfanwy at Oxford', to the Pipers the week before, afraid that it was going too far. This poem and 'Myfanwy' appeared in *Old Lights for New Chancels* (1940). 'Myfanwy at Oxford', also entitled 'Myfanwy' at that time, was published, with slight variations, in *The Lincoln Imp* (Vol. 9, No. 3), Trinity Term 1938.
> An opera top is a form of underwear, like a camisole, worn under evening dress.

To Clive Bell   Garrards Farm
                                                       Uffington
22 February 1938   Berkshire

Dear Clive,

I never can thank you adequately for those lovely meals you give me and that excellent company. I'm not sure that I didn't enjoy today's best of all – but I held forth and showed off far too much under the influence of drink.

I now repent of my behaviour. But here is a proof of one of my boasts. Two copies of Tom Moore's copies of *Old Moore*. As I have four, I can spare two. One is for you and in less than two years it will go the way of all printed pamphlets! It deserves to. The other, I wish you would give to Virginia Woolf – I don't know her address. The only proof I have that it is *the* Thos Moore's signature is that I bought all four from a shop in Stoke Newington kept by some people who said they were relations of Tom Moore and had some of his letters which they would not sell. The shop was round the corner beyond St Paul's church, Balls Pond Road. It has since disappeared. Besides, who would bother to forge such an oddity?

Question: Who wrote this?

> I'll not leave thee, thou lone one!
> To pine on the stem;
> Since the lonely are sleeping
> Go, sleep thou with them.
> Thus kindly I scatter
> Thy leaves o'er the bed,
> Where thy mates of the garden
> Lie scentless and dead.

Answer: T. Moore. *Irish Melodies*. 'The Last of Rose of Summer'.

Again thank you very very much for such a good and happy luncheon. Do come over again with the Colonel. Or come and stay in the spring. God knows what you and V.W. will do with these Almanacks.

Yours, John Betjeman

PS Penelope sends her love.

> C.B., the prolific art critic and historian and a member of the Bloomsbury set, used to ask JB to lunch on a regular basis. My brother and I were often taken as children to his Victorian house at Seend in Wiltshire.

To Charles D. Abbott   Garrards Farm
                                                          Uffington
10 March 1938   Berkshire

Dear Mr Abbott,

I am indeed flattered to be counted by you a poet of significance. I don't think anyone else thinks I am – unless it be Ellis Waterhouse, so give him my love. Weren't you something to do with New College?

I enclose for you here the only couple of rough drafts of poems I have written that I can find. I generally write on the backs of envelopes and flyleaves of cheap books and gather the material together – generally all in one day. Then I type the thing out and look at it the next morning, think it's very bad and forget about it, and it gets lost. This happens to much that I write in verse.

If I do not commit what I have written to the typewriter pretty well at once, I forget what I have written, as I cannot read my own writing – nor will God be able to.

The two drafts I enclose – one on Exeter which I rather like and one on Slough which I think is crude and poor – are, as far as I recollect, original drafts. I don't punctuate much, you will see. I leave that to the publishers.

I am to be found at Shell Mex-House (Temple Bar 1234) on Mondays, Tuesdays and Wednesdays each week from eleven to four-thirty, if you would care to see me.

With apologies for my delay in replying.

Yours sincerely, John Betjeman

C.D.A., US librarian (and Rhodes Scholar at Oxford in the 1920s), was founder and director of the Modern Poetry Collection at the Lockwood Memorial Library, University of Buffalo, NY. His book, *Poets at Work* (1948), mentions JB and Eliot.

To John Hayward   Garrards Farm
                                                    Uffington
25 March 1938   Berkshire

Dear John Hayward,

I meant to write to you yesterday to thank you for that delightful dinner party. I have seldom known Soame Jenyns in better form and your story of the ottoman is the best laugh I have had since the days of *Young England*. I hope the great poet [T. S. Eliot] was as happy as I was. Do you ever read the *Happy Mag* (sevenpence)? There is a very curious joke on the first page of *Hors d'oeuvres* this month on the right hand column bottom. If only I hadn't sent it on to someone else, I would have enclosed it. It is a most stimulating magazine in every way.

> So now that the skies are as blue as your eyes
>   And April is waving 'Cheerio'
> Oh, won't you decide to become a spring bride?
>   Oh, darling, please say it's a go.

And what goes for the poetry, goes for the ten complete stories every month. It is one of the only magazines which Percy Progress would read from cover to cover. The Editor is a Savage Club beer drinker who knows Jack Squire. The artists have wonderful signatures all over the foregrounds of their drawings:

What wonderful things to horrify us, there are.

I was reading a review in the *Edinburgh Review* of Abraham Hayward's editions of the Thrale-Piozzi letters the other day or his life of Mrs Thrale-Piozzi – I forget which. It said some nice things.

Once again, dear fellow, many thanks for such a delightful evening and for such charming company. The great poet is really one of the pleasantest people I have met and it is a treat to see him among his friends.

Yours gratefully, John Betjeman

> J.H. was a well-known literary critic. He was a great friend of T. S. Eliot and later edited his prose. J.H. was crippled with muscular dystrophy from the age of ten, and was cared for by Eliot for many years.
>   'Percy Progress CBE' was a fictitious creation of JB's who was eventually crystallized in a series of stories, the first of which appeared in *Lilliput* in 1944.

To Jack Beddington   Garrards Farm
                                                      Uffington
22 April 1938   Berkshire

My dear Beddi,

Thank you very much for your two rich postcards. I am sending you in exchange a photograph reproduction made by that old stinker Maurice [Bowra], of a poem by Maurice Bowra about Yellow and me. 'Dr Hinton' [the Revd F. P. Harton] is the neighbouring Anglo-Cat vicar [and] our friend, and the Pakenhams are also friends – Frank Pakenham is Longford's brother, very rich and married to Elizabeth Harman (late of Harley St). They are both Socialists and live in a horrible villa down the Iffley Road and eat Co-op food. This will explain any difficulties in the otherwise lucid Tennysonian idyll. It is a bit rude, so don't leave it about. It is a present for you and a breath of the Old Country.

[William] Mitchell says that Spendthrift [Beddington's secretary] is not so careful about her clothes since you have gone. And Spendthrift tells me that the Soul has left the Seventh Floor. How true! My darling Miss Turner has, I am happy to say, reverted to Roedean and she wears, at times, a thrilling, rather greasy, tweed coat and skirt. Sometimes she takes down my letters. Miss Codling ought to wear khaki shorts. Enough of sex. I am told there is none in Cape Colony. We miss old Pinder a great deal from our room, but happily the telephone people still think he is with us, so we cannot even forget him.

Paul Nash is staying with us. He is in much better health. He has to have seven pillows at night. John Piper and my Myfanwy came over yesterday. She is going to have a child in November. Ours is very well and noiseless. Not so the aeroplanes which are worse than ever. Pengellow has hay fever again. Stephen Spender is very fond of you indeed. All sorts of people tell me how nice you are. Isn't that nice?

The guides progress well. Those clever Batsfords forgot to order the maps. They tried to blame me. Fortunately I produced the letter I wrote last November telling them to order them. The crook printers are having a fine time making mistakes on purpose. I went down to Woking with Mr St-George Fisher one of the public school directors. On the way down we noticed in Esher a builder's shop with the name Christopher Wren over it. Further on was a new house among the pines bang on the main road and alongside it a huge board like this:

I have written a poem about Cheltenham.

Sir Henry Newbolt has died. His death will be felt in S.A. where the birds do not sing, the flowers have no smell, and the women have no virginity (*old Saw*). I look forward more than I can say to your return. Wilson wanted me to get a job for his daughter. I put her on to a Folk Dance Society as she was described by him as 'literary and musical and wanting to do cataloguing of some sort'. I also put her on to the Georgian Group. Nothing happened.

I have been sent a most interesting Social Credit paper called 'Prosperity', which says that D'Arcy was tricked out of his rights to the Persian Oil Fields by an RC priest who was a British Intelligence Officer and the Anglo-Persian Oil Co. (1909) was the result. It also says that all wars are the result of the fight between the Anglo-Americans and ourselves. How wonderful the world is. How nice too, to think that you will be able to tell me that Sir Herbert Baker is a good architect after all. Come back soon. Love to Mrs Beddioleman, if she is out there now. Yellow and Paul send their love. John B

J. Beddington had gone on holiday to South Africa.

To Walter de la Mare   Garrards Farm
                                                Uffington
1 May 1938 S[t] P[hilip] and S[t] J[ames]   Berkshire

Dear Mr de la Mare,
Forgive a letter from a stranger. I dare say you have received a letter
from Mr J. B. Jones and a typescript about the proposed RICHARD
JEFFERIES – ALFRED WILLIAMS memorial. We are both announced as
giving it support.

Can you or Mr Henry Williamson write a letter to *The Times* about it?
Mr H. W.'s address I do not know, but he is, I am told, likely to do
something. You may know him and be able to find out.

The point of writing to *The Times* is this. The Memorial is a pretty
daft idea – bronze plaques on a screen – and they would do much better
to preserve what is left of the lovely country round Swindon. But the
importance of it is this, it is the first time that Swindon, a strong,
self-satisfied and hideous town which is spreading all over the west
country in this neighbourhood, has recognised officially the existence
of Art or Literature. It should therefore be encouraged.

I so liked your notice of Sir Harry Newbolt in *The Times*. He wasn't
half so bad a poet as Bloomsbury would have us think. And what a
pleasant, cultivated man.

Yours sincerely, John Betjeman

> W. de la M., the poet, having just played an active part in erecting a sarsen stone to the
> memory of the poet Edward Thomas on the 'Shoulder of Mutton' Hill in Hampshire,
> wrote (4 May 1938), 'I am afraid I cannot take any active part in the project. I am not
> very familiar with the work of Alfred Williams. . . .'
> Richard Jefferies (1848–87), Swindon's famous son, wrote many books on nature and
> the countryside.
> Alfred Williams (1877–1930), whose poetry first appeared in the *Swindon Advertiser*
> and the *Wiltshire and Gloucestershire Standard*, was the author of numerous books about
> Wiltshire, including *Life in a Railway Factory* (1915).
> Henry Williamson was the author of *Tarka the Otter* and was a Richard Jefferies
> enthusiast.

To T. S. Eliot   Shell-Mex House
                                               Victoria Embankment
1 July 1938   London WC2

Dear and great poet,
This is to thank you for your speech which was an unqualified success.

The more I read your poetry the more I got a conscience about having let a sensitive person into such a predicament. But my eye! how well you acquitted yourself. The Directors were pleased, the audience was happy and still and Field Marshal Sir Philip Chetwode said to me, 'Who was that young man who made the speech?' Nothing I can ever do will repay you for your kindness.

Anyhow the article on the planning of London will be ready in time PROVIDED YOU CAN GET THEM TO LET YOU HAVE A COPY OF THE *BRESSEY REPORT* for me – either from HM Stationery Office or the LCC (Publications).

Sir Henry Newbolt, Sir William Watson, Lord Alfred Douglas, Edmund Blunden, Arthur Sharley Cripps, and Arthur Symons.

I found that I *had* asked John Hayward but my list of guests seemed to have been missed out. I have written to him.

Yours gratefully, John Betjeman

> T.S.E. opened an exhibition of original Shell advertising drawings at Shell-Mex House, after which there was a party.
>
>   JB had agreed to write an article for T.S.E. for the *Criterion* on the Bressey Report, commissioned from Sir Charles Bressey, highway engineer, and Sir Edwin Lutyens, architect, by the Ministry of Transport, to survey highway developments in the London area designed to keep pace with the expansion of road traffic. It was published in 1937.

To John Hayward

Shell-Mex House
Victoria Embankment
London WC2

4 July 1938

Dear Friend,
I am deeply indebted to you for your kind letter. The account of your meeting with the Woads is most interesting. Woad himself said at the party, 'If I were to meet any of these long-haired fellers in the street I'd be handin' them over to the police.' He left early and went home by UNDERGROUND but Mrs Woad stayed on as 'some people we know' started to come in after the 'bullay'. When told that the young feller that made the speech was Mr Eliot, the famous poet, Woad said, 'What's he written?' The only words his companion could remember were 'Oh the moon shines bright on Mrs Porter etc.'

Mr Jenkin was photographed between the Master and Lady Mary Pakenham.

I can't draw the Master.

I telephoned to Mr Jenkin as one of his directors the other day. This is a very good idea. You might do it. I chose McWhirter. A list of directors is given on the *Daily Mirror* writing paper.

I would love to have luncheon at Bina Gardens. No trouble from here. I only feared to trespass too often on your hospitality.

Yours, dear sir, William Lisle Bowles

Mr Jenkin, whom JB and J.H. enjoyed mobbing up, worked for the *Daily Mirror*.

To T. S. Eliot   Pakenham Hall
                                                     Castlepollard
21 July 1938   Co. Westmeath

Dear and great poet,
I got your letter forwarded to here today. I also got a letter on Tuesday the day I was leaving for Oireland from Brother George Every. I would have loved to undertake the subject. But I had to send a telegram refusing, to the Brother and giving the name and address of Frederick Etchells as an alternative BECAUSE:

1) My berth and passage was booked to Oireland.
2) My hosts here were expecting me and coming from Dublin on purpose to be here when I arrived.
3) I was taking with me a friend from Bristol whose annual holiday it also is, who had not met our hosts before. He was coming as a guest introduced by me.

So, you see, too many people would have been inconvenienced. If it had been only me, I could easily have held back my visit until next week. As it is, I feel a fearful cad to have let down you and your friend in a crisis, when you so kindly helped me out with Shell. I am writing today to your friend a further explanation.

What can I do in return for my delinquency? Finish the Bressey Report article in time for August 1st. That I will do. I have brought it with me and other necessary books.

The subject is most interesting.

In the silence here – a silence so deep one hardly dares speak in it and where there is no sound over the hills except at evening where you can hear the turf carts rumbling over the bog two miles away – I will be able to get it all in the right perspective. London seems like some mad dream in all this green, wet civilisation.

> In the city dusty
> Is the old lock rusty
> That opens rasping
> On the place of graves

Do you know Oireland? It is what England was like in the time of Rowlandson with Roman Catholicism thrown in. I can't think why we don't live here. If I had any competence of my own I would.

There aren't any aeroplanes.

The roads are too small for many motors.

The Church of Ireland is 1835 Gothic and 1835 Protestant.

The only disadvantage is the thought of men like Johnny Morton (Beachcomber) waking up Ireland and the Celtic Twilight and getting to know Yeats.

Once again I renew my apologies and my promise to get the Bressey Report done. As I look out of the window I see miles of beech trees winding down the avenue, small hills and fields, and the silver sky that hangs over Oireland when it means that the weather is going to be good. I am so happy that my conscience jabs at me for not having gone to Swanwick as I should have done.

I really was honoured to be asked to talk among such distinguished people – broad church though the whole thing seemed to be. Canon C. Raven, John Strachey, Joad. But it would have been most interesting. I will willingly go next year if they ask me.

Love to South Kensington and John Hayward and the unhappy Mr Jenkin. Yours in the name of Bishop Mount, John Betjeman

JB was forgiven and met his deadline for the article on the Bressey Report.

'Beachcomber' was J. B. Morton, the humorous and influential columnist on the *Daily Express*.

To Gerard Irvine

30 September 1938

Garrards Farm
Uffington
Berkshire

Dear Mr Irvine,

I would prefer a Wednesday in December if you can fix it and I *would* like to stay the night, as I shan't be able to get back here on the same evening.

[J.P.] Gandy-Deering was a genius and I love Wilkins' work – if it is Wilkins – at Haileybury, Downing and King's.

I think I am Catholic in a low way. Red velvet and a couple of candles for illumination. Prayer book version of the Mass. In fact Georgian 'High' Church. Frequent mass, celebrated in a long surplice and black scarf at a red velvet covered communion table. Clear glass. Box pews. There was once a man at St Mary-le-Bow, who thought like that.

I like England's Glory for the jokes, yes. Wasn't it frightful when they gave up the jokes and had reviews of the Cabot Tower, Drake's Statue etc!? I wrote and complained. They said it was only an experiment and now I'm glad they've gone back to the jokes again.

Yours, John Betjeman

> G.I., a prefect at Haileybury College, unknown to JB and at the instigation of Paul Miller whom he had taught at Heddon Court, had asked him to talk at his school.
> William Wilkins, the Greek revivalist architect, had done work at Downing and King's Colleges, Cambridge, as well as Haileybury.
> England's Glory are makers of matches who put jokes on their matchboxes.

To Bess Betjemann

3 October 1938

Shell-Mex House
Victoria Embankment
London WC2

Darling Bessie,

Thank you very much for your letter. I am sorry you're now saddled with a Rock Bungalow. Of course it is sad to think of poor Undertown no longer being ours and that we will no longer sit on that slate terrace and look across to Bray Hill. In fact I feel as though I had lost an important part of me. But I think, in view of the ruination of the place, there was nothing else to be done. I hope you made a proviso that the purchaser should build nothing south of the house. By so doing, he could block out any view from our remaining fields towards the sea and Bray Hill. I think three thousand, two hundred and fifty pounds was a pretty good price and I doubt if you would have got much more, even in the scare. If what you say is true about the widening of the lane and the cliff road – forty feet is not very wide for a road, by the way – then that will make things worse. We were protected in the past by being a dead end. I suppose I feel so unhappy now that it is gone, because of childhood memories and all the Cornish saints and tufts of grass and rocks and pools that I shall always remember. And in the winter the place was worth living in again.

But I really think I stand by my original idea of going to Ireland and buying a small property there. I can get a decent sized house and demesne for about twelve hundred pounds. I shall spend eight hundred on repairs. That is two thousand. I shall borrow the money on a reversion. Won't want to do it with P's money, because the Chetwodes would kick up a fuss, as they hate Ireland and the Irish. How I am going to afford to live in Ireland, I neither know nor care. All I do know is that away from aeroplanes and motor cars I at once expand. I have written all that I have written which was worth writing in Ireland, and I regard it as salvation. I think it possible that should Europe collapse, Ireland will become what it was in the seventh century, the last house of civilisation in the Dark Ages. P likes horses and the country and religion. She will get all three. Anyhow I intend to buy *now*, before people discover Ireland. Already prices are beginning to rise. Ten years ago, I would have got all I want for three hundred pounds, but I had not the money. Nor have I now, but I am in a position to borrow on a reversion, thanks to your admirable management of the estates.

Goodbye St Enodoc, goodbye Corkscrew and the Mablys and everyone. I am sorry to go, but England is no longer habitable – war or no war.

The Longfords have been looking out for places for me for the last six months and I have several prospective houses. I should like the Plym [PSGB] to be brought up in beautiful country, as I was. Cornwall – for all that it is now – was an ineffaceable memory. Ireland is like what Cornwall *was*.

I will tell P to write to you about taking SAN-DUNES (God, what a name!) for next year. The Plym is very well indeed and says ra ra ra da da da ta ta ta za za za and that's about all beyond filling his pants every half hour.

Why don't you build a small house for yourself, with the money from Undertown? Or get tight on it?

Thank God the 'crisis' is over for a bit, at least.
Much love from John

Ernie and Bess Betjemann had built Undertown in Trebetherick in the late twenties.
The architect was a golfing companion of Ernie's, Robert Atkinson.
    Edward Longford had written to JB (24 August 1938), 'We are ever so pleased you
want to settle here. It ought to be possible to provide quite a decent place for two
thousand pounds. . . . I should fancy Tipperary would suit you.'
    'Corkscrew' was JB's nickname for Elsie McCorkindale, who lived at Torquil and
whom we called 'Aunt Elsie'.
    The Mablys lived at Trenain Farm.

To Elizabeth Bowen   Garrards Farm
                                                           Uffington
29 October 1938   Berkshire

Dear Authoress,
That book of yours *The Death of the Heart* is a winner – an absolute
winner, a stunner, a topper. How did you think of it? I lay in bed with a
bad cold all yesterday and read it and clean forgot about my cold while
doing so. I had just finished *Pendennis*, an odd conjunction. But I
noticed that both you and Thackeray, have the same richness. A phrase
– eyes like 'urgent poached eggs'; the wonderful sense of class
distinctions – the little nudges – the complete transition of atmosphere –
are common to you both. Malihilt's letter with the PS. 'Should you
wish anything be sent, no doubt you would write. A picture postcard
would be sufficient.' All those little touches of supreme importance,
occur on every page. Your book seems to be full of excellences on each
page which spread over any average novel would ruin it to distraction.
You are most generous with your writing just as Thackeray is. I
suppose Eddie is Goronwy [Rees]. The bit I liked best was Waikik's. I
have loved that life myself in Cornwall and at Littlehampton, for
months at a stretch. Dear God and how I loved it. How well you did it.
Dickie that Fascist, I notice you said so once: Daphne I know well: the
Corona Café I have often been to.
    Your book goes to prove my contention that the Anglo-Irish are the
greatest race of western civilisation. Thank you so much for your book.
My favourite characters are the first Mrs Quayne, Daphne, Dickie, and
Major Brult (a young Major Connolly?)
    Yours sincerely, Eric E. J. Brult (John Betjeman)

E.B., the distinguished and prolific novelist and short story writer, who had already written *The House in Paris*, *Friends and Relations* and *The Hotel*, was born in County Cork.

To John Sparrow   Garrards Farm

[Undated – late October 1938]

My darling Pansbury
And Likewise Hanbury
As old Lord Wrenbury
    Used for to say
Tis I'm inditing
In my own hand*writing*
This handsome letter to
Your chambers gay.

As I opened *The Times* sheet
That fluttery rhyme sheet
That political crime sheet
    I chanced for to see
A letter signed Pansbury
And likewise Hanbury
On Czecho-Slovakia
    And ould Liberty.

Now God Bless Hanbury
Likewise Lord Wrenbury
May they go to Tenbury
    For to aid their gout
May He bless their experiments
In all sincerity
And send them to Parliament
With the People's shout.

May PARR's kind phantom
Chant Freedom's anthem
From Cork to Grantham
    And bless their souls
May 'God save Pansbury'
And 'Long live Wrenbury'
Be the constant prayer of
    The Ghost of BOWLES.

But the point of this letter which
I am inditing
Is about a matter which
    Concerns my wife
And, kind sir, capitulate
And likewise osculate
And likewise copulate
    For to end all strife.

You said you'd get for her
But haven't yet for her
A choice Edition of
    The Tours of Young
His tour of Ireland
Of the Bog and Mireland
Is in Thorpe's Catalogue
    For the merest song.

Yet I did hesitate
The book to commandate
And with the heavy weight
    Of it in the mail
Because Thorpe's catalogue
(The Guildford branch of them)
Is sure to come to you
    Without much fail.

I should have sent for it
Unless you'd meant for it
Thorpe's to offer what
    They do beseech
But I with selfishness
In which I'm well finished
Instead did buy from them
    A book by Leech.

Now lest this letter
Should get much flatter
With each verse I utter
    From my fountain pen
I will endeavour
Right now or never
To end palaver
    With the best of men.

For you dear Spansbury
And your friend Wrenbury

And all those Wykehamists
    Who come to call
When playing at football
Art oh so beautiful
And in the changing room
    Art is best of all.

Accept the parentage
Of my brave narration
And the explanation
    As a fearful cold
I am lying in bed with it
'Tis not in my head as yet
And in this torment
    Tis but two days old.

I'm imbibing lotions
And pills and potions
Which cause commotions
    In my lungs and bowels
I use all handkerchiefs
Of linen from Lancashire
And soon will be using of
    The bathroom towels.

As my health gets better
The thoughts I'd utter
I could not enter
With the written word
    On this virgin page
But were I Pope-Hennessy
Or Alfred Tennyson
'Twould be much easier
    For to engage.

Farewell sweet Pansbury
The Friend of Liberty
Likewise of Literature
    And the Unemployed
In shorts or flannel bags
Or on a channel boat
Or with the Jenner and you
    Are the masochist's joy.

J.S. was one of JB's absolute best friends and stayed at and visited Garrards Farm more frequently than anyone else. JB's early letters to him, except for this and the next one quoted, have not survived.

JB called J.S. either 'Hanbury', his second name, or 'Spansbury', a conflation of 'Hanbury' with 'Sparrow'.

J.S. had written to *The Times* (27 October 1938) pointing out that the leaders of the Third Reich did not want war, provided they got what they wanted, as in Czechoslovakia, by threat of war. He listed their methods: 'Control of the press, violent mob-oratory, secret police, mock trials, concentration camps and almost every form of physical and mental torture.'

Lord Wrenbury was a judge and member of Lincoln's Inn.

J.S. collected books about Dr Parr.

J.S. thought that Jenner referred to Richard Jennings.

To Sir Giles Gilbert Scott   Garrards Farm
                                            Uffington
16 December 1938   Berkshire

Dear Sir Giles,
I am intensely interested in the work of George Gilbert Scott Junior who was, Mr Comper tells me, your father. Having just finished his *Essay on English Church Architecture*, I am prepared to travel as far as my purse will allow in search of his buildings. The only ones I have seen are the ones known to be his: All Hallows Southwark: St Agnes Kennington: Milverton: RC Church, Norwich: Pembroke Chapel (Cambridge) East end. Can you give me any information of more of his work? I can find no full list of his buildings and he was clearly a great architect. I have been reviewing Basil F. L. Clarke's *Nineteenth-Century Church Builders* and came across this sentence 'Churches of a somewhat Bodleian type were built by other architects. George Gilbert Scott, Junior, built St Agnes Kennington. . . .' Should have thought it was just the other way about 'Churches of G. G. Scott Junior type were built by G. F. Bodley. . . .'

I have incidentally quite a collection of Scottiana, from a first edition of *The Force of Truth* (Thomas Scott) onwards, and I saw, on a visit to the Isle of Man, your exquisite RC Church and priest's house at Ramsey.

I am sorry to bother a busy man on this matter and would not have done so had I been able to find full information of your father's works: if you can help, you will greatly oblige.

Yours sincerely, John Betjeman

Sir G.G.S. (1882–1963), the architect of Liverpool Cathedral, was the grandson of Sir George Gilbert Scott (1811–78), who designed St Pancras Station, and the son of George Gilbert Scott Junior (1839–97).

'I was very interested to get your letter,' replied G.G.S. (19 December 1938). 'I always think that my father was a genius; the pity is that he did not do more work. He was certainly the best of the group who broke away from dead arch[itecture] and began to feel instead of think.'

St Agnes's, Kennington, was one of JB's favourite churches.

To John Bryson   Garrards Farm
                                                            Uffington
Epiphany 1939   Berkshire

> Ow Mister Broyson
> Yew are a noice one
> Oi 'aven't done with yew yet
> Ow you entoice one
> Yew can't put a proice on
> Yer saucy little hondergraduette
>   x   x

How the old jokes wear. I don't believe I ever sent to you this Oirish pohm Oi wrote. Here it is for you. Court place Squire. Fir god's sake make some effort to see

Your old chum, Sean O'Follain

J. Bryson and Nevill Coghill were 'real dons' wrote JB (in *W. H. Auden, A Tribute 1975*), 'who read Anglo Saxon, Finnish and probably Swedish and Faroese as easily as I read the gossip column of the *Cherwell*.'

Court Place was J. Bryson's house in Iffley.

Sean O'Faolain was the editor of *The Bell*.

To Dr Francis Carolus Eeles   Garrards Farm
                                                            Uffington
20 February 1939   Berkshire

Dear Dr Eeles,

I must ask your help in a matter which has given me sleepless nights.

Uffington Parish Church (St Mary's) of which I am People's Warden has recently had an oak partition screen of excellent plain early eighteenth-century design by F. Etchells put into the South transept chapel. The whole effect is excellent and the plans were specially commended by the Diocesan Advisory Board. Money for the improvements was collected in the village. Everyone is pleased. Mr Etchells offered to provide us with a design for a 'kneeler' for nothing. Kneelers seem to be necessary for rheumatic old women and men. *And here the trouble starts*: without consulting Mr Etchells, or the churchwardens or a village Women's Guild, which had collected money for a kneeler, two excellent spinsters [Miss Molly and Miss Edmée Butler] of the squiress order in a neighbouring hamlet whose chapel of ease is united with Uffington, have sent for some oak and are having a kneeler made of their own design. They are incorporating some perfectly hideous 1860 oak communion rails which were turned out of the church many years ago. They were, I think, early [G.E.] Street. Clumsy church furnisher's stuff. They are putting a step to these of oak and calling the horror a kneeler. It will, probably, look like this:

Awful cusped and flimsy 'supports' at 'A'. They say there is no need to get a faculty as the oak communion rails belong to the high altar of the church and are merely going back into the church. By removing the supports and substituting square upright stays something less offensive could be made. But these good ladies are very touchy, very autocratic, and very kind and will brook no interference. What is to be done? If only you can tell me that a faculty is necessary for putting in a kneeler, irrespective of what it is made, then we can make them show plans of what they intend to do. They seem to be under the impression that if you are a squiress and intend to pay for a church fitting, you can design it and give it and no one else is to have a say. If they would only employ Mr Etchells, whose work they will be slighting with their intended kneeler, or even another architect, that would be something.

Then I must point out to them tactfully that they must get a faculty and I have made enquiries. If you say a faculty is necessary, I will get the Vicar to write to the Diocesan Advisory Board to ask whether a faculty is necessary and they can reply. You might tell them the situation. You see the ladies are friends of ours and very nice. We only do not see eye to eye on aesthetic matters. I am sorry to bother you about village details, but ours is a magnificent church and we are doing all we can to repair the damage Street did to it in 1852.

The sooner I can get going, the better.

Yours sincerely, John Betjeman

Dr E. was secretary to the Council for the Care of Churches. The delicate situation was overcome and J.B. received the appropriate letter saying a faculty (permission from the Diocesan Advisory Board) was necessary.

To Roy Harrod   Garrards Farm
                                                   Uffington
25 March 1939   Berkshire
5th Sunday in Lent

My dear Roy,
At last, though hampered by 'flu, I have a moment to write an answer to
your long, neat and interesting letter. I very much like to think of you,
you dear old thing, giving a daily thought to the mysteries of mind and
body. No one is less of a philosopher than I am, and they still remain
mysteries and I would be the last person to attempt an intellectual
defence of Christianity as practised by Catholics. Father d'Arcy can do
that or C. S. Lewis.

But your letter, despite this, leaves me puzzled. 'What I feel about
theists is that on the whole in modern times they are bores, throw no
light on the situation, tell us nothing of interest' . . . 'The inspiration
has not been handed down to the modern world' . . . 'Revealed
religion, even if one could accept it, leaves most of the great problems
unsorted.' What are the great problems? For you, economic ones? That
someone is worse off than someone else? That

> After two thousand years of mass
> We've got as far as poison gas?

That people are tortured and unhappy mentally and physically? That
time and space are so inexplicable? That one new dimension leads to
another? You put your attitude clearest when you say that revealed
religion leaves most of the great problems *unsolved*. *Unsolved*. What is
the solution of any 'problem'? I suppose it is knowing how it is done,
with one's mind and being able to solve future problems of a like nature
for other people, if they cannot solve them themselves.

Now I quite agree with you that the church is imperfect, that many
problems can be solved and aren't solved because of human slackness
and weakness. For instance, there should be no slums, bullying should
be curbed, armaments should be abolished, hysterical people should be
psycho-analysed, prisons should be reformed. Those are some of the
thousands of problems which could be solved by the human mind. But
the problem behind it all, and the one I expect you are referring to is
'Why aren't these reforms made?' And that brings everything down to
the fundamental 'Why aren't we perfect?' and that goes down to 'What
is perfection?' and that goes back to theism and theories of good and

evil. And as soon as one talks of good and evil, one is bound to set up a criterion and then comes the time for one to choose a way of life.

I choose the Christian's way (and completely fail to live up to it) because I believe it true and because I believe – for possibly a split second in six months, but that's enough – that Christ is really the incarnate son of God and that Sacraments are a means of grace and that grace alone gives one the power to do what one ought to do. And once I have accepted that, the questions of atonement, the Trinity, Heaven and Hell become logical and correct. Of course my attitude to them is different from that of an Italian peasant, but that is because words can never explain mysteries, my *knowledge* of them is the same as that of the peasant. By knowledge I mean knowing with more than the intellect. You would not hold this possible. You believe that the intellect is our highest faculty and that mind and body are all we have. If you throw in spirit, then even a thing like positive, almost tangible evil becomes possible. Then one's spiritual life becomes the activist of one and we are racing in an arena of witnesses living, dead and unborn into the world.

I feel this will shock you, you dear Liberal intellectual old thing. And for every book you can produce which disproves the existence of the spirit, I can produce one which proves it. It boils down to the alternative, materialist or Christian. For intellectuals the materialist standpoint is the obvious one and the easiest. The second is harder, but I hold that it is the most satisfactory, especially when one comes up against injustice, birth and death. But there is no argument. The intellectual is too proud to surrender to this seemingly ridiculous story when viewed from outside. But there are comparatively few intellectuals. A course of Von Hügel will show you, though, that there is plenty of room for the intellect in Catholicism.

I fear this letter sounds arrogant, proselytising and smug. It's bound to do that, because it is written from one point of view, whereas your kindly letter was tolerant of everything. As I know that you are intolerant of unreality, avarice and indeed the Seven Deadly Sins (New Inn Hall Street), I know that you are an Agnostic Christian. So am I for most of the time. But I know that Christianity is not a negative force but may even do some service by immunising people against worse creeds, such as Fascism. I believe it's positive and can alone save the world, not from Fascism, or Nazism, but from evil. If I did not believe that I should live in the present and squeal at death all the time, instead of most of the time.

God is not mentioned in Eliot's new play *Family Reunion*. But do go and see it and regard the Eumenides as Christianity and then see the variety of planes we live in. It puts what I mean far more clearly than I can. Love to Billa, John B

> The economist R.H. had married Billa Cresswell in 1938.
> Father Martin d'Arcy, SJ, was one of the kind of Catholics Evelyn Waugh liked to think he was fond of. He wrote books under the name Martin d'Arcy. There was a famous verse about him that went:
>> Are you rich and nobly born
>> Is your soul with anguish torn
>> Come to me, I'll heal it all
>> Father d'Arcy, Campion Hall.

To Sir Hugh Walpole   Garrards Farm
                                                        Uffington
4 April 1939   Berkshire

Dear Sir Hugh,
Do not bother to answer this. I thought I would write to tell you that I have just re-read *Mr Perrin and Mr Traill* and thank you for writing it. Never have the horrors of common room life been so well portrayed. Many thanks. Oddly enough I nearly got drowned in Cornwall on a rock by the tide coming in when I was a small child. My companion on the rock was Betty Plumb (Perrin's daughter). She has since gone off the rails, they tell me.

   Yours sincerely, John Betjeman

To Sir Kenneth Clark   Garrards Farm
                                                        Uffington
14 April 1939   Berkshire

Dear Sir Kenneth,
How very nice of you to write to me in so kindly a manner when you are just as badly down the drain as I am. It looks as though this Ministry of Information is in for a bit of re-organisation after its series of blunders. It is understood that the Premier was not carrying his umbrella yesterday.

   Now something positive seems to be being done by Paul Nash (anxious to find a job for himself and with his usual business acumen) at 7 Beaumont Street, Oxford. He has somehow got the ear of Sir Ernest Swinton of All Souls who is in charge of military camouflage and has persuaded Sir E. to allow him (Paul) to compile a list of categories in which artists and writers may be employed and to produce a list of artists and appropriate categories into which each falls. He is also trying to do the same for us writers. He has founded a committee consisting of himself as chairman, a man called Leonard Huskisson, an artist, John Piper, self and P. Morton Shand who all happen to be in the neighbourhood of Oxford. He wants me to ask you to join or at any rate to lend your name and vet lists when we get them – and if we get them. Paul makes no mention of his committee – when dealing with Sir E. Swinton. I don't know if anything will come of it.

Meanwhile I have been to old G. M. Young and he and P. and John Piper have drafted this statement on behalf of writers. I hope we will be able to get something done. Would you come to help us? This statement is being given by personal friends to Lord Macmillan, John Hilton – but it should go further. If you could get some influential signatures and ourselves on to a committee if it is not too late – we may be able to save a few lives for after this war, if it ever ends.

Yours, John Betjeman

> K.C., whom JB had met at Oxford, was at that time evacuating art from the National Gallery (of which he was director) to North Wales. G. M. Young, the historian, was a member of the Standing Commission on Museums and Galleries.
>
> Paul Nash's series of lists, with which JB became heavily and inextricably involved, turned into a sort of employment agency for the artistic, called the 'Art Bureau in Oxford for War Service.'
>
> Lord Macmillan was a trustee of the British Museum.
>
> John Hilton was director of Home Publicity in the Ministry of Information.

To Mr Boswell   Garrards Farm
                                                   Uffington
18 May 1939   Berkshire

Dear Mr Boswell,
I enclose the Railway voucher which is cancelled in favour of the return one from Oxford.

I feel I am entitled to a few expenses incurred on these architectural tours. Can I claim for them? For instance, I have had to make explorations in Bristol, Plymouth and Exeter before doing my talks. I have had to visit the two latter places in order to fix up what we're going to say with local residents. I shall be having to do the same thing for Salisbury and will have to go to one small town for my last talk. Is there some sort of research fee? It takes time I might otherwise be spending in writing, travelling about to these places, visiting buildings and people and employing the usual bonhomie when I don't feel like it.

Yours sincerely, John Betjeman

> JB had an extensive and often hilarious correspondence with Ronald Boswell, the model BBC Talks booking manager, who was calm, courteous, firm and equable. He never wasted time or words and his memoranda were commendably brief. He was allergic to meetings. JB received a guinea extra for each research visit. 'Believe me I am not making a profit,' he wrote to Mr B. 'So sorry to hear you have lumbago, try therapeutics or Droitwich Spa.'

To Geoffrey Grigson [Ireland]

19 June 1939

Dear Fellow,

I am so distressed and embarrassed that I can hardly bring myself to write to you. Yet if I do not, I will not be able to continue the final week of this tour in Oireland with a clear conscience.

Five years ago I wrote a short story which was based on an experience in an hotel in Barnstaple. It was a very bad story, and rather pretentious. Then, about three years ago, when I was just thirty, a man called Michael Harrison wrote and asked me to send a MS story, if I would, to a book to be called *Under Thirty*. This I did and pointed out that the story was written when I was twenty-eight. As the story had been rejected for the *Cornhill* you can imagine how bad it was and I was glad to be able to get a few guineas for it. Now the tragedy of the thing is this, the story was about Commercial Travellers and as I could not think of any suitable names I chose all the names of modern poets I could think of, including yours. But the story opens up with your name and the character to whom it is ascribed, though he is not a villain, is argued about by the other commercial travellers who cannot remember what he is called. He turns out to be someone who has received money from the Commercial Travellers' Benevolent. All the characters are inoffensive except one called Spender and another whom I called Auden and then altered to Crossman because Auden is a rare name and I really bore no ill will when writing the story, to anyone. I merely wanted a sequence of names. Now I would have altered all the names if I had been sent a proof of the tale, but if I did receive a proof – and I have no recollection of it – it was at least two years ago. Witness my horror then when I received a copy of this book *Under Thirty*, the week before last while you were still in France. I could not get hold of you. There is your name in cold print and if I found my own name in such a position I would be furious. The only consolation is that no one will buy the book or see it and there will probably be a war and we will all be killed. Dear God, though, to think of the trouble and misgivings I have suffered. Writing this letter has been like making out one's first confession for [Father] Freddie Hood at Pusey House. I would like your absolution.

We return next Saturday (June 24th) to Uffington. We go to Mt Mullory today and on to various other houses. I am going to buy this house which is perched above the wide [River] Suir and looks over beech trees to mountains. It has bathrooms and lavatories, winding walks and dry walls, but not much architecture. A mere squire's house, in the best position I have yet found in Ireland.

John P and I have finished our guide to Salop and I am turning my attention to West Country churches. I must make certain I have got the counties right – Cornwall, Devon, Somerset, Dorset. Would it not be a good idea to include Bristol or shall I leave it out?

I went swimming with Myfanwy in the Thames at Henley and was able to see her do the crawl and to feel the strength of her arms in the water. A memorable experience. She is getting very sunburned. Penelope looks like a hazelnut on sticks.

We went to Morning Prayer here yesterday in an 1820 church with blue-washed walls and that bare wooden Holy Table which makes the Church of Ireland such a happy refuge from Romanism. I read the second lesson.

Lord Ashtown has some fishing up the river here. It was he who was committed for trial for curious behaviour with two boys on the loop line train between Amiens Street and the Broadstone. But he got off.

A postcard from you of absolution or anger sent to Garrards Farm, Uffington, Berkshire, will relieve the mind of yours ever,

John Betjeman

G.G. lived in Uffington in the late thirties and was a great friend of the Pipers. He forgave JB. 'Dear Butiboox,' wrote JB (6 July 1939), 'many thanks for your kind and undeserved absolution letter.'

Under Thirty (Rich and Cowan Ltd, 1939) contained JB's story 'Move with the Times' which began, 'Now 'oo was the old boy as used to be with Consolidated Dried Fruits before Lemon come on? Grogson was it?'

'No not Grogson – let me think . . .'

The house JB refers to that he might buy was Glenahiry Lodge in County Waterford, a secondary house of Lord Ashtown (the 4th Baron b. 1897) whose seat was Woodlawn in County Galway.

To Edward and Christine Longford   On the Midland Railway
                                          but as from Garrards Farm
                                          Uffington
31 July 1939   Berkshire

Dear Edward and Tine,

The journey was terrible: the crossing rough in the extreme, but I had managed to get some seasick remedy in Dublin which saved me from being sick, but my stomach is only right this morning and my head didn't cease to ache until yesterday (Sunday) evening.

You may guess how much I enjoyed myself at the Swanwick S[tudent] C[hristian] M[ovement] camp from the fact that here on this train back to London at an hour when no one else is awake, I am *pleased* to be going to Shell-Mex House. It was the ideal antidote to Ireland. Because even after Ireland, London seems pleasant, as a result of sandwiching the Swanwick in between the experiences.

I must give you some details, as our prophecies were nearly all right. After a cross country journey lasting from eight twenty-five till three p.m. and mostly sitting four a side in third class smokers with children's buckets and spades scraping my face, I arrived at Derby. A typical young man in a tiny battered car met me, with spectacles, long nose, khaki shorts and a dull, respectful manner. He was not able to find his way out of the town. The interesting thing about Swanwick, where 'The Hayes' (the Mansion converted into a conference place) is situated, is that although it is twelve miles from Derby, there are houses down every road, coal tips on every hill and mineral lines down every valley. We all wore labels, little round discs of various colours (because mine was pink people called me 'Sir') with our names written on. The young man who took me, had 'JACK BRIGGS Home Student, Newcastle University' or something like that written on his disc. When I got to the camp it had been arranged that I should sleep in a tent – round about forty in a tent. I set on the excuse of a rough crossing, and managed to get into 'the hostel' where I was given a cell with a window which wouldn't open.

The food was very, very plain and in the camp, one had bits of last meal's butter on our knife and some cabbage on the spoon for tinned apricots. Then all the spoons would be beaten on the table and the students would shout, 'We want a story from JIM DOWSER.' Up would stand old Jim and tell us a funny anecdote about the Archbishop of York or a verse from the *Bab Ballads*.

SOME OF THE 'DELEGATES'

Professor P. B. SINGHE
Travancore Technical College

NORMAN HINCHCLIFFE
Theological Student
London College of Divinity

Mr L'OMAHOOBA
MAMBOSA UNIVERSITY

JIM BOGSWORTH
Chaplain of
Sidney Sussex College
Cambridge.

Professor Robinson D.D.
University of S. Wales.

The Woman Doctor
Girton

Miss Ann Pantry

SOME MORE 'DELEGATES'

JANET
MACDONALD
Presbyterian Medical
Mission Jubbulpore

BROTHER PHIL REEVES
Waltham

Enquiry Officer

Miss Björng
Norway

One of the 500
Women Students

One of the 500
Men Students

'Art and Values in the Conservatory' were a complete failure. I was too doped to notice many of the questions. But I remember one, 'Will Mr Betjeman explain his theory systematically?' I could not remember what my theory had been. On the spur of the moment I had decided to judge architecture by the criterion of the Seven Deadly Sins. It seemed as good as anything else, though Lust was a bit difficult.

After the International Sing Song there was some humorous entertainment and a woman with a foghorn voice conducted singing of 'Green Grow the Rushes Oh' and I could not help noticing the blacks singing 'Three-three, the lilywhite boys, clothed all in green-oh'. At the beginning of meals in the hostel, all the women burst into singing 'Let us with a gladsome mind' and then sat down to corned beef and little bits of potato which had dropped into each glass.

What it was all about I never discovered. The girls fell in love with the Kelham students in their black habits. The services were very broad and inter-denominational. Presbyterians and Baptists and Central Churchmanship predominated. There were about six Anglos. [C.S.] Lewis I saw, who was most effusive, but I managed to avoid him. He dazzled pipe-smoking chaplains and embryo missioners with High Table jinks. Miss Eleanora Iredale, as Tine supposed, was from the Sorbonne and had written a treatise. She wanted me to join a group to discuss the relation of Christian[ity] with Public Life in Caxton Hall. Very nice.

I feel a little sick and my headache is coming on again. Many, many thanks for Ireland. It made Swanwick more awful than ever. Oh God to be back in Castlepollard. Give the Colleen Peter Powell's love from me. Thank you both again and again.

From yours in the S.C.M. (Uffington Branch), Jack Betjeman

E. and C.L. had been friends of JB's since the late twenties when he went to stay with them in Ireland.

T. S. Eliot had begged JB to lecture at the Student Christian Movement summer camp.

To T. S. Eliot   Garrards Farm
                                                            Uffington
3 August 1939   Berkshire

Dear Poet,
These poems enclosed, were written by a friend of mine C. J. Pennethorne Hughes of the BBC Bristol. He has written one or two

sketches and lyrics which come out in highbrow reviews. He is in charge of the talks dept of the West Regional. These poems enclosed he wrote over a period of years. I think some of them are rather good. He is spoiled by being painfully self-conscious and self-critical. But he does not seem to be like anyone else (except, in youth, the Sitwells) and I'd like to know if you think any are worth publishing. For instance I like 'Revival', 'Wrong Three Times', 'Conversation after a Virgin Kiss', 'For Dr Arnold', 'Euphrosyne at the Seaside', 'Provincial' (1) and (2), 'Sand Castle', 'Poem in Competition Style about Parties'. But knowing the man well, I cannot judge of the poetry. All I know is that many of them are very satisfactory to me. The man has a genius for writing for the wireless, composes superb ear-entertainments of words and satires and really Cole Porter lyrics, but English. Perhaps his heart lies more in that way.

Don't forget our Dulwich ramble. I have you down for a provisional Saturday and Sunday in September. Which is it?

Yours, JB

PS Oh God! The Student Christian Movement Camp.

> T.S.E. replied, 'I return herewith the poems of your friend Mr Pennethorne Hughes, which I much enjoyed reading. . . . I find the poems themselves very uneven. . . . possibly his diffidence gets in the way.' JB persisted with poems of his friend and colleague on the BBC and they were eventually published: *38 Poems by Pennethorne Hughes*, chosen and with an introduction by Geoffrey Grigson with recollections by John Betjeman (J. Baker, London, 1970).

To T. S. Eliot   Garrards Farm
                                                         Uffington
9 August 1939   Berkshire

Dear Poet,

How very kind of you to take all that trouble over C. J. Pennethorne Hughes. I feel exactly the same about him. There is obviously something there, but it is swamped in diffidence. He must be encouraged and I will encourage him. He is torn between writing for the air and writing for himself. He must separate the two functions and try each. I will forward your remarks.

I cannot give you any picture of the S.C.M. camp, situated as it was among those mineral lines, bus route, coal tips, terraced villas and trodden grey-grim fields. And the jokes and Mr C. S. Bloody Lewis, the tutor who sent me down from Oxford, hiking off to a Central Holy

Communion at seven in the morning and playing High Table small talk with pipe-smoking Central churchmen all with hearts of gold. I liked Bro George [Every] very much, but not even my liking for him will bring me to that awful place again. I dare say you have been there. I liked Mary Trevelyan immensely, despite 'Green Grow the Rushes-oh'.

MR MOSQUITO
LIMPOPO COLLEGE

MR DULEEP-AHMID
Travancore University

JACK BALFOUR-
STEWART
Chaplain St Catharine's
College, Cambridge.

NORMAN
HINCHCLIFFE
Homerton Bible College

JANET MACDONAL
Presbyterian
Mission to
Central
Asia.

But have I drawn these delegates for you already? My memory is failing. I look forward to September 16th. That is fine. We must remember Dulwich. I will be up on Mon, Tue and Wed each week. Today I have blasted A[ir] R[aid] P[recautions] stuff here, watching for aeroplanes in a field and telephoning if I see any.

    Yours, John Betjeman

> T.S.E. had written (3 August 1939) that he imagined JB 'in khaki shorts sitting round the campfire, singing sea shanties under the direction of Mary Trevelyan'.

To Gerard Irvine

11 August 1939

Garrards Farm
Uffington
Berkshire

Dearest little chum,
I have been up all night on the blasted Observer Corps and I don't like my new fountain pen.

    Yes. Schoolmastering is so lovely in retrospect, that I wish I were a schoolmaster again. If I ever can get one, I will.

    This is very interesting about Ezra Pound. I wonder what they have printed in USA. Beastly swizz, beefy good, wizard, swop or swap, swot or swat, quis? Ego. Ego non. I.d.t. Iced ink. French architect. Middle and leg. Square leg. Slips. Corner point. Lobs. Bowl over arm, man. Chuck it in. Bags I. Favis. Oh Irrrrrrrrvine. Swot-pot. Mug it up. Force. Quaker Oats. Treacle.

I am getting morbid.

Write to me a little now and then.

I can't write back adequately. My heart is too full or too constipated or too palpitating or too tired.

There have been Protestant rows here at P[arochial] C[hurch] C[ouncil] meetings. Does your mother agree with us that PCCs should be abolished? I want to start a campaign against them and at any rate in country villages. All the wrong people get on and use them as a doctrinal debating ground.

Keep your faith, despite Oxford. Write again.

Love to your pupil

Love to your family

Love to you

Love from Cecil Sharpe and Cecil Rhodes

> G.I. had reported with some pride that Ezra Pound was said to have expressed admiration for a poem of his which had recently appeared in print.

To Michael Rosse   Pakenham Hall
                                      Castlepollard
10 September 1939   Co. Westmeath

BY A LOCAL POET (MS REJECTED BY THE OFFALY CHRONICLE)

Those castellations
Like Constellations
And wide plantations
        Mid crags and moss
Do guard Birr Castle
A fine example
To all and sundry
        Like the Earl of Rosse

'Tis he abides there
Likewise he hides there
And entertains there
        At his own expense
He's built an arbour
With his own labour
Of beech and maple
        For a defence

The green arbutus
And greener yew there
In plann'd confusion
        Do sweetly grow
And there the dahlia
Like royal regalia
With never a failure
        For ever blows

'Tis there the telescope
Just like a periscope
Or Grecian Penelope
        So loyal and grand
Waits twixt its arches
For all researches
Of astral bodies
        The Earl's command

Were I the Keeper
Or e'er the creeper
About each window
        And antique boss
I would embrace them
And interlace them
Those ancient buildings
        For the Earl of Rosse

TUNE 'THE GROVES OF BLARNEY'

10 September 1939

Dear Michael,
I hope you like the foregoing poem – a tribute for the rest of Birr and I
ought to have put in a verse about croquet but rhymes, for it, even in
such lax poetry as this, are hard to find.

We returned to a somewhat electric atmosphere here after seeing the
Municipal Gallery at Dublin. It contains the world's worst Lavery.
Love to Patrick and Roy [Sambourne] and very many thanks for a grand
time. How I like Watson and his footman and what an intelligent
chauffeur – and what very rare trees. If you are in England please come
and see us and stay – Uffington, Berkshire – Uffington 46.

John B

To Oliver Stonor   Garrards Farm
                                                       Uffington
14 September 1939   Berkshire

My dear Morchard,

Your wise and comforting letter came in the knick of time. Or is it nick?
I never got the house in Ireland. My wife opposed and money became
awkward – at least the borrowing of it for the purpose.

I was seriously contemplating joining the RAF because I AM TOO
OLD TO FLY and was going to the recruitment office on the day you
wrote in order to escape from myself. I went to the office, but only to
make enquiries not to join. I have you to thank.

If you can get anything for me when you get in as a surveyor I shall be
enchanted.

I have now started a scheme of getting a list of authors prepared with
suggested billets for them. G. M. Young and I have drafted a statement
to this effect:

> Writers are in the unfortunate position of having no single corporate
> body to protect their interests – or, in the present case, to direct their
> activities. Architects have the RIBA, Actors have Equity, Journalists
> their Union etc.
>
> It follows that many writers may therefore be allowed to engage in
> duties for which they are no better qualified – often worse – than
> others, at the same time their natural or cultivated talents are not
> employed.
>
> It is suggested that some body be formed to deal on their behalf
> with Government.
>
> In the first instance, a register *raisonné* should be made, with the
> help of the Authors' Society, indicating different qualifications.

Many writers may not be willing or competent to participate on positive propaganda. But they could all be used in many ways: drafting, précis-making, translating, censorship and clerical work.

If you agree with this, will you let me use your name? If you do not, amend it as you think fit, I am trying to get it before influential people. God knows if we succeed. But it seems a positive thing to be doing.
    Yours with gratitude, John Betjeman

> O.S.'s occasional pen-name, Morchard Bishop, had been taken from a village near to his home in Exeter.
>   JB wrote jokingly (13 July 1939):
>
> > Hail fair Devonia, Morchard Bishop's maid,
> > Salute the Duchy, fling the hand grenade
> > Lift up the ceilings, make an arch of blue
> > And choc-o-late to Queen Victoria true
> > Let the most fearsome and most dangerous hounds
> > Relieve themselves about the Darley grounds
> > Hail fair Devonia; let the South wind try
> > To make the Green Tree (ilex sombre) dry.

To Alan Pryce-Jones   Garrards Farm
                                                   Uffington
17 September 1939   Berkshire

My dearest Bog,
What a joke about your being a Captain, if it is really true. But how distasteful for you, having to go over to France. Abroad is so nasty. I would rather die in Wolverhampton than Aix-la-Chapelle. But then you prefer abroad, don't you? I hope your job is as nice as it sounds and I hope you will end up as a Colonel and come through quite safely. I would very much like to see you and will motor over to you, if you will give a date this week and a time. I will brave the dark. Alton Barnes and Priors I know. Both have box pews. Bishop's Cannings is good too. A lovely tract of country [the Pewsey Vale]. Hardenhuish [Wilts] (pronounced Harnish) is by the Younger Wood and Ricardo of *Rent Theory* is buried in the churchyard.
    Tuesday I cannot manage, and I have bloody dull Observer Corps duty on Wednesday and Saturday, but I could come over on Thursday, if you have a free moment.
    Private Spansbury Sparrow of the Ox and Bux L.I. will have to salute you when you meet.

We are all very depressed. Now don't go and get killed. Propeller sends its love. Hope Poppy and David are in nice military quarters at Camberley.

A.P.-J. subsequently became a Lieutenant-Colonel and J. H. A. Sparrow a Colonel in the Coldstream Guards.
    Alan and Poppy had a son called David, born in 1936, known as 'Baby Bog'.

To Kenneth Clark   Garrards Farm
                                                      Uffington
20 September 1939   Berkshire

Dear Sir Kenneth,
I can just imagine that interview with Paul [Nash]. Asthma, 'when I was an official artist', dossiers, classifications, schedules, 'when are you having lunch?', 'ah, well. . . . Oxford as a cultural centre. British artists. . . . Government Grant. . . . Board of Trade. . . . Sir Ernest Swinton . . . I . . . I . . . I . . .'

So in order to make things easier, I send you a list of young archaeologists made out by Stuart Piggott, himself one! A list of artists made out by John Piper: a list of writers made out by me, T.S.E. and Siegfried Sassoon – all are incomplete, but may help. They are of men only, and men of military age.

I have taken the liberty of putting you and me on.

Who the hell is Gordon Porteous? He is Randall Swingler to me – that is to say just a name from a back number of the *Criterion*.

I am getting Geoffrey Grigson to add to this authors' list and will also approach John Lehmann.

This may help to supplement the list you and Humbert Wolfe have made. We can get 'dossiers' of most of these people.

I think we should get E. J. Carter, Librarian of the RIBA to do the same for architects. I would help – but I don't think I know as much as he does on that subject. Many thanks for your nice letter. *Ora pro nobis.* [Pray for us.]

Yours, John Betjeman

John Lehmann was the editor of *New Writing* and a friend of JB's.
    Humbert Wolfe was a poet and literary critic.
    K.C. wrote of T. S. Eliot's list (29 September 1939), 'I am prepared to accept his opinion on poets and writing generally, but I am rather rattled to find out that he thinks H. Gordon Porteous is the best art critic in London.'

To Kenneth Clark   Garrards Farm
                                                Uffington
5 October 1939   Berkshire

Dear Sir Kenneth,
What a bloody fool I am. Here is the second half of the list of artists
which I omitted from the letter I sent to you. It is very nice of you to
take notice of it. John Piper is staying here and doing superb
water-colours of the neighbouring churches. I really think they are the
best modern water-colours I have ever seen. He can do Gothic Revival
or genuine Norman or the most complicated Geometric tracery with
equal facility, he gets all the texture of lichened stone and no niggliness
and lovely deep recessions. We are getting right round to Genuine
E[arly] G[othic] now. Today we are going to sketch in Mildenhall
Church near Marlborough – box pews, two three-deckers, red velvet,
clear glass, west gallery, whitewashed walls, hatchments – 1815 and
Mediaeval. The best church in Wilts. I send you a photograph of a bit of
it to keep you in touch with things, now you are in London.
    I agree that old Paul's dossiers are comical. What is the point of
making all those categories, unless you know what the jobs going are to
be? I want to get into the map section of the Air Force. I like the Air
Force, it is so horrible that no one has thought of going into it. I advise
you to consider it. We are both too old to fly. When I come up to
London, I will let you know more about it. Did I send to you the
archaeologists' list?
    Yours, John Betjeman

To Oliver Stonor   Garrards Farm
                                                Uffington
6 October 1939   Berkshire

My dear Morchard,
Congratulations on your letters my dear fellow – misprints or no
misprints. And congratulations on your job. Manchester is lovely. The
bleak City Art Gallery (a lovely thing by Sir Charles Barry) has the best
pre-Raphaelites in England. I hope it is open. The Cathedral is not bad.
I wrote a poem about Cheshire once which started:

> Infirmaries by Aston Webb
> On every hill surmount the pines
> From two miles off you still can see
> Their terracotta Dutch designs.

If you find a duration job for me, I will take it however humble.
   Yours, John Betjeman

To Ninian Comper
                                                 Garrards Farm
                                                 Uffington
12 October 1939
                                                 Berkshire

Dear Mr Comper,
What a treat to hear from you. I was going to write to you today, because I read several letters written by your father to the Bishop of St Andrews (or Aberdeen?) yesterday in a back number (1860, I think) of the *Union Magazine*. All about his using lights and a coloured stole. Very funny. Oddly enough, too, I was reading the letters of John Mason Neale and at night I still read part of his *Readings for the Aged*. What a wonderful man! As you say, those Victorians did believe.

    I have just come out of a strenuous three days' Ignatian private retreat in Oxford with the Cowley Fathers. It was good to see your lovely east end to their chapel. I like it white, as it is, and think it looks better than it would if it was coloured. Someone told me you designed the very charming church schools for Cowley SS Mary and John. Is this true? they certainly are very good and before I was told you did them I put them down to either you, Leonard Stokes, Temple Moore, or F. C. Eden.

    I would keenly like to see *The Cicestrian* with your paper and it should certainly be printed in *Theology*. I will send a copy, if you will let me have one, to my friend T. S. Eliot, the poet, who has much to do with that periodical.

    I am here in a silly thing called the Observer Corps, and hope to get into the RAF. But only if I can persuade myself it is right to fight at all. At present fighting in a war seems to me to be committing a new sin in defence of an old one. But I am not bothering. I feel that when my conscience is clear on the point and my mind made up, I shall know what to do and have no qualms about doing it. Unfortunately my income from Shell ceases (six hundred a year) in four months' time and I shall be hard put to it to make it up. No one makes money out of criticism to keep a wife and child and two maids and two evacuees! But let it all wait. There are many worse off than me – including you.

This is very bad news about Aberdeen. Heartbreaking, in fact. Far worse news, I think, than that you have a whacking great overdraft and work at a loss. In fact that is almost good news, for it shows how you love your work to the exclusion of everything else. And I do not think it matters that there is no one to carry on quite as you do. There never could be. A strongly individual architect, like you are, is bound to stand alone. No one carried on from Soane or Hawksmoor or Gibbs. But something evolved from each of these people in most unexpected ways. Your work is being more and more appreciated by the laity as [Dr] Eeles gets more and more in with the clergy and as pseudo-modernism and uncomprehending imitations of your own work flourish. What matters is not what other people will do in an imitation, but what you have done and are doing yourself. There is no doubt that you have transformed church architecture in England and you stand on your own as the only creative genius in that sphere – with F. C. Eden a little lower down the scale. That is something which is its own reward and a greater reward than is given to other people in your art because your work has all been to the Glory of God. I know, for myself, that you solved for me an architectural puzzle I could never understand. I would see an aeroplane or underground train and think 'lovely architecture' and I would see Greenwich Hospital and think the same thing. How can I like them both? Why is the new Regent Street bad? It wasn't until I saw your work and knew at once this was great architecture that I solved the puzzle. I saw then that it was not the question of the age we live in, but of the creative gift in an architect and the sincerity of the man. I saw as I sat in St Cyprian's, proportion, attention to detail, colour, texture and chiefly the purpose – the tabernacle as the centre of it all. This is as much of the present age as the aeroplane. It is not aping a past age, that is bad; or what pretends to be modern and is not; that is worse.

So you have brought many people to God by your buildings. I know how satisfying a Comper church is to worship in, how distracting a Cachemaille-Day. This news of your being financially down is therefore good news. No one who works sincerely for God as you do, need expect worldly advancement or even comfort of 'success'. Who am I to preach a sermon? No one. But I have just come out of retreat. In fact I regard it not as a chastisement but as a blessing to you that you have these setbacks. To me, as a spectator, they show how little the world thinks and how much God cares. And the world is waking up to

Catholicism. To be 'Church of England' now is not a mere form as it was in Edwardian days. People who go to church, go because they believe. I wonder how many hundreds have been instructed in Catholicism by your planning, delicacy of proportion, texture and colour? Many, I suspect – me for one. So it does not matter who succeeds you in doing the work of beautiful church building. God will look after that. Someone will come along. So long as you go on doing what only you in England can do, you will be doing God's will.

I say – this is really awful me preaching to my better, my senior, my superior in every way, but that, to think you are depressed. There is no need to be. There will always be work for you to do. Someone who is a missionary, as you are, for the Faith, is bound to be tried, in fact their path could not be easy. So it is all right really. And if you have no work at all, go on planning newer and newer churches and I will help to see to it that they can be built if I survive this war, and someone else will if I don't.

I hope you will forgive this outburst. It's meant to hearten you when you must be feeling very low.

Yours, John Betjeman

This is one of the only two surviving letters from JB to his hero N.C., the celebrated church architect. N.C. was in a state of despair on learning that his plans for the refurbishment of the Episcopal Cathedral in his native Aberdeen had been unexpectedly rejected. He had written to JB, worried about his overdraft and expressing his fears.

John Mason Neale, one of the leading post-tractarians, was godfather to N.C. He was the founder of an order of nuns, the Society of St Margaret at East Grinstead. He wrote, or translated from the Latin, many of the hymns we know.

The church schools for Cowley SS Mary and John are, in fact, by Leonard Stokes.

The Cicestrian was the diocesan magazine of the diocese of Chichester. Bishop Bell, a great friend of Eliot, edited it.

N.F. Cachemaille-Day built a number of unconventional churches, e.g. St Saviour Eltham in 1933, which was influenced by German expressionism.

To Cyril Connolly

19 October 1939

Garrards Farm
Uffington
Berkshire

Well, old man,
It was good to see how this spot of bother is affecting you. *Horizon*, eh? Some sort of highbrow journal eh? Well chaps, it's going to give Jerry what for. Teach him to take a slosh at the British Lion by giving him as good as he gives, gets, gives, gets – which is it?

My missus is a Red Cross Nanny brave little woman and I hope your missus is doing something equally daring.

We must all do our bit. *There's a war on, you know*. But if the best you can find to do is some highbrow paper with a communist-poet fellow, then take my advice and chuck it up and get a job in the Sussex Light. *There's a war on you know*. And tell that fellow Peter Watson to strip off his 'artistic' poses and get down to real work. Has he ever emptied latrines from the C/O into the GHO, I wonder, with the Quartermaster Sergeant bellowing at him every five minutes? Till he's done that, he is not a man. *There's a war on, you know*. Tell him that.

Of course I understand your kindness in asking me to write for your journal. I appreciate it. But we are fighting for LIBERTY to make the world fit to live in for Democracy, to keep our splendid system of Local Government going, to make the world safe for Slough to go on and to see that every John Citizen gets a square deal so that he can pay up his instalments into the Building Society without having to go without his Ovaltine. Am I justified, then, in taking up the pen when so many gallant lads like Lord David Cecil are doing their mightiest to take up the anti-aircraft gun? I enclose a poem, to hearten our lads 'somewhere in France'. Of course none of us wanted a scrap, but now it's here let's keep smilin' through. *There's a war on you know*. I shouldn't be surprised if that fellow [George] Schurhoff you mention isn't a German spy. Look out. WRITE SOON again. God bless you. Jolly, all this, isn't it?

JB

Yellow sends its love. We have two schoolmasters living in the house. I rather like them. They are left wing.

Peter Watson financed *Horizon*, the magazine Cyril Connolly had just founded.

The schoolmasters were evacuees from London.

Later JB wrote (27 October 1939), 'I don't like the title *Horizon* much, though I can't think of a better one myself. But *Horizon* rather smacks to me of Roger Boughton or of the Romilly Boys. I feel sure you will find somewhere around Red Lion Square, that a magazine called *Horizon* is already published by the Communist Nature Ramblers Club, printed at the [illegible] offices, Glasgow . . .'

To John Murray   Garrards Farm
                                                    Uffington
20 October 1939   Berkshire

My dear Jock,
I enclose my poems to-date. 'Sir John Piers' was merely fifty copies
privately printed for circulation among friends, three of these copies
went to Libraries. Two poems appeared in the *New Statesman and Nation*
('Pot Pourri from a Surrey Garden', 'In Westminster Abbey'), one in
The Listener ('Cheltenham'), one in *Yellow Jacket* – an undergraduate
ephemeral ('Holy Trinity Sloane Street'), one in the *Lincoln Imp* – the
magazine of Lincoln College, Oxford ('Myfanwy at Oxford'). The rest
have never been submitted for publication.

If you do publish them, I should like to write a short preface pointing
out that they are not satirical. I had enough encouragement from
reviews last time to do this and it might save me from being reviewed by
professional humorists. I could say some funny things about people's
reactions to my verse, backed by quotations. 'Sir John Piers' will need
the prose extract printing with it.

I have a feeling that 'The Heart of Thomas Hardy' is below standard,
also 'A Drunk Scottish Nationalist looks at Cleopatra's Needle' is pure
parody and might do better elsewhere. I hope you will like them and
not find them too indecent.

As to production, I should like to see a small, chaste octavo printed
very simply in exact imitation of William Pickering's books of the late
thirties or of the Aldine Poets. Binding dark blue cloth. Paper creamy
brown. White label on spine. A sort of pocket book. No illustrations
beyond a Pickering tailpiece at the end of the preface very wide margins
8 or 6 point modern face or Baskerville. But you may not want to
publish them.

Yours, JB

Suggested Title: *The Negligent Incumbent* or *Poems, Amatory and
Topographical*

William Pickering was a famous publisher active in the early nineteenth century. His
books were renowned for their clarity of print.
The Aldine Poets was an early nineteenth-century series of books, well-printed and
slightly deluxe, containing the most obscure poets as well as the well-known ones.

To John Murray   Garrards Farm
                                                          Uffington
From John Calvin, *John Betjeman*,   Berkshire
John Wesley, John Knox

2 November 1939

My dear Jock,
I am returning to you the proof and, though delighted with the news
that you will publish the poems, am not too keen on Plantin as the type.
Do you remember how they printed Robert Bridge's *New Poems*? The
type there seemed absolutely right for poetry. Plantin is too heavy and
looks like *The Shropshire Lad* to me.

In fact, on this proof, far the most suitable type is that which Butler
and Tanner use for their remarks on how much space they will take up
etc. If they would use that type, only a point or two larger, use a
perfectly enormous margin, I think the forty-eight pages could easily be
filled and don't forget I want to write a preface. I am sending to you a
copy of [H. F.] Lyte's Poems by this post. It seems to me the ideal way
of printing poetry. Could not that type for the text and arrangement of
the title page be copied. Send it to Butler and Tanner and ask them to
copy it as closely as possible, leaving rather broader margins top and
bottom, especially bottom, and I think we have a criterion for printing
poetry which will be something like the old one. No one prints poetry
right now that Bridges is dead. I hope I am not presumptuous in saying
all this, but *I hate* Plantin. I shall have another poem on Sunday
morning in Swindon in a day or two.

I think this binding of Lyte's poems is very pretty. I would like the
book bound in the serviceable school book manner and Rivington's
could give you some suggestions. The cover of early copies of *North and
Hillard* comes to my mind.

'Blackfriar's' is coming out in *Horizon*, old Cyril's projected paper,
and he and Stephen Spender want to publish a whole lot more of my
poems of which they have the MSS. I will tell them that they can
publish no more without your permission and will ask them to write to
you or see you. I have a cold. I hope you haven't.

Are you printing a posthumous volume of Newbolt? If so, where? I must
review it. His later poems are very good.
   Love, JB

Henry Francis Lyte (1793–1841), author of *Poems, Chiefly Religious* (published by Rivington's), was a hymn-writer, poet and priest.
    Rivington's, an old-fashioned firm, were in those times the leading religious publishers.

To Cyril Connolly   Garrards Farm
                                                         Uffington
8 November 1939   Berkshire

Dear Cyril,
Your letter from the Yeo arrived a day or two ago with the bit on the back of the envelope about your having got my Murray news. I hope you have had satisfactory dealings with J.G.M. [John Grey Murray] about my poems. I'm sorry to be such a bloody nuisance.
    I cannot tell from the proofs of 'Lambourne' yet, if you are printing it in the first number – but if I may give general advice tell the men to use Modern Face types or Baskerville and no SANS SERIF, no pseudo-modern, no Beton [Victorian typeface] (as in your letter heading), no playbill and all the contemporary fussiness. Your paper should look as much as possible like the *Quarterly Review*, the *Gospel Magazine*, or *Blackwood's*, if it is not to look dated in a few years. These periodicals alone, almost, maintain the English printing tradition.
    Just look at *Contemp[orary Review]*, *Poetry and Prose*, *London Mercury*, *Wheels* or any other of those things to see what I mean by datedness. The only good-looking modern periodical that has started in our time is *New Verse* and you do not want to copy its format, so back to *Blackwood's* old boy.
    I have told a man on the BBC at Bristol – G[eoffrey] G[rigson] knows him – Pennethorne Hughes to send along a rather good play he did for the BBC called *Search Light on Chester Cave*. It seemed v. good to me as an example of wireless writing. He writes poetry too and the best stuff he does is for music and may sound odd without it. His *White-tie Worker* was good.
    Yours with love, JB

    Now let us turn to literary men
    To start with I will give a list of ten
    Auden (that's eight) and [Frederick] Prokosch (that's two more)
    And Archibald MacLeish, that's twenty-four.

John Piper wrote to JB (18 November 1939), 'The *Horizon* office is impressive, and S. Spender, C. Connolly and P. Watson all very charming. Tony Witherby the printer told me he thought your "Lambourne" poem not only one of the best poems of modern times, but of *all* times. . . .'

To John Murray   Garrards Farm
                                                      Uffington
23 November 1939   Berkshire

Dear Jock,
Thank you very much for yours of November 20th.

Creamy was the word I meant, or at any rate off-white, perhaps a faintly bluish tinge like an old fashioned bankers draught, or a letter from a firm of country solicitors.

Oh no, do not keep to the *Westmeath Examiner* style for 'Sir John Piers'. Keep it like the rest of the book.

What title shall we give the book? *An Old Clergyman and other poems*? There is no poem called 'An Old Clergyman' which would make it interesting. Or *The Negligent Incumbent** or *Sir John Piers* or *Topographical and Amatory Verses*? or *Nave and Chancel**? or *The Baptistery*? *Stained Glass Windows*? or *Squint & Squinch*? *Decay*? *Damp Rot*? or *Death Watch Beetles*? or *The Cemetery Gates*? or *From Holloway to Mullingar*? or *Holloway to Multyfarnham**? or *Multyfarnham*? or *Upper Holloway**? *The Tortoise Store**? *Heating Apparatus*? *Oil and Gas*? or *New Lights for Old Chancels*? or *Old Lights for New Chancels***? or *By Southern Electric and Great Southern*? *The Parish Room***? I favour those marked with a star. Perhaps you can think of others. Second title should be *Topographical and Amatory Verses*.

You will, by now, have received the silhouette [by John Piper] and one more poem and the dedication.

I enclose the Preface and acknowledgements. Longer than I feared, the first. I trust not too long.

I hope you are happy in married life. My compliments and love to your wife, whom I have not yet seen.

Believe me, my dear Murray,
Yours affectionately, George Crabbe

Old Lights for New Chancels was the title finally chosen for the book.
J.M. married Diana Ramsden James on 23 November 1939.

To Myfanwy Piper   Garrards Farm
                                                     Uffington
23 November 1939   Berkshire

Dear Goldilocks,
At the analyst's yesterday I went *right back to the pram* and thought I
would like to be wheeled by you up Swain's Lane past the Cemetery
Chapel round by South Grove and down West Hill and round Merton
Lane, along the edge of the Heath and back to West Hill by Brookfield
Lane. Then I would like to be taken out and breastfed. Then I would
like to be led to school at Byron Haven by you and get into a scrape.
Now I had better stop.
    I enclose the Preface for my poems which I would like you and John
Pahper to see and let me know what you think. Cut and criticise
ruthlessly. The opening sentence is, so far as you are concerned, a lie.
    Love, darling, and longing for Tuesday, JB
    PS John Bryson has called with Clapham, Kendrick and Gardener.
Not in person. But has brought their books.
    Mr Pahper is acknowledged in Tom Kendrick's preface.

> M.P. thinks that JB never saw an analyst and that this must have been one of his jokes,
> but there is evidence to suggest that he did. My mother never stopped saying he had
> 'persecution mania'.

To Richard Buckle   Garrards Farm
                                                     Uffington
24 November 1939   Berkshire

My dear Private,
How very brave of you to go back to school again. I hope the boys are
nicer than they were at the Old School. Of course I remember you now.
It was in the tea car on the five fifteen, shall we ever see tea cars again?
No. Yes. I wish I had known Cyril Arapoff earlier.
    I don't see how I shall ever get to Warwick. The town is beautiful.
Particularly the Beauchamp Chapel in the church. Could sit in it for
hours.
    This letter enclosed was sent to me by Maurice Bowra. It's, I think,

from the Headmaster of Wellington (Somerset). Rather a rough school, I suspect. But rather fun, don't you think? I mean the school. I think I should have *enjoyed* myself there.

Leamington is very beautiful. I used to sit in the Jephson Gardens sometimes. The waters are delicious.

Keep safe and thank you very much for your letter.

Yours, John Betjeman

> R.B., the writer and eminent ballet critic, a fan of JB's, was at Marlborough.
> Cyril Arapoff was a photographer specializing in portraits of actors and ballet dancers.

To C. S. Lewis   Garrards Farm
                                                    Uffington
13 December 1939   Berkshire

Dear Mr Lewis,

Since I have just expunged from the proofs of a preface of a new book of poems of mine which Murray is publishing, a long and unprovoked attack upon you, I wonder whether you will forgive my going into some detail with you personally over the reasons for my attitude? I did not get an opportunity of speaking to you at that dreary Swanwick affair.

You were kind enough to say in a letter to me of about one and a half years ago that you had always regarded ours as a purely literary battle. I must say that it may have become that now, but it started on my side as a rather malicious personal battle. I think it only fair to explain why. When I was finally obliged to leave Magdalen, it was necessary for me to get a job to keep myself because my father had quite rightly washed his hands of me. In order to obtain a post in the inevitable prep-schoolmastering to which all unsuccessful undergraduates of my type are reduced, I needed written testimonials from the President of my college, the headmaster of my school and my tutor. I applied to you for a testimonial and you told me you could not say anything in my favour academically (at tutorials you frequently told me I had 'no literary style', and would only get a third and I certainly did little or no work for you as a consequence). So on this testimonial the only thing you said was that I was kindhearted and cheerful. It lost me three decentish jobs before I realised that I would be wiser not to show this testimonial in future so I got another and a good one from my only Magdalen friend, Revd J. M. Thompson!

Naturally I was inflamed against you and thought, with the impulsiveness of a young man, that you had done it out of malice from the easy security of an Oxford Senior Common Room. The tragedy of it was heightened by the fact that I have always had a great love for English Literature – and none for philology – and that it was my ambition to become a don and read English Literature to the accompaniment of lovely surroundings. I thought of you as reading philology in surroundings which you did not appreciate. I visualised that white unlived-in room of yours in New Buildings, with the tobacco jars and fixture cards from Philosophy clubs and the green loose covers on the furniture which always depressed me. And when I was working in various far more repulsive surroundings in suburban and industrial England, I often thought of those rooms and envied you a good deal.

It was not until I got on to the subject of your tutorials with Henry Yorke (who, as Henry Green, has written novels which are better than anything I shall ever do) that I found a fellow sufferer and managed to get the whole thing more in perspective.

In those early days I remember you condemning Uncle Tom Eliot to me, and I admired him greatly then, and I still do. In fact you were going to make a parody of his poetry and send it to the *Criterion* or some such paper. Now I see from *Rehabilitations* that you take him seriously. It is from signs such as this, that I feel your attitude to poetry, if not to me, will have changed a little, so that you will be willing to attend to my side of the 'literary' battle which has emerged from a personal antipathy.

It seems to me that we have two different approaches to poetry. Both, I hope, have a sense of the sound of words and of metre and stress in common. After that there is no common ground. Your approach is philosophical, or metaphysical or abstract or something I do not understand. Mine is visual. The difference of our views comes out clearly in your book on Spenser. Nowhere in that excellent book do you say anything appreciative or discerning of Spenser's amazing powers of topographical description, which are best appreciated when one has visited the neighbourhood of Clonmel, Waterford and Youghal. Of course, you may rightly reply that that had been done enough already. In that case I would cite a bit of your own poetry – a poem called 'The Planets' which opens with the line:

Lady Luna in light canoe.

I don't see how anyone who has looked at the moon can think of it as 'cruising monthly' in a light canoe. I can't even see that the excuse that this is an experiment only justifies such an opening for a poem given some prominence in your book. If we are going back to the days of my lack of style, what 'style' is this? if such a thing as 'style' exists. It seems to me as out of touch as your talk about Dragons with Tolkien in a Berkshire bar must have seemed to the Berkshire workman. I know something of Berkshire workmen by now! Probably to you, the opening of Tennyson's 'Princess' is just funny, while to me it is moving and good. Probably you prefer the 'Wreck of the Deutschland', which I cannot understand, to the 'Epithalamion' on p. 89 of the Hopkins book. But there is no object in continuing this speculation. You confessed yourself to me in your kind letter I referred to of one and a half years ago, as not quickened in architectural matters and it seems to bear out my point. For I don't see how anyone with visual sensibility can live in Magdalen and be unmoved by architecture, if their job is partly that of teaching an appreciation of English Literature. A mathematician would certainly be moved, how much more someone who reads English poetry?

I was a very usual type of undergraduate, caught up with the latest fashions in 'art', pretentious and superficial. But all that, I have since discovered, is quite right in this type. Indeed it should be encouraged, for it argues an awareness of what is going on and an incipient sensibility which can easily be crushed or misdirected for ever by an antipathetic tutor. As you said in your letter, 'I was a very young tutor'.

I would not like you to think I was blaming you for this lack of visual interest, which you would probably be the first to confirm. But if you still lack the sense, I expect you now know when other people have it. And here I am afraid you will think me very rude. When one of the Betjeman type comes to you now for tutorials, are you able to send him on to someone else? I should suggest Nichol Smith or Blunden or old John Bryson or Nevill [Coghill] as suitable tutors. Not a Mr Mac-Farlane, whom I remember with disgust as making easy game of Dr Johnson for an undergraduate audience. In my day there was no escape.

I feel I have been unpardonably rude in this letter. But the subject is one on which I still feel deeply and this all certainly reads like a heart to hearter from someone who has just joined the Oxford Group movement.

There is just one more thing that itches which I would like to display. When I went in for the English group I had a viva from a Mr Brett Smith. My answers on eighteenth- and nineteenth-century writers were not, I suspect, bad and Mr B.S. asked me at the viva, 'Why are you not in for the Honours School?' You were at the same table with him.

Having now completely explained the causes of my former annoyance, I can put this in the post and sleep contented – for I still sometimes wake up angry in the night and think of the mess I made at Oxford. This letter has taken about two hours to write. I hope you will not give it more than two minutes. It was written largely as a self-vindication and requires no reply, if you do not feel inclined to make one.

Yours sincerely, John Betjeman

C.S.L., JB's English tutor at Oxford, was the author of a mediaeval study, *The Allegory of Love*, and several popular religious and moral works, though he later became famous for his 'Narnia' series of children's books.

Nevill Coghill was a great Oxford personality: Tutor and Fellow in English Literature at Exeter, producer of many plays in Oxford and the West End, and a lively translator of Chaucer's *Canterbury Tales*.

It is doubtful if JB actually sent this letter for it remained in his papers. He did find various ways of getting back at C.S.L., however. In the acknowledgements of *Continual Dew* he writes that he is 'indebted to Mr C. S. Lewis for the fact on page 256'. There is no page 256.

To Stuart Piggott
GREETINGS CARD FROM JB
[Christmas] 1939

THE NEWPORT 'RISING', 1939

Left Wing! Left Wing! Again I say, Left Wing.
To Peggy and poor old Stuart let me sing
Uffington Workers from their sloth arise
A light of Marxist frenzy in their eyes
Send MARXIST GREETINGS to the Captain too
And Communistic grunts and groans to you
Bold Mrs Piggott. Now no Malvern Lays
Shall charm away the Workers' Day of Days
Miss Butler's barns are blazing! Wheeler's ricks
Crackle and sport: and see the bright flame licks
The Vicarage! the Church! the School! the Pubs
The Institute, the Fellowship, the Clubs.
Workers arise: throw off your servile chains
And smash the Piggotts as you smashed the Danes
And crush the Betjemans and kill their maids
Burn the McIvors, send to Hell's red shades
The motley bourgeoisie. The Day is bright
With Revolution. Uffington Unite!

S. and P.P. met my parents in Uffington where his father had a cottage.
   The Misses Butler lived at Woolstone Lodge.
   John Wheeler was the tenant farmer of the Craven Estate who sub-let Garrards Farm
to my parents and farmed its land.
   Mr McIvor was the Craven Estate agent who lived at the manor.

To John Murray   Garrards Farm
                                          Uffington
10 January 1940   Berkshire

Dear Jock,
I return the Revise herewith. Just a few corrections I have marked.
p. 7 last line 'Moving' instead of 'canter'
p. 8 delete the commas in last line but one
p. 17 last line 'Bickerdike' *not* 'Bikerdike'
p. 20 3rd line 'drift' *not* 'friff'
p. 60 insert 'Gwylim' under Welsh poem
   There are a few missing and misplaced letters which the proof reader
should correct. I have marked them.
   The title page is a great improvement. But I honestly do not like the
title. I would much prefer CHELTENHAM AND CLIFTON or merely the
subtitle. I feel the present title is too humorous and cancels out my
preface. I hope it is not too late to alter it.
   In case you have space at the end, I enclose a new poem which could
go under 'miscellaneous'. It is a good answer to what would become the
penultimate poem. In that case you would have to cancel your advert
and put it on the page facing the contents and remove '1940' to the title,
where, I think, it would look much nicer. 'First Edition' is a bit like
counting your chickens before they're hatched. But probably this is too
late. I like the 'St Cadoc' poem, though.
   Love to all, Robert Southey

   Old Lights for New Chancels was at proof stage.

To Michael Rosse   Garrards Farm
                                          Uffington
25 January 1940   Berkshire

Dear Michael,
Until I am definitely engaged in some job that will get me speedily

killed, I would like to help all I can about this Irish Committee which is far, far more important than our Georgian Group since Ireland has something left to save and good architecture goes on until the sixties and seventies there – *vide* Kingsbridge Station, the Broadstone, Court houses and Chapels in every town.

Do you think you could get Edward Longford into the Committee? He knows a lot about Georgian Classic and Gothic. And then I should like to see the Committee realise my ambition of a complete list of the works of Francis Johnston, that great Irish Pioneer of Gothic and master of the Classic – a man beside whom the Morrisons are mere amateurs.

Love to Anne and oh God, to be in Ireland again and happy as we once were.

Yours, John B

'The Committee' was the Irish Architectural Records Association of which Lord Rosse was chairman.

JB was a founder member of the Committee (along with Lady Wicklow). It was designed to collect and catalogue Irish architectural drawings. When in Ireland JB located and collected Francis Johnston's drawings which culminated in a pioneer study published in *The Pavilion* edited by Myfanwy Piper.

The Morrisons were Richard and William who worked in Ireland. A book on their work was published in 1989 by the Irish Architectural Archives.

To Gerard Irvine   40 Avenue Road
10 February 1940   London NW8

My dear Prefect,
Thank you so much for your letter – and a very nice one too. I wish I could see you and tell you a thing or two. But I can't, I have been absorbed – until I am sacked like every one else – by the Ministry of Information – and I am in London except late on Saturday evenings when I can get back home to the Egg [PSGB] for Sundays and to Propeller.

I am returning by Monday's post *Bachelor's Hall* and apologise for the delay. I am very interested to hear about the English Catholic Hymn Book and wonder who the publishers are.

Narcissus would be a very nice paper.

I should not worry about Sex's Ugly Head. 'The years from eighteen to twenty-two are years of ungovernable lust,' an old aesthetic friend of mine used to say. So are the years later on, unless one is careful. Afraid the only solution is to make acts of Faith, Hope and Love until one falls asleep. But it is not really so bad as one's upbringing has led one to believe – far worse the city shark, the ungenerous, mean, petty schemer, the proud and the spiteful and the cruel. At least you recognise the devil when you meet him. Bed is such a pleasant meeting place – alas. Write to me more on this fascinating theme if you like. But it really is a Ministries job. I am tinged with Irvingism again.

    Yours lustily, John B

> *Bachelor's Hall* was a sentimental and absurd novel with a homosexual theme, which inspired JB to write 'Monody on the Death of a Leeds Platonist Bank Clerk'. It was published by the Fortune Press, which along with publishing works by aspiring poets (including Philip Larkin), also had a list of books then denominated 'curious'.
>
>   'Irvingism', the Catholic Apostolic Church, was a religious body founded in the early nineteenth century by followers of the Revd Edward Irving, which combined charismatic and adventist beliefs with a strongly ritualistic and 'high church' form of worship.

To Jack Beddington   114A British Grove
                                          Chiswick
[? February 1940]   W14

Dear Jack Beddington,
Paul Nash has told me to write to you as someone likely to be in sympathy with the UA and WRRC (United Artists' and Writers' Rumanian Relief Committee) which we are trying to found on a workable co-operative basis. The idea is to give a series of bottle parties, say once a fortnight, at Julian Trevelyan's studio on the Mall. One artist shall contribute a picture to be discussed and a writer shall read a paper or recite a poem. Eventually the pictures and writing will be collected in a book – title not yet chosen – and the profits on the sales will go to the UA and WRRC. We thought you might be able to help us with financing the book scheme, which Batsford have agreed to publish if we can guarantee five hundred pounds towards initial cost of production. Also you could introduce artists to the parties such as Grace W. Pailthorpe, Peter Scott, Reuben Medrickoff and E. McKnight Kauffer, if you can persuade him. Pearl Binder had promised to do a wrapper for the book, if it is published. Do you think you could persuade either Robert Byron or Mabel Constanduros to write a foreword?

    Yours sincerely, Lillah Kzurt

This was a joke letter making fun of Paul Nash, who was becoming over-serious about the 'Arts Bureau in Oxford'.

Dennis and Mabel Constanduros were both prolific writers and adapters for the radio.

To William Plomer   Garrards Farm
                                                        Uffington
17 March 1940   Berkshire

My dear fellow,

It was most awfully good of you to have written so eloquently and kindly of my verse in dear poor Joe's paper. I don't care what other criticism I get now. I know that the whole point of my writing is understood by someone for whom I have deep admiration. I cannot be more pleased and it has made writing poems and publishing them worth while, simply to have had your review.

I still laugh when I see that bit of Dr Bradford – and what a choice bit. I hope the old boy sees it. He is just the man to subscribe to a press cutting agency. It is awfully good to have got him in quite seriously, as though he were as well known and respectable as Proust or Brooke or Eliot or Auden. What *will* people think? I hope they will buy his books as a result. Digby Neville is in *The True Aristocracy* isn't he? I have the whole set at home here. *The New Chivalry* is the most outspoken.

John Piper met you the other day. Poor old Joe saw him a lot. He's a nice man isn't he? Poor old Joe must be getting a little happier.

Do let us meet. I am at the shameful M of Information, Euston 4321 ext 517 all this week.

Yours my dear [illegible], John Betjeman

JB met W.P. through his work with the Society of Authors, and with their mutual friend, Gerald Berners. 'Poor old Joe' was J. R. Ackerley, the Literary Editor of *The Listener*.

The Revd E. E. Bradford (1860–1944) wrote very funny poetry about young boys. JB used to read the risqué poems out loud, and make everybody laugh. He visited him in Norfolk. Bradford had been forced to move out of his vicarage when its foundations collapsed after he had attempted to dig a swimming pool too close to it in order that he might watch the village boys swimming from his dining room window. He had the appearance of an innocent old man with eyes like a little squirrel. He wore a frock coat and a top hat. Bradford's books were nearly all novels in verse centring around sentimental friendships between older men and boys. His name appeared in Auden's and MacNeice's *Letters from Iceland*, casually dropped in along with those of the greatest writers.

To Douglas Cleverdon   Garrards Farm
                                                 Uffington
Palm Sunday 1940   Berks

Dear Douglas,
How very very kind of you to send me those books which I deeply
appreciate. You and I know what is nice. *Long Ashton* is quite good here
and there.

I have sometimes thought of writing a long blank verse description of
Swindon, street by street in the manner of the Bristol and Clifton
poem.

I ought to send you some freak copy but I haven't got one. I'll sign the
ones you've ordered, old boy – but not if they are for sale or Murray's
will be angry.

It was nice to get from you such heartfelt appreciation. I feel it is
worth writing poems when I get a letter like yours. I wonder if the
Inskips will have me up for libel? It would be rather fun if they did.
What would they say?

I am ashamed to say I am in the M of I. If you come to London let me
know. I am there all the week. Euston 4321 ext 517.
    Love, John

> D.C., who had started a bookshop in Bristol on leaving Oxford, had sent JB a long
> Victorian poem about the house and estate of Long Ashton near Bristol.
>   JB's new volume, *Old Lights for New Chancels*, had just come out. In the poem 'Bristol
> and Clifton', the line 'I know the Inskips very well indeed' appears; the Inskip family
> stood for many years at the apex of Clifton social aspirations.

To John Murray   Garrards Farm
                                                 Uffington
17 April 1940   Berkshire

Dear Jock,
It was most awfully nice of you to ask those chaps to lunch. I *did* enjoy
myself. It was very nice to see so many kind people. I was
overwhelmed. As Father H. [probably Harton] said to me this evening
about John Murray's, 'It's so nice to be dealing with *gents*.' He was
thrilled by the intellectual life he saw at the lunch and when he went on
to see John Piper at his exhibition he could not see the pictures for the
dazzle he was in from the lunch.

Your velvet edition arrived at the Woadery this morning. Thank you so much. Woad opened it by mistake. 'Hello someone's sent me a present. A book of poems. How curious.' I said, 'Oh I think that must be meant for me.' 'By Jove, yes' – then he went up to tell Mrs Woad of the odd happening.

He was very puzzled.

William Plomer has done me proud in *The Listener*. This kindness is too great. I cannot believe it and certainly do not deserve it. I have written to Plomer to thank him.

Propeller is making out a list of friends etc which she will send you.

Yours, my dear chap, John B

The Revd F. P. Harton, Vicar of Baulking, was my parents' great friend and spiritual director. They nicknamed him 'Father Folky'. He had an enormous effect on them both, particularly on my mother. His book, *Elements of Spiritual Life*, was her favourite, which she referred to constantly.

J.M. produced a deluxe velvet-bound edition of *Old Lights for New Chancels*. There were only three copies – one for the Queen, one for JB and one for John Murray. Velvet editions were not done for any of JB's other books.

JB sometimes stayed with the Chetwodes at Avenue Road, St John's Wood ('the Woadery').

To Hugh Walpole   40 Avenue Road
19 April 1940   London NW8

Dear Sir Hugh,

I was most flattered and delighted by your kind notice of my poems in the *Daily Sketch*. It has helped them to sell so that poor Mr Murray will get his money back. I am so glad you approved the production. It is a great relief to me to be taken as a poet at last and not as a comic verse writer, a sort of Sitwellian A. P. Herbert, which has mostly been my fate until this volume appeared. But to have the poems liked by you is a very great pleasure for your books are some of the only modern books I read with enjoyment. I still think Messrs Perrin and Traill (John Piper asked me to tell you, by the way, that he was at Epsom and hated it), *The Old Ladies, Fortitude, Jeremy* are among the best novels going. They were being praised to me at lunch today by my new friend, 'Bartimeus', who is rather a good writer, don't you think?

Would it be possible for Rupert Hart-Davis, who knows you, to let me come and see you one day? I would dearly like to see some of your books and pictures and to meet you. I am ashamed to say I am in the

Meenistry of Information, and bludgeoned by the Scottish Civil Servants into Insanity, and the prospect of meeting you would help to keep me sane for a week or two more.

Again with many thanks for your appreciation and kind notices. I am delighted to be coupled with Kipling and very honoured. I think with you that he will be read as long as reading lasts.

Yours sincerely, John Betjeman

'Taffrail' is also in the Ministry of Information – but is not so nice, or so good a writer as 'Bartimaeus'.

> H.W. had written in the *Daily Sketch*, 'It is not dry poetry, nor is it anywhere obscure. It does not preach at you, as Auden does, nor condescend to you as so many younger poets . . .'
> Bartimeus was the pseudonym for the naval writer, Capt Sir Lewis Anselm Ritchie, who later became press secretary to the King.
> Taffrail (pseudonym of Commander Henry Taprell Dorling, 1883–1963) was a writer of low-brow adventure stories.

To Douglas Goldring   Garrards Farm
                                               Uffington
5 July 1940   Berkshire

Dear ill-used and excellent writer,

How very good of you to send me *Facing the Odds*. A damn good title. The Georgian Group story is horrifying. I'm not a bit surprised. Who are Mr Everett and Mr (Stopford) Adams? Little did I realise all the intrigue that was going on – not till months afterwards.

You have hit the nail on the head exactly. That is how the country is governed and how this war is being conducted. The only difference from the Georgian Group is that in this instance we are at the mercy not of the Old Etonians (who sometimes turn out excellent) but of the Permanent Civil Servants (who never do). The Permanent Civil Servants are men who were never first at school and never third. Always second. Always jealous of those who are really clever and envious of those below them who don't bother to work but enjoy themselves instead. The Permanent Civil Servant did not get a scholarship but an exhibition, not a Fellowship, but a position in the GPO. Life for them is one exam in which as they get on, they set their own questions and answer them themselves. This MOI has stacks of such second-rate, factious gymnastics. Indeed there is a file room left over from the London University and called 'The Gymnasium'. They hate us temporaries and call us 'intellectuals' because we use our instincts and our hearts and not our brains only.

I wish you were here to write a book on it. You are the man for the job, for you have the gift which none of the rest of us have of writing well and readably. Thank you *so* much. I particularly liked 'The Cockney Pilgrimage'. I WILL SEE THE BOOK IS NOTED BY THE GG [Georgian Group].

Yours, John Betjeman

'The Cockney Pilgrimage' is the title of chapter four of D.G.'s book *Facing the Odds*, published by Cassell in 1940. This chapter is a sort of conducted tour of parts of London, particularly the lesser-known suburbs, emphasizing literary associations as well as architecture.

To Geoffrey Grigson

St Anne [26 July] 1940

Garrards Farm
Uffington
Berkshire

My dear Geoffrey,

So sorry about today. The thing was that Propeller had dawn patrol at four thirty a.m. this morning until twelve, riding on the downs as an LDV and then was meant to give a talk at two to a Mothers' Union at Ashbury and then go on to dinner at night. She would never have done it. So I had to give the talk at Ashbury to relieve her. I forgot all about it and so did she when I telephoned. Hope you did not kill the chicken and that you got my telegram in time.

I very much liked your poem on Hampstead Heath in *The Listener*. The adjective 'yellow' was most happy. It looked quite like a Constable in print, that poem did – or a David Lucas engraving.

Have you ever tried your hand at writing a short incident for the cinema? The M of Inf. is doing five-minute films on various subjects prescribed for by other ministries. All that is needed is a visual sense which you have. You do not write it as a film script, but just as though you were writing a story for the *Evening Standard*. It must have a bit of a climax or point the moral required.

If you feel you would like to try, do let me know and I will read you a subject to be turned into a film. It really is most exciting work, especially when you see what you have devised on the screen. I've done one and it is quite a success. I am most surprised.

Love to B.
Love, Sean O'Betjeman
PS Les Casey is not a bad poet. 'The Rising of the Moon' is his.
JB

'The Rising of the Moon', the patriotic ballad, is the theme line of the famous play by
Lady Gregory.

To Dick Girouard   Garrards Farm
                                                      Uffington
3 October 1940   Berkshire

Dear Dick,
I don't know how to write and console you about Blanche's death,
which I read in *The Times* yesterday. The chief consolation for you is
that death is never so awful when the person who has died is a really
saintly character, like she was, with a firm faith such as she had and you
have. It is only very sad for you and those delightful children and it will,
at any rate, have the effect of making this infuriating war seem
unimportant to you. But I do know from personal experience, that
nothing is too hard to bear.

I wish we had seen more of each other of recent years. There are few
things I remember more vividly or pleasurably than the jokes and
conversation you and Blanche and I used to have in that nice gloomy
house in Upper Berkeley Street. She had every sort of merit – she liked
our kind of jokes, she wrote extremely well, and she radiated out
goodness and kindness so that I remember looking on those Upper
Berkeley Street days, when I was pretty homeless, as an oasis of
laughter and congenial talk and security.

Propeller asks me to tell you how sorry she is for you and the
children. We are both remembering her and you in our prayers.

If you are alone and would like to come and stay for a day or two, do
let us know. We have a bedroom and should be delighted to see you.
Yours, John Betjeman

To Gerard Irvine

19 October 1940

Garrards Farm
Uffington
Berkshire

My dearest Prefect,

Thank you so much for your letter. Would I were a prep schoolmaster instead of a bumbaroo in London doing distasteful wasteful stupid work with a lot of second-class men and a few swamped firsts. I did not realise what Beta meant until I saw the Civil Service.

Indeed I know Lydiard Tregoze and Lord Bolingbroke and the house. The whole story is very interesting. When next I see you I will tell you all about it. The vicar is North Country and Low and nice.

An Air Force Mess is, I believe, hell. They scrimmage on the floor. An Army Mess is like Bloomsbury after it.

I cannot write the Penguin book. I have lost all the MS and daren't confess it and can't find it.

Propeller is very active and the Egg [PSGB] talks a bit. Religion comes uppermost. It was heard saying the other day:

> Ding dong Bell
> Pussy's in the well
> Who put him in?
> The Lord Jesus.

Archie is very well and pro-Hitler, I am sorry to say. It is Nuremberg manufacture that must have done it.

I know Montgomery's 'Oxford'. It has a good description of a fire, I seem to recollect.

You should read *The Letters of Edward Fitzgerald*. He had our tastes and was as good a letter writer as Comper.

I will come and see you in Oxford next term. Univ. used to be very tough. The Gothick between the hall and the chapel (N. Front) is by the man who sent down Shelley – a Head of the college called, I think, Griffiths. I don't blame him for sending down Shelley. I very much like your prep school gossip and conversations. Give me some more.

Love, JB

A bumbaroo or bummaree is a middle man in the fish trade of Billingsgate or a licensed porter at Smithfield meat market, London.

At the memorial service of old Lord Bolingbroke, who had lived alone at Lydiard Tregoze, his heir, a cousin, who was a don at Oxford called St John, went into the Lord of the Manor's pew in the wonderful church outside Swindon. The housekeeper and two stable-boys pushed their way through the crowd and the housekeeper announced, 'No, I'm Lady Bolingbroke and these are his sons.' Apparently he had married her secretly and the youngest son was legitimate. The son became the new peer. He was very knowledgeable about nature, and particularly butterflies. But because of his simple background and lack of education he was ashamed to mingle in society and lived a very reclusive life.

JB had contracted with Allen Lane of Penguin to do a Pelican book called *Old Churches*. It did not materialize.

Robert Montgomery's poem 'Oxford' (1831) describes a fire:

Upon her walls there hung a crimson glare,
And red fires raven'd on the breezeless air . . .
Then feed thy gaze with agonies of fire
As limb by limb, the tortur'd saints expire!
In serpent writhings, lo! the flames awake,
Hiss as they whirl, and riot round the stake.

9a Mary St Clair-Erskine
(later Dunn).

9b Alan Pryce-Jones.

9c Bryan Guinness
(later Moyne).

9d 'Cracky' William Clonmore
(later Wicklow).

10a Archibald Ormsby-Gore and Jumbo.

10b Maurice Bowra.

10c 'Colonel' Kolkhorst.

10d Lionel Perry.

10e Diana Guinness
(née Mitford, later Mosley).

10f Pierce Synnott.

11a Camilla Russell
(later Sykes).

11b Patrick Balfour
(later Kinross).

11c Edward Longford.

11d Wilhelmine 'Billa' Cresswell
(later Harrod).

12a P. Morton Shand.

12b Jack Beddington.

12c John 'Jock' Murray.

12d Kenneth Clark.

13a Myfanwy Piper.

13b John Piper.

13c Gerald Berners.

13d T. S. Eliot.

14a Gerard Irvine.

14b Ninian Comper.

14c John Summerson.

14d Cyril Connolly.

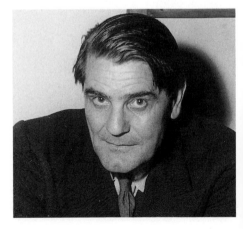

14e John Sparrow.

15a Geoffrey Taylor.

15b Douglas Cleverdon.

15c Evelyn Waugh.

15d William Plomer.

16a George Barnes.

16b Anne Barnes.

16c Patrick Cullinan.

16d Anthony Barnes.

16e Osbert Lancaster.

Seven:

In the Kingdom of the West

January 1941 to August 1943

Bells are booming down the bohreens,
White the mist along the grass.
Now the Julias, Maeves and Maureens
Move between the fields to Mass.

'Ireland with Emily'

In January 1941 JB travelled to Dublin and settled into his job as Press Attaché to Sir John Maffey, the British Ambassador, whilst waiting for my mother and brother to arrive. Apart from reporting to England on the state of affairs in Ireland, his brief was to further the rather shaky relationship between the two countries, many of the Irish being pro-German. He could hardly have done better, though he professed the job was of little consequence and continually frustrating. He said the only reason we had a Press Attaché in Dublin was because the Germans had one and a 'damn nice chap he was too'. He also insisted that what he was doing was of no importance but that he had to sign a form saying he would never divulge anything. Sir John Maffey advised JB not to fraternize with his German counterpart, Karl Peterson, because then Sir John wouldn't be able to cut him dead in the street. 'It was a difficult time,' remembers Sir John's daughter, Lady Aitken, 'and the British Government came out of those war years very well-liked because of my father's clever understanding of [Eamon] de Valera [later President of Ireland] with whom he exchanged poems and rhymes in the margins of official papers and of course John B who charmed a very important section.'[1] JB's 'section' was chiefly a cultural one and his attempts to improve Anglo-Irish relations were effected with a light touch. Frank Gallagher, the Director of the Irish Government Information Service at the time, remarked, 'To be an interpreter of two different people at once is not the easiest task in the world. John solved it by finding something to hurroosh for in all of us, disappointing as that may be to some of us who wondered what on earth he found to hurroo at in the other fellow.'[2]

JB painted his lightless back room on the third floor of the office in Upper Mount Street 'boudoir pink'. At the same time he determined to learn Gaelic. Gallagher put him in touch with his teacher, but imagined that JB would be tired out by all the homework. Instead he revelled in it and used to practise expressions from the phrase book out loud on top of the bus going to and from work. Invariably fellow travellers would help out and by the time he left Dublin he could write whole letters in Gaelic, and later taught my brother to count in it before he could in English.

Soon after his arrival JB began to look for a house to rent for the family. He borrowed a car on a long loan from M. J. Macmanus, the literary editor of the *Irish Press*, for the purpose. Mr Doody the estate agent wrote, 'There is a house near Killiney Railway station which might possibly meet your requirements. It is however close to the sea and I think you mentioned that Mrs Betjeman didn't like such proximity.'[3] He went to look and turned it down. My mother wrote (1 February 1941), 'If you manage to take a small furnished house before we arrive, do let me know if there is linen in it.' A week later, however, having worked out that between them they had an overdraft of one hundred and eighteen pounds, she decided, 'We can only afford P.G. rooms, we cannot possibly take a house at present. . . . I believe the cost of living in Dublin is twice as high as here so p.g.ing is bound to be expensive. I expect it will come to about ten guineas a week for all four of us. If Bett returns at the end of three months I can easily look after the Egg myself if we are hard up.' JB eventually found a place to stay for twelve guineas a week. 'HOW clever of you,' wrote my mother (13 February 1941), '. . . how perfect having a field for Moti [her Arab gelding was shipped from England a week after her arrival]. Could you possibly arrange to have six truss straw, six truss meadow hay, and a sack each of bran and oats delivered. . . . Phoenix Park is lovely to ride in. . . .'[4] On 21 February my mother, Paul and the nursemaid Betty Evans were driven in Mr Packer the Uffington blacksmith's van to Swindon station, whence they travelled to Bangor, and stayed the night with my mother's aunt, Marjorie Anglesey at Plas Newydd. JB sailed over to meet them and bring them back to Dublin.

For six months they lived as paying guests at Dunsinea House in Castleknock, near Dublin. Their landladies were Miss Eva and Miss May Hamilton, the two eldest of five sisters of an impoverished aristocratic family, whose family seat was Hamwood in County Meath. Their father had not allowed them to marry beneath them and subsequently only one daughter, Lily, married. Miss Eva and Miss May were painters and their connections in both the Dublin art world and that of the old landed gentry were limitless. This was invaluable to JB at the outset of his time in Ireland.

Poor as they were, the Misses Hamilton had kept their fur coats, which they inevitably wore indoors to stave off the cold. JB minded the intense discomfort and my mother minded the socializing. 'As John has probably told you, we are both madly homesick and loathe all the social life here,' she wrote to Myfanwy Piper (20 May 1941). 'We have to go to large cocktail parties, dinner and lunch parties and, worst of all, a special brand of Dublin party when you arrive after dinner: about nine p.m. and are expected to stay till at least two a.m. . . . John is at least doing something positive in his job which he is excelling at, according to Sir John Maffey and others.'[5] Frank Pakenham had seen JB in Dublin and reported his success back to a mutual friend in the Air Force, F. MacNeice Foster, who wrote to JB (6 May 1941), 'He [Pakenham] formed the impression quite clearly that in a short time you had carved out a niche for yourself in a way which no other Englishman had done, and had won the confidence of a number of extremists who normally were quite proof against British blandishments. He was, quite seriously, immensely impressed with the work you were doing.'[6]

JB took his work more seriously than he pretended in letters to his friends. In his reports and dispatches to the Ministry of Information he explained how difficult it was to convince even sincere Catholics of German atrocities. He urged a symbiotic union of the North and South to achieve the Republic's military co-operation. He thought that de Valera believed the interests of Ireland would best be served by a British victory – and concluded that de Valera was Britain's best friend in Ireland. After the war JB received a letter from a member of the IRA in which the sender admitted that he had been deputed to shoot him. Luckily JB was out of Dublin for a spell when the hit-man arrived. Later, on reading some of JB's poetry, he decided that he could never have been a spy and so his life was spared.

In July 1941 my parents found a house to rent called Collinstown, near Clondalkin, which lay among farmland crossed with narrow winding lanes. (The house is now demolished and the land built over.) My parents worshipped at St John's Church, Clondalkin, and JB called the area 'Ireland's answer to Essex'. Collinstown was a large, late-Georgian house which belonged to Major Kirkwood, a friend of the Misses Hamilton. It came with a maid called Maeve, who used to sprinkle holy water onto JB's car bonnet in the mornings in an effort to make it start. The house stood in its own little park with wonderful gardens around it. It had no electricity and to the east side was a large orangery with a shallow goldfish pond at one end into which my brother frequently fell. At the other end there was a table for ping-pong, a game at which my mother excelled.

During that first summer my mother made seventy pounds of jams and jellies, including plum, raspberry, and gooseberry and elderflower. She broke in a Connemara filly called Tulira in the field in front of the house, where a donkey called Queenie was already *in situ* belonging to the Captain. Meanwhile my brother Paul went off for lessons with the children of a family called Warham who had a governess and lived a few miles away at Johnstown. He travelled on the crossbars of the gardener's bike along Black Ditch Road which was said to be haunted, or in my mother's four-wheeled dog cart pulled by Moti. JB wrote a nonsense rhyme which went:

> There is a Paulie with no head,
> he runs about at the bottom of the bed
> There is a Paulie with no feet,
> he runs about at the bottom of the street
> There is a Paulie with no arms,
> he runs about and plays with the Warhams.[7]

Perhaps JB's greatest friend and kindred spirit during those Dublin years was the poet, Geoffrey Taylor, whose gentle wit, quiet scholarship and extraordinary knowledge of beetles and plant life JB found so appealing. Mary Taylor, Geoffrey's widow, remembers how, 'like so many others who were thrown into new situations, it affected John's feelings about being a poet – he was even ashamed of writing poetry at all. The moment Geoffrey and John met they clicked and Geoffrey told him that poetry was the most important thing in the world.'[8] Geoffrey, a conscientious objector, had returned to his native Ireland at the outset of war, becoming poetry editor of *The Bell*. He and Mary rented his brother's house, Airton House, Tallaght, a few miles from Collinstown. 'Penelope and John used to come over sometimes in the cart and John and Geoffrey would closet themselves up and read poetry to each other for hours at a stretch, while we sat in another room playing the piano and singing "Brother James's Air" with a descant. I remember going in with some sandwiches once or twice and the atmosphere was absolutely electric – never did I encounter two people having so much serious FUN.'[9]

In the end they decided to edit an anthology of landscape poetry together: *English, Scottish and Welsh Landscape* which came out in 1944. 'It will have to be *your* anthology, because yours is the selling name,' wrote Geoffrey Taylor (17 October 1941), 'but it will be fun to divide the work. . . . I've been all through Heber and found nothing to our purpose – though plenty of good stuff. Some of the right stuff in Ingelow, I also got an 1864 selection from Wordsworth. . . .'[10] The books from which they chose their poems were bought mostly in second-hand shops like Mr Fenning's, on the quay below Christ Church Cathedral. 'He was always in there, on Sundays,' remembered his daughter Eithne. 'We used to give him paraffin to take home and soap which a friend made; we just loved him.'[11] Maurice Craig, who was a twenty-one-year-old poet at the time, remembers JB wobbling on top of a ladder in the dusty recesses of Edward Massey's shop, yelling, 'I've got impetigo,' by which he meant vertigo. Later JB and Geoffrey Taylor edited *English Love Poems*, which was published in 1957.

JB's power of generating enthusiasm was limitless and the cultural links he set up between Ireland and England bore fruit long after he left. His friend, John Lehmann, the editor of *New Writing*, published pieces by the poet Patrick Kavanagh as did Cyril Connolly in *Horizon*. JB's friendship with Kenneth Clark, the director of the National Gallery, which had grown through their mutual friendship with the Pipers, proved invaluable for getting Irish artists known in England. Jack Yeats, the brother of the poet, W. B. Yeats, had never been shown in England until JB pressed Clark to put on an exhibition. Although it was part of JB's job to promote the arts across the Irish sea, this way and that, his involvement in Irish culture was deep and his desire to help heartfelt. He was prepared to listen to the poems of the outrageously conceited Lord Dunsany (to whom JB always referred as 'Lord Insany'), who kept his most recent compositions in his top pocket and brought them out at a moment's notice. He even sent the manuscript of one of Dunsany's novels to Hamish Hamilton. Literary criticism was not all that Dunsany begged of him either. He wanted help with 'an export licence for the shotgun cartridges from England; I can neither work nor exist without any sport or exercise,' he wrote (3 November 1942).[12]

JB's capacity to get on with people and put them at their ease made him popular with Dublin's small and aspiring literary world. He opened the BBC door to many, including Patrick Kavanagh, who used JB mercilessly to help him promote his work. After my birth at the Rotunda Hospital, Dublin, he wrote the poem 'Candida' and later wrote to JB (undated), 'My poems are being considered by T. S. Eliot for Faber's. The one I wrote for Candida I left – not to flatter or please you (which it may not) but because it happens to be a good poem. . . .'[13] Terence de Vere White and his wife Mary were great friends and would spend days at Collinstown, as would the brilliant

Father Paddy Browne. JB was also well in with the two powerful personalities and leading dissidents against censorship and the tyranny of the church, Sean O'Faolain, editor of *The Bell* (Ireland's premier literary magazine), and the bombastic Frank O'Connor the short story writer who often erupted like a grumbling volcano.

JB's energy during this time was phenomenal. He wrote a long and lighthearted centenary ode to the old Gaiety Theatre (17 November 1941) which was read out by Andrew McMaster as a prologue to a performance of Shaw's *Caesar and Cleopatra*:

> Only those floreated golden walls
> Can recollect the hundred curtain calls
> Of Hilda Moody's O Mimosa San
> In '97 when the Geisha ran.

Meanwhile he wrote reviews for *The Dublin Magazine*, found jobs for people who were out of work, and helped Eddie Toner and Liam O'Leary of the Irish Film Society to obtain films from England, secreted in the diplomatic bag. He opened art exhibitions, helped with a survey of architecture for the Tourist Board, drank with newspapermen in pubs and entertained visiting celebrities at Collinstown such as the actor, Leslie Howard, who had come to make a film. Beverley Nichols came to stay but left after only one night because there were mushrooms growing on the wall of his bedroom. In 1943 Laurence Olivier arrived to film *Henry V* amidst a blaze of publicity and excitement, which resulted in JB getting hundreds of telephone calls at his office from people wanting to be extras in the battle scenes. The filming went on in the grounds of Powerscourt, the huge Georgian mansion not far from Dublin, until the horses developed a virus which spread like wildfire and Lord Powerscourt ordered everybody off his estate. The filming was consequently held up and in the meantime my parents entertained Olivier and his producer Henry Bower at Collinstown.

JB's involvement with Irish architecture was, not surprisingly, fervent. Michael Rosse who, together with Professor R. M. Butler and Dr R. I. Best, had formed the Advisory Committee for the Recording of Irish Architecture in 1939, roped JB in to help almost as soon as he had set foot in Ireland. Maurice Craig, writing an appreciation in 1984, remembered that JB 'became quickly involved with Harold Leask the scholar, T. J. Cullimore and Eleanor Butler [now the Countess of Wicklow] in rescuing from neglect and disorder the Murray Collection of architectural drawings by Francis Johnston and others which had long been languishing in No. 8 Merrion Square and elsewhere and are now the core of the collection in the National Library.'[14] As a result of this JB published a pioneer study of Johnston in *The Pavilion*, which Myfanwy Piper edited. He also made an extensive survey and gave a long lecture on 'The Fabrics of the Church of Ireland'.

This Dublin life was a far cry from the short sojourns he had spent a decade before at some of Ireland's great houses. Nonetheless he continued to visit the Longfords at Pakenham Hall, as well as staying with my mother's relations the Chetwood-Aitkens (who spell their name differently) at Woodbrook, near Portarlington in Queen's County (Laois).

In July of that summer my parents spent the weekend at Dunsany, a great reconstructed mediaeval castle with a Wyatt-style staircase, swords and helmets, tigerskins and ancestral portraits, set in an undulating park of ancient oaks. JB's favourite place to sleep was in the small attic room decorated with Celtic *art nouveau* designs of twisted snakes. On Sunday morning he went to the morning service in Trim Cathedral and fell for Mrs Perry, the Dean's wife, who sang in the choir wearing a blue gown. He wanted to buy flowers for her, but instead they were picked by the gardener at Dunsany and sent round.

During that particular time in Ireland it was the Hemphill stronghold, Tulira in County Galway, towards which he was most drawn and Lord Hemphill's ravishing American wife, Emily, with whom he struck the greatest chord. She was a breathtakingly good horsewoman, who had met her husband in 1926 while riding with some friends in the Borghese Gardens in Rome. Emily had fallen from her horse, and this handsome stranger had ridden by, leapt off his horse and rushed to her assistance. She fell for him instantly and they married within a year in New York, later moving into Tulira, an eccentric Victorian house built by the literary figure, Edward Martyn, around an earlier tower. It was famous as Martyn's house in George Moore's *Hail and Farewell* and JB told the present Lord Hemphill that it was his favourite house in Ireland.

JB's poem 'Ireland with Emily' was written after a bicycle ride through the strange primeval-looking landscape of the Burren in County Clare. In July 1944 Emily wrote to JB from Tulira to thank him for sending her the poem. 'I have read it – and read it again and last summer has come back . . . and there has been a week here just like the one when you came to stay and I went again to Aran Quay to swim. It was just the same, only I kept thinking you would suddenly appear – but you didn't.'[15] JB was stunned by Emily's extraordinary beauty but, though he worshipped her, it was only from afar, for she was in fact in love with Ion Villiers-Stuart, whom she later married. JB continued a correspondence with Emily from England, telling her he would cross the ocean for her. 'I wish you could,' she replied (1 November 1945). 'It is so lonely here and so queerly like the Burren, only that the remoteness is of distance and not of misty atmosphere.'[16]

JB kept up with his English friends and wrote home an inordinate amount, often wishing he was back across the water. 'I would give ten years of my life for a month in a don's back garden in Cambridge or for a week's bicycle tour in North Oxford,' he wrote to John Hayward (17 September 1942).[17] Whenever JB had to go back to England on Ministry business he stayed with the Pipers at Fawley Bottom ('the bum'), which had become a second home to him.

During his Irish stint, JB often saw William Plomer and J. R. Ackerley on his trips back to England. He had met the tall, discreet and bespectacled Plomer, already an esteemed writer, with Gerald Berners at Faringdon and also through his work for the Society of Authors. Ackerley he had long known from when the latter had overseen a series called *Conversations on a Train* for the BBC, which were held between people with opposing views on controversial subjects, with train effects in the background. (The programmes were always causing trouble. JB and Raymond Mortimer asked, 'What's wrong with Public Schools?' and caused ruffled feathers in some quarters of the BBC.) Ackerley became a brilliant literary editor of *The Listener* and published JB's poems 'Cheltenham' and 'Margate, 1940' in the magazine, in addition to countless radio talks. Plomer became a close friend of Ackerley when he moved to live near him in Maida Vale to be in the thick of what he called 'the Canal school of literature'. Stephen Spender and his companion, Hyndman, as well as L. E. O. Charlton and Tom Wichelo, already lived there. JB always referred to Ackerley in his letters to Plomer as 'Poor Old Joe', and there is seldom a letter to Plomer without mention of him.

JB and Plomer had a high regard for each other's poetry. Plomer wrote (21 September 1941), 'The other night I was dining with some canal acquaintances and my host suddenly recited "A Subaltern's Love-song" with the utmost zest. I ventured to remark that you were writing an epic but were worried about the plot. "All epics have the same plot," said a fellow guest. "The hero goes down, and then up." This seemed true. Difficulties, then a happy ending. What could be simpler or better? I said I would repeat the remark to you. I can't tell you how I look forward to seeing or hearing more of the epic. . . . It is most important that you should go on. . . .'[18]

Although JB had complained to some soon after he had arrived in Dublin that his muse had 'dried up', he began writing what he referred to as his 'Epic' which, after various incarnations, was to become part of *Summoned by Bells*. In 1943 he sent an extract of it to Geoffrey Taylor at *The Bell* and asked that it be published under a pseudonym in case his mother might come across it or the names be recognizable and cause possible offence. Geoffrey Taylor wrote (16 March 1943), 'After all that, we are not printing your poem in *The Bell*. It seems I ought never to have accepted it as a pseudonym poem – your name and fame being, apparently, the important thing; not the poetry. Damn Sean [O'Faolain] for not having said so sooner.'[19] Part of the 'Epic' later appeared in *Selected Poems* in 1948 under the title 'North Coast Recollections'.

Despite O'Faolain's unfavourable judgement of the 'Epic', JB had become so popular in Ireland by the time he came to leave that the announcement of his departure made the front page of the *Irish Times*. He received over seventy letters. His old Irish friend (and my godfather) Edward Longford wrote (17 June 1943), 'This is a great blow and a sudden one. I haven't been thinking about much else this week. It will be an awful gap in my life.'[20] Maurice Craig wrote saying how sorry he would be to see JB go (14 June 1943), 'When one counts the souls as I do upon the fingers of one hand, it goes hard to see a finger amputated.'[21] Cyril Cusack, the actor, whose integrity kept him performing in Dublin and who never missed a chance to lobby JB about England, for making it almost impossible for less renowned Irish actors to act there, wrote (24 June 1943), 'John, dear old boy, this is to say two things: first, that I am sorry you are about to leave us, and secondly, that I continue to regret the UK official attitude towards Irish actors invited to act in England. As to the first, you have a knack of making it possible for people to miss you from amongst them. . . .'[22]

Of my parents' leaving party in a room in Dublin Castle, Terence de Vere White remembers, 'The *gardaí* controlled the traffic as it piled up in the Lower Castle Yard, and there must have been a sinking in the hearts of many who had seen themselves as choice spirits.' Frank Gallagher's farewell speech ended, 'Sure the Betjemans will, across the water, carry on their work of levelling out the peaks and valleys in the estimation of us into one sweet and pleasant plane. We shall remember them. One thing they will carry with them as proof of Irish hospitality is that they came three and went four. . . . To the four of them we wish the Irish blessing, *Dia go deo libh* [God be with you].'

At the end of his long and detailed address, 'Fabrics of the Church of

Ireland', which he gave in Dublin in 1943 to a meeting of clergy, JB said, 'After more than two years' residence here I shall return to England, with the profoundest gratitude to Ireland . . . where everyone – Roman, Anglican, Nonconformist – believes in another world and where everyone goes to church. . . .'[23]

1. Lady Aitken, letter to CLG.
2. Frank Gallagher, extract from notes for speech made at JB's leaving party (1943).
3. JB's papers, University of Victoria, British Columbia.
4. PB's papers.
5. Myfanwy Piper's papers.
6. JB's papers.
7. CLG's papers.
8. Mary Taylor, CLG interview (1993).
9. Mary Taylor, CLG interview (1993).
10. JB's papers.
11. Eithne Fenning, letter to CLG.
12. JB's papers.
13. JB's papers.
14. Maurice Craig, 'An Appreciation', *The Irish Times* (21 May 1984).
15. JB's papers.
16. JB's papers.
17. JB's papers.
18. JB's papers.
19. JB's papers.
20. JB's papers.
21. JB's papers.
22. JB's papers.
23. CLG's papers.

To John Piper   Collinstown Park
                                                  Clondalkin
Nine a.m. 10 January 1941   Co. Dublin
1st Sunday after Epiphany

A chara [Dear friend],
Your letter was a plank thrown to a drowning man – a refuge – *o Cor
Mariae, refugium peccatorum, ora pro nobis!* [Heart of Mary, refuge of
sinners, pray for us.] Sacred Hearts; the gas-lit convent chapels;
Benediction; tiled passages; Arundel prints; Munich glass; very very
bad copies in oils of Italian masters; palms in pots; the Legion of Mary;
the Sodality of the Sacred Heart; the Sodality of St Joseph, Her Most
Chaste Spouse; enormous enlarged photographs, on elephant folio
developing paper, of pontiffs; the art of Sean Keating; Charles Lamb;
Paul Henry; and, high up, the stained glass of Eric Home; and, lower
down, episcopal portraits by Leo Whelan; extreme cold and no fuel;
damp on stencilled walls; pitch pine bookcases: *Chronologia Martyrorum*,
*The Order of St Benedict in Central Africa, What Father O'Loghlin preached in
the Caribbean*; *Metaphysics and Moral Theology*; Astely; Spenser; 'Is that
Mr Belcherman? Oi were after speaking to Mr Doyle who told me to
give you a ring. Joost a little proivah matter.' 'Is it about a permit?'
'Well, listen neow, it is and it isn't. It is for me married sister that's after
wanting to join her husband in Kilkenny.' 'Well, why shouldn't she join
him?' 'She's in Liverpool, ye see. Wait now and Oi'll tell ye.' 'Is that
John Betjeman?' 'Yes, who is it?' 'Can't you guess?' 'No who?' ''Tis
myself – Séan.' '*A Séan, a chara! Conas atá tu? Go maith?*' ['Séan, my
friend! How are you? Well?'] '*Go maith.*' ['Well.'] 'Now what about
some golf?' 'Yes now – that'd be fine.' 'Hello John, is that you? I wonder
if you'd do me a favour?' 'I doubt if I can.' 'Well the Friends of the
Friends of the Irish Academy of Sculpture has staged a debate on
Michelangelo and the Future of Gaelic Sculpture. Austin Clarke's
going to open it, with Paddy O'Reilly – you know him don't you – a
[illegible] – in the chair. We want to know if you'll take a hand.'
   'Hallo, is that John Betjeman? Oi'v just heard that England's had a
licken.' 'Who told you?' 'Karl [Peterson].' 'Did you read moi review
naow?' 'I did. Was it the one in the *Irish Times*?' 'It was not. It was in the
Capuchin Annual.' 'Ho yes. Very subtle. I read it.'
   'Oh Mr Betjeman. I wonder if you know of anything at the Ministry
of Information. I'm completely pro-British. Ewart Milne said I was to

give you a call.'

I certainly will try and come over in Feb, to be with you at the time of the birth and to see Goldilox [Myfanwy Piper] with the baby at her breast.

Propeller is very well. Books I get from England – *The Luftwaffe Raid* by Eric Linklater; *The Defence of Calais, From Dunkirk to Benghazi, The Soul of Czecho-Slovakia, England's Navy, Sailors Ahoy!, Twenty-four Weeks of Nazi Oppression, Engines of the Modern Army, Bomber Command, Fighter Pilot, Wings over Palestine, A War Journal, A War Diary, A War Record.*

And here Neutrality, harps, art exhibitions, reviews, libels, back-chat, high-tea, cold, no petrol, no light, no coal, no trains; Irish language, partition, propaganda, propaganda, propaganda, rumour, counter-rumour, flat Georgian façades, – Guinness, double Irish, single Scotch, sherry, Censors, morals, rain home to all. God bless you. What a relief to think of Etchells and the old Marlburian.

Love, JB

Leo Whelan was a portrait painter quite well-known at the time.

The *Capuchin Annual* was edited by Father Senan, a Franciscan. It was an RC literary magazine.

Sean Keating, Charles Lamb and Paul Henry were popular Irish painters of the time.

Austin Clarke was a current Irish poet, as was Ewart Milne.

Karl Peterson was JB's German opposite number.

To John Lehmann   Collinstown Park
                                                       Clondalkin
27 January 1941   Co. Dublin

A very good six pennyworth, my dear fellow. My address in future (Hitler permitting) will be The Office of the UK Representative to EIRE, 50 Upper Mount Street, Dublin. I would be pleased to look out for any good Irish authors for you: if you will let me know any you would like me to see, tell me. It all helps, don't cher know, the great cause of Anglo-Irish Amity.

John Betjeman

The 'six pennyworth' refers to *New Writing*, founded and edited by J.L. He was a partner in the Hogarth Press, which had published JB's *Antiquarian Prejudice* (1939).

To John Lehmann   United Kingdom Representative to Eire
         50 Upper Mount Street
         Dublin
12 February [1941] Private and Confidential

Dear Sean Lehmann,
I enclose a copy of *The Bell* in which there may be stories or articles to interest you for *New Writing*. If there are, I should write direct to Sean O'Faolain, the Editor. There is no need to mention that I put you on to the idea or I will be accused of doing propaganda and I do not think that the accusation would be justified.
 It is raining.
 Yours, Sean O'Betjeman
They are all very fearful of British propaganda here. I don't blame them. This will be merely cultural exchange, old boy – if you find anything worth getting. PS *The Bell* cannot be sold in England – some HMG paper regulations. JB

To John and Myfanwy Piper United Kingdom Representative
            to Eire
           Dominions Office
2 March 1941   Whitehall sw1
1st Sunday in Lent

Darling Goldilox and Mr Pahper,
I have got *The Church Builder* 1860–1880 with extra illustrations but few of interest.
 I went over to Holyhead on Friday last to fetch Propeller, 'Bet' [Evans] and the Egg who all got over safely. While in Anglesey I saw Llanbeulan Tal-y-llyn chapel (Church of Wales). Mediaeval, plastered inside and outside, open benches dated 1786, untouched except for some red baize on the Holy Table. First class. Very remote.
 Oh God! I miss you both. Do both pour out your hearts to me at the above address and you will miss the censor for the letter will go in the bag.
 I wish I cared more about the war, then I would care more about my job. All able-bodied pro-British have left Ireland for the English services and we are at the mercy of people who are either anti-British,

anti-German and pro-Irish (faintly a majority) and there are pro-Irish and pro-German (about forty-eight per cent) and two per cent pro-German above everything. The Irish papers are all anti-British and the best-selling writers are pro-German. I am beginning to hate Ireland and the Irish.

We are in an 'Ascendancy' house (c. 1830 in a demesne outside Dublin four miles, at Castleknock) kind landladies – Anglo-Irish – very expensive – *very* cold – the Egg has already caught one – bath water hot once a week and then not hot enough for Propeller. It is the house of a mediocre artist called Eva Hamilton but she is very kind. We are two miles from Dublin Zoo. That is nice. I had a long delightful letter from Griggers [G. Grigson] which I will answer soon. Also one from Comper. He says Cosham has been 'bombed'. Oh heaven!

The G[othic] Revival is very dull here, but I am getting quite interested in Irish Mediaeval Gothic – fifteenth-century. But I have no time. It is all drinking in pubs with journalists and keeping in with people I probably never want to see again.

I really don't think I will be here above three months. I don't see what I can do. We are not allowed to do 'propaganda' anyhow. The drink will enlarge my brain.

The I[rish] C[hurch] is quite a standby. It is going higher; the nearest eight o'clock H[oly] C[ommunion] is three miles away on Sunday.

Propeller presided at a luncheon I gave to sixteen fifth columnists the other day. It was funny but sad. We all went in taxis to look at a church afterwards – double bluff.

If you can ever get over let me know and I can easily fix a permit for you both and arrange a lecture to cover it. Could you do this? How I long for you both and for churches at the Bum [Fawley Bottom] and for an English altar in any over-restored transept in E. Berkshire or Surrey – or even SUSSEX.

The British Legation here is a great joke. No contact with the Irish at all. I don't blame 'em. If only I had more time I could write at greater length on the subject of Ireland and the Legation. But do write to me in the bag. God bless England. God Save the King. Up the British Empire. The C of E (High) for Ever! Pray for us.

Love, Sean O'Betjeman

JB and PB lodged at Dunsinea House with Miss Eva and Miss May Hamilton when they first arrived.

'Ascendancy' refers to the Protestant regime which lasted from c. 1660 to c. 1900. JB meant that the house was Protestant 'Anglo-Irish'.

Myfanwy wrote (8 March 1941), 'Oh how I miss you, it's really awful.'

To Frank O'Connor   United Kingdom Representative to Eire
                            50 Upper Mount Street
7 March 1941   Dublin

Dear Poet,
Delighted to hear from old Sean O'Faolain that you are back. Look at
me, a bloody British spy (open) Press Attaché here. Now can you *both*
come in to Dublin for lunch one fifteen Friday next (March 14th). The
O'Faolains are coming. If you can't or can come or would like another
date let me know.
    Did I tell you that Lord Wicklow was once taken to the opera in
London to hear Wagner. He fell asleep and his hostess said to him,
'How do you like it?' He woke up and replied, 'Sounds to me like
Willesden Junction!'
    That first poem by R.F. in this month's *Bell* is a winner. Only two
images spoil it for me a bit. He is a real poet.
    Love to you both.
    My wife, Propeller, is over here now. We are p. g.s with Miss Eva
Hamilton. Her sister Connie (Anglo – St John's Sandymount) is ill in
bed with frostbite contracted *inside* the house.
    Yours, John Betjeman

> F.O'C., pseudonym of Michael O'Donovan (1903–66), writer and journalist, was a
> powerful personality with a deep West Cork accent which he made the most of.
>   Sean O'Faolain, editor of *The Bell*, was a man of letters and a lover of Elizabeth Bowen.
>   R.F. was Robert Farren (Roibeard O'Farachain), author of the nature poem, 'All That
> Is, and Can Delight'.
>   St John's Sandymount had the reputation of being the 'highest' church in Dublin.

To Kenneth Clark   United Kingdom Representative to Eire
                            50 Upper Mount Street
                            Dublin
14 March 1941   *Secret*

Dear Director,
    Art Liaison in Eire
This is a ridiculous title for this letter, but it helps the Registries.
    a) Mrs James MacNeill (Josephine) has approached me with a request
that you should lecture on art to the National Art Collections Fund.
Will you let me know if you can come, and what dates you have free

after Easter? Your visit will be invaluable for I shall be able to enunciate the difficulties here far more clearly than in a letter and you will be satisfying the craving for attention that there is in artistic and literary circles in Dublin. At present the German Minister has rather a monopoly of art and gave a dinner to old Jack Yeats recently.

b) There is an exhibition on Stephens Green of the work of a girl (twenty-seven, red-haired and awkward and not cognisant of any modern artists) called Miss Nano Reid. Her water-colour landscapes are, if you will take my word for it, really beautiful and something both Irish and underivative. It would be a great thing in this city of gossip, if you could get for me a London gallery to consider hanging say eight of them which I will select here when the exhibition is over. Will you act as agent and let me send the pictures to you?

Now, for heaven's sake, come over. I long to see you. I heard from the Pipers who enjoyed themselves immensely staying with you and, like the rest of us, fell in love with Jane [Clark].

Love to Miss Arnold and Miss Gibb,
Yours, Sean O'Betjeman

K.C. liked a few of the Nano Reid (1905–81) paintings and suggested exhibiting them at the Redfern or Leicester Galleries. Nothing came of it at that period, but in 1946 she took part in a group exhibition *Living Irish Art* at the Leicester Galleries. In time she became well regarded as one of the foremost Irish painters of her generation.

To John Piper   United Kingdom Representative to Eire
                                               Dominions Office
17 March 1941   Whitehall SW1
St Patrick's Day

My dear Mr Pahper,
Thank you so very much for your long letter. It was a breath of healthy valour-scented air after all this Guinness with journalists and high tea at Killiney with the Editor of the pro-German Catholic paper. Never was I aware before that I was serving my country and only memory glimpses of a nice J. O. Scott tower, for which I long, or a box-pewed, oil-lit hamlet interior, make me go on. Perhaps in some way I am preserving that.

I have discovered one quite good artist here. Miss Nano Reid – not someone one can talk to, for she is rural, awkward and hasn't even heard of Cézanne. But her landscapes in water-colour are curious and rather nice.

The two Gothic revivalists here of our date are G. C. Ashlin and J. J. McCarthy. The latter has a certain Venetian merit. Both were Romanists.

Miss Eva Hamilton, our landlady – boring but good hearted – is an artist. So is her sister L. May Hamilton or Letitia Hamilton. They paint mirror Paul Henry.

I had tea with Jack Yeats on Thursday. He was very good value. A man to talk to, but I miss you very much. There's no one else to fire one with enthusiasm. Here it is giving out all the time and then the fear that one is doing propaganda and then one remembers one is British and feels an itch for a decent transept with a Mowbray side chapel.

I enclose a cutting of the sort of life I lead. I am home to a meal about once a week. Never worked so hard in my life and, seemingly, to less purpose.

A woman who is pro-Nazi and thinks she is a spy has made a pass at me and I have been through embarrassing scenes in motor cars. I didn't know beech trees could shade one, brown streams rush and cattle have foot and mouth disease in neighbouring fields and yet one could be in hell. I am in hell. A hell of my own choosing. I begin to hate Ireland and feel it is all playing at being a country. My colleagues are decent golf-club types, in the office. But this eternal lunching out is getting me down and dining out and drinking and high tea and no petrol at all – public buses to go everywhere and walks through suburbs. It feels like St John's Wood in Leicester.

Thank goodness Propeller and the Egg and 'Bet' are happy enough. They like the country and Moti has arrived to cheer Propeller.

I have not written a line of poetry.

Now for your journey with K. Clark. I've seen Dodington, we once did it for the *Archie*. The photographs were unsatisfactory. Were Woolley and Langridge any good inside? Someone else told me Didmarton was worth it. I have that Bristol book *The Church-goer*, but never thought of reading it.

I am quite interested in Early Gothic Revival here. There is a Protestant chapel to a female Orphanage which is rather good – narrow gas pipes, fluted columns, queer capitals and grey and white colours, galleries all round three sides and the orphans wear eighteenth-century dress like Dolly dyes. I went there for mass today – very low [see over page].

The Zoo is quite near and is very bad. Like a circus after hours. I have taken up membership so the Egg gets in when it likes.

I am losing money fast. Exceeding my income. I bought a coloured [John] Plaw for about fifteen shillings – and had such conscience afterwards I stopped buying any more books, but not before I got all the illustrated Supplements to the *Architect* for 1876–9. Quite a lot of churches. Too late for Basset Keeling, alas.

So glad old [John] Summerson is there. But he ought never to have let in Sir Dan [Godfrey]. I hope and pray we all may meet again. A conscience tells me I must go on here for a bit. I begin to see what may be done and perhaps it helps to keep what we want intact.

I wonder whether I could fix it that you come over here for a day or two? Would you come? It is most interesting. They are just getting to rococo by Osbert's *Homes Sweet Homes*. The young architects are *very* modern. How is Heddi [Edward]? The Egg fell into a pond this afternoon.

I have just completed an article on Voysey for Max [?] I will certainly be able to do Mildenhall – never more in the mood – *when* I have time. Love to K[itty Church] and A[nthony West] and Jackson and the Imperial and that girl who is learning farming down at the crossroads.

JB

Love to Miss Holly.

J. O. Scott was an architect, the second son of Sir Giles Gilbert Scott.

G. C. Ashlin was a partner of E. W. Pugin, the son of A. W. Pugin.

J. J. McCarthy, the Victorian church architect, has been referred to as 'the Irish Pugin'.

The female orphanage, where the children dressed up on Sundays, has been demolished. The building was by William Farrell.

Enoch Basset Keeling (1837–86) built St Mark's, Notting Hill.

John Summerson had been installed at the RIBA.

Sir Dan Godfrey was the conductor of the Bournemouth Symphony Orchestra. *Walter* Godfrey is meant.

Mildenhall, Wiltshire, was one of JB's favourite churches. He wrote about it in *First and Last Loves*.

To Oliver Stonor   United Kingdom Representative to Eire
                           50 Upper Mount Street
19 April 1941   Dublin

My dear Newtown Mount Kennedy,
How very nice to hear from you and how wonderful of you to have completed a book between the intervals of surveying. Your passion for Biblical titles I sympathise with. It is also a means of getting the scriptures known to pagans.

Just over two months ago I got the job of Press Attaché here. I did not want it, as I was just beginning to enjoy myself at the M of I and had made many friends and was actually making films. I made great friends, by the way, with 'Bartimeus', author of *A Tall Ship*, *Naval Occasions* etc. then this job came along. I move now in diplomatic circles and have moved Propeller and the child over to here, where I find myself very pro-British and absolutely longing for the darn old blitzes. It is most surprising. I would give ten pounds to see a nice over-restored church in England and would embrace the first piece of polychromatic brickwork I could clap eyes on. I have to see pro-Germans, Pro-Italians, pro-British and, most of all, anti-British people. The German Legation here is pretty dim and repulsive. I have to see journalists, writers, artists, poets. I have to go about saying 'Britain will win in the end' and I have to be charming to everyone and I am getting eaten-up with hate of my fellow beings as a result. The strain is far greater than was that of living in London during the blitz. I have no time to write or think at all or feel. This is a respite I am enjoying now in an 1878 country house in Monaghan (Shane Leslie's father's house). It is a lovely place with a lake, terraces, daffodils and beech trees. This morning I feel revived. It is the first leave off I have taken and it ends after tomorrow.

Now less about myself and more about you. What is the new book about? Have they destroyed much decent Georgian and Gothic Revival your way? Does Chester Castle still stand? Write to me c/o UK Rep to Eire, Dominions Office, Whitehall, sw1 and it will go in the bag and so avoid the Censor.

Is mise le meas mór [I am, with great respect], Séan Ó Betjemán

> JB called O.S. by the names of many different towns and villages.
> Newtownmountkennedy is a town in County Wicklow.
> The house JB was staying in was Castle Leslie in Glaslough.
> The book Oliver Stonor wrote in 1941 was called *The Star called Wormwood*. He wrote it under the pseudonym of Morchard Bishop.

To John and Myfanwy Piper   United Kingdom Representative
                                                              to Eire
                                                    c/o Dominions Office
20 April 1941   Whitehall sw1

Dear Mr Pahper, darling Goldilox,
I am writing this on the G[reat] N[orthern] R[ailway] (Ireland) in a flash-jazz cocktail bar on the train. Propeller and I have been staying on the border. It is perfectly easy to cross it with no interference. [Illegible] was bicycling to and fro the whole time and jumping hedges from Eire into Six Counties fields. We were staying with Shane Leslie's parents, each is over eighty. The old boy remembered meeting Edward Lear in Berkeley Square. The old boy (Sir John Leslie) was with his father. 'This is Mr Lear.' The child looked up at him and Edward Lear took off his hat and showed him his initials inside. Landseer often stayed at the old house (1878 Jacobean in a lake-studded demesne) and was known as 'Lanny'. There were many of his sketches in albums as also sketches by Dicky Doyle, John Luck and others.

I am now back in Dublin. We also went to Caledon over the border, a superb house, Thomas Cooley 1779, with chinese papers and contemp. hangings and a dimmish homo peer and two wings by Nash, not very good, and a huge library of colour plate books, mostly natural history, including that elephant folio *Audubon's Birds*.

We have got Robert Donat coming over next week to perform to the newspaper men in the Theatre Royal. I can give you no idea of how hellish difficult my life is here and how much it makes one hate the enemy to see the Italian flag waving down the street outside their legation today when we have not even a flagpole. That word up there is Italian. I go to a lot of third-rate art exhibitions and I am consoling myself for the foolish decision I made to come here with thinking out a real heart searcher about Mildenhall which I hope to put to paper within the next few days.

I have had a queer letter from Mr Oliver of the Georgian group and another from Anthony Squire and another from [William] Mitchell who wrote it with a quill pen in the Clifton Club and ends 'I can't write any more because the quill is now squeaking so much that two members have left the room'. I am joining a Dublin club. The food is very bad at it and I shall ask people to lunch. The Miss Hamiltons here who are our landladies refer to K. Clark as Sir Andrew Clark of the Municipal Gallery out of ignorance not malice. He is coming to give a lecture, thank God. They are shocking bad artists with kind hearts and loud voices and give me nervous attacks at breakfast every morning. I think I have told you about them before. There is an early Brangwyn in my bedroom. Fungus grows on all my dark suits in two days as the house is so damp. Maurice Bowra tells me that Sir Andrew has 'been promoted sideways again'. I gather that Beddi is nearing knighthood.

Let me know about damaged churches and if you write c/o UK Rep to Eire, Dominions Office, Whitehall and put 'per diplomatic bag' on the top the censor won't see it and I will get it much sooner. Comper has had 'flu. I have had a sad letter from him. He says that Hutch [Father C. W. Hutchinson] has let the demolition squad into St Johns and they have wrecked the whole building. My mother was bombed at West Kington but not damaged. Hope to God the Bum is intact.

I am afraid I often think of Goldilox's figure, hair and face and it compares very favourably with all colleens.

Martin Travers' daughter Sally who acts over here with a repertory company is pro-German and sleeps with my opposite number. He is so unpopular here except among politically minded tarts and stockbroking and lawyer place-hunters that he does his cause more harm than good. I am a little sunbeam and very pure in contrast.

I am being renewed for another three months, worse luck.

I have had a letter from the Vicar of Stratton, Swindon. He has been appointed to Whissonsett with Horningtoft, diocese of Norwich.

Love to Heddi and Beddi and all friends.

Is mise le meas mór [I am, with great respect], Sean O'B

Caledon, County Tyrone, was the home of Eric, the reclusive fifth Earl of Caledon and brother of Lord Alexander of Tunis.

Thomas Cooley (1740–89) was an English architect who worked a lot in Ireland and designed the Royal Exchange in Dublin.

Robert Donat was a British actor.

Father C. W. Hutchinson was a famous confessor, especially to those in the arts and on the stage. He was a wonderful priest and a bit of a socialite. He was vicar of St Bartholomew's, Brighton and then of St John the Evangelist, Waterloo Road, next to the Old Vic Theatre, where he had a tremendous influence.

Martin Travers, the architect, later wrote (7 June 1941), 'It would be nice if you could get in touch with my daughter [Sally] who I have not seen for two years. You could then, if so minded, write and tell me what sort of a creature she has developed into.'

To John and Myfanwy Piper   United Kingdom Representative
             to Eire
             c/o Dominions Office
             Whitehall
26 May 1941   SWI

Dear Mr Pahper, darling Goldilox,

Thank you so much for your letters, postcards etc. What a blessed relief it was to hear from you and what a relief it is to be able to write to you. Good food and no bombs are poor compensation for no friends and intangible balderdash. Yet if conscription is introduced into the Six Counties area, which it probably will be, I shall resign this job with a clear conscience. I cannot go into it now, the subject will be too boring. But believe me, if it is done and if it means that our government is so damn silly over Ireland, then God help its tactics in the rest of the world.

I have not had time to write letters to friends, to you first of all, because I have been so busy. As to a poem – one has never entered my head, but for some *Old Lights for New Chancels* the other day and when the book arrived, I could not believe I had written it. It seemed to be part of another man – someone who writes poetry.

Those were such happy days, when one could choose who we wanted to know and who bored us. Now it is our *job* to know *everyone* – to go to dinner and to supper parties with them, to have tea in suburban houses with reproductions of Van Gogh and have the law laid down to us on Milton, to listen to sycophants, to talk about the war, to minimise defeats, to magnify victories, to give the official line, to be attached, and never to be thought of as a poet, or writer, or man of any sensibility at all. It is like being in a cartoon. And what is worse, there is no home life to go back to – only this wet, cold house and mad, kind, blue-eyed spinsters continuing the same sort of conversation. All this is worse for Penelope than for me – she hates parties at any time and knows nothing about Irish politics and cares less. Only the Egg is happy, for there are streams and waterfalls.

Most of all we miss any church life. We have to bicycle three miles to a N[orth] side eight o'clock H[oly] C[ommunion] and no church life at all surrounds us and the Protestant church identifies with politics and class and the Catholics are incomprehensible to such as us, used to the cold, pure English liturgy.

To crown all this, we are absolutely broke, for I am fully taxed and have to keep up state and entertain every day.

Enough about myself. Conscription may settle things for me – unless they make some sort of compromise in which case I will have to go on – for given any *chance* of friendly relations between Eire and England they must be promoted, and I can help and it is a nice positive kind of war work.

I am sure that this job at Medmenham, looking at photographs, would be rather nice for you. In fact it would be so good, that one despairs of your getting it. If you do get into the RAF let me know at once when you are applying and I will write to the Air-Commodore, so that in case you fail for Medmenham, you get in to Abingdon or Benson.

K. Clark and Jane came over here – thank God for them, they worked very hard with the Irish and created the most wonderful impression and talked to Dev for two hours – and K. told me he was going to try to keep you. I pray God he will.

There are quite a lot of funny things here to tell you about when I return and I will anyhow be coming over for a few days soon. I hope and will, if I may, come and stay. It will be nice to see swelling, sturdy Goldilox again, the golden swimming blue, and there will be bathing in Boulter's Lock and a rest among the fritillaries afterwards. I suppose Heddi can talk a bit. I had a sad letter from Poor Old Joe – flat bombed and all his friendship books – while he was visiting W. Plomer.

'Bet' (Betty) has gone very Irish and very Roman. Bought a statue of the Sacred Heart and a Rosary. Joined a camogie team. Propeller is reading [Baron] Corvo. I only read telegrams and talk smilingly to bitches and journalists – but there are a few friends – none like the old ones.

My love to you all three, Sean O'B

J.P. had written (26 April 1941), 'Is poetry as impossible in your present surroundings as painting will no doubt be in camouflage? I think of you always as by many miles the most valuable, sensitive and original poet in the British Isles, and therefore certainly at present in the world; and I ask with the combined tentativeness and earnestness of a Canon Dixon addressing a G. M. Hopkins.'

J.P. never went for the job at Medmenham (RAF) because he was asked to do the Windsor job (see footnote of letter of 12 October 1941).

Camogie is the women's version of hurling, a field sport not unlike hockey.

To Kenneth Clark   Collinstown Park
                                               Clondalkin
6 July 1941   Co. Dublin
3rd Sunday after Trinity

My Dear Director,
I expressed to Jane last week, in a letter, thanks that are due to you also
for the lovely time I had in England. I shall not forget those moments of
hot weather looking at major works of art in the panelled cool of Upton,
nor our beer at Tetbury and the Charlotte M. Yonge Chapel of ease in
that town.
    I expect Jane has told you of my discovery in the RIAI here.
    I enclose some notes about country houses which may be of use to
you. They are bald, but, I think, they give the gist of the thing. Now if
there is any chance of your getting me over to work on this, I will be
delighted to come. It would be nice to work under you again, to fight
the Civil Servants again and to have our own way – as we always do in
the long run. It would be nice to put in J. P[iper] and to have you
headman and to have some laughs. I am devoted to Maffey, but many
more months here being jolly with the second-raters will anyhow send
me off my head so that I will apply for a transfer. I have one or two
people in mind who could take my place.
    We are now living in style *on our own*. Next time you come, if I am not
already working with you again, you will be able to stay in this very
nice house in a kind of Essex of Dublin.
    Do let me know:
    1) how you get on with this scheme
    2) if you can get me into it. My heart is completely in it and further
from Eire than ever.
    Love to Jane.
    Love to Miss Arnold and Miss Gibb.

        James Lees-Milne remembers that K.C. was always being asked to make lists of
        paintings, works of art and buildings. It is uncertain what happened to the list alluded to.
            K.C. was living at Upton House, Tetbury Upton, Glos. The house was built in the
        Palladian style in 1752 with one enormous room of double height.

To John and Myfanwy Piper

12 July 1941

Collinstown Park
Clondalkin
Co. Dublin

Dear Mr Pahper and Goldilox,

Well that's very interesting about a new Heddy being on the way. Congratters. I long to see it at the breast of its mother. Call it something Daily and then it will be Daily Piper. That will be a great advantage in the new world of after the war when an accent of any sort will be a means of getting a job.

We are one degree less miserable than we were – only one degree – because we are in quite a nice Georgian House (to hell with Dublin Georgian) and on our own. The furnishing is all orange and yellow. There is a huge orangery, four gardeners and a *Country Life* garden all kept up for us by the landlord. Hot water once a week owing to fuel shortage. There is a large and very third rate Maini Jellet abstract in the hall. Detective novels in the few bookshelves. But the place has a nice atmosphere and we are away from the old women who plagued us before. Bett has come back in a sulk and will have to go. Very sad as she was such a comic character and adores the Egg. But she is being impossible. We have mad elderly Irish servants, so poor girl, she must be lonely, and it is probably for the best. The Egg is pretty independent now.

At Clondalkin Church (Father Madden) there is Communion once a month and there it is at eight a.m., ten fifteen a.m. and seven thirty p.m. Rather a bore as petrol is short for going elsewhere. I frequently mention you in my prayers – especially since we have turned a studio at the top of the house into a chapel.

I am at last on a poem again. A blank verse Tennyson Epic about Trebetherick. Three pages only written so far, but I am sure that, with God's grace, I shall go on.

I have told Maurice Child to apply to you for a revised version of his *History of Cranford Church*. I cannot get over there to do it. He is a very nice man and I rather like the Martin Travers-ery in the church.

The War looks a bit more as though the British Israelites may be right. Ask Osbert [Lancaster]. He'll know. My love to him and to dear quiet Karen and to you both and Heddi and to all my friends. Dear God, I have not forgotten them. Will I ever see you all again? I am lost in grass and blarney and diplomatic disadvantages.

Write to me when you have a moment. I am not the correspondent I was for I have neither the time nor the stimulated mind to write letters. All I do is gloomy.

Thank God for the Maffeys. They are very nice.

Love from us both, JB

PS And, by the way, thank you very very much for all your hospitality. You've no idea how much new life it put into me to be met on the five fifteen again. We loved your letter.

Betty Evans soon went home to Uffington to marry her fiancé George Packford.

Though *Summoned by Bells* was referred to later as 'the Epic', JB might also have been referring to the poem 'Beside the Seaside' which was published in the *Strand* magazine in August 1947.

Maurice Child was vicar of Cranford, Middlesex. He made worldliness and Christian piety meet and was the acknowledged leader of the baroque Anglo-Catholicism movement which tried to restore baroque decorating, music, ceremonial and liturgy. Sam Gurney backed the movement financially and treated Child as his alter ego.

To Douglas Goldring   United Kingdom Representative to Eire
                                    50 Upper Mount Street
14 July 1941   Dublin

Dear Goldring,

Thank you so much for your letter of July 10th. Now could it be that your letters are being destroyed by the Bordon postmistress? There is no doubt in my mind that I wrote a long and fascinating letter to you a few days after I received your last. I am taking the opportunity of using our slap-up writing paper with this one, so that there is no risk.

Oddly enough, by the same post as your letter, came one from W[illiam] G[aunt] at Farnborough, Wantage – low inclined to broad – the church I mean. He tells me he has finished his book on the Pre-Raphaelites. I do hope the dear old thing gets a job. There are few people I like more.

I would to heaven I were in England. One feels very exiled here at times. The glory seems to have gone off the old and the new glory is so small in the bud, it is hard to see it – but it must be there. Anyhow it is so bloody political, dividing itself into these categories in descending order of magnitude:

1) pro-British with relations fighting, but above everything pro-Irish

2) pro-Irish and not caring who wins, so long as Ireland survives as a united nation

3) pro-Irish and anti-British, but also anti-German

4) pro-Irish and pro-German.

But it doesn't really matter what they think. One friend gained for England, is one enemy for Germany and that is my job.

Yours, John Betjeman

The Pre-Raphaelite Tragedy by William Gaunt was published in 1942.

To Kenneth Clark United Kingdom Representative to Eire
50 Upper Mount Street
19 July 1941 Dublin

Dear Director,

I have seen Jack Yeats and told him of your proposal to have an exhibition of his pictures in the London National Gallery. He is not averse to the idea and says that many of his latest things are with Harry Clifton, Lytham Hall, Lancs.

I have also obtained from Mr R. R. Figgis permission to have his picture of that strand on the West coast. We might with your permission get either Con Curran or Figgis to collect some more of Jack Yeats' from Ireland, but I do not like to do this until I get dates from you indicating when the exhibition will occur and by what time you want them,

Yours devotedly, Séan Ó B

Love to Miss Arnold and Miss Gibb.

Jack Yeats was shown at the National Gallery in 1942, in a joint exhibition with William Nicholson.

R. R. Figgis known as 'Bobs', a member of the bookselling family, was a noted member of the Irish art scene.

Constantine Peter Curran was an author and expert on Irish eighteenth-century plasterwork and a close friend of James Joyce.

To William Plomer   Collinstown Park
                                            Clondalkin
24 August 1941   Co. Dublin

My dear poet,
It really has been a pleasure to receive your *Selected Poems* and I have
forborne writing until I had read and digested them all.

I didn't know you had been abroad so much – I was never a one for
abroad myself – and it is not easily that I read about landscape abroad.
You have completely conquered my natural repugnance and I enjoy
your S.A., Greek and Jap poems as much as the ones on more familiar
subjects.

Some stand out and there are bits I have committed to memory. My
dear fellow, you make MacNeice and our other friends look silly.
There's no journalism here. This is felt and horrible. I read some out to
my wife Propeller who never listens much to poetry, and she was
entranced. This is very rare.

Now of the S.A. ones 'Jo'burg II' and the beginning of 'ULA
MASONDO'S DREAM' appealed to me most, the latter is a lovely poem,
the thing we always wanted to feel when we read Rider Haggard and
somehow just didn't. The nature poem, too, on Namaqualand after
rain, gives a very good picture of the natural history of S.A. – curiously
unlike everything English, and sinister and too rich, as I now feel S.A.
is. The last verse of 'The Scorpion' is wonderful – one of the best in the
book.

Maru is just like the Jap consul here – a frightening little man, a kind
of Eastern Strict Baptist, with a taste for sport.

The 'Two Sonnets on Grace' are very *sympathetic*. Also that nice
sense of impending doom we all know so well, the rich luxuriance of
nature one always notices when in love and gets guilt about.

'Vagabond Love' is a winner, especially the opening lines.

'Armistice Day' might have been written by Wilfred Owen had he
survived, on the same lines as yours.

The opening of 'The Silent Sunday' is marvellous and I like the
whole poem. But the best poem in the book is 'September Evening
1938'. There's no doubt of it.

> Lights in the bungalow,
> A constant hum of cars;
> Mallow flowers in the grass;
> One or two stars.

That transition to mallow flowers and stars – again that rich goodness of God and the sense of impending doom. This time perfectly brought off.

'The Death of a Snake' is v. horrific and v. memorable, with its neat purposeful conclusion.

'The Russian Lover' got past the Censor all right then!

'A Traveller's Tale' at the end is very moving – your iteration of the pearl in the palm, effective.

As to the Ballads – they are up my street. Certain phrases I shall always remember:

> Who strolls so late, for mugs abait
> In the mists of Maida Vale
> Sauntering past a stucco gate
> Fallen, but hardly frail?

V. memorable.

And in 'The Widow's Plot', this lovely stanza:

> But mostly stayed at home and dusted
> Crooning early, crooning late,
> Unaware of being distrusted
> By her mate.

It is a most extraordinary and comforting thought to me, that I see things very much as you do and obviously feel rather as you do. I would I had the genius to produce 'The Travellers Tale' and 'September Evening 1938', particularly that last. Dear fellow, thank you very much for the book. And love to Poor old Joe. I am sure he is proud of his friend. So am I.

My epic progresses slowly for want of a plot.

Dia dhuit. Is mise do chara dhílis [God be with you. I am your dear friend], Séan Ó Betjemán.

The poem referred to as 'Jo'burg II' is 'Conquistador', the second of three 'poems of Johannesburg'.

W.P. replied (21 September 1941), 'I wish I could understand the Gaelic ending to your letter. It's Greek to me, but I hope it's civil. . . . I don't know when anybody has taken such trouble as you have done to tell a creature of his responses to the creature's book.'

To Father Hutchinson   United Kingdom Representative to Eire
                                50 Upper Mount Street
6 September 1941   Dublin

A chara [Dear friend],

I cannot tell you the exigencies and irritants of the very tricky work I find myself doing here.

But this is to tell you of a new addition to our church – or rather the return of an old one. She is Miss Helen Kirkpatrick, 26 Wilton Row, SW1, Sloane 6519. She is a famous American journalist, was brought up Episcopal Church in America (the one that is Catholic and in communion with us), she came over here to do some work and I had a long talk with her. She now writes to me at the end of a letter about Anglo–US–Irish relations, 'I think you are right about Confession. Where and whom do you recommend in London?' I took the liberty of recommending you and told her I was writing to you in a letter sent by the same post as this one. I gathered from her that she is now single (and moral) and had divorced her husband. I may have been wrong, but I thought that as she was not married to anyone else, she was probably after confession, entitled to communion. But you will know. She is just the sort of person we want for the church and I hope something can be done about her. Will you get in touch?

We are all well here – the Egg (my son) is recovering from whooping cough. Penelope is schooling horses. If you write, address me c/o UK Rep to Eire, Dominions Office, London SW1 and mark the envelope 'by Diplomatic bag'. You will escape the Censor's delays.

My prayers are often for you and the Waterloo Road. Father Cyril T[omkinson] seems to have resumed work again in *his* bombed church.

Yours, John Betjeman

PS Wait till I send you a nice long letter about the Church of Ireland. What an institution! JB

Fr H.'s church, St John's Waterloo Road, had been destroyed in the blitz.

Father Cyril Tomkinson was a priest with a reputation comparable to Fr H.'s. When his church, All Saints Clifton, was blitzed, he became Vicar of All Saints Margaret Street, London W1.

To Frank O'Connor

Collinstown Park
Clondalkin
Co. Dublin

Domhnach Meadhon Foghmhair 6dh 1941
[Sunday 16 September 1941]

A chara, a Eoghain [Dear Owen],
(I can't find Frank in O'Growney ['s dictionary] so I use O'G's Christian name instead.)

Loike the bloody fuil Oi ham Oi did not luik in the *Oirish Toimes* yasterdee for to see that yez was churmun fo' the Day Lewis lecture and so when Oi met Day Lewis on the hairoplane, Oi did not think ter be takin' him along ter see yez before the meeting. In fact it was not until owld *Pádraig Cábhanagh* [Patrick Kavanagh] was after a-telephoning to me, that Oi realised the omission Oi had made. *Verzeihen sie mir, mein lieber freund* [Pardon me, my dear friend]. British diplomacy has made another blunder.

But Oi got into touch with him last noight and he said he was going for ter see yez *inniu* [today]. I even was after talking about yez ter Day Lewis and he was after hadmiring of your writing and Oi was after saying yez was sure to be after seeing him at the lecture.

We have been away in Queen's County with some very very dim Irish relations of Propeller called Chetwood-Aitken who live at Woodbrook, Portarlington, I may have told you about the house.

Propeller brings this note on her way to or from St John's S[andy]mount (to which I hope Evelyn, the lovely creature, will be after going regularly) and is going to fix up with you a time to be coming out to us and that right soon.

God bless you and looking forward to seeing you all,
Is mise do chara dhílis [I am your dear friend], Séan Ó Betjemán

Cecil Day Lewis, who later became Poet Laureate, worked for the Ministry of Information at this time and came over to Dublin to give a lecture. He was a friend of JB. F.O'C.'s wife, Evelyn, was formerly married to the actor Robert Speaight.

To John Piper

Collinstown Park
Clondalkin
Co. Dublin

12 October 1941 and 20 December 1941

My Dear Mr Paaper,
Your letter from YE OLDE HAYCOCKE [Fawley Bottom] was an

inspiration to me and reading it again this evening by the electric light with the curtains drawn, I am imagining myself back in England.

I only made a very peremptory tour of Stamford and only saw one church (St Mary's) and then saw Uffington (very low, as you say) and went back into Rutland. Peterborough is lovely. But singularly soulless inside. 'The Dead Sea', do you remember, in Bishop Glyn's time? Crowland is a winner. So is the much-etched tri-partite bridge.

I felt sure Apethorpe was up to scratch. I hope you drew and photographed it. I enclose a most interesting piece of *Little Guide*, of which I am sure you could make some abstract use, which came to me covering a simply vile anthology by C. Day Lewis and L. A. G. Strong, published by Methuen's, combining two poems of mine for which I never recollect being asked permission and which I would not myself have chosen. However I am now equal in rank with Mew, Allott, Zwingler, Madge, Clarke, Spencer, Bottomley, Whickham, though not so high as Thomas (Dylan), Auden, S[pender], MacN[eice], D[ay] L[ewis], W. B. Y[eats], T. S. E[liot], D[orothy] Wellesley and others. I'm getting on.

I had a very nice letter from William Plomer.

I expect you will by now have received my drawings of you at work at Windsor and of Goldilox. I often think about her and the new Heddi. God bless them both and an extra blessing for Heddi and you.

The temptation to rush off in a vein of self-pity gets me these damp October Irish evenings. But it is only dull. I will have some quite exciting stories to tell you (of a war nature, alas) when I come back, which should be in November, for a week.

I have been reading James Hogg, *The Ettrick Shepherd*. His ballads, especially those in *Songs of a Mountain Bard*, are very good. His prose stories are very good straightforward accounts in the style of an old newspaper, of ghosts and murders. He writes as though he were Shelley and a Scotch Shepherd, full of clouds and spirits.

I have also read an Angela Thirkell, *Balls* – like *Punch* without any jokes. Very 'nice'. Worth reading for sheer horror. The other side of the blanket to Dornford Yates. *Mrs Miniver* stuff.

I have also been reading Jean Ingelow. She is worth looking at.

We have a neighbour in Geoffrey Taylor – a Chiswick intellectual who is sorry he left for Ireland, his native country, at the beginning of the war. We have found excellent nature poetry in [William Lisle] Bowles, especially in his *Village Dialogues*.

I opened an Art Exhibition in Dublin today. A fat lot I know about Art. It is ridiculous. This is the second time I have done it. A young priest artist, under the influence of Dufy, called Fr Hanlon.

I have been given an assistant. A woman called Miss [Joan] Lynam. Nice enough. She pronounces every foreign word in the language in which it is spelt and she reads Kafka, Rilke, Putsch, Lorca (pronounced Lewerthieer), Stefan Zweig, Houdini, Rimbaud, Colbert, Querido, Borodini; she is left, and has of course read Auden, Spender, MacNeice, Day Lewis, Maxim Gorki, Karel Čapek, Edouard Bono, Edouard Roditi. On the other hand she is Irish and more pro-Irish than any of us and has met Arthur Griffiths, Redmond, Flaherty, O'Higgins, Kevin Collins, Michael Drayton, Michael Collins, Wilkie Collins, Maxim Gorki, Horace Plunkett, Yeats, Hilda Doolittle, Father Finlay; she has of course read Browning, Wordsworth, Byron, Shelley, Cowley, Shakespeare, Spenser, Lyly, Lely, Leland, Lillie, Nash, Naish, Nish, Nice; but for all that she is very nice and efficient, thank God.

Propeller has had her hair washed – it looks very straight and funny. She attracted a priest at the art exhibition today.

The Egg is now in the psychological state Heddi used to be in. Those were lovely photographs of Heddi Goldilox sent. By the way, isn't his birthday getting near? I have forgotten the date. Do let us have it.

We are going to Belfast for a week next week to Maureen Dufferin (née Guinness). It will be nice for Propeller to get into an atmosphere of war and rations again and she is looking forward to it. So am I.

I have found one rather good Ashlin and Pugin church in Dublin: French Gothic, with iron screens, mosaics and vaulted roof of stone. Nothing else.

The Francis Johnston drawings keep on turning up until I feel quite overwhelmed by them. Some are lovely. But all too early for us.

Ever heard of a poet called Ewart Milne? He writes the sort of poetry that I don't know about.

Love to Goldilox and Heddi.

Séan Ó Betjemán

J.P. and Myfanwy had just been on an all-day tour of Stamford's churches in September.

Kenneth Clark arranged for J.P. to paint Windsor for Queen Elizabeth and be deferred from the Armed Forces. J.P. wrote to JB (27 August 1941), 'I follow unworthily in the footsteps of Paul Sandby, who did two hundred water-colours for George III, which I am instructed to look at earnestly before starting.' (The illustrated story of J.P. at Windsor is reproduced as an Appendix.)

Father Jack Hanlon had a one man exhibition at the Waddington Galleries in Dublin. He exercised his priestly role, moved easily in social circles and was a talented painter.

Maureen Dufferin was married to JB's Oxford friend Basil 'Bloody' Dufferin and Ava and lived at Clandeboye.

JB collected F. Johnston's drawings for the Irish Architectural Records Association. Ewart Milne wrote about a dozen books of poems.

To Cyril Connolly   United Kingdom Representative to Eire
                             50 Upper Mount Street
30 December 1941   Dublin

A Cyróil, a chara [Dear Cyril],
I have written to Denis J[ohnston], Capt MacC and Flann O'B[rien] to tell them they are too late. By now you should have received Sean O'Faolain's article and the last part of T. H. White's (a nice man whom you have brought into my life – looks like Arthur Elton and talks like him).

I'm so glad you are printing Paddy [Kavanagh]'s poem. It's very good, I think. The total effect is grand. But probably too long for you to use. Very sad. But he'll be delighted if you can use some of it. The more he is paid, the better. He is dirt poor.

Frank [O'Connor]'s article I talked to him about. He says the Moral Censor alone is concerned with the Ku Klux Klan and birth control passages, but that the Irish Press Censor might object to the remarks about US troops in Eire and loyalist corruption. The former Censor is your responsibility. He can (though he may not see it) ban the number in which the KKK and BC references appear. The others you would be wise to consider from the point of view of the Irish Press Censor.

I have strongly urged the old Doctor who, with little Dufferin, has also strongly urged that you get more paper. Good luck.

Sean should have telegraphed the *Bell* copy by now.

All here send you their love.

Beverley N[ichols] is over here. Doing very nicely.

Le meas mór, do chara dhílis [With great respect, your dear friend], Séan Ó Betjemán

Denis Johnston was a dramatist and war correspondent.

Flann O'Brien was one of the pseudonyms of the humorous writer and journalist Brian O'Nolan (also known as Myles na Gopaleen).

We used to holiday with T. H. White on Alderney in the fifties. He wrote *The Sword in the Stone*.

JB promoted the poet Patrick Kavanagh to the English literati and became his friend.

In January 1942 there was an Irish number of *Horizon* which included work by Patrick Kavanagh, M. J. MacManus, L. T. Murray, T. H. White, Kenneth Clark, Sean O'Faolain, Frank O'Connor, Edward Sheehy and Jack Yeats.

To Myfanwy Piper   Dunquin
                                                        Dingle
                                                        Co Kerry
28 May 1942   (the most westerly bungalow in Ireland)

My Dear,

I simply had to write you about my one Cocktail Party, though heaven knows it seemed to me, incredibly, like five. I always said the house was Too Small for that sort of thing and with the Nursery turned into a Ladies and the Spare Room with the Gents it looked as though all the whole, perspiring, and oh-so-pi-dog population of St John's Wood had collected in Mulberry Terrace. I had taken the precautions of ordering plenty of Eats and a most divine man from Gunter's said he knew all about drinks and a lorry came up at the last minute with sherry and gin and maraschino and lovely squishy ices and pale pink creams in little containers, all from Gunther's too. Heaven knows what the bill will be! I thought, though it's me as sez it, that our front garden looked a treat and the clipped bays on our tiny railed terrace did full justice to themselves. Ineffably, Cedric chose that evening to bring home from the office some Lord or other – he seemed a sweet old gentleman – a client of his at Heal's. And as I knew someone was going to try to bring Amabel Williams Ellis, who lives near us, I was afraid of a *crise* as she is as red as a beetroot. But all went swimmingly when she did arrive and I steered the Lord, who loved gardens and enthused over our poor patch, straight to the eats and left him to the mercy of Aunt Celia who is a secretary of the Overseas League and so has plenty to talk about. The Craven Prichards came and brought Ruthven Todd with them, a young man of whom, they say, we shall hear much. And then we had to have his woman, who proved herself to be Cedric's Assistant Saleswoman in the Kiddie Department. Rather awkward. *Memo*: Does business mix with pleasure? Only at times and not on Gin and T and Gunther's ices.

The Gloags were there, of course, and stayed right to the end where he had a lovely time munching the eats and pulling everybody to pieces. Wells Coats made some *delicious* scrumbly, tumbly, scrambled eggs in the kitchen at three a.m. Cedric and I didn't get to bed till five a.m., and as it was too late for Norman Cameron to get back to Chiswick – the Manges hadn't room to take him in their Hispano – we put him to sleep on the sofa in Cedric's study. Today the whole place is a litter of cigarette ends, tiny sausages on sticks, and I see a fearsome collection of smashed glasses in the dustbin which betokens over-hasty clearing up by our Ermyntrude, who is sure to blame it on to Gunther's men. But I think it was all worth it. Cedric said he thought he had established good will for the business.

How is your John and your Edward and I mustn't forget the littlest one! Yours rather hectically, Christine (Jope-Slade)

> JB went to Dingle for a brief holiday (which he described as 'rocks, rocks, corals, curraghs, pipes, jugs, tartans').
>   M.P. later commented, 'I think Cedric, along with the rest of this letter, was an invention. John thought that it was a nice, garden suburb, Heals-y kind of name. Of course the other names are genuine.'

To Cyril Connolly   Portarlington

6 June 1942
5th Sunday after Trinity

My dear Cyril,
Thank you so much for putting me up on my last night in England. I caught the aeroplane very comfortably and saw Miss Hunter Dunn at breakfast and thought of her a good bit in the warm aeroplane.

Tell Peter Q[uennell] I told Quintrell all his messages. He took them well.

In Belfast I took a tram to the zoo and there were only two peacocks, six monkeys and a donkey in the whole place. But the tram journey was lovely, a blaze of rock gardens and glittering new perambulators and at one house the owner had had his crest painted on the glass of the lamps at the entrance to his carriage drive.

I did enjoy seeing you and that lovely girl.

We are staying at the house of Propellor's little known Irish relations the Chetwood-Aitkens. Swift used to visit their home and I found a book signed by Swift and with his notes in it in an attic. The house is rambling, the demesne weed grown with a choked lake and all around bog and burnt-out houses in this the dimmest county in Ireland. It is my only convalescent home over here. Major C-A and his wife have one daughter in the ATS.

Propellor sends you her love. The Egg is very well.

There they are at play with Propellor in a deck-chair – v. difficult to draw.

Love and many thanks, dear Cyril, JB

To Jane and Kenneth Clark

Woodbrook
Portarlington
Queen's
County

6 July 1942
5th Sunday after Trinity

Dear Jane and K,

I felt I must write to thank you for that unforgettable evening at *Façade* and the strawberries and fish and the view over windy Middlesex at sunset afterwards. It was the highlight of my 'refresher course' – as broad church clergy always refer to retreats – in England. I was very sorry not to be able to go to dinner with Princess Von Hard the evening you were to be there. My mother had decided to stay near Hanley with friends of hers – bridge and racing people named Cunliffe with an 1820 house done up by the Misses Frith, no books and a big wireless set and patience packs for each guest – and she wanted me to dine. So I had to.

I brought Comper to dinner with the Princess on the evening after the one you were there. But as Archie Harding and an intellectual girl from the BBC (Administrative Policy Section) were there, they were not quite the people for the old boy. Archie Harding found him too right wing and too churchy and the intellectual girl was not the sort of girl who would be interested in the things which interest you and me and Comper. The Princess was puzzled, I fancy. He [Comper] is getting on with the Berkeley Memorial, and is profuse in his thanks to you and his admiration of your admiration of him. Lady Berkeley seems now to be thinking she will have no money to execute it.

Comper has produced a superb design for a nave altar for Westminster – an altar away from the choirscreen; approachable from four sides, with a baldacchino above and on the screen itself, a device something like (though not much like) what I have drawn, for a rood. The effect is of altar and baldacchino and rood being one and the same object. The Dean is vague and not too keen about it.

Unknown Warrior
hurt

His plan elevations for the rebuilding of [G.E.] Street's St John the Divine, Kennington are, I think, in his best style and wildly original. He is adding a clerestory to Street's E[arly] G[othic] arcade and above the clerestory a plaster Gothic roof with pendants. The screen in front of the chancel has two pulpits, N[orth] and S[outh] with sounding boards. The organ is to be in the West gallery. The vicar and churchwardens have approved. I will ask him to send you the drawings.

I am writing from the one rest house I have in Ireland, the house of Propeller's dim Irish cousins, the Chetwood-Aikens. Swift used to come here and I found some books of Knightly Chetwode's here in an attic with Swift's notes in them.

There is a daughter, an AT, the two old people, all surrounding houses either nunneries or burnt-out ruins, and bog in all directions in this, the dimmest county of Ireland.

Again, many, many thanks and God bless you both.

Yours, John B

> *Façade* is the sequence of poems by Edith Sitwell set to music by Sir William Walton.
> Alice (nicknamed Princess Von Hard), born Astor, was enormously rich and charming. She first married Prince Obolensky, then Raimund Von Hofmannsthal, then JB's friend Philip Harding (her least-known husband) and finally David Pleydell-Bouverie.
> The memorial to the 8th Earl of Berkeley who died in 1942 was erected by his widow in Berkeley Church, designed by J. N. Comper.
> AT: a member of the ATS, the women's Auxiliary Territorial Service.

To Benjie Nicolls

United Kingdom Representative to Eire
50 Upper Mount Street
Dublin

19 August 1942

A Nicolls, a chara [Dear Nicolls],

Pat Hillyard [BBC] is over here and I have seen him and am very grateful to him for fixing up something about *Mr Michael O'Higgins* and to you for forwarding the stuff about Michael O'Higgins to him.

I have put him in touch with *Captain Michael Bowles* of the Irish army who is also the Director of Music for Radio Eireann, and who was one of the people who arranged for Sir Adrian Boult to come over here and conduct. Captain Bowles is a friend of mine and I have told him to tell Pat Hillyard a few good Irish songs and singers of a popular nature but at the same time very Irish. I have told Pat that the line to take with Bowles is the desire of the BBC to preserve a sense of being Irish in Irish listeners to their programme for the Forces and in Britain. That always goes down well.

While on the subject of Bowles it occurred to me to remind you of the possibility of Bowles being asked over to conduct or something for the BBC as a sort of return compliment from the BBC to Radio Eireann. I am sure this would be an excellent thing to happen and should be done through Sir Adrian Boult. What do you think?

Yours, John Betjeman

> B.N. was Programme Division Controller at the BBC. He and Sir Adrian Boult asked Bowles to conduct. 'The effect of the Bowles invitation has been stupendous and all that could be desired,' wrote JB.

To John Piper   United Kingdom Representative to Eire
    50 Upper Mount Street
11 September 1942   Dublin

Mah dear Mr Pahpa,
I long to do the book on you and have written as much to Lord Clark. I *did* get your illustrated letter and another the other day and God bless you for them. I am now fully determined to return even if it means Libya for me. But I must wait until after the birth. This is to be a caesarian in the Rotunda Hospital at the end of next week or the beginning of the week after. Then there will be, I suppose, about a month before Propeller recovers – which, pray God, she will. The doctor who is doing the operation is doctor to the German Legation and the Italian Legation. His sympathies are said to be that way. I hope he will do the operation in a neutral manner.

I am too miserable and anxious and frustrated even to write a letter. This is the lowest I have ever reached. Do forgive me for not replying at greater length to you. My deep love to Goldilox and Heddi and Clarissa. They tell me Gerald B[erners] is still in love with Clarissa Churchill.

Sean O'Betjeman

PS Evie Hone has had a commission to do a window for Chetwode Church. Why? JB
PPS Someone has given me a *Pleasures of Memory* with Gilpin's beautiful booklet in it. JB
PPPS Fine attack (anonymous) on Batsford in *N[ew] S[tatesman]* the other week.

Yours, JB

JB's *John Piper* for the Penguin Modern Painters series was published in 1944.
    CB was born on 22 September 1942 in the Rotunda Hospital.
    Evie Hone was the leading Irish stained glass designer. 'Do you really mean that Evie Hone is doing a Windsor at Chetwode? [She had designed windows for Eton College Chapel, Windsor.] Are they removing the thirteenth-century glass to accommodate her?' wrote J.P. (7 October 1942).

To Hamish Hamilton   United Kingdom Representative to Eire
                                  50 Upper Mount Street
18 September 1942   Dublin

PERSONAL

Dear Publisher,
I do not believe you ever send review copies of books, whether war or non-war subjects, to the *Irish Press*, the government paper here, whose literary editor, M. J. MacManus, is a great friend of mine and personally friendly to us. Believe me it is well worth sending him copies for review. His paper and the *Irish Independent* have the biggest circulation in Ireland and the *Irish Press* reviews are good. It happens now and then that the Censor does not pass the review of a very anti-Nazi publication, but you may be sure that the book itself passes through countless hands in Dublin. I know that paper and review copies are now very short, but believe me, with a list like yours, no copies sent to Irish papers are just sent for charity, but are extremely useful, both in keeping up good and thereby useful relations with Eire and putting across our point of view. *I attach a list of other papers which are always delighted to receive books whether on war or non-war subjects.*

    Yours sincerely, John Betjeman

To the Editor, Times Literary Supplement   Garrards Farm
                                           Uffington
21 November 1942   Berkshire

Sir,
A book has appeared in some bookshops recently under my name called *Vintage London* ('Art Colour Series').
    Though I cannot deny having written it at a time of financial stress three years ago, nor that I received fifteen pounds for all rights to the manuscript and no royalties and that for this fifteen pounds I also had to come up from the country and select illustrations and write the captions, I wish to dissociate myself entirely from the very poor reproduction of the majority of the illustrations. At the time (about three years ago) that I was shown proofs of the coloured illustrations I protested strongly and said I did not wish my name to be associated

with the book. I was never shown proofs of the black and white illustrations, which are even less like the originals than the coloured ones, until I saw the complete book by chance a month ago in London.

I saw the publishers, to whom Messrs Adprint, who are responsible for the reproductions, had sold the completed book, and these publishers kindly agreed not to send out any review copies. Despite this concession, I feel I must further disassociate myself from any responsibility for the reproductions. I would not be taking this trouble were the book not primarily an illustrated one.

Yours etc., John Betjeman

The letter, when published, was slightly redrafted. Copies also went out to the *New Statesman and Nation*, the editor of the series and to Collins.

To Edmund Blunden   United Kingdom Representative to Eire
                             50 Upper Mount Street
Advent Sunday 1942   Dublin

Dear Mr Blunden,
Oh God to be in England. Oh God for a nice whiff of paraffin oil and hassocks. Yes even for a glance at [C. S.] Lewis striding, tweed-clad to Headington.

And now for the scholarly part of the letter. You very kindly told me during our short drink in the Mitre with poor old John Bryson, that you would let me have the names of some eighteenth- and nineteenth-century landscape poets of merit and you mentioned Sir John Hanmer. Can you let me have others?

We have discovered one or two knockouts – Geoffrey Taylor and I – but we expect you know them all. Dean Alford, Father Faber, William Holloway (Dorset or Suffolk), bits in [William] Allingham's remains edited by his wife, Cunningham (John), Scott of Amwell etc. etc. But you are the man. On you we pin our hopes. And do you know Dr Habberton Lulham of Brighton (dc. 1939)? In the *Book of Sussex Verse*. He is up to [James] Hurdis at his best and in the Hurdis manner. I wish I knew something about him.

Yours in the name of W. Price who did the E. Window at Merton, which they demolished, and of Butterfield, whom they scorned,
        John Betjeman
        PS I enclose a copy of our list of selections as far as we have gone. JB

JB and his closest friend in Ireland, Geoffrey Taylor, were already collecting for a landscape poetry anthology. E.B. suggested J. H. Reynolds, Leigh Hunt (whom JB and Taylor had originally discarded), the Revd C. Strong, Dr Dorastin, Mundy and W. S. Rose.

John Scott of Amwell near Ware, Herts, was a particular favourite of JB's and G. Taylor's.

Dr Edwin Percy Habberton Lulham was the author of *Devices and Desires* (1904), *The Other Side of Silence* (1915) and others.

James Hurdis (1763–1801) was a pastoral poet in the Cowper vein.

To John Piper   United Kingdom Representative to Eire
           50 Upper Mount Street
Advent Sunday 1942   Dublin

Dear Mr Pahper,
I forgot to tell you in my last hurried note with the MS how delighted Geoffrey Taylor and I are that you will do the landscape pictures. We did not know anything about Faber and Faber being the publishers. I hope they won't use that blasted Beton [typeface]. Just do whatever pictures come into your head. They will be the same as the poems we have submitted. The anthology is now being typed. Tell Goldilox to look at Head's poem on a storm at St Leonards or Hastings. She had better take a look too at *A Book of Sussex Verse* (Cambridge 1920s). It is most useful. Swinburne, of course, she won't forget. Nor Tennyson. Nor Allingham. Nor Hardy: nor all three Dibdins; nor those dim Scottish poets of the Scott period: nor Hartley Coleridge: nor Longfellow 'The little wars, with this soft white hands': nor Keble: nor Bryson: nor Aubrey de Vere: nor Heber 'The Ground Swell': nor Campbell: nor Thomas Bailey Aldrich: nor C. Tennyson Turner ('The quiet tide near Ardrossan'): nor N. T. Carrington ('Frigate at anchor in Mt Edgecombe'): etc.: I can't go on.

I feel very discontented with what I have written about you. There is too much of Charles Piper and not enough jokes and characters. I kept thinking about K. Clark and then about what Raymond [Mortimer] might have written.

Love to all, JB

English, Scottish and Welsh Landscape (1700–c. 1860) with poems chosen by Geoffrey Taylor and JB, illustrated by J.P., came out in 1944 (published in the end by Frederick Muller in their series New Excursions into English Poetry). It was produced by the hated Adprint.

Graham Sutherland was to do the illustrations but J.P. wrote (5 November 1942) that he had 'stolen the job of illuminating the landscape anthology from him. It came over me after you had gone that the anthology was the best of its kind ever made and that G. Sutherland would miss the point. . . . I wanted to do nothing else so much.'

Myfanwy Piper was compiling an anthology of poems of the sea.

To Brinsley MacNamara   Collinstown Park
                                                       Clondalkin
St John the Evangelist's Day   Co. Dublin
[27 December] 1942

My dear Brinsley,
It was very kind of you to send me *Othello's Daughter* for Christmas, together with a card. I have just settled down to it. You have a wonderful gift of creating the atmosphere of your story straight away; it goes with slow, swinging strides, just like Hardy does and a pleasurable sense of melancholy descends on me as I read – as it did in that fine book *The Valley of Squinting Windows*. I suppose this time we are reading about the Chapmans and certainly about Devlin. I am very grateful to you. I have only just started the book, but it has cost me quite an effort to put it down to write this letter. I suppose Lady Marlay is Lady Chapman?

I hope you had an enjoyable Christmas. I was going down to Sandymount and glanced at the Star of the Sea Church on Christmas Eve and thought you might have been taking a walk thither.

You can have no idea of the benefit and pleasure you conferred on me with your present of *Good Words*. Almost daily I pore on those volumes. Oh if only we had all been born and died in the nineteenth century!

Again with many thanks and best wishes for the New Year,
Yours, John B
PS W. B. Maxwell is very good – *In Cotton Wool* is the best I have read – I have read ten.

B. MacN. (real name John Weldon), was an Irish novelist who worked at the National Gallery of Ireland.

JB sent B.M.'s collection of short stories to John Lehmann the following week. He published *The Cuckoo Clock*. JB later sent them to Jonathan Cape.

'The Chapmans' are T. E. Lawrence's family.

W. B. Maxwell was an Edwardian novelist.

To Hubert de Cronin Hastings   United Kingdom Representative
                                         to Eire
                                   50 Upper Mount Street
1943[?]   Dublin

My dear Obscurity,
I have just bought in Dublin *Towards a New Britain* which I suspect you
wrote. It both shocked and delighted me.

   Delighted because it will help to make people think beyond the local
district council: because it was clear and full of instruction. Shocked
because it put up so poor a show for contemporary building. The
drawing on the cover for instance. Between you and me I would rather
live in that paltry town where the chimneys are made of wine bottles
and T. squares, than in that summer 'land labourer's cottage' with the
Goldfinger paving and hints of glass looking over on to the still
skyscrapers. And so would you. Why do we both live in farmhouses
and not at High Point? Oh my dear Obscurity, we *must* make
contemporary domestic architecture according to rules of proportion
and with textures which will fit in with the buildings we have got. Is
there no map of buildings which are built up to, let us say, 1850? And
of better ones after that date? And of sky lines? And trees and prevalent
materials and in building? Is the flat roof essential in the pre-fabricated
house? Though Ansell writes [illegible] at the beginning, I know what
he means and I am beginning to sympathise with him. And ought not a
lot of industrial building and the housing connected with it, to be
temporary and capable of being removed and set up somewhere else? If
you can show one decent domestic unit – NOT A BLOCK OF FLATS – and
not from Arizona or Sweden: if you can show it in *wet* weather in the
photograph and if you can guarantee by juxta imposing it on a
photograph of a street of old houses, that it is the sort of house you
wouldn't mind living in with a family, and living opposite, then you
will have done more than all your book can do, for you will have
appealed to the heart as well as the head.
If bricks and stucco made this:

which fitted in with mountains
or marshes from 1800 to 1830,
why don't we find its equivalent for the present time in *England*? I
haven't seen it yet!
   Love from all to all. Shall be back for good in August. John B

H. de C.H. had been JB's loved and revered mentor at the *Architectural Review*.
   Towards a New Britain was probably a propaganda pamphlet. No trace of it can be found.

To John Piper

1 March 1943
St David's Day

United Kingdom Representative to Eire
50 Upper Mount Street
Dublin

A few objects for worship (drawn from memory):

LITANY DESK

Dear Mr Pahper,
Thank you very much for your letter re:

1) Anthology.
Geoffrey T. and I have discovered over two hundred poets whose names begin with letters from A to G, the titles of whose books in Allibone [Dictionary of Authors] sound promising such as 'Blog, Elijah: "Ipswich", A descriptive poem, 1803 8vo', which we see no chance of reading, as all the books are lost in Trinity Library [Dublin]. How many more poets there may be between 1790 and 1860 who have written descriptive verse, God knows. Therefore it seems that our anthology must be somewhat unrepresentative in that it contains only those poems which we have discovered in second hand bookshops. But even with this amount, we want as much space as possible. Now will you find out from Oliver Simon how many pages we can have and how many lines a page? This is most important; I don't want the thing to be a sort of hotch-potch art book that I'm sure Adprints visualised. Your pictures will redeem it from ever being remaindered. But it would be nice to publish something that was in a way authoritative or at any rate gave an inkling of the enormous, untilled extent of the field. It is really thrilling work, reading the stuff. The best is mainly always in Cowper-style blank verse. Perhaps it will finally lead to an *Oxford Book of Descriptive Verse* 1780–1860. Longfellow in *Poems of Places* hardly touched the subject. We are first and I don't think Det. Insp. [John]

Arlott clashes at all. So will you find out from Oliver Simon for me about the maximum space and lines per page he can allow. I want, even as it is, at least two hundred pages: if I can get them. The terms seem to me OK – poor pay for you if you decide to split the hundred pounds. I intend to make them use Geoffrey T's name along with mine on the title page. He has done more than me on this work.

2) You can have no idea what a comfort to me the Britwell Sal[ome] water-colour is. I look at it and want to cry whenever I get an evening at home.

I have written by this post to Comper urging him to give stuff to your exhibition. When he understands that it is to do in Eeles and Maufe, he will probably come round. I seem to have heard of Ellery Anderson.

3) You will probably by now have got the *How to* [remainder of letter missing].

> Oliver Simon was a well-known typographer.
>
> John Arlott was then in the Police Force and brought out *Landmarks* with G. Rostrevor Hamilton (1943) and *Of Period and Place Poems* (1944).
>
> Britwell Salome is a village in Oxfordshire.
>
> JB objected to Dr Eeles' over-academic approach to his work on the Council for the Care of Churches, and did not admire Edward Maufe as an architect at the time.
>
> J.P. put together a travelling exhibition 'The Artist and the Church' under the auspices of the Council for the Encouragement of Music and the Arts (CEMA). It included a water-colour by Comper of Cuddesdon Chapel (unexecuted).

To Oliver Stonor   United Kingdom Representative to Eire
                                      c/o Dominions Office
                                      Downing St
27 March 1943   sw1

My dear Sturminster,
It was very nice to hear from you. What a pity that book is reproduced in urine by those filthy Austrian Crooks Adprints Ltd. I only chose the John Piper and the Swindon illustrations. The rest I left to them, since I am so cut off here.

We live in a large wet, partly furnished house, near Palmerstown – Collinstown Park. Just now the daffodils are out on the 'lawn' and the avenue beeches are budding. It is what one would dream of as the ideal existence – if it weren't for Irish politics – and what I often longed for. But what is my reaction? Acute nostalgia for Wolverhampton, as you divined. I have never worked so hard in my life and with so little tangible result.

I don't think you need worry too much about mental splintering and unproductiveness. A long period of inanition always means in the end a terrific fruition time. Your accumulated experience will result in something remarkable quite soon.

I wish I was at Corfe Castle. Do you see Fra. Newberry there of the Glasgow School of Art, or is he dead? A wonderful link with the past – E. A. Walton, George Walton, C. R. Mackintosh etc.

I see Frank O'Connor quite a lot. He is the best writer here. Very frustrated and unhappy and pro-us. I go through Chapelizod every day on my way to work.

It is late at night and I am very tired with a ghastly day before me tomorrow. Write again. This is an unworthy letter of thanks for your charming piece which has set me up as I am getting very interested and parochial over here.

All pubs are the same. Guinness Good. Sherry good. No wine. No coal. No petrol. No gas. No electric. No paraffin.

Yours, my dear Sidling, Sean O'Betjeman

O.S. had reviewed JB's *English Cities and Small Towns*, the production of which he so abhorred.

To William Rothenstein   United Kingdom Representative
                                                                   to Eire
                                                           50 Upper Mount Street
20 April 1943   Dublin

Dear Sir William,
It was exceedingly kind of you to have written to me about my book [*English Cities and Small Towns*] and exceedingly rude of me not to have replied sooner. Your son [Michael]'s drawing looked particularly well in the *TLS* when it was reproduced larger than in my book. Those Adprints people are filthy reproducers. They seem to soak everything in yellow acid or Prussian blue. They are crooks, too.

I have been here since the end of the Blitz and it is a sort of mental blitz. But I am thankful for having my wife (who sends her affection) with me. I have discovered that the real cause of the differences between these two countries is spiritual and will not be cured until God wills it.

The Irish have always, since pagan times, lived in two worlds. They are a spiritual people without much visual sense and they are governed by their intellects and logic. The English live in our world and have an awe and fear of the other when they think about it. They are governed by their wills and their sense of moral obligation (i.e. duty) and are not logical. They like compromises. The Irish hate them. The English are the poets, the Irish are the non-dreamers.

Yours ever, G. K. Chesterton.

I know those little Stroud valley mills. I should have mentioned them. Oh to be on the banks of the Coln at Quenington.

Again, with many thanks,

Yours sincerely, John Betjeman

> Sir William Rothenstein (1872–1945) was an artist, art historian, author and father of JB's friends, Michael and John.

To Myfanwy Piper   United Kingdom Representative to Eire
                        50 Upper Mount Street
3 May 1943   Dublin

Oh darling Goldilegz I often wish
That you were Margaret Short. I seem to see
Your strong blonde body curving through the reeds
At Shiplake while I await you in the punt
And Mr Piper sketches in the fields
Oh darling Goldilegz I write this down   SPECIALLY
Dunsany-wise, straight off, so full of sex
That as I write even my fountain pen   DESIGNED
Becomes symbolic to me. Goldilegz   TO SHOCK THE
Still do you sweep your short hair off your brow? CENSOR WHO
Still do you run barelegg'd across the yard?   HAS TAKEN TO
Still would you pillow with athletic curves
My bald, grey head upon your breasts?   READING OUR
Your stalwart body still excites me much   LETTERS
The thought of you, now spring is coming on,   JB
Requires that I should exercise control.
So now I'll thank you for the Browning bit.
I'm proud to say that I have known it long
It was the furthest point I ever reached
In *Red Cotton Night-Cap Country*. We enclose
(Do Geoffrey Taylor and myself) some bits
Which we liked very much and hope that you
Will entertain for your anthology.

The Noel Carrington is too divine
And earlier than his arty namesake's work.
And William Holloway is wonderful.
We nothing know about him but that he
Was friends with Robert Bloomfield though he wrote
Of Dorset mostly. Do not fail to look
At Charlie Tennyson Turner – he's complete
In one big volume that Macmillan did.
I have it and could loan it if you like.
It has some lovely sonnets on the sea
The best sea sonnets that I ever saw.
Propeller interviewed a maid for you
A nasty bitch that Collinson had found
And quite unsuitable, two pounds a week
And most refined and very Catholic
Do let us know facilities for Mass
They're most important here in getting maids
(I mean Italian Mission Mass, not ours).
We have a maid ourselves called Margaret Long
Not similar at all to Margaret Short.
I will be over on the twenty-fourth
To try and fix myself for work at home
Before September when I quit this isle
(But keep this information to yourselves).
I hope to God the ballet will be on
With Mr Pahper's sets and tell him too
That Eric Newton gave a lecture here
With slides and mentioned him and showed a slide
All very friendly. Love to Mr P
To Eddie and Clarissa and to you
My golden-hearted, golden Goldilegz
   Sean O'Betjeman

Margaret Short was JB's secretary.
   Lord Dunsany wrote spontaneous verse.
Red Cotton Night-Cap Country is by Browning.
   Noel Carrington (1777–1830), a Devonshire pastoral poet, had a namesake on the fringes of the Bloomsbury set – the brother of Dora Carrington.
   William Holloway was an early nineteenth-century poet (*Scenes of Youth*, 1803) and Robert Bloomfield a late eighteenth-century ploughman poet.
   JB very much liked the verse of Charles Tennyson Turner (1806–79, the elder brother of Alfred Lord Tennyson) and later wrote an introduction to *A Hundred Sonnets* by C. T. Turner, selected in collaboration with his great-nephew (1960).
   Eric Newton was art critic of the *Guardian*.

To Jane Clark   United Kingdom Representative to Eire
                                    50 Upper Mount Street
3 June 1943   Dublin

Dear Jane,
Thank you so much for having me to stay the other night in that quiet luxury.

The journey back was interrupted for me – I had some W. B. Maxwell novels to read which I hadn't read – by the presence of L[aurence] Olivier and old [Henry] Dallas Bower who was on the train bound for Eire to direct *Henry V* at Powerscourt. That nice lesbian-looking chauffeuse you secured for me was very pleased to see Olivier at Euston and shouted out, 'Hi-di-ho! Larry! My brother was at school with you.' There was a very attractive secretary with L. Olivier, a Miss Cathcart, who had been in the tennis team of Malvern Girls College. Tell K of this.

I see Beddi has got a CBE,
whatever that is. He *will* be pleased,
dear old Beddi. I had thought
the war was ageing him a bit.
This should rejuvenate him.

They've finished the repainting in Burlington Road and some dreadful jazz light fixtures, visible from the road, have been put up in the first floor bedrooms intended to be our dressing tables.

Love to K.
Love, John B

JB wrote to Myfanwy Piper (3 June 1943) about the evening, 'I have never seen Jane looking lovelier and have become very keen on her. More keen even than I was and I have always been a bit keen. But you are still paramount if I may borrow a film phrase.'

Henry Dallas Bower was the producer of *Henry V* and had got Olivier released from the Fleet Air Arm to make the film.

To Frank Gallagher   United Kingdom Representative to Eire
                            50 Upper Mount Street
16 June 1943   Dublin

Dear Frank,

Thank you so much for your kind letter. It all sounds rather like a bereavement and it is one. I am very depressed at going. So many friends made, so much kindness. But I'm not leaving until the middle of August, so far as I know, so we will meet again. And Propeller will not leave until September.

The reasons for my going are not hard to explain to you, though they might be to some people. When I was over in London last I was urgently asked for by Minnie [the M of I]. I suppose I could have said 'no' and been backed up from here. But then it occurred to Propeller and me that we would either have to remain here permanently (and the job is unlikely to go on after the war) or go back when we were wanted. We both have responsibilities in England. First our village life where the Vicar (Anglo-Catholic) [Revd Bridle] is old and ill and wants us to help with the church life of the village as we used to do; and second, the need to be in England during all the post-war reconstruction schemes and to put in a word, everywhere possible, for Christian bases. Living in Ireland has been a wonderful experience, because it is a wholly Christian country. I am sure it is my duty to go back and help to remake England one so far as I can. It would be not so easy to carry any weight either in the village or in public work and writing, if people were to have justifications for saying, 'You lived on eggs and bacon in comfort in Eire for the war and now you come and tell us what we ought to do.' We obviously must share some of the unpleasantness with them of wartime life. So that was why we decided I had better accept the job offered me. Rough luck on Paul and Candida.

Might as well take this opportunity for thanking you for all the kindnesses you have done me – dealing with those journalists for me, getting interviews with the *Taoiseach* [Prime Minister] – to whom I am greatly indebted and do convey my thanks to him – and for hospitality and gaiety in the past.

I would, by the way, very much like to see the Prime Minister before I go. But there's plenty of time for that. Oh dear, I am sad.

Yours, John B

JB was preparing to leave Ireland.
    F.G. was an Irish journalist and author (pen-name, among others, 'David Hogan'), member of the Irish volunteers, and Director of the Government Information Bureau. He gave the speech at JB's farewell party.

To Alan Pryce-Jones   United Kingdom Representative to Eire
                                  50 Upper Mount Street

15 August 1943   Dublin

My dearest Bog,
I am coming back on August 30th. Pipers until Sept 4th, then I want to come to you for a night or two (Min of Inf during the day). Is this going to be possible?

    Propeller going straight from here to Uffers [Uffington] at Michaelmas with kids – baby has a cold, Powlie [PSGB] very like Ernie. But has no expression on his face and a Dublin accent very useful for post-war world where accents will give a chap a start in life.

I saw a lot of the Captain [R. Shaw] who was charming and who wrote two damned good articles on Ireland in *The Toimes* as a result of his visit. I have known his Anglo sisters for two and a half years. Very grateful to you for telling me of him. We got on well.

    Red ink rather vulgar what? Cracky called the other day. Longing to see you. WRITE and tell me if September 4 is OK.

    Simpson – of course, I remember now.

    Love, John B

Shaw was political secretary to the Hon. John Astor and chief proprietor of *The Times*.

Eight:

Dear old, bloody old England
Of telegraph poles and tin

September 1943 to September 1945

Greyly tremendous the thunder
Hung over the width of the wold
But here the green marsh was alight
In a huge cloud cavern of gold,
And there, on a gentle eminence,
Topping some ash trees, a tower
Silver and brown in the sunlight,
Worn by sea-wind and shower,
Lincolnshire Middle Pointed.

'A Lincolnshire Church'

In February 1943 JB gave a talk on the Home Service about coming back to England: 'It is something really terrible, this longing for England we get when we are away. . . . I do not believe we are fighting for the privilege of living in a highly developed community of ants. That is what the Nazis want. For me, at any rate, England stands for the Church of England, eccentric incumbents, oil-lit churches, Women's Institutes, modest village inns, arguments about cow parsley on the altar, the noise of mowing machines on Saturday afternoons, local newspapers, local auctions, the poetry of Tennyson, Crabbe, Hardy and Matthew Arnold, local talent, local concerts, a visit to the cinema, branch line trains, light railways, leaning on gates and looking across fields; for you it may stand for something else, . . . something to do with Wolverhampton or dear old Swindon or wherever you happen to live. . . .'[1]

My parents returned to Garrards Farm in Uffington in the autumn of 1943 but things could never be the same as they had been before the outbreak of war. A sadness hovered. After the silence of Ireland the noise of aeroplanes was deafening. My brother remembers that some of the planes pulled gliders behind them. My mother, whose grasp of modern science was non-existent, asked Maurice Bowra, 'Are the ones in front pulling the ones behind?' 'No,' replied Bowra, 'the ones behind are pushing the ones in front.'

Gradually village life resumed its idiosyncratic pattern and as usual 'The Folkies', my parents' name for the selfless and deeply holy

Revd and Mrs Harton, played a large part. My mother wrote to JB (undated) in London, 'Mrs Folky has been very irritating lately. I said to her at Woolstone Fête, "My God, Watley-White's a good organizer!" and she said, averting her head, "Oh darling, you mustn't use that word." I thought I'd like her to hear some of *your* blasphemous language in the mornings. Then next time I saw her I said THANK GOD – the first words I spoke. She had been telling poor Mrs Matthews [an overworked and busy farmer's wife] that she ought to take on the Mothers' Union Young Wives' Group. . . . Mrs M. protested and Mrs Folky said, "It doesn't rest with you, it rests with God, and if He wants you to do it He will give you the Grace of time." Mrs Matthews then suggested that Mrs Harton ran the farm for twenty-four hours; *then* she could talk about Grace.'[2]

JB continued to be involved with the Workers' Educational Association and even taught drama for a few weeks at the social centre in Lambourn on Monday evenings, after he caught the evening train home to Challow. My brother attended Mrs Rintoul's school in the village and went birds'-nesting with Roy Weaver, who lived in Pear Tree Cottage next to Garrards. His sister, Sally, became *my* best friend. I played with her in the yard between our two back doors for long hours. Whenever I got into trouble, I was put to sit on a tied-up horse, unable to get off. (JB and I went to Sally's wedding in Uffington in 1958, after which JB wrote the poem 'Sally Weaver's Wedding', first published on 11 July 1959 in *The New Yorker*.)

Florence May Weaver, Roy and Sally's mother, nicknamed 'Queenie', since she was the first baby born in Uffington after Queen Victoria's death in 1901, remembers how JB hated horses and always sat in the back of the four-wheeled dog cart in case he wanted to bale out quickly. My mother tried to interest JB in riding. She gave him a course of lessons with Miss Joy Bassett, who ran the stables at Ashdown House, a remote place on the downs a few miles from Uffington. 'At one stage he asked me to teach him to trot,' recalls Miss Bassett, 'but he was one of those types who leans forward and flaps his elbows in and out and we gave up trying in the end.'[3] Years later my mother discovered that JB had often persuaded Miss Bassett to walk him out of sight behind a hedge where they dismounted and read poetry. Finally she took JB out herself but when they found themselves in a field of bullocks JB screamed at her, 'You've brought me into a field of bulls to kill me.' He never rode again.

'He used to read poetry to Mrs Betjeman while she was cooking,' remembers Queenie. 'I remember the day you got back from Ireland with the new nursemaid from Dublin, Pauline Fergusson. You all had lice you'd caught on the boat. Your mother had to bicycle to Faringdon to get delousing apparatus and swathed everyone's heads in capilline bandages for days.'[4] Pauline Fergusson (now Mrs Morton) remembers her time at Uffington as 'lots of fun; there were endless picnics and Mr Betjeman used to parody everything and make fun of the local people. Paul was the apple of his eye. He used to make up poems in railway stations and he was endlessly looking at churches. There was lots of socializing; the Pipers and John Sparrow were always visiting. Of the locals, they saw a lot of the Hartons and the MacKenzies.'[5] Arthur and Eileen MacKenzie, he a sculptor and she a textile designer, lived up the village street in the Old Bakehouse. She had hand-printed the bedcovers for the spare room at Garrards, in a bold modern design of shocking pink and black flowers. My brother and I sometimes stayed the night with them if my parents went to London, and marvelled at the smell of goats and fresh bread. Eileen MacKenzie remembers, 'I first met John at the top of the church tower where he was showing the bells to Arthur. He had just persuaded him to join him as a bell-ringer and we saw a lot of him after that. He used to bring the Pipers round to the Bakehouse and we'd go to supper parties at Garrards. Both John and Penelope seemed to know about *everything* – but what impressed me most of all was his rendition of "Do you remember an inn, Miranda" in the village hall. The Packers, the Weavers, the Baileys and the rest of the village were spellbound. I think he was shy of the village, though. I never saw him walking down the street in the middle of the day – he felt self-conscious – instead I'd see him lurking early on damp misty Sundays when no one was about, with people who were staying at Garrards, like Bob Boothby.'[6]

When on leave John Sparrow visited Garrards as often as he could. He wrote to my brother (12 April 1944), 'Dear Paul, you must learn to like Rimes (or rhymes). It will help you to read. Here are some Rhymes:

Bell Mice Ride Pin Dust
Hell Vice Pride Sin Lust
Sell Nice Fried Inn Trust

With love from your Godfather John.'[7]

On his return to England JB reported back to the Ministry of Information in Malet Street, London, to resume his work in the Films Division with Arthur Calder-Marshall, his friend and colleague from before the war, and his new friend, the humorist, Honor Tracy. The Crown Films Unit made documentaries from British newsreels about the war effort, which were distributed all over the world. They also intercepted German newsreels and other foreign material of enemy origin, edited them and built up evidence on the war atrocities. Among other films, JB was in charge of a series of positive propaganda documentaries called the *Pattern of Britain*. When he left, his secretary, Hazel Sullivan, wrote (19 July 1944), 'All your nice films were taken from us. . . . Our new films are very good for our morale as they include *VD*, *Infant Mortality* and *Borstal Boys*. . . . I have no doubt that you will appreciate to the full just what you are missing. . . . Ann Woodley still looks very nice in slacks. . . . She has asked me to say that she would like to send her love but is peeved with you because you did not kiss her goodbye as promised. Since you have gone Miss J.H.D. [Joan Hunter Dunn] no longer smiles at me. . . .'[8]

Hazel Sullivan also recalls in a letter to Lord Arran, 'Our office was a new one built in the Cloisters and when 17th March dawned and the MOI completely ignored it, Mr Betjeman decided that he would make a stand for the glory of Ireland. After lunch he returned with a very large flag of Ireland which I had to drape around him toga-wise. Somehow he had also got hold of two highly coloured stuffed South American spiders, beautifully coloured but terrifying, and one of these was fixed as a brooch on his shoulder and the other was perched precariously on his then small bald patch. He announced that he was going to see the Minister, and had a mild bet with me that although people would turn around and look at him as he passed by he would not excite any undue attention. I was instructed to follow at a discreet distance. He left the Cloisters and proceeded with great dignity along the open path flanked with the large pillars that lead to the Senate House, thence through the doors and up the grand staircase (Julius Caesar entering his Senate could not have done better). As he said, many looked but went on their way unconcerned and without comment.'[9]

In January 1944 JB had begun writing book reviews for the *Daily Herald*, then under the editorship of Percy Cudlipp, his erstwhile colleague on the *Evening Standard*. JB's agent, Edmund Cork, had negotiated a fee of fourteen guineas a week, increasing to eighteen in July 1945. Once a week he had to look through about thirty books, select six or seven, read them and write about them in eight hundred words. This job was to become the bane of his life and he never stopped complaining about it to my mother and all and sundry. But now that he had two children and my brother was set to go to the Dragon School in Oxford, he could not afford to pass up the wage even though he had to write what he referred to as 'vulgar telegrams'.

In March 1944 JB was moved to the 'P Branch' of the Admiralty who were stationed at the Empire Hotel in Bath. During the week he lodged in a bed and breakfast in Macauley Buildings on Widcombe Hill. In April 1944 Honor Tracy wrote, 'Please send me your Bath address because I am writing a farewell poem for you. At present I am drunk, I was picked out of the canal last night by PC Smith at two a.m. Case coming up on Tuesday. . . . How I love you. I am very drunk. There is no need to read this letter to everyone who comes into your office. Don't tell Arthur [Calder-Marshall] about the canal.'[10]

In his Admiralty post, JB was in charge of two publications which were circulated to various branches around the country (there were twelve Rear Admirals dotted about): the 'Green 'un', as it was called, supplied current bulletins about the best places to find supplies of labour, steel and wood etc.; and the 'Pink 'un', which was top secret, gave bulletins about recent damage, for instance: 'Don't try to find labour in Acton because it's been bombed.' JB had three people working directly under him in his office, including Arnold Weinstock (now Lord Weinstock). He remembers JB well. 'He looked frightfully scruffy; he chain-smoked and always had a cigarette hanging from his top lip. He was working for the *Daily Herald* at the time and he used to get all these trashy books sent to him. He'd give them to us to read and we said which ones we liked and he then reviewed our selection which he got to keep. He had this friend called Bryan Little who was in another section of the Admiralty and they'd bicycle off on architectural excursions all the time.'[11] JB's and Bryan Little's time in Bath culminated in the latter's book, *The Building of Bath*, published by Collins in 1947. (In his foreword he writes, 'I have had much help and encouragement from Mr John Betjeman and Mr John Summerson.') JB and Little often visited Fortt's restaurant in Bath, which had a ground floor like a corner house where you could get tea.

There were many other activities which ran concurrently with his official war job. Geoffrey Taylor wrote from Ireland (13 April 1944), 'I see you are rising to a sort of froth of fame, which is fun but irritating because it obscures intrinsic seriousness.'[12] JB had already made two television appearances and even become the new question-master on *The Brains Trust*, both on radio and television. His time at the Ministry of Information had given him a knowledge of film-making and by now he had made well over fifty radio broadcasts which gave him a head start over many newcomers, when it came to being relaxed on air. Percy Popkin, JB's fastidiously correct accountant from Romford, Essex, wrote after his first performance (29 September 1943), 'The wife and I do hope you will be chosen frequently for *Brains Trust* Master. It was, to our minds, a first-rate performance on your part and the session went through smoothly enough to the listener and one could not have expected it better even if it had been rehearsed.'[13]

JB's guiding star at the BBC was Douglas Cleverdon. They had met at Oxford, both first-generation university students. The son of a wheelwright, Douglas arrived at Oxford as a shy eighteen-year-old from Bristol Grammar School and was plunged straight into the artistic and aristocratic set. Harold Acton introduced Cleverdon and Betjeman and theirs was to be one of the most mutually fruitful friendships for the rest of their lives. On leaving Oxford, Douglas became a bookseller with a glamorous shop in Bristol where Roger Fry made a hanging sign and Eric Gill designed the name-board. This became famous because it was the first use of Gill's 'sans-serif' typeface. JB bought books from his shop and sold his first book, *Mount Zion*, there. In the late thirties Douglas joined the BBC and began to commission JB. He was responsible for putting on 'How to Look at a Town', which proved extraordinarily popular. 'My recent increasing interest in architecture,' wrote David Gurney (Samuel's nephew) in his diary (7 July 1943), 'led me to listen to a BBC broadcast last night by John Betjeman in the "How to . . ." series. This was one of the best broadcasts the BBC have ever undertaken.'[14]

Cleverdon was an impresario to poets, writers and actors: he was like a top trainer running a string of racehorses. He got things out of them that they never knew they could do. He used to shut Dylan Thomas in the BBC library with a supply of beer and sandwiches (and a tin waste-paper basket) until he had produced a script to meet a deadline. This method led, amongst other things, to the writing of *Under Milk Wood*. He helped JB endlessly. 'How greatly you have improved my script. . . . You brought the whole thing to life and I am profoundly grateful to you,' wrote JB in the summer of 1943.[15] After the war, Cleverdon persuaded JB and Osbert Lancaster to take part in extempore conversations which went out live. They were hysterically funny since both men got the giggles on air, so badly that the administrator wrote a stiff letter to Cleverdon asking him to keep Betjeman and Lancaster under control.

Publishers, editors and literary ladies began to hover around JB's burgeoning fame like moths around a flame. Graham Greene, who worked for Eyre and Spottiswoode, asked him to write an introduction to Oliver Onions's novel, *In Accordance with the Evidence*. Edith Sitwell wrote to him (1 November 1943), 'Isn't Hardy's "Tolerance" a wonderful poem? I wish we had a great many lives and no bores, so that we could devote all those lives to poetry, and nothing else. I *would* if I had my way.'[16] The firm of Hamish Hamilton wanted their fifty pound advance back for the undelivered book of Graham Robertson's letters which JB had agreed in September 1939 to edit. He tried to assuage Hamilton's anger by offering him a book of his 'Percy Progress CBE' stories, to no avail (the first appeared in *Lilliput* in late 1944 and the series was not continued). Michael Sadleir of Constable proposed a book on John Oliver Hobbes. Joyce Grenfell asked him if he always answered his fan letters. 'I do,' she wrote, 'even if they are addressed to Miss Joan Grenville.'[17] *Time and Tide* commissioned an article on Bristol. Christina Foyle, who ran the Lecture Agency, asked JB to be on her list of lecturers and Collins were desperate for him to help with a new series of architectural guide-books, using colour photography, against which JB had strong views. Berta Ruck, the novelist, wrote a letter of grateful thanks (24 January 1945) for a review he had written on *Intruder Marriage*, in the *Daily Herald*: 'After so much of the unadulterated contempt to which I am now hardened, it is quite breath-taking as well as pleasant to receive in *print* kind, sympathetic words about mystery telling.'[18] Cecil Day Lewis pressed him for an article on Dublin for his esoteric literary magazine *Orion* and he went to Kettner's for a lunch organized by John Sutro to launch his friend Peter Quennell as editor of *Cornhill*.

But, despite approaches from other publishers, it was to Murray's that JB remained faithful, and he now set about revising their *Handbooks*. Together with John Piper, he began to explore the well-hedged lanes of leafy Bucks for *Murray's Guide to Buckinghamshire* (published in 1948). Meanwhile, since his return from Ireland he had written a few new poems and collected up older ones which had already been published in periodicals in order to make up enough for his fourth volume of poetry (and his third with Murray's), *New Bats in Old Belfries*, which came out at the end of 1945. The poems, which Nevill Coghill had helped to select, had detectable inspirations. His time in Bath inspired 'In a Bath Teashop', his operation on a sebaceous cyst, 'Before the Anaesthetic or A Real Fright', and during his recuperation, while staying with Arthur MacKenzie's father at Beaulieu in Hampshire, he wrote 'Youth and Age on Beaulieu River, Hants'.

In October 1943, a month after he left Ireland, JB was elected to the exclusive Kildare Street Club in Dublin and paid his two guineas to be an overseas member. He forgot none of the friends he had made in Ireland and in some cases he tried to further their careers. Geoffrey Taylor and JB shared a love of insects and JB arranged for him to do a book on insects for Collins's 'Britain in Pictures' series. (Later Taylor also wrote a King Penguin on the subject.) Geoffrey suspected it was JB who had got him the job and wrote (8 November 1944), 'Nice of you. And a nice book I've done. All about the English clergy, really. They were *all* entomologists as well as poets.'[19] When Desmond Fitzgerald wrote a play, however, it was read by JB's agent and deemed to be too tragic. Patrick Kavanagh's constant outpourings and demands were hard for JB to keep up with: 'I have a headache due to having been drinking Scotch. . . . I write to inform you with some regret that I didn't get married yet. . . . Can you help me with a job?'[20] he wrote on one occasion (11 January 1944). My mother had already given him some cooking pans for a wedding present, which he sent back to Reggie Ross-Williamson, JB's successor as Press Attaché. Kavanagh's demands for a job continued throughout 1944 but JB was unable to find him anything regular.

Although JB had been thinking of getting 'a nice dim job in the BBC'[21] (he wrote to Hamish Hamilton 24 September 1944), when he was released from the Admiralty towards the end of 1944, he changed his mind and in January of the following year he accepted a post with the British Council, the recently formed organization designed to spread cultural propaganda overseas. His friend from Oxford days, Jack Yates, already worked there. The books and periodicals which were for export had been removed to Oriel College, Oxford and JB was to be in charge of the whole department of nearly two hundred women. 'The buzz went round that this rather distinguished poet was to join us,' remembered Daphne Shackleton. 'Since I was a small cog in the periodicals department, I did not imagine my life would be greatly altered until Diana [Craig], one of the girls with whom I shared a flat, was picked to be his secretary. . . . He had *asked* for her.'[22] The flat where Daphne, Mary Brocklebank and Diana Craig lived was in the Banbury Road. Diana was seventeen, plump, blonde and tennis-playing, with an irresistible giggle. 'I remember meeting him in the signing-on room, we had a laugh and the next thing I knew I was his secretary. He was tremendously unstuffy and completely approachable about anything. He used to lie on his back on the floor to dictate letters. I have never met anyone who was such fun in my whole life. He took me everywhere – all around the colleges and to Sunday lunch at the Colonel's [Kolkhorst].'[23]

During the summer the office moved from Oriel to a wing of Blenheim Palace. JB organized a competition of sketches of Blenheim by the staff and got John Piper to judge it. It was won by a girl called

Clementina Fisher. JB stayed at Yarnton with Kolkhorst for much of that summer and bicycled on the back roads past Bladon Heath and through the park to the palace each morning. Yarnton offered a familiar and eccentric background to JB's hectic life. There was no petrol to get back to Uffington as much as he would have liked and Yarnton proved a comfortable compromise.

'You were either in the Colonel's set or out, there was no half way,'[24] said Gerard Irvine, who used to bicycle over at weekends from St Stephen's House in Oxford, where he was training to be a clergyman at the time. Kolkhorst had a square head, a cleft chin, a huge forehead and the famous nose of his Magee forebears. His circle were a motley crew – including aesthetic dons, such as John Bryson and Toby Strutt, the old aesthete and great Anglo-Catholic; Hedley Hope-Nicholson, a Firbankian figure – quarrelsome, snobbish and difficult – and Stuart Hill, who spent an hour and a half doing his make-up every morning. The point about the kind and avuncular Kolkhorst was that he was a great listener; it was hard not to use him as a confessor.

My parents were heartbroken when their landlord, John Wheeler, said he needed Garrards Farm for his son Peter to live in. Early in 1945 they began looking for other houses: first, a red brick farmhouse at Stanford in the Vale, which fell through, and another house at Avebury. It was Robert Heber-Percy who first found the Old Rectory at Farnborough, near Wantage, a mid-Georgian red brick house seven hundred feet up in the Berkshire Downs. In May Lord Chetwode paid three and a half thousand pounds for the house and gave it to my parents as a belated wedding present. My mother wrote to JB at Yarnton (25 June 1945), 'We may have bitten off more than we can chew with Farnboro' but I regard it as a last stand against the slave state. If by taxation and filling in forms they make it impossible for us to live there then we shall have to emigrate to St Helena as you once suggested.'[25] My mother was desperate for JB to be happy at Farnborough. He would have a library (which he had never had before) for the myriad books he had bought over the years. She imagined he would give up his job at the *Daily Herald*, whose weekly deadlines put him in such a bad temper. She knew that living at Farnborough would be hard work – the house was four times the size of Garrards – but she determined to create a happy home.

1. JB, 'Coming Home', BBC talk (25 February 1943).
2. PB's papers, Beinecke Library, Yale University.
3. Joy Bassett, CLG interview (1993).

4. Queenie Weaver, CLG interview (1993).
5. Pauline Morton, CLG interview (1993).
6. Eileen MacKenzie, CLG interview (1993).
7. JB's papers, University of Victoria, British Columbia.
8. JB's papers.
9. JB's papers.
10. JB's papers.
11. Lord Weinstock, CLG interview (1993).
12. JB's papers.
13. JB's papers.
14. JB's papers.
15. Mrs Douglas Cleverdon's papers.
16. JB's papers.
17. JB's papers.
18. JB's papers.
19. JB's papers.
20. JB's papers.
21. JB's papers.
22. South African Broadcasting Corporation.
23. Diana Peel, CLG interview (1992).
24. Gerard Irvine, CLG interview (1993).
25. JB's papers.

To Bess Betjemann   Films Division
                                             Ministry of Information
                                             Malet Street
10 September 1943   London WC1

Darling Bessie,

May I come down and stop a night with you at ye olde Rose Cottage [West Kington] on Saturday next (Sept 18). I should not be able to leave London until after luncheon. That is to stay Sept 18th. I shall have to go back on Sunday, alas!

I arrived here last week. After two days I felt so ill – probably due to the change of climate – that I had to go to bed. I stayed with a friend, Arthur Elton, in Hampstead. Now I am up again. I don't like to stay with friends nowadays, because of food shortages etc., for any length of time. So I have installed myself with the Cowley Fathers, Edwards House, 22 Great College St, Westminster, SW1. But this is, I think, more than I can stand. We have to be in by nine-thirty p.m. Clean our own cells, make our own beds, sweep floors, help with the washing up and then I bicycle up to this place feeling like a rag. The food is, of course, communal and awful. But it is all very holy. Awakened at five forty-five a.m. No, I don't think I shall stick it. I am wanted to help there because twenty people are coming for a retreat this weekend and they are short-handed. I feel obliged to stay because after all it is hospitality and not expensive. But oh how I long for Rose Cottage and to see you again. So does Archie and Bill who will be coming with me. DO GET SOME STUFF FOR ARCHIE'S NOSE.

It is like this at present:

Longing to see you.

Much love (and remember me to Katherine), from John

'Bill' alias 'Jumbo' was Archie's dim elephant companion who never spoke. Mending Archie's nose was something all the women in JB's life have had to do. PB always did it with lisle stocking material.

To Maurice Bowra   Garrards Farm
                                                Uffington
17 October 1943   Berkshire

Dear Maurice,
Thank you so very much for the Russian Book [*A Book of Russian Verse*].
It reads grandly. I didn't deserve your flattering reference.
   Your essay at the beginning is most illuminating. I never realised
Russian poetry was so recent – and, of course, I never realised there had
been more of that business about Augustans, Romantics, etc. I think
about the best thing is 'I loved you once, and in my soul maybe'. There
is one omission which I suggest you rectify in the next edition. Do put
in a brief biography of each of the poets – only about six lines each,
saying when they lived and how they lived and how they died. All the
translations, I believe, retain the Russian metres. This is worth
mentioning too.
   Good luck to the book, old boy. I am sure it will do well. I trust the
party will not condemn it for being pre-1917.
   It is the best piece of production I have seen come out of Macmillans.
W. A. Morison's 'When o'er the yellowing corn . . .' is a nice piece of
translation.
   Propeller is mad – she thinks only of chickens, cooking and horses.
Powlie has made a crucifix. Candida still has no expression. I long to see
you.
   Love, John B

   This is the only one of many letters to M.B. which survives.

To Cecil Beaton   Personal
13 November 1943   Films Division

Dear Cecil,
I have discussed this question of your movie camera (which would have
to be 35 mm) with the Director here and he has seen Francis [Williams].
   There is no possibility of getting a camera from a British unit,
desirable though that would be. There simply aren't any to spare and
they are all turning round madly, the cameras I mean. But a large
American film unit is going out to Lord Louis Mountbatten's command

for the express purpose of filming China and I think it would be best for you to approach Major Irving Asher of the US Army at Denham Studios and see if you could get one from him. This is a purely personal suggestion and I myself don't know Major Asher, so do not regard this as a Ministerial direction, it is just a piece of personal advice from

    Yours ever, John Betjeman

> Francis Williams was Controller of News and Censorship at this time.
>
>   During the early forties the Films Division of the Ministry of Information (where JB worked on his return) was known as Crown Film Unit and was making propaganda films about the War Effort and exporting them overseas.

To John Arlott   Garrards Farm
                                                  Uffington

27 December 1943   Berkshire

Dear Mr Arlott,
I am delighted with *Landmarks* and shall review it in the bloody old *Daily Herald* which is employing me for reviews now.

My goodness! what a discovery Lewis Morris is. I never knew he had it in him. 'The Epic of Hades' is such a bore. I never realised he had done much else. I immensely like, too, that Colchester man.

Alas, at Christmas I had a present from a friend which would have been invaluable to you – *Londoners' Song*. Edited by Wilford Whitless in 1898. Full of unknown stuff.

I've never appeared beside Wordsworth before and feel very honoured.

I am back home but being KILLED by the Min of Inf in London. A sadist in charge of the Films Division is trying to do me in. I am under him. Oh God! I have not time to do anything. That is part of his system of torture – trying to take work of a regular nature from me, so as to discredit me, while I have to fight to keep it.

A happier New Year than you expect to you.

Yours sincerely, John Betjeman

PS You don't cut across Geoffrey Taylor's and mine except in M[atthew] Arnold, who can't be printed too often anyhow.

> As a policeman in Southampton in the Incident Room in 1940 doing night duty, J.A. read everything JB had written. He wrote to him out of the blue asking if he would collaborate on an anthology. JB politely refused and J.A. collaborated with George

Rostrevor Hamilton instead. *Landmarks* was published in 1943 including his own poem, 'Cricket at Worcester'. His poems were very much in the manner of JB's. J.A. would have remained a provincial policeman had JB not introduced him to Geoffrey Grigson, who was a BBC Radio producer in Bristol in the forties. JB told Grigson he had met a policeman who was mad about poetry who might make an amusing broadcast.

To Gerard Irvine

2 January 1944

Garrards Farm
Uffington
Berkshire

My dear Prefect,
On the contrary I am ABSOLUTELY DELIGHTED with it [*True Aristocracy*] – a most learned little book with a lot of good stuff from Praed and Hood and some unknown eighteenth-century poets, I am most grateful to you. It was very kind indeed and I did not even send you a Christmas Card. Oh heaven! The guilt I feel.

I am a slave. I sit here writing letters for the few hours I get back or reading tripe to be reviewed by me in the *Daily Herald*. Failing that, I never leave Malet Street and very dull it is. I am trying to get a free-er job.

I have a postcard view (as Bradford would say) of Wardour Castle Chapel – but have never seen the chapel itself. Whose book plate in the *True Aristocracy*?

I fire watch with Canon Demant of St Paul's. Most interesting my evenings are, with him. The Dean is keen on having short services, but Canon Alexander, a recluse and tractarian-ish, won't hear of it. He is very old. The archdeacon is Lib Evangelical and Canon Cockin is the other one at St Paul's. St Martin's Ludgate is nice and lazy.

I met a woman in Min of Inf whose father was a retired clergyman (Broad) in Wotton-under-Edge. She knew you. I don't know her name. I spotted she was a clergyman's daughter before she told me she was.

A Happy New Year. Write again.

Your loving friend and schoolmaster, John B

True Aristocracy was a novel in verse written by Revd Dr E. E. Bradford, published in 1923 by Kegan and Paul, Trench and Trubner.

Canon Demant, who held the Moral Theology chair at Oxford, became a close friend and often stayed at Farnborough. JB's letters to him do not survive.

JB's enthusiasm for his old idea of starting a periodical called *The Church* was rekindled by his conversations with Canon Demant.

To Geoffrey Taylor   Garrards Farm
                                                       Uffington
2nd S[unday] after Epiphany 1944   Berkshire

Dear Geoffrey,
I thank you for yours of Jan 7th. I've had page proofs. It seems short of
the *Landmarks* but is infinitely better. Still, when they see Piper's
drawings the reviewers will think the text is any old stuff put in to fill
up. But we must suffer proudly. Ours is v. good indeed.
    I think you and I might do a book of Clergymen's verse 1700–1900.
    I've just found a wild and mad and ridiculous poet – Theo Marzials,
A Gallery of Pigeons (1873) – he was a friend of all the Pre-Raphaelites
and had a life 'tragic in the extreme' which is all I can find about him. I
should think he was ultra-decadent. Here are his most silly four lines
and funniest:

MARJORIE MINT AND VIOLET

A-DRYING ROUND US SET,

'TWAS ALL DONE IN THE FAÏENCE-ROOM

A-SPICING MARMALET

Love to Mary. Love to Sarah. Love to Reggie and Eileen – their lectures
to us are wonderful.
    Propeller *is* coming over. In April, I think.
    There are too many aeroplanes here. Too many people, too.
    Love, John B

> JB refers to the proofs of the poetry anthology, *English, Scottish and Welsh Landscape*,
> which he had edited with G. T. and compares it to John Arlott's anthology, *Landmarks*.

To Sir Giles Gilbert Scott   Uffington
                                                       Faringdon
27 January 1944   Berks

Dear Sir Giles,
Would you have any objection, should the war ever end and should I
ever have the opportunity of writing a book again on something that
interests me, of my undertaking a chronicle of the life of your family
over the past century and a half?

On the religious side I should say that I am at present what is known as Anglo-Catholic, but this has not prevented me from reading and admiring the work of Thomas Scott. My grandfather left me a huge bible with Scott's commentary attached and I have today bought William Cowper's copy of Thomas Scott's *Force of Truth*, a work of which I already possess a less attractive copy, and which I have read and recommended to many people.

On the architectural side, I think I possess and have read all Sir Gilbert's publications. I have an autographed copy of his book on Church Restoration. But more than this, an examination of Sir Gilbert's buildings whenever opportunity arises, convinces me that he is much traduced. I am sure that I could obtain illustrations of such jobs of his as the Martyrs' Memorial, St Mary Abbots, St Pancras, that church by Westminster Cathedral and St John's Chapel at Cambridge, which would convince people of his merit. As for his son, your father, I have in the past written to you about him and told you what unbounded admiration I have for his work. There is also John Oldrid to be considered. Finally there is yourself.

Would you object to my investigating this project (I do not anticipate any difficulty over a publisher, but I have made a rule for myself not to get commissioned by publishers until I have finished a book . . . bitter experience of getting an advance and not being able to complete the book and having to return the advance has taught me this). Also do you know where I am most likely to find letters, papers and drawings connected with your family?

Yours sincerely, John Betjeman

> Thomas Scott (1747–1821), a well-known commentator on the Bible, was the grandfather of Sir George Gilbert Scott (1811–78) and great-great-grandfather of Sir Giles Gilbert Scott (1880–1960).
>   'I am much interested in your proposal,' Sir G.G.S. replied (2 February 1944). Although JB's admiration for the Scotts never diminished, the book never happened.

To Mr Foges   1 Holly Place NW3
                                                  No, I mean
                                                  Min of Information
                                                  Malet St
1 February 1944   London WC1

Dear Mr Foges,
I have been thinking over our conversation of yesterday afternoon and I

should like to take this opportunity of explaining my position and conclusions in letter form. You were kind enough to suggest that I should consider writing or editing a series of guide-books to be illustrated with colour photography and published by Collins.

First as to my personal position. I have been asked by John Murray to edit a reissue of their famous handbooks which went out of print at about the beginning of the last war. This I feel I must accept not only because the task will be congenial to me, but also for two other weighty reasons: the handbooks themselves are ranged in a set manner and convenient format together with invaluable material which will form a basis for revision and gives Murray a flying start in the production of a really thorough, scholarly and readable guide-book to each county of England. I owe first loyalty to Murray who have been the publishers of [my] poems at considerable risk in the past and who are personally old friends of mine.

But even were I not committed to Murray, I should not like to undertake the editing of a series of guide-books with coloured photography as illustration for any publisher. First there is the initial inadvisability of breaking into the guide-book publishing world with yet another series. Ward Lock and Co. have produced a thoroughly serviceable and, if hideous, at any rate informed and excessively full, series of illustrated guides to all the seaside resorts and principal inland towns of England, Scotland and Wales. Methuen's have produced the *Little Guides*, which cover every English county and Wales. In each volume the county is treated alphabetically, parish by parish. The illustrations are poor and the information is aggressively antiquarian, but the series catches the church-crawling public and the growing numbers of amateur archaeologists. Finally there are *Burrows Guides* which are purely local and beneath contempt, a mere advertising racket to catch the local shopkeepers. You will see from this that there is no field open for a new series of guide-books, unless that series has something exceptional about it. The only chance I can see for such a projected series is one with exceptional illustrations. This has been tried in monochrome with the series financed by the Shell Oil Company which I edited and which came to an end with the outbreak of war. This series, despite excellent notices and good sales for certain counties and poor sales for others, could never have been produced profitably without the commercial backing it received from the Shell Company. Arthur Mee produced a few guides with, I think, Hodder and Stoughton, which had better monochrome photographs than most guides, but which did not look like succeeding. It is natural to conclude

therefore that a series of guides which depended on a new form of
illustration in colour, produced cheaply, *might* be a success, even
though the text covered well-tilled ground. But I do not regard it as a
certainty. And this brings me to the second reason for my not wishing
to edit such a series – colour photography.

After careful examination of the colour work, both in actual negative
and in half-tone blocks from the negatives which you showed me in
your colour photography work, I feel bound to conclude that colour
photography is excellent for detail work but useless for general views.
Batsford's produced a book of general views of England in colour
photography called *The Coloured Counties*. It was so frightening that
even they allowed aesthetics to get the better of finance and did not
advertise it unduly. Though I think the examples of general views
which you showed me are a slight improvement on this book, I think
that a series of guide-books illustrated with coloured photographs
would be prejudicial to a medium which, within its limitations of detail
work, has made so many improvements lately – bad for your reputation
and disastrous to Messrs Collins. At present in the general views those
objects in the photograph which are in focus are all right, though even
these have a certain sameness of colour and absence of selection and
emphasis, while the rest of the photograph, which is out of focus, is
covered by a mist of chemical-looking green for trees and grass and blue
for sky. Nor do I think, because it cannot see the multitude of colours
which the human eye sees, perhaps unconsciously, in let us say a tree in
leaf or a field, that the camera will ever replace the selective eye of the
artist when working in colour. It is just because the photographer works
in monochrome that he can get good landscape effects. Colour is a
handicap to him for this type of view. So it is if he wants to take a
general view of a building or a street. The only alternative to coloured
photographs which occurs to me for a series of guide-books is the
reproduction in colour of the work of artists, on the lines of the old
Black's *Colour Books*. It is up to Collins to consider whether such a
venture is worth undertaking. Personally I doubt it. And in case I
should here seem to allow personal prejudice in favour of the Murray
Guides let me say that I do not think such a series would in any way affect
the Murray series. I simply think it would be unoriginal and dull.

I do, however, see a most interesting and beautiful series of books
which Collins could produce in a field not dissociated with the original
guide-book suggestion and which I should be pleased to edit for them.
This series would make full use of colour photography at its best, that is
to say in detail work. Instead of producing books about places, let a

series be devised about things. For instance: English stained glass; furniture in its different periods; glass; stonecarving materials; and regional styles of architecture (perhaps as experiments in colour photography went on it might be possible to produce whole buildings in colour photography); country crafts; county types of farm cart and agricultural implement; geology; church towers; needlework; pottery; algae; marine animals; wall paintings; plasterwork, etc. It is merely for Collins to consider the subject this way round for it to be comparatively simple to find subjects and authors. The text would have to be scholarly and somewhat of the final word on the subject, none of this Batsford business of running up something in the office to justify the re-issue of a haul of old blocks called the 'Spirit of this' or 'the Heart of that' or the 'Magic of something else'. If you think this letter worth considering you might care to arrange a meeting for me with Collins to discuss it.

This is the longest letter I have typed for years and the first I have typed for a long while and I fear I cannot correct my typing errors without making an even worse mess than exists at present. You will have to use your imagination over words which appear difficult and remember that my typing though inaccurate is sincere.

Yours sincerely, John Betjeman

> Mr Foges was an editor at Collins. JB did not take on the editorship of the guides and was subsequently asked to write a book on Bristol. This did not materialize either, but in 1945 discussions about *English Parish Churches* began with Collins and the Shell Guides began again after the war.

To Edgar Anstey   Films Division

5 February 1944

You Dear Old Thing,
I hope you had a jolly time in leafy Devon.

Would you take it amiss if I composed a little note for *Documentary Newsletter* on the writing of commentaries? It would be done in all humility, but I have seen so many commentaries now that I am beginning to get the hang of what is wrong with some of them and I think I might make some helpful practical suggestions.

Will you come to dinner on Tuesday, 15 February, Holborn Restaurant at seven o'clock?

Yours ever, John Betjeman

E.A. was an author and also a military correspondent at the time.

The Documentary Newsletter was owned and published by Film Centre Ltd, 34 Soho Square and was published from January 1940 to November/December 1947. It continued as *Documentary Film News* (1948–9).

To Miss Coleman

14 February 1944

Dear Miss Coleman,
Yours was such a charming and kind letter, that I feel I must answer it. I am thereby helped to clarify my own position and may enlighten you.

First, about poor [A.E.] Coppard. My original review was twice as long as this one that appears and did not make the same sense (or lack of it). I was so horrified by the way it had been cut in the *D[aily] H[erald]* that I wrote to Coppard last week and tried to excuse myself.

You must know, however, that there are two things for a married man with children to do, in the present slave state: 1) to earn his living 2) to do what he knows he can do – in my case, write poetry.

I am employed in fearful work in a Government office which does not give me enough to support my family and keep up my commitments. I have therefore to earn outside money. This reviewing of second-rate books (and most are third-rate) was, I thought, confined to the Great British Public, to whom, I prayed God, I would be unknown as a writer. Your letter is a disillusion[ment] and I do hope that you are the only person who reads the *Daily Herald* who knows of me as a poet. I think you must be. Now if I continue with this *D.H.* job, I will be able – if the war ever ends – to retire to the little house where my family lives in the country and write the reviews better (for having more time to do them) *and* write poetry. I had a long fight with the *Daily Herald* over anonymity. I wanted to be anonymous just in case someone like you should see my writing therein.

I think the whole thing points a moral – there is no compromise with Mammon. Then I am faced with this – my family or my poetry? My physical comfort or my peace of mind? And those four factors do not fall into two divisions but four.

I am very grateful, once again, for your salutary letter. Yeats said you should never do journalism unless you did it so superlatively well that you could print it in a book afterwards. I do not agree with this. Journalism is woodwork, literature is sculpture. I must get better at woodwork and make my handwriting clearer for luckless souls and my matter palatable, if not for you, at least for the G.B.P. [Great British Public].

Yours, John Betjeman

Miss Coleman was a *Daily Herald* reader unknown to JB. JB's review of the poet and writer Alfred Edgar Coppard's book *Ugly Anna* had suffered in the cutting.

To George Barnes   Garrards Farm
                                                          Uffington
21 April 1944   Berkshire

Dear Prawls (a generic term for all three of you),
So long as I live I shall not forget that romantic visit to the Marsh.

The first sight of the farm, the LIKEN on the red tiles and the brick, the view over the Richard Wilson hills – gold Richard Wilson looking West, red and green Randolph Caldecott looking East. And then I shall never forget the next morning with that sea of mist below the island and the sheep bleating up through it. And breakfast and Tenterden and talks with you and All, including Anthony Prawls, to whom my affection.

The Kent and East Sussex [Railway] was rather cold but very beautiful. They did not take my ticket at Headcorn.

I enclose a W. B. Maxwell. Not the best, but quite a good one. The place for books of fiction is the Red Cross Book storage depot (where I got this) next to The Times Book Club in Wigmore St. Tons of stuff.

My address in Bath will be: P. Branch, Admiralty, Empire Hotel, Bath, whither I go May 1st. I will keep in touch.

Yours gratefully, John Betjeman

JB had first met the brilliant and funny G.B., who became Talks Director at the BBC in 1941, before the war. He and his wife Anne became great friends of JB's.

Prawls was the name of the Barneses' house in Kent.

During the weekend JB spent there they argued over the pronunciation of 'lichen'. The argument was to run and run, and on 26 July 1948 Evelyn Waugh wrote:

'I lie itchin'
Because of the imperfections of my kitchen
While you are bikin'
Round Berks studying the lichen.'

JB replied, 'Of course it is lityen not lycken'. Presumably he had mispronounced it on the radio in a reading of his poem 'Ireland with Emily'.

Anthony 'Prawls' was George's son.

To Nancy Mitford   16 Macaulay Buildings
                                      Widcombe Hill
16 May 1944   Bath

Darling Nancy,
I must say I like being here. Extreme Protestant household, lace
curtains, regular hours, rain over elms and chestnuts, crumbling Bath
stone, wallflowers and lilac and a feeling that one is on the edge of the
West Country.
    My work is so wonderfully boring that I am fascinated (temporarily)
by it.
    I hope you read *The Flute of Sardonyx* before you sent it to me. By Jove
it's decadent. I'd like to see Diana and Co. Give them my love. One
form of state control is as bad as another.
    Love, John Betjeman

> *The Flute of Sardonyx* by Edmund John (1913) was a collection of poems in the vein of E.
> E. Bradford.
>> I give my white-skinned boy a pearl,
>> Fair as his body . . .
> It caused a contemporary critic to write, 'The credit of English poetry is at stake, and
> sanitary measures are imperative.'
>   By now Diana and Oswald Mosley had two sons together.

To John Murray   P Branch
                                      Admiralty
                                      Empire Hotel
21 June 1944   Bath

Dear Jock,
I fear you may not have been able to read my last letter. This one is not
crossed.
    I hoped to be able to come up on Wednesday next. Now it will have
to be Wednesday week. The Head of my branch has been summoned to
his father's deathbed, which will mean I shall probably have to remain
here on Wednesday.
    I have written to the same effect to the Pipers.
    As regards the J. Summerson proposition – once again I say fine: but
I think it is too confining to make the picture books entirely
architectural, I think the pictures should include other objects e.g.

carts, trees, cairns, lichen on stone, even scenery when it cannot better be illustrated by line, railways, horrors etc. I see the books as one illustration per page and fairly small – a sort of picture equivalent of the guides. I think you should put old J. S. as head of the architectural pictures, but leave me in charge of the *general* editorship of both books, so as to avoid overlapping.

I have a rough format in mind of the picture books which I would like to get your opinion on when we meet on Wednesday week. I shall be up all day, so we might make a date. I shall be at the Admiralty I expect.

The War will never end.

Love to Diana [Murray], John B

PS Have written one more lyric.

> JB was to edit a reissue of the Murray's *Handbooks* which had gone out of print in the 1900s.
> JB and John Piper edited the guides to Buckinghamshire (1948) and Berkshire (1949) and gave them a completely new look. Summerson mooted one on Kent.

To Mabel Fitzgerald

Garrards Farm
Uffington
Berkshire

20 August 1944

Dear Mabel,

Many thanks to you for Desmond's play [*De Profundis*]. Yes, I will be some time reading it. My hours at the Admiralty are nine a.m. to seven thirty p.m. Hellish. Good old Dublin and its right sense of time. My mornings are spent reviewing rubbish for the *Daily Herald* – once a week my articles appear and I thank God none of my friends see the paper. So Desmond's play will have to be sandwiched into a free moment. But I look forward to reading it. I will hand it on to the BBC.

We are all well here – save that Candida has a slight cough. I get home on Sundays which is very lucky.

We miss Dublin a lot. More than words can express. I feel a fierce desire to be travelling in the train from Dalkey or going on the hill train round Howth. What a wonderful book *Dubliners* is to an exile, such as I now feel myself.

Love to Desmond and D[?] and family and all of you. Oh to be by that white marble mantelpiece with the croquet lawn outside and tea and cakes within!

Yours ever, John B

M.F. and her husband Desmond were great friends of JB's in Ireland. He had been Minister of Defence and written several plays, one of which, *The Saint*, was produced at the Gate Theatre, Dublin. He wrote a number of others which were never put on.

To Cyril Connolly   Garrards Farm
                                                         Uffington
14 September 1944   Berkshire

A Cyróil, a chara [Dear Cyril],
I did like to hear from you. I'm so bloody overworked at the Admiralty on the most crashingly dull stuff that I wouldn't like to promise an article on the tempting subject (which I should make BRISTOL, the loveliest city in England – only beaten by Edinburgh) if I had the time. But my hours are nine a.m. to seven thirty p.m. daily. I was trying to rid myself of the Admiralty by the end of this month. But I fear the Slave State has got me in its clauses (newspaper intellectual pun). The people, however, are nice and honest with whom I work.

I enclose a poem for you, if you would like to print it and can read the writing. The town name is DUNGARVAN. It's a bit simple.

Bath is a joy to be in. I've firewatched over the Kimble Memorials on Thursday nights. I've told lots of people that they are your relatives. Bath Abbey is very low and lazy. They had a 'religion and life' week in Bath lately – one of those absurd low church and non-conformist get-togethers, where everybody sacrifices a bit of what they believe for the sake of 'unity' and the resultant faith amounts to nothing or the L[owest] C[ommon] M[ultiple] of all those present – and I found after firewatching, to my amazement, that there was a weekday celebration of H[oly] C[ommunion] in the Abbey going on. I said to the curate afterwards, 'I'm sorry I was late for the service: I would have turned up in time if I had thought there was going to be a service.' He replied, 'Oh well, there isn't normally a service but this is Religion and Life week.' He didn't see that his remark was rather funny. I'll certainly do the 'Where shall John go' if I can get out of the Ad[miral]ty. I'd enjoy it. But it would depend on that. I see no end to the wars, and greater troubles still with the plansters if they ever do end.

Love to L. Propeller sends her love. John B

The poem JB sent was 'The Irish Unionist's Farewell to Greta Hellstrom in 1922'.

To G. A. Kolkhorst   Garrards Farm
                                                       Uffington
17 September 1944   Berkshire

Darling Colonel,
Thank you very much – notice *I* thank you very much – it is vulgar just
to write 'Thank you very much' – for my happy night, a prelude, please
God, to more happy ones, at Ye Olde Manor.

The train journey was crowded, cold and long but when I returned I
found I had to get my own tea.

The weather continues inclement. We are planting mangels this
season and replacing them with wurzels in August and crossing them
next Christmas so as to get mangel-wurzels.

My love to Mrs Trelease and to Sister.

A Happy Christmas from John Betjeman

> Mrs Dolly Trelease was an impoverished cousin of 'Colonel' Kolkhorst. She took over
> from 'Sister' and ran the house.

To Geoffrey Taylor   Garrards Farm
                                                       Uffington
18 September 1944   Berkshire

My dear Geoffrey,
It's not Adprints but the Curwen Press who deserve the credit. And *we*
got the Curwen Press to do the job – I mean J. Piper did. How odd
being reviewed by A. A. Milne. He was fair puzzled, wasn't he?

I don't think I have ever been so miserable in my life as I am now. I
have not had the *time* to write one line of poetry since May. I have had
the urge time and again but not the time and now all my perceptions are
blunted. We are in a slave state here and I am beginning to think I would
as soon be in prison or dead. Everything one loves threatened by
post-war plansters of different types. Satire impossible owing to the
law of libel. No redress, just arrogant destruction by keen young
careerists left and right. I don't see any end to the war – not for two
years at least in Europe and another three for Japan on top of that.

I've found Canon Rawnsley's *Book of Bristol Sonnets* with v. good

C. Tennyson-Turner-style stuff. Also I have netted a fine haul of nineteenth-century wood engraved anthologies in mint-ish condition in Bath.

Your mother and I see your cousin P. Morton Shand, who holds our views. Love to Reggie and Eileen. Love to Mary. Propeller would send her love if I was to bother to go to one of the loose-boxes and ask her.

Love, John B

English, Scottish and Welsh Landscape had just been published.

To J. C. Trewin   P. Branch
6 October 1944   Bath

Dear Mr Trewin,
I thank you very much. I return the proof and I hope you are able to read my corrections.

It is a great and unusual pleasure to be allowed the leisure to correct a proof.

I will indeed let you know if any book comes along which seems in my line. ENGLISH CHURCH ARCHITECTURE, ENGLISH SCOTTISH WELSH AND IRISH ARCHITECTURE, anything about Ireland except archaeology, I can always do for you.

I suppose my opening para[graph] in the review could be omitted – though I rather like it. The only other thing would be to cut out the whole T. L. Dale book.

Yours, John Betjeman

J.C.T., the dramatic critic and author, was Literary Editor of the *Observer* at the time. He had praised *English, Scottish and Welsh Landscape* and asked JB to review for him.

To Mabel Fitzgerald   St Austell (Cornish Calendar)

16 October 1944

Dear Mabel,
There's no doubt that *De Profundis* is a fine piece of work. It is full of ideas and the sense of sin and guilt in it is terrific.

But I have tried it out on my agent (Hughes Massie) who is

particularly good at placing things like this and his reader says that 'there is no chance of its stage production because there is no opening for a play of ideas' and that 'though it shows a most sensitive apprehension of things it would be regarded by many people as too tragic without the uplift of great tragedy'. In fact it is a play to be *read* and it should obviously be published is what I say. But had my agent considered placing it as a *book* he would have said so.

I am v. sorry. But I am v. glad to have read it. Of course, Desmond is a lovely writer. Why on earth doesn't he do more of it now? It's maddening that he should not have published and written more. If he can write this, he can write a great prose book – why doesn't he turn it into a novel?

Love to you all from us all, John B

To John Piper

5 November 1944

Garrards Farm
Uffington
Berkshire

Dear Mr Piper,
I was entranced – enraptured with Hassell's *Grand Junction*. A superb piece of generosity, superb aquatinting, lovely copy in rich morocco. God bless you and reward you. I send a feeble return of the compliment. I can't tell you how nice it was to get a book as a present and NOT FOR REVIEW. Particularly so as I once had the book and had to sell it, owing to poverty.

I was going to write to you to tell you that I thought the Devizes illustrated article one of the best things you had done. Knowing the town well, I travelled over it again and found myself reminded of all I had liked in it. The baby is, as usual, yelling and I cannot concentrate much on what I write.

Re Tuesday: Wednesday would be easier. I've to spend Tuesday in Swindon on my way back from opening a Coolmore [Summerson] exhibition in Bath. I suppose you wouldn't be free to do a church crawl? I shall be free *all day Wednesday* and part of Thursday. I will be in Bath on Monday.

Love to Goldilegz, Heddi and Clarissa, John B

Hassell's *Tour of the Grand Junction – with an historical and topographical description of those parts through which the Canal passes* (with hand aquatints) was published in 1819.

To Geoffrey Taylor   Garrards Farm
                                                       Uffington
24 November 1944   Berkshire
St Minver (Cornish Calendar)

My dear Geoffrey,
I thank you deeply for your letter and for the beautiful manuscript
book. If anything will encourage me to write again that will. I enclose a
poem I have written lately and hope you like it. I have sent it to old Cyril
but I doubt if it is up to his standard.

Yes, who is that bitch Cressida Ridley? Describing Crabbe as
'humourless' and Matthew Arnold's 'Scholar Gipsy' and 'Thyrsis' as
'literary'. It is just the New Stateswoman feeling she must be different
and giving it to a friend of Cyril and Raymond at a smart party in
Bedford Square, if such a party can be called smart. I was pleased
really; the whole thing was so characteristic. What was shocking was
the ignorance displayed.

I am delighted to hear you have done insects for those crooks. I saw
no reviews. I never get press cuttings owing to persecution mania. I
don't like them.

Norman Nicholson is an untechniqued poet. Marie Stopes is not. I
become swamped with verse nowadays as these silly fools like to see
themselves in the *Daily Herald* but the *Daily Herald* doesn't.

I have left the Admiralty. I got guilty about my unsuitability for that
sort of work. I was able to do it all right and the people were charming
and so was Bath. But I got a sense of futility. I dare say I shall have it
more, looking after a hundred quarrelling women in the British
Council, which I do next week probably.

We are quite servantless. But we are well and very much older in soul
and appearance. Love to Mary and Sarah.

How I agree with you about the C of E. But even that is selling the
pass-all for union at the expense of unity which of course means the
LCM of belief as there can be no HCF as there is only one faith.

Yours for ever, John B

John Piper and I went to Nottingham this week and put bicycles on
the train and went out miles through red foggy cemetery-sprinkled
suburb to a church called Tollerton which we thought had not been
touched since 1775 when it was rebuilt. It had had thousands spent on
ruining it in 1909. The next day we bicycled miles up hill to a church
called Papplewick which we saw from the 1938 *Kelly* had not been

touched since 1795. Outside it was a dream of bold Strawberry Hill. Inside there were the white Chippendale Gothic delicate N[orth] and W[est] galleries and an enamelled East Window after Lawrence. But the whole of the nave and chancel had been mucked up with unstained oake in NINETEEN FORTY. JB

Cressida Ridley had reviewed *English, Scottish and Welsh Landscape* for the *New Statesman and Nation*.
G.T.'s book *Insect Life in Britain* was published by Penguin.

To Alan Pryce-Jones   Yarnton Manor
                                                   Yarnton Junction
11 January 1945   Near Oxford

My dear Bog,

Simpson must be a very long road to have 332 houses in it. I have become very keen on Kent, especially that part round Romney Marsh. Randolph Caldecott near to and Richard Wilson from a distance.

I never get any decent books sent to me at the *Daily Herald*, only Hutchinsons and a few dreary little left wing sterilities. I have a look at your reviews and use them, I fear, to prompt my own brain. I never enter the *Daily Herald* and don't always see even my own balls in it. I hate reviewing. Money.

But all this is to tell you that at last I am for a month or two the most fortunate man in the war. I have been put in charge of a hundred and twelve quarrelling women (and a few Q's) situated in the Rhodes Building Quad of Oriel (St Mary Hall) and I am staying with the Colonel. Sister is there and that nice dim relation, Mrs Trelease. Toby [Strutt] comes on Thursdays and Sundays. There is a good deal of ill feeling because Toby has an 'hon' staying with him (Gainsboro' family) and won't share him with the Colonel. The carpets on the landing are now four deep. A man came to value the china yesterday and told the Colonel that he (the Colonel) had been overcharged. The man was an expert on Chinese china, so I took the opportunity of slipping in among the Chinese stuff a few of those little china ducks for salt and pepper, from Beaumont Street, which I found in the pantry. I think the house is more fantastic than ever. My suggestion is that you come over here from Simpson. After all, it isn't much of a journey from Bletchley, and stay a night. That will be easier than meeting in Kent. I go to London about twice a week – or shall be doing so – but I never know when.

I long to hear about you and Li in Norm[and]y and I long for you to
come to the Colonel's.

My love to Poppy. Propeller is v. overworked as the children – at
least Candida – had whooping cough and Prop has her cooking;
chickens; horses; theology and Paul to attend to as well.

Ah Captain (I'd better keep to Capt. till Col. is out), how I *long* to see
you.

Love, John B

A.P.-J had a war-time house in Simpson Road, Bletchley.

At the beginning of January JB took the job as principal of the Books and Periodicals
section of the British Council which had been evacuated to Oxford.

Toby Strutt (sometimes called St Ruth) was a member at Exeter College common
room, whom Kolkhorst liked very much but whom his entourage found dull. He became
the butt of friendly jokes.

A.P-J. had been promoted to Lieutenant-Colonel.

To Alan Pryce-Jones   Yarnton Manor
                                               Yarnton Junction
24 January 1945   Near Oxford
Conversion of St Paul

Dearest ,

The Airedales which the Colonel has, instead of those bigger ones
which tried to eat him and had to be shot, are called such because they
pass so much air – especially at meals. It is a thing you must be prepared
for.

The Colonel says he would very much like you to come. But next
Monday my chief is coming down from London and I will have to be
there in Oxford, probably all night or till late. Could you make it any
other day? Telephone to the Colonel.

Did I tell you that a man had been to value the China? He was a
Chinese China expert so I put those birds for pepper and salt that the
Colonel keeps in the pantry from Beaumont Street days, in among the
Chinese objects. The expert thought the Colonel had only paid a
hundred and seventy-five per cent too much, not two hundred per cent,
as I had feared.

Do try for a day other than Monday next. I long to see you.

Love, JB

(Dear Alan,
I shall be pleased to see you when convenient to yourself and John.
Yours sincerely,
Colonel)
Rather formal what? [JB]

> Apart from having one of the finest collections of oriental carpets in England, Kolkhorst also had an important collection of Rhodian and Majolica ceramics, which his friends jokingly considered to be false.

To John Murray   British Council
                                                     St Mary Hall
6 February 1945   Oxford

My dear Jock,
I enclose the Lincs Poem finished. I have made the acquaintance of A.
L. Rowse since I have been here and I find that he thinks a lot of my
work. He says I ought to publish the broadcasts, articles etc. I have
written on topography and architecture in a simple illustrated volume.
He says it would sell like hot cakes. What do you think? Of course some
of the broadcasts may not be bad. In fact one of them is in a little
horrible text book of *Selected Modern Essays* by Macmillan. It looks very
funny with schoolmaster's 'notes' at the end. Osbert is in the same
book, equally dottily annotated.

If you think you would like to publish such a book I could certainly
produce – if the BBC, *Listener*, *Evening Standard*, *Archie Rev*, *Studio* etc.
have them – a corking fat volume which we could then start to cut
down.

Let me know what you think.
Love to Diana and children, Sean O'Betjeman

> The poet and historian, A. L. Rowse, had known JB at Oxford but they later became close friends through their mutual love of Cornwall, churches and poetry.
> J.M. thought the idea of a prose book was a good one. This did not, however, come about until the publication of *First and Last Loves* (1952).

To Evelyn Waugh   The British Council
                                                St Mary Hall
                                                Oriel Street
27 May 1945   Oxford

Dear Evelyn,
I could not resist seeing who was writing to John Piper from White's. I
have enclosed a letter to him with yours telling him he bloody well
ought to do it. I fear it only went off today – your letter – because I have
been away in Edinburgh and only today am back here.

You are very much in my thoughts, for I am reading for a second time
Brideshead Revisited since it has come in to me for review in the bloody old
Daily Herald. It will get a spanking good notice. To me it is a great treat
to read a book with a standard of values behind it, Christian values what
is more. I shall have somehow to hint this fact to readers without letting
it be apparent to the Editors, since recently I had a letter from them to
say that I was using this paper for *Roman Catholic propaganda* and that
'The *Daily Herald* finds itself in conflict with the Catholic Church on
several points'. I was also accused of 'Jesuitry'. This made me rather
proud. Of course, I have not altered my tactics. I find that there is no
longer any left or right but merely those who want to run a Slave State
(your phrase, which I now always use) and those of us who don't want
to be run.

Propeller's father has just bought Farnborough Rectory, Nr Wantage for us:

1730-ish. Red brick seven hundred feet up on the downs. No water, no
light, no heat. Beech trees all round. We shall be at Uffers till
September at least.

I would very much like to see you. Edinburgh is the place for our sort
of book, particularly James Thin on South Bridge and John Grant and

J. Orr. Worth a visit, cheap as you could wish. They haven't got to illuminated books yet and are chock-a-block with them.
   Love, John B

E.W. and JB had long been friends by this time, having met at Oxford.
James Thin, John Grant and J. Orr were bookshops.

To William Plomer

The British Council
St Mary Hall
Oriel Street
Oxford

2 June 1945

My dear William,
I am simply delighted to receive 'The Dorking Thigh' and you will be interested to hear that I read out your poem on Tottenham Court Road at a lecture to some cultivated characters in Edinburgh the other day where it was received with rapturous applause. As you say in your preface, the poems are made to be read aloud: that is an excellent test and all yours pass it. I very much like 'A Ticket for the Reading Room' which is new to me. Once again, my dear William, many many thanks. I am going to try to persuade the bloody old *Daily Herald* to let me review it. They don't like me writing about poetry. Love to you and poor old Joe.
   From John Betjeman

JB often read the poem 'The Dorking Thigh' out loud to my brother and me, when we were older.

To Geoffrey Taylor

Uffington
Faringdon
Berkshire

8 June 1945

My dear Geoffrey,
Of course now that I have given myself a moment to write to you, I am feeling so ill and tired that all I would say does not come out. I hear your book on insects is v. good and beautiful but I have seen no sign of it yet. It would be very nice if you could come to England and stay with us. I would take a holiday to see you again. I am happier than usual at the

British Council and I am in Oxford all this week and find the excellence of the buildings a compensation for the work of the day. I am v. lucky to be here and shall resign as soon as we leave Oxford or its neighbourhood. I will never live in London again. It is death. Curious hangovers from Eire survive – Ewart M[ilne], Muriel MacSweeney and one or two dim Trinity men appear here. I see that till I die Eire is part of me. What of Reggie [Ross-Williamson]? I do not envy him. Yet here, with the Slave State looking nearer every day, things are not much better. Love to Mary and Sarah. I see your mother no longer – she being in Bath and me in Oxford. I spend a lot of time defending Dev. here, for his consistency, if not for his tact.

John B

To John Murray   Garrards Farm
                                                      Uffington
11 July 1945   Berkshire

Dear Jock,
I enclose what, with two other poems which I must ask you to get, should be enough to make a book. They are lettered A to L so that they shall not be lost.

The two missing poems are 1) 'Lincolnshire Tale' which you printed in the *Cornhill* 2) 'A May Day Song for North Oxford' which I rather like and which Cyril (C) can let you have. I have no copy.

I prefer the version of the water-colour sonnet which I include among the corrected page proofs and marked M, to that which is printed by Butler and Tanner. And will you ask these gentlemen to set up all sonnets I have written in this book correctly. The correct method is that given on the proof of 'Planster's Vision' enclosed (B) – they are to notice the indentation which is identical in all my sonnets.

There *might* be another poem if you wanted one. If we are cutting down, I think we could sacrifice the 'Bank Clerk Monody' and 'Cheshire Lines' which are very early work. And do you think the 'Poultry Farm' ballad too indecent?

Ask B and T not to settle the order of the poems yet and so not to number the pages.

You know that book on churches for *Britain in Pictures* I told you about. Well I put the matter in my agent's hands in order not to be diddled by Adprints. And he went to W. A. R. Collins and said this ought to be a full length book. W.A.R.C. agreed and wants it. But, though nothing is signed, it should morally go first to Allen Lane and next to you. I have told my agent (Cork of Hughes Massie) this fact. About half of it is written, I should think. But as I wrote it before the war, I probably would not agree with it now.

I told my agent that if he could square Allen Lane and *Britain in Pic[ture]s* I should inform you as I did not want you to be done out of the book if you want it and I said my first loyalties are always to you, as you ran the risk of publishing my verse. On the other hand, I don't want to do in W.A.R.C., a nice man who will call off *Britain in Pictures*, I expect, whose offer I had accepted in writing. I think I must leave things in Cork's hands, it's so bloody touchy. He will be seeing you.

Am getting better slowly and going to Beaulieu (c/o J. L. MacKenzie Esq, Friar's Oak, Beaulieu, 224 Hants) on Friday for a week. Love to Diana. I will write from there about the *Bucks* list which requires a little excision and revisions which a minute will reverse.

Yours, John B

This collection of poems became *New Bats in Old Belfries*.
JB's agent was Edmund Cork.
JB did not do the churches book for Allen Lane.

To Penelope Betjeman

22 July 1945

Friar's Oak
Beaulieu
Hampshire

WABA STAND ON WABA'S POWNIE TINKY BULL

Darlin Nooni,
Oi expect whoi there is naow boox from Bath this week is because there was ownlee oone for mee tew send last week tew Bath.

Re moi arrangements. Oi ought to see [Doctor] Stenhouse on my return as he alone can determine my convalescence. Oi am gowing ter stigh 'ear oontil Wednesday and Oi 'ave written the Colonel ter sigh can ee 'ave me Thursday. Oi would propowse travellin back on Wednesday and then if yew was gowin' owver ter Farnborough yew could pick me oop at Great Shefford or, if not, could get trap to meet me at Lambourn. That would mean Oi would be owm on Wednesday noight and could yew fix an interview with Sten'ouse fer Thursday mornin on moi way tew Oxford – Oi could gow boi a boos from Farin'don liter in the digh.

Oi will fown yew Tewzday – noight at six p.m.

Yorz trewely, Tewpie

> 'Waba' was CB's nickname for a time. Her pony was called Tinkerbell.
>
> JB had been in the Acland Nursing Home, Oxford (where he was nursed by Mary Renault) having a sebaceous cyst removed from his stomach. To recuperate he went to stay with his friend Arthur MacKenzie's father and stepmother, Jack and Vera, whose house was beside the river. There he met a neighbour, Brigadier Buckland, and his daughter, Clemency, who lived across the water from Friar's Oak. The sojourn inspired JB's poem 'Youth and Age on the Beaulieu River, Hants'.

To Martyn Skinner   Oxford Preservation Trust
                                         The Painted Room
                                         3 Cornmarket Street
26 August 1945   Oxford

Dear Old Top,

How sweet of you to send two guineas. An official receipt will be sent when the accounting staff comes back from the bathing beaches late in Spetmebber (sic) and so please take this as an unofficial one.

As to the botanic garden there would of course be no point in pulling down the present buildings unless the traffic in the High has been reduced to a few bicycles and unless Sharp's plan has that as its chief object I see no pjont (sic) in the plan. Like you I don't like plans. But what I wanted to say was that although I have not read *Malaya 5* yet I have bought a copy and will. I was simply delighted with that unknown mediaeval piece of yours which you presented to me at Sanders. My dear boy, it is full of the most mellifluous and highly coloured poetry and although it may not have so much story about it so far as narrative power go (sic) it is packed with real poetry. Poetr (sic), old boy, yes poetry so rare now and so individual too. typing (sic) here is by me today, hence errors.

Yours till death, JB

> JB and M.S. had arrived at Oxford as freshmen on the same day. Much later they became friends and JB dedicated a poem to him in *High and Low*, 'Lines written to Martyn Skinner before his departure from Oxfordshire in search of Quiet – 1961'.

To John Murray

21 September 1945

c/o Colonel Kolkhorst
Yarnton Manor
Nr Oxford

My dear Jock,
I return the:
A) POEMS AND ACKNOWLEDGEMENTS
corrected in so far as it is within my ability to correct them and I suggest we omit CHESHIRE LINES – it is facile undergraduate stuff, written too long ago and not enough thought in it – MONODY as being a little facile and unkind and UFFINGTON RINGERS as being a bit too Georgian and *Sunday Times* Solemn thanksgiving in style.

1) I think that with the CLEMENCY poem (taken I fear by the N[ew] S[tates] *woman*), YOUTH AND AGE ON BEAULIEU RIVER and the re-arranged Little Bloody poem in perpendicular fashion on the page so that it looks more like BEFORE THE ANAESTHETIC except that most alternate lines will not have initial letters, will fill up the gaps the omission of these three other poems will create. I don't like to publish the Little Bloody poem without Maureen's permission and so I am sending it to her for approval.

2) As to the order of the poems which seems to be that of Butler and Tanner, I don't mind it except that:

a) PARLIAMENT HILL FIELDS and BRISTOL should not be next to one another as they are in the same rather tittupy metre and were not written in the same year.

b) SOUTH LONDON SKETCH 1844 and SOUTH LONDON SKETCH 1944 should be opposite one another and their connection, the one following on the other, be typographically emphasised by the titles.

c) Do you think SUNDAY AFTERNOON SERVICE is unduly prominent as third in the book? I should have thought the end of the book was a better place for it. But I am indifferent.

d) Ought I not to open with the Little Bloody poem?

3) I am still unsatisfied as to title and would like a title which conveyed the impression of a moonblanched country church tower of the Perpendicular period. For this reason STARLIT STEEPLES, which I had thought of, is a bit too alliterative and untechnical. What about MOONLIT PERP? or YARNTON BELLS? or BELLS ACROSS WATER? or BELLS OVER WATER? or BERKSHIRE BELLS? or STARLIT STONES? or MOONLIT ARCHES? or SQUINTS AND SQUINCHES?

4) As to a) printing and b) binding.

a) it seems to me that Butler and Tanner are poor in their imposition – just hold a page up to the light and see how the margins vary; and they seem poorer still in the way they print the poetry and I would commend that they take a look at a Pickering book or an Oxford Press book just to see how lines should over-run. But I suppose it is all part of Progress that we can have no readable printing of poetry done now, and there is not the skill or labour to do the work.

b) The binding should be of the same material as *Old Lights* (nail file Rivington style) only RED instead of blue, and with a white label as before. I hope this will be possible. Had you thought of a double printing on title pages – blue or black? Too long and expensive? Probably.

B) MURRAY'S PICTORIAL GUIDES

1) SALOP I cannot regard our photographs (J. P.'s and mine) as a comprehensive record, but some of them show how photographs should be taken for this purpose. As I am still laid low with what the doctor calls SCIATICA, I have not been able to get to the N[ational] B[uildings] R[ecord] stuff of Salop, but hope to next week if it is not too late. J. P. proposes an expedition to Salop with which I greatly agree but must square the British Council first. I think the NBR photograph will chiefly serve as guide to what there is to photograph that we have omitted.

2) BUCKS AND SALOP I am not hopeful, I fear, that [Marcus] Whiffen will produce good photographs of Bucks. I fear he is primarily a *writer* – and, as such, very good. It is agreed that these Guides shall be, primarily, visual records of the county and I am sure that if you stick to NBR or even a preponderance of NBR photographs you will produce something halfway between Batsford and *Country Life*. I am quite sure J. P. is right in saying that they must depend primarily on the photographer's eye for their effect and that they must show the County as it is, rather than as the S[ociety for the] P[rotection of] A[ncient] B[uildings] or the Fine Arts Commission or anything else would like it

to be. But they must show what is beautiful in it, regardless of date, association or antiquity. It so happens that the old buildings are the most beautiful, but you can, with a camera, make even an old building look dull and ugly as NBR and Whiffen show. However, I feel that we must give Whiffen his chance. But I think you must be prepared to risk a loss there and use him only for captions. Don't publish the book just for the sake of getting it out and beating Batsford's to the post. It won't be worth it. And it won't beat them. It will be Batsford's.

Yours, John B

New Bats in Old Belfries was published on 19 December.
Marcus Whiffen did the preliminary survey for the guide to Buckinghamshire.

To John Piper

23 September 1945

c/o Colonel Kolkhorst
Yarnton Manor
Nr Oxford

Dear Mr Pahper,
I am more indebted to you than you can know for the efforts you and Goldilegz have made and are making to remove me from these absurd bonds in which I am now needlessly shackled. A visit to Percy Cudlipp filled me with dismay at the thought of having to depend for most of my income on the *Daily Herald* when I am out of the British Council. But if I can only get a bit of self-confidence, that will come all right. You have been a true friend to me in my war years and lying back in bed in the Colonel's luxury I fully realise it. I have sciatica and shall be in bed for about a week more I gather – I only hope the NBR has not yet left its All Souls Office. As I told Jock in a letter today, there is little likelihood of the NBR providing adequate photographs for the Guides; most likely, though, it will indicate to us what ought to be photographed. I am therefore most anxious to do the tour you suggest in the late October sunlight, having first seen the NBR. I think we should concentrate on Ancient buildings, don't you? I have not yet resigned from the British Council, I am ashamed to say, nor do I wish to until my chief there is back from leave, as I have anyhow to give a month's notice; the time I spend in Salop in October is bound to have to count as leave and I may only have about seven days owing to me. But let us definitely fix a week in late October – when you say. The bore about the BC is that the people are so nice, though the job is so awful.

On the Bucks guide, I told Jock that he must not expect much of Whiffen's photographs and that it would be better for him not to publish the Bucks guide at all rather than try and beat Batsford to the post with just another Batsford book. I have rarely, by the way, seen an uglier book than *The Changing Shape of Things* (with [John] Gloag's blessing) Murray four and six, sub-*Archy* layout, words by Paul Redmayn, music by D. I. A. arranged by arty Noel C[arrington]. On the other hand the *Murrays of Elibank* that they have published is in the true Sir John [Murray] style. There is a very nice photograph (full page and in the slant and not quite in focus) of Colonel The Hon Arthur Murray as an Officer in the last War outside his dugout, against which a notice is leaning marked 'BROOKS'S' – these Murrays were liberals or worse, in Campbell-Bannerman's bat.

The Colonel is very anxious to see you and would commission you to paint the house. He also would like to see Goldilegz. Would you come over here this week while I shall be here and probably up and convalescing?

John B

> *The Changing Shape of Things* was an educational series of books for schools on such subjects as transport by sea and air and how it changed over the ages. The reference to music by D. I. A. must be a joke because there was never any music associated with the series.
>
> The Murrays of Elibank were distant relatives of Murrays, the publishers.
>
> 'Campbell-Bannerman's bat': his baggage (as in 'batman').

Nine:

Up the ash tree climbs the ivy

November 1945 to June 1949

Feathery ash in leathery Lambourne
Waves above the sarsen stone,
And Edwardian plantations
So coniferously moan
As to make the swelling downland,
Far-surrounding, seem their own.

'Upper Lambourne'

In October 1945 my mother wrote from Farnborough to JB, who was still staying with Colonel Kolkhorst at Yarnton, telling him how grateful she was that he was being looked after. 'Until the stoves are lit here, I certainly think we would die of the cold. Packers [the builders] seem to have deserted us, they have never even finished painting the kitchen.'[1]

The new house, a beautiful eighteenth-century rectory of red and blue brick, faced out across a wide lawn and ha-ha to the distant blue horizon of Watership Down above Kingsclere. Farnborough is the highest village in Berkshire, seven hundred and twenty feet up on the downs. From my attic bedroom window the great wide view northwards was of endless undulating downland; as a child I thought I could see the whole world. To the east of the house was a small wood of the tallest beech trees through which a path led to a pond among snowdrops, followed in spring by wild garlic. The drinking water had to be fetched daily in a bucket from a communal tap in the village street and the washing water was pumped up from a well in the scullery for half an hour every morning between seven thirty and eight o'clock by Mr Abbot who lived in the lodge. Mrs Abbot remembers us all arriving. 'Mr Betjeman came in to see me and he said, "You'll never be able to spell our name so I'm going to write it out for you," and he wedged a card behind the clock on the mantelpiece.'[2]

Each evening JB prepared the paraffin lamps, trimmed the wicks and lit the fires. Evelyn Waugh wrote in his diaries, 'In the late afternoon I went to stay with the Betjemans in a lightless, stuffy, cold, poky rectory among beech woods overlooking Wantage.'[3] Years later my father remarked, 'How very Evelyn, to write so readably and inaccurately.'

The Rectory was certainly cold but it was neither lightless nor poky nor could you see Wantage from it. In the winter we lived in the inner hall, where there was a coke stove along with the harness, saddles and bridles, or in the kitchen, a large room adjoining the main body of the house. It had originally been the village schoolroom and contained another huge stove, behind which the cats we had brought from Uffington, Kitty Fritz and the tortoiseshell Kitty Curl, slept continuously. There was a huge kitchen table and a dresser painted pale blue.

It was JB who generally chose the décor, although my mother sometimes made mild protestations about his predilection for ecclesiastical designs. For Farnborough, he ordered the wallpaper from the London firm of Green and Abbott; an ivy trellis for the main bedroom, a blue art nouveau design for his dressing room, a reddish Gilbert Scott design for the dining room (which was never used as such). His library, painted cornflower blue, was next to the bedroom. It was a dark room with an added Edwardian window, whose leaded panes faced east onto the beech trees.

On the days when JB sat at his desk with books for review in high piles on every surface, it was forbidden territory to my brother and me. His own books were his passion and in the evenings he taught us how to handle them, how to turn a page at the top right-hand corner. 'I *say*, look at this,' he'd say, drawing in his breath with a whistling sound, on opening some book of aquatints, or showing us the illuminated pages of a Kelmscott Press volume. In his radio talk 'How to Look at Books' (1939) he had said, 'Books are, to me, the last link with the beautiful in England. English books are still the best printed and bound in the world. English literature is still the greatest reading. In the old days they took such care about the production of a book. I took one down from my shelves . . . a little-known poem called *The Favourite Village*, by a Sussex clergyman called James Hurdis, who lived about a hundred and fifty years ago. My copy is gilt-edged octavo in a sumptuous leather binding. The binding is tooled with a beautiful design in the Adam style, all wreaths and borders. Even the gilded edge has tooling on it. The pages have faded to a soft cream colour. . . . And then as I smell its pages, I smell the England that has gone: a slightly musty smell, which all old books have, and which makes me think of the golden leather backs of the rows of shelves in a country-house library, of the deep silence of the fields outside. . . .'

'Polishing old books is much more enjoyable than writing them, don't you find?'[4] JB wrote to the historian Arthur Bryant, with whom he had become friends (15 January 1948). He had just been given *Views of Bath* by J. C. Natt (folio 1806, Bulmer) by his mother for Christmas. 'I am STAGGERED. . . . It cost one hundred and thirty-two pounds,'⁵ he wrote to Evelyn Waugh on the same day.

Going into JB's library was a treat. For me the most exciting thing was to open the right-hand drawer of his desk where he kept an enormous dead centipede in a glass case and also a cardboard cut-out souvenir which concertina'd into an optical illusion of the Crystal Palace in miniature. JB loved reading aloud and read us every book by Mrs Molesworth, every poem in Coventry Patmore's *A Child's Garland* and all M. R. James's ghost stories. We asked for these last again and again and once enacted one of them, *Lost Hearts*, in the hall and at the bottom of the stairs while an amazed village audience looked on.

Compared to Uffington, the village was very small with only a hundred or so inhabitants, few of whom went to church. There were two main farms at either end of the street, Chandler's and Laurence's; a village school; a rather daintily converted smithy where the Granger-Stuarts lived; a village hall; a shop; and a mixture of tiled and thatched cottages. Florrie and Pearl Wilkinson were the sisters of Bob, Sis, Peter, Stella, Christine, and Billy. They all lived in a tiny cottage by the watertap and worked in the house. Florrie was blonde and eighteen, Pearl red-haired and sixteen.

> God save me from Florrie's sister, Pearl,
> She puts my senses in a whirl,⁶

wrote JB, stunned by Pearl's beauty. The girls had been working on the next-door farm and were sunburnt and always singing the latest hits from the radio. Florrie remembers what a temper JB got into if anything went wrong in the morning: 'He lost his newspaper once, which he wanted to take on the train, and he said there were evil spirits in the house hiding it from him. We found it after he had left, on his chair which he had pushed in to the kitchen table. But most of the time he was kindness itself. He used to take us to look at churches. There was one church called Inglesham we went to and he rowed us up the Thames from Lechlade in a boat and we had to climb up a bank to get to it. Then we would have a pub lunch and a spot of sloe gin to go with it.'⁷

Sometimes JB joined the bell-ringers in the church, which he reached by walking on a path under beech trees to a small gate in a paling fence and crossing the road. Stan Sprules remembers JB taking all the bell-ringers to Uffington on Mondays to ring the bells there: 'That used to be our best day out. We must have gone in two cars, me and my brother Alfred, Bill, John and Tom Groves, Bill Dearlove and Bill Wilkins. We'd always go and have a drink in the White Horse afterwards.'[8]

The village shop was run by Mr and Mrs Dowkes who came from the Midlands.

> Hiccory Diccory Dowkes,
> I'll tell you some Birmingham jokes,

was what we were taught to recite by JB. We never knew the nursery rhymes we quoted were any different from other children's.

> Ba Ba centipede,
> Have you any jelly,
> No sir, no sir, it's all gone smelly.

We were also brought up to call the lavatory the 'Lavery', after the Edwardian artist. (JB's own phrase for going was 'standing up'. He'd say, 'I must go and stand up.') Both I and my brother (until he left for the Dragon School in Oxford) went to the village school and spoke broad Berkshire. Most of the village children of our age, who numbered around a dozen, almost lived at the Rectory – except for Johnny Willoughby, who was kept indoors, and the Marshall girls, who lived two miles away in a remote farm cottage. Juney White became my best friend and Terry Carter my brother's. They all loved my parents, even after JB flew off the handle when Terry Carter and I fell between the rafters in the roof loft through the lath and plaster ceiling of his dressing room, making a gigantic hole. All the village children came on the trolley cart pulled by the Connemara mare, Tulira, who had come with us from Ireland, to lunch picnics on remote tracks and lost valleys around the Ridgeway, the ancient grass track that runs along the Downs.

During the winter of 1947, when the village was cut off for a month, with snowdrifts as high as houses, my mother became the local heroine, riding Tulira down to Wantage to collect the mail and provisions, pulling a large sleigh behind, on which Florrie and Pearl rode to act as brakes. Miss Whitaker, the new schoolmistress, arrived the day before the snow came, but her furniture which was following on in a Pickford's van got trapped on its way from Newbury. She came to live at the Rectory for a month until the roads were unblocked. 'I remember Mr Betjeman scurrying about carrying buckets of wood to light the fire in my bedroom.'[9] My brother and his schoolfriend Paul Knapp-Fisher were also trapped by the snow and couldn't return to the Dragon School, where they were both boarding. Paul remembers, 'There was a wonderful feeling of joy when confronted by a colossal drift about fifty yards down the Wantage road. Dadz gave up trying to get back to Oxford and turned the Vauxhall around.' Paul Knapp-Fisher, whom JB always called 'the quietest boy at the Dragon', went missing for several hours and was found by JB asleep in a snowdrift, suffering from hypothermia. 'How tough we were in those Farnborough days,'[10] JB wrote to Miss Whitaker nearly forty years later.

It was inevitable that Paul would go to the Dragon School because of JB's ties with the Lynam family. He liked the school's defiance of convention and its generally liberal leanings which made it such an individualistic place, where tidiness came a long way after Godliness – it was nothing like its neighbour, Summerfields.

Some days JB travelled to Oxford in his grey Vauxhall saloon to work at the British Council and subsequently at the Oxford Preservation Trust. On others he drove to Didcot, which the station-master pronounced 'Deed Coat' on the loudspeaker system, and from there took the train to London. The distances were farther than they had been at Uffington and by the time he got home in the evenings he was often exhausted. My mother was too, for she had created a miniature smallholding which was arduous and time-consuming. Apart from keeping poetically-named horses, such as Lalla Rookh and Dirk; rabbits called Perseus and Andromeda; and goats and chickens, she also kept Jersey and Guernsey house-cows, called Buttercup and Daisy, which she milked both morning and evening, and made bright yellow butter, which my brother and I hated. We longed for the whitish substance which came from the shops. (I thought it was called 'shock' butter. JB never corrected me.)

At weekends my mother produced large meals which, if they couldn't be taken to some idyllic picnic spot, were eaten in the kitchen. Her food was famously good; she took tremendous trouble and cooked simple things perfectly. Diana Mosley had by now long been married to Sir Oswald Mosley and they often came over for Sunday lunch from their beautiful house, Crowood, near Ramsbury, with their two sons. Having been imprisoned during the War for their involvement with the National Socialist Party they were, at that time, virtually ostracized by polite society, but my parents' loyalty to Diana did not waver. JB helped get her sons Max and Alexander into a prep school. Diana wrote (24 May 1946), 'You really are an *angel* to have found a school which might accept Alexander and Max as pupils – or should I say a genius. . . . Thank you *so so* much for all the trouble you have taken. I was beginning to despair, as I had had so many furious refusals. Isn't it odd in a way, if I had a school I should welcome reds, in the hope of converting them.'[11] (In the event, Alexander lasted less than a term, he hated the school so much. The boys were taught by an old recluse, and later by a tutor at home.)

The Pipers continued to visit from Henley, as did Osbert and Karen Lancaster, and John Sparrow and Maurice Bowra from Oxford. There seemed to be more clerics of varying denominations than there had been at Uffington, including the Jesuit Freddie Ling, who was much loved by JB, but not by my mother who accused him of deflecting JB from Catholicism. In the meantime, JB's weekday life was filled to the brim. William Plomer, who had been particularly frustrated at not seeing enough of JB, wrote (3 November 1948), having just received his *Selected Poems*, 'I think, like a Stage Door Johnnie, I shall stand in wait for you, with the book in my hand, outside one of your Homes and Haunts, late at night, and press you for your autograph.'[12]

On top of the *Daily Herald* job, JB was fast committing himself to more work. Jim Knapp-Fisher (Paul Knapp-Fisher's uncle and guardian), a friend from Oxford days, had bought the publishing firm of Sidgwick and Jackson and asked JB to edit a series of children's books called *The Watergate Classics*. He was a tall, bald man, of great good humour and charisma, who lent us two Holman Hunt paintings, one of an amaryllis, the other of a girl holding an urn, which hung in the hall at the Rectory. JB always referred to Sidgwick and Jackson as 'the hygienics', because they published a number of extremely dull specialist textbooks on chemistry and medicine.

In May 1946 JB left his job at the British Council and later in the year started working three days a week as Secretary for the Oxford Preservation Trust in their offices in the Cornmarket. He took with him his beloved Diana Craig from the British Council, and the two of them ran the Trust, which had been founded by Lionel Curtis and was guided by a voluntary committee of Oxford worthies, such as JB's old tutor, the Revd J. M. Thompson. JB, by now well-used to being actively involved in conservationist causes, worked tirelessly but, as was his wont, became frustrated and bored with office routine and left in 1948.

The number of talks he gave on the radio increased, as did his appearances on television – activities which Evelyn Waugh decried but in which he engaged with even greater skill. Terence de Vere White, his friend from Ireland, wrote (18 December 1946), 'I had the pleasure of listening to you on the Third Programme. You have a very charming voice. Everyone says that and they have never noticed the tiny substratum of petulance until I point it out.'[13] Alan Pryce-Jones, who now edited the *Times Literary Supplement*, persuaded JB to write a column, while the tall, willowy beauty Anne Scott-James, editor of *Harpers* (who later was to marry Osbert Lancaster), persuaded him to write verse for her magazine. He declined to write for Gordon Spencer, the editor of *Sun Bathing Review*, who wrote to him in the autumn of 1946, 'It occurred to me that your views on one of the social phenomena of our time – nudity – would be most stimulating, and I wonder if you would care to communicate them in an article for this magazine. . . . I do not think that any responsible critic can fairly object to social nudism on moral grounds.'[14]

Wystan Auden, who was living in Long Island, New York at this time and kept in regular touch with my parents, selected and wrote the introduction to an American collection of JB's verse, *Slick But Not Streamlined* (a title which JB detested), which came out in 1947. Auden wrote (9 August 1947), 'I was furious about the title they gave your book but the sales department insisted. . . . Don't be too modest about your poems. I think my favourite is "Sunday Afternoon Service at St Enodoc Church". "The Attempt" in *Sir J. P.* [*John Piers*] is one of the most beautiful love lyrics in the language.'[15] He had wanted to call the book *Betjeman's Bust* and had written on New Year's Day, 'I can't tell you how I have enjoyed reading through all your work, though it made me very nostalgic. I've just finished a long poem I've been working on for two and a half years, *The Age of Anxiety*, which I would like to dedicate to you. May I have your permission?'[16] Auden's introduction to *Slick But Not Streamlined* began, 'It is difficult to write seriously about a man one has sung hymns with or judiciously about a poet whose work makes one violently jealous. Normally when I read good poetry, for example Mr Eliot's line, "The place of solitude where three dreams cross", my reaction is one of delight and admiration; a standard of excellence has been set in one way which I must live up to in mine; but when I read such lines of Mr Betjeman as:

> And that mauve hat three cherries decorate
> Next week shall topple from its trembling perch
> While wet fields reek like some long empty church

I am, frankly, rather annoyed because they are not by me. My feeling is similar to that one has when, on arriving at some long-favourite picnic spot in the woods, one finds that another trespasser has discovered it too.'

In 1948, JB's *Selected Poems* was published, chosen and with an introduction by John Sparrow. The *Murray's Guides* to *Buckinghamshire* and *Berkshire* which came out in 1948 and 1949 respectively, were the culmination of JB's and John Piper's pleasurable journeying around those counties. 'We have visited every parish in the county and entered every church and many houses,' they wrote in the introduction to the *Buckinghamshire Guide*. But perhaps the most important contract JB landed during that decade was to edit the *Collins Guide to Parish Churches*. Although he assumed he might accomplish it in a fairly short time, the book took over a decade to complete.

If JB's routine was erratic, our holidays at Trebetherick in Cornwall were constant and completely regular, the highlight of our year. But the journey became an agonizing test of patience to Paul and me, as JB wanted to stop and look at churches in nearly every village and town we passed through. It made no difference if he had seen them many times before. Exeter Cathedral became our biggest dread, for it involved waiting and sighing for at least half an hour while JB craned his neck upwards in silent concentration. I remember my brother saying in an angry voice when we stopped at Lifton, so near Trebetherick, 'Not *another* auld church, Daddy!' It wasn't only the churches, however, which slowed up the journeys to make them last two and sometimes three days, but the friends whom we visited or with whom we stayed. I looked forward to stopping off at Anthony and Violet Powell's house in Somerset, because they had a magic grotto in the garden. At Christopher Hollis's nearby, there were a lot of very tall sons who hit their heads on the doorways and much talk of cricket and religion, and in Reynolds and Janet Stone's rectory garden at Litton Cheney in Dorset there were huge ferns around a mesmerizing and secret pond. JB enjoyed driving as fast as his car would go. If he got behind a slow driver he would curse and shake his fist. But once we were there, safely tucked away down Daymer Lane at the Bodare Hotel, Trebetherick, we seldom got in the car again until the return journey.

We led exactly the same summer days as JB had done as a child with his parents. We learnt to swim in the same rock-pools and shrimp in the same sandy ones. We collected cowries in exactly the same places as he had been taught to collect them by his mother. We watched big seas by the same blow-hole and dammed the same freshwater stream under Bray Hill; we took the ferry to Padstow and walked up to Prideaux Place; we bathed at Daymer, Jutty, Gully, Greenaway and Big Cave Bay; we walked through the woods to Shilla Mill and we surfed daily on Polzeath Beach when the tide was right. Once JB came in on a particularly thunderous wave right up the beach into the shallowest water until the board stuck onto the sand. He stood up triumphant only to discover that his trunks had been pulled off by the surf miles back and he was forced to walk across the rest of the beach holding the board close in front of him in a state of painful embarrassment until he regained his towel. We picnicked with the children of JB's childhood friends – the Walshams and the Kunzers (Joan Larkworthy's children). We had tea with 'Aunt' Elsie McCorkindale at Torquil and Mrs Oakley at Whitebays and we sat around camp-fires on Daymer beach with Dragon School masters.

Perhaps once during each holiday, JB would venture inland either to lunch with old Lord and Lady St Germans at Port Eliot in St Germans, or with the reclusive and eccentric Revd Densham at Warleggan, having first listened to his sermon. Sometimes JB visited his friend A. L. Rowse near St Austell. 'John knew North Cornwall better, and I South Cornwall. So, in return, I took him to see places nearby like Luxulyan, and Victorian churches like Charleston. He recognized Caerhays Castle at once as Nash's. Hence our later cooperation on photographs for the book *Victorian Cornwall*. We had friends in common, close friends like Gerald Berners, Maurice Bowra and David Cecil. . . . We had so much more *in common* than practically all his other friends. For example, we had all Oxford and most of its denizens. We had all Cornwall. We were both very churchy, loved the church and church-crawling together. Though I was not a religious believer, I always respected John's religion, he was a true Christian and had Christian charity and compassion – as did not Evelyn Waugh who was a bad Catholic for being so very uncharitable and *unChristian* (and I was sad at Evelyn's influence on Penelope and bullying John).'[17]

Waugh's interference in my parents' affairs during this time when my mother was desperately wanting to go over to the Church of Rome has become something of a *cause célèbre*. Perhaps this is because all three sets of their long and serious letters, each propounding their religious beliefs, are still in existence. In actual fact it was my mother who made up her own mind to become a Catholic. Waugh only confirmed her decision, managing to exacerbate the wounds on both sides in the meantime.

JB and Waugh had been friends since the early thirties. 'I can't remember through whom I first met him. I think it was probably the hangover from the Hypocrites Club at Oxford – David Talbot Rice, Richard Plunkett-Greene and Cracky William Clonmore. . . . It was that set, there was a lot of drink.' They met frequently over long weekends with Bryan and Diana Guinness in Wiltshire. 'We used to love hymn singing at Biddesden,' JB remembered. 'The maid there was a great evangelical and used to have wonderful hymn singing in which Evelyn took part. Those were in what were called unregenerate days. . . . I remember Evelyn saying to me how he hated writing, like I hate writing. . . . That was a great bond. We had tremendous laughs about Libertys and Arts and Crafts. It was an affectionate laughter.'[18] Their mutual respect was total and undeniable. They had similar tastes in literature, book collecting, art and architecture. This was their saving grace, for whatever the world may say, JB harboured no malice against Waugh for mischievously entering a religious debate when, as a close friend of both my parents, it was clearly none of his business. Of Waugh, JB later admitted, 'I never thought his religion had much to do with my idea of Christianity.'

The religious rift between my parents was not purely doctrinal. The village life which centred around the church had been a strong bond between them, from the early days of their marriage over a dozen years before, in Uffington, involving so much happiness and laughter, to the 'socials' in the Farnborough village hall, when the whole village did the hokey-cokey, the conga and the Gay Gordons together. Suddenly, all that changed. 'I had thought that however much Penelope and I quarrelled, at any rate the Church stayed the same – rather like old Archie, something you can always turn to. And Penelope was really very Anglican by temperament – the sort of person who always quarrels with the vicar.'[19] Now my mother went to a hideous Roman Catholic church in Wantage every Sunday, even though she had no respect for the incumbent Father Wixted. The times of the C of E and RC services always seemed to conflict so that Sunday lunch was often eaten at unusual times. My mother gathered around her a gaggle of Irish farm labourers' children, whom she brought to Farnborough to stay, and spent much of her Sunday mornings fetching Italian servants of the local nobility who had hitherto been excused from going to Mass, since they were out of the official five-mile radius, and ferrying them to Wantage. Her activities did not mean that she gave up running the Farnborough Women's Institute or organizing fêtes and gymkhanas. But JB felt hurt that she could have forgone something as strong as the physical side of the Church of England for the sake of such a small difference in beliefs. After all, his Anglo-Catholicism involved confession, Mass on weekdays and prayers morning and evening.

My brother and I did not notice a thing, apart from a step-up of the number of rosaries in the house, the arrival of a statue of Our Lady in my bedroom and my awareness of the 'Hail Mary' after the 'Our Father' at our nightly prayers kneeling beside the bed. I remember JB making fun of the 'Hail Marys' and reciting them in a broad Irish accent, which I assumed, not unnaturally, was how we were meant to say them – 'Hooley Merry, methyr of Guard. . . .' Occasionally my mother took me to Mass in Wantage or to the deeply pious Lady Agnes Eyston's chapel at East Hendred. I paid no attention and didn't know the hymns. Far more familiar were the services at Farnborough in the unassuming and familiar church beside the bumpy meadow.

When my mother was having her Roman Catholic instruction with the Dominicans at Blackfriars in Oxford, JB had meanwhile befriended George Barnes and his wife Anne, who were to be his great comfort during this disquieting time. George Barnes had met JB before the war, and was now Head of Talks at the BBC. He had indulged JB and let him make the programmes he wanted to. He was a brilliant, cultivated and funny man, who knew both Yeats and Eliot, was an intellectual without taking himself seriously, and a faultless organizer. His wife Anne, a confidante to many, had made their house, 'Prawls' near Tenterden in Kent, into a cosy family home. It was small, unpretentious, four-square and clapboarded and JB found it to be a glorious, peaceful, private and unpompous haven in which to relax. JB and the Barneses had few mutual friends; the social pressures were non-existent and over the next few years JB was to spend more and more time at Prawls. He even holidayed in France each September with his new-found friends. George Barnes wrote (undated) about a typical proposed sojourn, 'Would this suit you for Sunday next? Bike. Fairfield, Brookland, Old Romney, New Romney, St Mary in the Marsh, Ivychurch, Brenzett, Snave, Snargate, Appledore, Stone. This is twenty-seven miles: we can take the whole day. Then on Monday, when I shall have left, A & A [Anne and Anthony] can take your aching limbs by bus to Ashford and Woodchurch and places, either putting you in a train or bringing you back for Mon. night.'[20] Their son Anthony, a little older than my brother Paul, was already at Eton and JB instilled into him a love of church architecture and introduced him to his great hero, Ninian Comper. Paul often went to stay at Prawls and was particularly thrilled by the enormous Bassett-Lowke electric train set which George Barnes had set up in the loft. It was highly superior to the beaten up Hornby set we had at Farnborough.

Despite his private unrest, JB's public face was as jaunty as ever and his popularity, firstly as a broadcaster and secondly as a poet, rose towards the end of the decade. He was asked to perform, read poetry or lecture, by a host of provincial societies such as the Salisbury Poetry

Circle, the Tamworth Arts and Science Club, and the Irish Railway Record Society. He was by now a member of both the London and the Oxford Diocesan Advisory Committees (which dealt with matters architectural), and his advice was beginning to be sought, as it was for ever afterwards, on both literary and architectural matters, as though he had some sort of official post. For instance, in 1948 the Marquis of Bath wrote, 'I am opening Longleat to the public in April next year and I want to produce a small book about it which I will sell to the public for two and sixpence. . . . The point is will you *please* do it for me.'[21] Who else was there to ask?

1. PB's papers, Beinecke Library, Yale University.
2. Mrs Abbot, CLG interview (1993).
3. Mark Amory (ed.), *Evelyn Waugh Letters* (Weidenfeld and Nicolson, 1980).
4. JB's papers, University of Victoria, British Columbia.
5. JB's papers.
6. 'Florrie' was subsequently changed to 'Thelma' in the published version.
7. Florence Sprules, CLG interview (1993).
8. Stan Sprules, CLG interview (1993).
9. Joan Whitaker, CLG interview (1992).
10. Joan Whitaker's papers.
11. JB's papers.
12. JB's papers.
13. JB's papers.
14. JB's papers.
15. JB's papers.
16. JB's papers.
17. A. L. Rowse, letter to CLG (September 1992).
18. JB, Christopher Sykes interview, Georgetown University, Washington DC.
19. JB, Susan Barnes interview, 'Betjeman I Bet Your Racket Brings You in a Pretty Packet', *Sunday Times Magazine* (30 January 1972).
20. JB's papers.
21. JB's papers.

To Eileen Molony

3 November 1945

c/o Colonel Kolkhorst
Yarnton Manor House
Nr Oxford

Ah my darling dark yellow-stockinged Amazon,

So you have come back to me and I cannot even remember what the P.E. looked like for thoughts of your large eyes (see 'The Chapel-Organist, A.D. 185–' by T. Hardy for a description of yourself, in his *Collected Poems*).

Thank you so very much for *The Bookman*. A real bumper number with Dora Sigarson Shorter and others in as well as RSH.

I lent it to a clergyman who used some of it for notes for a sermon on [The Revd R.S.] Hawker and now I have it back again and shall treasure it.

I shall CERTAINLY come and see you in London. But whyever leave Bristol?

Love, John B

E.M. was the BBC Talks producer in Bristol, who then moved to London.
    Hardy's poem contains the following lines:
        'A handsome girl,' he would murmur, upstaring (and so I am).
        'But – too much sex in her build; fine eyes, but eyelids too heavy;
        A bosom too full for her age; in her lips too voluptuous a dye.'
        (It may be. But who put it there? Assurdly it was not I.)
    E.M. replied (12 November 1945), 'Your letter beginning "Ah my darling dark yellow-stockinged Amazon", not being marked "Personal", bounced its way merrily from hand to hand through BBC Registry, and eventually ran me to earth in the Talks Department. Little did you know what a champagne bottle you were breaking across my bows as I was launched into London life. The whole organisation is humming with interest and speculation as a result.'

To John Murray

2 December 1945

The Old Rectory
Farnborough
Wantage
Berkshire

My dear Jock,

I enclose the other half of the contract and thank you and Mr Murray for the unexpected but BY NO MEANS UNWELCOME cheque for fifty pounds. I will now be able to buy Christmas Presents with the half the Slave State does not take to pay such people as those who mismanage the petrol coupons in Reading.

I will come up on Monday or Tuesday next week to sign the special editions. I hope to hear you have not printed more than two thousand copies. You will never sell them. By the way do ask your advertising people not to refer to me as a SATIRIST in future. I spent a long time in the last book's preface explaining I wasn't a satirist then; I am even less of one now. What I write may not be poetry to TAMBIMUTTU, whoever he may be, but it is certainly not SATIRE.

Hope to be out of [the] B[ritish] C[ouncil] by February.

Yours, John B

M. J. Tambimuttu (1915–83) was quite influential in the London literary life of the forties. A poet himself, he edited *Poetry London*.

To Nancy Mitford   Farnborough Old Rectory
                                            Wantage
19 December 1945   Berkshire

My dear Nancy,

Cold from the G[reat] W[estern] R[ailway], in which I have just been finishing *The Pursuit of Love*, I write to tell you on this lovely *writing* paper how v. greatly I enjoyed it.

You have produced something that really is a monument to our friends. It is exactly how we used to talk at Biddesden. In the beginning of the book I wondered how you were going to keep it up to the high standard you had set. By developing Linda as a character you subtly and gradually changed the key of the thing. It starts as a sort of *Diary of a Nobody* about the upper classes instead of the lower middles, as does that immortal work, and it develops into a very moving love story. You look down like a goddess on the world. It cannot be that the wonderful, unforgettable Uncle Matthew is really like Lord Redesdale, can it? He is my favourite character in the book. Gerald and particularly Eddy are superb. Oh you clever old girl. How I am going to break this lovely book to the drearies of the *Daily Herald*, I don't know. I shall enjoy trying. Clever, clever Nancy. I am proud to know you.

Propeller has all Nancy Catford's books. You have done full justice to Surrey – but I've got round to thinking Surrey the loveliest county of all and long for a garden like Sir Leicester's. It is not a poetical book, it is a clever one. Really clever and beautiful.

Love, John B

'Uncle Matthew' *was* based on Lord Redesdale, N.M.'s father.
'Nancy Catford' may have been a nickname for N.M.

To Cyril Connolly   The Old Rectory
Farnborough
Wantage
28 December 1945   Berkshire
Holy Innocents' Day

Dear Cyril,
You certainly have done us proud this Christmas and I doubt if we even
sent you a card. To begin with *The Condemned Playground* – it is a great
pleasure to have it. I re-read with as intense enjoyment as when I first
read them – the Aldous Huxley and 'Where Engels Fears to Tread'.
There is something, too, very pleasant about seeing one's own name in
print. Especially in print, old boy, which is certain to be printed again
and again. You say somewhere in one of those articles that you are a
lyricist. I think you are. I think these short articles are just your
medium – for you have a gift of parody which never goes on for too long
and which less talented writers would expand into a book. Then you
write so much that is devastatingly condensed that an article shows it up
in all its subtlety. I mean such remarks as 'All move in the psychologists'
wonderland which is revealed to us when we watch charmless people
trying to be charming'. My hat those articles *are* good. Dawkins (a
Professor) was telling me the other day about how delighted he was
with the title *The Condemned Playground*. What always surprises me is
that people I know notice such a lot. No one would think that you in
that huge coat and with no hat on your head and going off to Soho to
lunch would notice everything as you do. I must say, old boy, *The
Condemned Playground* makes me proud to know you, not that I wasn't
before. I'm sorry you didn't include the Irish article.
    But, as to the Richard Doyle, I'm equally delighted with that. It's a
book I've been trying to get for years for Paul (not Mark, though he
rather likes the name) *and myself*. I once saw one of the original water
colours for it in old Joseph Holloway's house in Dublin. It really is as
good a children's book as exists. The Prawn [PSGB] is delighted with it.
He is still half in the dream world and is very interested in fairies (the
Dicky Doyle sort) and was only talking to me about them on a walk the
day before yesterday and now comes your pictorial fulfilment of his

imaginings. It was most generous of you to part with it. I shall have to exercise great restraint not to take it from the Powlie's shelves.

You and Lys really must come here. It is bloody cold and rather like Collinstown and the house quite featureless inside. But if I can only get some drink and it is clear crisp weather, you will be enchanted with the place. Seven hundred and twenty feet above sea level, as I said in my last, and bloody draughty. Unluckily we have to fell fifteen beeches around the house. They have AMERICAN disease, which is INCUR-ABLE.

Well, I must close now. Love to Boot. We will have something Very Special for you when you come. *Prepare yourself*. Propeller is anxious for you to come and stay. She is more eccentric than ever.

Love, Felicity

C.C.'s *The Condemned Playground* came out in 1944. It was a collection of his essays, including a parody of Aldous Huxley, entitled 'Told in Gath', and 'Where Engels Fears to Tread', a parody of Brian Howard and Ronald Firbank.

Dawkins, Bywater Professor of Byzantine Greek, was an eccentric Oxford don, much revered and loved by JB. He laughed uproariously at his own jokes.

Richard Doyle, an artist and caricaturist who contributed to *Punch*, is best known as an illustrator of fairy tales. He illustrated Thackeray's *The Newcomes*.

Lys Connolly lived with C.C. from 1945 to 1950. She had changed her name by deed poll but never married him.

To Tom Driberg   The Old Rectory
                                                        Farnborough
                                                        Wantage
Octave of Epiphany 1946   Berkshire

My dear Thomas,

I thank you most warmly for your perspicacious and truly appreciative notice of my poems in *Reynolds*. Kindly note our new address: 1730-brick house, church restored, united benefice, is high-ish and muddled. Seven hundred and twenty feet above sea level. Corking scenery. No light, no water, no telephone allowed by Slave State – but what exquisite scenery; come and see your godson. He is charming and fair.

Love to the Houses of Parliament.

Yours, John Betjeman

T.D. reviewed *New Bats in Old Belfries* in *Reynolds News* (23 December 1945). 'Betjeman specialises in nostalgic, exact, topographical, metrically archaic, only half satirical

descriptions of middle-class life. . . . The thing about Betjeman that probably annoys
some fools is that they don't know if they are meant to laugh or not.'
  The benefice (living) of Farnborough was united with West Ilsley where the vicar
lived. He conducted services in both villages.

To George, Anne and Anthony Barnes   Windygates
                                                        Songster's Way
                                                        Sidcup
8 January 1946   Kent

Dear Stuart, Doris and Norman,
Howard and I did very much as you supposed we would, we caught the
jolly old train at Rye and changed at Ashford and again at Tub's Hill
and Howard couldn't see a tree at Pett's Wood nor could I. Such a pity,
it was such unspoiled country before the riff raff came there. Then we
changed at Orpington and I just had a sec to pop down to the Estate
Agents on the corner of Station road and then it was the eleven eighteen
to Penge East through quiet countryside parts until Bickley, where it
became all those ugly old grey brick houses – so suburban I think,
compared with the sun traps of today – and at Penge East we were quite
in a wilderness – *miles* from Crystal Palace Low Level Station so it was
bus, bus, bus, trolley bus, bus before we got to old Mr Comper's. The
old bird – Howard says he is early Victorian, positively. Howard and
he talked architecture nineteen to the dozen until I got heartily sick.
Then we went up to the old man's house on Beulah Hill. Such a funny
house, my dears, all sort of Tudor but not the *real* thing, you know, like
they build nowadays, but in *plaster*, did you ever? and perfectly
enormous and full of stained glass of what Howard says is a very bad
period – 1836 – too late to be real Regency, which I think divine –
Regency I mean. He lives there all alone and has a garden eleven acres
down a sort of precipice and a lake and a wood at the bottom. The silly
old man refused thirty-five thousand for it because he said it was the last
country left between London and Croydon. Certainly you can see miles
from his terrace but I would rather have had the oodles than the view.
There he and Howard jawed on all about St Alban's Holborn and those
Victorian churches which Howard says are hopelessly out of date and
should be pulled down for pre-fab designs, as you must have a house for
people first and proper sanitation and things like that before all this
nonsense about entertainment, museums and religion. But of course
Mr Comper is proper Victorian and doesn't see things like Howard
does.

Well we did enjoy ourselves with you, dears, at that weekend. Howard said he could have wished he could have converted you to the flat roof and suggests you put one on Prawls. Windygates seemed very lonely when we got back. The girl was out and the sun parlour window had been left open and smashed one of the vita glass panes which Serge Chermayeff gave us for a wedding gift.

I thought those parcels must have cost you something to send and so enclose a little something to cover postage.

That horrid man you had down – Benjamin or some such name – told Howard that if you had as much trouble in changing the P[ostal] O[rder] as Howard had had in getting it, then you would be quits. I don't like that smart kind of so-called humour.

Again thanks *ever* so,

So long, Darenth

> This is another of JB's letters written in an invented persona. On the way down to Prawls across the Darenth Valley, JB had invented a fictitious suburban couple, Darenth and Howard. JB called the Barneses Stuart, Doris and Norman when in his Darenth mode.
> Serge Chermayeff was an architect recommended by JB to the BBC for a talk in 1932 when he worked on the *Architectural Review*. By 1946 he had changed his view of him.

To Kenneth Clark

The Old Rectory
Farnborough
Wantage
Berkshire

28 January 1946

My dear K,

Comper is in excellent health and good spirits. His office is now in his parents' house which we visited, as the Slave State pulled down his studio to build flats on Knight's Hall SE27.

But Comper is, as you know, a member of no professional body, since he follows Bodley in his dislike of committees, professionalism and schools of architecture. So there is no infamous book which contains him, no official recognition of his work and Stanley Morison has just discovered that *The Times* prepared no obituary of him. R. Lutyens will now write one. I am supplying him with facts.

I wrote to Prof. Richardson saying couldn't he get Comper made an RA? But he tells me in a private letter that the RA can elect no one over seventy-five and Comper is eighty-three. The Prof. thinks he should be given an OM and is going to organise for the Fine Arts Commission.

Tom Boase does not think Comper 'enough guns' for an OM. I doubt if he knows Comper's work.

But I do think that in some way his country should recognise Comper's work. Not that he is worldly enough to care one way or another and not that I have consulted him.

I write all this to you in the hope that you may think of something that can be done to give him official recognition. Needless to say, I have said nothing to Comper about this idea.

Love to Jane. Whatever she may say, Norman Shaw *is* a good architect.

Yours, John B

> G. F. Bodley, Gothic Revival architect, was claimed by Comper as 'my master'.
> K.C. remarked that it was difficult to get an OM for someone who was not a public figure, but undaunted and single-handed JB began a long and time-consuming crusade, which culminated in Comper's knighthood. He was by then ninety but lived for another six years.
> Tom Boase was a History of Art professor and a director of the Courtauld Institute.

To Frank Gallagher   The Old Rectory
                                            Farnborough
                                            Wantage
28 February 1946   Berkshire

Dear Frank,
I am immensely grateful to you for your criticisms. I had not read the typescript which had gone to you. It was made from the MS which was handwritten.

Of course I agree with all your three criticisms of detail.

The remarks of Insany's certainly read as though I subscribe to them. The whole point of the paper was to show that I did not. But I will expunge them since they are liable to the interpretation you put on them.

The remarks about the nuncio should never have appeared and I will remove them. I agree with you, on reflection.

The Catholic argument with 'once a Catholic always a Catholic' was a footnote – not delivered in the address – but I see it has been typed in as part of the main text. It will easily come out.

You inspire me – though that was probably not your intention – entirely to recast the essay. You yourself once told me the main difference between England and Ireland – the sense of the presence of

God in the latter – and I think I have got that.

Open with remarks on the different sets of people likely to take offence whatever is written about Ireland – this will enable me to differentiate 'Unionists' and the like.

So taking as my main themes these points:

1) differences between England and Ireland
   a) Sense of presence of God
   b) logical natures of Irish thought, illogical English
   c) mob language i.e. mode of expressing oneself
   d) Celtic field and tribal system as opposed to feudal English system has altered look of country in past.
2) Popular misconceptions about Ireland in England
   a) Paddies
   b) Celtic Twilight
3) Popular misconceptions in Ireland about England
   a) that English people know Irish history
   b) that English people despise Ireland

Concluding with remarks on the advantages of a small, self-supporting nation as one in which a full life can be had as opposed to a large industrial one which is always being drawn into bigger and bigger [illegible].

It is my aim to avoid names as much as possible and tables of facts.

I shall recast and consult Frank Pakenham and hope the result will be something worthy of the position I held and far more competent than that, something which will inform the thousands of English visitors you will be getting, of how to get on in Ireland and how to appreciate the ancient nation Ireland is. Again many thanks, for you must be very busy.

Yours, John Betjeman

In F.G.'s capacity as head of the Information Service and writer on Irish politics, it seems that he got JB to write on Anglo-Irish relations in a positive way for some sort of public exposure. It is uncertain what came of it.

Honor Tracy, who was working for *The Bell*, wrote (14 August 1946), 'Reggie [Ross-Williamson] says you have a beautiful piece on the Englishman's approach to Ireland and that you have not placed it so far. Would you give it to me?' and then (28 August 1946), 'No doubt you hate my guts but I wish you would give me your article. We could pay fifteen guineas for it if it is four thousand words long.'

To William Collins   The Old Rectory
                                               Farnborough
                                               Wantage
10 March 1946   Berkshire
1st Sunday in Lent

Dear Collins,
I thank you very much for your letter of March 1st.

I would very much like a further talk on the book. I am all agog about it, but I cannot start until I am out of the British Council. I can get out of the British Council if Jock Murray can get the *Murray Guide* going. If he can't, I'm rather sunk. He will know next week.

My position financially is this. I am at present as rich as Croesus (for me) and miserable. That is to say I get about seven hundred a year from the *Daily Herald* and a thousand a year from the British Council. Both about halved by the Slave State, of course. I have got to earn about twelve hundred a year in order to keep my house and pay family school bills.

Now if I chuck the BC, I am at the mercy of the *Daily Herald* which may sack me at any moment for being a bloody reactionary and not the sort of reviewer they want. I don't trust them an inch. Then I am ruined, can't pay school bills and so on.

If I can assure myself of five to seven hundred a year writing on top of *Daily Herald* I would feel safer. Murray might do this if he gets the guide going. I could probably make about three hundred out of your Church book. The work would go together well with the guide.

To write your church book should take me about nine months and I shall want the summer weather and some exes [expenses] for getting about – particularly to the North of England.

I had hopes, as you know, of founding this monthly *The Church* – but I've no time to make the necessary preparation while I'm working at the rate I do at hack work and no paper is, I suspect, yet available (or ever likely to be) for periodicals – particularly Christian ones.

That is my whole position. I don't know whether [Edmund] Cork can do anything about it. I doubt it. And I don't see why you should. But if Jock fails to get his *Guides* back from the publishers who bought the rights, I am taking a grave risk if I chuck the British Council. If I hadn't a family, of course I would take it.

Yours sincerely, John Betjeman

W.C. was the chairman and managing director of Collins, the publishers, who had met JB through the latter's agent, Edmund Cork of Hughes Massie.

English Parish Churches, which JB thought would take nine months, took nearly a dozen years to complete.

To John Summerson   The Old Rectory
                                             Farnborough
                                             Wantage
15 March 1946   Berkshire

My dear Coolmore,

You are not the modern Ruskin. You are the modern Fergusson. I cannot do without Fergusson. I think *Georgian London* the most lovely book, lovely to look at and pithy to read. You have a wonderful acid style. I keep seeing you in my mind's eye with that curled lip and sudden laughter. You have long been one of my heroes. Now you are *the* hero. You are not a bit academic or pedantic. You are learned and stimulating and extremely witty.

Never shall I forget you coming out from under that Butterfield arcade with a measure.

Of course Goodhart-Rendel is right about Truefitt. A most original man. And what about Fred Deshone, who was cut off so early?

Give my love to your wife and Sir John.

Again I thank and congratulate you. I had to borrow a copy of the book for review in the *Daily Herald* (in my inevitable vulgar and superficial style designed for that paper), as the buggers didn't send it to me for review.

Yours ever, John Betjeman

James Fergusson (1808–86) was a prolific writer on architectural and archaeological topics. His best known work was a *History of Architecture for All Countries* 1865–67, noted for its accuracy and the excellence of its illustrations.

George Truefitt (1824–1902) published *Designs for Country Churches* (1850).

Frederick Chalmers Deshone was a church architect. He became insane and shot himself in 1877.

To Ninian Comper Clandeboye
20 March 1946 Northern Ireland

Dear Mr Comper,

Would you consider anything so humble as doing the lettering for a memorial stone? I write on this paper because I am with Lady Dufferin, whose address it is, and whose address until the 5th of next month is the Ritz Hotel, London W1 (Regent 8181). Her husband, a great friend of mine, was killed in Burma last year and she wants to put up a stone to him in the 'Campo Santo' at Clandeboye, near Belfast. The other stones there are of white Italian marble, including that to the famous Lord Dufferin, who was Viceroy of India. I have suggested to Lady Dufferin that she might avoid that precedent and use a local stone or slate. Lord Dufferin is not buried at Clandeboye, but she wishes to put up a stone in the family cemetery there – 'The Campo Santo' – as a memorial.

The words she and I have decided on are:

IN MEMORY OF
BASIL SHERIDAN,
4TH MARQUESS OF DUFFERIN AND AVA
CAPTAIN, ROYAL HORSE GUARDS

A MAN OF BRILLIANCE
AND OF MANY FRIENDS

HE WAS KILLED IN ACTION AT LETZE ON MARCH
25TH 1945 AT THE AGE OF THIRTY-FIVE,
RECAPTURING BURMA THE COUNTRY WHICH
HIS GRANDFATHER ANNEXED TO THE BRITISH
CROWN

I have given her your name and told her I would write to you. I said the architect would fix up the matters of the lettering, stone, stonemason and setting up.

Can you do this? If so, will you write to Lady Dufferin at the Ritz? I *did* enjoy my visit with K. Clark, etc.

Yours ever, John Betjeman

Comper accepted to do the lettering for the memorial and it was unveiled at Easter the following year, after Lady Dufferin and JB had exchanged several letters about materials and minor changes.

To E. O. Springfield   The British Council
                                                3 Hanover Street
3 April 1946   London W1

Dear Mr Springfield,
The worst threat I can hang over your head, is for me to refuse to leave
unless you remove Miss Tavendale either from this office altogether or
put her under me or my successor and me or my successor under you or
under Colonel Sullivan for administration matters. I fear the monthly
and all too short visits of Col. Sullivan and Mr Wilkinson are not going
to smooth out our administrative difficulties here. In the last two days I
have had complaints about Miss Tavendale from
   1) Miss Barton on the subject of her vacancies and the sort of people
she is given by administration.
   2) Miss Dinsdale because Miss T. refused to allow her to move some
of her typists to near a window in the library.
   3) Mr Elston because Miss Tavendale refused to allow him and his
four male assistants to go by a short cut to the nearest Gents to their
office.
   4) Miss Barton about priorities for the motorcar.
   5) Mr Yates because Miss Tavendale has disallowed a claim of his for
a taxi about which I wrote a minute of reasons for approval some
weeks ago.
Numbers 2 and 3 were solved after argument and discussion. Nos 1
and 4 have probably arguments on both sides. But the point of all this is
that I am very busy on our reorganisation here and Miss Tavendale is
not, as I have repeatedly pointed out, the right person to be in charge of
what is now a big organisation. Mrs Cousins is perfectly satisfactory
and works amicably with the rest of the staff and with,
   Yours sincerely, John Betjeman

   E.O.S. was JB's superior in the BC and later received an OBE.

To George Orwell   The Old Rectory
                                                Farnborough
                                                Wantage
18 April 1946   Berkshire

Dear Mr Orwell,
I have always thought you are one of the last living writers of prose. Let

me tell you how very much indeed I enjoyed and echoed every sentiment of your thoughts on THE COMMON TOAD in *TRIBUNE* the other day. Don't bother to reply to this. It's a Collins.

Yours sincerely, John Betjeman

G.O., author of *Animal Farm* (1945) and *1984* (1949), was for a number of years Literary Editor of *Tribune*.

To Anthony Barnes   The Old Rectory
                                                      Farnborough
                                                      Wantage
12 May 1946   Berkshire

My dear Little Prawls,
I am simply delighted with the Powlie's Progress. So is the Powlie. Thank you very much. The Prune at Prangmore Aerodrome touches very near the conscience.

By this post I am writing a belated Collins to Mrs Prawls. A terrible thing happened between my leaving Prawls and the present. I had to preach a sermon in a very large Gothic revival Church (1890-Perp) in Northampton. I had accepted to 'talk' and pictured a circle of earnest young men and girls before the vicarage fire and a cosy chit-chat. Not a bit of it. I was to *preach*. It was terrible. Quite six hundred people at Evensong. I sat in the choir and remembering that clergy always go down on their knees during the penultimate verse of the hymn before the sermon, I went down on mine. All I said was 'Oh God! Oh God!' and sweated. Then as I bowed politely to the altar and ascended the pulpit, the congregation was singing the last two lines of the hymn.

'And may the music of thy Name
Refresh my soul in Death'
I very earnestly echoed those sentiments and wished Death were at once. I read every word of the sermon in a very loud voice so as to be heard. I doubt if anyone was interested. My great enemy and ex-tutor Lewis had preached on the previous Sunday and been 'a great success'.

The only consolation was that Mr Bassett-Lowke, the model railway king was in the congregation and I met him afterwards. He told me that he did not regard the R[omney] H[ythe] and D[ymchurch] R[ailway] as a true model. It was just too big and had to be made by Paxmans who are, normally, full gauge Railway Engineers.

I hope life at Eton is not so awful as was my life at Marlborough.

Your intellectual progress is always in my thoughts.
Love, John B

A.B., the son of George and Anne Barnes, was a scholar at Eton College.
   'The Prune at Prangmore' refers to JB meeting George and Anne Barnes at a pub in
Hythe and entering with a limp. He then described in a loud voice, to embarrass them,
how he had 'pranged his aircraft'.

To Diana Craig

[May 1946?]

              Twas at the Miller-Manuels'
                 In a sumptuous Bloomsb'ry Hall
              Miss Dunlop and Diana Craig
                 Went to a dinner-ball,
              Soft as the heavy carpets
                 Their eyes betrayed their souls
              As they gazed across the napery
                 At well-selected Poles.
              'Oh Captain Miller-Manuel
                 I fear I'm dancing this
              With Major Dobrzynski
                 And *he* knows how to kiss.
              I like you very much indeed
                 And thank you all the same
              But I much prefer the Major
                 With the long and funny name.'
              Alas, the lush carnations!
                 Each *most expensive* bloom
              Was crushed against the Major
                 As he whirled her round the room.
              The chromium and the shaded lights
                 They both began to spin
              Like a glass of Lyons 'thirty-eight
                 Mixed with black-market gin.
              'Oh Captain Miller-Manuel
                 Miss Dunlop's very nice
              I know she'd like to dance with you
                 Her heart is made of ice.
              My next fifteen are promised
                 To the Pole that I adore
              But I like you very much indeed
                 As I have said before.'

The lights were switched to purple
    The wine flowed on in waves
And little jars of caviare
    Were handed round by slaves.
As Bloomsbury resounded
    To throbbings of the band
The Pole he gave Diana Craig
    His Castle and his hand.
'Oh Mrs Miller-Manuel
    It's been the greatest fun
I'm sure that I've enjoyed it
    Far more than anyone;
I cannot quite express myself.
    I'm tied in lover's knots.
But oh! I am so sorry
    About Sadie's horrid spots.'
'Two thousand pounds it cost me,'
    Said the Captain to his mate
'And there's our daughter, Sadie,
    And she hasn't made a date,
I fear we made the invites
    Far too wide and vague
When we asked that cold Miss Dunlop
    And that fast Diana Craig.'

D.C., young, plump, blonde, outgoing and tennis-playing, was JB's chosen secretary at the British Council and afterwards at the Oxford Preservation Trust. Her flatmate, Daphne Dunlop, also in the periodicals section of his department at the British Council, remembered how Diana told JB all her problems and how once 'goggle-eyed and full of superlatives, she told Mr Betjeman about a dance we'd been to, the Saturday night before . . . we were asked to bring partners – and did; but somehow, when the dancing began, Di became distracted by a number of elegant Polish army officers who were also attending the ball.' On hearing the account, JB gave Diana this verse the next morning.

To Janet Stone

Coolgrena
Trebetherick
Wadebridge
18 May 1946
Cornwall

My dear Janet,
So far as I can see Litton Cheney is about a hundred and thirty miles from here – that we are about four hours' travelling. That means we

should not get to you until about two if we started from here at ten, which is the earliest hour we could manage to start without feeling really ill on the journey. So I suggest we arrive about three, having stopped off for sandwiches with L[aurence] Whistler at Lyme, then back with you and tea.

   Love and thanks, John B

> It was an almost annual occurrence for us to visit Reynolds Stone, the engraver, and his wife, Janet, at their Dorset rectory on the way back from Cornwall.

To Anthony Barnes   The Old Rectory
                                             Farnborough
                                             Wantage
26 May 1946   Berkshire

My Dear Little Prawls,
I owe you a letter at least I feel I owe you one and so I have decided to write one to you without any punctuation at all for only last week John Piper and I on a tour to Metroland found ourselves going by way of Eton and had lunch at Ye Olde Christopher Wrenne House at Windsor and thought and talked of you we took some ravishing photographs of Sham Tudor in Chesham and Amersham including a house belonging to black marketeers and called *Olde Timbers* it was sprawled and oaken and uneven among birdbaths lily ponds and clipped macrocarpas and only the most debauched taste like ours could have appreciated it and Prawls Major would be horrified at our impurity I am going to write to him about it I have an idea that Woodyer's work at Clewer must be interesting but it is all behind high walls and we could not summon courage to ask the sisters to let us in perhaps one warm afternoon you will visit it Aberdeen was a great success but would take too long to describe in these art capitals
   Love from John B

> This letter was written in artistically wrought capital letters.
>   Woodyer was a Victorian architect (1816–96) who built the House of Mercy at Clewer.

To Mr Broad   The Old Rectory
                                                 Farnborough
                                                 Wantage
28 May 1946   Berkshire

Dear Mr Broad,
I only received your letter PU/103 of May 24 today. It was addressed to
me at the British Council, which I left a fortnight ago, although you
could not be expected to know that. It was further delayed because the
direction of the Council on the envelope was one which the Council left
in September of last year. I therefore make all haste to reply to you
because you will want to find someone else, to write the two
thousand-word articles for which you ask by June 7th.

I cannot undertake the work because

1) I do not know enough about the circulation and influence of *British
Ally* which you publish in Russia.

2) I could not write a 'rather important brief literary survey' on war
books that have appeared since the war ended, because in the first place
such books are too contemporary in the time sense to give one the right
perspective for balanced judgement and in the second place those
writers you mention as having been featured in your paper – George
Miller, Peter Scott and Lt John Davies – excellent as they may be as
propaganda in Russia, cannot possibly be considered as serious
literature.

3) I do not agree with you that most of our younger writers were at
the war and not writing. The numerous 'forces' publications that came
out during the war gave the lie to that. They were both at the war and
writing. I should add that if a man is a writer nothing will stop him
writing this side of eternity.

4) Though I think I see what you mean about the impression the
Russians may have of the preciosity of our writing, I think no good
purposes would be served by classing creative work (if there is any)
about war as 'masculine' and other creative work as feminine or
precious or by any other word which may express Russian distaste.

5) Even were I prepared to accept the thesis you offer me as guidance,
I could not afford to do so for five guineas a thousand words, for all
serial rights.

I suggest you ask someone simply for an article on books about the
war and to hell with literature. Several people come to mind who would
be willing to do the job. Most of them would probably want higher fees,

since, with present day taxes, ten guineas is virtually five. I am sorry I
cannot include myself among their number even at an increased price!
    Yours sincerely, John Betjeman

To John Murray   The Old Rectory
                                                    Farnborough
                                                    Wantage
8 June 1946   Berkshire

Dear Jock,
J. P. and I had two wet days and saw fifty churches and twice as many
villages. We took a few interiors. I've seen the negs. These just show
you some of what there is that [Marcus] Whiffen missed.
    The result of this tour has been to our minds that we must give
ourselves at least another week in Bucks (in fine weather); we must do
Metroland which is not half bad.
    I cannot come on Friday 14th to see Whiffen. I feel he comes in later.
The value of these guides will be *not* that they are comprehensive but
that they see the good and the characteristic with an artist's eye rather
than Herbert Felton's. In fact on these pictures only they stand. And so
far, we have not enough good pictures. I hope you do not disagree with
this view. One wants at once to please the scholars and to make the
public *see* with a new eye. So one has to look about a good deal more than
has been done yet and select. We are both very excited and interested
and it is only J. P.'s bloody opera at Glyndebourne which holds us back
– that and petrol and films. Can you help on the latter two items?
    Yours, John B

    Marcus Whiffen was the original designer of the Buckinghamshire Guide
    (recommended by John Summerson), but resigned from the project in the summer of
    1947, after it had been virtually hijacked by JB and John Piper. 'It is not merely that the
    selection of subjects has been altered, but the whole idea of the book has changed,' he
    wrote to Jock Murray (27 July 1947).
        Whiffen had been going to use photographs from the National Buildings Record and
    Herbert Felton was to have been employed by the latter to fill in the gaps.
        John Piper was designing sets for two Benjamin Britten operas at Glyndebourne, *The
    Rape of Lucretia* and *Albert Herring*.

To Alan Pryce-Jones

The Old Rectory
Farnborough
Wantage

8 June 1946

Berkshire

My dearest Captain Bog,

I do greatly appreciate your returning to me my spectacles as I know what hell it is first to do up a parcel and then to queue up at a Post Office for the privilege of paying for its despatch. It arrived safely.

We have had a visit from relations of yours who were house-crawling and their names were Miss Anne Loder (and a 'friend', I thought, called Miss Farrer or Farrell, whom I much liked) and Miss L.'s mother, Lady Wakehurst. They spoke very kindly of you. They were extremely nice and Lady W. was one of the most well-born and Vere-Pryce-Jones-ish persons I have ever met. Propeller never quite grasped who it was who had called.

I shall be wanting to come and stay with you. Collins have commissioned me to do a book on English Churches and I should like to use you as my Rochester Diocesan Correspondent and your area of Canterbury Diocese (ten guineas, I think). I am going to make the chief feature of the book *Un-restored churches*, but the book itself will list all churches, irrespective of period, from the Venerable Bede to J. N. Comper which persons like you and me think worth looking at.

Thus we will mention good Victorian buildings. For Mediaeval and eighteenth-century fabrics John Piper has devised this classification

1) 'Pleasing Decay'
2) 'Completely furnished'
3) 'Good examples of their time'.

Thus if you were considering London and district I can think of nothing under 1) but St M's Bd Street would have come under 2) and St St's Walbrook under 3). Can you contemplate such a list for Rochester? I could then call on you and we could visit together.

My love to Poppy and David.

Love, JB

St Mildred's, Bread Street, and St Stephen's, Walbrook, are both by Wren.

To Alan Pryce-Jones   The Old Rectory
                                               Farnborough
                                               Wantage
28 June 1946   Berkshire

Dearest Captain Bog,
If by this month and not July I can't, because there isn't time! But do
you mean August? or will you be there in August? I hope you will be.
Just let me know more clearly.

I wish I had known that about your cousin. I found myself rather
attracted by Miss Farrer. I like the manly type. They were staying in an
hotel in Newbury and hunting for a house – hence their visit to us.
Apparently they had contemplated buying the house.

Poor Mrs Woad is dying (Lady C.), two clots of blood on the heart.
No hope. I am very depressed, because with the years I have grown
most fond of her. Very generous, truly unselfish, not afraid of anything
and with a positive faith in her lack of faith. I am sure she has died, or
rather is dying, with courage. Penelope is up with her in Wales, where
she is at the house of a very little known Admiral brother [Admiral Sir
George Knightley Chetwode]. And this evening I have been looking
over Mrs Woad's photograph albums which have arrived here with a lot
of Woad furniture in the Louis Seize style which I am beginning to
admire. The albums contain photographs of houses, early motorcars,
huntballs and the great whacking signatures of Young Cadius from
1893–1904. Also a lot of Basil Blackwood letters. There is something
really terrifying looking at these photographs of a young girl when
geraniums grew in window boxes and gardeners raked the gravel in
front of the bedroom window before the guests got up and now to think
of her dying in a small house in Wales in pain, old and unwilling to live.
Really the only solution is to devote oneself to Christianity and look
forward – if *only* one can believe it for a split second – to Heaven and
meeting old friends.

I mean what I say about Rochester. It *is* your diocese, I suppose. If
not, choose the one that is. Yes I do want to see you both.

Love to you both, John

A.P.-J. remembers there was a joke about his cousin and Miss Loder living together.
Were they lesbians? No, they were not.
  Basil Blackwood (1870–1917), uncle of Basil Dufferin and Ava, was the 'BTB' who
illustrated Belloc's *Cautionary Tales*.

To Dr Francis Carolus Eeles   The Old Rectory
                                                      Farnborough
                                                      Wantage
29 August 1946   Berkshire

Dear Dr Eeles,

I thank you for your letter of August 26th. I agree. I will, if I may, come down when I have my material more in order at this end and know more precisely what I want in the way of individual places.

I do not believe I ever wrote to thank you for your and Miss Scott's kind welcome to me at Dunster. *I am certainly coming again.* And I will take Miss Scott to the cinema so that she will be able to clear some of those rood lofts out of her mind. And I will take you too because after one has been to an American film one realises how beautiful England still is, despite its wires and prefabs and tin signs and road houses and motor cars. I am suddenly shooting forward with the book and will know a lot more of what I want in a month or two.

> The Queen was in the kitchen
> Washing up the bowls,
> The King was in the cellar
> Shovelling the coals
> The Maid was in the garden
> Eating bread and honey
> And talking to a neighbour
> About getting more money.

I believe the Dean of Durham wrote that. I thought you might like it.

Yours sincerely, John Betjeman

JB was looking at churches in Somerset on a preliminary reconnaissance for *Parish Churches*.

Dr E., secretary for the Council for the Care of Churches, was based at Dunster in Somerset.

Miss Judith Scott was Eeles' assistant, to whom JB was slightly attracted.

The Dean of Durham from 1933 to 1951 was C. A. Alington.

To Evelyn Waugh   The Old Rectory
                                           Farnborough
                                           Wantage
17 September 1946   Berkshire

Dear Evelyn,
This broadcast about you – Maurice, the only person I would trust
beside myself to do it, is going to Greece and so I want to do it and will.
Two thousand five hundred words, including extracts. To be in by the
middle of November. May I come and stay with you and we can decide
what you want said? I am really no good as a critic where my admiration
is so wholly engaged as it is with your writings. I am fogged by my own
delight. As for stuff about 'trends' and 'influences', I find you can invent
any old trend and work it in and invent any old influence and work that
in too. The only influence I can think of is Ronald Firbank in the earlier
books. Am I wrong?
    As to colour books old boy, if I weren't so damned tired I would make
a complete list but the Atlas folio book I can give you details of:

THE CHAPEL

OF

ST ANTHONY THE EREMITE

AT

MURTHLY, PERTHSHIRE

THE SEAT OF

SIR WILLIAM DRUMMOND STEWART

OF GRANDTULLY BART

LITHOGRAPHED BY SCHENK & GHEMAR

FROM THE DESIGNS OF

JAMES GILLESPIE GRAHAM ARCHITECT

AND

ALEXANDER CHRISTIE A.R.S.A.

EDINBURGH

ALEXANDER HILL, PRINTSELLER TO THE QUEEN

LONDON PAUL & DOMINIC COLNAGHI & CO

MDCCCL[?]

My other big *coloured* lithographic books are Richardson's *Round Abbeys
of Yorkshire*, Beckford's *Lansdown Town, Crystal Pal[ace]* Nash Hyde and
Roberts (2 vols) Wyatts P.'s *Industrial Arts* (3 vols), Hackburn's
Decorative Painting of the Middle Ages (1847) and about twenty others but

it's so dark at the other end of the room with these oil lights that I can't trust my memory for more titles.

Now I feel I must give you that Chapel of St Anthony book. It's an RC chapel. But the book is so large. How can I get it to you? I would bring it to Oxford by motor car. Write and suggest means and say if I can come to stay, and love to Laura. John B

JB's talk on E.W. went on air on 14 December 1946.

To the Secretary of the Oxford Canning Club   The Old Rectory
Farnborough
Wantage
2 October 1946   Berkshire

Dear Mr Brown,
I am sorry not to be able to accept the kind invitation of the Canning Club to reply to a paper on the English Spirit. The politics would not have disturbed me as I am a non-political type. But I can't talk impromptu – have to write every word out and memorise. No nerve. But the crux of the matter is Wednesdays are hopeless for me. Again with many thanks for the invitation and regrets in having to decline it.
    Yours sincerely, JB

To Stuart Piggott   The Old Rectory
Farnborough
Wantage
16 October 1946   Berkshire

My Dear Stuart,
I had meant some time ago, when I read your tribute to Harold Peak, to write and congratulate you on becoming, rather unsurprisingly, a Professor. But how very pleasant it sounds. You are indeed lucky to be at Edinburgh and with Grant's bookshop so near which is quite the best in the British Isles. As for the city itself, I have always thought it the loveliest I had seen – more beautiful than Rome, even. The capital of capitals, the Modern Athens and the modern Abbotsford. Moreover, you will find as you go on seeing it, that Lorimer's work is good and you

will already have been connected to Scottish Baronial. Get Billings'
Antiquities of Scotland (2 Vols) – very good steel plates.

But of course people like Playfair and Hamilton and the Adams Bros.
are consummate archytex. I like their Gothick stuff too very much. Just
at the moment I am reading *for the first time The Heart of Midlothian*. And
my itch for Edina grows with every page of that superb book.

What I have *not* seen in Edinburgh is the Irvingite Church – which
has a painted interior and is probably worth seeing. The only building I
hate is St Andrew's House which replaced that lovely Calton Gaol. Old
Dorothy Trotter is rather good value on Edinburgh architecture. She
and Philip Trotter live there. Also I hope you will give a lecture or two
on the Modern Athens – outside your curriculum – for the sake of the
place and not in favour of the Classic. By the way the 'Barclay Church'
is a wonderful bit of Gothic original 1860-ish by a genius named
Pilkington, who deserves exploration. Oh my, I envy you.

OUR LOVE TO YOU BOTH
Yours ever, John B

S.P. had just written the obituary to his independent archaeologist friend Harold Peak in
The Times.

The Trotters had an art gallery in London in about 1930 and were in deep trouble for
exhibiting D. H. Lawrence's 'obscene' pictures, seized by the police. It was called the
Warren Gallery (her name).

To Evelyn Waugh

The Old Rectory
Farnborough
Wantage
Berkshire

30 November 1946

Dear Evelyn,
Just a line, as we say here, to tell you you are the greatest living novelist.
For my talk I am confining myself to your novels and this is my outline.

EW The greatest living English novelist. Why out of print so much?
Damn Mr Bale [of the publishers Chapman and Hall]. Why the greatest
novelist? because of
A) a) carefully written, economical, unslushy English.
   b) learning – quote
   c) observation – quote
   d) gift of story telling – explain
   e) ear for dialogue – quote and mention Firbank ancestry.
B) A resolved attitude to life, whose developments may be traced in his
novels.

a) Farce with substratum of Truth: *Decline and Fall*
b) Contempt of Modern World and also joy in it: *Vile Bodies*
c) Sorrow of world, sense of and profound sense of relations of human beings to our ancestors: *Handful of Dust*
d) Love of God and sense that people are only complete when considered in relation to God e.g. *Brideshead Revisited.*

Conclusion:
Compare this resolved person with the average slushy core of the polished surfaces of such good technicians as Priestley and Coward.

If you don't agree with this outline let me know. The *Strand* has sent me a very funny caricature of you by Osbert Lancaster. Have you seen it? I have to do five hundred words to go with it.

My dear Evelyn, I feel that when you have developed the technique of doing *Brideshead Revisited* style so perfectly as you did *Handful of Dust* humanistic style, you will have done all a man can do on this earth with pen and paper. As it is, each of your books is always an advance on the one before and the first was a masterpiece, and you have gone on with one masterpiece after another. God bless you. Love to Laura. Propeller is very mad on cows. John B

E.W. wrote (Immaculate Conception 1946), 'Too kind, too kind. It isn't Chapman & Hall's fault my books are out of print.'

To Arthur Bryant

17 December 1946

The Old Rectory
Farnborough
Wantage
Berkshire

Dear Mr Bryant,
A letter of appreciation is always a pleasure and should always be acknowledged. It is a double pleasure when the writer is a man of distinction, such as you are, whose works I have long admired and with whose point of view I find myself constantly concurring. What a damned pompous sentence. What I mean is thank you very much indeed. I am *greatly enjoying Postman's Horn.*

Yours sincerely, John Betjeman

A.B., the historian, had written to congratulate JB on *New Bats in Old Belfries.*
Postman's Horn was published in 1946.

To Lionel Curtis   Oxford Preservation Trust

17 December 1946

Having dictated the letters resulting from the plans committee I settled down to read your poems and then suddenly realised I had not thanked you for my very pleasant luncheon today which I now do.

And I now thank you for the poems (which I return) for, like Rowse, I have thoroughly enjoyed them. I am prejudiced perhaps in their favour for I have only to see the word 'anemone' or the word 'hay' in a poem to *want* to read the whole thing. But you have written, I think, your best poem in 'A Private's Complaint'. The penultimate stanza is lovely and its last eight lines are worth my deepest thanks for they conjure up a remote English country morning musically and memorably. I also like the verse at the bottom of page seven. Why you should sign 'To Mr Greatheart', 'Feeblemind', I cannot think. For me it is one of the best in the book. You should write a long, memorable, musical and closely observed autobiographical poem, full of the detail of a Pre-Raphaelite painting, describing the childhood places, scenes, people, toys, hedges, events of Herefordshire. You really should. Revd J. M. Thompson did it beautifully in his privately printed poem 'My Apologia'. You must record Victorian Herefordshire in verse. You could and you must.

Yours, John Betjeman

L.C. was a historian, political theorist and poet. His *Victorian Rhymes* was privately printed at the Oxford University Press in 1942.

To Evelyn Waugh   The Old Rectory
                                               Farnborough
                                               Wantage
12 January 1947   Berkshire

My dear Evelyn,
Herewith the F[rancis] J[ohnston] article. I like the stencils by Edward Bawden and the stained glass, and Anthony West writes well.

I'm very sorry you are in hospital. The excess in smoking of cigars such as caused the death of I. K. Brunel? I hope not.

As to your letter. I deeply appreciate your zeal on my soul's behalf. Indeed I have never been more exercised by a correspondence in my life. What you say amounts to this – I have doubts of the Truth of the Incarnation because the Church to which I belong is not Christ's Body on earth. At the time of writing this I am without any doubts. Also, like you, I am no mystic – I was not going through the dark night of the soul.

What I cannot believe – and this is a far more permanent carbuncle (you would call it) than my occasional doubts about the Resurrection – is that the C of E is *not* part of the Catholic Church. The Roman Communion could not have me unless I were convinced that the C of E was a heretical church. I do not doubt for an instance that the RC church is part of Christ's Body but I also do not doubt that the C of E is. For every heretical clergyman in the C of E (if by heretical we both mean Protestant or what is far worse 'modernist') you quote to me, I can quote back, I am sure, two Catholic ones. And as for the controversy on historical grounds about the C of E's claims to be part of the Catholic church, if I go to my confessor he will get me to read Pusey, Gregory Dix and heaps more Anglican protagonists. And what good will that be? As you yourself say, intellectual doubt is the least of all the causes of infidelity. I am sure I shall not be far forward.

If it is God's will that I see that the C of E is heretical, then with what eagerness I shall knock at the doors of Farm Street. If as you suggest, I seek instruction on the Catechism from a Roman priest, what will he teach me (beyond Papal Claims, on which there is plenty written in C of E literature, Catholic and Prot.) beyond what I have been taught in sixteen years of trying to be a Catholic in the C of E? The teaching on Sacraments, the Scriptures, Incarnation, Virgin Birth, even on the Immaculate Conception is the same in the church to which I go.

Of course, upbringing, habit, environment, connections – all sorts of worldly things – make me love the C of E. But this would not matter a straw, if I *knew*, in the Pauline sense, that Our Lord was not present at an Anglican Mass, even at a Mass celebrated by a heretical Anglican clergyman whose views on the Incarnation were the vaguest. Surely it would be a sin for me to leave a church which I thought, with all its faults, to be Catholic and for which I prayed, as I do pray daily, with the intention that it shall in God's time be wholly Catholic, so as to be reunited with other Catholic Churches?

It *is* possible to argue – though I have never read the arguments – that the strength of the C of E is the diversity of opinion which can be held in it. Such argument seems to me rather daft at first glance.

Before I go to Farm Street (it would more probably be Dominicans at

Blackfriars or Douglas Carter at Summertown) I must ask my own confessor at the Cowley Fathers about all this. I am really grateful to you for forcing me to look into all this, though it makes me very miserable. John B

> The article was 'Francis Johnston: Irish Architect', which JB had written for *Pavilion*, edited by Myfanwy Piper, in 1946.
> E.W. had written (22 December 1946), 'Your ecclesiastical position is entirely without reason. You cannot possibly be right . . . but every argument you can put forward for your little group in the Church of England is *a fortiori* an argument for me.
> Anthony West was Rebecca West's son by H. G. Wells.
> Farm Street was the Jesuit house in London.
> One of JB's confessors at the Cowley Fathers was Father Freddie Ling SSJE.

To Evelyn Waugh   The Old Rectory
                                                     Farnborough
                                                     Wantage
23 January 1947   Berkshire

Dear Evelyn,
I have delayed answering your letter, because I have been thinking about this a great deal. All I can do now is to read, pray and study the life of Our Lord. That I am doing. I feel that it is not so much a matter of which church, as of loving God and I still think [of] us as *both* right, which is why I emphasise the importance of the validity of our orders in the C of E. You are very kind to take so much trouble about the racked soul of
    Yours, John B

> E.W. had written (9 January 1947), 'If you accept an absurdity, as you do in pretending the Church of Wantage is the Catholic Church . . . you will naturally break out in boils!'

To Evelyn Waugh   The Old Rectory
                                                     Farnborough
                                                     Wantage
3 February 1947   Berkshire

Dear Evelyn,
I enclose with many apologies for delay, the *Life* article.
    As to your salutary and magnificent letter (prompted, no doubt, by

the virtuous Cracky who must have sent you the offending pamphlet) I am most grateful to you for it. I shall not be able to afford a year's freedom. But I will, I promise you, give thought to the claims of the RC church against the C of E.

What I find hard to believe are (1) the *certainty* of the Incarnation and Promise: sometimes I know this is true and sometimes I am assailed by doubt. But this doubt assails RCs too, as we know, and is not a matter of belonging to RC or C of E, Eastern, Baptist or any other church. I do know for certain that there is nothing else I want to believe but that Our Lord was the Son of God and all He said is true. (2) Can it really be that all my communions, confessions, prayers in the presence of the Reserved Sacraments have been false? Have all those monuments of loving God and being aware of His presence in Church been self-deception? And are all the Wantage sisters, priests, missioners and parishioners of the many hundreds of Anglican Churches which are Catholic that I have known, going to Hell? Surely the evidence of one's own spiritual experience and that of other Anglican Catholics is not false. And if Our Lord is present in the Anglican Church, it is my duty not to leave a sinking ship, but to go on in it until, in God's time, the Anglican Church is wholly Catholic and can be received in Communion with your church. If, on the other hand, I can inoculate myself with doubts about the C of E being part of the Catholic Church, as you suggest I should try to do, I cannot possibly remain in it. Pray for me. Ch[ristopher] Hollis, to whom I have talked, does *not* think Anglicans are in Hell!

Yours, John B

To Samuel Gurney

The Berkshire Cattle Trough and Drinking Fountain Association
Farnborough
Wantage
Berkshire

6 February 1947

Dear Sam,
I hope the snow won't hinder our coming on Saturday.
I return the David Gurney letter.
My comments would be useless. I think the Revd P. McLaughlin

is v. clever in suggesting he makes himself gloomier and more enquiring still.

To me, who has just been reading Father R. M. Benson's *Bible Teachings*, the purpose of God and His way of giving the Bread of Eternal Life seems so deep, disturbing and demanding of such surrender of will, that only the desperately hungry and tortured among 'educated' people could possibly even start to think of embracing it.

Yours ever, John Betjeman

> S.G. had inherited the sinecure office of Chairman of the Metropolitan Cattle Trough & Drinking Fountain Association, whose continued existence in the 1940s was a subject of great amusement to JB.
> S.G.'s nephew David Gurney was suffering from depression.
> The Revd P. McLaughlin, the Rector of Soho, was also Chairman of St Anne's House, a centre of Christian discourse and mission to the intelligentsia. A unique and influential institution, its Governing Body included such literary celebrities as T. S. Eliot, Rose Macaulay and Dorothy L. Sayers. In 1955 he became a Roman Catholic.

To Alan Pryce-Jones   The Old Rectory
                                                Farnborough
                                                Wantage
9 February 1947   Berkshire

Dear Bog,

The Acting Father Superior SSJE
The Mission House
Marston Street
Oxford
Telegrams Evangelist, Oxford

The Father Superior is away in India and the Acting one is Revd F. S. Playne SSJE. If you are proposing to have a retreat, he is the man to whom you should write. But a most human, holy and understanding man is Freddie Ling. The Revd F. Ling SSJE whom you may remember as being at Staggers with Cracky.

If you are deciding on a retreat give yourself three clear days and do the Ignatian one. First day is hell, second day hellish, third day heaven and you feel you must be a monk.

I am in London on Mondays and Tuesdays, staying the night in London whenever I can find a bed. On Tuesdays I go to Mr Comper in

West Norwood and catalogue his 'Wark' as he calls his work on 'charches'. He is now eighty-three and as active as ever. I would love to see you. You could come and stay here, couldn't you? There are some Vict[orian] churches in the Gospel Oak area of London that you and I must visit. Windows by real eccentrics of the latter half of the century. I am going to Cornwall for a fortnight's peace on Monday week (Feb 17th). Come before then if you can and if the snow permits. Telephone.

The Arthur Mee book starts *very dully*. If it is worth doing, I will send something. Prop could do Injun [sic] *Art* and archyteckture for you.

Love, John B

> Freddie Ling often came for lunch and cart picnics at Farnborough at weekends. JB wrote a nonsense rhyme:
>> Powlie came from Powlie land
>> And Waba came from Howlie land
>> And Father Ling
>> He came to sing
>> With both of them from Cowley Land
> above a water-colour of the three of us with my face flowing with tears.
> Staggers was St Stephen's House, the high church theological college.

To John Murray

Bodare
Trebetherick
Wadebridge
Cornwall

25 February 1947

Dear Jock,
Who is Farquharson?
Yours of 24th. I am here until March 3rd when I travel to London (d.v.) and stay with Woad. On Tuesday March 4th I shall be in London and have dates at ten thirty a.m. and at one p.m. I could manage sort of two thirty in the afternoon – I have to return to Oxford on the four forty p.m. from Padd[ington].

The Revd Sandys Wason, a famous clergyman of the eighties and still alive in his eighties is sending you his poetry which I think lovely in its 1890 way. Peter Q[uennell] probably won't like it. It is very religious. Wason wrote that famous book of nonsense poems *Magenta Moments*. Griggers knows all about Wason. He edited *The Spirit Lamp* either before or after Bosie Douglas. The story is told of Wason that he went into an undergraduate's room at Oxford who had an enlarged photograph of his father on the wall. Wason examined it closely through an eyeglass and then said 'A landscape, I presume?'

Love to Diana and Farquharson, Ian MacBetjeman

Farquharson was the Production Manager at Murray's.
Sandys Wason, Vicar of Cury and Gunwalloe in Cornwall, a wildly eccentric
Anglo-Catholic priest, was by process of law turned out by his parishioners but claimed
he was still the vicar. J.M. promised to look at Wason's poems carefully but nothing
came of it.

To Gerard Irvine   The Old Rectory
                                                Farnborough
                                                Wantage
20 March 1947   Berkshire

My dear Gerard,
Many thanks (1) for your letter (2) for the most instructive pamphlet.
Only yesterday I picked a pamphlet up in Mowbray's [religious
bookshop] refuting it. What schism! Crax thinks the Colonel's fall was
induced by apoplexy. When he heard this news Crax sent a telegram
from Dublin saying 'Hope not fatal'. The Colonel has to go to the
Wingfield again to have a pin or screw put in his leg, so I do not expect
you and the Incumbent saw him. He will enjoy the Wingfield and have
a lot to say about horses *if* he ever comes out.
     Your prayers are asked for a quandary I am in. Propeller is toying,
nay more than toying with Rome (keep to yourself) and I do not feel any
urge to go over. Indeed I think it would be *wrong* for me to go over,
mainly betraying the Church of God. But it will not be at all wise to live
in a divided family, as I shall, I suppose, have to do. For P will want the
children over too. The Motto is, my dear Gerard, celibacy pays.
     Yes, Royal Fort plaster – by Stocking, I believe – beats all Bristol
Plaster except the Arno's Grove Bath House.
     I am off to Bushy Heath to Lucy Kemp Welch tomorrow. She must
be ninety. Paints horses. Illustrated *Black Beauty*.
     Yours truly, John B

G.I. replied (1 April 1947), 'My advice is (for what it's worth) stay put. That is I know
sound; it is a principle of moral theology to stay where you are when in doubt. You can't
go over to Rome just because your wife has gone; or because it breaks up your family.
Nor even because the Church of England has proved itself a false church (if you were to
think that it had). You can only go over to Rome because you believe that what Rome
says is true about the extent of the church, and the Pope and Anglican orders and all the
rest. If you do believe that (and I suppose that you *don't*) you ought to go over whatever
Penelope does.'
     Thomas Stocking was a renowned plasterer in Bristol and the area.

To Alan and Thérèse Pryce-Jones   The Old Rectory
                                                     Farnborough
                                                     Wantage
27 March 1947   Berkshire

My dearests, Poppy and Captain Bog,
I never saw London look so lovely as it did that spring morning I left
you – silver Revived Dec[orated] spires coming up out of the red brick
houses and red brick Revived E[arly] E[nglish] coming out of the white
brick streets and the journey I made by a forgotten railway over the
housetops from London Bridge to West Norwood was one of the
loveliest journeys of my life. And I can put down my heightened
appreciation of everything to my admittance to the dolls house of the
night before. I am still feeling dotty from the happiness of all those
churches, tea at Binns' and then the pale pink walls and all that Regency
and drink and first class food. This is a red letter week for me, for
afterwards I went to Swindon and stayed the night at St Mark's
vicarage (very high) and today I am going to Solihull, the Esher of
Birmingham. My life for the moment, is a paean of praise to the
Almighty for the industrial works of man. I do thank you both very
much and I do solemnly warn you to take a villa in an industrial town or
a large house *in* a provincial town, but not to try squire's isolation in a
remote parish. It will kill you with overwork and anxiety.

I wish I lived with you both all my life. You both have a curious calm
about yourselves and peace. Uncle Tom Eliot has it. I think it must be
due to beauty of nature and keen intelligence and all that playing at
houses.

Bog MUST, whatever happens in the way of tempting and 'essential'
invites elsewhere, go to the Cowley F[athe]rs at Whitsun. He is of the
stuff saints are made of and it will just clinch the sainthood. Poppy is a
saint already. So is Bog. Oh I *did* enjoy myself.

One of the nicest Swindon boys, who used to be in [the] G[reat]
W[estern] R[ailway] works there, is now teaching Chemistry at
Tunbridge Wells Technical College. His name is Bill Still and he goes
to St Barnabas. *It would be a kindness if you were to ask him out one evening.*
He is full of humour and knows all about Church. He used to come and
talk to our Youth Fellowship in Uffington. He is a great golden-haired
God. My love and grateful thanks to you both,
    Love, JB

The P.-J.s were living at Castle Hill Farm, Tonbridge, Kent, rented from Henry d'Avigdor-Goldsmith, a mutual friend.

To Evelyn Waugh

           The Old Rectory
           Farnborough
           Wantage

3 April 1947
Maundy Thursday

           Berkshire

My dear Evelyn,

Many thanks for your kind letter. But also many many thanks for
FOREST LAWN which came today. I cannot believe it. My hat! What a
subject. Did you meet any morticians?

No I can't sleep either and I am very gloomy. Your letter started it, I
don't doubt.

As for house hunting in Ireland – a very nice idea. I go to Aberdeen
for a week 1st May. When do you propose going? TULIRA Edward
Martyn's house – Kildare Street (but done on the cheap) – is available.
Write to Lord Hemphill who owns it. He drinks, I believe.

Propeller very well. Children all ill.

Love to Laura, John B

JB had been scouting for houses for E.W. in Ireland for some months. He had written
(21 December 1946), 'The parts of Ireland to make for are those in the west – Kings and
Queens counties. No one ever visits them or ever will. They are flat, lonely bog, relieved
by islands of beech-clad demesnes.'

    Edward Martyn was a rich West of Ireland landowner with literary and artistic tastes.
He built Tulira, County Galway, a chunky, polychromatic, high-Victorian house,
around an existing tower, when a young man, and later regretted it when he became keen
on the Celtic Revival style of building. The Kildare Street Club in Dublin is built in the
same style as Tulira.

To Laurie Lister
4 May 1947

           The Douglas Hotel
           Aberdeen

Dear Mr Lister,

I thank you very much for the sweet little P.O. Will you please tell Miss
J. Grenfell that I am at last at work on a little monologue for her. For the
past three weeks I have been through some spiritual anguish which has

made all composition impossible and now I have a very bad cold in the head. As I am in an hotel and will be all this week (here in Aberdeen) I cannot shake it off by spending a day in bed. This is all delaying. But my idea is this – A lady who speaks in a rosy soft voice and loves all 'lovely' things and no sudden noises nor vulgarity. She will probably wear homespun and a necklace of painted cotton reels. Quite what will happen to her while she is talking this monologue, I have not worked out. It will be in blank verse and last for about five minutes. I cannot write to Joyce G. because I have not her address by me. Yours, I can always remember.

Yours sincerely, John Betjeman

L.L., actor, author, and artistic director of Laurence Olivier's producing company, was most famous for his directing of revues, including Joyce Grenfell's. (His revue *Airs on a Shoestring* ran for two years.) JB's invented lady for Joyce Grenfell was called Sylvia Paddington. They often collaborated and once compiled and read a poetry programme together called *Innocence of the World* on Blake and Wordsworth. Also they did a stage version of the *Face the Music* quiz at the Polytechnic in Kings Lynn. Joyce Grenfell had been at school with PB.

To Evelyn Waugh   The Old Rectory
                                                    Farnborough
                                                    Wantage
Whitmonday 1947   Berkshire

My dear Evelyn,

Religion first. Believe me I find it no pleasure. Indeed to worship here at Farnborough requires a great act of Faith. You say I have seen the light. I agree. But what I regard as the light which I have seen is the Catholic church of which the C of E is a part. I do not feel any doubt about that. You say that the C of E is not Catholic. I have never said this. It would be far *easier* (but against my conscience) to become RC. For in this village which has no Nonconformist chapel, the only bulwark against complete paganism is the church and its chief supporters are Propeller and me. If we were to desert it, there would be no one to whip up people to attend the services, to run the church organisations, to keep the dilatory and woolly-minded incumbent (who lives in another village) to the celebration of Communion services any Sunday. It is just because it is so disheartening and so difficult and so easy to betray, that we must keep this Christian witness going. In villages people still follow a lead and we are the only people here who will give a lead. I know that to

desert this wounded and neglected church would be to betray Our
Lord. Really you are wrong in thinking that I regard religion as 'the
source of pleasurable emotions and sensation'. I used to, as an
undergraduate, but it has been a stern struggle for the last fourteen
years. C of E village religion is *no* pleasure. Ought I, because you and
Cracky have proved to yourselves that the Roman Communion is the
only Communion with God on earth, to try to prove that to myself too?
Were I a non-believer, yes. Were I living in a town where the church to
which I belonged would not suffer from my defection, possibly. But
here? I doubt it. I can only go on praying and that I do daily, not for
myself, I may add, but the Catholic Church. Do let me beg you to think
twice about settling permanently in Ireland. The physical comforts,
the natural scenery, the morality and political outlook of the people is
far preferable to those in Britain. But you will always find yourself a
foreigner there. Do you mind being a foreigner? Take a lease of a house
for three years before you finally decide.

I am beginning to find that there is a lot to be said for sham
half-timber. I have been visiting during the recent fine weather, some
rich specimens in Metroland at Chesham and Amersham, sunk deep in
bird baths and macrocarpa down lanterned drives. They have much
more beauty than the flat mould stuff of the Atomic Age. My visit to
Aberdeen, Balmoral and Braemar paved the way to this appreciation,
by turning my mind towards conifers and heather.

Edinburgh is full of our sort of books – particularly John Grant of
George IV Bridge and Thin's opposite the old University.

Love to Laura, John B

PS I have just started Newman's *Apologia* for the last time in my life.

E.W. wrote (?April 1947), 'Awful about your obduracy in schism and heresy. Hell hell
hell. Eternal damnation,' but later wrote contritely to PB (4 June 1947), 'I am by nature a
bully and a scold and John's pertinacity in error brings out all that is worst in me. I am
very sorry. I will lay off him in future.'

To Ronald Buchanan McCallum   The Old Rectory
                                                 Farnborough
                                                 Wantage
3 June 1947   Berkshire

Dear Mr McCallum,
Pembroke is, as you know, my favourite college, because it is the last of

old Oxford left architecturally, vinously, socially and atmospherically. I was, therefore, genuinely upset to read of Dr Ramsden's death – that leaves only Messrs Drake, Salt and the Master, of the old regime. And I thought your obituary of Dr R. a beautiful piece of writing, in the *Oxford Magazine*.

I composed this little poem on Dr R.'s death:

Dr { Pocock / Ramsden } cannot read *The Times* obituary today,
He's dead.
Let { manuscripts on Virgil / monographs on silk worms } by other people be
Thrown away
Unread
For he who best could understand and criticize them, he
Lies clay
In bed.

The { body's waiting in his / body waits in Pembroke } College where the ivy taps the panes
All night;
That old head so full of knowledge, that good heart that kept the brains
All right,
Those old cheeks that faintly flushed as the port suffused the veins,
Drain'd white.

When they found him { Mr Bleak and Mr Blake / Mr Salt and Mr Drake } and looked upon
Him there
In his high forgotten room, he was lying sideways on
His chair
'Dr { Pocock / Ramsden } ! Dr { Pocock / Ramsden } !' – and they gave his arm a shake
He was gone
Past care.

Crocus in the Fellows' Garden, winter jasmine up the wall
Gleam gold.
Shadows of Victorian chimneys on the sunny grassplot fall
Long, cold.
Master, Bursar, Senior Tutor, these, his three survivors, all
Feel old.

They remember, as the coffin to its final obsequations
    Leaves the gates,
Buzz of bees in window boxes on their summer ministrations,
    Kitchen din,
    Cups and plates,
And the getting of bump suppers for the long-dead generations
    Coming in,
    From Eights.

The Revd J. M. T[hompson] wants to print it in the *Oxford Magazine*. Pencil alterations and clarifications are added which would disguise names, and I hope, avoid offence. Incidentally I know nothing of the circumstances of Dr Ramsden's death, but imagined Mr Drake and Mr Salt finding him dead.

I have told the Revd J. M. T. I am sending you [a] copy of the poem with pencil alterations and asking him to await your remarks. If you think that, thus altered, it might still give offence, then please tell Revd J. M. T. There is something so frail and so really valuable about Pembroke College that I would not for the world upset it by any verse-making of mine.

Don't bother to reply to me. And keep this MS as a small tribute to you for your charming obituary of Dr Ramsden. I apologise for bothering you on this, who must be so busy. Do come out again here with your family.

Yours, John Betjeman

R.B.M., a political historian, was Master of Pembroke College, Oxford from 1955 to 1967. He had been made a Fellow of the College in 1925.

The poem, 'The Death of Doctor Ramsden', as JB first called it, was published in *A Few Late Chrysanthemums* (1954) with the title 'I. M. Walter Ramsden ob. March 26, 1947, Pembroke College, Oxford'. The original version reproduced here contained an extra verse which did not appear in the published version. The alternatives to some of the lines which could render it impersonal to Dr Ramsden were removed.

To Miss A. M. Lorimer   The Old Rectory
                                                          Farnborough
                                                          Wantage
12 June 1947   Berkshire

Dear Miss A. Lorimer,
Forgive delay. I hope you like this new kind of writing of mine. I think
it looks very cultivated.

I certainly took all those meals you mention out and a lot of teas I took
out too – these will be on the bill. You will see I had two lunches, teas,
dinner and breakfast on the journey there and back. These should all be
included. But I don't remember what they cost. And of course I drank
myself silly because I had an awful cold. But we can't charge for that.
Say one and sixpence each for teas and about five shillings each for
lunches and five shillings for dinners and add them to the total. As I
have not the bill I can't work out which they are. Anyhow there will be
no risk of my *making* money on the trip if you do this for I also went on
tours by motor-coach and taxi. Of which I have long forgotten the
details.

Yours, John Betjeman

A.M.L. was in charge of Administration and Finance on the BBC Third Programme.
Christine Piggott had given JB a box of writing paper bordered with art nouveau
designs. While it lasted, his handwriting went arty to match it.

To Anthony Barnes and Jonathan Guinness   The Old Rectory
                                                          Farnborough
                                                          Wantage
12 June 1947   Berkshire

My dear Little Prawls (and Guinness),
I was very pleased to hear from you both and to receive the delightful
Ephemeral. I particularly like the drawing called *Listless*. I enclose
another (and older one) which you may have. I know nothing about its
origin. The Misses Butler of Woolstone, Berks owned it.

As to your poems, they are your children, as mine are, and we like
nothing said against them. I like the first two stanzas of Welwyn better
than the last two. I stayed in Welwyn lately in a house of old-fashioned
non-believers. The furniture was unstained oak, there were large Van
Gogh reproductions on the walls and the only photograph in the house

was a large framed 'common study' of Bernard Shaw. From my bedroom I looked over a chaste neo-Georgian array of houses and saw the freckled children bicycling to the study-clinic (school).

I can well understand the magic experience the sound of those bells must have been across the marsh. A few weaknesses, though, which might be corrected if you intend to repolish the poem (1) ringer's horny 'fist' – no not fist. They ring with their hands and fingers, one does not think of fists in connection with bell-ringing. (2) re-echoes like a bird. *Not* like a bird. They don't re-echo much (birds, I mean). (3) Tower and hour are not to my nice ear, true rhymes, and why was the Lord driving home asleep on a Sunday morning at presumably, ten a.m.? Because I like the feel of this poem, I beg you to re-write and polish it. I am sure it is worth it.

I am Scottish *Nationalist* not Scottish Unionist. I deplore the Union. Love from, Iain MacBetjeman

> J.G. is the son of Bryan Guinness and Diana Mosley.
> *Ephemeral* was the Eton rag.

To Miss Kallin   [Postcard]

July 1947

AIR the rose of Tralee
Shall we sing it??

Farewell Aberdeen 'twixt the Donside and Deeside
How oft have I strayed through the long summer day
On the fringe of the links o'er the wide spreading seaside
To see the pink pebbles caressed by the spray.
How gay as a student by King's rugged steeple
I loitered in archways and meadowpaths green
To my Jacobite sympathies kind were the people
Though deep in Balmoral dwelt Hanover's Queen.

From windows of dreamland I see the grey granite
All sparkling with diamonds after the rain
The Dee and the arch and suspensions that span it
And fir-covered forests that rise from the plain.
Down Union Street with majestical motion
Electrical tramcars go painted in green
The ships to thy quaysides come in from the ocean
But I leave forever my loved Aberdeen.

JB had been in Aberdeen to research his broadcast *Aberdeen Granite* which went out 28 July 1947 and sent this song on a postcard in microscopic handwriting to Miss K., Talks producer at the BBC.

To James Knapp-Fisher

5 July 1947

The Old Rectory
Farnborough
Wantage
Berkshire

Dear Jim,

I agree that *The Princess and The Goblin* will do better than *At the Back of the N[orth] Wind*. Also it has lovely Arthur Hughes wood engravings. We could use these. The full page pictures by someone else could be dispensed with as they are not so hot.

A Flat Iron for a Farthing is an admirable suggestion. The wood engravings by Helen Allingham (wife you know, of William Allingham) should also be used.

I will bring these books up on Monday.

Goldilegz (old fan of Piper J.) will be seeing you. Gissing time is kissing time. I won't on any account stand for an abridgement of *Ivanhoe*. Scott is far the greatest novelist we have and the whole point of him is that he is so long-winded. *Hereward the Wake* possibly. But I won't have Scott cut down, not even *Ivanhoe*, one of his worst books. On the whole I am against any abridgement. If a book won't stand as its author wrote it, we must have others that will.

Surely the engraving on p. 110 of your copy of *The Princess and The Goblin* is the purest poetry and so many more in that book. My! What a lovely thing we will make of it.

Yours ever, JB

JB had taken on the editorship of the *Watergate Classics* for Sidgwick and Jackson which was owned by J.K.-F., an Oxford friend of JB's. JB was offered a fee of one hundred guineas for the first six books.
  George Gissing had been a popular novelist.

To Evelyn Waugh   The Old Rectory
                                           Farnborough
                                           Wantage
25 July 1947   Berkshire

DONE IN MY NEW STYLE OF HANDWRITING

Dear Evelyn,
I was very sorry not to be able to go to the Pre-Raffs [Pre-Raphaelite
Exhibition] with you. I went with Propeller a week or two ago. They
are well worth it and I do hope you went.
   I want very much your opinion of a superb window here c. 1863 in
Brightwalton church. I am sure it is Ford Madox Brown's first effort for
Morris and Co. A brilliant thing in greens, pinks and purples with
kissing cherubs and women with hairnets on and not in the least
medieval or stylised. You could tell by the drawing. You must see it.
Come and stay. The Victorians must be protected from all this
Georgian smartness on the Right and Planning on the Left.
   John B

> John Piper painted a water-colour of a section of this window, he thought it so beautiful.
> Pevsner says of it, 'By an unfamiliar-looking hand. Mr A. C. Sewter, the foremost
> expert, attributes it to Burne-Jones.' It is now accepted as being by Ford Madox Brown.

To William Plomer   The Old Rectory
                                           Farnborough
                                           Wantage
26 July 1947   Berkshire

My dear William,
I am honoured, flattered and amazed. I am so glad you are doing it. I am
non-political. At any election I would vote for the candidate I liked best
as a person, irrespective of party. I am a Church of England Catholic. I
love the Church of England. Sex, architecture, topography, seaside and
fear of death are I suppose chief motives in my poetry. I am *not* a satirist
and dislike the few satirical poems I have written, 'Sagittarius' would
have done them better, e.g. 'Westminster Abbey' and 'Slough', both
'poems' of which I am now ashamed as they are cheap [illegible].

But you know all this anyhow. Poems I like are, I think, 'After the Anaesthetic', 'Pot Pourri from a Surrey Garden', 'Beaulieu River', 'Ireland with Emily'; there is also some blank verse about the seaside coming out in a day or two in the August *Strand* which you may like.

How lovely and leafy it must be in Linden Gardens when sad-eyed Joe comes round to see you, smiling through his pain at the world. I do not believe in progress, do you? Come down here and stay a night in our discomfort, if you have a moment. Oh, old boy, I am excited and honoured. Your constant admirer, John B

> W.P. was due to give a BBC talk on JB on 25 August 1947.
>   'Sagittarius' was the pseudonym of Olga Katzin, who wrote satirical verses for the *New Statesman and Nation*.

To William Plomer   The Old Rectory
                                             Farnborough
                                             Wantage
26 August 1947   Berkshire

My dear William,

I was DELIGHTED with your flattering remarks and judicious selection. You said just what I would wish to have said. Indeed after the insufferable misunderstanding my work has naturally received in America – the publishers called the US edition SLICK BUT NOT STREAMLINED! – your mellow and really sympathetic appreciation was as a reviving sea bathe. Talking of sea bathers, I very much enjoyed your tragedy in *New Writing*.

I was quite surprised yesterday at how many people I did not know had listened to your talk. I always think that the only people who know my name are those who know me personally. But in an optician's shop in Baker Street to which I had occasion to go, the assistant said he had been most interested by a talk about me last night and at the Garage [Murray and Whitaker] at Newbury it was just the same. Fame, old boy. Fame at last. *May I please have a copy from the BBC of your remarks?* Spansbury (J. H. A. Sparrow) is meant to be writing a preface to a selection of my verse he has made. But he has been months about it. I have suggested to Jock Murray to ask you if he can use your talk if Spansbury does not cough up soon.

LOVE TO POOR OLD JOE and you, John B

It was W. H. Auden's enthusiasm which had been responsible for getting JB published in the USA. He selected and wrote the introduction to what Doubleday's chose to call *Slick but Not Streamlined* which consisted of poems and short pieces and came out in 1947.

To Max Beerbohm   The Old Rectory
                                               Farnborough
                                               Wantage
13 October 1947   Berkshire

Dear Sir Max,
Your truly delightful present to me of a portrait of Smithers and its inscription has arrived for me down in Cornwall where I am sadly ending a holiday amid the plong of tennis balls over macrocarpa hedges, crack of croquet mallets and shouts of elderly schoolmasters in shorts organising rounders on the sands. I am overjoyed and immensely flattered. I have the only existing record of Smithers' personal appearance.
    Smithers, as you will see from the enclosed letter, has turned rather nasty. But I think you will be able to buy him off.
    With best wishes to Lady Beerbohm and you from us both and a multitude of thanks. I shall frame Smithers' portrait for my library.
    Yours more gratefully and more admiringly, John Betjeman

> JB had written to the essayist and caricaturist M.B. asking him about the publisher Leonard Smithers. M.B. had drawn a caricature of a rough-looking chap with no tie. 'What is his Christian name,' he had written below (September 1947). 'I doubt if he has one . . . a man without a tie might well have no Christian name.'

To Max Beerbohm   from Leonard Smithers
                                               Dealer in Exquisite Works of Art
                                               149 Rosebank Way
13 October 1947   Willesden NW10

Dear Beerbohm,
A friend of mine has sent to me a copy of your caricature of myself and I am considering whether to take legal action or not. Before coming to a decision, I thought I would give you an opportunity of purchasing some of my treasure for sale which I am listing overleaf. I was forced by circumstances I will not discuss with you, to change our address and

give up the little business which I last mentioned to you. Here are the books etc. you may buy and the prices. Your cheque will certainly make me reconsider the legal action I am considering now.

ORCHIDS by Theodore Wratislaw (unsigned but in nice condition) £300
CAPRICES by Theodore Wratislaw (with pencil correction, probably by the author, on p. 15) £700
RAFFALOVITCH's Breakfast Cup (slightly chipped) and Saucer £250
This interesting literary relic was frequently in the presence of Father John Gray and on that account I am adding a further £250 to the price = £500
WALTER CRANE's Walking Stick (very probably his) £700
THE PIPES OF PAESTUM by Dorian Lewbottle (bound in vellum 150 copies hand printed on Kelmscott Paper with decorations by Edmund Dulac). These rare and *curious* poems by a little known genius were published by me £1000

TOTAL £3,200
    Yours truly, L. Smithers

> JB wrote this letter in the person of Leonard Smithers, a rather shady publisher whose somewhat 'lush' books, which came out in the nineties, caused raised eyebrows.

To Anne Barnes
                                                    The Old Rectory
                                                    Farnborough
                                                    Wantage
13 November 1947   Berkshire

My dear Anne,
How very sweet of you to write to me. Recovery is setting in. I feel as though I am 'on the tiles' again. Indeed I fell in love with a woman glider pilot (George was a bit keen, too, I thought, when he met her at Jock Murray's party for his authors, one of the dimmest, of which she is, and was asked at my request and stole everybody's thunder by her wind blown simplicity) and find myself falling in love left and right every other day.

I met Little Prawls at George's awful office the other evening and showed him a Comper crypt in Paddington which he liked. He is heavenly company and I look forward to coming to Prawls next half or vacation or holidays or whatever it is called.

I went to Cambridge last Saturday and Sunday (seven parties in thirty-seven hours) and saw several of your friends. I liked very much Michael Oakeshott. King's Chapel took my breath away with the beauty of its newly whitened interior. John Piper and I are going to stay with the Dean (K. Harrison) on December 16–17th to look at the glass and the photographs he is having made of it. It keeps my mind off this female glider pilot. Religious difference kills family affection, that is the tragedy of this event at present. But it will come all right.

    Love, John B

       A.B. was the wife of George Barnes.
       The 'Comper crypt' is at St Mary Magdalene's.

To Mrs Arthur Bryant   The Old Rectory
                                              Farnborough
                                              Wantage
30 November 1947   Berkshire

Dear Mrs Bryant, or as I prefer to think of you, dear Rajah's niece, You and the historian shall have the first copy of the verses I finished in Rapsgate with my deep gratitude for the most peaceful interlude I can remember for months:

SUNDAY MORNING, KING'S CAMBRIDGE
File into yellow candle light, fair choristers of King's
    Lost in the shadowy silence of canopied Renaissance stalls
In blazing glass above the dark glow skies and thrones and wings
    Blue, ruby, gold and green between the whiteness of the walls
And with what rich precision the stonework soars and springs
    To fountain out a spreading vault – a shower that never falls.

The white of windy Cambridge courts, the cobbles brown and dry,
    The gold of plaster Gothic with ivy overgrown,
The apple-red, the silver fronts, the wide green flats and high,
    The yellowing elm-trees circled out on islands of their own –
Oh, here behold all colours change that catch the flying sky
    To waves of pearly light that heave along the shafted stone.

In far East Anglian churches, the clasped hands lying long
    Recumbent on sepulchral slabs or effigied in brass
Buttress with prayer this vaulted roof so white and light and strong
    And countless congregations as the generations pass
Join choir and great crowned organ case in centuries of song
    And praise Eternity contained in Time and coloured glass.

I'm not wholly satisfied with the last stanza. All stops out by Boris Ord and a bit of a discord I fear. But it is a framework if I am not too tired to go on working at it.

DUNTISBOURNE ROUSE. You must see it. Chaucer's England, fords and storm tiles and wilderness and a tiny little church like a weather beaten hare crouched on the hillside with a vaulted Norman crypt below it. In the twilight yesterday it staggered me, beating even Duntisbourne Lear and Daglingworth. Do go before you leave that wonderful country.

Will you say that I shall expect to hear from A.B. on Tuesday at my office (Oxford 2918). I may be having a Speculative builder to lunch whom he could influence if he comes and we can go to W[ater] Eaton afterwards. And you will be there too I hope.

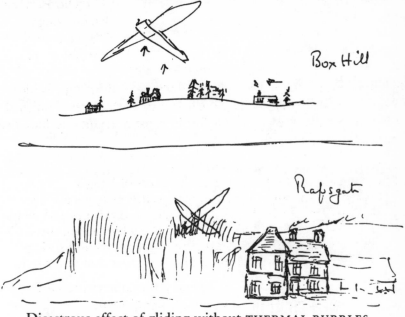

Disastrous effect of gliding without THERMAL BUBBLES.

Yours most gratefully, John Betjeman
PS Tell your husband it's nonsense his saying he has no visual sense.

He couldn't possibly have such an eye for the right sort of house and the feel of country if he had no visual sense.

Mrs A. B., wife of the distinguished historian, was born a Brooke, related to the White Rajahs of Sarawak.
The last line of the poem had never pleased JB and he had already changed it from

'And praise Eternity contained in walls of coloured glass.' When it came out in *A Few Late Chrysanthemums* in 1954, however, he only changed the first 'And' to 'To'. The Duntisbournes are villages in Gloucestershire.

To Arthur Bryant   The Old Rectory
                                                       Farnborough
                                                       Wantage
12 December 1947   Berkshire

Dear Bryant,

I am delighted with your long and interesting letter. I wish I felt the confidence about my poetry that you do about it. I always feel I am old fashioned and trivial.

The matter of *Water Eaton* first. The more I think about it – that wide waste of Cherwell meadow, that superb stone house, the still elms, the dark rooms, the remoteness and above all the architecture, the more delighted I am with it. I feel it is crying out to be rescued. I don't think the ghost matters at all. You can always have the house blessed by a priest (a nice high church one of which several are obtainable in Oxford e.g.: Revd W. Favell, St Paul's Vicarage, Oxford) which allays ghosts of an evil nature and makes the house a home. We have always done this ourselves when moving into houses e.g. at Uffington and here. Another thing is that it is wonderful to have your own chapel attached to the house. Half-an-hour's meditation per day, at any rate in summer, will compensate for everything you lose by leaving Rapsgate. I found that John Piper knows Duntisbourne (A. L.) Rouse and had drawn it. I will try to get hold of his drawing.

I will indeed try to come and see you when in. When in London do make a special journey to Comper's superb church (1899) of St Cyprian's, Baker Street. It is a red brick building near Clarence Gate, Regent's Park (near the Rudolph Steiner place) not much outside, but a Norfolk dream of gold and light within. Hugh Ross-Williamson is curate there. His other work in London is Carshalton Church, Surrey and a crypt in Paddington (eighteen eighty-something) which I will have to show you myself as it is very difficult to find.

We are delighted with the Jaydon paragraph and am incorporating it. So many thanks.

Yours, John Betjeman

We had the house at Farnborough blessed by the Bishop of Reading.

In 1945 the Bryants had moved to Rapsgate Park, a William and Mary manor house set above deep combes near Colesbourne in Gloucestershire. A.B. was not happy with it and had been looking for another house. He did not fall for Water Eaton, and after trying for Chettle, Cranborne Lodge, and Steepleton, he plumped for the manor house of Smedmore on the Dorset coast in 1948.

The irresistibly named Gloucestershire village, Duntisbourne Rouse, invited an allusion to A. L. Rowse.

To Kenneth Harrison

19 December 1947

Dear fellow or dear Fellow,

Words cannot express the wonder of my visit and the pleasure I had being conducted by you who really know and love the place, round the Chapel and then round Cambridge. My mind is still dizzy. I really mean it when I say that the expedition you took me [on] was the best I can remember in my life. It is worth having looked at architecture so many years to have the pleasure late in life of going round Cambridge virtually for the first time. But I also shall not forget those two delightful evenings. I am still QUITE WELL. I slept on the LNWR all the way from Bedford to Oxford long and deeply.

With the greatest hesitation and diffidence I am sending you a copy of my verses on King's Chapel. *You* will realise how feeble they are and how bombastic and inadequate. The building, music and glass are so much too great to be effable in verse or prose. I think the last stanza is a bit too much 'all stops out' and I will need to tinker with it, but am at a loss what to do yet.

I am writing a separate letter of thanks to Noel Annan who was, I gather, joint host yesterday evening. If I had time I would also write to: the Vice-Provost [Donald Beves]; G. H. W. 'Dadie' Rylands; The Provost [J. T. Sheppard]; Noel Annan; 'C. Stone' [J. R. N. Stone]; Michael Oakeshott; Christopher Morris; Boris Ord [organist and choirmaster]; Tim Munby [librarian]; the other Dean [the Revd A. R. Graham-Campbell]; to thank them for their existence.

Yours, John Betjeman

K.H., a fellow and lay dean of King's College, who had arranged things, recalls that JB's and John Piper's visit to King's on 17 and 18 December, 'took place in drifting rain. . . . JB's enthusiasm for the architecture of the chapel and its music extended to me in a manner that I did not deserve.'

King's College now hold three manuscripts of the poem in their library. The original
received by Mrs Bryant; the marginally altered version dated 'Christmas 1947' which JB
had inscribed for George Barnes 'and especially dedicated to Anne Barnes and to Little
Prawls', in which 'yellowing' in the fourth line of the second stanza had become 'golden',
and 'that' in the fifth line 'which'; and, finally, dated 1959, the version published in
1954, which he was asked to write out by the college.

To John Sparrow   The Old Rectory
                                                         Farnborough
                                                         Wantage
25 December 1947   Berkshire

My dearest Spansbury,
This Christmas Day is the first chance I've had to write about your
ADMIRABLE Preface. Most flattering. There is – and I must write to
you of it, for the sake of accuracy – one error in the first three pages
which really should be altered unless you honestly think what you have
said there is true. I am not primarily a poet of place. I never write of
place first and people afterwards (at least not nowadays) but of people
first and place as an inextricable part of them. Thus the quotations you
make are from poems of which the primary ideas in my mind were as
follows:

1) 'Henley-on-Thames' – Edwardian fashionable river life surviving
into Hitler Wartime with ATS where smart subalterns of the Brigade
should be, e.g. The incongruity of ATS among the Edwardian baskets
of geraniums.

2) 'Trebetherick'. The overwhelming effect of nature in a storm and
in its cruelty on a child's mind. Impotence and reverence of man for
nature.

3) 'Lincolnshire'. Lower plane altogether. An attempt to get an East
Anglian M.R. James.

4) An all-over picture of Ireland E[ast] and W[est] (leaving out
N[orth] and S[outh]) today with Irish Catholicism dominant and the old
Somerville and Ross Landlord Protestantism dead. Hence all the
references to deserted demesnes and to the Sacred Heart and to the
difference of Galway people from Midland (of Ireland) people.
Essentially a Social as well as a Topographical poem.

And that is one of the reasons, I think, why you do not like (and I do
not like) things full of a sense of period from the earlier poems. They *are*
poems of place, pure and simple. As for my satire I QUITE AGREE WITH
YOU.

So too when you describe my 'amatory' poems really it would be better to call them 'sexy'. All my better poems are Amatory in that they are written from a love of the people and place they describe. They are written from love and, I like to think, reverential understanding.

So I think I have something in common with Cowper (and Eliza Cooke, Jean Ingelow, Tom Hood) but nothing in common with Clare or Bloomfield. Those two last are poets of place only (Clare sometimes also of nature). Also my view of the world is that man is born to fulfil the purposes of his Creator i.e. to Praise his Creator, to stand in awe of Him and to dread Him. In this way I differ from most modern poets, who are agnostics and have an idea that Man is the centre of the Universe or is a helpless bubble blown about by uncontrolled forces. I dare say I don't show that much in my verse except in the choice of subject (in the non-sexy poems). But on the social plane, old boy, I know that is my motive for writing. I mean it comes out too in *Ghastly Good Taste*, whose only merit was that it related architecture to the social life of its times instead of to an aesthetic theory absolute and *in vacuo*.

But the preface is ADMIRABLE and could go as it stands, of course. It is only that I feel to describe me purely as a poet of place is to put me on the same level as Drinkwater's 'Mamble' (a place poem if ever there was one) and suchlike Georgians and to link me with Bloomfield than whom, I like to think, I am a better poet. And I believe why you and I don't like that *earlier* stuff, as I have said, is just because it lacks this social sense and sense of Original Sin and awesomeness of Natural phenomena. But I may be wrong.

Happy Christmas, dearest Spansbury. I enclose my comments on your most helpful ones on the 'King's [College Chapel]' poem. I only disagree with you on a few points which I hope you can read. I pronounce it Rénaïssănce, don't you? I think 'King's' is a corker of a poem and worth all the labour I can give on it and that you can; you have hit on the weaknesses in the last two lines, just as I knew you would, clever old thing. Also 'which' instead of 'that' for the middle stanza, last line.

JB

J. Murray wrote of the preface to JB (30 December 1947), 'I think it is a mistake to make you out a poet exclusively of either people or place. To my mind, the one reflects the other in most of your poems. I am sure you are right on those two points which make it impossible for you to be a satirist: I mean man's impotence and love. Myfanwy, I think, feels strongly about the latter, and I have asked her to send me her thoughts on the subject so that I can convey them to J.S.'

It is likely that JB was referring to Thomas Hood the elder, a pastoral poet, rather than to Hood the Younger known as 'Tom', a humorist.

J.S. excluded 'Sunday Morning, King's Cambridge' from *Selected Poems* in 1948, despite supplications from Jock Murray. It did not appear until *A Few Late Chrysanthemums* in 1954. JB did not change the last line in the middle stanza.

J.S. was a single-minded and forthright character. I was brought up to believe that his brain was twice as big as most other people's. He remained unconvinced by JB's arguments and in the preface to *Selected Poems* did not desist from describing JB as a poet of place, albeit alongside Crabbe, Cowper and Barnes. J.S. wrote, 'If there are figures in the foreground they are subordinate to their setting and somehow expressive of it.' Neither did he change the word 'amatory' to 'sexy'.

To Patrick Kinross

28 December 1947

The Old Rectory
Farnborough
Wantage
Berkshire

Dear Patrick,

I return, reluctantly, the cuttings about Perp: Peter and the First Baron. Very fine they are. It was delightful to see your easy flowing hand again and to think of you once more within easy reach of Drogo Castle and writing a book. I am very glad you are writing a book. But what is it about and who are the publishers? I should like to see the book you alone could write, an illustrated account of the parties of the twenties: factual and funny: Bunnie Tothsall, Babe Bosdah, Gawain [Gavin Faringdon], the Plunkett-Greenes, the Interior Decorators, the Yeo [Yeomans Row], the Police, the danger, the irresponsibility, the fast motorcars. I am fast going Scottish-Nationalist. I hope you are. I prefer Scotland now to any country on earth. Also I am Episcopalian. I wish I had been at King's, Aberdeen instead of Magdalen. Edinburgh is the loveliest city in the world. Strachan glass is hideous, though. Old Dorothy Warren is a great tonic and so is Philip Trotts. They are Edinburgh in excelsis. Up the New Club.

Cracky is off his head. Propeller is becoming RC. I minded. Now I don't. The C of E for me as it is in Communion with the Episcopalians. This has been a time of trial, all the same. The Lambeth Conference an exciting prospect. Not the kind of excitement I like.

I suppose the Cobwebs are still at Chagford. Love to them. Do come and look at Drogo Castle. It was illustrated in *Country Life* a few months ago and looked to me the greatest and most imaginative of all Lutyens' works, which is saying a lot.

I hope you have enough money to live comfortably. I haven't. Living here is so expensive. Do come and stay before we go broke. Name any time or date except March 18th for a week, when I will (d.v.) be in Denmark, the only abroad I can bear the thought of.

I wonder how Torphichen is? I often think of him. Love to the Baroness, Rosemary, Ursula and Pamela. Do you know my friend Molly Kidd, who married John Fernald? She is probably a relation of yours. I *am* Scottish Nationalist.

Love from us all. Woad is stayin' here this Christmas and can't understand why I don't read the daily papers.

Love, John B

Patrick Balfour had succeeded as 3rd Baron Kinross in July 1939.

    P.K. had sent some documents about his great-grandfather and grandfather. He was staying at Easton Court Hotel, Chagford, a haunt of the literary set, including Evelyn Waugh. He is likely to have been writing *The Ruthless Innocent* (1950).

    The then Lord Torphichen was an obscure Scottish peer, famous only for his obscurity.

To Kenneth Clark   The Old Rectory
                                                     Farnborough
                                                     Wantage
29 December 1947   Berkshire

My dear K,

I was infinitely touched to receive 'Hannah More'. I find her a refreshing draught for the soul and, unlike Karl Marx, easy to understand. I have just been reading Whyte Melville's *Kate Coventry*, which has several references to Hannah More, who was still popular with maiden aunts in the 1850s. WHYTE MELVILLE IS EVERY BIT AS GOOD AS HERMAN MELVILLE and a lot more interesting and deliciously class-conscious. Read *The Brookes of Bridlemere* and *Kate Coventry*. I told Goldilegz and Mr Piper the other day that I did not think I should ever see you again as I never go to London at any rate of an evening. But now I see that I have been elected to the Beefsteak and that you come between Randolph and Louis Clarke as a member so you and Ian Hay and I might have a yarn there one Monday at luncheon. Love to Jane and to Allan and to the twins. I enclose a copy of a poem I have written on King's Chapel which Spanzbury does not think good enough for his selection of my verse but which I think the best thing I have written. Mr Piper and I saw H. M. Brock and his paintings and wife and daughters when we were in Cambridge.

Love, John Betjeman

Hannah More (1753–1833) was a popular religious writer, poet, tragedian, novelist and philanthropist.

JB had been proposed to the Beefsteak by Evelyn Waugh, seconded by Christopher Sykes and Osbert Lancaster, and undersigned by nearly thirty members, including A. P. Herbert, Duff Cooper, Christopher Hussey, Osbert Sitwell, Lord Esher, the Duke of Wellington, Harold Nicolson, Lord Birkenhead and Clive Bell.

To Evelyn Waugh   The Old Rectory
                                                     Farnborough
                                                     Wantage
30 December 1947   Berkshire

My dear Evelyn,
I am delighted with (1) your present to me of [Ronald] Knox' book. Just my subject and just my writer. I look forward to reading it now that the misery of Christmas with Woad staying is over, though the old boy was far less trouble than I anticipated and lived in really fearful conditions here for a man of his age. (2) Your offer to sponsor my first visit to the Beefsteak. Friday 9th would suit me well. Whites c. twelve thirty or twelve forty-five. (3) Your postcard on that broadcast of mine. Very much to the point.

I have given away several *Scott King's* this Christmas. It is a winner.

I have asked Allen and Unwin's to send to you the TRAINS WE LOVED, I thought it a beautiful book both to read and to look at with coloured plates of pre-grouping days.

Do read Whyte Melville's *Kate Coventry* and *The Brookes of Bridlemere*. He's better than Housman and very upper class. More of Gliders and Gaitskell when we meet.

Yours ever, John B

The Rt Revd Monsignor Ronald Knox (1888–1957), the prolific theological writer of whom E. W. later wrote a *Life*, was a favourite of both my parents. He was widely known as 'Ronnie'.

Scott King's Modern Europe is a novella by Waugh.

JB was particularly keen on the work of Cuthbert Hamilton Ellis (*Trains that we Loved*) and wrote a preface in verse to *King Steam: Selected Railway Paintings and Drawings* (1971) which begins, 'Hail! poet artist of the age of steam.'

E.W. had written:
    What is this about Gliders,
    What was that about Gaitskell?

To George Barnes

[Undated 1948]

Fifty-five
High Point
London NW6

Dear Barnes,
Just a word of advice which all of us in the Party will be wanting to give you and which Edgell Rickword and Monty Slates decided in 'The Fitzroy' this evening, I was to do. We need a call to solidarity in the Steel-trade. There is, as you know, a dispute going on at present between the Bone-handle Makers Union and the Blade branch of the Cutlery Section of the Steel Trades General Union. This may well become a vital issue of some importance. I have been up to Sheffield addressing meetings of these fellows and I know *they are in earnest*. If we can raise their present slave rate under-capitalism by another twenty-three pounds a week we shall be on the way to a big Victory. The BBC hasn't been particularly friendly lately, but as I know we can count on you as a sympathiser, we expect better things –
Yours fraternally, Tambimuttu
PS Incidentally it is about time you broadcast some of my poems. I am having my book of them sent to your private address by registered post. Please return when you have used them by the same method. T.

JB wrote a series of spoof letters on G.B.'s appointment as Director of the Spoken Word in 1948.

To George Barnes

[Undated 1948]

Amalgamated Engineering Union
Runcorn Branch
Hon. Sec. Alf Hobson

Dear Sir,
I am instructed to communicate to you the following resolution passed by my branch, a copy of which has been forwarded to the Prime Minister and the Archbishop of Canterbury.
'I fear the appointment of Commander George Barnes as DSW is contrary to Democratic trades unionism and represents a victory for militaristic monopoly capitalism.'
Yours fraternally, Alf Hobson

To George Barnes   77 Charteris Close
                                                Finchley Road
[Undated 1948]   NW7

HOWARD OUTPUT – AUTHOR
– PLAYWRIGHT – JOURNALIST –
BROADCASTER – WRITER.
Contributor to all prominent
periodicals and national dailies.

Dear Sir,
As an experienced broadcaster, I offer my services to you in your new
capacity. I have just completed a play which several film companies and
three publishers are considering which will, I think, make an excellent
broadcast drama of the spoken word. The theme is topical, being the
triumph of democracy over dictatorship, with a human appeal in an
ex-Fighter Pilot who comes home to find his wife divorced. I have sent
it by registered post to your private address.
    Yours faithfully, Howard Output

To Gerard Irvine   The Old Rectory
                                                Farnborough
                                                Wantage
3 January 1948   Berkshire

My dear Gerard,
I thank you warmly for your letter. As to your poems, permit a *general*
criticism which you may apply to the particular. I rather agree with old
Bosie's dictum that 'poetry' consists of style and sincerity. Style is your
weakness, dear boy. Style means ear, conciseness and clarity. You have
vision and you have ideas and the beginnings of your poems (esp.
'Rycote Liberty') are often lovely but they tail off with Robert
Buchanan.
    Ear is only gained by reading and re-reading the ancient models who
appeal to you. For me that means Tennyson. Donne is not a model. He
had no ear. Conciseness is only gained by being strictly grammatical or,
failing grammar, so mellifluously and obviously associative that the
catalogue of words is as clear as a grammatical sentence. Clarity is part

of sincerity. You must know perfectly well what you are saying and balance the train of thought equally through the stanzas or keep the same attitude of soul throughout the poem.

Just to take 'Rycote' (I agree the best poem), the penultimate stanza on p. 41 has a weak rhyme in the 'B's and I do not like the diffuseness of running one stanza's grammar with the next. The stanza beginning 'Thus history . . .' on p. 42 has a third line faulty metrically. The last verse (cel*a*ndine, by the way) is lovely. Forgive all this. But I'm sure it's worth thinking about. The Anglos need poets and you are one. I have no temptations to Rome. We are the Catholic church. There are no RCs in England.

JB

G.I.'s book of poems, *Sunset and Eveningstar* (1946) was illustrated by the antique dealer Geoffrey Bennison and published by the Fortune Press.

To Myfanwy Piper
                                                          The Old Rectory
                                                          Farnborough
                                                          Wantage
6 January 1948   Berkshire

Darling Goldilegz,
I had to write to you to thank you for your criticisms of Spanzbury's Preface. I always knew you were a *clever* girl, but pondering over what you said about Spanzbury's Preface, I am enthralled to find that you are not merely clever but *profound*. Very unusual in a woman. Of course what you say about my poems, I had not realised myself – that they reflect my view of Man in relation to created things – until you pointed it out I only knew they were (most of them that Spanzbury selected) unadulterated me. I do thank you, dear clever Goldilegz and love to Mr Piper and all.

Yours, John B
PS This is the twenty-ninth letter I have written today and the *most important*. JB
PPS *A Ghost Story*. Last night I dreamt I went to a family party in Bardwell Road and my father was wheeled in in a chair, dying. His face was painted umber. My mother went out of the room to answer the telephone and I ran to my father to hold him up. His body had no bones in it and he cried out 'She loves answering the telephone more than she loves me.' And the desolation he felt swept through me and he died and

I woke up. I told P this dream at once. At breakfast, after, came a letter from my father's employer and business manager of whom I had not heard for twelve years. My father had died talking to him and he and I had had to go to the mortuary to identify the body. Like Dunne's experiment with Time. Purgatory, by the way, is IN TIME.
JB

To Anne Barnes   The Old Rectory
                                                       Farnborough
                                                       Wantage
15 January 1948   Berkshire

My dear Anne,
I do hope you will forgive so delayed a Collins as this and as you can see from the style of my opening words I am in a dazed state. This is because I have been tidying up my room and completing my correspondence. It is the Powlie's last night and when it leaves tomorrow the soul leaves this house or so it seems to me. I suppose you feel the same when Little Prawlz disappears to Eton. For Candida is still too young to be much more than an extension of Propeller and Propeller has drifted away into the arms of St Thomas Aquinas or St Teresa anyhow, well away from mine.

But I can look around my tidied room with satisfaction. Oh but I long for Snave [Church, Romney Marsh] and Prawls and Stone-in-Oxney. I think of all the enjoyable times I have spent at Prawls that last was the most enjoyable.

The Comper Luncheon was, I trust, a success. I longed to have a gossip about it afterwards with Little Prawlz but I felt he must be speeded off to catch his Cambridge train or he would be delayed indefinitely by a discussion of 'my wark'. He made a great impression on Mr Comper ('me') and [Comper] wrote to me yesterday in these words from The Priory, Beulah Hill, SE19: 'The gracious personality of your Eton friend has plunged me into an enchanted dreamland and created a great desire to meet him again.' I should explain that when Mr Comper is referred to by Mr Piper or me we always speak in the first person: 'But looks like one of my altars, doesn't it?' 'My work at the East End here, I think.' The Powlie asked me if Mr Comper could swim. I think it was a little bored but cheered up when it was sent into the garden where it tore itself on the brambles. It has continued to talk about Trains and 'the Betjeman-Barnes Express'. It has written to you I believe. It keeps talking about the Commander. I will send, when I can bring myself to do up the parcel, *The Brookes of Bridlemere*. I have bought a complete set of [Whyte] Melvilles (25 vols) for six pounds, ten shillings, as new, of course.

Love to Little Prawls and to the Commander and many more thanks.
Love, John B
PS The POWLIE left its bedroom slippers behind (dirty old brown ones). Could you very kindly post them to it?
P. Betjeman
Dragon School
Oxford

'My wark' was how Comper always pronounced 'my work'. His nineties accent was a source of much amusement to JB.

There was an incredible Bassett-Lowke model railways set out in the attic at Prawls which amazed and delighted Paul.

A.B. wrote (24 January 1948), 'We adored your visit and as you say it was happier than ever. Gin and giggles and the wonderful periodic entries of the Powlie to announce a new and "wizard" combination! This is just to *beg* that you will feel you can always come here, at any time, if you should want to get away for a bit.'

To Faith Compton Mackenzie   The Old Rectory
                                                  Farnborough
                                                  Wantage
22 January 1948   Berkshire

Dear Faith,
I have now gone entirely Art Nouveau and hope you will be able to read this letter. The Reynolds Window is saved and orders to put it back were given last week. The Warden of New College, inspired by Charles Peers and a bloody mediaevalist woman who was replacing the Med[iaeval] glass in the ante-chapel after this war tried to get it smashed or sold and to have a window consisting of Mediaeval fragments interspersed with bits of their own design put in its place. The college was divided, most of the Dons, being scientists, economists and civics-professors, were indifferent. The Warden opposed the Reynolds' window, David Cecil opposed the Warden; so did Major Radcliff the Bursar, Scouts and old members of the College and Sir K. Clark and T. D. Kendrick and I and quite unexpectedly David C. won. *Laus Deo*! There are ENORMOUS CENTIPEDES IN THE SEYCHELLES RED AND

POISONOUS. Tell him [Sir Compton Mackenzie] to be careful.

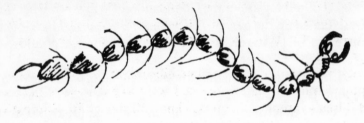

Yours ever, John B

> F.C.M. was the author of two autobiographical books, *As Much as I Dare* (1938) and *More than I Should* (1940), as well as many novels. She was married to E. M. 'Monty' Compton Mackenzie, author of *Sinister Street* and *Whisky Galore*.
>
> Sir Charles Peers was a historic buildings committee man.
>
> The West window of New College, Oxford was designed by Joshua Reynolds, and painted by Thomas Jarvis 1778–85. The main panels represent the 'theological' virtues of Faith, Hope and Charity.
>
> It was a grievous disappointment to Reynolds.

To Professor Geoffrey L. Bickersteth   The Old Rectory
                                               Farnborough
                                               Wantage
22 January 1948   Berkshire

Dear Professor Bickersteth,
On the strength of having met you but once and for only a moment when you were in the Company of Father Sedding outside St Matthew's, I am seeking your assistance in discovering the dates of birth and death of a poet of nineteenth-century Scotland. He is called WILLIAM RENTON and he wrote *OILS IN WATERCOLOURS – EDINBURGH/EDMONSTON AND DOUGLAS/1876*. These poems are, I think, exceptional – word pictures in a variety of rhythms closely observed and a pre-cursor of Hopkins. One of his 'Seascapes' in this book I have seen reproduced in a modern holiday annual for children. It is called 'Pool':

> Pool from sea,
> Sea-rocks slope
> Sea-weeds grope
> Into thee,
> Whose the opal-lemon is
> Above the blood anemones.

You probably know that. But many of the other poems in this book are even more vivid and unusual. I possess the book but no facts about William Renton beyond an advertisement on the flyleaf of *Oils and Water Colours* of a book by him called *The Logic of Style*, price six shillings, Longman's.

It struck me that in Aberdeen something might be available about his biography. I want his dates because I want to put some of his poems into a children's anthology. You may know all about him. Alternatively you may know some Scottish scholar who does.

Yours sincerely, J. Betjeman

G.L.B. was Professor of English Literature at Aberdeen University.
   Father Sedding lived at St Edward's House, in the Parish of St Matthew's, Westminster.

To Frederick Booker

The Old Rectory
Farnborough
Wantage
Berkshire

31 January 1948

Dear Mr Booker,
I am most grateful to you and your wife for letting me see her poetry. She is undoubtedly a talented person and I have been very interested reading the poems. I read them all at a sitting and then I read them again. So much poetry that I get sent to me has neither an ear for rhythm nor an eye for scenery nor a brain for thought. But I think your wife has all three.

I was interested to see that in her early poems, written at school, she had a great ear for rhythm and rhyme and that is always a sign of instinctive poetry in a person. I liked of them 'The Prospect of Leaving School' best.

Of course, like all of us, she is later moved by Gerard Manley Hopkins (I see she has copied out the beginning of his beautiful 'Binsey Poplars') and presumably Eliot. These, though great poets, are dead ends. Their influences on style, ear and syntax are deplorable. Enjoy them but eschew following their examples.

If I may apply a maxim of Lord Alfred Douglas's to these poems of your wife's, I would say, with him 'Good poetry is made up of two things: style and sincerity. Both are requisite in equal degrees.' Your wife's later poems are far more interesting in content than the earlier, but she has often (e.g. in 'The Vacuum') been so interested in the theme (e.g. 'sincerity') that she has forgotten the style and the poem is interesting reading but not the best of her poems as poetry. This is of course a personal criticism. I know what agony one feels when one's poems are in any way criticised. They are precious to one as children.

Now the two poems of hers I liked best were 'Tarantella for Today' because it was a cry from the heart and not merely light, and the 'Romance of the Road' because it was observed, neatly and sincerely expressed and particularly i.e. it was a thought that could never be so well expressed in prose. Why do you not send some of her poems up to the *The Poetry Review*? I do not know its address, but it is much better now than it used to be and is an admirable means of seeing oneself in print for the first time – if none of these poems have been printed already. I suppose the library at Newbury would know the address of that periodical.

Do let me advise a course of Pope. His *Essay on Criticism* is brilliant and so useful. And then turn straight to some master technician like Tennyson (particularly his 'Audley Court', 'The Lady of Shallot', 'In Memoriam', 'The Kraken', 'Aylmer's Field', 'The Dying Swan') and read them out *aloud*. Pope is like a dose to the mind for his clarity and conciseness and Tennyson is a new eye to nature with his freshness of perception of English landscape.

Yours sincerely, John Betjeman

F.B. had met JB briefly while working as an accountant in an office in Newbury. JB had come in asking if he could borrow two pounds because he had left his wallet at home. F.B. had lent him the money, and on the strength of that meeting had written to JB enclosing his wife's poems and asking for comment. This was his reply. Some years later Joan Booker wrote JB a poem for his birthday. Her poems were published in 1992 by the National Poetry Foundation.

To Evelyn Waugh   The Old Rectory
                                                      Farnborough
                                                      Wantage
28 February 1948   Berkshire

My dear Evelyn,
I must write to tell you what I find myself doing after each publication you make, that your last is the BEST THING YOU HAVE WRITTEN and that is the highest praise I can give since I think you the best living writer of English prose.

But what I like so much about it is its complete exposure of American materialism. It makes one almost pro-Soviet. It is an amazing thing to have described so shortly exactly what America obviously must be, not a country at all but a pool of ancient refugees lapsed into their antique paganism. The steam, the heat and the radio song assault the body and ears as one reads. Wonderful old boy. Wonderful. I am proud to know you.

I was lucky enough to buy two copies of *Orizonne* [*Horizon*] in Martin Secker's (Richards Press) last week. Old Martin Secker said he couldn't get the story out of his head. It was the most heartening thing he had ever read and the most horrifying. He ought to know, soaked as he is in the nineties and Arthur Machen.

I hear Cyril [Connolly] has had a heart attack. Poor old thing. I have written. I am going bankrupt or nearly so. Would I had your genius.

Yours, John B

> *The Loved One* had been first printed as a single issue of *Horizon*.
>
> E.W. replied (undated), 'It was very kind of you to write about *The Loved One*. I am pleased with it myself, but then I was pleased with *Brideshead Revisited*, which Cyril tells me was a great disgrace . . . I say it is good news about your bankruptcy. You will be sold up and I will get all your books.'

To Geoffrey Taylor   Farnborough
                                                             Wantage
6 March 1948   Berkshire

My dear Geoffrey,
I have *not* got *In Tennyson Land*, though I have seen it before. And I am v. pleased to have it as it makes excellent reading. I am delivering a paper on the old boy to the English Association in April.

For Propeller's 'reception' I am going away to Cornwall (Tuesday 9th) and for the recovery I am going to Denmark (paid for by the Danes) for a week the week after. I enclose a sonnet I wrote on this subject overleaf. I feel better about it now, though in the eyes of the Pope she is not, I believe, married to me now.

Love to you both, John B

> In the perspective of Eternity
>   The pain is nothing, now you go away
>   Above the steaming thatch how silver-grey
> Our chiming church tower, calling 'Come to me

My Sunday-sleeping villagers!' And she,
  Still half my life, kneels now with those who say
  'Take courage, daughter. Never cease to pray
God's grace will break him of his heresy.'

I, present with our Church of England few
  At the dear words of Consecration see
  The chalice lifted, hear the sanctus chime
And glance across to that familiar pew.
  In the Perspective of Eternity
  The pain is nothing – but, ah God, in Time.

This poem had been through several earlier versions, and when it reached the page proofs for *A Few Late Chrysanthemums* the third to last line read, 'and glance across to that deserted pew'. Jock Murray had regarded it as 'too personal' and it was pulled out at the last minute and never published.

To Roland Pym   Farnborough
                                             Wantage
6 March 1948   Berkshire

Dear Mr Pym,
I am flattered and delighted first with Ch[rist] Ch[urch] Meadows soon to be planned away and next to think you are doing a backcloth for my 'Subaltern's Love-song'. I didn't know it was being performed. Miss Hunter Dunn (*that* was her name, she is now Mrs Wycliffe-Jackson and lives in Ashley Gardens and you ought to go and see her, she is a lovely sturdy creole type with curly hair and strong arms and strapping frame and jolly smile and soft laughing voice, a girl to lean against for life and die adoring). Well anyhow Joan Hunter Dunn lived with her sister Betty and young brother (who went to Stowe) at The Red House, Farnborough (the Aldershot one, not this one), where her father practises as a doctor. I think you want to get a feeling of open-airness about the house – nothing Victorian – rather Letchworth and Welwyny, with toothbrushes airing at open bathroom windows and certainly rhododendrons and evergreens – and the wire netting of a tennis court enclosure. I have never seen the house. I have merely imagined it. I believe its date was 1910.

I expect it is a bit like this and rough
cast *vide Studio* Decorative Art
November 1906.

Alas poor Graham H! I was v. fond of him. I miss him as must many,
not least Ernest H. By the way, don't be guided [by] my impressions. I
am proud to think you are doing it as I know and admire your work. Do
what you like.

Yours, John Betjeman

Roland Pym, the artist, had written to JB asking him what Joan Hunter Dunn's house
might have looked like. He was about to paint the backcloth for the revue *Oranges and
Lemons*, which included a reading of 'A Subaltern's Love-song'. Despite the subsequent
elaborate set which showed the interior of the house and a tennis net in the background,
the poem was not understood in the provinces and was cut out by the time the revue
came to London.

Graham H. was Graham H. Shepard, son of E. H. Shepard, the illustrator.

To the Editor of The Times
9 March 1948

Sir,
The Radcliffe Observatory at Oxford is threatened with what amounts
to wanton defacement. It was built between 1772 and 1778 from
designs by Henry Keene, which were completed by James Wyatt.
Whether regarded for the delicacy of its sculptural details and the nice
relation of window to wall space or for its subtly arranged grouping by
means of wings with the Observer's house (Osler House), it is easily the
most outstanding late eighteenth-century building in Oxford and one of
the most satisfying and unpretentious architectural groups in the
country. The south frontage has already been built up with brick
buildings out of scale and out of texture with the Observatory. It is now
proposed to complete the destruction by obscuring the north, the best,
front, with a home for nurses.

The purpose of such a building is, of course, of great importance and we do not wish to question the necessity, but it seems difficult to believe that another site, or even one of the large houses in neighbouring North Oxford, cannot be found as an alternative.

President of St John's College – Austin Lane Poole
Warden of Wadham College – Maurice Bowra
FRCP Litchfield Lecturer in Medicine – Dr Alec Cooke
Nuffield Reader in Pathology – Dr Alistair Robb-Smith
Secretary of the Oxford Preservation Trust – John Betjeman
Secretary of the Georgian Group

> This letter, printed in *The Times* with a photograph of the Observatory beside it, had a profound effect. The scheme was dropped but Dr Robb-Smith and Dr Cooke received formal letters of reprimand from the Radcliffe Administrative Committee. The nurses' home was built on the Manor House Estate at Headington and is still in use today.
>
> JB also enlisted the help of Kenneth Harrison, the Dean of King's College, Cambridge, who wrote to *The Times* suggesting (as a joke) that the whole building be moved: 'Some years ago the Radcliffe Trustees sent their telescopes to South Africa; let them now be equally sensible and generous with the building, and send it to Cambridge. We would give it a good home, in really lovely surroundings.'

To Alan Pryce-Jones   Daymer Bay Hotel
                                                   Trebetherick
11 March 1948   Cornwall

My dear Bog,
I am really touched by your sweet letter. I am down here giving Gerald B[erners] a rest and there seems to be all Bodmin Moor between me and barbarity. Just lots of nice old conservative ladies walking about among the palms and euonymus and tamarisk, a blazing sun, white breakers, blue sea, great cliffs and a hush which not even aeroplanes can destroy. I am shocked to find how easily I can be consoled by place and I am quite sure it is all in the hands of God. If He has decided for some inscrutable reason, to still Propeller's restlessness in Rome, then He is right and I must accept it.

I feel very inadequate and your supposition that I can Give Light, though vastly flattering, makes me feel more so. *You* my dear Bog, are the Light bearer, you see the gunshot from [illegible, retreat?].

I return to F'borough Monday and fly to Denmark on Wednesday next week then back to the earth.

Love, JB

This letter was written two days after PB was received into the Church of Rome.

To Ronald Liddiard   The Old Rectory
                                               Farnborough
                                               Wantage
6 May 1948   Berkshire
Epiphany

Dear Ron,
How very kind of you to write to me. I have had many letters about that broadcast but none I enjoyed getting more than yours. Ah! that Gin and Ginger wine at Church Farm. Oft' do I think of it on cold winter days when the wind whistles through this house and blows the lamps out and freezes the lavatories and I pine for the outline of the old White Horse Hill. Do both of you or rather all of you come out here and see us. You can count it as farming. Telephone. We are always here except that I am away on Mondays and Wednesdays.
    Best wishes to you all – child, wife and your father and you.
    Yours ever, John Betjeman
PS I came across some drawings of the Observer Hut (x2) that I made. Fragrant with memories of Mr Long's keenness for observing, they were. JB

    R.L. and JB were members of the Observer Corps in Uffington during the war. R.L.'s 'Gin & Ginger Wine' mixture drinks were known locally as 'Berkshire Specials' or 'Longcot Thorns'.
    Mr Long was the head gardener at Kingston Lisle Park.

To Samuel Gurney   The Old Rectory
                                               Farnborough
                                               Wantage
14 May 1948   Berkshire

Dear Sam,
Looking at my diary I see to my dismay that I am to address an Oxford undergraduates' club on June 7th. I shall be honoured to be asked on a future occasion. As you see I have gone Art Nouveau with increasing age. I do thank you most warmly for keeping Penelope from severing all

connections with the true Catholic church in this country, our dear old C of E. She listens to what you say in its defence and I fear I simply cannot mention the subject.

Yours ever, John Betjeman

To Oliver Stonor   The Old Rectory
                                            Farnborough
                                            Wantage
7 August 1948   Berkshire

My dear Ottery Simmery,
How kind of you to write just the sort of letter I should have wished to receive. And how perceptive of you. Yes. Serious. That's me.

I well understand what you feel about your church. The clergy are often saints, the congregation devils. Here the clergyman is lazy and good natured, woolly-minded and useless and I go on going to church because I know that however awful my church is, it is Christ's body in this village and I can't rend it apart by leaving it. And for that reason you too will have to stick to your lay readers and go for the sacraments to the nearest Anglican church where you can get them. I think that if one goes on doing that, one gets one's reward (in the next world perhaps), but anyhow it *is* possible to receive the sacraments in England and one must go ahead despite all difficulties. It's never easy, the Christian life, and the more effort it demands, the more worth keeping up it is. I sound like a clergyman talking. Forgive me. I would indeed like to come and see you. But how to get there, how to find the time and the petrol – that is the problem.

Yours ever, John Betjeman

To Anne Barnes   Bodare
                                            Trebetherick
                                            Wadebridge
26 August 1948   Cornwall

My dear Anne,
How greatly I enjoyed myself, how much refreshed I was you can guess from the fact that we reached Wadebridge at seven forty-five p.m. the

day before yesterday and I was UNEXHAUSTED. Needless to say the Powlie was too and I enclose its letter to you.

It is VERY JOLLY HERE. I went to drinks yesterday with Joc Lynam, a housemaster at Sherborne, a housemaster at Eton (Walpole's), the Warden of St Edward's School, a retired official of the Bangkok and Shanghai Bank, the Dean of Trinity (Oxford). We had a little amateur cine show afterwards, technicolour but quite clear, of children bathing on the beach here.

The Walshams are down here and so is Miss McCorkindale and Miss Warren and Joan Larkworthy – in fact all the past is here, a bit shrivelled with its progeny too young to be interesting. It rains and blows. We go to Lundy this afternoon. Propeller is reading *South Wind* for the first time and is so enthralled I have to look after the children.

Love to you and Little Prawls and the old Commander, John B
PS I'll send Coulter later this week. JB

> Joc Lynam, the headmaster of the Dragon School, had a house in Trebetherick.
> JB meant the Hong Kong and Shanghai Bank.
> John Walsham was the 'John' of the poem 'Trebetherick'; Miss McCorkindale we called 'Aunt Elsie'; Miss Warren was a terrifying woman who played bridge all the time; Joan Larkworthy was JB's earliest chum.
> Lundy is a beautiful beach with caves.

To Anthony Barnes

The Old Rectory
Farnborough
Wantage
Berkshire

October 1948 (St Ervan)

Dear Little Prawls,
Four o'clock will be all right, dear Boy, but would you not like to come out to tea with me in my little motor car, if it is still working, and bring your little friends with you? I expect that would be easier and I should be very happy to go to church at St George's, Windsor to hear the Choir.

I was there last week talking to Canon Crawley in the afternoon. After dinner that evening he was dead of a heart attack. I wonder how I would have felt if I had known he was going to die so soon. I imagine I would have felt rather as though talking to the King, or perhaps something profounder than that for it would have been like standing on the threshold of eternity. Indeed, in retrospect, of course, it was, or do I mean is?

Love, John B

To William Plomer

The Old Rectory
Farnborough
Wantage
Berkshire

6 November 1948

Dear William,

I am sorry to be so long in answering your nice letter and in thanking you for the heavenly broadcast which I enjoyed, despite the pomposity of a man called Achew, Apew or something.

As you say, dear Spanzbury is not strong on 'mature femininity', but then all my girls can always be interpreted as big strong boys. I am writing a poem, 'Old Liberals on Boar's Hill', at the moment. Do you know, old top, it's appreciation like yours which makes me go on writing and the thought of *The Listener* that stops me. What you say of me is as though I said it myself and of course it was Jean Ingelow I was thinking of in 'Come up, Hupmobile, Delage' but you alone spotted it – and, I expect, Spanzbury. Certainly let's lunch on Jan 20th. Shall it be the Garrick at one p.m.? Unless I hear to the contrary, I shall take that as settled (DV). I have entered it in my diary.

We will go a bit tight to the Authors' Soc. disguised as Young Men of Talent. Love to old Joe. I don't include him in my *Listener* strictures. It's A. Clifton Taylor who gets me down. Do look at Meade Falkner's poems in *The Mint* No 2. I enclose for you a copy, as far as I have got, of 'The Old Liberals'. Off to Trebetherick (DV) next week.

Yours, John B

JB had just sent his *Selected Poems* to W.P.
   Jean Ingelow's poem 'High Tide on the Lincolnshire Coast' contains the lines:
       Come uppe, Whitefoot, come uppe Lightfoot.
       Come uppe Jetty, rise and follow,
   Jetty to the milking shed.
which are echoed by the line 'Come up, Hupmobile, Delage' in the poem 'Indoor Games near Newbury' which appeared in *Selected Poems*.
   'The Old Liberals' appeared in *A Few Late Chrysanthemums*, having first appeared in *Horizon* (April 1949).

To George Barnes

Bodare Hotel
Trebetherick
Wadebridge
Cornwall

17 November 1948

My dear Commander,
I am here (with a bad cold) until 27th.

I find on swapping our last year's Oxford University Diary with this one that I had asked out Lady Bridget Parsons to lunch on December 6th and I suggest, subject to your agreement, that we change our place of rendezvous to Athenaeum Ladies' Annexe, Carlton Gardens, and that *you come as my guest*. You will like Bridget P., as I know you have an eye for a jolly girl. She lives in Mount Street, in a flat of no character at all.

> Beautiful Lady Bridget
> What do you do in your flat?
> Ferret about and fidget,
> Polishing this and that?
> Or lie in bed with an *André Gide*
> And a *Cachet Faivre* in case of need
> And a Borzoi asleep on the mat?

Unless I hear to the contrary I shall take it that this is all right.
Your loving aunt, Irene Vanbrugh

> Bridget Parsons was the Earl of Rosse's sister, a great beauty, supercilious, affectionate and choosy of her friends. Many people worshipped at her shrine. She never married. *Cachet Faivre* was the headache remedy of the time, which came in a pretty box.

To John Murray

The Old Rectory
Farnborough
Wantage
Berkshire

27 November 1948

Dear Jock,
If my poems are doing well, can you let me have an idea of how much money I shall be getting by, let us say, December 31st? I ask because I am, I see, overdrawn on all sides and must probably consider selling a few colour plate books which, thank God, I have, as visible capital. I

don't expect much will be coming in from *Bucks*.

Yours, John B

JB's royalties on *Selected Poems*, published in October 1948, were £176.2s.5d by the end
of the year.

To Harman Grisewood   The Old Rectory
                                             Farnborough
                                             Wantage
9 December 1948   Berkshire

My dear Harman,
I have never done this before and I dare not do it to George [Barnes] so I
am doing it to you, since you are, I suppose, one shadow less important
than George. Though only a mere shade of a shadow less. Old Billa
Harrod last night gave such a good talk to our Women's Institute on
'The Psychology of Clothes' that I asked her to leave the manuscript
with me as I thought it was just the thing for the wireless. I therefore
enclose it and beg you to send it to someone in charge of the *Women's
Hour*. Old Billa's address is 91 St Aldates, Oxford. Communications
should be with her and they may like to get in touch with her direct.

I may tell you about the old girl, if you don't remember her, that she
has got a very nice voice and a winning manner and is full of humour.
What interests her is much more interesting than what interests old
Roy, with his statistics and population curves. She prefers the curves of
the bosom.

Yours ever, [JB]

JB and the novelist H.G. had been in the OUDS together at Oxford.
    JB also recommended Wilhelmine Harrod to George Barnes: 'Her voice is like sensual
treacle and her brain is sharp.' Wilhelmine Harrod never did the programme but
provoked a lot of correspondence through a letter she wrote to *The Times* defending the
'New Look' which had been publicly attacked as a waste of material in those lean times,
since it brought dresses down close to the ankles.

To James Knapp-Fisher   [Farnborough]
12 December 1948

My dear Jim,
I can't thank you enough for the cheque. It was unexpected and has

saved me from ruin this Christmas. Last week I was suddenly made horribly aware of my bank account and was wondering where on earth to turn for cash. Heaven Bless the Educational and Hygienic publishers. THE PRINCESS AND CURDIE is much better than AT THE BACK OF THE NORTH WIND though Arthur Hughes' illustrations of the last are terrific. It will be a job to find someone who will not compare unfavourably with Hughes. Really, you know, I think the best sort of artist would be John Austin, who excels in detail, or Margaret W. Tarrant, who does those sickly religious pictures for children that Mowbray's sell. Jack Yeats would be best of all if he would do it. You want someone old-fashioned and who has read the book. Jack Yeats would not be cheap as he is a most successful artist. I wonder if there is an old Scots artist who could do them. Try Jack Yeats (he lives in Dublin but I've forgotten his number in Fitzwilliam Square, and mention my name it might at least elicit a reply if not a favourable one). Then I will think again if he fails.

Love from your fellow, John B

JB and J.K.-F., Chairman and Director of the publishers Sidgwick and Jackson, had been at Oxford together.
JB often called Sidgwick and Jackson 'The Hygienics' because they published so many medical books.

To Emily Villiers-Stuart

January 1949 (Sunday)   *Off to the aeroplane*

Dearest Emily,
I thought the sooner you had the enclosed the better. You know how much I loved your coming up as you did. You know now you need never be lonely. You will be daily in my prayers and I will write to you soon and be looking about for some place to live in for you and something for you to do in England. God Bless you. My goodness! that scent you put in your hair! those wet woods! that stream! the sunset behind Dublin church towers! St Anthony pray for us. Dear Emily.

Love, John

JB sent E.V.-S. (about whom he had written 'Ireland with Emily' when she was married to Lord Hemphill and lived at Tulira, County Galway) a beautifully embroidered handkerchief, having posted it at Dublin airport on his way back to England after a brief trip to Ireland. Her second husband, Ion Villiers-Stuart, to whom she had only been married for two years, had just died of a heart attack.

To Evelyn Waugh   The Old Rectory
                                           Farnborough
                                           Wantage
17 January 1949   Berkshire

Dear Evelyn,
I am very pleased to have *The Month* and not so pleased to hear about my
'jaunty sub-aestheticism of the Third Programme', whatever that may
be! Though I hardly dare to tell you, I really do not think Edith Sitwell
is so good a poet as Mr Auden. I think she is vastly over-rated and I
should have thought Blunden and Ralph Hodgson, among living poets,
were better than either of them and, of course, Uncle Tom Eliot is. But
you may be quite right. I deeply respect your judgement and if you
have the time to tell me of some poems by Edith Sitwell which you
think magnificent, I shall immediately read them. She is much better
than most modern poets, but is she so good as all that?
    I am enchanted with the final paragraph of your review.
    We both send our love to you both, John B

> E.W. replied (18 January 1949), 'Jaunty sub-aestheticism' was a villainous phrase. What
> I meant was that BBC jauntiness of the Tom (glad he's dead) Handley sort was infecting
> aesthetics and pushing it below the surface into popular underworld. But how badly I
> said it. I don't think E. Sitwell a *great* poet; I think Auden a pathetically bad one.'

To The Society of Authors

1 February 1949

The Condition of Reviewing

Sir,
Mr Lewis Wilshire's timely and admirable letter deserves a reply from
one of those at whom his arrows are, presumably, directed.
    I imagine my position is similar to that of other reviewers in the daily
papers. My book reviews appear in the *Daily Herald* once a week. The
space allotted to me is generally about eight hundred and fifty words
long and even this may be cut down because something of 'News Value'
occurs at the last minute. I receive an average of twenty to thirty books
and it is obviously impossible to mention all of these in eight hundred

and fifty words or thereabouts. It is my practice, therefore, to spend at least a day and a half selecting which I shall review and then another day or two reading at length those I have selected, which are rarely more than six. Because many bad and sub-mediocre books are published, I disregard these altogether unless they are so frightfully bad that they deserve public castigation. It is natural, therefore, that the six books I do mention are at least mediocre ones. Good new books are, and always have been, rare. They may have, and indeed probably do have, grave demerits but the very fact that they have been selected is an earnest that they are not contemptible. There is not space in a notice of a hundred and thirty words to produce detailed criticism: the most I can hope to do is give the readers some idea of the subject and story of the book and use a few adjectives of a descriptive nature about how the work struck me personally. If the book strikes me favourably, so short a notice of it is bound to sound rather like a 'blurb'!

I think that as newsprint increases, so criticism, at any rate in the daily papers, will grow tarter because there will be the space which all reasoned criticism demands. It is fatally easy to write short, damning, funny reviews, but these rarely can be fair or even descriptive. At present I find reviewing is largely a matter of selecting and describing and I hope Mr Wilshire will believe me when I say that I find it as difficult as writing a love-letter in the form of a twelve-word telegram.

Yours faithfully, J. Betjeman

This letter was published in *The Author* in spring 1949.

To Emily Villiers-Stuart

The Old Rectory
Farnborough
Wantage
Berkshire

16 February 1949

Dearest Emily,
What do you think this is?
    1)

For answer see the end of the letter.

And what is this?   2)

See also end of letter.

And are there hopes of my writing poetry again? There are, thanks to you. So far I have only written some comic verses to Reggie about Glen Druid and the poacher and the wrongs of Oireland. Dear Emily, you know what a solace you are to me. Your presence made that round of social visits bearable. I daren't write down all I want to say. I put dots instead . . . . Fill them in with purple ink in that backward sloping hand. If you write to me regularly I will reply regularly. Not that it matters whether we write or not. But if I write regularly and know your needs, I will have some clearer notions of what I can do for you over here, what sort of things there are that you can do and would feel like doing. For instance you may want to live in London. You said you thought you would prefer a city. Well it is the only one where you would find old friends and enough congenial new ones. The one advantage of Ireland is that you have friends there and they are most important. The older one grows the less one wants, I find, to see new people. But that loneliness in which you must be at present, won't do at all. Come on a *visit* here first and stay here, for weeks – months – and see what you think of the strange drab atmosphere of England. You may find it too disquieting so that Ireland will seem less melancholy if you return. I pin my hopes on your coming over in April. The Summer Term at Oxford begins on April 24th. Don't think I will ever fail you. I haven't and I won't. Also it always happens that if one waits and trusts, most unexpected things happen. Something that will suit you perfectly will turn up, never fear. But it may [be] something most unlikely. I hope to goodness it will be something that suits *me* perfectly too! I shall try and see Peter Patrick again this term. He is so good and gentle, in the teddy bear fashion that

you are, that I shall probably get from him what he thinks of the idea of
your leaving Ireland for a bit. God bless you, dear Emily. I hope you
got the prayer all right and that it is useful to you. How very pious this
letter sounds. Write to me whatever comes in to your head.

   Love, John

   Answers (1) Your eyes   (2) The Augustinian Holy Picture

> E.V.-S. moved to Stradbally, County Waterford, in her recent widowhood and years
> later to London.
>   Peter Patrick was E.V.-S.'s son by Lord Hemphill. He was named after St Peter's in
> Rome, where his parents had met, and St Patrick's Cathedral in New York, where they
> married.

To George Barnes   Cunard White Star
24 February 1949   HMS *Caronia*

Dear Commander,
I held the blank paper you sent me to the fire and do not think you need
be worried at all by the message that came out in the invisible ink. Of
course, when you are in America and entirely on your own you do find
certain inclinations running away with you. Give them free play while
you are there, but only so far as your conscience will allow, though it
looks to me as though your conscience has allowed considerable latitude
already.

   Believe me, my dear Commander,
   Your old friend, JB

> In reply to a blank piece of paper G.B. had sent to JB by mistake, JB sent the above to the
> BBC which caused maximum embarrassment.

To Emily Villiers-Stuart   The Old Rectory
                                                      Farnborough
                                                      Wantage
1 March 1949   Berkshire
Shrove Tuesday

My dearest Emily,
Peter Patrick is coming to luncheon (DV) on Sunday next with the
Powlie from Oxford.

I am just about to go and lecture at Harrow. If I can buy some, I will send you postcards of it.

My mother is coming to stay here for Easter (Thursday April 14th to Friday April 22nd inclusive) so when you come to England come after or before that date. She will effectively disturb the house with demands for hot water bottles (it is sure to be cold) and special diets, poor thing.

Colonel Kolkhorst has had P.P. to tea. Colonel K. is the University Reader in Spanish and now Acting Professor. He says in a letter to me: 'P.P. came to tea. His charm is *devastating*. Less Ego this time and a little more *earnest* consideration of external realities in the world about one. What a relief it must be to *le bon Dieu* to succeed for once, with such a perfect specimen. One bull's eye in a million misses.'

This is high praise indeed from an Oxford don. I hope you will meet him when you come over. He is one of my greatest friends and one of my oldest ones. He likes being laughed at and, as he is very ridiculous, this is just as well.

If you ever go to Cork will you get me some postcards of St Finbar's Church of Ireland Cathedral there? Only if you go to Cork. Not important.

This village is full of tragedy as usual. A case of ill-treatment of children in a house opposite, yet not such as one can put the NSPCC on to it. Another case of a farm worker with a young family condemned to death by cancer. I think of that platitude of Dibdin's:

> Come, never seem to mind it,
>   Nor count your fate a curse,
> However sad you find it
>   Yet somebody is worse.

Write to me, write to me, write to me,
  Love for ever, from John

To Emily Villiers-Stuart

[13 March 1949]
2nd Sunday in Lent 1949

The Old Rectory
Farnborough
Wantage
Berkshire

Dearest Emily,
It was very nice to hear from you on that thin paper and in that immigrant writing even though you used blue instead of purple ink.

Your letter, moreover, sounded as though you were a little happier. Perhaps those *Paternosters* are working. I shall not forget them. What are these? That's right. They are the same as those in a former letter.

Peter Patrick came out for the day last Sunday and was very happy and we tobogganed in a field with a bull in it. Then I took him to dinner at my friend Colonel Kolkhorst's and he grew loquacious and earnest and fascinating, expanding in his happiness and the admiration we all had for his sincerity and good manners. And I realised that, like you, he is deeply interested in *politics*. It pains me a lot to think of all he may suffer from the Baron. But I think he is young enough (and old enough) to resist it now, provided he gains a measure of independence for himself at Oxford. In youth one can suffer without being scarred for life – by youth, I mean after childhood. Obviously P.P. is as strong as a horse mentally and spiritually. I have not talked to him about the Baron. But Propeller did. He is always welcome to stay here (P.P. I mean) for as long as he likes. He has won all hearts. But I expect that legally he has to go to Dublin. We could I expect arrange a plot with his Tutors – if you think it a good idea – for him to stay in England if Dublin becomes unendurable to him. Let me know. I'll talk to him about it next time I see him.

I had forgotten you liked gardening. I remember now there was a garden round Tulira. But wasn't it all *weeds*? I seem to remember walking round some beds with you and being given the impression (by you) that a lot of work had been put in to them (by you). Ah! that garden at Glenview! I see your gold hair bent over bushes shoulder high and your hands snipping off little bits and putting them in a delicate basket. Then it is time for you to get ready to dress for dinner. I know no one I like thinking about more than you and writing letters for during the day. How I long to see you over here so as to tell you some other ideas about you that have come into my head. I would like to find a post for you over here involving the use of the relief nib on paper, secateurs on dead flower heads and dressing for dinner. Do I go too far in all this mocking? It is my perverse form of affection. WRITE WRITE WRITE to me, for I am most anxious to help you and yours by all means I can for the love I bear you.

Love, John B

To Anthony Barnes   The Old Rectory
                                                Farnborough
                                                Wantage
19 March 1949   Berkshire

My dear Little Prawls,
Not for the life of me would I come to Eton anywhere near the 4th June.
The most unfashionable time of all for me, please. By the way, 4th June
is St Petroc's day and I shall be absorbed in prayer. I am very proud to
find you quoting me in the *Chronicle*. What a jolly depressing picture
that is of that poor Empire Builder!

I was also very pleased to read about the expedition to the City. I
never think the interior of St Paul's is quite up to the exterior and of the
exterior the dome is far the best thing. St Mary Woolnoth, now I agree
with you – there's a church. I long to take you on a tour of some lesser
known London churches. Quite a lot survive and the Hawksmoor
works in the East End are staggering. I am horrified to think that a
Plowden should become a Planner. Mr Piper and I came across their
house in Shropshire when we were doing a *Guide*. There have been
Roman Plowdens there since the Act of Uniformity and the Plowdens
are to Shropshire rather like what the Stonors are to Oxfordshire. If he
is a Planner you must *narrow* his outlook, not broaden it.

Yours till death and after, I hope,
John B

Edwin Plowden (later Lord) became Chief Planning Officer and Chairman of the
Economic Planning Board 1947–53. William Plowden, his son, was A.B.'s fag
at Eton.

To Anthony Powell   The Old Rectory
                                                Farnborough
                                                Wantage
7 April 1949   Berkshire

Dear Tony,
How very kind of you to write! A spontaneous expression of
appreciation like that, old top, really does cheer up someone like me
who feels increasingly out of date. There is a lot more of the long

17 Myfanwy and John Piper at their farmhouse
in Fawley Bottom near Henley-on-Thames.

18a Cecil Beaton as the sailor
and JB as the young clergyman
in their friend John Sutro's
film *The Sailor's Return*.

18b Evelyn Waugh
with JB (on roller-skates).

19a Marcelle Rothe (later Mrs Peter Quennell), JB and PB
in the garden at Garrards Farm, c. 1935.

19b JB captioned this picture
'Ectoplasm'.

19c JB at Brighton,
September 1935.

20a Collinstown House, Clondalkin, which JB and PB rented during the war when JB was Press Attaché in Dublin. The right-hand wing was added later.

20b PB, JB and friends in Fleet Street, Dublin, c. 1942, near the Palace Bar. This was Dublin's principal literary pub of the time, at which the editor of the *Irish Times*, Robert Smyllie (*sitting beside PB*), presided.

21 JB and PSGB on the beach in Ireland, 1948,
when visiting Father Paddy Brown.

22a The Old Rectory, Farnborough, near Wantage, Berkshire (now called 'Oxfordshire'), which the Chetwodes bought for PB and JB as a belated wedding present in 1945.

22b Family portrait in the garden at Farnborough with the neurotic dalmatian, Peter Pudding.

23a Tulira, the Connemara mare from Ireland, pulls the trolley cart containing most of the village: (*front row, left to right*) Bushel Wilkinson, CB, Geoffrey Grigson (who had to come to lunch), June White, Winnie Sprules, Billy Wilkinson, (*back row, left to right*) JB, unknown man, Bob Wilkinson, Terry Carter, unknown girl, Stella Wilkinson and Topsy White.

23b JB at Southampton Airport just before flying to Alderney to stay with T. H. White. To JB's left are Florrie Wilkinson, her brother Bob and (*far left*) Terry Carter who drove JB from Farnborough.
23c Auburn-haired Pearl Wilkinson who worked in and around the house.
God save me from Florrie's sister Pearl
She puts my senses in a whirl.

24 'Uneasy about abroad':
JB at Auxerre, 1949, while on holiday with the Barneses.

narrative piece about Cornwall but it is too intimate to be published.

Give my love to Violet. I am generally in London on Mondays and do let us meet and eat and drink.

Yours, John Betjeman

p.p. Henry Yorke, Lennox Berkeley, Vere Pilkington and all at Canterbury House, yours ever Jack Grotrian.

A.P. wrote (5 April 1949) about the *Selected Poems*, 'I must tell you how much I enjoyed them. They make Auden and Co. look very poor performers; though perhaps this is not very high praise. I hope we shall have more of the long narrative piece about Cornwall.'
   Henry Yorke, Lennox Berkeley and Vere Pilkington had been Oxford undergraduates who along with Anthony Powell had rooms in Canterbury House in King Edward Street.
   Jack Grotrian was also an Oxford undergraduate.

To Sir Giles Gilbert Scott   The Old Rectory
                                             Farnborough
                                             Wantage
27 April 1949   Berkshire

CONFIDENTIAL

Dear Sir Giles,

Forgive my bothering you but I have just seen that beautiful little church you designed at Bournemouth and it occurred to me that you might be willing to furnish me with a testimonial to the merits of another great church architect, Mr J. N. Comper, who will be eighty-four this year. He has, as you know, received no public recognition since he refuses to belong to any professional body, so the only way to do anything about it is by private enterprise.

The Prime Minister's secretary has told me that he will submit Mr Comper's name for the New Year's Honours List provided I can obtain testimonials. Would you be willing to send me one for forwarding to the Prime Minister? I am also approaching the Bishop of Chichester, the Dean of York, The Revd Mother Superior of Wantage, Mr Stanley Morison, Sir Charles Peers, Sir Kenneth Clark, Lord Shaftesbury, Mr John Piper and Mr T. S. Eliot. If you can think of anybody else who should be approached and whose name would carry weight, I should be most grateful. Naturally, I am not telling Mr Comper anything about this activity.

Yours sincerely, J. Betjeman

The church (RC) was The Annunciation, Charminster Road.
   'I am in complete agreement with your effort. . . . I have written a testimonial. . . . I
am so glad you like the church at Bournemouth. This was the first job I ever had, except
for Liverpool Cathedral,' wrote G.G.S. (29 April 1949).

To Lady Mander   The Old Rectory
                                                   Farnborough
                                                   Wantage
24 May 1949   Berkshire

Dear Lady Mander,
How very kind of you to write to me. I have put down tentatively
March 17th 1950, if I am still alive. November 18th is not possible for
me. I have written to the Secretary too.
   I would so like to see Wightwick Manor too. Old Mr Wyndham
Hope Hughes who taught Kempe how to make stained glass, died at the
beginning of this year aged a hundred in the Victoria Hospital,
Swindon. His son, Colonel Christopher Hughes, MC, Marlborough,
Wilts, could give you information about Kempe. I have always liked the
early glass of Kempe but his later glass and imitations of it, all green and
grey, have ruined so many churches for me that I would like to see the
good early Kempe which I have so often heard about at Wightwick.
   Yours sincerely, John Betjeman

   Lady M. wrote on nineteenth-century subjects such as Rosalie Glynn Grylls. She
   belonged to the Wightwick family whose house, Wightwick Manor (1887),
   Wolverhampton, is a celebration of the best Victorian artistry and craftsmanship,
   William Morris paper and hangings and Pre-Raphaelite pictures. Lady M. gave it to the
   National Trust on condition that she could live there part of the week.

To Mr Boswell   The Old Rectory
                                                   Farnborough
                                                   Wantage
25 May 1949   Berkshire

Dear Mr Boswell,
I have agreed to do eight of these seven-minute talks and the expenses
connected with them are likely to come in several instances to almost as

much as the fee you offer me. The places that have been decided upon are:

Hayling Island – this I have already written about, and it was necessary for me to hire a motor car from Newbury to go over the island because my own motor cannot be relied upon for so long a journey even if I had the petrol, and the train service from here to Hayling Island is impossible. (As I am a close student of Bradshaw and always go by train when I can, you may be sure that what I say is true.)

Freshwater – this can be done in a day by motoring to Winchester and hiring a car to Yarmouth, Isle of Wight.

Weymouth – I shall have to stay the night here.

Bournemouth – I had to stay the night here and have made all my notes.

Sidmouth – I shall certainly have to stay a night here, probably two.

Port Isaac – I can do this from memory without having to go to the place.

Clevedon – I will have to stay the night there.

This excludes any fares involved in coming up to do the broadcasts. My present arrangement with Mr Annand is that I shall record 'Freshwater' and 'Hayling Island' when I am in London on Monday next, and if possible I shall record 'Bournemouth' on that day too.

There is one other place and I cannot remember where it is. But rather than make a separate journey for each talk the idea is to record them in two or three lumps.

I cannot work out for you the expenses each time in advance. Will it not be best to allocate an overall sum? I am used to doing things at a loss when I enjoy them, as I am enjoying doing this series, but eight guineas plus my bare railway fares is going to be rather a strain on my pocket.

Yours sincerely, John Betjeman

To Penelope Betjeman Acland Nursing Home
2 June 1949 Oxford

Dear Peenalloppee,
I could not deal with your letter earlier. Have not been feeling up to the sustained effort. But intense pain, I now realise, has an excellent purifying and clarifying property and what I write down now, is, I hope, a truthful account of my thoughts under it so far as they affect

you, me, the children and the Father of us all, as the result of your letter.

Your letter had two things in it that it asked. First that Wubz [CB] should be brought up RC. Second that I should chuck everything if that would be necessary for me to do, so that you could show me how much you loved me. The second comes first, as it is really the more important. I think I must for a long time have been going through some sort of breakdown. Excessive bad temper is one of the signs. The peace of this place now I am out of pain makes me see how tiresome I have been and cruel and bullying. *Oi am very sorry*. Oi do think however that I have hit on the explanation. I do hope you will believe it. I hope you will also agree to the solution I propose.

I don't really mind doing degrading work like book-reviewing (I doubt if I am now fit for anything better) provided I have your love. And having your love doesn't mean being told I have got it 'underneath all our quarrelling'. It doesn't ever entail on your part mending my clothes. It means seeing you and being with you *alone* much more than I am.

Whatever the circumstances of our marriage in its beginnings, I had grown to love you so much by the time the Powlie was born, that you were more important to me than anything else. And you still are. I have always prayed in my heart that I will die before you because I feel that I could not live without you. And even the coming of the children has made no difference to that feeling for you.

My trouble has been jealousy. Not, thank goodness, of the children, but of the things that take you away from me. First there was the farm. It was all right – or at any rate easier at Uffington – because it was not so unwieldy and we could sometimes get away together and after a row we could always be 'snoungish' in no time.

Ireland was just hell. It was war work for both of us and was, so far as you and I are concerned, the beginnings of disaster for then *my* work took *me* away from *you* when you needed me most, and that made me ill-tempered.

Farnborough gets me down because the farm and the children between them have taken you away from me so much that I only see you alone late in the evening when you and I are both tired and touchy. Or rather I am touchy and you are tired.

Then came this third thing to take you farther away from me still – Rome. Of course it is God's will and we must leave it at that. But I was jealous of Rome and RC interests of yours, Rome as a Church, that is to say an organisation, for further pulling us apart. That is really why I have an 'obsession' about Rome, because I love you so much.

It's no good my just saying this. But I do mean it. If I could be with you alone – just you and me alone once a week for a whole afternoon including lunch and tea, I'm sure I should be happy and reasonable again.

Even if we quarrelled sometimes, it would still be worth it. I would even garden with you or ride with you, provided neither Wubz nor the Powlie nor anyone else was there. It will mean a certain amount of sacrifice of time and trouble on both our parts, but it is, I think, the only solution that we should see more of one another alone at regular intervals every week. Then, however busy you were with farm and RC, and however busy I was doing whatever demeaning things, we would always know that on a certain day – Tuesdays or Weds – we would have lunch and tea together and be on our own. And from that we might grow more united.

The business of Wubz's being brought up RC is not easy unless I explain to you my fundamental religious longing, which is very difficult. I long for Jesus as a Man, I long to see Him, to be lifted up to Him, to love Him, not to injure Him as much as I do all the time. I *try* to long for Him when I don't long for Him. Jesus is the centre of my faith and the Sacraments are one of the ways by which I try to know Him. I have never doubted our Sacraments in the C of E and I see in Farnborough that the only witness to Jesus is our church there. I see Jesus on the Cross there, very much more crucified and suffering than, say, at Wantage (C of E or RC). Each person who leaves Jesus here in Farnborough drives another nail in His Cross. That was how I felt (and I hope you won't mind my saying it) first when you left Farnborough for Rome. But I now know that it is God's will for you to go there, and so I must say I'm sorry I felt like that. But you do see, don't you, that if I let Wubz go I personally think I would be further wounding Our Lord in our feeble church in Farnborough, which one day may be a great one and a full one. It's just when things seem quite hopeless, as they do now, that they brighten. To let Wubz leave the C of E at present would, I think, be your will not God's will. She is down for St Mary's and with you RC and she brought up Catholic, she will probably in her own good time go Roman. But she is losing nothing now with the arrangements.

If we could only see one another more, then we could love one another. And if I come back to Farnborough, I must see you at least once a week for a whole afternoon together alone. Oi must do that because Oi loove yew. Oi will even loove the Centipede and the Broadwoods and Broazi when they are all shrivelled and grey. The alternative seems to be amicable separation so that we do not kill the love that remains between us. It is more important that we should love one another, than that the children should love us. They go off and marry and become separate entities, as you point out. But we go on together after they have left us. In my prayerbook I wrote ages ago that you and the children are part of God's working in me. I can't remember the exact phraseology, but its sense is that when I Sin I also wound that good part of me which loves you and the children. We are a complete family, beside which the question of whether Anglican orders are valid or what the Revd Steele thinks happens at the Consecration, are unimportant. And you and I are responsible for the family. We must be together *only* if we give ourselves a chance to love one another. Otherwise, far better apart. And I don't see how we can love each other if we busy ourselves so much with our own affairs and see so little of one another. The happiest day I can remember for a long time was our visit to Windsor. Let's have such days once a week, not always so grand as that, but when we are together and alone.

Believe me, very trewly yorz, Tewpie

JB was in the Acland nursing home in Oxford having a cyst removed.

My mother had written a long letter from Farnborough a few days earlier: 'You must be really honest and admit we were never religiously at one in the Anglican Church. I wanted to become RC when Fr Burdett tried to convert us both and you said, "You ought to try your own Church first." Then I was completely converted to Catholicism by Fr Folky [Harton]'s book. . . . When we went to Eire I became more and more convinced of the truth of the Roman claims and hoped that you were feeling the same way. . . . Life simply IS NOT long enough to go on like this and personally I think it would be idiotic to separate, we would neither of us be any happier and the children would be very *un*happy. Let us forgive and forget and both admit that we have colossal faults and different temperaments and different approaches to religion and have been very bad husbands and wives though I think we are BOTH good parents, and let us each lead our own lives as far as friends are concerned and not try to conceal things any more but let us LOVE AND BE HAPPY. Yours very truly, Morwenna Plym Woad.'

'The Centipede' was how JB referred to PB's parting, 'the Broadwoods' her legs, 'Broazi' her hair.

Ten:

In the perspective of Eternity

=

July 1949 to September 1951

Oh God the Olney Hymns abound
    With words of Grace which Thou didst choose,
And wet the elm above the hedge
    Reflected in the winding Ouse.

Pour in my soul unemptied floods
    That stand between the slopes of clay,
Till deep beyond a deeper depth
    This Olney day is any day.

'Olney Hymns'

Despite my mother's conversion to Roman Catholicism and his feelings of devastation, JB went on loving her until the end of his life. 'I *hated* her conversion,' he said many years later. 'Now I don't mind at all, because despite it, Penelope has remained Penelope.'[1] Alan Pryce-Jones remembers, 'He felt terrifically abandoned at the time and couldn't understand how Penelope could have dealt such a blow; he minded the suggestion that Anglo-Catholics were junior partners of Roman Catholics.'[2]

It was a watershed, for it saw the beginning of JB's being able to love other women whilst continuing to love my mother. In June 1949, he fell in love with Margaret Wintringham – who was blonde, full-bodied, beautiful and wind-blown. She lived in a cottage in Hinton Parva, a small village at the foot of the Berkshire Downs. She recalled, 'I had heard about this Poetry Society in Swindon and I was absolutely thrilled so I went along. John was talking about Lincolnshire poets, Tennyson and so on, and he said, "If there is anyone in the audience from Lincolnshire please put your hand up." I put up mine and we talked afterwards. Then he called in at the cottage in Hinton Parva and it went on from there. He used to come about once a week on his way back from seeing his mother in Bath. I used to tag along when he was thinking of writing a guide-book on Oxford with John Piper. I remember him saying, "Of course, Keble is the only totally beautiful building in Oxford." '[3]

In early autumn, JB had gone to supper with Margaret and her husband and had left his handkerchief behind. She returned it, washed and ironed, with a short note expressing how much she had enjoyed doing it. Sometimes they met for coffee in Swindon before JB caught the train to Bristol or London. He tried to get her a job with the BBC doing a commentary on one of his poetry programmes, and wrote to P. H. Newby, a Talks producer at the BBC (14 April 1950), 'It was a lady I was thinking of, who might be able to read in Lincolnshire dialect. . . . She is a Lincolnshire woman from the Tennyson area. She has never been tested on the wireless and her voice may be unsuitable.'4 She failed the test, but JB provided her with children's books to review for *Time and Tide*. He told his close friends about her. He wrote to Patrick Kinross, 'I have got a girlfriend who makes very funny poems and good ones. She *understands*. But then so does Propeller.'5 She wrote good poetry on the side and JB would read out loud to her his favourite eighteenth- and nineteenth-century poets in the hope that she would like them as much as he did. She, on the other hand, tried to convert him to communism. The branch secretary of the Communist Party, who lived in Harwell near Didcot, sent JB a persuasive letter together with a propaganda pamphlet. Both Margaret and her husband were stalwart 'Party Members'. JB forever referred to them as such, in an affectionate way. 'The Party Members are coming to lunch,' he would say or, when introducing her husband to a newcomer he'd always say, 'He's a Party Member, you know.' Eve Disher, the painter and girlfriend of JB's Marlborough chum Arthur Elton, wrote (24 October 1949), 'I hope she is plumpish and does rather *gaily* try to convert you. I suspect this is the worst attack you've had – isn't it? Worse than the flier?'6 (JB had taken a passing fancy to a lady glider, whom he had met at a Murray's publishing party a year before, but nothing had come of it.)

JB's intense devotion to Margaret lasted for over a year. She and her family were frequent visitors to Sunday lunch at Farnborough. My mother referred to Margaret as JB's 'Poitry Girl' and would take the children off in the pony cart so that Margaret and JB could be left alone to talk about poetry. He wrote to John Piper (11 April 1950), 'I saw Margaret Wintringham again today and it was like getting back into a warm bath after a good run on the Downs.'7 Years later JB wrote (13 December 1958), 'Darling Margaret Wintringham, I constantly see you in my mind's eye. I hear your fading voice. I look into your Lincolnshire blue eyes. I think of your curves. Longing springs. . . .'8

Life did not seem to change and the stream of visitors to Farnborough continued, the singing after meals becoming even louder. Edward

Long, who was helping JB with his guide to parish churches, came to stay a few times with his wife Margaret, an exceptional pianist. We all sang Theo Marzials's songs together, accompanied by Mrs Long: 'Go lovely rose . . .' and 'Stay steersman, oh stay thy flight – down the river of years. . . .' Sometimes my father played the harmonium in the kitchen but it was usually 'Mr Piper' who played Fats Waller and sang:

> Joshua Joshua,
> Sweeter than lemon squash you are,
> Yes by gosh you are,
> Joshu-oshu-a

on the piano in the hall; or my mother who could play every hymn and sight-read songs JB loved to sing like 'Drink to Me Only with Thine Eyes', 'After the Ball is Over' and 'Two Lovely Black Eyes'.

My mother continued to order clerics and Wantage nuns into the trolley cart with unerring determination, taking them for canters along the Ridgeway. Inevitably, when the trolley went over bumps several people flew out including, most memorably, the new incumbent for West Ilsley and Farnborough, Father Nash, who was projected a good eight feet into the air in his cassock. (His predecessor, Father Steele, had flatly refused to get on the trolley, giving 'nerves' as his excuse.) Miss Ruth Webb, JB's new secretary, also remembers being catapulted out several times. She had arrived on 1 October 1948, having heard about the job from her colleague at the Agricultural Research Centre in nearby Compton, Miss Eagle, who was a churchwarden at West Ilsley. Dark-haired, pale-skinned and reserved, she was put to lodge in the 'Indian room' on the north side of the house which was hung with thirty aquatints of India. 'I was glad of the opportunity to do something different; I used to help with the architectural books Mr Betjeman was doing with Mr Piper, as well as what he called his hack work – reviewing for the *Daily Herald*. Then I used to catalogue information about church architecture from his books, to help with the *Collins Guide*. Sometimes we would piece together a poem he had written on separate scraps of paper, which he produced from different pockets. He never liked me to type his letters, he felt he needed to write to his friends by hand for fear of insulting them. I got very little salary, but I learnt a lot. I was warned that he would be liverish in the mornings and in a very bad temper, but in fact it was only occasionally bad. (His biggest phobia was the possibility of getting marmalade between his wrists and his cuffs at breakfast, which seemed to be easily done and would make him shout 'Oh God, Oh God!') Sometimes I used to help Mrs Betjeman cutting kale from a nearby farmer's field in the middle of winter and bringing it back with a horse and trolley. I remember Mr Betjeman getting back late from London and calling out plaintively across the yard, "Penelope," and I knew things were all right. They both of them cared a lot about people. Often I would have to follow up trying to get a job for someone who Mr Betjeman had met on a train or for P. Morton Shand, and lots of others."[9]

Farnborough was my favourite place on earth, I seemed to have complete freedom. I remember no reprimands or anxieties. I recall JB constantly kissing me on the top of the head. Miss Webb remembers it very vividly too. He called me first 'Waba' or 'Wuba', then 'Wabz' or 'Wubz', then 'Wibbly' or 'Woebley' and finally 'Wibz', which was his and my brother's nickname for me thereafter – in consequence, mine for him was 'Dadz'. The thing I liked best about him was that I could make him laugh so easily. Having been influenced by the steady stream of ghost stories, I wrote macabre verse and my first poem made him throw back his head, open his mouth and rock with laughter. He often quoted it:

> Wibberly Wobberly Wib
> She blew up her dad with a squib
> And when he was dead
> She cut off his head
> And scratched on his face with a nib.

He made *me* laugh a lot too. In September 1949 he bought a stuffed crocodile in Tiverton and because my mother would not have it in the house, he kept it in the apple store and brought it out on fine days when he would put it in the long grass beside the path out towards Mr Laurence's farm. When people visited, he would walk them along the path and then suddenly clutch hold of their arm, feigning terror. Several people, including most of the villagers, were momentarily startled. He was also a good mimic; he could take off anyone and used to read stories to me in wildly differing regional accents – some days he would talk with an American accent in nothing but what he called Longfellow language, and by the evening we were all doing it:

> If you talk like Hiawatha
> You can talk for twenty minutes.
> Pass me please the bread and butter
> Is it time to go to school now?

This activity put me off *Hiawatha* for life. The poem that most impressed me and which I begged to be read again and again was 'I remember, I remember, the house where I was born', by Thomas Hood.

JB's enthusiasm for art involved a rapid filling-up of wall space at Farnborough. There were Rossettis, Alma-Tademas, Birket-Fosters and of course masses of Pipers. He never spent more than fifteen pounds on a picture but when he discovered that Charles M. Gere, who had illustrated Kelmscott Press books for William Morris, was still alive at eighty-three, he wrote to him, proposing that he should do a portrait of me. Mr Gere replied (28 February 1951), 'Are you thinking of a water-colour? Those I have done were about eight inches by six, just head and shoulders, the price being twenty-five guineas.'[10] Four times JB drove me in the Vauxhall to Mr Gere's house in Painswick in Gloucestershire and I sat, bored and irritable, while JB talked to Mr Gere about all his Arts and Crafts friends. Always on our way back, we would stop at the Tunnel Inn near Coate which, with its ruined and ivy-clad canal-tunnel entrance, excited me more than almost anywhere. (JB got terrific stick if he drank spirits at home and whenever we were on our own we would always 'stop off for a nip', while I had a packet of crisps, which were also illegal.)

A lot of my life at Farnborough was spent on the back of a pony, and although JB professed to hate horses, I was so proud of my achievements on a docked-tailed mare called Dinah at Mr and Mrs Glover's riding school, that I persuaded him to make his first and only venture to a hunter trials. Mrs Glover ran the event in fields next to her riding school at Chieveley, which now lie under the Services at Exit 13 of the M4 motorway. There was a young woman called Diana Russell who arrived in a horsebox from East Woodhay with several ponies and usually won everything. She was brusque, jolly and competitive. JB's 'Hunter Trials' followed, beginning with the lines:

> It's awf'lly bad luck on Diana,
>   Her ponies have swallowed their bits;
> She fished down their throats with a spanner
>   And frightened them all into fits.

In 1950 he sent the poem to Patrick Cullinan, adding as a PS, 'This is rhyming journalism and I don't think it is anything else my dear boy. It is designed for *Vogue* or *Harpers* and isn't my writing divine, my dear.'[11]

In late 1949 JB became Literary Adviser/Editor to *Time and Tide* (which he always wrote as *Tame and Tade*), under the auspices of a large and bossy Welshwoman, Lady Rhondda. He began to write letters to his friends using double and treble 'r's and 'd's and 'l's in a Welsh manner and signing himself 'Evan'. He wrote to Cyril Connolly (27 September 1950), 'For ten guineas a week I go to *Tame and Tade* from two-thirty to five p.m. Mondays and advise them on books to review and reviewers – where to send them. All the time I think:

i) that you ought to have my job
ii) that you ought to be approached but I dare not do it
iii) that you are the best critic and prose writer alive and *Tame and Tade* pays at the most ten guineas a thousand. Would you do a "middle" on Roman Catholic writers in England? They are a world of their own and an influence? or not? and if not why not? and if yes, how?'[12]

He also asked friends who needed the work, like Pansy Lamb and Karen Lancaster, to write book reviews, as well as established literary heroes like T. S. Eliot and Walter de la Mare to write poetry.

Some of the *Shell Guides*, which had been suspended during the war, were reprinted by Faber and Faber in 1950, being *Devon, Derbyshire, Gloucestershire, Oxfordshire, Somerset* and the *West Coast of Scotland*. The *Shell Guide to Shropshire*, which had long been hovering in the wings, and which JB and John Piper had had such fun compiling, was finally published in 1951, also by Faber. Meanwhile JB was writing poems and articles for *Horizon* and the *New Statesman and Nation*, as well as keeping up a regular output of radio talks which took him all over the West Country and involved constant use of Bradshaw. JB also chaired a programme called *Poetic Licence* and asked his friends like Edmund Blunden to be speakers. He wrote to him (28 February 1951) complaining about a script which had been prepared by the BBC: 'The beginning is terribly dull and sticky. Who the hell wants any of that silly youth parliament nonsense? I suggest we alter it at lunch at the Garrick at one o'clock on Monday. I have asked Osbert (Lancaster) and Frank O'Connor. . . . *We will go to the BBC tight.*'[13]

'Often, I took dictation in the evenings,' remembers Miss Webb, 'letters, articles, reviews. I soon developed an allergy to his cigarette smoke and coughed and wheezed and rather than dismissing me he gave up smoking.'[14] JB smoked Passing Cloud cigarettes, which came in a pale pink packet. His abstinence did not last long, for he took up smoking again when Miss Webb left.

JB took his onerous task on the Oxford Diocesan Advisory Committee extremely seriously from 1946 until 1978 when he resigned. The DACs were set up at the beginning of the century to safeguard against the overzealous restoration of churches by the incumbent or by parishioners. Plans to make changes to churches had to go through the DAC. The meetings were once a month and their deliberations might result in JB going to look at several village churches from Sparsholt to Minster Lovell to approve – or not – a font being moved, or to persuade an incumbent to abandon a scheme for new lighting. Michael Maclaren, who was a member of the committee from the late forties, along with JB and John Piper, remembers a verse JB wrote:

> We want a little tablet made of brass.
> Around the table murmurs of 'Alas!'
> If only it were much more widely known,
> How strongly this committee favours stone.[15]

Together with the Pipers, Osbert and Karen Lancaster were the most constant visitors to Farnborough. JB had been firm friends with Osbert since Oxford and had first introduced him to the powers that be at the *Daily Express*, in which his pocket cartoons were to make him a household name. JB had been writing a series of articles tracing the rise of civilization for the *Express* and had asked Osbert to help him with the archaeological bits. JB introduced him to the Features Editor, John Rayner, and he never looked back.

The Lancasters had bought a house on the London Road, leading out of Henley-on-Thames, less than two miles from Fawley Bottom (the Pipers' house). It was a tall white stucco terraced house with a long garden at the back and JB always joked that it was exactly like a London house. It certainly had sophisticated décor which impressed me terrifically as a child – white and gold starred wallpaper in the sitting-room and a green striped dining-room and black furniture. Karen, whom JB always called 'Kar-een' because he thought it sounded more like a car lubricant, was stylish, funny, gravel-voiced and darkly beautiful. Whereas John Piper was handy around the house, JB and Osbert were exaggeratedly hopeless, and shirked all pretence at trying to help their wives except by being wildly good at entertaining them. JB's 'helplessness' often manifested itself when the car broke down. Once we were driving along St Giles in Oxford and we saw a wheel rolling quite fast in front of us; then there was a thud and the car lurched over. We got out and walked to the Randolph Hotel. There was no question either of finding the wheel, which had by then run between several other cars, or of finding out why it had happened; JB simply rang up Coxeters, the garage, and ordered a nip at the bar.

If the Pipers and the Lancasters were the mainstays at Farnborough, the advent of Patrick Cullinan was certainly the chief excitement of

1950. Cullinan, now a celebrated South African poet, was then a sunburned seventeen-year-old schoolboy with a blond lock of hair which constantly fell over his blue eyes. The grandson of Sir Thomas Cullinan, who founded the diamond mine, Patrick lived in South Africa and had been sent to school at Charterhouse where he had first encountered JB at the Poetry Society. He began to write to him and came to stay in April 1950. I became completely transfixed by him and watched with fascination as he cleaned his teeth each morning with an almost supernatural vigour. JB wrote to Cullinan both at Charterhouse and when he went up to Magdalen College, Oxford and positively encouraged him to keep on writing. He wrote in 1950 (undated), 'You may not agree with me, but I think:

1) Poetry should not be private but easy for all to understand.

2) It should have tones of meaning beyond the surface one.

3) It should read out loud well.

4) It should be memorable.

5) It should very clearly not be prose. Rhythm helps to make it different.'[16]

'When I wasn't laughing with him, I was greatly in awe of JB,' remembers Cullinan. 'He was the first person to take my poems seriously and to believe that I was going to make it as a writer. John whizzed me all over England in his battered old Vauxhall. We went from churches to country houses, from county to county, talking for hours, reciting poetry and laughing. As you can imagine, John's world of writers and artists was a revelation to a seventeen-year-old; it was wildly exciting. The year before, my mother had died of a brain tumour and I had become deeply introspective. John was wonderful to me, never patronizing, always wittily provocative. He helped me get over my self-absorption and obsession with my mother's death. We visited Faringdon to cheer up Lord Berners who was ill in bed – a startling figure in a nightshirt and stocking cap. He was depressed but soon chirped up when John began to read *Eric, or Little by Little*. John hammed it up outrageously, inserting all sorts of smutty asides and monstrous double entendres; Lord Berners and I were weak with laughter.'[17]

A few days after their visit, Gerald Berners died. His death was a huge blow to both my parents, for he had been a pillar of their lives from their first sunny days at Uffington in the early thirties until those last darker ones in the late forties when his exotic and incomparably glamorous Sunday lunches still lasted long into the afternoons. He had been their true friend, loving them both equally. JB wrote his obituary in *The Listener* (11 May 1950): 'Let me recall Faringdon House ten years ago on a sunny summer evening. The bells of Faringdon church tower are playing "Now the day is over", across the grass terraces. Pigeons dyed blue are still strutting about in front of the limestone façade. A very old motor car, date about 1906, for containing one person and painted bright yellow stands in front of the entrance. All day, from early in the morning, Lord Berners will have been at work either composing on the piano in the dining room – a piano with a huge gilt fish perched on it – or he will have been writing in the drawing room where the stuffed birds are and the set of Ackermann's *Repository* and the early Corots, the Matisse seascape, the Constable paintings, the oil by Bonington of a sailor, the Dufy of the races. The furnishing of the house showed no sign of any interior decorator having been called in. Some of it was as his mother had left it, the rest had grown up gradually. A third thing Lord Berners might have been doing would have been painting the lake from the terrace below his drawing room or painting the elm trees of the park, whose grassy slopes descend to that willowy, flat valley of the Upper Thames with the Cotswold hills rising blue in the distance.' Diana Mosley wrote to JB immediately, 'Thank you for writing as you did about Gerald in *The Listener*, it was quite perfect. . . . I was beginning to fear that no one would say those things that you said.'[18] Anthony Barnes remembers going on a tour of the Cotswolds with Gerald Berners and JB. They were driving very slowly through the Barringtons looking at cottages when a man behind them got furious at being held up. When he was finally able to pass he drew up beside them and shouted, 'Why the hell are you driving so slowly?' JB, who was at the wheel, pretended to be infirm by contorting his face and Gerald said very calmly, 'I'm sorry but my friend is deaf.'[19]

In September 1950 a French girl called Françoise Allard arrived to learn English. She was intent on learning as many colloquialisms as possible. One afternoon she came downstairs after a rest and said proudly, 'I have just had forty wanks.' I didn't understand why JB and Maurice Bowra exploded into laughter.

By the autumn of that year JB had begun to run out of the steam that life in a remote place demanded. The time he spent in trains, or the car, particularly from Didcot to Farnborough, made him exhausted and when he got home there was likely to have been a crisis of the kind bred by large houses. My parents, for example, could not afford the estimate they received for putting electricity down the drive. In a desperate bid to escape, JB rented Kelmscott House, near Lechlade, but we never moved into it. In December 1950 Miss Webb left to become a nurse and missionary. JB wrote to her after Christmas, 'Alas, alas, on the day after Boxing Day Fritz peacefully died behind the boiler in the kitchen, we think he broke his heart when you left. Sixteen was v. old for a cat.'[20] I remember JB was very depressed when Fritz died. For my brother and myself one of our most vivid memories of Farnborough is of the morning when JB found Fritz lying there, stiff as a board. He had been with my parents since their first year at Uffington and had been named after a passing acquaintance.

If JB wanted to look on the gloomy side of life he could be particularly good at it. The group of elm trees outside the church at Farnborough had been felled and the ancient cathedral-like barn which bordered our garden pulled down by the farmer, Mr Laurence. JB minded intensely and although he and PB were loved by the village, they began to put the wheels in motion for selling up. 'We had some good times with the Betjemans,' remembers Miss Mabel Dearlove who taught my brother the piano. 'We had dances on the lawn at the Rectory every June and Mr Abbot hung up hundreds of fairy lights on the trees and the Iona Band came up to play from Wantage. They never had a wireless you know. Mrs Betjeman used to bring the Pipers and the Lancasters to listen to the set in my cottage if Mr Betjeman was on. . . . We loved the Betjemans, they were the best.'[21]

Lionel Perry wrote on 12 July 1951, 'I hear with uncertain feelings that you are leaving the Downs and establishing yourself in a country town. Of course many respectable burgher families have started in that way. Do not be over-ambitious, but perhaps we shall see you or your descendants "landed" again.'[22]

The whole family had uncertain feelings about leaving Farnborough. It was the end of nearly twenty years of village life. That September we moved the five miles down the long hills to alien territory in red-brick Wantage. On the last trip down with the last of the furniture, Paul and I travelled in the trolley cart with my mother driving. Terry and Maureen Carter, Billy Wilkinson and my best friend, Juney White, came with us. I cried all the way and once the village children caught the Reliance bus from Wantage market-place back up the slow, steep crawl to Farnborough, I knew that things could never be as happy again.

The ensuing decades were to see the unprecedented success of JB's *Collected Poems* and his emergence as a television broadcaster and film-maker. From now on he was to spend more and more time in London. The limelight had begun to glow around him.

1. JB, Susan Barnes interview, 'Betjeman I Bet Your Racket Brings You in a Pretty Packet', *Sunday Times Magazine* (30 January 1972).
2. Alan Pryce-Jones, letter to CLG.
3. Margaret Wintringham, CLG interview (1993).
4. Copy in BBC archives.
5. Lord Kinross's papers, Huntington Library, California.
6. JB's papers, University of Victoria, British Columbia.
7. John and Myfanwy Piper's papers.
8. Margaret Wintringham's papers.
9. Ruth Webb, CLG interview (1993).
10. JB's papers.
11. Patrick Cullinan's papers.
12. Cyril Connolly's papers, Tulsa, Oklahoma.
13. Edmund Blunden's papers, University of Texas, Austin.
14. Ruth Webb, CLG interview (1993).
15. Michael Maclaren's papers.
16. Patrick Cullinan's papers.
17. Patrick Cullinan, reminiscences sent to CLG.
18. JB's papers.
19. Anthony Barnes, CLG interview (1992).
20. Ruth Webb's papers.
21. Mabel Dearlove, CLG interview (1993).
22. JB's papers.

To Anthony Barnes   The Old Rectory
                                                Farnborough
                                                Wantage
3 July 1949   Berkshire

Dear Little Prawls,
EDWARDIAN SONGS
The drawing room ballad of the nineties had gone out and musical
comedy and variety had come in. I should say any songs from SAN
TOY[?] or THE GEISHA would be appropriate – e.g. one of my favourites
from the BELLE OF NEW YORK I think is

> Rhoda
> Rhoda
> Ran a pagoda
> Selling tea
> And syrup and soda

and a last line something about 'the pretty pagoda Rhoda ran'. I should
think all three of those light operas were recorded.

Variety is represented by songs sung by Harry Lauder (still alive),
Marie Lloyd, Gus Elen, all of which are recorded. But sometimes these
songs are Victorian.
EDWARDIAN NOVELISTS
Anthony Hope = The Dolly Dialogues, or is it Victorian? *W. B. Maxwell*
(the chapter on the River in the *Countess of Maybury* is perfect) see also his
Vivien and *Ragged Messenger* and *Guarded* for social scenes.
Miss MacNaughton (*A Lame Dog's Diary*, *The Expensive Miss Du Cane*).
J. C. Snaith.

All of which are to be found in Nelson's Sevenpenny Library, whose
catalogue at the back of most volumes is a superb guide to Edwardian
fiction.
EDWARDIAN POETS
Stephen Phillips. 'Marpessa' has a sort of lush beauty especially in its Art
Nouveau opening lines.
Sir William Watson. 'Wordsworth's Grave' is rather good in the
pontifical manner.

But both these men I chose as characteristic of their time, not as men
of genius like Yeats and Hardy, who were of course writing then.

I loved *Parade!* [An Etonian rag.]

I love Dorchester Abbey particularly the sculptured knights and glass.

I look forward to seeing you on my return from Isle of Man at 45 Gloucester Place Street Terrace Square Mews, w1 on Friday as near seven as I can make it. Off to c/o Mrs Cullin, Seaforth House, high teas a speciality, Crown St Peel, I. of M. today.

Love, JB

A.B. wanted to put on an Edwardian evening at the Praed Society, the Eton Poetry Society. JB was fond of music-hall throughout his life.

To H. S. Goodhart-Rendel   The Old Rectory
                                                    Farnborough
                                                    Wantage
13 July 1949   Berkshire

Dear Goodhart-Rendel,

I really cannot manage anything as early as November 29th on [G.E.] Street. There is all the getting together of the slides and finding out of pictures and re-reading of books on top of the fearful hack work I have to do to keep myself alive, and I see no chance of doing justice to Mr Street by November. So let us leave it vague and when I have completed something I will let you know and deliver the lecture to you in private at Hatchlands or in Crawford Street and then you can add and subtract from it.

The Isle of Man is really most interesting. There is a great deal of vigorous Abbotsford-style Gothic there. I say Abbotsford-style deliberately because Scott's novel *Peveril of the Peak* started a romantic craze for the Isle of Man. If you do not know the place already it is well worth a visit and so I am just going to give you a few reminiscences while it is fresh in my brain, on the chance that you may not know it.

The Castle Mona Hotel, once the house of the Duke of Atholl who sold the island to the British Government, was designed by George Stewart in a chaste Gothic style and is ashlar-faced, with lovely pale marble-looking slate. But the real burst of original Gothic came along between 1820 and 1835 and was all the work of John Welch who did the most dashing stuff in an Early English style in the way of churches with original spires and towers, the palace of the Bishop of Sodor and Man, the noble King William's College which you may see from the airport, and a series of castellated houses along the cliff tops of Douglas Bay and a romanic Tower of Refuge on a rock in the middle of the bay. In between these buildings at the same time were built Classic terraces in the Kemptown style, and these survive.

In the sixties, when Lancashire mill-workers seem to have started that mass migration for a fortnight in the summer (which still goes on), Governor Lord Loch caused five-storeyed, bay-windowed, stucco terraces to be built along the sea front itself and below the Classic and castellated work of the Georgian town. I must say I think it all blends together beautifully, and what with the narrow gauge railways, electric trams, horse trams, the glens, the fairy lights and the wild mountains and unexplored lanes among whitewashed Celtic cottages, where people still speak Manx, the island is all an old sensualist like me could desire. For instance, in one day I was able to get lost among blueberries on a mountainside looking for a Celtic chapel and then, after a long downhill walk, to take a bus and then a train to Douglas where I drank champagne at two shillings a glass and ate shrimps and mussels and then went to the biggest dance hall in Douglas to see thousands of couples dancing beautifully in a vast cavern of cream-coloured, White City Baroque.

Yours sincerely, J. Betjeman

JB had long admired the celebrated architect H.S.G.-R. Hatchlands was H.S.G.-R.'s handsome mid-Georgian (1750) house in Surrey with gardens by Repton and Jekyll.

H.S.G.-R. replied (19 July 1949), 'Douglas Loch, the son of the Manx Governor, was a very great friend of mine . . . there used to be lots of statistical-looking Manx literature in his Suffolk house.'

To Anne Barnes

16 July 1949

The Old Rectory
Farnborough
Wantage
Berkshire

My dear Anne,

Words can't express what a relief to me the visit to Prangs was. Of course, I have a strong feeling of guilt that I have offended The Commander. But guilt is *sometimes* enjoyable. Not this guilt nor my other guilt!

Like a fool I went there. With priggishness and self-righteousness, with fear and love, I insisted on doing nothing. She – oh God I can't put it down in ink or pencil or charcoal or anything – she put up with my priggishness. And now what have I? Remorse, internal writhings, detestation of everything here, inability to concentrate, fear of her revenge on me and the prospect of several more deliciously wonderful visits each with its sad ending. Sad for her, self-righteous for me, misery for us both. Yet if one 'went the whole hog' as we used to say at Marlborough, the guilt would be worse still and I wouldn't see her again.

I will say this about it all however. I am a bit of a puzzle at the moment to Propeller. The Stakhanovism (working out in four years, by working very hard, a plan designed for five years) resulting from the first thrill has died down. Sobotnick (working on Sunday) is likely to be a consolation.

Sobotnick, my Stakhanovist.

With the North Sea in your eyes – I can't go on with it yet but it is all so badly, thrillingly and attractively unattractive.

Much love and many thanks from

Lady Bates

PS I couldn't go to Little P.'s Praed Society on Friday for charitable and genuine reasons. I had to take a man by motor to a doctor in Swindon and so missed all possible trains to Eton. JB

'Prangs' was another nickname for Prawls, the Barneses' house.

JB first met Margaret Wintringham at a Swindon Poetry Society evening in June 1949. She came from Lincolnshire. He referred to her as 'his Stakhanovite' because she and her husband were members of the Communist Party.

Lady Bates was the widow of Sir Percy Bates, who ran the Cunard Line. Their only son, Eddie, was a close friend of A.B.'s.

To Anne Barnes   The Old Rectory
                                                    Farnborough
                                                    Wantage
19 July 1949   Berkshire

Dear Anne,

I am so very pleased to have your letter. I received a beautiful slap-in-the-eye from my Stakhanovite yesterday in the form of this quatrain:

> For J.B.
> Remember when in your philosophy
> Human relationships take second place

> Your chastity is founded on my charity
> And through my grief you reach your State of Grace.

Of course, she's quite right. If I'm not prepared to risk mortal sin, then I shouldn't go on with it. Anyhow she leaves today for three weeks in France and I shall begin to breathe again. She is very funny. But oh that Party line, that runs through her! It is shiveringly attractive and horrifying at once. There is always that delicious sense (which the Commander too manages to carry) that one has gone just a little too far.

I delivered my address on Tennyson on Monday last and Little Prawls made a sweet little speech of thanks afterwards. It had obviously been most carefully thought out and was delivered in halting and blushing turns and he looked just as though he was staying up late at Prawls when [the Commander], you and I wanted to have a nice sex talk after he had gone to bed. I have put square brackets round the Commander because, although he would very much enjoy a nice sex talk, he would not like to think we knew he would enjoy it.

My Stakanovite said to me yesterday, 'Your exaggerations embarrass and frighten me.' She is very funny – I mean she really does like jokes and doesn't mind being laughed at.

Give my love to Cambridge and to the David girl [Nora].

Much love from Joe Stalin

A.B. wrote (undated), 'What a mess you seem to be getting into. *If*, as we agreed, the Church is really after common-sense aims, preservation of saints and the Family etc., WHY is it more mortally sinful to go to bed than to do what you are doing, which involves you in frustration, self-righteousness, and detestation of your home? ALL or (preferably) NOTHING would be the advice of yours (unbelieving) truly.'

JB gave his address to the Praed Society.

To Mr Boswell

The Old Rectory
Farnborough
Wantage
Berkshire

20 July 1949

Dear Mr Boswell,
I enclose a receipt from Thos. Cook for my air journey to the Isle of Man. I arrived at Ronaldsway on July 4th and had to take a taxi from there to Douglas – one pound – in order to catch the last train to Peel – two and sixpence. I stayed in lodgings and had to share a bedroom with

a stranger on my last night on the island, which was Thursday night. But that did not matter as it is a Manx custom and does not seem unusual over there. And since your work must be very dull, dealing with people's expenses and with contracts, I will tell you some more about my lodgings in order to put some colour into your life.

There was only one bathroom and the queue for this in the morning was extraordinary, as there were something like twenty-four of us in the house. There was no hot water and only one water closet. All that is very Manx and explains why there are so many hundreds of public wash houses in every town on the island. On the other hand, the food was excellent – two eggs and three sausages for breakfast and heaps of butter and marmalade and toast and tea at a table with a nice large Lancashire family, three generations of it. High tea with Manx kippers cured in wood smoke at six o'clock, then off to the dance halls of Douglas by luxury coach or narrow gauge railway. And my bill for the four and half days I was in those lodgings, including food, was two pounds. I was only once in to high tea, however, and, of course, I spent most money travelling about the island, going to dance halls, travelling in luxury coaches and electric tramcars, and on the last day I hired a taxi for two pounds twelve and sixpence in order to visit the one part of the island I had not explored away up in the north and far from railway or luxury coaches.

I do not know how you would like to assess all these peregrinations. I have kept no accurate account. It would be a mass of sixpences and shillings and one-and-sixpences paid out about every hour of every day, and then of course there is what I had to pay for my outside meals. I think if you gave me the usual daily allowance I would not lose very much on it. And if you like to add to that the two taxis I took, I think I should come out all square.

It would be very nice to see you in person one day, when I am in London and you are too, about my expenses for these 'Coast and Country' broadcasts. Here again assessment is not very easy since I have to drive to the places in my own motor car, when it will go so far, and I wonder whether there is a flat rate.

Yours sincerely, John Betjeman

To H. S. Goodhart-Rendel

The Old Rectory
Farnborough
Wantage

7 August 1949

Berkshire

Dear Goodhart-Rendel,

J. B. Clacy and his wife had their latter lives saddened because their daughter made a runaway marriage at the age of fourteen.

Joseph Morris (of Morris and Stallwood) was articled to him. Joseph was Berks County Surveyor and then joined the Agapemone, taking his son Frank and two daughters with him. Stallwood put it about that Morris had gone mad and so Stallwood collared M's work. But Joseph made a recovery and got back some of it. Frank Morris designed the Pearl Assurance Building and McIlroy's, Reading, and died many years ago of enteric in a flat in Park Lane, W1. Joseph and Frank together designed the Agapemonite church at Clapton; Frank got Walter Crane to do the glass using James Sylvester Sparrow's patent process. The four beasts below the steeple were carved by A. G. Walter. Frank Morris found him. All this I had from Miss V. S. Morris who did Wokingham Police Station and much sub-Voysey stuff round Reading and is almost the last Agapemonite and dusts the Art Nouveau Temple at Spaxton, Somerset (and which she art nouveaued herself) and puts flowers on Smyth-Pigott's grave, which is under the polished parquet floor at the Ag. church, his body standing upwards, I believe. As you know, he thought he was Our Lord and so did Miss Morris think he was. I love a few facts and thought you would like these.

Yours, J. Betjeman

John Berry Clacy (1810–80) was Berkshire County surveyor, auctioneer and postmaster. He built a number of largely undistinguished buildings in the Reading area using both Gothic and Italianate styles.

The 'Church of the Agapemone' was a nineteenth-century religious sect founded by two ex-Anglican clergymen who claimed to personify the Holy Ghost. The 'Agapemone' (meaning 'love feast') was opened in Spaxton in 1849. The movement soon dwindled after a trial which disclosed how corrupt the morals of its members had become. In 1890 the sect came briefly back into being at Clapton with a new leader, J. H. Smyth-Pigott (who believed he was Christ) and a new name, 'the Children of the Resurrection'. The church at Clapton was called 'The Ark of the Covenant'.

Miss V. S. Morris was a hundred years old when JB met her.

H.S.G.-R. replied (12 August 1949), 'Your letter shall be treasured. I used to know the sculptor Walker who did the Evangelists' symbols at the Agapemone Church at Clapton. . . . I never can remember how disreputable the Agapemonites were.'

To H. S. Goodhart-Rendel   The Old Rectory
                                                         Farnborough
                                                         Wantage
16 August 1949   Berkshire

Dear Goodhart-Rendel,
Miss V. S. Morris is an architect and was apparently one of the first
women to practise the art on these shores. She wears a collar and tie and
one feels that she ought to have a straw hat and mutton chop sleeves and
a bicycle, it's that sort of collar and tie. She and her brother designed
Wokingham Police Station and there are several houses by her at the
Agapemone, including her own. Her style might be termed as
Voysey-Italianate with plate-glass windows.
    Yours ever, J. Betjeman

> H.S.G.-R. had written (12 August 1949), 'I always thought that the only female
> architect in practice in the days of my youth was Ruth Mercier in France.'

To T. S. Eliot   The Old Rectory
                                                         Farnborough
                                                         Wantage
23 August 1949   Berkshire

Dear Tom,
I have become 'Literary Advazer' to *Tame and Tade* which means going
in on Mondays from two-thirty till five and distributing the books.
    I CAN'T UNDERSTAND EZRA POUND. But you can.
    I hardly dare ask you, but if you have time, could you write about
those seventy cantos for *Tame and Tade*?
    Probably not – but oh I do hope so and if you say 'yes' I will send you
your publication. The pay is *awful*.
    Yorz ever, John Betjeman
    PS I am in bed with 'flu but go to Cornwall for a week this week –
BODARE, TREBETHERICK, WADEBRIDGE.

> JB had been taken up by the owner of *Time and Tide*, Lady Rhondda, and was Literary
> Adviser and then Literary Editor until December 1953, when he was fired.
>   T.S.E. did not review *The Pisan Cantos* by Ezra Pound, but Wolf Mankowitz did
> instead. 'Put simply, the situation of Pound seems to be that of an enthusiastic doctor
> beginning with an intense interest in the source and cure of a dangerous disease and
> finishing as a dreadful example of the disease itself.'

To Anne Barnes

The Old Rectory
Farnborough
Wantage
Berkshire

9 September 1949

Dear Anne,

It is hard to know which to thank the more – you, the Commander or Little P – for my happy stay in France. You, I think, did the most difficult things, like buying a ticket at Auxerre, the Commander on the other hand did the *organising*, Little P, as always, supplied the culture.

A terrible thing happened on the train. I found a carriage to myself (there were no firsts, only seconds and thirds) and a ticket collector climbed in as the train was moving. I gave him my first class ticket with some happy little phrases in French and he moved on. *He must have thought I was Frog* – for about twenty minutes later he came back to the compartment, settled himself down with a pipe and talked volubly and amiably to me – I did not understand one word. He left in a huff.

We had a happy time at Trebetherick and I was able to keep up a daily correspondence with Margaret Wintringham. It loosened the emotional strain and crystallised our relationship, if I may coin a few metaphors. We also went over to see Gerald Berners who was staying with Rowse in a small house outside St Austell and near St Just-in-Roseland. Anthony West, who came with us, called the house St Queer-in-Rowsland. Rex [Warner] and Ex [Lady Rothschild] have made a great impression on Gerald. I forgot to tell him about Mrs Reggie Warner.

I am happier and sillier than usual and drinking heavily. I would like to go to France again. That Vouvray! Those snails! Oh! It was worth the journey back.

Love to you all, John B

JB had been on holiday to France in July with the Barneses. He flew from Le Touquet to Lydd and saw Chartres and Vézelay for the first time.

'Ex' was Barbara, née Hutchinson, first wife of Victor Rothschild.

A.B. replied (11 September 1949), 'I was so glad to hear that you are happier and drinking – what could be nicer – and also that you enjoyed France. We *adored* having you.'

To Henry Sidney Rogers   Oxford

[September 1949 or 1950]

> Oh with what proud delight we hear
> From one whom greatly we revere
> A man who knows his Street from Scott
> Who knows what's good and what is not.
> Long may the bells of New St Old
> Ring words and changes manifold
> So that his Gothic office throbs
> With clients climbing up with jobs –
> Cathedrals, screens and heating plans
> And palaces for suffragans.
> And long may Inspiration come
> E'en when St Aldate bells are dumb
> From meditating in the night
> On Butterfield and William White
> Xccept our thanks and deep respect
> Dear Alderman and architect.

JP [John Piper] and JB

> H.S.R. of Oxford specialized in ecclesiastical architecture, including furnishing the
> military and Lady chapels of Christ Church Cathedral.

To Sir Leslie Scott   The Old Rectory
                                                            Farnborough
                                                            Wantage
9 September 1949   Berkshire

Dear Sir Leslie,
A Senior Engineer of the M[inistry] of H[ealth] called I. H. Hainsworth
M[ember of the] I[nstitution of] C[ivil] E[ngineers] is to hold the Public
Enquiry at Letcombe on 29th. Of MICE and men.

The S[ociety for the] P[rotection of] A[ncient] B[uildings] tells me
that the C[ouncil for the] P[reservation of] R[ural] E[ngland] is not to
employ counsel and that Mr Langley Taylor will represent the CPRE.
Is that all right?

I see the line the Government will take. It will be turned into an
inter-ministerial fight, the M of H scoring off the M[inistry] of T[own]

and C[ountry] P[lanning]. The M of H will be severely (and bogusly) 'practical' – sewage alone will be discussed. The value of the old houses and the life of the village will be deemed irrelevant. What ought we to do? I think we should protest against someone who is merely a glorified Sanitary Engineer being made judge of a case which is more than just sewage disposal. Will you write a letter to *The Times* to this effect? The announcement is public. The M of H will then feel it will have to consider other matters than sewage and so it will not lose face with the M of T & CP. To hell with these civil servants!

Yours sincerely, John Betjeman

L.S. had been a Lord Justice of Appeal and was a great figure in local Berkshire politics and agriculture.

Letcombe Basset, a village near Wantage, was considered to have had inadequate drainage and therefore the RDC condemned the cottages, arguing that the village was too small to be self-sustaining and thus the cost of installing a sewerage system would be unjustified. The case rose to national prominence when JB and the planner, Thomas Sharp, discussed it on the BBC on 1 February 1949. It became a *cause célèbre* because the same situation was foreseen arising in many other villages. A Ministry of Health inquiry was held in September 1949 but by April 1950 the RDC had backed down and agreed to install drainage and recondition some of the cottages. Etchells, who lived locally, kept a watching brief on the case for the SPAB.

JB persuaded Frederick Etchells to attend the inquiry. 'For goodness' sake do go. . . . It is a painful but necessary public duty,' he wrote (8 September 1949).

To Anthony Barnes

The Old Rectory
Farnborough
Wantage
Berkshire

6 October 1949

Dear Little Prawls,
Very nice indeed to hear from you. Sad to think of your ups and downs. I should have thought it was the *boredom* which was the worst thing about your ordeal. The Homo petty officer sounds interesting. I'm never very worried – not so much as I should be – about sexual irregularity. I find I hate *power maniacs* more than sex-maniacs or anyone else and will forgive the wildest sensual excesses for a spark of kindness, generosity and humour in the profligate. But those are my views and I doubt if God agrees with them.

The Corsham district is certainly rewarding. The Court itself is superb inside. Do go and see Clifford Ellis if you have a chance or Lord M[ethuen] so as to see the Saloon there. I enclose a letter of intro in case you have an opportunity of using it. Just say you are a friend of Penelope and me to the Methuens and that we asked you to call – that should be enough for them. There is much eighteenth-century work in Corsham behind that Vic-Jacobean exterior.

I hope you will enjoy Bradford on Avon. It is a winner of a place. So is Steeple Ashton and so is South Wraxall. The Manor House is where I found Ackermann's *Public Schools, Oxford, Cambridge, Microcosm of London* all in mint condition stacked under some golf clubs in the ground floor gents.

How enjoyable to sit in a transept in Redcliffe Church and dream of Chatterton during Evensong. [William Lisle] Bowles has some good sonnets about Redcliffe Church.

I must stop. This pen tires me out. It *will* not write clearly.

Love from us all – we all have colds except me. John B

> A.B. was serving in the Navy at Corsham. He sat in Corsham church porch weeping those first few days after his arrival. He visited most of JB's suggested places by bike, including Hardenhuish Church, St Mary's Street Chippenham, Lacock, Castle Combe, the failed spa at Melksham and Eddington.
>   Clifford Ellis was the princpal of the Bath Academy of Art, which was bombed out during the war and moved to Corsham, where it remained for some time afterwards.
>   PB's cousins, the Methuens, lived at Corsham Court. Also 'Admiral Woad, Propeller's very dim uncle is near, and there are lots of box pews in that curious county.'

To Anthony Barnes   Trefelix
                                                       Trebetherick
                                                       Wadebridge
15 October 1949   Cornwall

Dear Little Prawls,
Very nice indeed to hear from you. I am just here for two nights as I had to do some very silly broadcasting (at which I was a complete failure and will not be asked again) called *Any Questions* with brilliant FREDDIE Grisewood and a team of 'experienced broadcasters'. They were *so* nice to me afterwards, I knew I had not been quite up to the mark and not so good as they were.

I had better not write too openly on the subject you mention for fear that letters are read by your comrades in arms. But of course the affair is a splendid thing and probably will prove the deepest, purest and most remembered emotional incident of your life. One suffers more the younger one is; less the older one is. The compensation for suffering so much when young is that one recovers much more quickly. Don't bother yourself about the rights and wrongs of that sort of love in relation to the Faith. The whole question, so long as it is love, is Academic. When it turns into lust (and there often is a certain amount of lust can drive out love or an affair can be wholly lust) then whether it is heter or homo makes little difference. And anyhow the ages of eighteen to twenty-two are, as an old reprobate friend of mine used to say, 'years of ungovernable lust'. The fact that it is ungovernable makes it less of a sin at that age (eighteen to twenty-two), though it can be mortal of course if done deliberately and with full consent. In that case, confess it and receive absolution. But if you look at a self-examination form or read any Moral theology, you will see that lust is only one of the seven deadly sins. There are six others just as bad. I read 'Maud' in the train going down to Falmouth yesterday and thought how very fine the third part is – or is it the second – where he describes the sea shell on the beach. I also read 'Locksley Hall – Sixty Years After' with its amazing foresight into the future. Ah! but 'In Memoriam' has the grandest Tennyson of all – such descriptions of Lincolnshire! Don't be too bothered to try to make a consecutive argument out of the poem. I am certain it is a series of elegiac lyrics strung together in what is little more than a sequence of moods and chronology. If you can get a chance to read favourite passages aloud to yourself you will find they are heightened in meaning and melody.

I would like to know how long you will be in the Duchy [of Cornwall]. I have some books and maps which will be useful to you if you are there for any time. Today they were surf-bathing at Polzeath and I had a picnic on the Rumps with a creamy white sea below us and a blow hole spouting fountains of foam to the cliff tops. Write again – to Farnborough.

Love, JB

> JB made his first of many appearances on *Any Questions* on 14 October 1949 with John Arlott, A. G. Street and Lewis Hastings. Freddie Grisewood was the Question Master. JB referred to an affair A.B. had started at Eton with another boy.

To Candida Betjeman   The Athenaeum
18 October 1949   Pall Mall SW1

Dear Candida,
I am very pleased to have your nice letter and I am sorry I have not a

nice postcard to send to you like Mummy did. Here are some fairies:

but I think they are witches pretending to be fairies. I liked the drawing you did of trees and flowers and yourself.

Here I am sitting in this club.

Love from Daddy

To Mr Boswell   The Old Rectory
                                               Farnborough
                                               Wantage
26 October 1949   Berkshire

Dear Boswell,
The mileage from Wantage to Winchester and back is 80; Wantage to Bournemouth and back 199; Wantage to Weymouth and back 204. Wantage to Clevedon 97, Clevedon to Porlock 79, Porlock to Ilfracombe 45, Ilfracombe to Bridgwater 80, Bridgwater to Wantage 101. Wantage to Sidmouth 175, Trebetherick to Looe and back 90,

Trebetherick to Bristol (to give broadcast) 170, Bristol to Wantage 70.

These mileages are reckoned by placing a ruler across a 10-inch map and adding 10 miles in long distances to allow for curves and diversions. I have not got an AA book, which would be invaluable for working out these distances more accurately, and if you care to check them with an AA book I shall take no offence.

You tell me that I should not count my journey to Cornwall for my holiday as part of my expenses for these broadcasts and that the most reasonable thing to do would be to make a calculation of the loop out of my journey to Cornwall in order to reach Sidmouth. I find this very difficult to do since if I were to go to Cornwall the normal way from here, I would go via Marlborough, Frome, Taunton, Exeter, Oke-hampton, Launceston, whereas to go to Sidmouth I went via Marlbo-rough, Frome, Bruton, Yeovil, Honiton, Sidmouth, thence back to Exeter. Moreover, I forgot to tell you that my return journey was not straight home but involved going via Bristol and staying a night on the way in order that I might give one broadcast and record the other. I would not normally, if I were returning from Cornwall to here, go via Bristol. You will thus see that the journey to Cornwall by motor car, though it may have been convenient for me to have a motor car in Cornwall for my holidays, is convenient to you since it enabled me to keep, in far less time and at far less expense to you, three separate BBC appointments, i.e. Sidmouth, Looe and Bristol. I have, therefore, calculated the mileage on the principle of Wantage to Sidmouth single, Trebetherick to Looe return, Trebetherick-Bristol-Wantage single. This leaves for my poor basic the journey from Sidmouth to Trebetherick. Nowhere in my calculations have I been able to work out a detailed consumption of petrol because, obviously, when one is motoring from Porlock to Ilfracombe and back, the appalling hills, twists and bends used up years of my aged motor car's remaining life.

I fear I have no note of my rail and boat fare for Winchester-Yarmouth. At Yarmouth, I hired a taxi for the day, price thirty shillings.

You will not forget, will you, when making your calculations of my expenses, that on every journey I have had to buy meals and spend the whole day in the place visited and also to cruise around the neighbour-hood of the place, as a reference to my delicate little talks on the places described will prove to you.

Though it should be on a separate piece of paper, I should like to enter a protest about the Special Fee of eight guineas for my visit to Devonport. Although that talk was only for four minutes, the time taken up was infinitely more than that which would be taken up if I were to write a broadcast lasting thirty minutes. I think you should seriously consider revising your scale of payment for outside broadcasts. You remember that when we met I said I thought four guineas was absurd for four minutes when I had to go specially down to Devonport. You therefore said eight guineas and I agreed. I have had the cheque for that amount, including my expenses and I have decided not to cash it in order to register my protest more effectively and to show that, though I am not J. B. Priestley, I am at least sincere in my objection to this rate of pay.

In order to reach Devonport before three o'clock on the afternoon of October 19th, I had to leave London by a train from Paddington at seven thirty a.m. At Bristol I had to jump out of the train and telephone to the BBC to find whereabouts in Devonport or Plymouth I was supposed to appear in order to make this broadcast. I was told at the Devonport Column itself at three p.m. When I arrived at North Road, as I had my luggage for the night (incidentally, I also had to ask the BBC where accommodation had been found for me), I took a taxi to Devonport Column and arrived shortly after two thirty. It was raining and there was nobody about and the door to the Column was padlocked. Having had no lunch, as there was no restaurant car in the train, I went into a public house and drank whisky to keep out the driving cold. Eventually I found some engineers in the Police Station near the Column at Devonport and, although there was no producer, the engineers and I managed to work out a performance between us. I had to stand at the top of the Column, a hundred and twenty-four feet high, in an icy wind and with no protection from the weather beyond my own clothes, and I was expected to give a broadcast in the dark from this windy height. That would obviously have been impossible so the co-operative engineers and I faked it. They held some microphones up to the wind and I went down to the Police Station and pretended to be very out-of-breath and gave my broadcast from its snug comfort. I was meant to be describing Plymouth from the Devonport Column at night. I was due to have my script ready at eight eighteen and it was not dark until seven thirty. I wrote some preliminary stuff and then had to put in at the last minute, sentences about what the view was like. That meant dashing up the stairs of the Column as soon as it *did* get dark and coming down and writing the stuff against time and with a good deal of outside interruption. This I was able to do but I maintain not many people could have done so. If the broadcast is no good, and I am quite prepared to believe it is a failure (I have not listened to it), then the thirteen

pounds, six and threepence which you have paid me and which I have
not cashed is a fair price. But if the broadcast *is* any good, it is absurdly
small because the time involved was from seven thirty in the morning
until after ten at night. The exposure to weather which I endured on the
top of the Column while the rest of the recording that was being done in
Bristol was going on, and while I was meant to be preparing my first
thoughts on the view, gave me sciatica and a cold from which I have not
yet recovered. I then had to stay the night in a hotel and I did not get
back here until five o'clock the next evening. Just at the good old
piece-work rates and disregarding the discomforts and length of
journey involved, about thirty conscious working hours of my life were
spent on the BBC's behalf for eight guineas. This I think you will find,
works out at about five shillings and sevenpence an hour. What do you
pay your electricians? What do you pay J. B. Priestley? It would be
interesting to make a comparison with the rate you offer me.

Yours sincerely, John Betjeman

PS None of this should be allowed to reflect on the producer at
Bristol. He knew what he was doing when he asked me to make the
broadcast. It is simply an account of the amount of hours and work
involved. JB

To John Summerson

[November]

Bermondsey gas was bright in a very Low church in Nunhead
(The which, despite its name, is a Protestant quarter of London).
Forward I bent in my pew shading my eyes and waiting
For the Minister – not a priest no sacrificer at altars –
To give the blessing, when oh! such a pyrotechnic explosion –
Saxons and mines of serpents and Roman (shame on them!) candles,
Catherine wheels and rockets and that illegal mixture

Made of potassium chlorate and sulphide of arsenic, bursting,
Transcended what you would see at the Palace from Penge or Anerley
And all but subdued my sense. I clung to the upright standard
Ordered by Mr Vulliamy (I'm an architect by profession)
From Skidmore and Sons of Coventry ecclesiastical ironwork,
I clung to the bracket believing that stained glass windows by Hardman
Had let themselves out of their lights and were whirling about before
    me.
My fellow churchwarden started I took one look at a capital
Dear old middle pointed (I've done much better you'll notice
Although in a later style, in my work for the corporation)
I took one look at the cap and one at my fellow churchwarden
So this was the World. Goodbye. I glanced at the Holy Table
Thankful even in death that we took no Eastward Position
And then I was where I am communicating to you, sir,
Through the medium of Mr Betjeman poetaster and poet
Who possibly understands the loss of the world I lived in
Here by my windy graveside. I am buried in Norwood Cemetery.
Answer ....

> The answer was 'Sir Horace Jones' (*see following letter*). When published in 1950 in *The Harlequin* (along with his poem 'Late Flowering Lust') its name was changed from 'Sir Horace Jones' to 'The Corporation Architect'.

To John Summerson

The Old Rectory
Farnborough
Wantage
Berkshire

5 November 1949

My dear Coolmore,

You were right about Sir Horace [Jones] and he did not die in a church –
I put that in to make it difficult. But I think he must have been very Low
church as he was such a prominent Freemason. And Freemasons, as
you will know from your Harrow experience, are always Low. That is
interesting about him being so fat. Have you got a picture of him? I
expect Bunning was thin. I did not know he did that Egyptian
Columbarium at Highgate.

I am very interested in Sir Horace's work. I like the Tower Bridge so
much, especially since it was attacked by Gloag, and I like the Guildhall
Library, which was such a nice setting for Douthwaite.

Yours, John Rennie MacBetjeman

Horace Jone. (1819–87), architect and surveyor to the City of London Corporation, designed Tower Bridge 1886–94. In his lecture 'Honour Your Forebears', read to RIBA in January 1954, JB referred to Jones as one of his heroes.

John Bunstone Bunning was architect to City of London 1843–63.

JB's signature is a reference to Charles Rennie Mackintosh, designer and architect of the Glasgow School of Art.

To Martyn Skinner

15 November 1949

POETRY (BERKSHIRE LTD.)

Dear boy,

I said to myself, 'I won't write to Martyn S. until I've read his colloquies. I put the book on my desk and went to Cornwall without it. And now I have come back and read it. Now, my dear fellow, have you shown yourself a most complete master of the couplet. You can spring surprises on us with rhythm and rhyme as well as meaning yet always within the bounds of [illegible] demands. I cannot congratulate you too highly on these colloquies. Of course the first is just my subject. But you do not bring it to a conclusion. You leave that swine as satisfied with himself as when he started. But the second colloquy is after my heart and I think its end is superb. There are couplets in both that should be made immortal such as:

> And magic casements open on the foam,
> An inch below the scissors and the comb

Indeed the whole of that passage I think the best in the book.

You know, of course, you will not be read rapidly. Your reputation will grow and grow. There is prophecy as well as lovely descriptions in your lines. People will go on reading these poems and they will be popular with the few always, Crabbe is – o not Crabbe – your only resemblances to him are a love of worthy life and couplets – like Patmore is. Yet in this anthology-ridden age you won't be quoted much but you will always be delighted in by those who find you. I think you do yourself no harm by being scarce and curiously published. It would be nice to have one fairly cheap and widely circulated edition of the forty poems, the letters and these two colloquies to be kept in stock by our old publishers who won't mind a slow sale. Then us collectors can delight in little things like this which you have given to me. I am delighted by the recommendations and my blurb. Why on earth do the printers rush into a size too big a type on pages 39 and 25, in the first for a whole line, in the latter for a single letter? Oh *I do* like the book. A thousand thanks.

Yours, JB

M.S. wrote two books of poems, *Letters to Malaya* (three parts, Putnam, 1941–7) and *Two Colloquies* (Putnam, 1949). *Old Rectory* followed between 1970 and 1977.

To Jane Clark   The Old Rectory
                                         Farnborough
                                         Wantage
16 November 1949   Berkshire

Dear Jane,

I very much enjoyed my comfortable, contented, warmed, well-fed and stimulated evening last week with you and K. and Hanbury and Mrs Lamont at Upper Terrace House. My most vivid recollection after the reading from Peter, is of you on those Oliver Hill stairs with that Tartan shawl over the black dress, the black sleeves showing, the watered grey silk flowing out, your black hair and huge Irish eyes. It really was a lovely picture. You must wear the tartan with that grey dress, whatever K. says, and then take it off when ever you feel warm. Here is the Randolph problem in visual terms:

IDEAL SOLUTION

NEO-GEORGIAN COMPROMISE

GOTHIC REVIVAL COMPROMISE

Please, dear Jane, don't think I advocate this scheme because I think the Randolph is a masterpiece. I simply don't think there is any way of adding to it in order to get in the extra bedrooms which Trust House want to include without producing something that will agree neither with Beaumont Street nor the Randolph. You hit the nail on the head when you said that someone ought to be able to design something beautiful which would excel the buildings either side. But there is not space to do that and to maintain *scale* – even if a genius did exist with the courage of his convictions. I think the best our desiccated age can do with no contemporary style better than the prefab, is to do what will look least offensive. A continued Randolph for those few yards will soon look as though nothing has happened, while elongated Georgian or anything else will look pinched on the site. Anyhow, because I value your opinion, I give you all this in defence of Gothic Revival and hope you won't mind me doing it. I *did* enjoy my evening.

Love to you all, John Betjeman

The application for alterations and additions to the Randolph Hotel in Oxford was passed on 28 October 1949. The 'Gothic Revival compromise' was adopted.

To Kenneth Clark   The Old Rectory
                                        Farnborough
                                        Wantage
16 November 1949   Berkshire

My dear K,
I have written several lines to Jane as a Collins with a visual explanation
of the Randolph extension. But what I wanted to write to you about and
omitted to mention to her (kindly thanking you warmly for your
hospitality and appreciation of me in that preface) is to suggest a
temporary solution for Alan. You say he is a Christian and likes
adventure. Why not get him to stay, if he does not do so already, at the
Trinity Mission or any other mission in [the] slums of London,
Liverpool or Glasgow? All the adventure possible, all the outlets for
energy are there. Also one gets first hand evidence on crime. Also the
regular, almost monastic life in a mission house, is a sure steadying
effect and establisher of true social sense. I tried it myself for some
months at the Magdalen Mission after leaving Oxford. It was valuable
to me. I remember how marvellous Alan was in the Boys' Club at
Yarnton which he visited for about two minutes, joining in *boxing* – the
greatest asset for a 'social worker' – with terrific success. If you approve
the idea, I will get a mission to write to him and to ask for his help. It's in
the jungles of our barbarism at home that most adventure lies.
    Yours, John B

Alan Clark went on to become a Conservative MP and Government Minister.

To George Barnes   The Old Rectory
                                        Farnborough
                                        Wantage
18 November 1949   Berkshire

Intensely Private

My dear Commander,
The only regional branches of the Central Council for the Care of
Churches are the Diocesan Advisory Committees. I am on two –
Oxford and London. I think, speaking for both of them, I can safely say

we would be very annoyed at being thought branches of the Central Council for the Care of Churches. Dr Eeles and Miss Scott, who run the Central Council, are primarily antiquarians and cataloguers and not people whose aesthetic judgement we would ever think of seeking. Thus, if you want to know about the relative architectural merits of an Anglican church, you would be best advised to approach the Secretary of the Advisory Committee of the Diocese in which it is. His name and address will appear in the Diocesan Year Book and I expect all Diocesan Year Books are in your library. So you are back where you started from when you asked me the question. I cannot think why the Central Council for the Care of Churches did not immediately refer you to the Diocesan Advisory Committees concerned. Perhaps it feels as removed from these Committees as some of us do from it.

There is no authoritative body concerned with the architectural merits of Anglican churches. The nearest approach are the Central Council and Diocesan Advisory Committees I have mentioned. The only other solution would be to form your own Committee. I could name such people as Etchells, John Piper, John Summerson, Edward T. Long, Bruce MacFarlane, Peter Fleetwood-Hesketh, and possibly four more, who between them would know every church in England and whose aesthetic opinion would be worth taking. I think it would be wise to form such a Committee if you find you cannot work through Diocesan Advisory Committees. And, of course, the disadvantages of working through Diocesan Advisory Committees is that some of them are bad, particularly in the Northern districts where they are manned by people who are purely antiquarian with an outlook on Post-Reformation or at any rate, Post-Stuart work as prejudiced as the *Little Guides*. Again, other Committees may have got as far as Georgian, now it is so fashionable, and are blind to the merits of the better Victorian work. Miss Scott, for instance, of the Central Council has appalled us on the London Diocesan Committees by recommending incumbents to white-wash brick-faced interiors of Victorian churches.

I should like to hear more about this and to be able to have a finger in it. There are a great many churches which appeal for funds which don't deserve the publicity they get, and a great many others which get no publicity and which deserve it. I have left entirely out of consideration the more important side of this matter, the value of a church as a place of worship, High, Low or Broad, but I imagined you were only writing about architecture.

Yours ever, John Betjeman

G.B. was putting programmes together to display the frail state of England's churches. He was driven barmy by there being no central body.

To Cyril Connolly   The Old Rectory
                                                                 Farnborough
                                                                 Wantage
4 December 1949   Berkshire
II Sunday in Advent

Dear Cyril,
I have bad guilt at not answering your flattering invite, old boy, to put some verse into the 12 Oct Number. I had not any poems by me at the time, I had not written any. Since then I have written two but now I realise it is too late, for the *Church Times* says you are stopping *Horizon* and Capt Bog has written a monody in the *TLS*. I am very sorry about this indeed. I *must* tell you, even at the risk of appearing ridiculous, that the death of *Horizon* is like the death of a relation. You and Raymond M[ortimer] and Peter Q[uennell], but particularly you and Raymond M, set me a standard. I always thought to myself, 'What would Cyril think of this?' or 'This will puzzle old Raymond', and despite nerves and [the] slight infuriation I would feel at [the] thought of how much French you knew, I also knew that you were an essential encouragement. I knew that to appear in *Horizon* was a real honour. In fact I think I was taken seriously first (and therefore took myself more seriously) after you had the courage to print my poems in *Horizon*. For goodness' sake, old boy, don't give up criticising and editing altogether. Appear somewhere, somehow at regular intervals. You are essential. But that only on the literary side. I would like to see you again very much indeed to tell you about *Margaret Wintringham* and love. Please let me know your movements and if you can come here. We have got the house a little warmer and we have some good wine (claret). I must see you soon.
    With deepest sympathy,
    Yours, John B

Horizon lasted from 1940 to 1950. C.C. was principal editor, Stephen Spender associate editor, and Peter Watson the publisher. In his final issue Connolly wrote, 'It is closing time in the gardens of the West and from now on an artist will be judged only by the resonance of his solitude or the quality of his despair.'

To Arthur Bryant

Ye Olde Spynninge Wheel
The Cause Waye
Corfe Castle
Dorset

The feast of St Agatha
and the Sisters Penitentiary 1950

Dear Mr Bryant,
I wonder whether you have heard tell of the Dorset and Corfe Ladies' Literary Guild? Possibly not, for we have only been going a few years. And this is to say that we herewith summon, invite, bid, demand, *command* you to come judge our poetry competition this sennight of July 15th, 16th, 17th, and 18th when we will recite our works by permission of the Verderer of the Isle of Purbeck, within the Castle Ruines. I think you will enjoy it. We cannot of course offer a fee, but will gladly give you and Mrs Bryant tea on each of the afternoons.
    Sincerely yours, Elspeth Hartlepoole-Quile

> The Bryants had moved to Dorset in 1948.

To Patrick Cullinan

The Old Rectory
Farnborough
Wantage
Berkshire

27 January 1950

Dear Patrick Cullinan,
How very nice of you to write to me. How nicer still of you to send me your poem '*ENGLAND 1950*' and your story.
    If you knew what a treat it is to have something worth considering sent to one after the heaps of mediocre verse, you would know how grateful I am to you. I like '*ENGLAND 1950*' very much. I like its two opening stanzas and its last two lines, I would have liked, for formality's sake, to have seen the third stanza bring in Father since you have Son and Holy Ghost and to have compressed its meaning, not stanza length. But that is only a quibble. It is infuriating to have anything one writes criticised and I won't say a single thing derogatory, for anyhow there is nothing derogatory to say. Before saying more about your poetry I want to see more of it – much more. What you don't think any good now, as well as what you like. Old manuscripts are like an artist's sketch

book, you can tell what the poet really likes and really dislikes from them.

Your story is a most accomplished piece. I shared with you in memory that feeling for inanimate objects as a child. They did make a world of their own for themselves. I had forgotten they did until your story reminded me of it. Or perhaps it put the idea into my head. Anyhow I like it a lot – or rather am greatly upset by the story which is what you desire. I hope your nurse did not fall on top of you into a pit in that terrifyingly sensual way. I should like the story unvarnished one day from your lips. Please send more prose. In fact send a little bundle, if you can collect one and can bear to part with it. I will bring it with me when I come to Charterhouse which I do (DV) on February 27th to stay with Mr V. T. S. Russell.

And please write to me again, if you have the time and feel inspired to do so. I may not reply on the dot, but I will eventually.

Of course you will be a writer. Nothing will stop you whatever, not riches or poetry, nor being made to do something else, not anything but illness. I am sure of that.

Yours, John Betjeman

P.C. and JB met when JB came to address the Poetry Society at Charterhouse. JB invited anyone who wrote poetry to send it to him. Cullinan did and their correspondence began. P.C. became an acclaimed poet and short-story writer in South Africa. The poem 'England 1950' was never published though it circulated among Cullinan's contemporaries.

To E. W. Gilbert   The Old Rectory
                                                                      Farnborough
                                                                      Wantage
6 February 1950   Berkshire

Dear Gilbert,

I am most grateful to you for your paper. It came when I was in bed with one of my usual colds and within a few days of Antony Dale's book on the *History and Architecture of Brighton*. I could not help contrasting the two. The Dale book so conventionally written with such a smart Georgian point of view, your own paper better written than Dale's and so much more full-blooded and a much more accurate picture of the town.

I think Jock Murray is absolutely mad not to make use of your material. I shall talk to him about it and give him a last chance and then if you will authorise me, I will approach other publishers. It seems to me that your work impinges on architecture far more than people realise. I have recently had to write a big article on Swindon's architecture for the Corporation and, of course, there is no architecture in the Antony Dale sense of the word in Swindon beyond a house or two in the Old Town. On the other hand, there are many square miles of building, speculative and municipal, and this is where human geography comes in. I do not see why a Regency terrace in Brighton put up by one of the architect builders of late Georgian times should be praised to the skies when a terrace put up by a speculator in Swindon in the eighties and adorned with terracotta should be universally condemned. Both are products of their ages and, though the eighties may seem to us less civilised than the twenties, who are we to judge? Anyhow, I could not help noticing that in the Swindon Council Offices there was a room of records which would be a delight to someone studying the architectural side of human geography. They have there all the plans and elevations and contracts, with names of builders and landowners of all the streets in Swindon from 1871 to the present day. You can therefore trace the whole social history of Swindon in terms of building. The art historians do us damage by severing architecture from the life of the people and turning it into a matter of movement and façades.

I think your paper on Brighton is far more valuable 'art history' than Antony Dale's and far more interesting. Also you have put in a lot of jokes, which is most important. The kind of person who would understand what a great work you are doing is Kenneth Clark, and if you will send me another copy of your Brighton paper I will send it to him with an accompanying letter, unless by chance you know him and have sent one already.

Never fear discouragement! I am quite certain that when you are old and tired you will be inundated with requests for articles and lectures and histories of towns and you will be knighted and given freedoms of cities and imitators will come along who will do your work not quite so well as you have done it.

Again with many thanks,

Yours, JB

PS I say! What a fulsome letter.

E.W.G. was the author of *Brighton: Old Ocean's Bauble* (Methuen, 1954). JB, who probably met him when they both worked in the Admiralty, had long been his admirer. At the time he was the lecturer in Geography at Hertford College, Oxford and Reader in Human Geography.

JB wrote to K. Clark (2 April 1950) enclosing E.W.G.'s pamphlet on Brighton, 'You
are the only person I know who will see what a discovery this man Gilbert is. He is
lecturer in Human Geography at Oxford and a dim member of that dim college
Hertford. He looks like De Valera and he has a wife and, no doubt, a child, in Chalfont
Road. I once heard him lecture and he rose to such heights of eloquence that I thought I
must see more of him. He is not a mere protectionist, he is interested in the past growth
of English towns and has a keen eye for architecture. I am happy to say that he is now
moving out of the eternal Georgian. . . . There are three other people with his sort of
mentality: Arkell, who wrote about Oxford stone and whose book you so much liked, a
man called Hoskins of Leicester University, and Rowse's friend Jack Simmons, also at
Leicester University. Add to these the Principal of Leicester University, F. L.
Attenborough, father of Richard Attenborough the film star. . . .'

My brother, who was a keen geologist and read geography at Oxford, remembers how
JB was a great friend of Arkell's. 'He is the proper sort of geologist,' JB said.

To Mr Ibberson Jones   The Old Rectory
                                                Farnborough
                                                Wantage
15 February 1950   Berkshire

Dear Mr Ibberson Jones,
I well remember your telling me about the great Tennyson at the
Swindon Poetry Society and I am very pleased to have your letter. I
have had a pleasant time this morning reading your poems. Do not
believe that it is any disregard for their merits that makes me refuse to
write a foreword. I particularly liked 'Lone Rider' on page 9 and 'Prairie
Sunday' and the first half of 'Chance Encounter' and 'Ladyday' and
'The Lychgate', particularly the last stanza on page 35, and there are
other poems I liked too.

All the same, I still cannot undertake to write a preface. I never have
written a preface for a book of modern poems and I do not like the idea
of doing one. It is a publishers' ramp in order to get free advertisement
for something they are going to publish. Poems should sell on their
merits. If you were dead and I had undertaken to edit your poems that
would be another matter. And that is I think, the only excuse for a
living writer to write a preface for another one. The next best thing he
can do is to introduce him to publishers.

I am very glad to hear you have had an offer from the Mitre Press and
I hope your book sells well. Don't expect to make any money by it. No
one since Tennyson has made a living by poetry except, perhaps,
Masefield. And, if it is any consolation to you, I have never made more
than sixty pounds on any book I have written.
Yours sincerely, John Betjeman

There is no record of anything having been published by I.J. of the Swindon Poetry Society.

To Anne Barnes   The Old Rectory
                                                    Farnborough
                                                    Wantage
25 February 1950   Berkshire

My dear Anne,
I had delayed my reply to you re March 11th and kind invite, until I knew for certain what was on here then. I had hoped to be able to come away. But now I can't as Woad is comin' to stay and bringin' his manservant (thank heaven) as he is ill and has to be kept quiet and there is nothin' to do here. We have been waitin' to get an answer out of Woad whether he was comin' or not for the past week.

I am anxious indeed to see you. There is no one like you to discuss Love with. I hear you met Osbert Lancaster by the way and had a nice talk about his son William, whose eyes (blue-grey) are as big as his cheeks and who looks like a marvellous ad put out by a queer publicity agent for breakfast food. I wrote a long letter to little P. who has developed a first class letter writing style which rather reminds me of Maurice [Bowra]'s. He says a great many telling things shortly and in attractive opposition. But it was Margaret Wintringham I want to talk to you about. This Communism is a bit boring. I don't think she is really keen on it. It is loyalty to her hubbie which keeps her in the party and unless she is loyal to her hubbie, her relationship with me will collapse. It is what is known as a vicious circle up in 'the Street', as we Newspaper boys call it. She looks if anything *more* attractive than she used to and has now completely resigned herself to the idea that her charm is Lincolnshire wind-blown land girl and not smart literary. The Commander, I fancy, prefers land girls. His tastes are so like mine. Though he would never admit it, of course. I must do something to shock him soon.

I am getting on very nicely with Propeller who has gone in for a new hairstyle called, I believe, 'windswept'. She had it done in Wantage where 'Margarite' the perm-specialist is an RC. The brain and face beneath the hairstyle are happily the same.

She and Waba [CB] have gone away to London for two days to see the ballet and hear masses. The Powlie is doing a tiny bit better at its school but is still, I am glad to say, regarded as 'uncooperative' by Joc.

Is there any chance of seeing you in London or better still of you comin' to stay here? Please let me know your *mouvements et les mouvements du Commandeur.* I *should* have loved to have come on March 11th – damn. Of course, Woad may cry off and I may be able to come but at present it is hopeless.

Love, John B

To Mrs F. L. Attenborough   The Old Rectory
                                               Farnborough
                                               Wantage
8 March 1950   Berkshire

Dear Mrs Attenborough,
On Central Station I was held up at the barrier by a man looking like this:

I got a closer view of him at the bookstall when he again held me up choosing every daily newspaper. His lips were like this:

and the rest of his face was to scale.
He paid for his papers in halfpennies

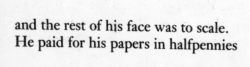

which he counted out one at a time and said to the gal in the bookstall, 'These afepennies are a nuisance to me at pontoon. You can 'ave them.' Then he held me up in the buffet selecting which chemical bun he would have and talking to a choom [sic] as he did so. When the train came in I heard a porter say to him, 'Here you are, Mr Hawkes.' I said to my porter, 'Is that the son of Alderman Hawkes?' He said it was and added, 'The spit of 'is father isn't he.' Thanks to the Principal's vivid story I was able to say 'yes'.

The train grew overheated on the way to Marylebone and we had twice to change engines. I was not surprised.

I *did* enjoy my visit to Leicester and have quite forgotten my terrors before and during the lecture, for delight in the memory of our food, conversation and jokes at your house.

A mad clergyman visited me today and I could not get rid of him until after lunch, so I am rushed for the post.

A thousand thanks for the happy time I had. I enclose a separate and short note of thanks for the Principal to whom the envelope of this letter will be addressed. Come and stay here on your way to the West. It is dirty; but classy-looking outside.

Yours, John Betjeman

> JB had lectured at Leicester University and stayed with Mrs and Mr F.L.A., its Principal, and an ardent photographer of churches. David Attenborough, his son, remembered, 'Alderman Hawkes – who was the proprietor of the city's gents' outfitters and who, I'm pretty sure, my father had been trying to extract money from to support the University College and who, I'm equally sure, saw little value in such an institution and had no intention of doing any such thing. . . .'

To Patrick Cullinan   The Old Rectory
                                          Farnborough
                                          Wantage
8 March 1950   Berkshire

Dear Boy,
Pray forgive my writing to you so late. I have been in Leicester (not hunting foxes but churches) and lecturing rather coarsely to refined audiences. And now I have returned to find your happy exercise in rhyme and metre. I hope you enjoy them both as much as your poem leads me to think you may. For rhythm Swinburne, for ingenuity Moore's *Irish Melodies*, for both Tennyson, for variety in monotony

Crabbe, for elegance Praed, others go back to dear decadent Dowson and don't flinch; or have a look at Flecker and even Rupert Brooke in places – i.e. 'Grantchester' and 'The Fish' and that ninety-ish pessimist A. E. Housman, whose *brevity* is his charm, not forgetting his recitability. I look forward to your coming here. But will you enjoy it? You who have always lived in luxury may be horrified by the squalor, the lateness of meals (eaten in the kitchen), the noise of children, the smells of cooking, the dullness of the surrounding scenery, and my early morning nervous irritability? Will you be able to stand it? I am anxious. I hope you will for a day or two. Try the inside of a week and stay on if you can stand it. Do you ride? We can provide plenty of that. You can be Pringle to my son's Bush boy. I dare not ride. It frightens me and makes me stiff. I am a coward to the very core in everything. All April is open to me, so let us know when you would like to come. I go to London on Mondays for the day and could bring you back on Monday. Stations are Newbury or Didcot. Send me more Poetry. Let's hear what (if anything) happens about Magdalen.

Yours ever, John Betjeman

> P.C. first stayed at Farnborough on 6 April. He later remembered 'a dark but friendly kitchen where we had our meals and I remember John opening and decanting the most delicious bottles of claret'.

To Gerard Irvine

The Old Rectory
Farnborough
Wantage
Berkshire

13 March 1950

Dear Gerard,

1) *Religion*. My experience is that there is no Faith in English villages at all, only convention, but that the convention can be turned into Faith. Of course there would be objections if you did the introducing tactlessly but you would have to do it at once and explain it as you did it. Easy. I will tell you about all that. It is a detail compared with the other matters you raise.

2) *Relations with Ye Olde and Village*. I don't know. I fancy the Colonel has, like all of us my dear except you, faint persecution mania and thinks there is more class war than there is. But I *don't* know. The answer is of course that you would have to side with (or represent anyhow) the people against the Colonel, if there was class war. But I

think the Colonel wouldn't mind. He prides himself on having reason and of course one could make use of reason.

3) There *is* an industrial village. But that is not the jungle work a country village is. Believe me I know. There is just ignorance in an industrial village. Not prejudice as well. It is big enough a place to bother about.

Finally, of course, it would not be nice. One knows that. *Not nice for you.* Nice for God. The Colonel, keeping up his dream of the feudal love and neighbour of the Duchess of Marlborough, would *in his heart* like another Father Aston, gentlemanly, lazy and appropriate to the village of his *Black's Colour Book* and as moderate as anything. The Colonel would insist on *Moderation.* That would be your first fence. And he doesn't know that essentials are nothing to do with incense, vestments and the like and, I am beginning to think, nothing to do with anything but obeying the rules and loving God that way.

I will pray. I thank you for your prayers. I am very fond of you and grateful to you and I wonder whether you ought to take so unenjoyable a job in order to save it from broad laziness or modernism. *Of course* if all the village went to church you wouldn't be able to stand in the aisles, let alone the nave. But it isn't numbers that matter.

I think I should just leave it in the hands of God. For your sake and from a worldly point of view I would favour keeping out. But *if* we can't find a good priest, then you must bother a bit about it. It is jungle work all right. Perhaps one insensitive, vigorous, middle-aged man is the answer. Don't worry. Pray and rest and so will I.

Love, JB

JB was keen for G.I. to take over the living at Yarnton, whose incumbent was dying. G.I. never seriously considered it. He knew that 'Colonel' Kolkhorst and the village didn't get on, and, lovely as it was, it would have been a terribly difficult situation because G.I. would have had to take the side of the villagers against the Colonel in any disagreements.

Black's Colour Book may have been one of those romantic books done by lady artists of English cottages and hollyhocks published in the nineteenth century.

To Lady Mander   The Old Rectory
                                                         Farnborough
                                                         Wantage
14 March 1950   Berkshire

Dear Lady Mander,
I am sorry to be so long in answering your nice letter of March 6th. I
have been away until this morning and no letters forwarded.

   I shall be coming from Oxford by train reaching Wolverhampton
Great Western Station at five forty-five (DV) on Friday. Alas, I shall
have to return by the ten twenty on Saturday morning. It is most
annoying, but I have a luncheon engagement near here which I cannot
avoid.

   I want to see as much as possible of what you think I ought to see.
Most exciting of all will be Wightwick. I have been reading the guide
book you sent to me. It sounds like the very best of Kempe. I suppose
Grayson, of Grayson and Ould, is the man who did 'High Meadow'
Claughton, Cheshire and the City Liberal Club, Walbrook, and
competed unsuccessfully for Brompton Oratory. I look forward to
seeing Wolverhampton and the theatre you mention if there is a chance
of getting into it before catching the ten twenty in the morning. There is
so much to see and so much to do and so little life to do it in. Oh dear, I
am excited!

   Alas, Penelope is away until after I leave for Wolverhampton. She is
in retreat for Lent. So it will only be me, the tired old prima-donna of
the early thirties.

   Yours sincerely, John Betjeman

To Patrick Cullinan   The Old Rectory
                                                         Farnborough
                                                         Wantage
3 April 1950   Berkshire

Dear Patrick,
I will meet you at Newbury Station on Thursday next April 16 at 7.10
p.m. *Unless I hear to the contrary*. There is a train which leaves
Paddington at 6 p.m. has Newbury for its first stop.

   A really clever boy (which of course you are) would work out some fascinating cross country route in *Bradshaw* e.g. this: Depart Chichester 3.02 p.m. Arrive Fratton 3.27 depart Fratton 3.40 arrive Eastleigh 4.28 (here I have a delicious cup of Southern Region tea in the Refreshment room) depart Eastleigh 5.13 arrive Newbury 6.40. You would by that obscure route avoid the Easter holiday rushes, as few people are clever enough to use any but obvious express trains and they avoid side lines. Anyhow whether you arrive at Newbury at 6.40 or 7.10 I will be there at about 7.05. Much look forward to seeing you. My aged father-in-law is staying with us and you will cheer us up. He was at Ladysmith or Mafeking or both or neither. Sorry about your 'flu. The picture was of Hans Andersen.

Yours, John Betjeman

> JB was one of the greatest *Bradshaw* (railway timetable) enthusiasts and there was nothing he enjoyed more than being asked how to get from Grimsby to Sidmouth or some such complicated journey.

To Wilhelmine Harrod

24 April 1950

Darling Billa,

Maybe I am in the train (Midland) but you can see where my heart is. Oh Breck, oh brecks, oh silver birches, oh pantiled barns and clunch work churches, painted screens the pedant searches, but my heart's in Reepham's square. Not that South Creake, thanks to a good ornate Roger Wodehouse of a Rector, isn't as good as Causton and lovelier for atmosphere and colour but not quite up to it for architects. You must see it, old girl. Audrey [Beecham] told me to tell you, when I met her at Gerald [Berners]'s gloomy cremation in that neo-Swedish crematorium, with its good view of the Headington pre-fabs – Audrey told me to tell you that she told Maurice's jokes about your foster children to Gerald on the Saturday before he died and he laughed a lot and wished he was up and about again.

Oh I *did* enjoy myself darling and a thousand thanks from us all. My diary (a red Oxford University one) I lost and it has made me very sad and helpless. It is probably at the Brecks (your house). Love to H[enry] and D[ominic].

Love, John B

We all stayed at Bayfield Brecks, which the Harrods rented from the Jodrell estate, a Dutch gabled red-brick farmhouse between Holt and the North Norfolk coast.

Roger Wodehouse was a patrician clergyman, high church, lovable, eccentric and at one time heir presumptive to the earldom of Kimberley.

Audrey Beecham was a poet. Maurice Bowra was in love with her and wanted to marry her but she refused him.

To T. S. Eliot   The Old Rectory
                                                    Farnborough
                                                    Wantage
25 April 1950   Berkshire

Dear Tom,

I enclose a letter I have had from Dr Eeles. I wrote to him horrified by the same sort of letter as the one you no doubt received.

Anyhow, I meant to write to you to tell you that I enjoyed reading *The Cocktail Party* so much that I have read it a second time. There is a terrifying clearness about it, like Wordsworth in front of nature. Oh my goodness! I wish I were a great man like you are. It is a fine piece of work. I do not know whether I want to see it as a play. I wonder whether actors will be able to convey the points so well as the printed page.

I am telling old Eeles that you have written to me and that I have taken the liberty of sending on his letter to you.

Love to Miss Dent and also to your secretary, who has very neat, small handwriting, and to all at Feebah and Feebah.

Love to John Hayward and tell him to give my love to the CRESSET Library.

Yours ever, John Betjeman

 PS It would be very nice to have you to stay here and to taste my claret. I am now a wine snob.

JB had received a clumsily worded circular letter about a new organization Friends of Ancient English Churches, started by Eeles under the Council for the Care of Churches umbrella. A fund raiser was installed to raise money for dying churches all over England. JB did not object in principle, but questioned the word 'ancient' and was miffed that he had not been consulted. Eeles wrote an apology to JB: 'I had in fact meant to ask your help, when the time came, in launching.' The organization did not get going but in 1952 the Historic Churches Preservation Trust was founded, based on the same ideals.

To Anne Barnes Sidney Sussex College
28 April 1950 Cambridge

Dear Anne,
Propeller says she will be delighted for you and Little P. to come on
June 10th. I have entered it in our diaries. We would like you both to
stay over to Sunday night and come on Friday if you like.

Little P. came out to dinner here last night. He was in very good form
and seems resigned to the futile waste of his time that Naval life must
be. We saw a few churches and read a ghost story.

I have been offered Literary Editorship of *Tame and Tade*. Shall I take
it? Kelmscott is going for a hundred and twenty five a year, rates and
repairs paid by University of Oxford. Do you want it? Shall I buy a
second hand Rolls (1929, 20 h.p.) for four hundred and sixty pounds
plus my Vauxhall? I have been offered Torquil, the house of my
dreams in Cornwall for eight thousand pounds. Propeller will not leave
here. Joad comes to stay tomorrow. I am taking him to an amateur
performance of *Dear Octopus* in Swindon in the evening.

Love, John B

Love to the Commander. I hear he has guilt about my not being able
to see him enough at that [illegible] dinner. Dear old thing. JB

JB was about to rent Kelmscott, William Morris's house on the Thames near Lechlade,
for three years. JB had misgivings for he wrote to P. Cullinan (12 May 1950), 'We looked
over Kelmscott yesterday, nine hundred and seventy-nine visitors last year. A serious
drawback. Sweating middle-aged Fabians and their mistresses and the like, call during
meals,' but he took it. PB refused to live there as it was haunted and damp. It was sub-let.

JB bought neither the Rolls nor Torquil, a secret slate-hung house on a sandy lane near
Daymer Bay, Trebetherick.

Dear Octopus by Dodie Smith was a long-running play starring Marie Tempest.

To Patrick Cullinan The Old Rectory
  Farnborough
  Wantage
2 May 1950 Berkshire

My dear Patrick,
I was enchanted to have your postcard and your letter written before
you left. I will *not* tear up the sonnet. There is too much in it that must
not be lost and that will interest you ten years from now, if we are both

alive. It is the sextet which needs clarifying, simplifying and ruling by laws of rhyme.

Your postcard is rich with gnomic utterance. It came just when the snow had fallen from an eyelid-unbatting sky here. There is one of those damned dogs barking here and I cannot think. This village is a hell. Thank God there is a chance of taking Kelmscott Manor House. Only a very slender chance, but still one worth taking. Then you, my dear Rimbaud, will be able to join Ned Jones and me and Dante Gabriel and you will write epics under the willows and I will paint pictures all to illustrate your long, Anglo-Saxon epics. I can't imagine less French behaviour! I say I do want to know what you are doing and thinking. The words on your postcard are gay, lucid, arresting and sound as though you were creatively happy, even if you aren't putting anything down on paper. Doesn't one work in spurts? – long periods of silence, then a painful burst of activity. With me it is mostly a long period of silence.

We all love you here and wish you were with us. But I think of you as self-sufficient all right with your romantic corduroy and your Dante and Milton. When you feel exhausted come here and rest.

That short story of yours is very good, you know. I opened a special folder for Patrick Cullinan MSS. I promise I won't tell anyone about it without your permission first. It will interest you in years to come to see it.

Love, John B

> At the end of April Cullinan had gone to France and Italy where he hitchhiked around, slept outdoors, and worked as a casual labourer.

To P. Morton Shand   The Old Rectory
                                                  Farnborough
                                                  Wantage
3 May 1950   Berkshire

My dear P. Morton Shand,
I am very pleased to have your letter; as you now see, my handwriting is so affected that it is incomprehensible to all but true art lovers like you and me and Dr Nikolaus Pevsner, Dr Christian Barman, Dr John Gloag, Dr Pritchard (J. Craven), Dr J. M. Richards, Dr G. Grigson and the rest of our little gang. I am horrified to hear of your unemployment.

But not surprised. If you were very busy and successful, I would at once be suspicious. Success is a sign of speciousness today. Nothing and nobody any good is doing well. I am, as usual, neither one thing nor the other.

Etchells is, I believe, 'flat out' as Hester expressed it on the telephone, two or three years ago when Propeller wanted to see Etchells and he had just come back from London. He is doing one of those cures eating nuts only for three months in a suburb of Bristol.

I am very glad to hear of Elspeth's athleticisms and Mary's job. I would very much like to come to Norland Square to lunch with you and Sibyl, Mondays if possible for me. What about Monday June 19th?

    Yours, Ian MacBetjeman

> JB is mocking his fellow 'art lovers' (particularly Pevsner), about whom he had mild paranoia. He thought they took themselves too seriously and found their fossilizing academicism stifling. JB was always apprehensive of 'experts' and 'doctors' (of the non-medical kind).

To Penelope Betjeman   The Old Rectory
                                               Farnborough
                                               Wantage

The first noight of your bein awaigh,   Berkshire
15 May 1950

Moi darlin Plymmi,
Nooni nooni, Oi nearly croied when Oi came back 'ere to foind now Plymmi.

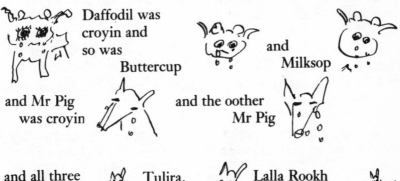

Daffodil was croyin and so was Buttercup and Milksop and Mr Pig was croyin and the oother Mr Pig

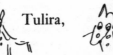

and all three powniz, Tulira, Lalla Rookh and Mercury.

And all becoz there was now Plymmi anywhere. Even the Rabbits was croyin' and of corse Rity and Kitty.

But Miss Webb was annoyingly calm and distant and Wubz said two decades with me for you and was very pleased to see the new hair ribbons I bought for her in B'bury pale pink and magenta respectively.

Oi am sow 'appy ter think 'ow muoch Oi loove yew. It was only your goin away to Italy that bore it upon me. Oi loove yew more than anything else in the world and Oi ate moiself for makin yew oonappy and for avin that sad unt little [illegible] yew gave me which Oi richly deserve. Ow Oi dew loove yew Penallerpee and when yew come back yew can introdejewce me ter all the animals again boi nime. Robut as joost roong up. Maurice has written a poem about Paddy Lee [sic] Fermor he is goin ter read ter me.

Give moi loove to the Frescows.

Ow Oi *dew* loove yew.

We *are* goin ter Corkscrew (Aunt Elsie) for Whitsun leavin 'ere Froiday returnin' Wednesday. 'Er address is Torquil Cottage, Trebetherick, Wadebridge, Cornwall. (Tel Trebetherick 109.)

Nooni nooni. Oi am now goin ter dew the boiler and gow ter bed and dream of Oi 'ave moi gentle ougli pretti lady loike little Plymmi with me agine and am never insooltin 'er any mur but loovin 'er with all moi eart and mooch more than Oi loove anywooon else (even than *God*).

Yorz trewely, Tewpie

PS Please let me know what yew think of Frescows in Florence and [illegible] there.

PB went to Rome for three weeks in May. Her primary reason for going was to gain JB's conversion through a Papal indulgence.

Miss Ruth Webb became JB's secretary at Farnborough and lived in the house. She worked in the dining room which was never used for meals anyway and JB would dictate to her in the mornings and then retire to his library upstairs.

To Anthony Barnes

The Old Rectory
Farnborough
Wantage
Berkshire

22 May 1950

My Dear Little Prawls,
Oh how sad that you on are on the sea instead of walking comfortably up and down in some old box pew. But if you go to Scandinavia, the churches! Oh my hat! I'm not sure that they aren't the best of the lot, so far as fittings are concerned and, in the bigger ones, so far as arshytexture is concerned.

Propeller is now in Italy and will be away for three weeks. Miss Webb is here but has to sleep out in order to avoid scandal in the village. Wabz is asleep, I hope, upstairs. The cows and cattle mourn for Propeller's absence. It is all curiously silent. I feel bereft. And now you are away. Am I alone on this island? Come back at once. Swim. I'll write where you want me to.

Love, John B

To Patrick Cullinan

The Old Rectory
Farnborough
Wantage
Berkshire

15 July 1950

My dear Patrick,
I loved your letter. You perceive a lot and it is surprising that you perceive so much so young. Your life at that University is the life of an exam-passer, is it? A student? Or is it University life as lived at Oxford or Cambridge? That is to say is it half as nice as Charterhouse or much nicer or worse? Have you made a bet with yourself that you must go through with it?

My old father-in-law, whom you met, died last week aged eighty. Very sad it will be for Penelope. Losing one parent is bad enough. When you lose both, you suddenly know you have stepped out into loneliness, there's no one to back you up or even to quarrel with, except other lonely people like yourself. I suppose husband and children are some consolation. But not much and they can't lessen the change. Don't think I didn't like that sonnet. It was explicit, vigorous and, like all your

writing, very much you. You are very young. May you always be so.
Send us your photograph as a rebel student translating St Francis. Let it
be on that nice deckle-edged printing paper they use in Italy. Oh I wish
you were here. It is pouring with rain. Just the weather for reading
poetry out loud. Send your most unfinished as well as finished work,
prose or poems. Artists' sketch books are often as good as and better
than the finished picture. Write as often as you like. No reply will not
mean I am neglectful. It will only mean overwork. God bless you.

  Love, John B

The Ever Open Door

To Alan Pryce-Jones   The Old Rectory
                                               Farnborough
                                               Wantage
  29 July 1950   Berkshire

My dearest Captain,
I deeply feel for you. That is the real question – is it true at all? Some
people are never bothered by it. I envy them. If it is true then nothing
else matters much. If it is not, life is not worth living, not even the sex
part of it. I am told that the desire to believe is counted very good etc.
etc. but in that case I *would* rather believe. Two thirds of the time I
don't. But I do remember having believed that Jesus was not a
'frightfully clean and nice man, my dear' nor just a peasant at an
interesting time of the western world's economic development – I do
remember believing He was God. And I have only to look round me at
various spires, towns, domes, hospitals, and ways of doing things to
know that other people have known He was God too. And I know I
have to go on practising the Faith by receiving the Sacraments and
sometimes, not immediately after H[oly] C[ommunion] by any means
but perhaps a day or two later, something has happened – I've been
talking to a Party Member or travelling on the G[reat] W[estern]
R[ailway] – and I've *known* (Pauline sense) that He was God, for just a
second. I'm sure that has happened to you. It is neither intellectual nor

emotional and perhaps no more than a strange desire for conviction. And how worthless one feels when one knows it is true and how one longs for the Truth to live in one for ever. And off it goes and somebody sends in a poem for consideration or rings up about lunch.

I don't think it matters a bit whether you are RC or not. So long as you are C[atholic] and have the Sacraments. The Validity of Anglican orders and all that sort of thing amuses but does not bother me. You, I know, won't be one of these cocksure proselytisers and will remain affectionate to the old C of E of your birth. Garrick's shut Monday I'm certain – I am working out, but do ring up *T and T ade* in the afternoon (after two thirty p.m.) and I will see you any T ame as I am staying the night in London.

R. A. Howden, an RC Queer psychotherapist, is your man, if you feel too dry to live. JB

'Like Penelope, I went over to Rome and people minded,' explained A.P.-J. (1993).

To George Barnes   Trebetherick
August 1950   return September 4

Dear Commander George and Prawlz and Mrs Prawlz,
Very sorry to be so long writing. I had 'flu. *La Grippe*. It gripped me by the throat in the *Wagon Lits*. It reached me on the Métro via Duroc to Invalides and on the aeroplane. It settled in deeply on the bus from Heathrow to Reading (Vincents) and I recovered enough to come down here on Thursday.

Jolly Joc's laugh rings over the tamarisk but I am too listless to respond to it.

I *did* enjoy myself. I caught my 'flu from the Armentières at Cordes, with the grapes and bare pink arms.

Love to you all and thousands of thanks, John B

Joc Lynam, the headmaster of the Dragon School, had a house in Trebetherick. Armentières was JB's name for French waitresses, as in:

> Mademoiselle from Armentières, parlez vous,
> Mademoiselle from Armentières, parlez vous,
> Mademoiselle from Armentières,
> She cut off her knickers for souvenirs,
> Inky pinky, parlez vous.

To Geoffrey Taylor

11 September 1950

Tame and Tade
Gorgeous Party Weekly Review
32 Bloomsbury Street
London WC1

Dear Geoffrey,
I wish you would review these two boox for *Tame and Tade* to which I have been temporarily made 'Literary Advazer'. The pay is awful (five or six guineas a thousand words) but the *honour* my dear – just think of it – also you can say what you like. Love to Mary.
    I am not myself any more but Mr Hyde
    If I ever was Jekyll
    Love, John Betjeman

To Evelyn Waugh

9 October 1950

The Old Rectory
Farnborough
Wantage
Berkshire

Dear Evelyn,
What a wonderful book HELENA is. I must write to tell you that what I like best are (1) the poetic descriptions of Colchester, Treves and Rome and its palace of retirement (2) that terrifying scene of Fausta's death (3) Helena's prayer.
    Congratulations too on the typography – it looks like Charlotte M. Yonge. You obviously told Bale how it ought to be printed. It looks like early Longman's and Macmillan novels. The only thing that puzzles me in the book is the saintliness of Helena. She doesn't seem to me like a saint. Not that it matters, for your point is, I take it, and this I have said in my jaunty, vulgar review in the *Herald* – written to attract the cloth caps as they hurry through to read 'Templegate' on the back page – your object is to show that things you can touch and see have as much and more power of saving souls than summons and arguments. I suppose it is because she saw that that Helena was a saint.
    I always knew you were a poet. I wish I had a chance of writing about your *Helena* at greater length in everyday language instead of the jaunty pseudo-simple style I have to use in the *Daily Herald*. *What* a good book!

Propeller must be proud of her dedication. Love to Laura. P. will write separately.

Yours, John B

> *Helena* is dedicated to PB and she was imagined by some to be the model for St Helena's character. E.W. had asked her for help with the 'horsy passages'.
>
> E.W. wrote (9 November 1950), 'I am delighted that you like *Helena*. It is you and six or seven others whom I seek to please in writing.'

To Patrick Cullinan

19 October 1950

'Sicirio'
Nr Farnborough
Wantage
Berkshire

My dear Patrick,
That was a very haunting afternoon in your rooms yesterday. The memory of that letter with its description of the hard light and the sense of the place watching the writer is still with me. Looking out at those still, misty elms from your window, I realised how exiled you must feel. You are obviously right to go back to South Africa. This is probably no abiding place for you. But abide for a term or two. I *think* I know you enough to be sure that the mixed experiences South Africa in vac and Oxford in term will be, in the end, a double inspiration. It is what you write that matters. Oxford will be a storehouse for S.A. and S.A. for O. I hope.

Love, JB

To John Hayward

27 October 1950

The Old Rectory
Farnborough
Wantage
Berkshire

Dear John,
I have had a letter from Sheila Wingfield asking me to write a preface for her book *Real People*. She tells me that you know about the book and that she has not got a copy of it and I am, apparently, to write a preface on what you tell me about the book. This is a bit difficult for you and for me. I like Sheila Wingfield's poetry. Do you? Can you let me have a copy of her book or the typescript or galleys or anything like that?

I wish I saw you more often. I am fast becoming a literary man and losing any spontaneity and enjoyment I had. Whenever I look at Edward Shanks in the Beefsteak Club I think I shall soon, like him, be fiddling about with folios and my poetical works, a waste of period dreariness behind me and nothing but cirrhosis of the liver and extinction in front of me. It is you and Tom [Eliot] and Mr Trimmings who can pull me out of my self-pity.

I have some poems by Sandys Wason which have a ninety-ish beauty and which I hope Martin Secker will print.

Yours ever, John Betjeman

PS I should say that I think I shall probably very much enjoy Sheila Wingfield's book. JB

PPS I have read that it is vulgar to have a PS or PPS to one's letter and to use exclamation marks.

JB wrote the preface to Sheila Wingfield's book.

E. Shanks (1812–1952), the author, was a figure revered by JB in his early days at the *Evening Standard*. He had written poetry in the twenties and thirties. His recreations in *Who's Who* were conversation, golf and playing with dachshunds.

To Anne and Arthur Bryant   The Old Rectory
                                                        Farnborough
                                                        Wantage
2 November 1950   Berkshire

Dear Arthur and Anne,

To say I am proud to have *The Age of Elegance* is to underestimate my emotions, to say I am delighted is also to be inadequate, to say I am enthralled – oh and etc; etc; etc; I am ENCHANTED to have it and *inscribed too*. You must work very hard to be able to write readable history. Most of the history I have read by modern writers (always excepting Leslie R[owse]) is unreadable, because the authors have not bothered to put it into decent, rhythmic prose. But your prose is lovely to read out loud and you make such vivid pictures and you explain battles clearly (surely very difficult) and you catch the atmosphere of places and situations equally accurately. I am very flattered indeed to think you like my poems, because I know what an eye and ear you have for writing.

I am wondering what policy to adopt for reviewing it in *Tame and*

Tade to which Ay have been appointed Literary Advazer. Would it be a good idea to put an historian on to it or would it be a good idea to put a good writer of prose on to it, with a sympathetic mind e.g. Ian Hay or Bastings. Which would you prefer? It deserves recognition both as history and prose style. I know of no reviewer (except A. L. Rowse who is probably bespoke for a high fee) capable of doing justice to both.

Would you care to review *The Journals of Mrs Arbuthnot* (2 vols) edited by Francis Bamford and The Duke of Wellington? Or do you hate reviewing as much as I do? Or would you do it for the joy of having the books? Anyhow, I will keep them at *Tame and Tade* just in case you would like them.

I hope Percy F. Westerman is well. Again a thousand thanks.

Yours,

Sean O'Betjeman

Ian MacBetjeman

Jan Trebetjeman

(Westaway Books Ltd)

Ewan Kewetjeman

Yours, John Betjeman

> *The Age of Elegance* was reviewed for *Time and Tide* by A. L Rowse under the title 'Regency Panorama'.

To Anne Barnes

The Old Rectory
Farnborough
Wantage
Berkshire

2 November 1950

Dear Anne,

I am sorry to write so late to thank you, the Commander and Little P. for that jolly time in Kent.

I have had a very coarse and funny letter from the Warden [Maurice Bowra] about Hugh Gaitskell, *Helena* and our tour in France: 'I was shocked to hear you had gone to France to look at churches and hope you did not enjoy it.' It is so coarse about Hugh Gaitskell that I cannot show it to people. Even Rupert Hart-Davis seemed shocked.

Margaret Wintringham is terrific at the moment. She broadcasts on the West. Her cheeks glow purple and her hair flies wiry in the wind and she wears a grey woollen jersey and a blue serge skirt and I have kept sex under foot as much as we can.

I get angry while I [illegible] when I think of Little P. being crucified by stupidity in the Navy. From one point of view it's worth it for the uniform but surely not from any other.

I am getting a copy of *The Priest and the Acolyte* from Fabes. Have you ever read it? If not, I will read it in a special voice next time we meet.

Any chance of your coming here after or before one of your visits to Cambridge?

Love to the Commander

Love to Little P.
What is his new ship?
Love, John B

The Priest and the Acolyte, a camp rarity, was written in 1908 by J. F. Bloxam.
    Gilbert H. Fabes was an antiquarian bookseller in Rye.
    A.B. often visited her family in Cambridge, where her father was Master of Trinity Hall.

To John Hayward   The Old Rectory
                                           Farnborough
                                           Wantage
2 November 1950   Berkshire

Dear John,
Very many thanks to you. When the proofs arrive (and may they be long in arriving because I loathe reading, don't you?) we will meet and have luncheon or tea.

I don't think you could have seen me behind that Iron Curtain. I hardly ever go about, I am so dim.

Those are very helpful little hints at the end of your letter. I suppose you know that fish knives are wrong and that every bedroom should have a waste paper basket and that however late the hostess comes down she should say 'Good morning' on first meeting a guest, even if it is late afternoon. On no account say 'Good day'. Lady Insany [Dunsany], the wife of the present peer, is the best example of unconscious correctness that I have met. She is also a saint.

Yours, John B
Ian MacBetjeman (Oliver and Boyd)
Jan Trebetjeman (Waterways Books Ltd)

> JB's catalogue of social errors, 'How to Get On in Society', was first published in *Time and Tide* (29 December 1951) as a competition. Competitors were asked to add a final stanza to five, which contained thirty-four 'social errors'. JB wrote, 'I have been so dazzled by yards of splendid verses from over a hundred entrants that I found it almost impossible to choose the best.' People got carried away and wrote whole poems, some of which JB admitted were better than his own, but in the end he gave first prize to 'H.M.B.' whose verse served as the best terminator to his own:
>
> > Your pochette's on the pouffe by the cake-stand
> > Beneath your fur-fabric coatie,
> > Now before we remove to the study
> > Let me pass you these chocs from Paris.
>
> JB never thought of his verses as anything but a journalistic joke.

To Anthony Barnes

The Old Rectory
Farnborough
Wantage
Berkshire

9 November 1950

My Dear Little Prawls,
I hear you are on the high seas. I like to think of this letter going up and down over them bearing my love to you.

Sir Ninian [Comper] came here with 'my' great-nephew John last week. They had been to have a look at my work at the East End of my old master, Bodley's chapel at Marlborow [sic]. I am putting on a lot of gold there and painting the roof blue with gold stars and my stars! What stars! What *will* they say, the old Marlburians?

We went back by arrangement and by motor cars, John driving Sir N.'s and me mine to tea here. We looked at Savernake Forest. Then we went to Mildenhall Church where I much admire the 'ambo' (two pulpits either side of chancel arch), 1814 Gothick box pews and 'condensed sigh-boreiyum' [sic] over the altar. As we were going out of Marlborough some hefty land girls thumbed Sir N. and me for a lift. One was wearing cord breeches, the others had khaki slacks, all wore scarves whirled round their hair. Sir Ninian averted his face and exclaimed, 'Oh! That uniform! It shows a lack of reverence to Our Lady.' When we got back here, the house was cold and empty. Propeller arrived an hour late and a fog had come up. Sir Ninian, by way of revenge I think, plunged straight into arguments against Papal Infallibility. 'Of course a great hero of mine is Pio Nono. He is going to be made a saint, is he not?' Propeller. 'Yes. They've discovered two miracles at his tomb.' 'I'm *so* glad. Such a great man. He condemned secession from the English church as a sin, you know. Oh yes. He pronounced it ex-cathedra.' And so on. Fortunately a master from Marlborough arrived, so he drew off some of the fire. Sir N. and his great-nephew then set off into the fog.

This must all seem miles away from you there in that Kingdom on the sea. All the more poignant and absurd, no doubt.

Love, John B

To Mrs Belt

24 November 1950

Dear Mrs Belt,
Three years ago you wrote to Martin Secker about Theo Marzials and you enclosed some beautiful poems by him and a picture of him by your father. I have composed the enclosed talk on Marzials for the Third Programme, which is to be illustrated with his songs, to celebrate the centenary of his birth. Its success very much depends on whether you will allow me to quote, as I have done on page 9, from that very touching letter which Marzials sent to you in 1918. I would also like your permission to have your father's drawing of Marzials reproduced in the *Radio Times*, if the *Radio Times* is able to reproduce it, or *The Listener*, or something like that.

Mr Skinner's essay on Marzials is a most wonderful picture and with your letter will bring Marzials back for the charming individualist he must have been.

I hope that I shall one day have the pleasure of being allowed to call on you and to see Marzials' relics which I understand from Mr Secker you have in your house.

I shall, of course, be pleased to make any alterations or additions to the script that you would like.

Yours sincerely, [John Betjeman]

Theophilus Julius Henry Marzials (1850–1920) was a poet, musician, artist and dilettante who wrote such songs as 'Go Pretty Rose' and 'The Miller and the Maid'.

Martin Secker had written to JB (21 September 1947) seeking advice on how to find out about 'that dim and mysterious figure', whose verse he wished to include in an anthology. After advertising for information they discovered the existence of Mrs Belt, whose father, Cyril Davenport, was Marzials' friend. Marzials doted on Davenport and became jealous when he married. He died sad and almost blind at Colyton in Devon at the age of seventy and left his papers to Mrs Belt.

Secker's *The Eighteen-Nineties: a Period Anthology of Prose and Verse* (Richards Press) came out in 1948 with an introduction by JB, whose fascination with Marzials burgeoned. His talk, *Theo Marzials*, went out on Christmas Eve 1950.

To Patrick Cullinan   The Old Rectory
                                                            Farnborough
                                                            Wantage
29 November 1950   Berkshire

Dear Patrick,
The Stanzas are indeed rhythmic and enchanting. Thanks to Margaret Wintringham I have of recent years become aware of sixteenth- and seventeenth-century poetry. The 'English School' at Oxford had killed it for me until then. I suppose the sameness of rhythm which you find in the Kraal among all those jolly Africans is because there is not, on the whole, a wide range of rhythms – not anything like even, the range of tunes – and so some of our verse rhythms have qualities like those other races. I have been in bed with a cold and am now full of whisky on an empty stomach, which is why I am not expressing myself as clearly as the Colonel would if he had as much to say.

But those S. day stanzas are enchanting. I wonder if Reuben de Rio is so good?

Talking of him, Dowson for rhythm is good and interesting and worth saying aloud. He is, I think, the best of the nineties and by that I mean the Colonel's poets.

It is the Powlie's birthday today. It is thirteen.

It would not do if the last view I have of you this time is scaling up that lamp post. But the only day I shall be free is Thursday evening, the next to last night of your term and then only on my way back with Penelope from Thame.

Is there a possibility of your coming here for a night before taking wing for S.A.? Let me know. Write or telephone. I miss you when you are not about. Don't stay in S.A. for ever once you get there.

Love, John B

PS I shall be in Taunton on Tuesday at Taunton School c/o Headmaster and home Wednesday evening. London tomorrow, Monday, and staying [the] night with Jennifer and Alan Ross, so this (Farnborough) is my only long anchorage.

To Patrick Cullinan   The Old Rectory
                                                   Farnborough
                                                   Wantage
13 December 1950   Berkshire

My Dear Patrick,
The snow and fog are thick here and the new secretary [Jill Menzies] has come to give the place the once over to see whether she can abide staying here. The sentimental memory opposite may stir up in you such distaste for your first term at Oxford that you never wish to come back. But oh please do. Did you remember to tell your father you had been to Douglas and smelt lunch cooking (Irish stew and cabbage and old biscuits fried in bat oil). I hope this reaches you by Christmas. I very much enjoy the Van der Hum this cold weather. Evelyn Waugh who has been staying with us told me he drank too much of it at the Wembley Exhibition in 1925 and was sick over the side of the Giant Racer. You will not remember those days. *Please send poems.* You can write much more than you think on these airmail sheets. I will write again later in the month. I wish I was swimming in cobalt blue water on the frontier. Love to Olifants and all on the Veldt.
    Love, John B

   The Death of the UNIVERSITY READER IN SPANISH
   (the late Col. George Alfred Magee Kolkhorst RSVP)

        The Colonel lies upon his bed
        And rests his dear old cube-shaped head,
        Above him, hanging on the frieze,
        Is carved the crest of the MAGEES,
        While underneath him there is not,
        The vestige of a chamber-pot,
        Because *the Colonel*, you must know,
        Is subject to no overflow,
        The food he eats is desiccated
        And subsequently sublimated

And so is he, and that is how
He comes to be where he is now.
   SODA is lying on the 'couch'
And so is FRED and so is SOUCH.
There is an air in every room
At least of Thought, if not of Gloom.
The Carpets shiver to themselves
The Plates are silent on the shelves
(And some of them are very old
And some of them are not, I'm told),
The toothbrushes in order ranged
Are all remarkably unchanged
(And these are older far in date
Than any rug or any plate),
The bits of sponge of various shades,
The fifty years of razor blades,
All these no evidence betray
That 'tis *the Colonel's* dying day.
She only mourns, the DAME TRALEES
Beside the bed of the MAGEES.
   What glimpse of the Eternal flashes
Across those long mascara-ed lashes?
What meetings with the blessed dead
Await that dear old cube-shaped head?
See like a spark from ETNA's Crater
The everlasting soul of PATER,
It flits about the room and rests
Beside *the Colonel's* woollen vests.
And what is that thing over there
With neither face nor form nor hair?
Just disembodied Intellect?
It's dear old PLATO, I expect.
It has departed by itself
To browse about the Youth Club shelf,
Till hark! A roll of Heavenly Drums,
The King of all, MAX PLOWMAN comes.
'Welcome, old Friend' MAX PLOWMAN cries
And, with a smile, *the Colonel* dies.
   'And now that you have got your wings
Let's test the Actualness of things.

Here, PLATO, what say you to this? –
Does that "Become" which yet not "Is"?
Can the intrinsic "Is" – potential
Invalidate the non-Essential?
Sed non, quod miles, Alma mater
Elaborate the thesis, PATER.
Come, KOLKHORST, help untie the Tangle!
WE'VE ALL ETERNITY TO WRANGLE.'
  Oh what a joy, *the Colonel* finds,
It is to be with First Class minds.
Instead of silly sexy patter
He joins in Things that Really Matter
As PATER, PLATO, PLOWMAN talk
He goes one Endless Country Walk
Along the bare *Elysian Fields*
Where not a Dog its Nuisance yields.
  But she, poor luckless Mortal here,
The DAME TRELEASE, lets fall a tear.
She gazes on the Corpse and sighs
And puts some pennies on its eyes,
And then, tiptoe-ing down the stairs
Sees HONEST TOBY at his prayers
And FATHER HUGH, beside him kneeling
Both overcome by decent feeling.
  Before them lying white and still,
Behold *the Newly-Opened Will*.

This verse was written as a joke while 'Colonel' Kolkhorst was very much alive. It was
originally sent to many of JB's friends.
  Magee was the surname of Kolkhorst's mother. The Magees were an Ulster family
who produced a Victorian Bishop of Peterborough.
  Soda was Kolkhorst's favourite dog.
  Fred and Souch were domestics at Yarnton, reputedly surly and dishonest.
  Kolkhorst's interest in the nineties led him to idolize Pater.
  The Revd Hugh Bridle was a Church of Ireland priest, and a close friend.
  The content of the will was always a matter of joking speculation.

To Edmund Blunden   [Postcard]
                                                Cold Arches
                                                Farnborough
3rd Sunday in ADVENT 1950   Wantage

> And where is SPEX HALL? I have quite forgot.
> It is some dim East Anglian beauty-spot.
> The church, I notice, has been much restored.
> And I should say the services were 'Broad'.
> I would not like to be its manor's Lord.
> Its War Memorial is a standard one
> Bought in the Euston Road from MAILE & SON.
> But this is really to say I share
> With you a love for Walter de la Mare
> And much enjoyed the tribute that you paid
> To him within the current TAME & TAIDE
> Oh thank you, thank you very much indeed,
> True poet of the Weald, true Friend in Need.

John Betjeman

Spexhall is a flat parish of scattered farms in East Suffolk.

To Alan Pryce-Jones   The Old Rectory
                                                Farnborough
                                                Wantage
25 February 1951   Berkshire

Personal

My Dear,
I never wrote to thank you for a very jolly evening at the Travellers. I
drove home very fast indeed from Reading and only by the Grace of
God am alive. I wish you would let me send you a contribution towards
it and will discuss it with you when you come to lunch, as I hope you
will, with Lady Rhonnddaa at the Lladdies Annnnexxe of the
Aththennaeaeumm on Mmarchch 20th St Cuththbbertts DDay. Also
ppressentt will bbe JJooccellynn Brookke and SSSttepphhenn
SSppenndder and Theodora Bosanquet. I will have bubbly to make up

for the bad food. Lady R is so u.c. [upper class] in her talk and ways that she will see we are having bubbly at luncheon out of ssopphistication. Have you read FINISTERRE? My *dear*! Never read anything so outspoken in my life. It will be banned (Gollancz) for certain. Love to Poppy. Love to Ole Pa'rick.

Love from your loving brother, Adrian Pryce-Jones

> JB drove as fast as his Vauxhall would go at every given opportunity.
> Lady Rhondda, the owner of *Time and Tide*, was Welsh.
> *Finisterre* by Fritz Peters, published by Gollancz, had just come out. It was one of the first English homosexual novels and rather gloomy because everyone in it committed suicide. Later books would be described as 'in the tradition of *Finisterre*'.

To Martin Secker   The Old Rectory
                                                Farnborough
                                                Wantage
28 February 1951   Berkshire

Dear Secker,
That Turner book has a hundred and twenty-seven pictures and seventy-two of them are inaccurately captioned. The text is so capricious and ill-informed that it is comic. I don't think the book ought to be offered for sale, and am going to say so in a review in the *Sunday Times*.

Chief friends of [Gerald] Berners were Robert Heber-Percy, Faringdon House, Berks, Constant Lambert, Clarissa Churchill, the Hon. Lady Mosley, the Hon. Nancy Mitford, Freddie Ashton, William Plomer, Lord Inverchapel – oh, but I could go on with the list for another twenty minutes. I don't think it is any good writing to each of those. I will come and talk to you about it soon. I think that is the easiest way of dealing with it. Comper says that Garner and his wife were the only people who were known to have gone over as a result of the Papal Bull on Anglican Orders.

Yours, John Betjeman

> Reginald Turner's book was *Nineteenth-Century Architecture in Britain*, published by Batsford in February 1951. 'It dismisses the Gothic Revival as a disease and does not even understand Norman Shaw,' JB wrote to Anthony Barnes.
> JB had discussed with the publisher M.S. the idea of writing a memoir of Gerald Berners. In the end it never materialized.

To George Barnes   The Old Rectory
                                                      Farnborough
                                                      Wantage
11 May 1951   Berkshire

My dear Commander,
Dylan Thomas is very much in need of regular employment. I like him
all right myself, and I like some of his poetry, and I know that he really
understands poetry, and reads it and interprets it beautifully. He used
to be employed by the BBC. Now for goodness' sake have a look into his
past record and see whether he is employable. Every allowance must be
made for him.

    Margaret Taylor is going to see you on his behalf next week. Dylan
Thomas is more important than I am. He can't provide for his family. I
at least can do that.

    Yours ever, my dear Commander, and we didn't get a bid for this
house. Sean Betjeman

> In 1951 Dylan Thomas resumed regular poetry readings on BBC's Third Programme
> but once turned up drunk and was reprimanded by G.B. A memo of 1951 refers to fees
> paid to Thomas suggesting that he should not be regarded as 'celebrity class' and that he
> would never be employed on a staff job. Thomas pleaded with G.B. but Laurence
> Gilliam, the Head of Features, said that he wouldn't take a chance with the drinking
> problem.
>   Margaret Taylor was the wife of the historian, A. J. P. Taylor.

To John Foster-White   The Old Rectory
                                                      Farnborough
                                                      Wantage
24 May 1951   Berkshire
Corpus Christi

Dear Mr Foster-White,
What a coincidence – the very week before I had your letter John Piper
and I did a tour of Middlesex, seeing Canon's Church (Whitchurch),
Northolt (a winner), Perivale, Greenford, Harrow and modern
churches at Belmont, Kenton, Eastcote and S. Harrow. Eastcote was
like most of the modern ones.

    I have long loved Middlesex. I was at Cranford on Sunday for a Sung
Mass in the Parish Church and then drove through that ghost country
to Hampton Court amid the gravel pits and bungalows.

You obviously love Middlesex too. Will you write twelve hundred words on Middlesex for me for *T and T*. I am 'Lit Adviser' to *T and T* and would see that it got in. You would do it beautifully. Pinner, Ruislip and Perivale call you. Dear country of its Country boxes of the 1800s and the semi-detacheds of the today.

> Gaily into Ruislip Gardens
> Runs the Piccadilly train
> With a thousand 'ta's and 'pardon's
> Daintily alights Elaine.

Yours, John Betjeman

J.F.-W. was Editorial Director of Macdonalds (Publishers) at the time and wrote to JB saying, 'We have a bear in the office, I think it's time he went home.' This persuaded him to come to the office and pick up the MS of *Archie and the Strict Baptists*, which JB had illustrated with his own water-colours. The book was published by Murray's with JB's illustrations forgone for those by Phyllida Gili.

JB's poem 'Middlesex', the first few lines of which are in this letter, was first published in *Punch* without its second stanza because of 'advertising' complications. It subsequently appeared in *A Few Late Chrysanthemums*.

J.F.-W. pointed out to JB that Ruislip Gardens, unlike Ruislip, was not on the Piccadilly Line, but the Central – so JB later changed it to 'red electric train'.

J.F.-W. did do the article for *Time and Tide* and many other reviews, besides, during JB's time.

To Miss Webb   The Old Rectory
                                                  Farnborough
                                                  Wantage
May 1951   Berkshire

Dear Miss Webb,
Found. Just where you said it would be. Thank you very much. What a wonderful memory you have.

We wait apprehensively here for May 9th when we are sold up. Daffodils flood the edges of the lawn. The trees are just becoming a misty green. Your successor was nice but so barmy she had to go into a loony bin, where she now is. Someone comes on May 7th. I have put things back to your neatness awaiting her arrival.

I hope you enjoy your nursing. I should be frightened seeing death near and so often. Does it, I wonder, prepare one for one's own death?

Wibz [CB] is being painted by an old man of eighty-three who illustrated Kelmscott books for William Morris. The Powlie goes to

Eton next week. We unite in sending you our affection. Come over if you ever are free.

Yours, John Betjeman

JB's secretary, Miss W., had left in December 1950 to become a nurse and missionary.

To Patrick Cullinan   The Old Rectory
29 May 1951   Farnborough

Dear Patrick,
Well I *am* pleased to hear from you about the University Reader in Spanish's conducting your USA chums round his lovely old house with all its lovely old things lying on top of one another in hopeless *déshabillé* (ask Toby the meaning of the underlined word). Come here after your exam. That will be lovely.

I am writing this opposite to her and dare not show her your letter. One gets a sudden cold jab if one goes too far. We looked at the Festival on S. Bank last night. In her ecstasy at the illuminations she laughed and smiled at me and touched my hand.

Love, John B

'The University Reader in Spanish' was G.A. Kolkhorst. 'She' was Jill Menzies, his new secretary, for whom he developed a grand, long-lasting, platonic passion.

To George Barnes   The Old Rectory
                                               Farnborough
                                               Wantage
3 June 1951   Berkshire

My Dear Commander,
I am coming to Ally Pally on Tuesday morning for a lot of underpaid tripe I am doing with Griggers. I hope I shall see you.

I *did* enjoy the launch party. Even Propeller enjoyed herself, though she did not look at anything, as she can only think about Aylesbury ducks.

On Tuesday I will be accompanied by my new Scottish-Canadian C of E Secretary with freckles, grey eyes, tip-tilted nose and grey flannel

skirts and cream shirts and furry
skin. As you may be in, I will
call on you with her. It may
be a slight return for so jolly
a party.

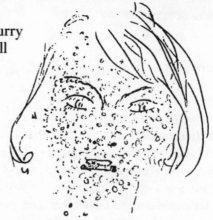

Love to Anne
Love to Little P
Love to Ally P
Love, Sean O'Betjeman

'Ally Pally' was Alexandra Palace, the BBC's television studios.

To Patrick Cullinan   The Old Rectory
                                                   Farnborough
                                                   Wantage
9 June 1951   Berkshire

My dear Patrick,
I write this to you at three p.m. while the above is being auctioned
down the hill at the Bear Hotel, Wantage. We have put a reserve of
eight and a half thousand on it and I don't think it'll reach the reserve.
But the woodlice still walk on the landing here unperturbed. And what
am I more than a woodlouse? I long to hear of you. My new secretary
who came on Sunday is a knockout. And very cool and calming in these
anxious times for Propellor and me.
     Come and see us when you like.
     I was caught by Paul Vine (your friend) on the telephone to speak to a
society – any date offered. I wish you had been here. I need your help
and stimulus to have the guts to make decisions.
     Love, John B

Patrick and Molly Lawrence bought the Old Rectory for eleven thousand pounds.

To Wilhelmine Harrod

The Old Rectory
Farnborough
Wantage
Berkshire

26 June 1951

Darling Billa,
The thought crossed my mind the same time as it crossed yours and when I received your postcard I had already had *Tame and Tade* send you Wyndham's book. Very much look forward to your review.

I was sad to read of the General's death, sad for your mother and all of you, for I remember him when I stayed there as such a dear old thing and neither alarming nor patronising nor narrow. I read all through his obituary in *The Times* and thought how little a recital of deeds like that gives an idea of a person's worth or character.

Love, John B

> W.H. reviewed *Country Neighbourhood* by Wyndham Ketton-Cremer, the Norfolk writer, in *Time and Tide* (14 July 1951).
> The General was General Sir Peter Strickland, W.H.'s stepfather.

To Anne Channel

Farnborough
Wantage
Berkshire

29 June 1951

My dear Anne,
V. pleased to hear from you. Am going broke. You must be sad at selling Sparnal Stitch. We have sold this house for a smaller one in Wantage. I am not so sad. A bit sad, but dread the move. Don't you?

I do want to buy a house in Trebetherick. Nowhere else. Not even Rock or Polzeath. There is hope for me of getting Old Barn from the Allins. It is surrounded by our land. But I will have to borrow money on the reversion of my mother's will, so I can't borrow much. If I *did* buy a house like Old Barn, would you live in it? What I want is somewhere to escape when life here is too much and somewhere for the children and Propeller in summer – less expensive than Bodare and somewhere to retire to with old friends and old hills around – so it's bound to be Trebetherick for me. Write and let me know how things go.

Love, John B

JB had met the glamorous, bridge-playing, much courted A.C. in the 1920s. Already thrice married, she had left her third husband, Herbert Channel, in 1924 and fled to Rock, near Trebetherick, the scene of their honeymoon. She bought a cottage, Sparnal Stitch, and in 1951 moved to Tresevens in Trebetherick. From the thirties onwards, she wrote regularly to JB about local gossip and politics. In his poem 'Old Friends' JB wrote:

> Where is Anne Channel who loved this place the best,
> With her tense blue eyes and her shopping-bag falling apart
> And her racy gossip and nineteen-twenty zest
> And that warmth of heart?

JB did not buy Old Barn in Trebetherick in the end.
The Bodare was the hotel we usually stayed in, if not with friends.

To Samuel Gurney   Farnborough
19 July 1951

Dear Sam,
This is the answer to your letter of St Swithin's Day.

1) I think that Purnell's prescription for washing the walls sounds good. As to the colour, I believe it is white with a dash of grey. On the other hand you don't want to use it in the chancel all round and spoil those paintings which I think are very attractive.

2) I don't know about the tester. Do you mean over the side altar?

On the other points I can't advise without coming and looking, but obviously if you colour-wash the walls you must colour-wash the roof the same colour. It is indeed poor, and is better for not being noticeable. I am not sure that I don't like the walls the colour they are, for the outside of the church being white there might be too much white if the inside were white and grey as well.

I think the font cover is one of the features of the church, and I don't really think it is out of proportion when you think of what those Norfolk font covers are like, such as Trunch. The only objection that there could be would be if it got in the way of people seeing the altar from the back pews, but I don't think it does that. The rood is lovely. Don't touch it. Anyhow I am so used to the church that I'd be very nervous of altering anything in it at all. More on my next visit to the church.

Yours, John Betjeman
PS I DID enjoy the service.

The church at Compton Beauchamp, where S. G. lived, is in a magical place tucked under the Berkshire Downs.

To George Barnes

The Old Rectory
Farnborough
Wantage
Berkshire

30 September 1951

My Dear Commander,
I made it, thanks to your unselfishness, and reached home by nine p.m. having caught a good (and the only) train from Ashford via Redhill where I changed for Reading – carriage to myself all the way.

Oh *wasn't* it fun! The best ever, ole man. And Bourges. I shall remember that all my life. Oh ta ever so. My breath is still bad from all that overeating.

My mother is, alas, dying and I shall have to go to Bath to visit her in her Nursing Home as often as possible.

This is the last letter I shall write from the house (the Old Rectory) which you have never seen. Now tell me all about yourself. But tell me by writing to the Mead, Wantage. Tel. Wantage 150.

Yours, eternally gratefully, and very excited about whether Little P's photographs will have come out.

I am, dear boy, yours devotedly, B.E. Nicholls

JB had been on holiday to France with the Barneses.
JB took me to Bath several times that autumn to see Granny Bess, Bess Betjemann. She sat, frail and elegant, looking out of the window onto Lansdown Crescent with her grey hair in beautiful neat waves. I remember thinking I had never seen such thin wrists in my life. She died the following year.
Benjie Nicholls was a director of the BBC and G.B.'s *bête noire*.

Appendix

John Piper at Windsor
(an illustrated story for Myfanwy)

In 1941 Kenneth Clark arranged for John Piper to paint Windsor for Queen Elizabeth and be deferred from the Armed Forces, and JB produced the following illustrated story to commemorate the event. In his letter to J.P. of 12 October 1941 he writes, 'I expect you will by now have received my drawings of you at work at Windsor and of Goldilox.'

Once upon a time there was a great magician who lived in a beautiful office surrounded by Cézannes, pointillists, pens, abstracts, soft carpets and all manner of lovely things. This magician had a magic wand. Many a down-and-out artist came and slumped into one of his comfortable chairs and he had only to wave his wand and the artist's dream was realized.

On some occasions he was able to command the presence of the KING HIMSELF. And so it happened that one poor artist came and the kind magician waved his wand and said, 'All this is yours.'

When the artist got home from his visit to the magician he told his lovely swimming-blue wife, who was, as usual, washing the dishes, of the good fortune the magician had promised him.

But she only sighed and cried a little into the sink, for she thought he would forget her.

So every day the poor artist went out and painted a lovely old ruin in the beautiful park of the King's palace.

And one day, the Queen herself peeped out behind one of the old ruins in the park and the poor artist jumped to attention holding his paintbrush nervously to his side.

'Don't bother to stand up,' said the Queen and soon they were on friendly terms.

After a few days, the Queen brought her own little sketches for him to
see. They were pointillist. But the artist, no longer poor, was so
absorbed in his work that he hardly noticed her, or bothered about her.
Meanwhile, what was happening at home?

His lovely swimming-blue wife was very unhappy, and the washing-up piled higher and higher in the little kitchen. She did physical training to prepare herself for the ordeal she felt she was about to face, to go and see the King and ask him to dismiss her husband and send him back to her.

But before she took an irretrievable step, the poor artist's wife decided to consult her Auntie Lena. Now Aunt Lena had magic knitting needles and whatever her nieces wished she was able to grant.

Aunt Lena is Lena Playll, Myfanwy's aunt on her mother's side. A splendid character who had been to Cheltenham College and taught history and Latin all her life.

So one day, as the Queen and the artist were painting a Gothic ruin in the park – the one pointillist and the other pen and wash – the King appeared through an archway bearing on his arm the artist's wife whom he had made a BARONESS IN HER OWN RIGHT. The Queen had the artist knighted (with the aid of the great magician) but that, of course, was not so good.

Dramatis Personae

Ackerley, J. R. (1896–1967): Playwright, novelist, poet and literary editor. Fought on the Western Front in the First World War which formed the basis of his controversial play *The Prisoner of War* (1925). Joined the BBC in 1928, where he eventually became literary editor of *The Listener* which he transformed into a forum for the best in contemporary criticism. He held the post for twenty-five years.

Arlott, John (1914–1991): 'The Voice of Cricket', also in his time a police detective, television interviewer, poet, author and teacher of modern history. Though best known for his cricket commentaries and books on the sport, he also wrote hymns and published several anthologies of poetry: *Landmarks, Of Period and Place, First Time in America*.

Ava, Basil see Dufferin and Ava.

Balfour, Patrick see Kinross.

Barnes, Anne (b. 1905): Daughter of Dr Henry Bond, Master of Trinity Hall, Cambridge. Married George Barnes in 1928. The confidante of many of her own and her son's generation.

Barnes, Anthony (b. 1931): Son of George and Anne Barnes, a scholar at Eton and King's College, Cambridge. Worked for various companies before becoming Director of the Redundant Churches Fund, from which he retired in 1992. He moved to Norwich and is now Secretary to the Norfolk Churches Trust.

Barnes, Sir George (1904–1960): One of the most eminent BBC figures of the century. Long career, starting in the Talks Department in 1930 and becoming its director in 1941. Finally director of BBC TV in 1950. In 1956 appointed Principal of University College of North Staffordshire. Knighted 1953.

Beddington, Jack CBE (1893–1959): Educated at Wellington and Balliol College, Oxford. Served in First World War. Publicity Director for Shell-Mex where he was responsible for launching the *Shell Guides* with JB. Left Shell-Mex to join the Films Division of the Ministry of Information.

Beerbohm, Sir Max (1872–1956): Essayist, satirist, caricaturist. Published several books of essays: *The Works of Max Beerbohm; More Max Beerbohm; Yet Again; And Even Now*. *Zuleika Dobson* was his satirical novel about life at Oxford but he was best known for his caricatures and flourished briefly before First World War, then left for Italy with his first wife.

Berners, Gerald Hugh Tyrwhitt-Wilson, 14th Baron (1883–1950): Musician, artist and author. Worked as an Honorary Attaché in the Diplomatic Service, then turned his attentions full-time to music and writing. Many musical works include *The Triumph of Neptune, A Wedding Bouquet, Cupid and Psyche*, written for the ballet. Two autobiographical volumes, *First Childhood* and *Distant Prospect*, and for his fantastic novels that parodied English social life: *The Camel, Far from the Madding War, Count Omega, Percy Wallingford, Mr Pidger* and *The Romance of a Nose*.

Betjemann, Ernest (1872–1934): Sportsman, tradesman and proprietor of G. Betjemann & Sons, 'Inventors, Silversmiths, Fancy Cabinet Makers, Dressing Bag Makers'. Ernest's Dutch ancestors, who spelt their name 'Betjeman', had emigrated in the eighteenth century and settled in the East End of London, where the business was founded. The extra 'n' in the name had been added in the nineteenth century, when there was a fashion for all things German. In 1902 he married Mabel Dawson (1878–1952), the daughter of an artificial flower maker, who for a short time ran a millinery and dress business in Buckingham Street, London.

Bishop, Morchard see Stonor.

Blunden, Edmund (1896–1974): Poet, teacher, critic and biographer. Fellow and Tutor in English Literature at Oxford, Professor of Poetry 1966–68. Fought in First World War for which he was awarded the MC. Literary journalist for the *Athenaeum*. Contributor to *Times Literary Supplement*, biographer of Shelley and Thomas Hardy. Married three times and had a successful educational career in Japan after Second World War. His most famous books were *Cricket Country* and *Undertones of War*.

Boswell, Ronald (d. 1960): Educated Harrow and Balliol College, Oxford. Talks Booking Manager at the BBC during JB's time and foundation member of Programme Contracts Department of BBC which grew enormously during his tenure. A much admired man in the BBC and former director of The Bodley Head.

Bowle, John Edward (1905–88): Historian and writer. Worked with JB on the *Heretick* at Marlborough. Later became a history master at

Westminster School. Held many professorships in overseas universities and wrote over a dozen books including *England – A Portrait, The Concise Encyclopedia of World History, Henry VIII: A Biography, The English Experience, Napoleon, Charles I: A Biography*.

Bowra, Sir Maurice (1898–1971): Classical scholar and writer. Dean and later Warden of Wadham College, Oxford, he was renowned for his wit and humour. Spent his entire life at Oxford (where he took up JB), and became famous for his conversation, influencing a generation of English intellectuals. Published over thirty books. Knighted 1951.

Bryant, Sir Arthur (1899–1985): Distinguished and prolific historian, also a First World War pilot and barrister. Wrote books on history, including biographies of Samuel Pepys (three volumes) and Charles II and succeeded G. K. Chesterton in writing 'Our Notebook' in *Illustrated London News*. Knighted 1954.

Buckle, Richard (b. 1916): Writer, critic, exhibition designer. Ballet critic of the *Observer* and *Sunday Times*. Staged numerous exhibitions of ballet. Wrote *The Adventures of a Ballet Critic*, as well as biographies of Epstein and Nijinsky, and edited the *Diaries of Cecil Beaton*.

Byron, Robert (1905–1941): Traveller, art critic, historian. Had a passion for Greece where, as a member of the family of Lord Byron, he was well received. Travel correspondent for the *Daily Express* in 1929 and went on a special mission to India which formed the basis of *An Essay on India* (1931). Worked as a sub-editor in the Overseas News Department of the BBC in the 1930s. His books include *Europe in the Looking Glass, The Road to Oxiana* and *Byzantine Achievement*.

Chetwode, Field Marshal Philip Walhouse, 1st Baron, OM (1869–1950): From an ancient English family who owned the manor of Chetwode in Buckinghamshire since the early 1400s. At the end of one of the most glittering army careers of the first half of this century, he became Commander-in-Chief of the Army in India. JB's father-in-law. Married Hester Alice Camilla in 1899, the daughter of Colonel the Hon. Richard Stapleton-Cotton.

Churchill, Randolph (1911–68): Journalist and son of Sir Winston. Educated Eton and Christ Church, Oxford. Vigorous supporter of his father's cause until 1935 when he stood as an Independent Conservative candidate. MP for Preston 1940–45. Compiled the first three volumes of his father's biography but died before completing the rest. Autobiography: *Twenty-One Years*.

Clark, Sir Kenneth, later Baron (1903–1983): Patron and interpreter of the arts. Educated Winchester and Trinity College, Oxford. Director of the National Gallery 1934–45 and Chairman of the Arts Council

1953–60. Books on art include *The Nude, Landscape into Art, The Romantic Rebellion* and *The Gothic Revival*, all published by John Murray. His TV series *Civilization* made him a popular public figure.

Cleverdon, Douglas (1903–87): Publisher of finely printed books and Radio Director of BBC. Educated Bristol Grammar School and Jesus College, Oxford. Joined BBC 1939. War Correspondent, Burma 1945. From 1947 Third Programme productions include radio works by Max Beerbohm, David Jones, Ted Hughes, Stevie Smith, Dylan Thomas (*Under Milk Wood*) and many other poets and composers. Directed first stage production of *Under Milk Wood* in Edinburgh and London in 1955 and in New York in 1957. Directed innumerable Poetry Festivals. As a publisher he produced a series of magnificently printed books, illustrated by David Jones, Michael Ayrton, John Piper, Anthony Cross, Eric Gill, Laboureur, and others.

Clonmore, Viscount see Wicklow.

Comper, Sir Ninian (1864–1960): The most distinguished pupil of the Victorian architect, George Frederick Bodley. The leading and most original ecclesiastical architect of his time. Refused to become registered which made his knighthood, for which JB pressed relentlessly, difficult to achieve. His principal works were the nave windows, Southwark Cathedral, and Warriors Chapel at Westminster Cathedral. Knighted 1950.

Connolly, Cyril (1903–74): Literary journalist. Educated Eton and Balliol College, Oxford. Wrote for *New Statesman* before Second World War. In 1939 he founded *Horizon* magazine which he edited until 1950. Lead reviewer in *Sunday Times* for over twenty years. Wrote *Enemies of Promise* and *The Unquiet Grave*.

Craig, Diana see Peel.

Cresswell, Wilhelmine see Harrod.

Cullinan, Patrick (b. 1933): Poet, critic and short story writer. Born in South Africa, he was sent to England to be educated at Charterhouse and Magdalen College, Oxford. Returned to South Africa to farm in the Transvaal and in the seventies founded the Bataleur Press for young South African writers. Has published three collections of poetry: *The Horizon Forty Miles Away, Today is not Different*, and *The White Hail in the Orchard*.

Curtis, Lionel (1872–1955): Scholar, poet and political writer. Served in the South African War. Very influential in the creation of the Union of South Africa and the progress of India towards self-government. Similarly played a major role in the drawing up of the Irish Treaty of 1921. Founded the Oxford Society and the Oxford Preservation Trust.

Driberg, Tom (Thomas Edward Neil), MP (1906–76): Journalist and politician. At Oxford with JB. Wrote the 'William Hickey' gossip column for the *Daily Express* (1923–43), and subsequently employed by *Reynolds News* and the *New Statesman*. A life-long Anglo-Catholic and Socialist, he entered parliament in 1942, and became Chairman of the Labour Party in 1957. His homosexual promiscuity (paraded in his posthumous autobiography, *Ruling Passions*) inhibited further promotion in the Commons. Nevertheless in 1975 he was created a Life Peer under the title of Lord Bradwell.

Dufferin and Ava, Basil Sheridan Blackwood, 4th Marquess of (1909–45): Styled Earl of Ava from 1918 until 1930 when he inherited his father's title. Married Maureen Guinness in 1930. Held various minor political appointments in 1930s. Served in Royal Horse Guards in Second World War, killed in Burma March 1945.

Dunn, Lady Mary, née St Clair-Erskine (1912–93): Daughter of the 5th Earl of Rosslyn. Exceptionally charming and spirited young woman, she was JB's first girlfriend. A friend and inspiration to many young writers and painters. Married Sir Philip Dunn in 1933 and had two daughters, Serena and Nell.

Eeles, Dr Francis Carolus (1876–1954): Liturgical scholar. Founder and first Secretary of the Council for the Care of Churches, a post he held until his death. Author of many booklets and articles on church buildings and Anglican and Scottish liturgy. Initiated a documentary and photographic archive of Anglican Churches. His own library formed the nucleus of the Council's reference collection.

Eliot, T. S. (1888–1963): Poet, playwright, critic, editor and publisher. Perhaps the most influential poet of the twentieth century. A prolific writer, his most famous works were *The Waste Land, The Four Quartets* and *Old Possum's Book of Practical Cats*, and his best known plays include *The Cocktail Party* and *Murder in the Cathedral*.

Elton, Sir Arthur (1906–73): One of the pioneers of documentary film-making. Publisher of the *North Somerset Mercury*, Governor of the British Film Institute 1949–50, Director of Shell International Petroleum Company in charge of films and television 1957–60 and wrote books on the history of technology. Lived at Clevedon Court, Somerset. Ran a private press in the early twenties.

Etchells, Frederick (1887–1973): Architect, artist and typographer. Specialized in ecclesiastical architecture. Writings include *The Architectural Setting of Anglican Worship*. Translated Le Corbusier's *Vers Une Architecture* and *Urbanisme*. Designed one of the first modern buildings in London, the Crawford block in Holborn.

Gilbert, E. W. (1900–73): Social geographer. Lecturer at Hertford College, Oxford 1953–67 and was for a number of years a Trustee of the Oxford Preservation Trust. As well as writing *Brighton: Old Ocean's Bauble*, he contributed to many geographical periodicals. Was in a forward thinking clique with Frederick Levi Attenborough (David and Richard's father) of Leicester University.

Goldring, Douglas (1887–1960): Novelist. A Founder and Secretary of the Georgian Group. A popular propaganda novelist in the twenties and thirties, his most famous book was *The Fortune*, one of the few pacifist anti-war novels of the First World War. His other books, of which there were over sixty, included *The 1920s*, a portrait of the time, and his autobiography, *Odd Man Out*.

Goodhart-Rendel, H. S. (1887–1959): Musician and architect. Studied music at Cambridge, but practised as an architect from 1910. Professor of Fine Art at Oxford 1933–36 and Governor of the Architectural Association and RIBA in the forties. Vice President of the Royal Academy of Music in the fifties. Wrote on architecture and fine art.

Grigson, Geoffrey (1905–85): Poet, critic, anthologist. Founder of *New Verse* poetry magazine in the thirties. A ferocious critic, he wrote for the *Guardian, Observer* and *New Statesman*. Wrote the *Shell County Book* in 1962 and the life of Samuel Palmer.

Grisewood, Harman (b. 1906): Novelist. Member of OUDS at Oxford where he met JB. Started working for the BBC in 1929 and became Chief Assistant to the Director General. Wrote several novels including *The Recess, Last Cab on the Rank*, and his autobiography, *One Thing at a Time*.

Guinness, Bryan see Moyne.

Gurney, Samuel (1885–1968): A rich bachelor, of ecclesiastical tastes, member of the Norfolk banking family. Lived at Compton Beauchamp near Uffington. Despite his Quaker ancestry he was a devout Anglo-Catholic and used the means at his disposal as Chairman of Medici Society, Fine Art Dealers, to produce liturgical books and church furnishings in the baroque style.

Harrison, Kenneth, P. (b. 1913): Fellow of King's College, Cambridge, and biochemist. Lay Dean 1945–8. Authority on the stained glass of King's College Chapel.

Harrod, Sir Roy (1900–78): Don at Christ Church, Oxford 1922–67. As a leading economist, worked on Churchill's private staff. Wrote many works on economics and a life of John Maynard Keynes. Married Wilhelmine Cresswell in 1938. Knighted 1959.

Harrod, Wilhelmine, née Cresswell (b. 1911): Known as Billa. A keen conservationist, she has been involved with the Council for the Protection of Rural England, Oxford Preservation Trust, Historic Churches Preservation Trust and was briefly secretary of the Georgian Group. Wrote the *Shell Guide to Norfolk* (1957). Founded Norfolk Churches Trust in 1970. Awarded OBE 1992.

Hart-Davis, Sir Rupert (b. 1907): Author, editor and publisher. Director of Rupert Hart-Davis publishers. Married (first) Peggy Ashcroft in 1929. Director of Jonathan Cape in the thirties. Edited the letters of Oscar Wilde and the diaries of Siegfried Sassoon. Published six volumes of the Lyttelton Hart-Davis letters. In 1960 published the poems of Charles Tennyson Turner, edited by JB. Knighted in 1967.

Harton, F. P., The Very Revd (1889–1958): Dean of Wells. Before his appointment to this office he had been Vicar of Baulking, near Uffington. An authority on ascetic theology, and author of the important book *Elements of the Spiritual Life*, he was Commissary for Religious Communities to the Bishop of Oxford.

Hastings, Hubert de Cronin (1902–1986): Editor of *The Architectural Review* which was created by his father, Sir Percy Hastings. Much admired, if feared by his staff. Gold Medal winner RIBA though he refused to receive it in public.

Hayward, John (1905–1965): Author, critic, anthologist and bibliophile. Handicapped by muscular dystrophy from childhood, he nevertheless achieved much. Founder of the quarterly journal, *The Book Collector*. Compiled anthologies of the works of T. S. Eliot, Samuel Johnson and John Donne. Cared for by T. S. Eliot for many years.

Hemphill, Emily see Villiers-Stuart.

Irvine, Gerard, The Revd Prebendary (b. 1920): Priest of the Church of England. Ordained in 1945, he ministered in various parishes, including St Thomas', Regent Street (where Dorothy L. Sayers was churchwarden) and finally St Matthew's, Westminster. Installed a Prebendary of St Paul's Cathedral 1985.

James, Edward (1907–84): Publisher. Educated Eton and Christ Church, Oxford. Godson of Edward VII and fabulously rich. Published JB's first volume of poetry, *Mount Zion*. Married the actress Tilly Losch and was a notable patron of the Surrealists, especially Magritte and Dali. Ended his days living in Mexico and designed buildings there.

Joad, C. E. M. (1891–1953): Author and philosopher. University Reader in Philosophy, he worked at the Ministry of Labour before retiring to write. Prolific writer of philosophical books including *God and Evil, Common Sense Ethics, The Meaning of Life, Decadence – A Philosophical Enquiry, The Horrors of the Countryside* and *The Pleasure of Being Oneself.* Chairman of the BBC Radio Brains Trust.

Kinross, Patrick Balfour, 3rd Baron (1904–76): Author and journalist. Worked in Fleet Street in the thirties on the editorial staff of various newspapers including the *Daily Sketch, Weekly Dispatch* and *Evening Standard.* Travelled extensively in Africa and the Middle East. Met JB at Oxford and later served with him as a member of the Georgian Group. Wrote seventeen books including *Society Racket, Europa Minor, Portrait of Greece, Attatürk: The Rebirth of a Nation* and *Portrait of Egypt.*

Knapp-Fisher, James (1905–76): Publisher. At Oxford with JB. Bought Sidgwick and Jackson and became its Chairman and Director. A gregarious man who loved to travel, he had a wide circle of friends and was a very popular figure.

Kolkhorst, George Alfred (1898–1958): Referred to as 'Gug' and then as 'The Colonel'. Oxford University Reader in Spanish who held a Sunday morning salon in his Beaumont Street rooms. A rich bachelor dedicated to the preservation of aesthetic standards of the nineties. In the mid-thirties he bought Yarnton Manor near Woodstock, Oxon.

Lancaster, Sir Osbert (1908–86): Artist, cartoonist and writer. Educated Charterhouse and Lincoln College, Oxford. Best known for his famous series of pocket cartoons in the *Daily Express* through which he became a national institution. He was also one of the most stylish writers of his generation, and wrote light-hearted architectural books, designed a lot of theatre sets at Covent Garden, Sadlers Wells, Glyndebourne etc. Wrote two volumes of autobiography. Married Karen Harris 1933 (died 1964), Anne Scott-James 1967. Knighted in 1975.

Lehmann, John (1907–87): Writer, poet, publisher. Editor of *London Magazine* from its foundation, also founded *New Writing* and *Orpheus.* Partner and General Manager of The Hogarth Press. Founded his own publishing house in the late forties. Wrote many books, including *Virginia Woolf and her World* and three autobiographies, and edited the *Selected Poems of Edith Sitwell* and the *Chatto Book of Modern Poetry* with C. Day Lewis. Brother of the writer, Rosamond, and the actress, Beatrix.

Lewis, C. S. (1898–1963): Writer and scholar. From 1925 Fellow and lecturer in English Language and Literature at Magdalen College, Oxford where he taught JB. Won the Hawthornden Prize in 1936 for his study of courtly love, *The Allegory of Love*. Famous for his *Narnia* series of children's books, *A Grief Observed*, published in 1961, and *The Screwtape Letters*.

Liddiard, Ron (b. 1913): Farmer and writer. In Observer Corps with JB in Uffington during Second World War. In 1971 wrote a book about the racehorse, *Baulking Green*, with a foreword by Lord Oaksey. At present writing his memoirs.

Longford, Christine, Countess of, née Trew (1900–80): Married Edward, 6th Earl of Longford, in 1925. An extremely active woman, she worked alongside her husband producing plays at the Gate Theatre, Dublin, and entertaining at Pakenham Hall. Wrote several books including *Dublin*, *Printed Cotton* and *Making Conversation*.

Longford, Edward Pakenham, 6th Earl of (1902–61): Playwright. Author of plays produced in London and Dublin. Chairman of the Gate Theatre, Dublin, and a friend of JB's from Oxford and Ireland. Pakenham Hall (now Tullynally Castle) was the venue for many Oxford students for long weekends. His plays include *The Melians*, *Yahoo* and an adaptation of Sheridan Le Fanu's *Camilla*.

Miller, The Revd Canon Paul (b. 1918): During Second World War fought in the Far East, made POW by the Japanese; helped build the Burma Road, and held in the notorious Changi Camp. Ordained in 1951, he was Canon Residentiary of Derby Cathedral 1966–83 and Chaplain to the Queen 1981–88.

Mitford, The Hon. Nancy (1904–73): Writer. Eldest daughter of the 2nd Baron Redesdale. Published her first novel in 1931 and continued to write light fiction in the thirties, but made her name in 1945 with *The Pursuit of Love*. Also wrote biography and history. Is well known for her editing of *Noblesse Oblige* which popularized the concept of U and non-U.

Mosley, Diana, The Hon. Lady, née Mitford (b. 1910): Writer. Third Daughter of the 2nd Baron Redesdale. One of the greatest beauties of her generation and very funny. Married Bryan Guinness 1929 and Sir Oswald Mosley 1936. Spent three and a half years in Holloway Prison under the wartime Defence of the Realm Act 1940–43. Books include *A Life of Contrast* and *Loved Ones*.

Moyne, Bryan Guinness, 2nd Baron (1905–92): Poet, novelist and playwright. Educated Eton and Christ Church, Oxford. Called to Bar 1930. A Governor of National Gallery of Ireland. Wrote many books and published several collections of poetry. Books include *Landscape with Figures* (1934), *A Week by the Sea* (1936), *The Children in the Desert* (1947), *Priscilla and the Prawn* (1960). His plays were *The Fragrant Concubine* and *A Riverside Charade*. Married Diana Mitford 1929 and Elisabeth Nelson 1936.

Murray, John (1909–93): Educated Eton and Magdalen College, Oxford. Universally known as 'Jock' he was in fact John Murray VI in England's oldest dynastic publishing house, founded in 1768. He published JB's *Continual Dew* in 1937 and from then on was JB's main publisher. He became a close personal friend of JB and others of his stable, including Osbert Lancaster, Kenneth Clark, Patrick Leigh Fermor and Freya Stark.

Nash, Paul, (1889–1946): Painter, designer and poet. One of England's most celebrated landscape artists. Educated St Paul's and Slade School of Art. Official war artist in 1917 and 1940. Exhibited widely throughout his life, sometimes with his brother John. Wrote the illustrated *Shell Guide to Dorset*.

O'Connor, Frank (1903–66): Irish playwright, writer and journalist. Librarian by profession, he wrote many books including *The Saint and Mary Kate, Fountain of Magic, Towards Appreciation of Literature, The Book of Ireland* and *Stories by Frank O'Connor*. His plays include *The Invincibles, Moses Rock* and *Time Pocket*.

Ormsby Gore, Archibald (b. 1908): Archaeologist. Strict Baptist, and very easily shocked. JB's constant friend and mainstay. Has suffered many operations on his nose and has lived all his life with Jumbo, who hardly ever speaks.

Peel, Diana, née Craig (b. 1927): Worked for JB as his secretary on the British Council 1945–46 and followed him to the Oxford University Trust 1946–48. Married Tony Peel, Headmaster of Amesbury School. JB attended her wedding wearing Henry James's morning coat.

Perry, Lionel (1905–81): The grandson of a Church of Ireland clergyman and son of J. F. Perry, a Fellow of All Souls College, Oxford. At Magdalen College, Oxford, before being sent down for failing preliminary exams. Volunteered as Air Gunner in the War. Lived in County Donegal, Ireland, from the fifties, looking after his ailing mother.

Piggott, Professor Stuart (b. 1910): Archaeologist and expert on European prehistory and Oriental prehistory. Educated Churchers College, Petersfield, and St John's College, Oxford. Assistant Director of Avebury excavations 1934–38. Trustee of British Museum. Author of many books including *British Prehistory, William Stukeley: an Eighteenth-century Antiquary, Prehistoric India, Neolithic Cultures of British Isles, Scotland before History, The West Kennet Long Barrrow, Ancient Europe* and *The Druids*.

Piper, John (1903–92): One of the greatest English artists of the twentieth century, he was painter, water-colourist, ceramicist, engraver, printmaker, stage designer, photographer, writer, deviser of firework displays and stained-glass artist. His many church windows include one for the new Coventry Cathedral and the memorial glass in Farnborough for JB. Collaborated on *Shell Guides* and illustrated many of JB's works including *Church Poems*.

Piper, Myfanwy, née Evans (b. 1909): Read English at St Hilda's College, Oxford. In the thirties she edited *Axis*, journal of French and British *avant garde* art and *The Painter's Object*. Married John Piper 1937 and had four children. Author of *Frances Hodgkins* for Penguin Modern Painters series. Wrote the librettos for operas by Benjamin Britten: *The Turn of the Screw, Owen Wingrave* and *Death in Venice*, and others for Alan Hoddinott.

Plomer, William (1903–73): Poet. President of the Poetry Society 1968–71. Founded and edited *Voorslag* with Roy Campbell and Laurens Van der Post. On the fringes of the Bloomsbury Group. Literary consultant to Jonathan Cape where he discovered Ian Fleming, creator of James Bond. His collected poems were published in 1960 and he wrote several librettos for Benjamin Britten.

Powell, Anthony (b. 1905): Novelist. Educated Eton and Balliol College, Oxford. His novels include *Afternoon Men, From A View to a Death* and the series *A Dance to the Music of Time*. Wrote four volumes of memoirs and was a Trustee of the National Portrait Gallery 1962–76. Married to Lady Violet (*née* Pakenham), sister of Edward Longford.

Pryce-Jones, Alan (b.1908): Author, critic, journalist. Worked on the *London Mercury* 1928–32. Contributed to the *Times Literary Supplement* and became its editor in 1948. Critic on *New York Herald Tribune* 1963–66. The title of his autobiography, *The Bonus of Laughter*, is taken from a line of JB's poem, 'The Last Laugh'.

Rosse, Lawrence Michael Harvey Parsons, 6th Earl of (1906–79): Educated Eton and Christ Church, Oxford. Vice-Chancellor of the University of Dublin 1949–65. Trustee of the Historic Churches Preservation Trust 1961–76. President of the Friends of the National Collections of Ireland and Ancient Monuments Society. Chairman of the Georgian Group 1946–68.

Russell, Camilla see Sykes

Scott, Sir Giles Gilbert (1880–1960): Architect. Son of George Gilbert Scott the Younger and grandson of the famous Sir George Gilbert Scott, he continued the Gothic tradition into the twentieth century with Liverpool Cathedral. He also designed Battersea Power Station. A bold and original designer. Knighted 1924.

Secker, Martin (1882–1978): Publisher. After working for Eveleigh Nash and unsuccessfully recommending Compton Mackenzie's *The Passionate Elopement*, he set up his own publishing company in 1910 and had a huge instant success with it. Went on to become London's most fashionable publisher and published Kafka, Thomas Mann and D. H. Lawrence. Output declined in the thirties and he briefly joined forces with Frederic Warburg and several other small companies before drifting out of publishing.

Shand, P. Morton (1888–1960): Writer. Educated Eton and King's College, Cambridge. Wrote books on food and architecture including *A Book of Food*, *A Book of Wine* and *The Architecture of Pleasure*, and translated *The New Architecture* and *The Bauhaus*. Influential contributor to *The Architectural Review* during the early thirties.

Skinner, Martyn (b. 1906): Writer. Winner of the Hawthornden Prize in 1943 and Heinemann Award in 1947. Wrote *The Return of Arthur*, *Letters to Malaya I and II*, *Two Men of Letters* and *Alms for Oblivion*.

Sparrow, John (Hanbury Angus, 1906–92): Warden of All Souls College, Oxford 1952–77. Educated Winchester and New College, Oxford. Double first. Elected Fellow of All Souls 1929 (aged 23); re-elected 1937 and 1946. Called to the Bar 1931. Distinguished military career. Various reviews and essays in periodicals. Publications include *Independent Essays*, *Controversial Essays*, *Sense & Poetry*, *After the Assassination* and *Visible Words*.

St Clair-Erskine, Mary see Dunn.

Stonor, Oliver, alias Morchard Bishop (b.1903): Writer. Edited James Boswell the Elder's *A Tour to Corsica*, *The Complete Poems of Samuel Taylor*

Coleridge and the *Poetical Works of Shelley*. Translated *The Way to Succeed* by Bernard de Verville. A secretive character who has spent most of his life in and around Exeter writing novels under pseudonyms but registered on the electoral roll as Frederick Stonor.

Summerson, Sir John (1904–90): Architect and architectural historian. Lecturer in History of Architecture at Architectural Association 1949–62. Various other lectureships and professorships in the UK and USA. Curator of the Sir John Soane Museum. Wrote on architecture including books on the work of Sir John Soane, Sir Christopher Wren, Inigo Jones and John Nash. Knighted 1958.

Sykes, Camilla, née Russell (b. 1912): A society beauty whose father, Russell Pasha, was head of the Cairo Police. Married Christopher Sykes, a well-known writer and Evelyn Waugh's biographer. Designed the original cover for JB's *Mount Zion* which was never used.

Synnott, Pierce (or Piers, 1904–82): Civil servant. Educated Oratory School and Balliol College, Oxford (double first). Inherited Irish estate, Furness in County Kildare, 1920. A dandy at Oxford where he wore cloth-of-gold waistcoats. Served in 60th Rifles during Second World War. Joined the Civil Service and retired as Deputy Under-Secretary of State, Ministry of Defence, 1965. President of Kildare Archaeological Society 1971–82 and Chancellor of Irish Association of Order of Malta 1971–81.

Taylor, Geoffrey (1900–56): Born Geoffrey Phibbs, but later took his mother's name. Writer and editor of anthologies, whose principal works include *English, Scottish and Welsh Landscapes* and *English Love Poems* (both edited with JB), *Insect Life in Britain, Some 19th Century Gardeners, The Emerald Isle* and *The Victorian Flower Garden*.

Thompson, The Revd J. M. (1878–1956): Scholar, historian, poet. Son of the Revd H. L. Thompson. Educated Dragon School, Oxford, Winchester and Christ Church, Oxford. Ordained in 1903 and a Fellow of Magdalen College, Oxford, in 1904. A broken career and the advent of First World War led him towards agnosticism. Tutored in Modern History at Magdalen from 1920 where he taught JB, and in 1935–37 was its Vice-President. Retired in 1938 to write poetry and edit the *Oxford Magazine*. Trustee of the Oxford Preservation Trust.

Villiers-Stuart, Emily formerly Hemphill, née Sears (1901–89): An American beauty and great horsewoman from Webster, Massachusetts, who married Lord Hemphill in 1929 and moved to Tulira, County Galway, with him where they had a son, Peter Patrick, who became master of the Galway Blazers. She later married Ion Villiers-Stuart who died after two years.

Walpole, Sir Hugh (1884–1941): Novelist. Son of the Bishop of Edinburgh. Published many books and plays including *The English Novel, The Secret City, The Bright Pavilions, The Killer and the Slain, Mr Perrin and Mr Traill* and the *Rogue Herries* sequence of novels.

Waugh, Evelyn (1903–66): Novelist. Educated Lancing and Hertford College, Oxford. Major works include *Decline and Fall, Vile Bodies, A Handful of Dust, Put Out More Flags, Brideshead Revisited, The Loved One* and *Helena*, which was dedicated to Penelope Betjeman. Became a Roman Catholic 1930.

Wicklow, William Cecil James Philip John Paul Howard, 8th Earl of, formerly Viscount Clonmore (1902–78): A zealous Anglo-Catholic. On leaving Oxford worked at the Magdalen Mission in Somers Town, and was ordained deacon before proceeding to the priesthood. Converted to Roman Catholicism and thereafter lived as a layman. Served in the Second World War as a Captain in the Royal Fusiliers. Succeeded to the Earldom in 1946 and in 1959 married Eleanor Butler, a Senator in the Irish Parliament.

List of nicknames

Beddioleman	Jack Beddington
Bess, Bessie	Mabel (Mrs Ernest) Betjemann
Billa	Wilhelmine Cresswell (*later* Harrod)
The Colonel, Gug	G. A. Kolkhorst
Coolmore	John Summerson
Cracky, Cracky William, Crax, Dotty	William Clonmore
The Egg, The Prawn, Powlie, Paulie	Paul Betjeman
Erney, Ernie	Ernest Betjemann
Father Folky	The Revd F.P. Harton
Mrs Folky	Sybil Harton
Goldilegz, Goldilocks, Goldilox	Myfanwy Piper
Griggers, Butibox	Geoffrey Grigson
Hideous, Bog, Captain Bog	Alan Pryce-Jones
Little Bloody, Bloody	Basil Dufferin and Ava
Little Prawls	Anthony Barnes
Malpractice	Maurice Hastings
Obscurity	Hubert de Cronin Hastings
Philth, Filth, Yellow, Propellor, Plym, Plymouth, Plymroad, Plymstone, and many other variations on similar themes.	Penelope Chetwode (*later* Betjeman)
Mr Piper, Mr Pahper	John Piper
Poor Old Joe, P.O.J, Gloomy Old Joe	J. R. Ackerley
Prawls	George Barnes

The Sarcophagus, Sarx, Schurfy	George Schurhoff
Scudamore	William Mitchell
Spansbury, Spanzbury, Hanbury	John Sparrow
Uncle Sam	Samuel Gurney
Waba, Wuba, Wubz, Wibz	Candida Betjeman
Woad	Philip Chetwode
Mrs Woad, Star, Bimbi	Hester Chetwode

Index